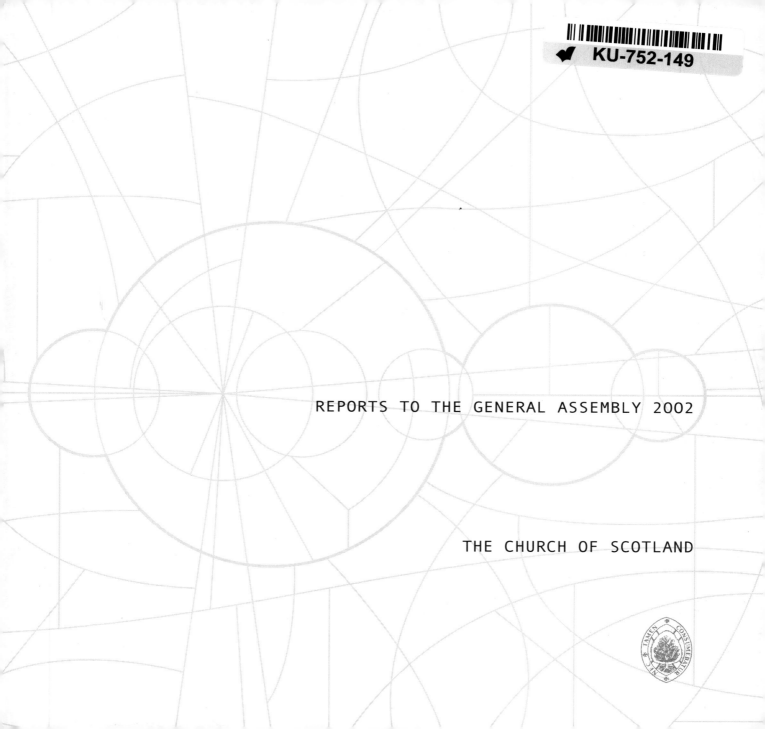

REPORTS TO THE GENERAL ASSEMBLY 2002

THE CHURCH OF SCOTLAND

Published in 2002 by
THE CHURCH OF SCOTLAND BOARD OF PRACTICE AND PROCEDURE
121 George Street, Edinburgh EH2 4NY

© The Board of Practice and Procedure of the Church of Scotland 2002

ISBN 0-86153-341-0

British Library Catalogue in Publication Data
A catalogue record for this book is available from the British Library

All Copy Keyed by the Church of Scotland
Type Design, Formatting, Printing and Binding by Lothian Print, Edinburgh
Cover Design by Pointsize Associates, Glasgow
Indexer Peter B. Gunn

CONTENTS

PRACTICE AND PROCEDURE
MAY 2002

PROPOSED DELIVERANCE

The General Assembly:

1. Receive the Report.
2. Record their appreciation of the Very Rev Dr John D Miller as Moderator.

ASSEMBLY ARRANGEMENTS
3. Approve the Order of Business for the first three days (Order of Proceedings).
4. Agree to apply Standing Order 103 to allow for electronic voting in place of voting by papers.
5. Authorise the Board to make all necessary arrangements for Assembly services in 2003.
6. Appoint the Rev R A Baigrie to edit the verbatim record.

LEGAL QUESTIONS
7. Pass an Act anent Granting and Signing of Deeds as in Appendix A.
8. Amend SO 34 as follows:
   (a) amend 34(i) to read as follows: "One person between the ages of eighteen and twenty-five on the opening day of the General Assembly shall, if possible, be appointed by each Presbytery to serve as a Youth Representative; each Representative shall be regularly involved in the life and worship of a congregation within the bounds of the Presbytery, and the minister of the congregation shall provide confirmation of this involvement if asked by the Board of Parish Education";
   (b) add a new 34(ii) and renumber: "The National Youth Assembly each year shall appoint ten of its own number, being between the ages of eighteen and twenty-five on the opening day of the following General Assembly, to serve as Youth Representatives to that General Assembly" (section 7a).
9. Amend Standing Order 32.3 by the addition of "the Personnel Manager" to the offices listed there (section 7b).
10. Pass an Act anent Church Courts as set out in Appendix B (section 7c).
11. Pass an Act Amending Act III, 2001 as set out in Appendix C (section 7e).
12. Pass an Act repealing Act XVI, 1933 anent Insanity of a Minister as in Appendix D (section 7f).

REMITS OF ASSEMBLY BOARDS AND COMMITTEES
13. Continue the remit given by last year's General Assembly on the review of remits and constitutions of Assembly Boards and Committees (section 8).

CONGREGATIONAL STATISTICS
14. Approve the inclusion of three additional questions in the Persons and Agencies Schedule as detailed in the Report (Section 10).

PRESBYTERIES OF EUROPE AND JERUSALEM
15. Receive the Report on the Presbyteries of Europe and Jerusalem set out in Appendix F and approve the recommendations contained therein.
16. Pass an Act anent the Church of Scotland in Europe as set out in Appendix F.

TOMORROW'S PRESBYTERIES
17. Receive the Report of the Inter-Board Group on Presbytery Boundaries and approve the recommendations contained therein.
18. Pass an Act anent Co-operation between Presbyteries as set out in the report (Appendix G)

SCOTTISH CHURCHES' PARLIAMENTARY OFFICE
19. Receive the Report of the Scottish Churches' Parliamentary Office (Appendix H).

THE SCOTTISH BIBLE SOCIETY
20. Commend the ministry of the Scottish Bible Society to the prayers and liberality of the Church (Appendix I).
21. Commend the Society's efforts to work with the churches in Scotland to promote the reading of the Bible through the **HomeWORD Bound** programme.
22. Commend the Guild for its significant and generous support of the Bibleworld project and Scripture distribution to ethnic minority peoples in Siberia.
23. Appoint Rev Andrew F Anderson, Rev H. Warren Hardie, Rev Norman Maciver, Rev Andrew McGurk and Rev Martin Allen to The Scottish Bible Society Council of Church Representatives.

GENDER ATTITUDE PROJECT
24. Encourage ministers, Kirk Sessions and congregations to study the publication *The Stained Glass Ceiling* (Appendix J).
25. Instruct the Board of Ministry and the Central Co-ordinating Committee to devise a written and enforceable code for ministers and employees of the Church in relation to sexual harassment, for approval by the General Assembly of 2003, and remit to the Board of Parish Education to keep awareness of sexual harassment and sexual misconduct before the whole Church in its gender-related work.
26. Thank and discharge the Gender Attitude Project.

REPORT

1.　The Very Rev Dr John D Miller

John Miller's nomination as Moderator was received with eager anticipation throughout the Church and it was no surprise when it was warmly confirmed by last year's General Assembly. Those with high expectations of this moderatorial year have not been disappointed. Modest and unassuming by nature, John Miller brought to the office a powerful blend of intellectual rigour, spiritual depth and the rich practical experience gained in thirty years of housing scheme ministry in Glasgow. He and his wife, Mary, are very much a team ministry in Castlemilk and that team has worked hard and well during this past year on behalf of the whole Church. Moderatorial duties have taken them overseas to Australia, Zimbabwe, Nigeria, Canada and mainland Europe where they have proved excellent ambassadors for the Church. One of the highlights of the year at home has been a series of weekend visits to housing scheme charges around

Scotland and these have brought great encouragement to these urban priority areas.

One of the great pressures upon Moderators is the expectation that they will cope and help others to cope with the unexpected. The 11 September 2001 is a date that will live in history and how fortunate we were to have someone of John Miller's spiritual capacity to help the Church's membership and many beyond it to work through the ensuing crisis. His wise and measured words conveyed grace and truth for all who had ears to hear.

Now the Church releases John and Mary to return to their beloved Castlemilk and it does so with profound gratitude to them both.

2. Assembly Arrangements

(a)   Clerkship
Following the nomination of the Rev Dr Finlay A J Macdonald as Moderator, the Board has made interim provision to cover his duties as Principal Clerk and Secretary to the Board. It is expected that the Depute Clerk should act in the absence of the Principal Clerk and the Board had no hesitation in arranging for the Rev Marjory MacLean to act as its Secretary and to undertake the duties of Principal Clerk until Dr Macdonald takes up these responsibilities again after his moderatorial year. To cover Miss MacLean's role as its Depute Secretary the Board has appointed Mr John McCulloch to be Assistant Secretary with the Rev Ann Inglis acting as Secretary to the Legal Questions Committee. In addition, the Board recommends the appointment of the Rev Matthew Ross as Acting Depute Clerk of the General Assembly. Mr Ross is minister of Ceres and Springfield and a member of the Board, particularly involved in the work of the Legal Questions Committee. Before studying divinity he worked as a House of Commons Research Assistant. These three appointments will be on a part-time and honorarium basis.

(b)   Assembly Services
The Assembly Service has been arranged in St. Giles' Cathedral on Sunday 26 May at 10 am with the Gaelic Service on the same day at 12.30 pm in Greyfriars Tolbooth and Highland Church. The Assembly Communion Service will be on Monday 27 May at 9.30 am in the Assembly Hall.

(c)   BBC Assembly Coverage
In response to a comment from a commissioner last year on Assembly television coverage the Vice-Convener undertook to take the matter up with the BBC. This offer was warmly received by the Assembly.

Many Church members have remarked that they want to see debates from the General Assembly itself and this point was conveyed at a meeting with the BBC last summer. In response the BBC explained the technical and financial constraints in which it operates and the difficulties in making the Assembly accessible to the more general audience. At the time of writing this report a further meeting is in process of being arranged.

The Board readily acknowledges the commitment of the BBC over the years to covering the General Assembly and the many appreciative comments which are passed on the nightly radio programmes.

3. Presbytery Representation

The Presbytery returns show that there are, in all the Presbyteries 1,262 charges, whether vacant or not, and that there are 221 other ministers (excluding retired ministers) who are members of Presbyteries. Representation is calculated for each Presbytery, in accordance with Act III, 2000 and the total number of Commissions is 861 made up as follows: 411 ministers, 411 elders and 39 deacons.

4. Business Committee

The Board recommends that the Rev David W Lacy be appointed Convener of the Business Committee and that the Rev William C Hewitt be appointed Vice-Convener. The names of others nominated to serve on this Committee will be found in the Order of Proceedings.

5. Commissioners' Subsistence and Travelling Expenses

The Board recommends the following rates for payment of expenses:

Overnight subsistence
not exceeding £38.00 for each night

Daily out-of-pocket Expenses
not exceeding £9.00 per day

Mileage rate, when no
public transport is available   22p per mile

6. Presbyterial Superintendence

Reports from Presbyteries show that Quinquennial Visitations have produced no case requiring action by the General Assembly; and also that Presbytery records are being properly kept.

7. Legal Questions

Courts of the Church

(a) *Youth Representatives*
Attention has been drawn within the Board, and by members of the General Assembly more widely, to the tendency of some Youth Representatives to attend in this capacity in consecutive years, and some have done so more than twice. The impression is that in some Presbyteries other young people are losing the chance to attend and one of the purposes of the Youth Representative system is being compromised. The Board is aware of the able and generous contribution made by individuals willing to serve the Church in this way for several years, and does not intend any personal criticism by this comment. The Board recommends that Presbyteries try to vary from year to year its youth representation, just as it should its complement of commissioners.

Further, there has developed a system whereby Presbyteries unable to produce a Youth Representative have another individual assigned to them. In geographical terms this is artificial, as the appointed individual is unlikely to be able to represent the allocated Presbytery.

The Board therefore proposes an amendment of Standing Orders, taking effect in the preparation for the General Assembly of 2003, to ensure a true connection between the individual and the area represented. The Board anticipates that the proposals regarding the size and function of Presbyteries will provide opportunity to secure a more proportionate distribution of Youth Representatives in due course.

A pattern has emerged of some overlap between the membership of the National Youth Assembly (now an annual event) and the Youth Representatives to the General Assembly. The connections between the two Assemblies are strengthening year by year, and the Board is keen to foster ways in which the debates of the Youth Assembly can inform the thinking of the Church more widely. The Board therefore suggests that a small number of Representatives should be elected by the Youth Assembly each autumn to represent the youth people of the Church as Youth Representatives to the next General Assembly. This will, incidentally, help to compensate for the reduction in numbers of Representatives likely to result from the change outlined in the previous paragraphs.

(b) *Corresponding Members*
Last year's General Assembly established the Central Co-ordinating Committee and agreed that it should appoint a corresponding member to the Assembly. The new Central Co-ordinating Committee incorporates the former Personnel Committee which had previously appointed its own corresponding member. Given that the purpose of having corresponding members is to ensure that relevant expertise is available to the Assembly there are compelling reasons for the Personnel Manager being so appointed in his own right along with other office-holders, such as the General Treasurer, the Director of Stewardship and the Editor of "Life and Work".

Accordingly the Board recommends that Standing Order 32.3 be amended with immediate effect by the addition of the Personnel Manager to the offices listed there.

(c) *Membership of Presbytery*
(i) Following an Overture and a Petition brought to the

General Assembly of 2001, the Board was instructed 'to consider the criteria for Membership of Presbytery, and in the light of such consideration, to review the relevant sections of Act III, 2000, and report to [the] next General Assembly.'

Until recently, the application of section 14 of Act III was complicated by the relationship between membership of Presbytery and the continuity of pension accrual of those not directly in the service of the Church. Since the last General Assembly the Pension Scheme Rules have been amended, largely removing this difficulty. It has become easier therefore for the Board to consider its remit, knowing that the desire to serve the Church in its superior courts is the only possible motivation for a minister or deacon to seek membership therein.

The Board observed that the General Assembly of 2001, in determining one Petition, took into consideration the experience and potential contribution of the individual petitioning, and not only the particular office that was added to Schedule I. The Board further observes that the offices listed in the Schedules may rarely be held by Church of Scotland ministers and deacons and so lose their relevance over time, and that the lists there appear somewhat arbitrary and extemporised. The Board accordingly concludes that section 14(11) (petition direct to the General Assembly) is a more desirable method to address occasional cases than section 14(9) (designation of an office through amending legislation).

The Board is of the opinion that the proper criterion for a minister or deacon to be admitted to membership of a Presbytery should be the nature of the post held as one involving ordained or diaconal ministry within the Church or unambiguously on its behalf; it should not include posts beyond the jurisdiction of the Church that do not require to be occupied by a minister or deacon.
(ii) On a slightly different matter, the Board takes this opportunity to invite the General Assembly to make explicit the intention of the Act, that a retired minister, having resigned his or her seat in a Presbytery occupied in terms of section 16(1), cannot later apply to have it restored.

An Act effecting these conclusions is set out in Appendix B.

(d) *Congregational Constitutions* - The Board of Practice and Procedure on the Report of the Special Commission anent Review and Reform, was given a remit from the General Assembly, 2001, to examine the constitution of congregations in the following terms:

"Instruct the Board of Practice and Procedure to examine whether the present "model constitution" represents the best and most flexible way of managing a local congregation".

The Board noted that the thrust of the Commission's report was to free the Church for mission and to develop local patterns to achieve this.

The current Model Constitution does not deal with the relationship of the Kirk Session and Congregational Board, and this has been an occasional cause of conflict. It could also be, as the Special Commission suggested, a "cumbersome and inflexible" process to co-ordinate the two bodies.

The concept that spiritual and temporal affairs should be separated as they are in the Model Constitution was examined. There seemed, now, to be no good reason for maintaining this separation and it was noted that it does not exist in the higher courts of the Church. The Board agreed with the view expressed by the Director of Stewardship,

"Christian stewardship is often seen to be concerned first and foremost with money. For this reason stewardship is regarded as a matter for the Congregational Board. This presents us with a fundamental problem. Money in the Church is related to the giving of members, which in turn is related to the commitment of members. We regard commitment as a matter for the Kirk Session, which it certainly is when we also consider the giving of time and talents. The basis of Christian stewardship and promotion is biblical and theological. It is concerned with God's gifts and our use of these. From this perspective stewardship belongs with the Kirk Session. We find the division between spiritual and temporal, and consequently between the Kirk Session and the Board, unhelpful."

The conclusion reached by the Board was that a single

tier decision making process, whereby the body making strategic decisions could also allocate the necessary budget, would help to achieve the aim of the Special Commission and could be of benefit to the Church. The making and implementation of decisions would be more easily co-ordinated. It was also agreed that the element of election by the congregation should be retained. Any new constitution on that basis would have to be sufficiently flexible to be useful to congregations of all sizes and locations.

Based on these conclusions, it was clear that the single body envisaged would have to be the Kirk Session. The present *quoad omnia* constitution, however, contains elements that do not fit well into a 21st century context and the Board considered what elements a new constitution might contain.

A new constitution should provide a pattern for the working of the Kirk Session that will be flexible and adaptable to local needs. There should be a minimum of prescription, only things which would be legally required. It would promote accountability and transparency in the administration of congregational affairs.

It is proposed that a new "Standard Constitution" be made available to the Church, in which the Kirk Session will have oversight of the whole life and service of the Church within its Parish; responsibility for the spiritual and temporal oversight of the Congregation's affairs; and in particular for the development of a missionary strategy in the Parish.

It is recommended that, under this Standard Constitution, all members of the Kirk Session will be elected by a free vote of the congregation and a fair system of voting will be devised. Those elected will serve as members of the Kirk Session for a limited period, possibly five years, and be eligible for re-election. Anyone elected to serve on the Kirk Session who has not already been ordained as an elder will be ordained in the usual manner and for life. It is proposed that the Kirk Session would no longer have the right to veto such an election, but that the general right of 'objection regarding life or doctrine' be retained.

The arguments in favour of a stated period of service for elders were set out in the report of the Panel on Doctrine in 1989, and referred to in the Panel's Report to the Assembly of 2001. This makes clear that this is not a new idea, but has been allowed for from the beginnings of the Scottish Reformation and that it works in other Reformed churches. The advantages are seen as making it possible to include younger people, who may find a more short-term option fits in with modern work patterns; permit periods of refreshment; and allow elders to make realistic decisions about how they might best serve the Church. In 1989 the Panel on Doctrine concluded its report on the 'Ministry of the Eldership' with these words,

> "We hope it is a pattern which loosens the rigidity at present surrounding the eldership, which liberates more members' gifts for service in the Church's courts, and which allows more members of the body of Christ the opportunity of guiding the Church's affairs for a while rather than requiring the same few to do it for life".

The Board agrees with the Panel's assessment, in 2001, that these 'options, which were regarded negatively in the past, are increasingly viewed with a healthy realism'.

It is envisaged that Kirk Sessions would work with a Committee structure, tailored to local needs. The opportunity would be given to the Kirk Session to encourage the giving of members' skills and abilities in appropriate ways by co-opting people with particular skills to its Committees.

If this approach proved acceptable to the Church, a decision would have to be made about how it could be carried through. One option would be to make the Standard Constitution the only possible one within the Church. This would replace the current mixture of Deacons' Courts, Boards of Management, *quoad omnia* Kirk Sessions and the majority operating under the Model Deed. There would be certain administrative advantages to this and it would tidy up a situation left unresolved at the Union in 1929. However, the Board inclined to the view that the Standard Constitution should be the form of congregational management recommended by the General Assembly, as the Model Deed is now, but that it should not be a change to the existing Model Deed. This is a more cautious approach than the other and would allow congregations to opt in if they saw advantages in the new Standard Constitution for their own mission. The

General Assembly could, of course, make the Standard Constitution mandatory in the future.

A set period of service for new elders, which would be included in the Standard Constitution, is already possible and can be found in examples of best practice. The Board believes that, by combining existing elements in this way, there is an opportunity for a better and more flexible way to manage the local congregation.

The Board now seeks the advice and comment of the Presbyteries, Kirk Sessions and Congregational Boards of the Church and, in particular, on the advantages and disadvantages of:

1. having a single body to oversee all the work of the congregation.
2. the direct election of elders as the sole method of appointment to a Kirk Session.
3. elders serving for a stated period.

It would also be helpful to have comment on how a new constitution, if approved of by the Church, should be introduced.

Presbyteries will find these issues for consultation included in the consultation process proposed by the Assembly Council, to whom responses should be sent as indicated in their Report; and the Board is grateful to the Council for this typically gracious assistance in avoiding duplication of consultation.

Ministry matters

(e) Suspension of a minister
Act III, 2001 anent Discipline of Ministers, Licentiates, Graduate Candidates and Deacons, s.5(2)(b) declares that a Presbytery is entitled to impose on an individual an administrative suspension at the point at which formal investigatory proceedings are initiated by its Committee. The question has arisen whether the specification of this entitlement at such a point implies that the Presbytery would be *ultra vires* in imposing such a suspension at an earlier stage.

In practice, administrative suspension is imposed to protect the privacy or reputation of the individual, or of his or her congregation or other sphere of ministry, or to secure the good name of the Church during the initial period of a controversial situation or allegation. The passage of time between an initial scandal and the reaching by the Presbytery's Committee of section 5(2)(b) renders the latter point far too late, in many cases, for an effective and useful suspension to be imposed.

The Board accordingly believes that it was not the intention of the General Assembly of 2001 to qualify the general responsibilities and related powers of the Presbytery. For the avoidance of future doubt, it proposes the amendments to the Act set out in Appendix C.

(f) Insanity of a minister
Since the passing in 2000 of the Act X anent Long-term Illness of Ministers in Charge, it appears to the Board that Act XVI, 1933 anent Insanity of a Minister is now redundant. Since Act XVI is in any case badly out-of-date, the Board recommends that the General Assembly repeal that measure, and the repealing Act is set out in Appendix D. The Board is satisfied that Barrier Act procedure is not required to repeal the Act though it was invoked for its initial passing; since the provisions are substantially repeated in Act X, 2000 no major change of principle is involved in the repeal.

8. Remits of Assembly Boards and Committees

The General Assembly last year instructed the Board of Practice and Procedure, in consultation with other Boards and Committees, (1) to review the remits and constitutions of all Boards and Committees of the General Assembly, (2) to give consideration to introducing a procedure to advise Boards and Committees on proposed amendments to remits and constitutions, and (3) to report to the General Assembly of 2002.

The Board seeks a continuation of this remit on the following grounds:

(1) it seemed sensible to await the outcome of the Presbytery Boundaries consultation since it has been acknowledged that this will have implications for the shape of the Church's central administration;
(2) the Assembly Council and the Co-ordinating Forum are engaged in identifying priorities for the Church with a view to moving to a point where Mission and Aid Funding follows areas of work as distinct from being given to Boards and Committees on a historical

budgeting basis. This too could have implications for the Board and Committee structure.

Once some outcomes of this thinking are known the Board will begin work on this particular remit and would hope to be in a position to report to next year's General Assembly.

9. Remit on "culture and timing of the General Assembly"

Last year's General Assembly, on the report of the Special Commission on Review and Reform, instructed the Board "to review the culture and timing of the General Assembly in order to increase the quality of reporting, participation and decision making".

The Board began this task by studying the most recent review which resulted in a number of changes being adopted by the General Assembly of 1997. The previous review had taken place some twenty years before that.

The 1997 changes followed a full consultation with Presbyteries and dealt with the following matters:

(a) *Numbers attending.* The number of commissioners was reduced from around 1100 to around 850 by adjusting the formula for Presbytery representation from one minister in three to one in four. The feeling was that to go further could result in ministers attending the Assembly as infrequently as one year in seven.

(b) *Briefings.* In response to a desire for briefing of commissioners arrangements were made for briefing sessions with Committee Conveners prior to their reporting. It has to be said that demand has been variable and some Committees have already abandoned the practice.

(c) *Conference Sessions.* In response to a desire for less formal sessions of the Assembly Conference Sessions have been introduced and have been found to be helpful.

(d) *Youth Representatives.* The inclusion of youth representatives in the Assembly was a significant innovation following the last review, though it is disappointing that not every Presbytery has been able to make such an appointment each year.

(e) *Cases.* The removal of cases to the Commission has eased pressure on the Assembly timetable and allowed more time for these cases to be dealt with. This has been recognised as a helpful change.

(f) *Duration of Assembly* The 1977 review led to the present Saturday to Friday Assembly to allow it to be contained within a "working week" and so make it easier for elders in employment to attend. Previously the Assembly had met from a Tuesday until the Wednesday of the following week. The 1997 review saw no need to change the present Saturday to Friday duration.

(g) *Reporting.* The length of the "Blue Book" and its availability before the Assembly have long been issues. The 1997 review called on Boards to impose a strict editorial discipline on their reports and the Board of Practice and Procedure continues to monitor this. The aim is to have the Book in the hands of commissioners a month before the Assembly.

(h) *Worship.* The last review encouraged some development beyond the traditional psalm, reading and prayer and this has happened. In recent years Assembly worship has offered a blend of the traditional and the more contemporary.

(i) *Venue.* During the last review only four Presbyteries favoured a change of venue from the Assembly Hall in Edinburgh and that was before the refurbishing of the Hall for the Scottish Parliament. Travel and accommodation were major considerations. That review also found no strong desire in the Church for a fully residential Assembly.

(j) *Timing.* The most recent review considered the case for a summer or autumn Assembly but found no compelling argument for change. The principal considerations were cost and availability of accommodation in Edinburgh, summer holidays and the annual cycle of congregational life.

(k) *Frequency of meeting, attending and reporting.* The last review considered whether the Assembly should continue to meet annually and concluded that it was in the best interests of the Church that it should. With regard to attendance, it is for Presbyteries to determine who should be their commissioners. However, the last review asked Presbyteries to consider whether individuals should be commissioned in successive years, and elsewhere in this report the suggestion is made that they should not. As far as reporting was concerned the review identified difficulties in operating a rota system for Board and Committee reporting, and this has not been introduced.

The foregoing is a summary of the most recent review (which is fully reported in the Board of Practice and Procedure section of the 1996 and 1997 volumes of reports) and the Board found it helpful to study this.

The Board believes that change is not introduced to the General Assembly only at points of formal review like this, but that the culture of the Assembly is gradually changing each year. The distribution of gender and age has noticeably changed even over a very few years, the variety of style adopted by Moderators is becoming more pronounced, and the use of audio-visual technology has transformed the amenity of the Assembly Hall, to name but a few visible signs of development. The Board believes that this evolution in the life of this court is far-reaching, and every bit as important and dramatic as more sudden, artificial change would be.

At the same time the Board is mindful of the ongoing discussions within the Church arising from "Church without Walls" and "Tomorrow's Presbyteries" and the potential for these discussions to lead to changes within the Church's structure and organisation that have not yet fully emerged. In view of these considerations, and also to allow for the further consolidation of the most recent changes, the Board asks for more time to reflect on the remit concerning the culture and timing of the Assembly.

10. Congregational Statistics

Following consultation with the Board of Parish Education, the Board proposes the inclusion of three additional questions in the Persons and Agencies Schedule, considering that the answers to them will provide a fuller picture of congregational life than is given by simply recording the number of communicant members. Subject to Assembly approval these will be included from the end of 2002.

The information sought is as follows:

(1) Number of children and young people aged 17 years and under who are involved in the life of the congregation.

(2) Number of people aged 18 years and over whose names are not on the Communion Roll but who are involved in the life of the congregation.

(3) Number of children who receive Holy Communion in terms of Act V, 2000, Section 15.

11. Loyal Address to Her Majesty the Queen

As one of a number of "privileged bodies" the General Assembly of the Church of Scotland was invited to present a Loyal Address to the Queen on the occasion of her Golden Jubilee. Similar invitations were extended and accepted in 1952 and in 1977. The Board considered the invitation and appointed a delegation to attend the ceremony at Buckingham Palace on 21 March. In the absence of the Moderator overseas the Board appointed the Very Rev Dr James Harkness to lead the delegation. Dr Harkness was Moderator of the General Assembly of 1995 and is Dean of the Chapel Royal in Scotland. Along with Dr Harkness the delegation comprised the Convener of the Board, the Principal Clerk, the Depute Clerk, the Procurator and the Solicitor of the Church. The text of the Loyal Address can be found in Appendix E.

12. Presbyteries of Europe and Jerusalem

For the convenience of Commissioners this section of the report on the Presbyteries of Europe and Jerusalem with its appendices is set out as Appendix G

13. Tomorrow's Presbyteries

For the convenience of commissioners the Report of the Inter-Board Group of Presbytery Boundaries is set out as Appendix G.

14. Gender Attitude Project Review

As agreed by the General Assembly of 2001, the Project had been continued for a further year in order that the

Research Project could be concluded and its findings published, and in order to bring budgeted proposals for the future of this work to the General Assembly of 2002.

The Review Group continued to meet throughout the year and presented their findings to the Board at its January 2002 meeting. Its main tasks were identified as assessing how the work undertaken by the Project had been carried out and what impact, if any, there had been on the life of the Church as a result. The Review therefore sought to determine whether or not the issues around gender attitudes had been satisfactorily addressed by GAP and integrated into the ongoing life of the Church.

Areas considered by the Project have included:

- Attempts by congregations and Presbyteries to address gender attitudes
- Preparation of educational resources for use in local Churches
- Discussions with Boards and Committees regarding attitudes and values about gender
- Reports from ecumenical and international bodies or conferences on gender awareness
- Topics such as violence against women; trafficking of women; women in leadership; theological education and gender; participation in the courts of the Church and experiences of women who are ordained

This work has been carried out systematically throughout the life of the Project and has resulted in a mix of satisfaction and frustration. There was satisfaction that issues of importance were being formally addressed, researched and debated within the Church. However there was frustration at the lack of resources committed to the work and the lack of general awareness of the need for it. Many in the Church regarded the issues as ones for ticking off boxes and filing as "attended to", rather than seeing gender attitudes and values as being an integral part of the ongoing, developing life of the Church both locally and nationally. Gender acceptance seems, in a public sense, to be regarded as the norm, yet the experience of many individuals still suggests a lack of acceptance and equality, however difficult the feelings may be to substantiate and document in a definitive manner. There is an abiding sense either that the Church

sees itself as having an accepted patriarchal inheritance, which it is unworthy to suggest is unsatisfactory, or that the Church is somehow "above" - or immune from - such considerations, due to its pursuit of a higher calling.

From the mid-point in the Review Group's deliberations, a strong feeling emerged that it would be neither appropriate nor acceptable to conclude that the work of the Gender Attitude Project should be regarded as complete. The history of the work within the Church of Scotland began with a period of theoretical consideration of the complementary roles of women and men within the life of the Church. GAP came to a decisive choice that - however much value there might be in considering such matters on an ecumenical basis - there required to be a rigorous consideration of the Church of Scotland's will to play its part in demonstrating how this could be worked out in practice; and the group came ultimately to a clearly defined attempt to quantify and implement this in relation to the structures of the Church. To this end, the association of the Project with the Board of Practice and Procedure has provided a platform for considering how the letter of the law relating to gender awareness and issues could be matched with the spirit of acceptance and implementation. Where the Church has legislated for such contingencies there requires to be an intrinsic will to carry it forward.

As discussions continued a resonance was detected between the emerging conclusions of the Review Group and its awareness of the vision of the Board of Parish Education, with its emphasis on relationships and leadership within the Church. There were clear links between the Project's conclusions and Parish Education's growing realisation that, within the Church, the resourcing of the work of women is often done substantially, if not exclusively, through the leadership of men. The opportunity was now presented to tackle the issues on educational and relational rather than legal and procedural grounds.

To this end the Board of Practice and Procedure agreed that the future of the work presently carried out by the Gender Attitude Project should pass to the Board of Parish Education, with the recommendation that funding be sought for the establishment of a post amounting to a minimum of 0.5 to 1.0 of a person (equivalent); the appointee(s)' responsibility would be to carry forward issues of gender awareness within the context of the Board of Parish Education's developing remit. The overall timetable, and an illness of one member of the Review Group, prevented the completion of the work in time to make a submission for funding to the Co-ordinating Forum meetings in 2001. The Board therefore agreed to recommend that an initial approach should be made to the Board of Stewardship and Finance by the Board of Parish Education, for a Special Grant to facilitate this development during 2003, and with a view to having ongoing finance included within that Board's Budget from 2004 onwards.

15. Assembly Hall Development

The Board continues to tread water and gird loins. The Scottish Parliament has confirmed its intention to relinquish the Assembly Hall in April 2003. The Board is, however, unable to enter into commercial commitments with potential clients until there is greater certainty that this intention will be realised and is very grateful to its proposed partner, the University of Edinburgh, for its continued understanding of the problem. The position should become clearer in the next few months.

Once confirmation of the re-entry date is received, it will be necessary to add on between six to twelve months for re-conversion work before the Hall will become available for commercial use. The nature of this work will depend on the outcome of discussions this year between the Church, Scottish Parliament, Heritage Scotland and various contractors. At the very earliest, the Hall could become available in early 2004, but a more likely date would be the middle of that year, possibly even later. But the clock is ticking. Conference organisers usually work on at least a two year horizon, and many will currently be firming up their 2004 commitments, and even now we could be at the back of the field for the conference market of that year.

Meanwhile the Board continues to develop its plans. The University (through Edinburgh First) has prepared a schedule of promotional events which would commence just as soon as confirmation is obtained of re-entry and consequent re-opening dates. EF has also identified target markets and developed drafts of promotional material. Joint heads of agreement for the formal partnership contract have been prepared and are currently in process of being firmed up. When the starting gun fires, whenever that is, the Board plans to be ready.

16. Presbytery Clerks' Project

During the year work was completed on the new Presbytery Information Management System (PIMS) for use by Presbyteries and it was sent out to every Clerk. PIMS, as well as providing a tailor-made database at a very reasonable cost, will enable the electronic transfer of data such as statistics and names of General Assembly Commissioners. It is envisaged that such transfers will become commonplace in the future. A change of internet service provider (ISP) at the Church offices has enabled a saving since all Clerks were added to the new ISP with no monthly charge as had been applied previously.

17. Inspection of Records

In accordance with the arrangements set in place by the General Assembly of 2000 the Board has examined the relevant records of Assembly Standing Committees. These have been found, generally, to be in order. Where deficiencies have been identified steps have been taken to remedy them.

In the name of the Board

DAVID W LACY, *Convener*
WILLIAM C HEWITT, *Vice-Convener*
FINLAY A J MACDONALD, *Secretary*

APPENDIX A

ACT ANENT GRANTING AND SIGNING OF DEEDS

The General Assembly, in view of the fact that property belongs to the Church at home and abroad, in respect of which it may be necessary that deeds and other documents should be granted and signed by parties officially representing the General Assembly, hereby authorise and empower the Moderator of the General Assembly, whom failing the Moderator of the previous General Assembly and the Principal Clerk of the General Assembly, whom failing the Depute Clerk, to sign on behalf of the Church all such deeds and documents as may be required up to the date of the meeting of the next General Assembly.

APPENDIX B

ACT AMENDING ACT III, 2000 ANENT CHURCH COURTS

Edinburgh 25 May 2002, Sess 1
The General Assembly declare and enact as follows:

(1) Act III, 2000 anent Church Courts is hereby amended as follows:

(a) by the deletion of subsections 14(7), 14(9), 14(10) and 26(2) and Schedules I and II.
(b) by the addition, at the end of sub-section 14(11) of the words '… in order to avoid a manifest anomaly in the constitution of the courts of the Church and having regard to the personal qualities, as a minister or deacon, of the petitioner'.
(c) by the addition, at the end of section 17, of the sentence 'For the avoidance of doubt, a retired minister who has resigned his or her seat in a Presbytery may not apply for its restoration'.
(d) by the deletion of all references to subsection 26(2) occurring in sections 26 and 27.

(2) Any minister or deacon whose membership of a Presbytery at the time of the passing of this Act was conferred in terms of any sub-section herein repealed shall retain such voting membership for the duration of his or her appointment, and upon retirement therefrom in terms of section 16 (1) or section 26 of the said Act.

(3) No minister or deacon shall lose his or her seat in a Presbytery by virtue of the passing of this Act.

APPENDIX C

ACT AMENDING ACT III, 2001

Edinburgh 25 May 2002, Session 1,
The General Assembly enact and ordain that Act III, 2001 is amended as follows:

1. Add a new subsection 1(4): "For the avoidance of doubt it is declared that nothing in this Act shall reduce the general power of the Presbytery to impose an administrative suspension on any individual subject to its jurisdiction in terms of this Act at any time".
2. Add the following sentence at the end of paragraph 5(2)(b): "This entitlement shall be without prejudice to the general power of Presbytery described in section 1(4) above".

APPENDIX D

ACT REPEALING ACT XVI, 1933 ANENT INSANITY OF A MINISTER

Edinburgh, 25 May 2002, Session 1
The General Assembly enact and ordain as follows:

1. Act XVI, 1933 anent Insanity of a Minister is hereby repealed.
2. Act I, 1988 anent Congregations in an Unsatisfactory State (as amended) is hereby further amended as follows:

Amend section 3 to read:
Proceedings shall not be commenced under this Act, or if already commenced shall be sisted, if it is found that grounds exist for action under (a) Act VI, 1984 anent Congregations in Changed Circumstances or (b) Act X, 2000 anent Long-term Illness of Ministers in Charge.

APPENDIX E

LOYAL ADDRESS PRESENTED TO HER MAJESTY THE QUEEN ON 21 MARCH 2002

To the Queen's Most Excellent Majesty

MAY IT PLEASE YOUR MAJESTY

On behalf of the ministers, elders, deacons and members of the Church of Scotland, we, Your Majesty's most dutiful and loyal subjects, beg leave in this Golden Jubilee Year to present to Your Majesty an expression of our warm appreciation and deep affection.

In a Loyal address presented by the Church of Scotland on the occasion of Your Majesty's accession to the Throne, the Church acknowledged "the many evidences already given of Your Majesty's high sense of public duty". The past fifty years have borne ample witness to the truth of that judgement. Throughout that period You have reigned over Your people with wisdom and grace, providing coherence and continuity to our national life and fulfilling countless royal duties in ways which have brought pleasure to many at home and overseas. Furthermore, we pay tribute to the dignity with which you have unfailingly fulfilled the duties of your vocation, often in the relentless glare of the modern media.

One of Your Majesty's first actions on succeeding to the Throne was to affirm the Accession Oath and it is a cause of continuing happiness to us that in Your letter to the General Assembly the promise enshrined in that oath, to maintain and preserve the rights and privileges of the Church of Scotland, is annually renewed. It has also been a joy to us that on a number of occasions Your Majesty has attended the General Assembly in person and we look forward to that pleasure again in this Jubilee year. When, due to the many other demands upon Your Majesty's time, You have been unable to attend the General Assembly in person You have been ably represented through the historic office of Lord High Commissioner and we recall particularly the fine fulfilling of that role in 1996 by Her Royal Highness, the Princess Royal and in 2000 by His Royal Highness, Prince Charles, Duke of Rothesay.

Over the past fifty years much has changed in the life of Church and nation. During that period neither Church nor Crown has been afraid of change; indeed both have positively embraced it. Yet at the same time both have, in their distinctive ways, borne witness to underlying values which endure. The Church of Scotland remains committed to its role as a national church, a role which we understand as placing a real obligation and responsibility of service upon us, service not just to our own members but, through a territorial ministry, to all the people of Scotland. We also continue to be mindful that we are called to labour for the advancement of the Kingdom of God throughout the world and so we cherish enriching links with partner churches overseas, recognising that many of these were established by the missionary endeavours of our forebears. At the same time, in obedience to Christ's prayer that all his followers might be one, we continue to play our part within the ecumenical movement, both in and beyond Scotland and we rejoice in the mutual enrichment this movement has brought and continues to bring to all Christian people. We are glad to contribute also to developing dialogue and understanding with and amongst the faith communities of other religions and are pleased that these communities, along with the churches, will be represented at the Jubilee service to be held in Glasgow Cathedral in May.

Your Majesty has maintained a fine example of quiet Christian witness over the years and we were deeply touched by the stress placed on the role of faith in Your most recent Christmas Day broadcasts. Your regular attendance at family worship in Crathie Kirk is an encouragement to us all and the associated hospitality of Balmoral Castle extended to visiting preachers remains for many a truly memorable experience. At a time when some would seek to identify religion as the root of all evil, how important it is that people of faith should together affirm those principles of love and peace which lie at the heart of all true religion. We are deeply grateful to Your Majesty for Your personal commitment to those things which are "lovely and of good report".

We would also, with loyal respect, pay tribute to His Royal Highness, Prince Philip, who is such a loyal and supportive consort to Your Majesty. The Duke of Edinburgh's Awards Scheme has provided wonderful opportunities by which generations of young people have developed gifts of initiative, self-reliance and resilience. Through his encouragement of the scheme and by his support of many other good causes His Royal Highness has contributed significantly to the nation's life. We recognise also the dedication to public service of Your Majesty's children all of whom, with their own families, we also hold in warm affection.

May it please Your Majesty,

Your Majesty's most faithful and loyal subjects,

THE MINISTERS, ELDERS, DEACONS AND MEMBERS OF THE CHURCH OF SCOTLAND

Signed in our name by

THE RIGHT REVEREND JOHN D MILLER
Moderator

APPENDIX F

PRESBYTERIES OF EUROPE AND JERUSALEM

1. Remit

1.1 The General Assembly of 2000 received a report from a Special Commission which had been set up the previous year to address a number of issues relating to the Board of World Mission. One of the recommendations of that Special Commission was that the Board of Practice and Procedure "should carry out an analysis of the Church of Scotland in Israel and should consider dispensing with the Presbytery of Jerusalem and placing the work of the Church's institutions there under the aegis of the Board of World Mission; that the Board of Practice and Procedure should reflect whether the sanctioned charges of the Presbytery of Europe should continue to form a Presbytery or be added to Schedule A of the Act anent Overseas Charges; that the Board of Practice and Procedure should consider the relationship between the Presbytery of Europe and the Board of World Mission, if the Presbytery remains in existence in the long term".

1.2 The General Assembly adopted all the recommendations of the Special Commission and, accordingly, the Board of Practice and Procedure was given this remit. The Board, in turn, remitted the matter to a special Committee under the convenership of the Rev David Arnott, with the Principal Clerk as secretary. The membership of the Committee is listed in Appendix One.

2. Methodology

2.1 The Committee decided to approach its task in the following ways:

(1) to consult individuals and groups within the Board of World Mission, the relevant Presbyteries and others involved in the work in mainland Europe and in Israel/Palestine;
(2) to seek information, through correspondence and (where possible) conversation with representatives of European Churches operating within Scotland;
(3) to make visits to both Presbyteries and meet with individuals and groups within the local context.

A list of all those with whom representatives of the Committee met in these ways can be found in Appendix Two and the Board would like to place on record its appreciation of the assistance given in this way.

2.2 The Committee regrets that it is unable to bring to this year's General Assembly a report on the Presbytery of Jerusalem. Whilst considerable analysis of the Church of Scotland in Israel/Palestine has been undertaken, it has not been possible, for a variety of reasons, to complete the research at this time. The Committee's work in this area will therefore continue and a full report will be presented by the Board to next year's General Assembly. What follows, therefore, relates only to the Presbytery of Europe.

3. The Presbytery of Europe

3.1   In addressing the Europe part of its remit the Board was quite clear that this did not involve an evaluation of the work being done by the Europe charges and their role within the mission of the Church, or the question of whether these charges should continue. The issue remitted to the Board of Practice and Procedure was a very simple one. Should the charges continue to form a Presbytery or should the Presbytery be abolished with the charges relating directly to the Board of World Mission through Act VI, 2001 anent Overseas Charges?

3.2   As it began its work the Board was also aware that what lay behind the remit was a frustration identified by the Special Commission on the part of both the Presbytery of Europe and the Board of World Mission in their working relationship.

3.3   The Church of Scotland has a number of congregations throughout continental Europe and these are grouped together under the Presbytery of Europe. At the same time these charges and the Presbytery itself relate to the Board of World Mission through that Board's Europe Committee. The Board acts as employer of the ministers, something which immediately puts the Europe ministers in a different category from ministers serving in Scotland, the former being employees, the latter holders of an office.   Moreover, while home-based parish ministers are responsible to the Presbytery in all things, Europe based ministers are responsible to the Presbytery in terms of life and doctrine and to the Board for the conduct of their duties. These factors have been the cause of tensions and difficulties.

3.4   A number of the European charges also relate to denominations within their respective countries. For example, the Budapest congregation is simultaneously a Church of Scotland charge and a congregation of the Reformed Church of Hungary and the minister of the Amsterdam Church is a member of both the Church of Scotland Presbytery and the local court of the Netherlands Reformed Church.   The congregation in Malta is a joint charge with the Methodist Church and, while not hitherto formally one of the sanctioned charges within the Presbytery, its minister over the past twenty-five years, being a minister of the Church of Scotland, has had a

seat in the Presbytery. These "dual membership" arrangements can and do create legal complications in terms of property titles and state recognition in some countries.

3.5   As well as being involved in Europe through the various "Scots Kirks" the Church of Scotland also has a network of partnership relations with various European Churches. These relationships are dealt with entirely by the Board of World Mission and do not involve the Presbytery at all. For example, the Board recently responded to a request from the Waldensian Church for assistance in obtaining an English speaking minister for their congregation in Turin by seconding a minister of the Church of Scotland.   It was a matter of some grievance to the Presbytery that, notwithstanding preliminary involvement in the initiative by Presbytery members, it had no *locus* in the process. The minister concerned now has a seat in the Presbytery.

3.6   As far as funding is concerned, some of the Europe congregations are entirely self-supporting (even aid giving), others require central funding in part and some are totally dependent on such funding. In the year 2000 the net cost to the Church of retaining the charges in Europe was £286,000. This cost was met from the Board of World Mission's co-ordinated budget which includes income from the Salvesen Trust. The Board has a duty to ensure that income from the Salvesen Fund, whether used in Europe or elsewhere in the world, is utilised in accordance with the terms of the bequest. The *cy pres* scheme (1991) relating to the Salvesen Trust states that the Board of World Mission should apply the fund for any purposes (including where appropriate, the rendering of financial assistance to indigenous Churches) which, in the opinion of the Board, provide or assist in providing the ordinances of religion to Scots in any part of the world outwith the UK. A number of the European charges are developing as 'international congregations' with excellent and vital work being done, not least with immigrant communities from Africa, students living far from home etc. However, if this approach, while commendable in itself, is taken to a point where there are not significant numbers of Scots in the congregation, the Board could find itself in the position of being unable to use part of its income generated from the Salvesen Trust for these charges. However, at present a strong core of Scots lies at the centre of each of these charges.

3.7 In its deliberations the Committee spoke to and corresponded with ministers from foreign language Churches who are living and working in Scotland and elsewhere in the UK. There is no one pattern for their relationship with their own parent bodies and indeed some expressed similar frustrations as expressed by the Presbytery of Europe. What is revealing, however, is that those parent Churches have not suggested that their ministers become mission partners working with local Church of Scotland congregations, nor indeed is the Committee aware of any formal links or recognition of these congregations at Presbytery level.

3.8 There is one school of thought within the Board of World Mission which argues that the Europe charges should integrate completely with local partner Churches. Certainly this would be in keeping with the general policy of the Board of World Mission over the years to encourage former colonial charges to become part of the indigenous Church, something which most have done. However, this is a minority view and, in any case, as noted in 3.1 above, was not a question which was remitted to the Board of Practice and Procedure. Accordingly, the Committee proceeded on the basis that the Europe charges should continue within the Church of Scotland and addressed the question which was raised by the Special Commission, namely should they continue to form a Presbytery or be added to the Schedule of the Act anent Overseas Charges? (Note: this Act was in preparation at the time the Special Commission reported and was passed by the General Assembly of 2001. It provides a framework for supporting the few remaining overseas charges other than those in the Presbyteries of Europe and Jerusalem, and which cannot realistically be grouped into a Presbytery, namely the congregations in Bermuda, the Bahamas, Trinidad and Sri Lanka).

4.   To Continue the Presbytery or Not

4.1 Although the reasons for having a Presbytery of Europe are historical the Committee is of a mind that the presbyterial system still offers a suitable framework in which the charges can exercise God's mission in their location, through their services of worship and their involvement with local congregations. It also offers a mechanism whereby that mission can be enabled and encouraged.

4.2 The Rev David Arnott (Convener of the Special Committee), the Rev William Hewitt (Vice-Convener of the Board) and the Principal Clerk attended a meeting of the Presbytery of Europe held in Malta in March 2001. Mr Arnott also attended the Presbytery meeting in Budapest in October of that year.

4.3 The programme for the Malta meeting had been arranged to allow for a substantial consultation between the Presbytery and the Committee. The Committee began by conducting a SWOT Analysis (Strengths, Weaknesses, Opportunities and Threats) with the Business Committee and this provided much material for discussion over the next two days with the Presbytery as a whole and in groups.

4.4 From this it emerged that the greatest strength of the Presbytery, as perceived by its members, was the fellowship it fostered and the greatest weakness was its sense that it lacked any real authority as a court of the Church. Opportunities for developing new reformed English speaking congregations were recognised (eg. in Berlin). Perceived threats included a feeling that they were viewed by many in Scotland as obsolete, representing an "ex pat" culture and Caledonian Societies.

4.5 There is no denying the strong sense of fellowship which exists within the Presbytery. Meetings are held twice a year, moving round the various locations, and are residential. Spouses frequently attend and have their own programme and there is a strong social element alongside the business. Indeed, it is suggested that, in this respect at least, the Presbytery of Europe is not so much an anomaly as a model! It seemed to the Committee that it would be unwise to destroy that which the Presbytery had identified as its greatest strength.

4.6 Over the past decade, particularly through the clerkship of the late Rev James McLeod, the Presbytery has organised itself with a committee structure and a pattern of well organised meetings where real business is done. This involves the usual items, such as congregational supervision and consideration of Assembly remits and those attending from the Board of Practice and Procedure were impressed with the rigour and attention to detail with which the Presbytery did its work. It is clear to the Committee that the Presbytery is adopting a more business-like approach and is tackling the issues it faces in Europe. At the same time the Committee was concerned to learn that the Presbytery felt it lacked authority and took the opportunity of emphasising that this was far from being the case. Act 1996 anent the Presbytery of Europe makes it quite clear that the Presbytery "shall have similar powers to those of Presbyteries in Scotland" (s.5) and "shall have direct access to the General Assembly" (s.8). This means that if the Presbytery feels strongly about something, eg. the development of some new work, and is unable to persuade the Europe Committee or the Board of World Mission to share its enthusiasm, it can take the matter directly to the Assembly by way of Overture or Petition. What is apparent, however, is that the decision making structures in the interface between the Presbytery and the Board of World Mission are not clear-cut and often lead to delay and frustration within the Presbytery.

4.7　There is a sense of excitement and expectation about the Presbytery of Europe and its charges. This is reflected by the fact that many of the charges are filled by ministers with young families who are committed to the new Europe and the vital presence of the Church within it. One congregation has outgrown the building in which it currently meets, another is redesigning some of its interior to make room for a crèche, others again find themselves at the forefront of mission and evangelism with those seeking refuge in Europe from other continents.

4.8　Presbyterianism has been the system of our Church government since the Reformation. It is also the system of Church government for large swathes of European continent. Its very adaptability has helped to ensure the continuing presence of the Church. That the charges in Europe form such a Presbytery strengthens the hand of the local congregations and reminds those worshipping they are part of a greater whole.

4.9　The Committee reached the conclusion that the Presbytery of Europe should continue on the grounds that:

(1)　the Church of Scotland is a Presbyterian Church and should operate in Presbyteries, unless in exceptional circumstances. The distances involved in Europe do not preclude this as they do with some other overseas charges;

(2)　the Presbytery offers valuable fellowship and support to those ministers and their families working in Europe and to the congregations;

(3)　it offers a natural forum to discuss matters affecting Churches on mainland Europe and in Scotland;

(4)　it gives the Church of Scotland a voice in Europe as a whole rather than just individual countries;

(5)　as we are becoming increasingly involved in Europe through the European Union the Church should be able to have a local voice reflecting issues and concerns that affect the Church;

(6)　the mission of the Church would be hampered were the Presbytery to be disbanded. The ability to reflect European issues back to Scotland would be dissipated, the strength of the fellowship and of belonging would be weakened and there could arise the danger of encouraging the congregations to sink into some form of narrow, parochial congregationalism.

4.10　To have placed the Presbytery of Europe under any other Board would have necessitated creating anew or 'borrowing' from the Board of World Mission such expertise as is required in areas such as overseas appointments, language training, family support, ministerial support and Presbytery delegation work. It would also require a change in the stewardship of the Salvesen bequest, some of which is used to provide the ministers in the Presbytery of Europe. To leave the Presbytery of Europe under the aegis of the Board is, however, not without its drawbacks. The Committee acknowledges that the Board of World Mission is an employer while the Board of Ministry deals with holders of an office (parish ministers), which it is recommended ministers in the Presbytery of Europe should become. The Committee is aware that the Presbytery does not sit happily with the ethos of the Board which prefers to employ mission partners and have all overseas personnel on the same footing. It is the Committee's contention that not only is this not possible, it is not desirable. If the Presbytery is an "anomaly", it is one worth retaining and maintaining, for reasons given elsewhere, no matter that it does not conform to the preferred pattern of the Board. This is not something which is being created, but it is something which requires to be managed in an ever-changing situation.

4.11 It is evident that much good work is being done by and through the Europe charges and that the Presbytery provides a forum in which those who live and work in various European centres can come together for fellowship and dialogue on matters of common concern.

5.   Continuing the Presbytery

5.1   In recommending that the Presbytery of Europe continue to be the means by which the Europe congregations are linked and supported the Committee has a number of consequential recommendations.

5.2   The Presbytery is slowly becoming more self-confident and is beginning to recognise that it does have the powers of a court of the Church.

5.3   Ministers serving within the Presbytery of Europe should, as far as possible, be subject to that Presbytery in the same ways as a minister serving within a Scottish Presbytery is subject to his or her Presbytery.   In particular, such ministers should no longer be considered employees of the Board of World Mission. They should continue to be appointed as at present, but with the congregation being able to vote for or against the applicant's suitability. This is in effect the current arrangement, for the Board does not proceed with an appointment unless the congregational representatives on the interviewing panel are in favour. This pattern would, in fact, be along the lines of New Charges where there is a congregation already in existence (see Act XIII, 2000 section 12). Rather than five year renewable contracts, the basis of appointment should be five year reviewable tenure, where the ministers will be office-holders rather than employees of the Board of World Mission. For the avoidance of doubt, the Committee further takes the view that the review process should be led by the Presbytery with participation by relevant personnel from the Board of World Mission, and that this should provide opportunity for discussion with Kirk Session and congregation without the minister being present. A 'Terms and Conditions' document, similar to that issued by the Board of National Mission to Associate Ministers, would be drawn up. This would set out those financial and other arrangements for which special provision would have to be made because of factors due to location – ie health, travel, education and the like. Each minister on an existing contract would be given the opportunity to decide whether to remain on that contract or change status.

5.4   There should be changes to the composition of the Europe Committee which is the body through which the Presbytery is linked into the Board of World Mission and these are detailed in Schedule 1 to the proposed new Act anent the Church of Scotland in Europe.(Appendix Three).

6.   The Europe Committee

6.1   The Europe Committee in its present form dates from the review of the then Board of World Mission and Unity conducted by the Assembly Council in the early 1990s. As currently constituted it has a membership drawn from the Board and the Presbytery, together with representatives of a number of Assembly Committees. Experience has shown that, while this representation may make sense in theory, in practice it does not work well. Busy people serving on other Committees are just not able to give priority to the Europe Committee with the result that attendance at meetings is irregular and that, in turn, creates difficulties of continuity. Difficulties also arise due to the status of ministerial members of the Presbytery as employees of the Board with a potential conflict of interest in policy-making discussion and decisions. As a result they are, in practice, prevented from participating fully in all aspects of the Committee's remit. There can also be a sense that the Committee is some kind of "parent body" to the Presbytery in a way which would never be true of any other Assembly Committee in relation to any other Presbytery.

6.2 In view of these considerations the Committee recommends the establishment, within the Board of World Mission, of a new Europe Committee as follows: three members from the Board of World Mission (one to be Convener), and two from the Presbytery of Europe (one to be Vice-Convener who shall also be a full voting member of the Board of World Mission *ex officio*), with powers to co-opt two additional members who will have voting powers. The Assistant Secretary (Europe) will service the Committee in a non-voting capacity and the Assistant Treasurer with relevant responsibility will attend in an advisory and non-voting capacity. The Assistant Secretary (Personnel) will attend as required. The Committee will be a Committee of the Board of World Mission with responsibility for partnership relations with European Churches and, as such, will parallel the Board's other area Committees. In addition the Committee will act as a "one stop shop" for the Presbytery of Europe in areas such as deployment of resources, appointment and reappointment of ministers, property and legal matters and such other areas as require home Presbyteries to liase with Assembly Boards and Committees. In this second capacity the Committee will have a measure of autonomy to take decisions provided that these do not breach budgets previously agreed by the Board.

6.3 For avoidance of doubt, Church and society issues relating to Europe will continue to be dealt with by the Church and Nation Committee.

6.4 In recognition of the growing autonomy of the Presbytery, the Board of Practice and Procedure also recommends a change in the procedures for appointing a minister. The Europe Committee at present works with congregational representatives in appointing a new minister. It is not considered feasible for the European charges to operate the same vacancy procedure as operates at home. The final responsibility for making such an appointment, however, belongs to the Europe Committee not to the congregational representatives. It is the Board's view that the time has come for these roles to be reversed. Personnel from the Europe Committee would be present to offer guidance and advice to the congregational representatives but the decision as to which candidate goes forward would effectively rest with the congregational representatives. Other procedures would remain as at present. It is also the view of the Board that membership of all Boards and Committees of the General Assembly be open to members of the Presbytery of Europe. There is much talent in its membership that could be of value to the Church. With airfares being comparatively cheaper, the overall cost to the Church is no longer the deterrent it once was.

Appendix One

Membership of the *Ad Hoc* Committee on the Presbyteries of Europe and Jerusalem:

Rev A David K Arnott (Convener), Mr James Dunn, Rev William C Hewitt, Rev David W Lacy, Rev Anne R Lithgow, Rev Matthew Z Ross, Rev Valerie G C Watson, Mrs Janette S Wilson (Solicitor), Rev Dr Finlay A J Macdonald (Principal Clerk).

Appendix Two

List of those with whom representatives of the Committee have consulted:

Rev Ian Alexander: Assistant Secretary (Europe and Middle East), Board of World Mission

Rev Alistair Bennett: Convener, Israel Centres Committee, Board of World Mission

Rev Walther Bindemann: Pastor, German Speaking Protestant Congregation, Edinburgh

Mr Bill Blair: Elder, Lausanne, Former Moderator, Presbytery of Europe

Rev Robert Calvert: Minister, Rotterdam

Rev John Cowie: Clerk to the Presbytery of Europe, Minister, Amsterdam

Rev Maxwell Craig: Formerly Minister, St Andrews Jerusalem

Rev Elisabeth Cranfield: Vice-Convener, Board of World Mission

Mrs Moira Cubie: Formerly Teacher at Tabeetha School

Rev Malcolm Cuthbertson: Formerly Convener, Overseas Charges Committee, Board of World Mission

Mr Walter Dunlop: Board of World Mission

Rev Ray Gaston: Formerly Minister at Geneva and formerly Europe Secretary, Board of World Mission

Rev Alan Greig: Vice-Convener, Board of World Mission

Rev Fred Hibbert: Minister, St Andrews, Galilee

Sheriff John Horsburgh: Convener, Special Commission

Rev Norman Hutcheson: Convener, Europe Committee, Board of World Mission

Mrs Anne Macintosh: Assistant Treasurer with responsibility for Board of World Mission

The late Rev Jim McLeod: Late Clerk to the Presbytery of Europe and Minister, Geneva

Very Rev Professor Alan Main: Convener, Board of World Mission

Rev Colin Morton: Formerly Minister, St Andrews Jerusalem

Rev Clarence Musgrave: Minister, St Andrews Jerusalem

Rev Iain Paton: Formerly Minister, St Andrews Jerusalem

Rev Professor Kenneth Ross: General Secretary, Board of World Mission

Rev John Renton: Convener, Middle East and North Africa Committee, Board of World Mission

Correspondence with:

The Danish Church in London
The Swedish Church in London
The International Evangelical Church in Finland

Appendix Three

Act anent the Church of Scotland in Europe

The General Assembly enact and ordain as follows :-

1. For the purposes of this Act the following terms shall be deemed to have the meanings hereby assigned to them:

"The Board" shall mean the General Assembly's Board of World Mission or any successor body assuming the responsibilities, functions and interests of the Board.

"The Europe Committee" shall mean the Europe Committee of the Board of World Mission, the membership and remit of which Committee being as set out in Schedule 1 hereto.

"The Presbytery " shall mean the Church of Scotland Presbytery of Europe.

"A Sanctioned Charge" shall mean a sphere of pastoral duty to which a minister or ministers based in Europe but outwith the United Kingdom and the Channel Islands is or are inducted, said Charges being as specified in Schedule 2 annexed hereto as from time to time amended as provided for in this Act.

"A Kirk Session" shall for the purposes of this Act only be or be deemed to be a Court of the Church with spiritual oversight over the congregation of a Sanctioned Charge (and that notwithstanding that it may be known by another name and may function within the constitution of another European Church by such other name).

2. The Presbytery shall, except as otherwise provided for in this Act or in any other legislation of the Church, have the same powers as Presbyteries in Scotland. Membership of the Presbytery shall be in accordance with Act III, 2000 save that, notwithstanding the provisions of Sections 23 – 25 of the said Act, the appointment by the Kirk Session of its Presbytery Elder may be made for specific meetings of the Presbytery rather than annually.

3. The membership of the Kirk Session and such functions as are applicable shall be in accordance with Act III, 2000, it being declared for the avoidance of any doubt that its members shall have been ordained to the office of Elder according to the practice of the Church of Scotland and shall have signed the Formula.

4. From the date when this Act comes into force, special arrangements involving the Committee shall apply with respect to the Sanctioned Charges and the Presbytery as hereinafter specified:-

(a) The appointment of Ministers shall be in accordance with the provisions of Schedule 3 hereof, it being declared that such Ministers shall be the holders of the office of a Minister of a Sanctioned Charge of the Church on the terms and conditions applicable from time to time with respect to that office.

Ministers currently employed by the Board to serve as such ministers may either retain that status for the remaining term of their contract (their existing terms and conditions being fully conserved and section 3 of Schedule B to Act III, 1996 being deemed to continue to apply to them and to remain in force for this purpose only) or may elect at any time during the said term to change status and become the holder of the said office on giving three months written notice to that effect to the Board.

(b) The Financial arrangements applicable to the Sanctioned Charges shall be as set out in Schedule 4 hereof.

(c) The arrangements for the reviewing of Sanctioned Charges and for readjustment, including the creation and suppression of a Sanctioned Charge shall be as set out in Schedule 5 hereof. The Board shall report any changes required to the said list to the next General Assembly, it being declared for the avoidance of doubt that the General Assembly may amend Schedule 2 hereof without reference to Presbyteries under the Barrier Act.

(d) The arrangements in regard to the heritable properties owned by the Church and used by a Sanctioned Charge shall be as set out in Schedule 6 hereof.

5. It is accepted that having regard to:

(a) some Sanctioned Charges having constitutional relationships with other European Churches

(b) the specialities arising from the Presbytery and the Sanctioned Charges operating within countries having different local conditions and legal systems; and

(c) the role of the Committee in regulating certain functions which would within Scotland generally devolve solely on the Presbytery or a charge within the Presbytery;

questions may arise from time to time as to the operation of this Act in particular circumstances and as to the application of the law and practice of the Church anent the Presbytery, the Committee and the Sanctioned Charges. In the event of any such questions arising, they may be referred by the Committee or, in the event of a difference of view between the Committee and the Presbytery, they shall be referred by the Committee to the Board of Practice and Procedure which shall decide the question and whose decision shall stand unless and until the General Assembly or its Commission shall decide otherwise on the petition of either the Board acting on behalf of the Committee or the Presbytery. The Board of Practice and Procedure shall report all such decisions to the General Assembly.

6. Nothing in this Act shall affect the relationship in which ministers and others appointed to non parochial appointments by the Board and serving in Europe stand at present to the Board.

7. This Act shall come into effect on 1 September 2002 and Act III, 1996 shall be repealed on that date.

Schedule 1

The Europe Committee Membership and Remit

1. The Europe Committee shall be a Committee of the Board of World Mission, reporting to that Board and serviced by the Board's departmental staff.

2. The membership of the Committee shall be as follows:

(a) Convener appointed by the Board of World Mission from amongst its membership;

(b) Vice-Convener appointed by the Presbytery of Europe from amongst its membership, such Vice-Convener, if not already a member of the Board, to become a full-voting member of the Board, *ex officio*;

(c) two additional members appointed by and from the Board of World Mission;

(d) one additional member appointed by and from the Presbytery of Europe;

(e) the Committee may co-opt up to two additional members for their particular expertise who shall have full voting powers;

(f) the Assistant Secretary (Europe) shall service the Committee and attend in an advisory and non-voting capacity;

(g) the Assistant Treasurer with relevant responsibility shall attend in an advisory and non-voting capacity;

(h) the Assistant Secretary (Personnel) shall attend, in an advisory and non-voting capacity, as required.

3. The Committee will have two connected areas of responsibility which will inform and complement each other, namely:

(i) all partnership relations with European Churches, including:

(a) developing and maintaining links with partner Churches and other bodies;

(b) identifying opportunities and recruiting staff;

(c) participating in selection of bursar and faith share partners;

(d) receiving visits from and visiting European partner Churches;

(e) budget and stewardship matters;

(f) raising policy issues with the Board of World Mission;

(g) highlighting Europe Committee work in Scotland;

(h) advising on issues relating to mission partners.

(ii) The Presbytery of Europe with particular responsibility for:

(a) financial arrangements;

(b) buildings;

(c) ministerial appointments;

(d) support for the ministry of the sanctioned charges within the Presbytery of Europe and assistance in relating to the Church in Scotland as a whole;

(e) support for ministers who are working in Europe and their families.

Schedule 2

Sanctioned Charges

Amsterdam	Costa del Sol	Lisbon	Paris
Brussels	Geneva	Lausanne	Rome
Budapest	Gibraltar	Malta	Rotterdam

Schedule 3

Appointment of Ministers to the Sanctioned Charges

1. Those eligible for appointment to be ministers of the Sanctioned Charges shall be the categories of persons listed in section 13 of Act IV, 1984 (or in any legislation enacted to replace the said section as being persons eligible to be nominated, elected and called as minister of parishes in the Church of Scotland) except in the case of Malta where the minister may be a minister of the Methodist Church. When a minister of the Methodist Church is so appointed, it is expressly provided that such minister shall be inducted by the Presbytery and the Methodist Church, shall retain status as a minister of the Methodist Conference and shall have full membership of the Presbytery of Europe with all the rights, privileges and duties associated therewith and, in particular, shall be authorised to moderate the Kirk Session of the charge of Malta. He or she shall at all times be subject to the law and discipline of both the Methodist Conference and the Church of Scotland. On ceasing to be minister of Malta he or she shall lose membership of the Presbytery and shall not retain any ministerial status within the Church of Scotland, nor be entitled to a practising certificate in terms of Act II, 2000.

2. In the case of new appointments being made after the coming into effect of this Act, the following procedures shall apply :-

(i) The Committee shall consult with the Presbytery and Kirk Session of the Sanctioned Charge concerned and, provided it is agreed that a new appointment shall be made and that the procedures set out in Schedule 5 hereof shall not apply, the Committee will, in consultation with the Kirk Session decide on the salary and on any other special terms applicable to the appointment. Before the appointment is made, the Committee shall be satisfied with the housing arrangements for the manse family.

(ii) The Kirk Session shall draw up an Electoral Register in accordance with the provisions of Sections 6-8 of Act V, 1984. An interviewing panel shall be formed which shall consist of 1 representative from the Committee and 2 representatives of the Congregation, each person to have one vote. In addition, the Interim Moderator of the Sanctioned charge shall be a non-voting member of the panel. The Assistant Secretary (Europe) shall act as the Secretary of the panel but shall not have a vote. The panel shall bring a nomination to the Committee.

(iii) If both the Committee and the appropriate Committee of the Presbytery are satisfied with the nominee, the interim moderator shall arrange for the nominee to preach to the congregation.

(iv) The Interim Moderator shall then invite the congregation to indicate whether or not the nominee is acceptable to it, only those whose names are on the Electoral Register being entitled to vote, and shall intimate the outcome to the Committee.

(v) If the Committee is satisfied that the nominee is acceptable to the congregation, it shall make the appointment, subject to the concurrence of the Presbytery, which shall then induct him or her to the Sanctioned Charge on the basis of reviewable tenure.

(vi) In the event of the Minister appointed being a probationer or a minister without charge, the Presbytery shall take the necessary steps for ordination, if required, and induction to the Sanctioned Charge.

(vii) In the event of the Minister nominated being unacceptable to the Committee, the Presbytery or the congregation or should the nominee decline the appointment, his or her nomination shall fall. The panel shall then bring forward a new nomination and the same procedure shall be followed as with the first nomination.

(viii) In the event that no appointment has been made within one year of the Sanctioned Charge falling vacant, the Committee shall have the power to appoint a minister to it without requiring the concurrence of the Congregation by way of a vote in terms of sub-section (iv) hereof.

Schedule 4

Financial Arrangements applicable to the Sanctioned Charges and to the other work of the Committee

1. The Committee, in consultation with the Presbytery, the Sanctioned Charge concerned and the Assistant General Treasurer with responsibility for the finances of the Board, shall assess and determine for the following year, the amount which each of the Sanctioned Charges shall contribute towards its ministry and related costs.

2. The Board shall thereafter in consultation with the Committee fix a budget to fund the work of the Committee for the following year in relation to (a) the discharging of its responsibilities for all partnership relationships with the European Churches and (b) the costs of funding the work and witness of the Presbytery and the Sanctioned Charges. The said budget shall include such sums as are necessary to meet ministry and related costs

(under deduction of the amounts payable by the Sanctioned Charges towards such costs as fixed in terms of section 1 hereof) and to fund non parochial appointments of staff employed by the Board to work in Europe and all related work of the Committee, including the Committee's own expenses. The budgeted amount shall be made available to the Committee which shall have full powers to deal with the funds so allocated to it and shall require to operate within the amount budgeted. Should extraordinary and unexpected expenditure arise whether in regard to property repairs or other matters, the Committee shall be entitled to apply to the Board for additional finance.

3. The Presbytery shall require those of the Sanctioned Charges which are, or which become, self supporting to contribute towards the Mission and Aid Fund, such contributions to be allocated by the Presbytery in consultation with the said Assistant General Treasurer.

4. The Financial Board (or equivalent body) of the Sanctioned Charge shall be responsible for the finances of the congregation and shall be responsible for the preparation of annual accounts which shall be prepared, audited and approved in accordance with Regulation 1, 1994 (Regulations anent Congregational Finance) as the same may be adapted in individual cases and as approved by the Presbytery to take account of local conditions. A set of the accounts of each of the Sanctioned Charge shall be forwarded to the Committee as soon as received by the Presbytery to which (rather than the Board of Stewardship and Finance) the Presbytery shall report as to its diligence in examining the said accounts.

Schedule 5
Arrangements relating to the Reviewing of the Sanctioned Charges

1. It shall be the duty of the Presbytery to keep under review the Sanctioned Charges by conducting an appraisal thereof every six years. The Presbytery shall thereafter agree a report which shall narrate in respect of each charge the outcome of the appraisal conducted which it shall transmit to the Committee.

2. On a vacancy arising for any reason in a Sanctioned Charge or in the event of the Committee and the Presbytery concurring in the need for the Charge to be reviewed at any other time, a Special Committee shall be appointed which shall consist of the Convener and 1 representative of the Committee (with the Convener of the Committee acting as Convener of the Special Committee) and 1 representative of the Presbytery (neither of whom shall be from the Sanctioned Charge concerned) which shall confer with the minister (if any), and the office bearers and which may consult with members of the congregation. All meetings with office bearers and with the congregation shall be called by the Special Committee and a member thereof shall act as Convener for the purpose of conference. In no case shall a minister preside at or attend any meeting called for review purposes where matters in which his or her interests are involved are discussed or decided.

3. The Special Committee shall thereafter report its recommendations regarding the future of the Sanctioned Charge to the Presbytery and the Committee and if both bodies concur, the Special Committee's recommendations shall be implemented forthwith subject to the right of appeal or dissent and complaint. If either or both bodies do not accept the Special Committee's recommendations, there shall be further conference between the Presbytery and the Committee and, if after such conference, no agreement is reached, the decision then reached by the Committee in the matter shall be reported to the Board and, provided it is confirmed by the Board, shall be final and shall be implemented by the Presbytery, subject to the right of appeal or dissent and complaint.

4. If, as a result of the aforementioned review procedures, it is decided that the Sanctioned Charge cannot continue as previously constituted, all the

forms of readjustment provided for by Act IV, 1984 (or in any legislation enacted to replace the said Act) and as adapted to take account of local conditions shall be competent. In the event of the readjustment decided upon requiring the termination by the Presbytery of the minister's tenure, the minister, subject to the disposal of any appeal in the event of the minister exercising his/her right of appeal to the Commission of Assembly, shall on the date of termination be deemed to have demitted his or her charge. The minister shall in such circumstances be entitled to require the Committee to pay (a) the full cost of him or her and the manse family returning to any place on the mainland of Scotland and (b) following his or her return to Scotland the Minimum Stipend (*pro rata* for part time ministries) for the period of six months from the said date of termination or until obtaining another charge or other paid employment, whichever is the shorter period.

5. If the Board, the Committee and the Presbytery all agree that circumstances exist which would justify the creation of a new Sanctioned Charge, the Committee in consultation with the Presbytery shall proceed to take all steps necessary to constitute and establish the new Sanctioned Charge, including the providing of suitable buildings and the appointment of a minister.

6. The Board shall, on behalf of the Committee, report any readjustment or the establishment of any new Sanctioned Charge carried out in terms of the above procedures to the next General Assembly and shall seek appropriate amendment be made to Schedule 2 hereof.

Schedule 6

Heritable Property

1. The heritable property pertaining to a Sanctioned Charge ("the property") shall be held by the Financial Board and the Trustees in whom title is vested for the use of and occupation by the Sanctioned Charge concerned.

2. Matters relating to the day to day management of the property shall be dealt with by the Financial Board of the Sanctioned Charge. It shall be the duty of the Financial Board to maintain the fabric of the property in proper order and repair and fully insured against loss or damage by fire and also against loss or damage by such other risks or perils as are from time to time deemed appropriate by the Financial Board.

3. Without the consent of the Presbytery and the Committee and, in the event of title to the property being vested in the Church of Scotland Trust ("the Trust"), also of the Trust, it shall not be lawful nor in the power of the Financial Board nor the Trustees (if other than the Trust) in whom title is vested to make any extensive alterations to the property nor to sell, let (other than on agreements which do not grant security of tenure of more than one year), convey, exchange or otherwise dispose of and deal with the same nor to give and execute mortgages, charges pledges or other securities over the property. For the purposes of these Regulations, "extensive alterations" shall have such meaning as shall from time to time be determined by the Committee and, where title to the property concerned is vested in the Trust, by the Committee and the Trust acting together.

4. Without the consent of the Presbytery and the Committee, the Financial Board shall not purchase or take on lease for a period in excess of one year any additional heritable property and, except where all the funds for the purchase or to meet the obligations under the lease are being provided by members or other persons associated with the Sanctioned Charge or from the disposal of property, title to which is not vested in the Trust, title or right to the additional heritable property being acquired or leased shall be taken in name of the Trust, unless the Committee and the Trust determine otherwise.

5. The Financial Board and the Trustees (if other than

the Trust) in whom title to the property is vested shall each year submit a written report to the Presbytery and the Committee concerning the property which shall include details of their management and maintenance thereof and summarise the details of the insurance cover in force with respect to the property.

APPENDIX G

TOMORROW'S PRESBYTERIES

REPORT OF THE INTER-BOARD GROUP ON PRESBYTERY BOUNDARIES

In 1999 the General Assembly remitted to the Board, in consultation with the Boards of Ministry and National Mission to "undertake a fresh examination of Presbytery boundaries". The following year the Board reported that in undertaking this remit it had become apparent that the issue was not simply to do with boundaries "but with the effective operation of the Presbytery system and the critical role of Presbyteries in supporting local churches". Accordingly, the General Assembly of 2000 agreed "that the work be developed by an Inter-Board Group drawn from the Boards of Ministry, National Mission, Parish Education and Practice and Procedure, with the Board of Practice and Procedure as the lead Board with responsibility for servicing the Group". Subsequently the Director of Stewardship was co-opted to the Group and meetings were also attended by representatives of the Assembly Council, the Special Commission on Review and Reform and the Committee on Ecumenical Relations (Membership list - Appendix 1).

The Inter-Board Group brought a report to last year's General Assembly which offered a radical re-organisation of the Presbytery structure. Following the reception of this report by the Assembly a major consultation process was in August 2001. This involved a series of "roadshow" meetings around the country followed by discussion within Presbyteries and Kirk Sessions. Thirty-eight Presbyteries submitted comments, as requested, by mid-November. In addition, seventy-one submissions were received by Kirk Sessions, congregational groups and individuals.

The Inter-Board Group met over two days in early December and gave very full consideration to the comments which had been received. It was apparent that the broad thrust of the Group's proposal had not captured the imagination of the Church. The Group's vision was of a different kind of Presbytery – larger, but with more powers. It was suggested that the Church might be organised with as few as seven to twelve Presbyteries, each gathered round a regional centre. Such Presbyteries would control substantial budgets, manage resources, employ and deploy appropriate regionally based personnel and generally oversee the work of the church in their areas. Within each Presbytery area congregations would be grouped into districts, which would not be "courts of the church" but less formal gatherings with a focus on local missionary and ecumenical activity. As a consequence of this new approach there would be a reduction in the role and size of the Church's central administration.

This, in outline, was the concept on which comment from the wider Church was sought, both in the August meetings round the country and in returns from Presbyteries. As it embarked upon this consultation process the Group was particularly encouraged by the support its thinking had received from the Special Commission on Review and Reform which in its Report had stated: "We have kept open communication with the Committee on Presbytery Boundaries and discovered that the logic of our "upside-down" Church has led us to similar conclusions".

In the event the outcome of the consultation was that, while a majority of responding Presbyteries (23 out of the 38) affirmed a need for change and there were a number of positive comments, overall there was little enthusiasm for such a radical approach. There were also complaints that the timetable for consultation was too rushed, though it should be pointed out that this was deliberately approved by last year's Assembly in face of a proposal to allow a longer period, a proposal the Group's Convener indicated a willingness to accept.

The main substantive concerns expressed were as follows:

(1) Fewer and larger Presbyteries would become remote from the congregations and there would be no sense of fellowship.

(2) Decisions would effectively fall to be taken by small executive groups within Presbyteries.

(3) Too much time and money would be spent on travel.

(4) Districts would become "talking shops" with no real power.

(5) There would be no guarantee that the development of regional centres of administration would lead to a reduction in the central administration. Indeed, many functions would need to be maintained at national level.

(6) The Group had failed to produce any detailed plan with indicative costs.

(7) The consultation process was too rushed and should be slowed down so that the issues raised could be considered within the context of "Church Without Walls".

At the same time a number of smaller Presbyteries indicated an openness to explore ways of co-operating across boundaries and one larger Presbytery offered to pilot the new scheme. It was also acknowledged that, while the Group's thinking was certainly imaginative and creative, judgement should be reserved until more detail was produced.

At its meeting in December the Group accepted that it clearly had no mandate, in the words of last year's Assembly report, "to bring a more fully developed scheme to the General Assembly of 2002". The Group debated long and hard whether it should simply report that its ideas had not been well received, or whether it should still attempt to fufil the instruction of last year's Assembly and "draft a further consultation document that would take into account the submissions of Presbyteries". In the end, it was the latter course which was followed, with the new document arriving in the Christmas post. This slim booklet was in three sections: (1) a summary of responses to the first consultation; (2) a fuller exposition of the Group's thinking regarding districts and (3) a series of open questions designed to assist Presbyteries in a process of self-analysis. This last element was a response by the Group to the often expressed view that change

was needed. If Presbyteries are saying change is needed, though not the radical changes suggested by the Group, then the Group would find it helpful to know what needs to change and in what ways.

By the mid-February deadline 36 Presbyteries had sent in further submissions and the Group readily and gratefully acknowledges both the efforts made by Presbyteries and the quality of the submissions prepared. In particular the observations made in response to the series of questions about the role and function of Presbyteries are extremely valuable. However, it was again clear from the second set of comments that it was not going to be appropriate for the Group to bring a developed scheme, based on its initial thinking, to this General Assembly. On the other hand, it is evident that the issues raised in the consultation process have stimulated much lively and fruitful discussion throughout the Church and that needs to continue in a less pressurised way and within the wider context of "Church Without Walls". Accordingly the Group brings the following recommendations to the General Assembly:

(1) that the responses of Presbyteries and others to the "Tomorrow's Presbyteries" consultation process be remitted for full consideration to the Board of Practice and Procedure and the Assembly Council as part of the process instructed by last year's General Assembly that these bodies should study the sections of the Special Commission anent Review and Reform, on "The Shape of the Regional Church" and "The Shape of the Central Church", the Board and the Council to establish between themselves a mechanism for taking this work forward and to report progress to the General Assembly of 2003;

(2) that the Board of Practice and Procedure enter into discussion, (a) with those Presbyteries which have indicated their readiness to explore possibilities of more formal co-operation and realignment of boundaries with neighbouring Presbyteries, and (b) with other Presbyteries as appropriate;

(3) that in recognition of the comments made by a number of Presbyteries on cross-boundary co-operation, the General Assembly pass an Act anent Co-operation between Presbyteries as set out (Appendix 2).

(4) that the Inter-Board Group as presently constituted be discharged, with thanks for its work in initiating the debate on the effective functioning of the Presbytery system;

(5) that the General Assembly record their appreciation of all who have engaged with the process and devoted considerable time and thought to it

ALASTAIR H SYMINGTON, *Convener*
DAVID W LACY, *Convener*
Board of Practice and Procedure
FINLAY A J MACDONALD, *Secretary*

Appendix 1
Membership of the Inter-Board Group
Board of Practice and Procedure
Rev Alastair H Symington, *Convener*
Rev David W Lacy
Mr Michael Gossip
Rev Marjory A MacLean
Rev Finlay A J Macdonald, *Secretary*

Board of National Mission
Rev James M Gibson
Rev Arthur P Barrie
Rev Douglas A O Nicol

Board of Ministry
Rev Professor William F Storrar
Rev John P Chalmers

Board of Parish Education
Rev John C Christie
Mr Iain W Whyte

Board of Stewardship & Finance
Rev Gordon Jamieson, Director of Stewardship

Some meetings of the Group were also attended by:

Mrs Helen McLeod (Assembly Council)
Rev Tom Macintyre, (Ecumenical Relations Committee)

Appendix 2

ACT ANENT CO-OPERATION BETWEEN PRESBYTERIES

Edinburgh, 25 May, 2002 Session 1
The General Assembly enact and ordain:

1. Subject to the provisions of this Act, a Presbytery may appoint to a special committee or commission of the Presbytery a voting member of an immediately neighbouring Presbytery.

2. Such appointments shall be made only to committees established by the Presbytery to fulfil the purposes of Act II, 1984 (as amended), Act IV, 1984 (as amended), Act I, 1988 (as amended) or Act III, 2001.

3. Such appointments shall not be made to any standing committee of the Presbytery, nor shall any appointee be granted a seat in the appointing Presbytery.

4. An individual appointed in terms of this Act shall retain membership of his or her own Presbytery for the duration of the appointment.

5. The task and function of an individual appointed in terms of this Act, and his or her responsibilities and the privileges of membership of a committee or commission, shall normally extend only to those necessary to fulfil the allocated task.

6. The reasonable expenses of an individual appointed in terms of this Act shall be met by the Presbytery making the appointment.

7. Nothing in this Act shall be taken to be an amendment or qualification of Act V, 2001.

APPENDIX H

ANNUAL REPORT OF SCOTTISH CHURCHES' PARLIAMENTARY OFFICE 2001

2001 might have been expected to be a year of consolidation for the Scottish Parliament, but matters political rarely turn out as planned. For the second year running, the autumn saw a change of First Minister, with resulting Ministerial and Committee upheaval; like any two-year-old, the Parliament is still struggling to find its feet, and continues to feel under severe pressure from the media.

Problems of their own making, some would say. Those who believe that our politicians locally and nationally are all "at it", feel their cynicism has been justified, while those with more resilient faith in the new politics are more likely to be persuaded by the claim that events have demonstrated a robust and effective level of accountability. Although there is something to be said for the latter view, public perceptions of Parliament and its politicians have taken a severe knock.

Without exciting any great public interest, Parliament's Procedures Committee has been reviewing how the Parliament is working, against the criteria set by the Consultative Steering Group - openness, accountability, power-sharing and equal opportunities; the experience of the Scottish Churches Parliamentary Office provided the basis for some input into that process, appreciating new opportunities and some imaginative approaches to getting people involved while expressing concerns at Committees meeting in private and changes in Committee membership to suit political party managers. We contributed as "stakeholders" in our Parliament, with a commitment to making it work better for the "common weal".

The bulk of the Office's workload lies in monitoring - formally and informally - what is happening in Parliament, and ensuring that the churches (locally and nationally) are well-informed about that. Around 500 people receive our monthly updates and briefings, as a resource for Bishops, Boards and Committees, for discussion and prayer groups, and for personal reflection. As well as working with churches at national level, the Office also provides practical advice on an *ad hoc* basis to local churches and groups in expressing their concerns, whether simply suggesting whom to write to or helping to set up meetings. I have also tried to stimulate interest in the churches' engagement with Parliament by accepting invitations to speak to local groups; however, as the work of the Office becomes better known, I would

expect that this will become less of a priority.

One key outcome from the monitoring process is in responses to consultation papers. It is not generally the role of the Office to write such responses, but to encourage and service churches, through their own structures, in doing so; the Office has also arranged gatherings where Scottish Executive proposals have been presented and Church representatives have been able to discuss responses, and on some topics the Office resources an ongoing ecumenical group to engage in continuing discussion with Parliament and/or Executive (eg on land reform and debt); the Scottish Churches Social Inclusion Network, for which the Office provides support, is also appreciated as a fruitful means of exchanging views and experience. Other meetings have been convened at the request of MSPs to enable them to consult with the churches on issues including sectarianism and organ transplants, and the Office regularly advises Parliamentarians on contacting the churches.

One key issue in (and beyond) 2001 has been community care, with an Executive commitment made, though not yet implemented, to ensure free personal care for all elderly people who need it; this debate has gone on in parallel with discussions on the regulation of care and on the gap between what local authorities pay for care and what that care costs voluntary care home providers (again unresolved at the time of writing). The Office has worked in partnership with the Board of Social Responsibility as well as the Salvation Army and other care providers on this.

The Office's involvement in advising and assisting with the following up of General Assembly reports and deliverances has this year also included those statements issued by the Scottish Ecumenical Assembly which were addressed to the Scottish Parliament and Executive. The range of issues on which churches express interest continues to be wide, from sex education to water charges, from asylum to civil marriage. In all these areas, the Office seeks to build expertise (in how to engage effectively with the Parliamentary process), relationships of trust, and an enhanced credibility for the contribution the churches can make.

Of course, there remain frustrations when churches

and politicians still work from behind walls, but the challenge of helping them work together to make a difference remains an exciting one.

GRAHAM K BLOUNT,
Scottish Parliamentary Officer

APPENDIX I

REPORT OF THE SCOTTISH BIBLE SOCIETY

The Scottish Bible Society's Board, staff and volunteers had a productive year, which began by renewing their vision and learning how better to tackle the challenge of bringing God's Word to the people of the world in a language they can understand, at a price they can afford and in a format they can use.

Fundraising for international Scripture needs continued with major appeals linked to Bolivia and Malawi, the second enhanced by an imaginative children's pack. The Bible-a-Month Club again stimulated substantial prayer and financial support for a range of projects, and the Guild of The Church of Scotland provided significant help for outreach among Russia's ethnic minority communities.

It is clear, however, that the challenge is not confined to overseas work. In Scotland, as Church attendance dwindles and electronic means of communication take over from traditional literacy, the Scriptures are seen as outdated and irrelevant. In response, the Society launched, in co-operation with the churches of Scotland, **HomeWORD Bound**, a five-year programme to help our *own* people rediscover, and in many cases discover for the first time, the Bible message.

Building on the success of *Faith Comes By Hearing* (Old Testament cassettes have recently been introduced) and *BIBLEWORLD* – over 65,000 children have now visited the permanent and mobile versions – fresh initiatives have been developed, including:

- *'Conversations'*, a method of 'contextual' group Bible study to help people explore how the message relates to life today;

- large posters in bus shelters, featuring Juan Sara, of Dundee United;
- adaptation of The Danish Bible Society's *'Bible Journey'* CD-ROM for use in Scottish schools;
- simple packs of Scriptures, available free for those enquiring about the Christian faith;
- Ministers' Packs, providing Bible resources to parish ministers to meet different situations, includes Scripture selections relating to the Year of the Child;
- fund-raising campaign to enable children in economically challenged areas to visit Bibleworld I and II;
- new Gaelic-English diglot published this Spring;
- plans for a brand-new, enlarged *BIBLEWORLD Experience* that will serve not only school-children but also adult groups and even tourists (this will entail major alterations to Bible House).

The **HomeWORD Bound** programme has been publicised by a Resource Pack for church leaders, a dedicated website, special window displays in Christian bookshops (linked to special **HomeWORD Bound** discounts) and public events in key cities. The speakers at two open-air presentations included the Right Reverend John Miller and other Church of Scotland leaders.

As The Scottish Bible Society looks forward, it took time to remember its past along with the local parish church in Burntisland, Fife. It was during the General Assembly in Burntisland 400 years ago, that King James VI authorised a new translation of the Scriptures.

The Society continues in the same spirit of King James, who sought to make the Scriptures accessible to all people. The Society and its friends are convinced that only by bringing the Bible to the attention of our own people through every possible medium can we challenge the widespread disengagement with the Bible and the Christian faith.

There was a time when the Scriptures spread from this island around the world; Scottish missionaries (including translators) made a vital contribution in many countries. We believe that as God's message permeates again into our individual and national life, we shall once more be better able to share it on an international scale.

APPENDIX J

THE GENDER ATTITUDE PROJECT (GAP)

This is the final report to The General Assembly of The Gender Attitude Project (GAP). Through these reports, discussions with groups and individuals within the Church, at workshops and in producing resources for the Church, GAP has endeavoured to raise awareness of gender issues. In essence, the work of GAP has been in fulfilment of the great command of Jesus - to love one another - in the conviction that sexism, discrimination, violence based upon gender and exclusive practices are all failures to obey that command. In a changing culture and church there are encouraging signs of the Church becoming a community of respect, equality and justice. There are still, however, sexist attitudes held and comments made which would immediately be seen as unacceptable and offensive if they were directed at black people, disabled people or children. Yet, because women are the 'targets' these attitudes and comments are thought to be acceptable and often viewed as hilariously funny.

The work of GAP has been reviewed by a small group appointed by The Board of Practice and Procedure. This has been a valuable exercise for the members of GAP and a summary of the report of the Review Group is found at Section 10. GAP believes that the style of the review is unique and perhaps worthy of noting by other groups within the Church who wish to review where they have come from, where they are going, and what has happened on the journey.

GAP Research Project

Much of the work of GAP in this last year has been the production of the Research Project, now published and distributed around the Church under the title 'The Stained Glass Ceiling'. Its publication attracted a good degree of press interest, largely due to a feature in 'Life and Work.' GAP welcomed this coverage and debate for much of it confirmed the necessity of gender awareness work.

GAP is very grateful to the research student, Susan Wiltshire, and to all who completed questionnaires or agreed to be interviewed by her, individually or in focus groups. The Research Project took 'snapshots' of urban and rural situations and looked for attitudes towards gender in these pictures.

Part of its value is the fact that a relative 'outsider' is looking at an institution and seeing it with eyes undimmed by familiarity. In this report it is possible only to draw attention to some of the conclusions:

- women in rural areas seem subject to more acute forms of sexism than those in an urban setting;
- sexist and discriminatory practices can be clandestine and taken for granted, such as in the use of language;
- theology is used as a basis to oppose female ministers, especially by male ministers and elders;
- Church culture continues to be imbued with maleness, possibly to a greater extent, but certainly not less so than culture generally;
- women ministers are seen as 'better' in some roles.

The process of producing the Research Project also gave rise to features of note. First, there was the difficulty in securing funding and, while finance is tight in all corners of the Church, there was a feeling that research into an area easily dismissed as 'women's issues' was not worthy of funding. Secondly, some people responded to approaches to be interviewed, and to the request for questionnaires to be completed, in rather dismissive ways: gender 'is not an issue,' 'a total waste of money,' 'a load of feminist nonsense'. It is unfortunate that a subject which is one of major debate in all Christian churches and in society at large - the roles women and men occupy and how they relate to one another - is of so little concern to some in the Church. Thirdly, many individuals, particularly women, when approached to give an account of their experiences within the Church, agreed to do so only with the safeguard of their anonymity. GAP believes that a culture within the Church in which people are afraid to talk about their lives is a culture that is unhealthy, dishonest and has to be challenged. It is apparent that to try to raise awareness of gender issues in the church is often to be faced with hostility, rejection or isolation. A concerned attempt to engage with the issues - or even simply to acknowledge hurt and anger - would be preferable. (In contrast, people outwith the Church often tell GAP members to 'keep up the good work!')

A disturbing feature of the research were the quotations from individuals. Here is a small selection, from men and women:

'I'm sorry that women do feel they have to work twice as hard as a man to prove themselves, I think that's a sad fact but I think it's real'.

'I think perhaps there should be a gender discussion in the Church because ... there are still gender problems between ministers and I mean that's not just the new ones, that's the older ones as well'.

'In one instance, a man had said. 'women shouldn't be ministers because they menstruate ... [And] if women in class [at university] asked a question, men would always laugh'.

'At Presbytery level it's still the men that tend to rule the roost ... it's a group of men who tend to exercise the bulk of the power both in terms of how people speak in meetings as well as what happens behind the scenes'.

Challenging this is difficult: 'they see you as being a freak'.

The underlying issue is that of power - a subject currently under examination by The Panel on Doctrine. Who holds power in the institution of the Church and how is this power used? A contribution to 'The Stained Glass Ceiling', written by student Rachael Barber, offers these comments:

The first influence on gender relations is the concept of power. Respondents were uncomfortable with the notion of power within the Church, yet could identify its existence. ...... In addressing the issue of power and achievement it is important to note that power was widely recognised within the Church. If The Church of Scotland fails to face up to its existence and association with particular roles then it cannot properly address the question of whether there is equal access to these roles.

Secondly, to some extent we can regard the existence of such power as embedded within the institution. Statistically, the Church leadership is still male dominated and from speaking to ministers I think it is still a largely patriarchal institution in its organisation. This does not reflect the make up of the congregations but plays out strongly in relation to how power is expressed.

In discussing 'The Stained Glass Ceiling,' the concerns it awakes and the questions it poses, GAP felt that there were two key areas requiring the attention of the Church:

- **Education and Awareness Raising**
- The Church of Scotland, through The General Assembly, has made clear what the law of the Church is in regard to the participation of women in the structures of the Church. But the law of the Church cannot change attitudes or encourage people to rethink their theology and the reasons why they hold certain views. This requires forms of education and awareness raising - not necessarily with the aim of everyone believing the same but certainly with the aim of nurturing relationships of respect, mutuality and justice between all people within the Church.

- **Ministerial Formation**
- Ordained ministers of Word and Sacrament do have a large influence upon the ethos of the church and its congregations. It is crucial that the ministers are aware of gender issues, sensitive to the differing pastoral needs of women and men and trained in good practice. GAP is encouraged by the overall tone of recent Board of Ministry reports on ministerial formation and the content of conferences for trainee ministers.

Sexual Harassment

'After having been asked about my marital status, I was then asked about my sexual habits as part of a 'normal' conversation'.

'A married clergyman kept 'phoning and calling round expecting to be invited in'.

1. What is sexual harassment?

The United Kingdom Equal Opportunities Commission web site offers this definition:

It is usually taken to mean unwelcome physical, verbal or non-verbal conduct of a sexual nature including

- *comments about the way you look which you find demeaning*
- *indecent remarks*
- *questions about your sex life*
- *sexual demands by a member of your own or the opposite sex*
- *any conduct of a sexual nature which creates an intimidating, hostile or humiliating environment for you.*

In the majority of instances it is women who are being sexually harassed; men can also be subjected to sexual harassment, although this is not so common. Additionally, both men and women can be sexually harassed by persons of the same sex.

2. Sexual Harassment and The Law

Under the United Kingdom Sex Discrimination Act all employees have a legal right not to be sexually harassed while at work. Other relevant legislation includes the Employment Rights Act and The European Commission's Code of Practice on The Protection of The Dignity of Women and Men at Work. It is possible for supposed victims to use the law to exercise power over another: people have been accused of sexual harassment or abuse who were in fact innocent. These abuses of the legal system do not destroy the validity and necessity of the system itself.

Many organisations who have a responsibility of care towards others - which includes their employees - deem it important and appropriate to have procedures in place which allow for victims and perpetrators to know their rights, to know what is unacceptable behaviour and know that investigation and discipline will be enforced. Some employers, such as universities and NHS Trusts, have made clear statements on sexual harassment and will not countenance behaviour in their workplaces which, sadly, ministers can suffer in theirs and which church members can suffer within congregations. The unusual status of ministers within employment law should not exempt churches from tackling this subject which is one of justice and dignity.

3. The Churches and Sexual Harassment

Sexual harassment is not only about employment rights and the legislation designed to protect all parties. For the churches there is the important matter of the professional integrity and conduct of clergy and the formation of Christian congregations as safe places. Sexual harassment can and does happen in the contexts of pastoral counselling and care, youth work, social gatherings and Church meetings.

In their leaflet <u>Sexual Harassment and Sexual Abuse - Affirming Human Dignity</u> the World Alliance of Reformed Churches (WARC) places this subject in a theological context. Based upon the basic dignity of all humankind as created in the image of God sexual harassment is identified as a form of violence against people - predominantly against women. Sexual violence, in all of its forms, is one aspect of the brokennness of the human family. Sexual harassment often takes place within the context of unequal power relationships and as such is an abuse of power by one person over another; it is *'the treatment of people as sexual objects which demeans and destroys their dignity'*.

WARC goes on to say: *'Sexual harassment is defined as any form of sexual advance that is uninvited, unwanted and unwelcome. These advances come in the forms of obscene gestures, inappropriate closeness and touching, suggestive looks and pressure for dates or activities with sexual overtones'*. WARC confesses *'that even within its gatherings, our families and churches, sexual harassment does occur'*.

In the light of these realities WARC is committed to establishing policy, guidelines and a process to deal with the incidence of sexual harassment ***and encourages its member churches to do likewise.***

In many places in the Christian Church action has been taken. The **Church of England** has been challenged on this subject following a report (Feb. 1998) by the trade union MSF (Clergy and Church Workers Section) - <u>Are Anglican Women Priests Being Bullied and</u>

<u>Harassed</u>? This survey, from which the two quotations above are taken, found, for example, that 40% of the women questioned had experienced verbal abuse and 10% some form of physical abuse and that in the majority of cases the perpetrator was a clergyman. It was apparent that some ordained women had suffered sexual harassment; unfortunately the experiences of lay women were not surveyed. Clearly, the context of The Church of England is very different to The Church of Scotland but the attitudes revealed are remarkably similar to the experiences of women in *'The Stained Glass Ceiling.'*

The Presbyterian Church (USA) has an extensive document outlining policy and procedures on sexual misconduct, seeking to safeguard *'the integrity of the ministerial, employment and professional relationship.'* Many Presbyteries of the PCUSA have created their own policies. **The Methodist Church in the United Kingdom**, at its Conference in 1997, received a report on Sexual Harassment and Abuse. This led to the development of the 'Safeguarding Policy' which is chiefly in relation to work with children and young people but work on sexual harassment is continuing. **Churches Together In Britain and Ireland (CTBI)** will shortly be producing a document on sexual abuse which will call for reflection and action by its member denominations.

4. *The Church of Scotland*

The Church of Scotland has met its legal obligations and produced policy and procedure to protect its children and young people but it is also the case that adults in the Church - whether volunteers or employees - can be subjected to inappropriate behaviour usually by persons of trust and authority. GAP believes that the unacceptability of sexual abuse and sexual harassment is self-evident but it is not enough to simply pass motions of condemnation. It is also necessary:

—to create an awareness of attitudes which are discriminatory and of language, gestures and touches which may insult the dignity of others;
—to make the Church a place of safety where victims feel able to speak out in confidence that they will be respected and listened to;
—that the community and processes of the Church seek justice and restitution for all parties.

This requires transparent, workable and fair codes of conduct and disciplinary procedures.

Within the 'secular world' there is good practice which often the Church is slow to follow. In contrast, the Church ought to be setting an example to society of best practice and to put in place policies, guidelines and procedures to deal with the incidence of sexual harassment.

The GAP Closes

This final report of The Gender Attitude Project closes with the hope that the work it has done will continue in some new form and also closes with words of thanks: to the men and women who have given of their time and insights, either for a short while or for the whole life time of the group; to Sheilagh Kesting and Marjory MacLean who have served as Secretaries; and to the Committee on Ecumenical Relations, the Committee on Church and Nation and the Board of Practice and Procedure for their support.

THE BOARD OF MINISTRY
and
THE CHURCH OF SCOTLAND PENSION TRUSTEES
MAY 2002

PROPOSED JOINT DELIVERANCE

The General Assembly:

1. Receive the Report.

2. Note the improvements and approve the necessary integrated changes to the Ministers' Pension Scheme Rules as described in Sections 2 and 3 of the Report.

3. Agree that the improvements to the Ministers' Pension Scheme will be introduced in 2004 when the National Minimum Stipend Scale is implemented ('the Implementation Date').

JOINT REPORT

THE CHURCH OF SCOTLAND PENSION SCHEME FOR MINISTERS
AND OVERSEAS MISSIONARIES

1. Introduction

1.1 The Pension Trustees reported to the 2001 General Assembly that, following the improvements to the pension payable from the Main Pension Fund, the original target pension of one half of the Minimum Stipend and Service Supplement had been reached, at which point the intention had been to phase out contributions to the Insured Pension Fund. Accordingly, the 2001 General Assembly noted that the Pension Trustees will commence discussions with the Board of Ministry regarding the Insured Pension Fund.

1.2 Whilst primarily setting out to consider the future of the Insured Pension Fund, the opinion was that this could not be done in isolation from the other pension benefits and from proposals for a National Minimum Stipend Scale. Furthermore, it was felt that the manse, which is a substantial financial benefit during a Minister's employment, should be reflected in the amount of the pension.

1.3 It was decided to consider the Parish Ministers' complete benefit package and to link any pension proposals to the implementation of the proposed National Minimum Stipend Scale. This Joint Report sets out the pension proposals which would be implemented at the same time as the Stipend Scale.

2. Proposed Amendments to the Main Pension Fund Benefits

2.1 Pension from the Main Pension Fund

The pension from the Main Pension Fund is currently based on service multiplied by 1/40th of the Standard Annuity. For some years, the Standard Annuity has been one half of the Minimum Stipend and the Maximum

Service Supplement. It is proposed that the Trustees no longer declare a Standard Annuity but that the pension from the Main Pension Fund be based on the National Minimum Stipend Scale and, for a Minister living in a manse, the Manse Allowance as specified by the Inland Revenue (currently £7,119).

The inclusion of the Manse Allowance, for Ministers living in a manse, means that the financial benefit of the manse is carried forward to the pension calculation in respect of service after the implementation date.

Based on current factors a Minister with 30 years' service would, under the current pension formula, have a pension of £8,589 (=30/40 x £11,452 (Standard Annuity in 2002)). Under the National Minimum Stipend Scale at the maximum level and once the Manse Allowance applies for the whole service, the pension would be £12,312 (=30/80 x (25,713 +7,119)).

2.2 Incapacity Pension

If a Minister has to retire on the grounds of ill health, and subject to medical evidence, an enhanced pension based on service to age 65 is granted. Under the new proposals, the pension in respect of future service would be based on the higher rate including, for a Minister living in a manse, the Manse Allowance leading to improved incapacity pensions.

2.3 Death in Service Benefits

2.3.1 Lump Sum Death Benefit: At current rates, the inclusion of the Manse Allowance produces a potential increase of £21,357 making a total benefit of £77,568 on death in service prior to the Normal Retirement Age up to age 75.

2.3.2 Widow(er)'s Pension: On a Minister's death in service prior to age 65, the widow(er) will become entitled to a pension based on the Minister's potential service to age 65. Under the new proposals, the widow(er)'s pension in respect of this future service to age 65 would be based on the new higher rate including, for a Minister living in a manse, the Manse Allowance leading to improved widow(er)s' pensions.

3. Contributions

3.1 Ministers' Contributions: It is proposed that the present payment by Ministers of 2% of the Minimum Stipend to the Insured Pension Fund would cease and instead all Ministers would contribute 2½% of their National Minimum Stipend into the Main Pension Fund. Ministers, whose compulsory contributions are paid to the old Endowment Contract at various rates depending on their date of commencement, would be allowed to continue their contributions to these policies on a voluntary basis, if they wished.

3.2 Congregational Contributions: Under the National Minimum Stipend Scale, the employer's contribution rate to the Main Pension Fund is 20% of stipends paid to Ministers. All congregations will contribute towards this requirement based on their recurring income level, subject to the Board of Ministry's policy relating to allowances during vacancies. (See Board of Ministry Report, Section 5.2.6.4). Congregational contributions to the Insured Pension Fund would cease from the Implementation Date.

4. Conclusion

4.1 The proposals would lead to higher pension benefits based on the final Stipend according to the National Minimum Stipend Scale and including the Manse Allowance.

4.2 All Ministers would contribute towards the higher pension benefits but the compulsory contributions to the Insured Pension Fund would cease. The overall contribution rate of 2½% of stipend is not significantly higher than the rate of 2% Ministers are currently required to pay to the Insured Pension Fund.

4.3 Although the employer's contribution rate to the Main Pension Fund remains at 20% of stipends paid to Ministers, those congregations who contribute currently to the Insured Pension Fund will see a reduction in their total pension contributions.

4.4 The Insured Pension Fund would be purely for Ministers' own Additional Voluntary Contributions (AVCs) after the Implementation Date. However, any proceeds in respect of Ministers' compulsory contributions and any congregational contributions paid on Ministers' behalf prior to the Implementation Date will be used for the Ministers' own benefit subject to the overall limits set by the Inland Revenue.

4.5 Under the current arrangement the Insured Pension Fund provides a tax-free cash sum from Ministers' compulsory contributions and congregational contributions, subject to the overall limits set by the Inland Revenue. This cash has been perceived to be useful towards the purchase of a house at retiral. However, with the Funds available as cash from these contributions varying in practice from about £7,000 to about £45,000, the overall help in this regard is limited and unequal. Under the new proposal, a Minister who wishes to use the Pension Scheme to provide capital could still do so by commuting, subject to Inland Revenue Rules, part of the higher Main Pension Fund pension.

4.6 The Board of Ministry and the Pension Trustees believe strongly that the pension proposals will lead to an improved and simplified Pension Scheme for Ministers, which would allow the benefit of the manse to be taken into account in the pension. Above all, the proposals would ultimately eliminate the problems of inequality and unfairness inherent in the current system where Ministers with the same service can receive widely differing benefits from the Insured Pension Fund.

In the name of the Board of Ministry

WILLIAM F STORRAR, *Convener*
R DOUGLAS CRANSTON, *Vice Convener*
CHRISTINE M GOLDIE, *Vice Convener*
WILLIAM GREENOCK, *Vice Convener*
IAN TAYLOR, *Vice Convener*
RUTH MOIR, *General Secretary*
ALEXANDER McDONALD, *Senior Adviser
for Pastoral Care*
JOHN CHALMERS, *Depute General Secretary*

In the name of the Pension Trustees

WILLIAM D B CAMERON, *Chairman*
JOHN W McCAFFERTY, *Vice-Chairman*
SIRKKA DENNISON, *Pensions Manager*

GENERAL TRUSTEES

MAY 2002

PROPOSED DELIVERANCE

The General Assembly:

1. Receive the Report and Accounts of the General Trustees.

2. (a) Record their appreciation of the contributions made by Mr Roderick Macdonald and Mr Stewart Tod to the work of the General Trustees and thank them for their service.

   (b) Re-appoint Mr William S Carswell as Chairman and Rev. James H Simpson as Vice- Chairman for the ensuing year and authorise the making of a payment of £1,158 to each of them for their services during the past year (1).

3. Urge the Scottish Ministers to make available to Historic Scotland significantly increased funding for the provision of grants towards the cost of maintenance of buildings listed as being of special architectural or historic interest (2.5).

4. Remind congregations of the availability of the Better Heating Scheme under which skilled advice can be obtained in the matters of saving money on heating bills and improving the standard of comfort in buildings (4).

5. Encourage congregations to give the General Trustees authority to act on their behalf to agree or terminate electricity and gas supply contracts (4).

6. Approve and adopt the Amendment to the Guidelines for Reallocation of Endowments as set out in Appendix 2 to the Report (5).

7. Remind Fabric Committees of congregations that manses must be inspected at least once a year and any necessary remedial works undertaken timeously (8).

REPORT

1. Introduction and Composition of Trust

The Church of Scotland General Trustees submit to the Assembly their seventy-seventh Report since the passing of the Church of Scotland (Property and Endowments) Act of 1925.

The Trustees regret to report the retirement at this Assembly of Mr Roderick Macdonald BSc, MSc and Mr Stewart Tod RIBA, FRIAS. Roddy Macdonald who had previously been a member of the Land Court was appointed a General Trustee in 1993 and has been particularly involved in the work of the Glebes Committee where his wise counsel and negotiating skills will be greatly missed. Stewart Tod who was appointed to the Board in 1982 is one of Scotland's leading architects with particular expertise in relation to historic buildings. His contribution to the work of the Trustees' Fabric Committee has been immense and many Congregations up and down the country have benefited from his practical advice.

The Trustees recommend that Mr William S Carswell MA, LLB and Rev. James H Simpson BD, LLB should be re-appointed Chairman and Vice-Chairman respectively for the ensuing year and that for their services for the past year they should each receive remuneration of £1,158 as authorised by Section 38 Sub-Section 1 of the 1925 Act.

2. Fabric Matters

2.1 Central Fabric Fund

The following is a synopsis of grants and loans made from the Central Fabric Fund during 2001. In cases where a grant or loan has been made in respect of work at more than one building, the amount involved has been apportioned and the apportioned amounts treated as separate grants and loans for the purpose of the numbers given. In view of falls in interest rates the General Trustees resolved in October 2001 that in the case of future loans and loans which had been voted but not taken up the normal rate of interest should be reduced from 6% to 5% and that the rate of interest on bridging loans should be reduced from 2% to $1^1/_2$% above base rate. Where the circumstances were considered to justify this, loans were made at the rate of 4% per annum or on an interest free basis.

| | Total | | Churches | | Manses | | Halls | |
	No.	Amount	No.	Amount	No.	Amount	No.	Amount
Grants	155	£654,822	84	£374,782	35	£147,000	36	£133,040
Loans free of Interest	11	£87,397	6	£30,062	2	£44,135	3	£13,200
Loans at Interest of 4%	24	£356,000	14	£219,500	4	£58,000	6	£78,500
Loans at Interest of 6/5%	68	£2,062,950	38	£993,625	10	£232,200	20	£837,125
Bridging Loans	6	£745,000	1	£18,000	5	£727,000	-	-

Against the figure of £654,822 voted by way of grants in 2001 has to be offset the sum of £57,715 being grants voted which have lapsed or been cancelled. This means that the net figure which the General Trustees made available by way of grant in 2001 was £597,107 – the equivalent figure in 2000 having been £640,430.

Although the Trustees have been able to give valuable assistance from the Fund in many cases, they are concerned by their inability to assist in a meaningful way congregations with limited resources, particularly those in Urban Priority Areas, facing significant fabric expenditure. Such congregations do not have the resources to repay even an interest free loan of any magnitude and a grant of £8,000 which has been the normal maximum from the Fund during 2001 is little more than a token gesture in such cases.

2.2 Care of Ecclesiastical Properties

In terms of the relevant legislation, Presbyteries have to report diligence to the General Trustees on fabric matters by 31st December each year. The returns to hand at the time of the preparation of the Report revealed that in 43 Presbyteries, 1322 Property Registers out of 1334 had been examined and all had been found satisfactory. In the same Presbyteries, the properties of 224 congregations had been inspected during the year to 30th June 2001.

A Sub-Committee of the General Trustees is currently reviewing the working of the Act anent Care of Ecclesiastical Properties.

2.3 Consolidated Fabric Fund

The Consolidated Fabric Fund was created with effect from 31st March 1996 when the value of each share was £1. The share value at 31st December 2001 was £1.17.

2.4 Millennium Project Fund

In 1999 following receipt of a non-recurring and exceptional payment from the Church of Scotland Insurance Company, the General Trustees set up a Millennium Project Fund and, as reported to last year's Assembly, the Trustees invited all Presbyteries to put forward for possible assistance imaginative and creative schemes which would enable officebearers with vision and enthusiasm to make a real difference to their congregation's work and witness. By the date fixed for submissions, 58 schemes had been proposed and a group of Trustees has, in consultation with representatives of the Board of Stewardship and Finance and the Committees on New Charge Development and Parish Reappraisal, been sifting through the submissions and examining in depth those considered to be of particular merit. At the October 2001 meeting of the Fabric Committee the following awards were made:

Duntocher Trinity —demolition of halls and internal re-ordering of church	£300,000
Monkton and Prestwick North —provision of multi-purpose facilities at Monkton	£130,000
New Deer St Kane's —completion of Church Centre	£150,000
Skene —extension to Westhill Church	£175,000

A number of other submissions were being investigated further at the time of the preparation of this Report and it is anticipated that by the time of the General Assembly further awards will have been made.

The General Trustees have been impressed by the imagination shown in the proposals put forward and by the enthusiasm of the officebearers concerned. They are sorry that the finite resources at their disposal mean that they will not be able to give assistance in as many cases as they would have liked.

2.5 Historic Buildings

The General Trustees are becoming increasingly concerned about the ability of the Church to meet potential liabilities arising from the ownership of a significant number of buildings listed as being of special architectural or historic interest. They do not believe that it is one of the prime purposes of the Church to assist in maintaining buildings which are no longer required for Church purposes but remain part of the nation's built heritage. They are finding, however, that significant amounts of our resources are being consumed to that end.

The Assembly of 2001 instructed the General Trustees to enter into discussions with the Scottish Executive and/or the Government at Westminster with a view to increasing the funding of Historic Scotland to allow grants of up to 95% of the costs of repair to Church buildings listed as Category A. On the basis that any approach would carry more weight if it was not from a single denomination, the General Trustees have asked the Scottish Churches Committee which is representative of the main Christian Churches in Scotland to take this matter up and they hope to be able to report further at the General Assembly.

Coincidentally a Consultation Paper was issued last year by Historic Scotland on Grants for the Repair of Historic Buildings, comments being invited by 30th November 2001. The General Trustees submitted a detailed response to this Paper stating *inter alia* that Historic Scotland was being asked to fulfil a remit which could be done properly only if significantly more funds were made available and opposing a proposal that grants to places of worship should be capped. In furtherance of the initiative taken through the Scottish Churches Committee, the Trustees ask the Assembly to urge the Scottish Ministers to make significantly increased funding available.

The General Trustees welcome the Government's Listed Places of Worship Grant Scheme under which grant aid equivalent to a reduction of the rate of VAT from 17.5% to 5% is available towards the cost of repairs and maintenance of listed buildings which are used principally as places of worship. They trust that it will not be too long before the scheme is replaced by an actual reduction in the rate of VAT to the lower figure.

3. Determinations Under Act VII 1995

The General Trustees report that they have under Act VII 1995 made 89 determinations as set out in Appendix 1 to the Report.

4. Heating, Lighting and Sound Systems and Water Charges

Mr Andrew W MacOwan who was appointed the General Trustees' Energy Consultant in January 2000 has been retained in that capacity and continues to carry on the good work previously undertaken by Mr Brian Marks and Mr Archie Strang. At 31st December 2001, 1655 surveys (including repeat surveys) of church buildings had been carried out under the Better Heating Scheme and 153 surveys of manses. The Trustees again ask the Assembly to remind congregations that for a modest fee towards which the Trustees offer a subsidy and which is a fair charge on monies held for a congregation in the Consolidated Fabric Fund, Mr MacOwan will provide a survey of buildings incorporating advice on how to save money on heating bills and improve the standard of comfort.

The General Trustees also retain Argyle Energy of Stirling to advise them on energy prices and to negotiate with suppliers with a view to ensuring that congregations obtain advantageous terms for electricity and gas. During 2001, a new arrangement was made with Northern Electricity for the supply by that Company of gas and agreement was reached with Scottish Gas on terms for the supply of electricity over the two year period from March 2002.

In a volatile market, decisions on suppliers may have to be made speedily and the General Trustees have been hampered in their negotiations by the fact that while they may recommend a particular deal the approval of the individual congregation is required to any change of supplier. In an effort to strengthen their position with suppliers, the General Trustees have contacted congregations and asked for authority to make decisions on suppliers on their behalf for, say, a three year period. The Trustees ask the Assembly to encourage congregations to give such authority.

The General Assembly of 2001 instructed the General Trustees to arrange for expert advice to be available to congregations on how to minimise their liability for water and waste water charges in view of the proposed withdrawal of remission. The Trustees have made an arrangement with Argyle Energy under which they will provide a telephone helpline through which guidance will be given at a modest cost. Advice is also available from the Water Authority.

In addition to their Energy Consultant the Trustees have a Lighting Consultant, Mr Hugh J Nicholl and a Sound Systems Consultant, Mr John McDonald who can provide advice to congregations for reasonable fees. Further information regarding heating, lighting and sound systems surveys and the telephone helpline on water charges is available from the Trustees' Secretary's Department.

5. Reallocation of Endowments

The Regulations anent the Application of Stipend and Fabric Endowments (Regulations 5 1995) provide a machinery for the possible reallocation of endowments held by the General Trustees for the benefit of congregations. The effect of the Determinations made during 2001 was as follows:-

(i) Blantyre: Old: Income on 28,670 unallocated shares in the Consolidated Stipend Fund applied to the benefit of the Minimum Stipend Fund.

(ii) Cairngryffe: £50,000 reallocated from fabric to stipend.

(iii) Edinburgh: St Andrew's Clermiston: £60,000 reallocated from fabric to stipend.

(iv) Elderslie: £15,033 reallocated from fabric to stipend.

(v) Farnell: £20,000 reallocated from fabric to stipend.

(vi) North Knapdale: £6,816 reallocated from fabric to stipend.

The Guidelines for Reallocation of Endowments which were approved by the General Assembly of 1995 provided that in the case of stipend monies reallocations were to be reallocations of capital while in the case of fabric monies reallocations might be of capital or of revenue. The rationale for this was that in the past there had been cases where income on Special Funds held for fabric purposes had, for a period, been allocated to assist with stipend. It was not, however, envisaged that income on holdings in the Consolidated Stipend Fund would be applied for fabric purposes. In a case which arose in 2001 the Board of Ministry felt that it might be appropriate, because of a possible change of circumstances in the future, for income on monies held for stipend purposes to be made available to assist on the fabric side. The Board suggested that the Trustees might request the Assembly to alter the Guidelines to cater for such circumstances. The General Trustees were happy to take the matter up and a suggested alteration to the Guidelines is set out in Appendix 2.

6. Stipend Matters

6.1 Consolidated Stipend Fund

As reported to last year's Assembly the General Trustees commissioned a firm of Actuaries and Consultants to review the investment policy which the Trustees had been following in connection with the Consolidated Stipend Fund. The Consultants came down strongly in favour of continued and, indeed, additional investment in the Growth Fund of the Church of Scotland Investors Trust. Against a background of lower longer term interest rates and the progressive loss of tax credits which will by 2004 reduce the total income from UK dividends by 20%, the Consultants concluded that the current level of support to stipends from the Fund could not be sustained in real terms without running a high risk of depleting the capital. They indicated, however, that by operating the Fund on a total return basis it might be possible in the medium term of ten years to sustain the present rate of dividend. After consultation with the Board of Ministry the Trustees, having obtained an estimate of the income likely to be available in 2002, agreed to hold the dividend for that year at £0.1830 per share. This represents an income yield of 4.5% on the share value at 31st December 2001 and although it does involve the paying of a dividend greater than the estimated income on the Fund for the year it is not considered that it is likely that there will be any encroachment into capital.

The Trustees are continuing to monitor the position and the investment policy will be reviewed in 2003 or earlier if need be.

The following statistics reflect the position over the past five years.

Capital	Total Value	Value of Share
31st December 1997	£50,883,313	£4.0401
31st December 1998	£55,601,217	£4.3764
31st December 1999	£60,573,638	£4.7116
31st December 2000	£59,278,098	£4.5708
31st December 2001	£54,141,935	£4.0657

Revenue	Net Income	Shares Issued at 31st December	Rate of Dividend
1997	£2,154,014	12,594,559	£0.1675
1998	£2,388,528	12,704,692	£0.1717
1999	£2,452,284	12,856,323	£0.1803
2000	£2,516,281	12,968,756	£0.1830
2001	£2,399,302	13,316,896	£0.1830

During 2001 the sum of £1,504,327 was admitted to the Fund in exchange for 357,182 shares.

6.2   Glebes

The difficult times through which farmers have been going during the past few years were compounded in 2001 by the outbreak of foot and mouth disease. The Trustees reacted (a) by agreeing to cancel contracts in cases where land had been let on a seasonal grazing basis but the taker had not been able to stock it and (b) by issuing with the rent notices sent out to agricultural tenants in May a paper indicating that they were prepared to look sympathetically at requests for a possible remission of rent where the circumstances of the individual cases so justified. A number of such requests were received and dealt with accordingly. This and the cancellation of seasonal grazing contracts resulted in a loss of income for stipend purposes of £15,168 but in order that congregations were not disadvantaged the Board of Ministry generously agreed to make available an equivalent sum.

In view of the current agricultural climate, the General Trustees have suspended the normal reviews of agricultural rents.

In 2001 the net income (including the subvention from the Board of Ministry) from Glebes was £307,718. The comparable figure for 2000 was £312,674.

7.   Finance

The General Trustees' Accounts for the year 2001 audited by the Auditor of the Church will be laid on the table at the General Assembly. A synopsis of the position at 31st December 2001 based on the most up-to-date information available at the time of the preparation of this Report is as follows:-

	2001	2000 Restated
	£	£
Stipend Funds	54,130,591	59,272,991
Glebe Funds	222,377	96,650
Consolidated Fabric Fund	31,889,040	32,872,812
Individual Funds	7,195,315	7,954,470
Central Fabric Fund	8,352,444	6,803,949
General Fund	2,217,582	7,232,841
Millennium Project Fund	1,232,376	1,500,000
Subsidiary Company Fund	4,357,900	—
	109,597,625	115,733,713

During 2001, £158,746 was received in respect of the redemption of feuduties and standard charges.

The General Trustees intend that the Accountants appointed to audit the Accounts of the Assembly Boards and Committees for 2002 should also be appointed to audit their Accounts for that year.

8.   Manses

As will be seen from Appendix 1, during the year 2001, the General Trustees passed twenty-six determinations authorising the sales of manses. In some of these cases the sale followed upon reappraisal but in seventeen instances the object was to provide a more suitable house for the incumbent. The General Trustees welcome the provision of better accommodation for our ministers either by the acquisition of a more acceptable property or the upgrading of an existing one. They are concerned, however, that not all manses are being satisfactorily maintained and they ask the Assembly to remind Fabric Committees of congregations that manses must be inspected at least once every year and any necessary remedial works undertaken.

9.   Land Reform

The Trustees reported to last year's Assembly on the Abolition of Feudal Tenure etc (Scotland) Act of 2000 commenting that the majority of the substantive provisions were not to come into operation until an appointed day which had not been fixed but which was likely to be within the following two or three years. The appointed day has not yet been set and it has been indicated that it will not be set until further legislation relating to title conditions has been enacted. It is believed that the date is unlikely to be earlier than 2005.

Meantime the Land Reform Bill has been introduced into the Scottish Parliament. It deals mainly with the creation of rights of pedestrian access over all land apart from certain categories of exempt land and with the community and crofters' right to buy. As indicated by the Chairman at last year's Assembly, the General Trustees had responded to an earlier Consultation Paper expressing particular concern about the impact of the so called "right to roam" on land on the outskirts of towns and villages and pressing for the establishment of a properly funded paths network in urban fringes. The issues in the Bill are proving controversial and it remains to be seen what the exact provisions of the eventual Act will be.

10. Administration

The Assembly of 2001 instructed the General Trustees, in consultation with the Boards of Ministry, National Mission and Stewardship and Finance and in the light of what was said in Appendix 9 to the Report of the Special Commission anent Review and Reform, to consider how best the properties and funds vested in them or under their control could be applied and invested to further the aims of the developing Church and to report to the Assembly of 2003.

In the first instance the General Trustees obtained an Opinion from the Procurator on what, if any, limits there were on their powers to follow through the type of proposal made in Appendix 9 and at the time of the preparation of this Report the Trustees were in consultation with the three Boards mentioned above. The Trustees will report fully on the matter to next year's Assembly.

11. Insurance

The Church of Scotland Insurance Company, which is owned by the General Trustees, continues to insure Church of Scotland properties, including those vested in the General Trustees. The Company, either by itself or as agent, provides cover for all classes of insurance.

Congregations are encouraged to have their properties professionally valued for insurance purposes. If such a valuation results in a substantial increase in the sum insured, then the Company will usually agree to restrict the additional premium for up to two years to assist the congregation concerned. Valuations can also result in the sum insured being reduced. This is because each year the Company, after taking professional advice, indexes sums insured on the basis of the cost of reinstating a stone-built church. In the case of a modern building this may give some scope for shading the sum insured. The General Trustees commend those Presbyteries which have had all buildings within the bounds valued. As well

as ensuring that buildings are insured adequately this also means the cost of a valuation is lower than it would be if individual valuations were commissioned.

Congregations are reminded that it is their responsibility to ensure that their particular sums insured are regularly checked and remain adequate. An automatic increase can never correct a sum insured which is fundamentally inaccurate.

The Company continues to grant discounts for churches insured for more than £2.5m with a further discount for buildings insured for more than £5m. There are also discounts for manses insured for more than £250,000, with an additional discount if insured for more than £500,000.

The number of fire claims is small, being fourteen last year, but malicious fire raising and vandalism remain the most common cause of loss having been responsible for eleven losses with one, which is thought to have been caused by children, settled for a sum in excess of £100,000. Most of the claims were caused by children or young persons on an opportunist basis and all buildings should be inspected regularly to ensure that there are no gaps in doors or windows through which matches or lighted paper can be pushed. All doors and windows should be lockfast when buildings are not in use. One of the other claims was caused by an electrical fault and two by lightning strikes.

Fabric Conveners are reminded to insist that contractors working with heat on buildings comply with the recommendations of the Loss Prevention Council so that claims arising from this source can be reduced, or even eliminated. The loss of a roof can take up to three years to restore with consequent disruption to the work and witness of the congregation. It is also important that Fabric Conveners, or their professional advisers, ensure that any tradesman working on a building has Public Liability insurance with a minimum limit of indemnity of £2m. A recent loss caused by a tradesman using heat on a roof cost over £1m but because Liability insurance was in place the Company was able to recover almost 85% of its outlay.

To ensure that delays in rebuilding are kept to a minimum, if plans of buildings no longer exist, it is worthwhile for a comprehensive photographic record to be made, especially of those parts which are not normally seen such as the roof construction and the interior of spires and steeples. Such records assist in restoration and should be lodged in a place other than the church building.

The Trustees' Quinquennial Insurance Conference was held in Edinburgh in October. Most Presbyteries were represented and other parties with an interest in historic buildings, architecture and our heritage also attended. The topics discussed included "The Vulnerability of Buildings from Fire" by the Head of Fire Safety at Lothians and Borders Fire Brigade, "Disaster Recovery Planning" by a speaker from the Ecclesiastical Insurance Company, Gloucester, "Health and Safety and the Church" by a representative of the Norwich Union, Perth and "The Valuation of Church Buildings" by a Director of GAB Robins, Chartered Loss Adjusters, Glasgow. The Conference was well received by delegates and the General Trustees trust that congregational Fabric Conveners have been made aware of the topics discussed.

The claims experience on classes of insurance other than fire has improved slightly over the last year. This is to be welcomed as it enables the Insurance Company to resist increases in rates which are being applied to other sections. Nevertheless the insurers involved still pay out over 90p for every £1 collected in premiums.

The Company continues its scheme for Household Buildings and/or Contents Insurance under-written by the Ecclesiastical Insurance Office. This scheme is available to members and adherents of the Church of Scotland in respect of cover over their own properties. Not only is it competitively priced but also when a policy is taken out, the Insurance Company will issue a voucher for £20 which can be passed to the Congregational Treasurer and used to offset the congregation's insurance costs.

A number of congregations now run cafés and coffee shops on a permanent basis. The Company has arranged a policy which covers Contents, Stock and Frozen Foods as well as Liability.

The Insurance Company made a profit on technical account of £627,450 (2000: £627,172) in the year to 31st October 2001. However, largely as a result of unrealised losses on investments of £1,047,475 (2000: gains of £369,887) with the appropriate release of deferred taxation, a loss of £56,973 resulted (2000: profit of £1,169,929). There was no dividend declared in the calendar year 2001, whereas the figure in 2000, including tax recovered was £90,750. Gift Aid donations and payments under Deeds of Covenant during 2001 totalled £610,394, the comparable figure for 2000 having been £513,730. Such payments are, of course, at the discretion of the Directors and depend on profitability. If equity markets remain depressed, recent distributions can no longer be assumed. The General Trustees record their appreciation of the significant financial contribution made by the Company to assist the operations of the Trustees and of the work done by the Directors of the Company. The Directors receive no remuneration for the responsibilities undertaken by them although the firm of Insurance Brokers of which the Chairman of the Company is a Director receives an annual payment of £6,000 in recognition of the time spent by him on the work of the Company.

On behalf of the General Trustees

WILLIAM S CARSWELL, *Chairman*
JAMES H SIMPSON, *Vice-Chairman*
ALAN W COWE, *Secretary and Clerk*

APPENDIX 1

Determinations Made Under Act VII 1995

1.   **General Sales:** In the following cases, the General Trustees made determinations authorising the sale or letting of the property concerned and directed that the proceeds should be credited to the benefit of the congregation in the Consolidated Fabric Fund:- Aberdeen: Woodside – strip of ground near church, Anwoth and Girthon – Anwoth Church, Auchterderran St Fothad's – Cardenden St Fothad's Church, Ballingry and Lochcraig – Lochcraig Manse, Birsay, Harray and Sandwick – ground at Harray Church, Black Mount – Dunsyre Church, Bridge of Allan: Chalmers – manse, Buchlyvie – Buchlyvie: North Church, Chryston – hall, Clydebank: St Cuthbert's – manse, Coatbridge: Clifton –

ground at halls, Coatbridge: Old Monkland – ground at hall, Cranstoun, Crichton and Ford – hall, Culter with Libberton and Quothquan – manse, Cupar: Old and St Michael of Tarvit – manse, Dalbeattie – property in Burn Street, Dalbeattie, Dalkeith: St Nicholas Buccleuch – apse and sacristy at church, Dirleton – former manse, Dundee: Broughty Ferry St James – manse, Dundee: Lochee Old and St Luke's – manse and retirement house, Dundee: Trinity – hall, Dunfermline: Townhill and Kingseat – ground at manse, Eday – Eday New Manse, Edinburgh: Kirkliston – manse, Edinburgh: St Martin's – ground at church, Elgin: St Giles' and St Columba's South – South Church and Halls, Ellon – ground at former Slains Manse, Falkirk: Camelon Irving – manse, Fintray and Kinellar – Kinellar Church, Gargunnock – hall, Glasgow: Colston Milton – church, Glasgow: Mosspark – church, Glasgow: St Andrew's East – hall, Glasgow: Yoker St Matthew's – ground at church, Glenaray and Inveraray – ground at manse, Innerleithen, Traquair and Walkerburn – manse, Inveraven and Glenlivet – manse, Keithhall – manse, Kilmarnock: St Ninian's Bellfield – hall and youth centre and manse, Kiltearn – hall, Kingussie – ground at manse, Kinloch – Arivruaich and Balallan Mission Halls, Kirkcaldy: St Bryce Kirk – Kirkcaldy: Old Manse, Kirkpatrick Irongray – manse, Lesmahagow: Old – manse, Leven – Scoonie Manse, Lochgoilhead and Kilmorich – manse, Netherlee – manse, Northmavine – manse, Perth: Moncreiffe – Rhynd Church and Hall, Rathen West – manse cottage, South Ronaldsay and Burray – Herston Hall, The Stewartry of Strathearn – Dunning Manse, Stichill Hume and Nenthorn – hall, Stirling: Church of the Holy Rude – retirement house, Tarbert (South Argyll) – manse, Tarves – manse, Turriff: St Ninian's and Forglen – warehouse and store at former manse and Whithorn St Ninian's Priory – ground at former manse.

2. Glebe Sales: In the following parishes, the General Trustees made determinations authorising the sale of glebe subjects and directed that the proceeds should be credited to the benefit of the congregation in the Consolidated Stipend Fund:- Acharacle, Athelstaneford, Brechin: Cathedral, Cardross, Contin, Earlston, Edinburgh: Corstorphine Old, Ellon, Fowlis and Liff, Glenelg and Kintail, Insch Leslie Premnay and Oyne,

Iona, Irongray, Lochrutton and Terregles, Kirkconnel, Kirkmichael, Tinwald and Torthorwald, Lismore, Lochbroom and Ullapool, Lochgoilhead and Kilmorich, Middlebie, New Machar, Oathlaw Tannadice, Portnahaven, Tingwall and Whithorn St Ninian's Priory.

3. Miscellaneous: The General Trustees made the following miscellaneous determinations:-

a. Acharacle – Sale of manse and amendment to Scheme No 49 of Scottish Ecclesiastical Commissioners.

b. Ballingry and Lochcraig – Demolition of Lochcraig Church and Hall, sale of part of site and crediting of proceeds to benefit of congregation in Consolidated Fabric Fund.

c. Dunfermline: St Paul's – Sale of manse, proceeds to be credited to Central Fabric Fund.

d. Innerleithen, Traquair and Walkerburn – Sale of former William Cree Memorial Chapel and application of proceeds to meet the cost of transferring memorial window to Traquair, to maintain this window and to keep the buildings of the congregation in proper order and repair and fully insured.

e. National Mission – Sale of ground at North Kessock Mission Hall and transmission of proceeds to Board of National Mission.

APPENDIX 2

Amendment to Guidelines for Reallocation of Endowments

(as approved by General Assembly of 1995 and amended by General Assembly of 1996)

Section 3 of the matters which Presbyteries should bear particularly in mind when considering reallocations will be deleted and there will be substituted the following:-

Reallocations may be of capital or of revenue. In the case of a reallocation of revenue this may be of a fixed amount or, if the circumstances justify it, at a rate of so much per annum, of a particular percentage of income per annum, for a fixed term or indefinitely.

NOMINATION COMMITTEE

MAY 2002

PROPOSED DELIVERANCE

The General Assembly:

1. Receive the Report
2. Make alterations to Standing Committees and Boards as set forth in the Report.

REPORT

The Committee recommends the following appointments: -

Board of Practice and Procedure

Ministers Retiring Colin Brockie, Melville Crosthwaite, William Hewitt, Rodger Neilson
Ministers Appointed Loudon Blair, Colin Brockie*, David Mill, Iain Thomson
Member Retiring Terence Thompson
Members Appointed Carole Hope, Elizabeth Fox

David Lacy, *Convener*
Alastair Symington, *Vice-Convener*

Board of Nomination to Theological Chairs

Member Retiring Lesley Macdonald, Moyra McCallum, Doris Meston
Members Appointed Kenneth Anderson, Moyra McCallum (3 years)*, Doris Meston (3 years)*

Robert Davidson, *Convener*
John Stevenson, *Secretary*

Committee to Nominate the Moderator

Member Retiring Jean Fowler
Member Appointed Catherine Nelson

Principal Clerk, *Secretary*

* Denotes second term

Judicial Commission

Ministers Retiring Robert Andrew, Jack Brown, James Crichton, Peter Graham, Ann Inglis
Ministers Appointed Fiona Douglas, Barry Dunsmore, Christine Goldie, Gordon Kennedy, David Lunan, Andrew MacLean, Tom McWilliam, Andrew Stewart, Graham Thain
Elders Retiring Alexander Bell, Joan Cape, Helen McLeod, Iain Macmillan
Elders Appointed Jean Broadwood (3 years), Myrtle Gillies (3 years), William Gordon (3 years), Alasdair MacFadyen, John Mitchell (3 years), Walter Muir (3 years), Hugh Neilson (3 years), Bob Nimmo (3 years), Audrey Salters (3 years), Walter Simpson, Grant Wood (3 years)

Douglas Allan, *Chairman*
Alastair McGregor, *Vice-Chairman*

Nomination Committee

Ministers Retiring Fraser Aitken, Erik Cramb, John Kellet, Ian McLean, Norma Moore, Matthew Rodger, John Russell, Gordon Savage
Ministers Appointed David Easton, Robert Glover, Willie-John Macdonald, Ian McLean, Mark Malcolm, John Russell (2 years)*, Pauline Steenbergen
Members Retiring Kathleen Forsyth, Myra Goskirk, David Haggart, Fiona Lynn

* Denotes second term

Members Appointed Kenneth Anderson, Walter Blair, Jean Broadwood, Robin Easton, Elma Farr, Elspeth Kerr, Maggie Lunan, Christine Smith

Keith Hall, *Convener*
Iain Cunningham, *Vice-Convener*

Assembly Council

Members Retiring George Hart, Eleanor McMahon, Mary Morrison
Members Appointed Ian Black, Morag Crawford, Frank Ribbons, Richard Wallis

Helen McLeod, *Convener*
David Dennistoun, *Vice-Convener*

Board of Stewardship and Finance

Ministers Retiring Colin Sutherland
Ministers Appointed Ian McInnes, Colin Sutherland*
Members Retiring Iain Dingwall, Linda McLean, Frederick Macleod
Member Appointed Iain Dingwall*, John Mackie, Kenneth Maitland

Colin Caskie, *Convener*
Vivienne Dickson, *Vice-Convener*

Church and Nation Committee

Ministers Retiring Fred Booth, Ronald Johnstone, Alistair McGregor, David Strachan, Margaret Yule
Ministers Appointed Fred Booth*, William Clinkenbeard, Ronald Johnstone*, Alistair Keil, Stuart MacQuarrie, Roderick McNidder
Members Retiring Marjory Clark, David Fergusson, Alan Millar, Isabell Montgomerie, David Miller, Vi Robertson
Members Appointed Judith Aitken, Margaret Anderson, David Clipston, David Fergusson (3 years)*, Karen Muir

Alan McDonald, *Convener*
Morag Ross, *Vice-Convener*

* Denotes second term

Panel on Doctrine

Ministers Retiring Iain MacRitchie, Kenneth Walker
Ministers Appointed Donald MacEwan, Kenneth Walker*
Member Appointed John Davidson, Alec Elliott

John McPake, *Convener*
Norma Stewart, *Vice-Convener*

Panel on Worship

Ministers Retiring Albert Bogle, Duncan Forrester, David Kellas, William McLaren, Peter Neilson, Pauline Steenbergen
Ministers Appointed David Kellas*, Douglas Lamb, Ann Winning
Member Retiring Diana Lamb
Members Appointed Andrew Barr, Liz Kemp, Lyn Peden, Colin McAlister, Ian Murphy

Gilleasbuig Macmillan, *Convener*
Ian McCrorie, *Vice-Convener*

Board of National Mission

James Gibson, *Convener*
Fiona Campbell, John Matthews, *Vice-Convener*

Parish Reappraisal Committee

Ministers Retiring John Anderson, John Brewster, Neil Dougall
Ministers Appointed Neil Dougall (3 years)*, Gary McIntyre
Members Retiring Elizabeth Cormack, Roberta Macdonald, Rita MacKenzie, Jean Macrae, Ishbell Watt
Members Appointed Rita MacKenzie (3 years)*, Jean Macrae (2 years)*, Ron McCabe, James Michie, Isobel Reynolds, Tom Stephen

Arthur Barrie, *Convener*
David Clark, *Vice-Convener*

* Denotes second term

New Charge Development Committee
Ministers Retiring Elizabeth Fisk, Michael Frew
Ministers Appointed Betty Smith, Norman Smith

Andrew Ritchie, *Convener*
John Collard, *Vice-Convener*

Mission and Evangelism Resources Committee
Minister Appointed Iain Sutherland
Members Retiring Jack Campbell, Guy Douglas
Member Appointed Colin Hyslop

Colin Sinclair, *Convener*
John Berkeley, Howard Taylor, *Vice-Conveners*

Chaplaincies Committee
Ministers Appointed Colin Anderson, Marian Cowie
Member Retiring David Hannan
Members Appointed Maureen Jones, Cameron Meikle
Elinor Arbuthnott, *Convener*

Parish Assistance Committee
Ministers Appointed Dane Sherrard
Member Retiring Moira Alexander
Member Appointed Diane Ashton
Stanley Brook, *Convener*
Alison Henderson, *Vice-Convener*

Iona Community Board
Minister Retiring Stewart McPherson
Ministers Appointed Mark Foster
Member Retiring Marilyn Shedden
Members Appointed Kenneth Fleming, Stephen Harding

Tom Gordon, *Convener*

Committee on Artistic Matters
Ministers Appointed David Beckett
Members Retiring Alan Dale, James Dempster, Donald Smith, Rosalind Taylor

* Denotes second term

Members Appointed Muir Austin, James Dempster*, Fred Giffen, Maurice Jones, Leonard Maguire, David Manson

Douglas Laird, *Convener*
Richard Frazer, *Vice-Convener*

Board of Ministry
Ministers Retiring Glenda Keating
Ministers Appointed James Dewar, Robert Hamilton, Glenda Keating*, Peter White
Member Retiring Janie Martin, Hamish Montgomery
Member Appointed Janie Martin*, John Spooner

William Storrar, *Convener*
Alan Downie, John Paterson, *Vice-Conveners*

Committee on Chaplains to HM Forces
Minister Retiring Christopher Ledgard, Bruce Neill, Iain Torrance, Gillian Weighton
Ministers Appointed Bruce Neill*, Gillian Weighton*
Members Retiring John Evans, Stuart Tickner, Robert Watson
Members Appointed Ian Shepherd, Stuart Tickner*

Herbert Kerrigan, *Convener*
Vice-Convener

Board of Social Responsibility
Ministers Retiring Alexander Glass, Douglas Nicol, Elizabeth Robertson, Ramsay Shields, David Souter
Ministers Appointed Alexander Glass*, Ramsay Shields*, David Souter*, Iain Torrance, John Watson
Members Retiring Alexander Bennie, Sheila Cormack, Michael Ellis, Mairi Lovett, Ruth McManus, Isabel Morrison
Members Appointed Alexander Bennie*, Ruth Middleton, Isabel Morrison*, John Swinton, Scott Watson, William Wilson

James Cowie, *Convener*
David Court, Gilbert Nisbet, *Vice-Conveners*

* Denotes second term

Board of World Mission
Ministers Retiring Norman Hutcheson, David Molyneaux, Alan Main, Margaret Muir
Minister Appointed Gavin Elliott
Members Appointed Shirley Brown, Janet Cant, John Milne

Alan Greig, *Convener*
Elisabeth Cranfield, Andrew Anderson, *Vice-Conveners*

Committee on Ecumenical Relations
Minister Retiring: Thomas MacIntyre
Ministers Appointed Norman Maciver, Sheila Mitchell
Members Retiring Lewis Rose, Andrew Sarle
Members Appointed Lewis Rose (3 years)*, Andrew Sarle (3 years)*

Erik Cramb, *Convener*
Christine Tait, *Vice-Convener*

Board of Parish Education
Ministers Retiring Ian Dryden, Catherine Hepburn, Christopher Kellock, Donald McCorkindale
Ministers Appointed Marc Bircham, Alastair Cherry, Ian Dryden (1 year)*, Steven Manners, Norma Moore
Members Retiring Gillian Braid, Ray Dely, Ann Lyall, Janett MacNaughton, John Ritchie, Bruce Sinclair, Margaret Varwell, Irene Woods
Members Appointed Bob Chalmers, Lesley Diack, Gavin Drummond, Nancy Gilmartin, Janette Henderson, Donna Hislop, Helen Malcolm, Ruth Sturgeon, Irene Williams

John Christie, *Convener*
Lorna Paterson, *Vice-Convener*

Committee on Education
Minister Retiring Iain Whyte
Minister Appointed Bill Armitage
Members Retiring Ronald Riddell, Eleanor Spalding,

William Weatherspoon
Members Appointed Elaine Carey, Nancy Gilmartin, George Ross, Maureen Simpson

John Laidlaw, *Convener*
David Alexander, *Vice-Convener*

Panel of Arbiters
Member Retiring Marina Brown, Glyn Taverner
Member Appointed Liz Kemp, Peter White

Graham Philips, *Convener*

Board of Communication
Minister Retiring Alister Goss
Ministers Appointed Sharon Colvin (1 year) Peter Graham, (1 year), Ian Hamilton (1 year)
Member Retiring Marjorie Lawrie, Richard Williamson
Members Appointed John Henderson, Kate Keter, Richard Williamson*

Jean Montgomerie, *Convener*
Iain Paton, *Vice-Convener*

In the name of the Committee

FRASER AITKEN, *Convener*
KEITH HALL, *Vice-Convener*
FINLAY MACDONALD, *Secretary*

* Denotes second term

* Denotes second term

CHURCH OF SCOTLAND TRUST
MAY 2002

PROPOSED DELIVERANCE

The General Assembly

1. Receive the Report and thank the members of the Trust for their diligence.
2. Note Miss Karina T McTeague resigned as a member of the Trust on 29th October 2001.
3. Note that in accordance with the constitution of the Trust, the Very Reverend James L Weatherhead and Mr Robert Bow retire as members on 31st May 2002 but are eligible for re-appointment.
4. Thank the Very Reverend James L Weatherhead for 16 years service to the Trust.
5. Re-appoint Mr Robert Bow as a member of the Trust from 1st June 2002.

REPORT

The Church of Scotland Trust, which was established by Act of Parliament in 1932, submits its Seventieth Report to the General Assembly.

1. The Work of the Trust

(a) General

The function of the Church of Scotland Trust is to hold properties outwith Scotland and to act as trustee in a number of third party trusts. During the year it has dealt with various matters which have arisen regarding these properties and trusts.

(b) The Scots Kirk, Paris

The new building on the site of the former Scots Kirk in Paris is near completion and the interior is in the process of being refurbished by the local congregation. Title to part of the ground floor and the basement of the building will be held in the name of the Church of Scotland Trust on completion of the legal formalities.

(c) Sea of Galilee Centre, Tiberias

The Trust has been represented at meetings of the Israel Centres Committee, a Committee of the Board of World Mission and the Tiberias Negotiating Group which was appointed by the Board of World Mission to negotiate a Joint Venture Agreement with the Cousins Foundation in Atlanta, USA.

(d) Sialkot, Pakistan

The Trust, in consultation with the Board of World Mission, has authorised the sale of various plots of land in Sialkot to realise the payment required by the Government in Pakistan to secure denationalisation of the schools in Sialkot. At denationalisation the titles to the schools will be held in the name of the Sialkot Diocesan Trust Association.

The Trust and the said Board had previously authorised the transfer of these plots to the Sialkot Diocesan Trust Association in terms of the Church of Scotland Trust Order Confirmation Act 1958 but the lawyer acting for the Trust Association had not effected the transfers.

2. Accounts for 2001

The Trust's Accounts for the year to 31st December 2001 have been audited and copies thereof are available on request from the General Treasurer.

3. Membership

Miss Karina T McTeague resigned from the Trust on 29th October 2001 due to business commitments. In accordance with the constitution of the Trust, the following two members retire by rotation on 31st May 2002 but are eligible for re-appointment: the Very Reverend James L Weatherhead and Mr Robert Bow. It is suggested to the General Assembly that Mr Robert Bow be re-appointed. The Very Reverend James L Weatherhead does not seek re-appointment and the members would like to record their gratitude to him for his service to the Trust since his appointment in 1986.

In the name and by authority of The Church of Scotland Trust

JOHN M HODGE, *Chairman*
CHRISTOPHER N MACKAY, *Vice-Chairman*
JENNIFER M HAMILTON, *Secretary & Clerk*

CHURCH OF SCOTLAND INVESTORS TRUST

MAY 2002

PROPOSED DELIVERANCE

The General Assembly:

1. Receive the Report.

2. Approve the re-appointment of Mr S R Auld, Mr D M Fortune and Mr J Skinner as members of the Investors Trust from 1 June 2002.

3. Ratify the co-option of Mrs I Hunter on 26 February 2002 and approve her appointment as a member of the Investors Trust from 1 June 2002.

4. Receive the Annual Report and Financial Statements of the Investors Trust for 2001.

REPORT

The Church of Scotland Investors Trust, which was established by the Church of Scotland (Properties and Investments) Order Confirmation Act 1994, submits its Eight Report to the General Assembly.

1. Introduction

The function of the Investors Trust is to provide investment services to the Church of Scotland and to bodies and trusts within or connected with the Church. The Investors Trust offers simple and economical facilities for investment in its three Funds: (a) Growth Fund; (b) Income Fund; (c) Deposit Fund. Investors receive the benefits of professional management, continuous portfolio supervision, spread of investment risk and economies of scale. In deference to the wishes of the General Assembly investments are not made in companies substantially involved in the tobacco, alcohol, gambling or armament industries.

2. Investment Performance in 2001

The terrorist attacks on 11 September 2001 hit a world economy that was already fragile and slowing down. Investment returns in 2001 were disappointing, with the UK FTSE All Share Index falling by 15.4%. This was the worst annual return since 1974 and impacted on the equity based Growth Fund. Under the newly appointed managers, Henderson Global Investors, the portfolio diversified into the property sector, in an effort to improve yield. Whilst over the year, returns were negative, given the fact that property, the best performing asset class, was not held for most of that period, the overall performance was a respectable return of –8.6%, compared to the Growth Fund's benchmark of –9.0%.

The Income Fund does not have an overall benchmark but the managers, Baillie Gifford & Co, benefiting from corporate bond market returns of some 3.4% above Gilts, achieved a positive total return of 6.0% in 2001.

In a year which saw sharply falling interest rates, the managers of the Deposit Fund, Noble Grossart Ltd, achieved a favourable average rate of 5.34%, compared to last year's 6.11%.

3. Income Distributions

As indicated to last year's General Assembly, the Growth Fund's income distribution was reduced from 16.0p for 2000 to 14.5p for 2001. Against a background of gradual loss of dividend tax credits until 2004, the Growth Fund projections over the same period indicate earnings continuing to fall short of the target distribution level of 14.5p per unit. It is hoped that projected shortfalls in earnings can be covered by reserves, thus avoiding the necessity of a further cut in distributions.

It is anticipated that the distribution from the Income Fund will be maintained at 73.0p per unit in 2002 but the effect of substantially lower interest rates means that the levels of income generated in the past will be difficult to sustain in the future.

Numerous reductions in Base Rates during 2001 impacted on the rate of interest paid by the Deposit Fund. This was, to some extent, cushioned by the prudent placing of funds by the managers. The rate payable in 2002 by the Deposit Fund will be dependent of movements in the money market. Currently base rate is 4% and while there is no certainty that rates have bottomed, markets already imply rising levels later in the year.

4.   Annual Report and Financial Statements for 2001

Copies of the Annual Report and Financial Statements for the year to 31 December 2001 are available from the Secretary.

5.   Membership

In accordance with the constitution of the Investors Trust the following three members retire at 31 May 2002, but are eligible for re-appointment: Mr S R Auld; Mr D M Fortune and Mr J Skinner.

It is recommended to the General Assembly that Mr S R Auld; Mr D M Fortune and Mr J Skinner be re-appointed as members.

Mrs I Hunter was co-opted as a member of the Investors Trust on 26 February 2002. It is recommended to the General Assembly that this co-option be ratified and that Mrs I Hunter be appointed a member of the Investors Trust as from 1 June 2002.

In the name and by the authority of the Church of Scotland Investors Trust

J B M DICK, *Chairman*
D M SIMPSON, *Vice-Chairman*
F E MARSH, *Secretary*

THE CHURCH OF SCOTLAND PENSION TRUSTEES

MAY 2002

PROPOSED DELIVERANCE

The General Assembly:

1. Receive the Report.

2. Note that the Actuarial Valuations of all three Pension Schemes were carried out as at 31 December 2000.

3. Note that a separate Joint Report by the Board of Ministry and the Pension Trustees has been issued covering proposals for amendment of the Scheme for Ministers and Overseas Missionaries.

4. Note that the Church has arranged two Stakeholder Pension Schemes through Standard Life to provide access to a Stakeholder Pension as necessary for any employee who is not eligible to join any of the three Pension Schemes. Also note that existing Scheme Members can contribute to these Stakeholder Pensions as an alternative or in addition to paying Additional Voluntary Contributions.

5. Note that all pensions in payment were increased by 1.7% from 1 January 2002.

6. Note that Reports and Accounts for all three Schemes for the year to 31 December 2001 are available from the Pensions Manager.

7. Re-appoint Lisle Pattison as a Trustee.

8. Appoint as a Trustee Arthur James Priestly, who is nominated to fill the vacancy created by the retiral of Roma Mary Hutchison Roy.

9. Note that Rev George M Philip retired as a Member Trustee of the Ministers' Scheme in October 2001 and that the Board of Ministry elected Rev Willam J McMillan as a replacement.

10. Thank Roma Mary Hutchison Roy and Rev George M Philip with gratitude for the services they provided to the Church as Trustees.

REPORT

1. Pensions Schemes in 2001/2002

It is difficult to remember another year as challenging as this for anyone involved with pension schemes in the United Kingdom.

The continued slump in the world equity markets combined with the new regulatory burden caused by the pensions accounting requirement FRS17, led to a number of employers closing their 'final salary schemes'. However, final salary schemes are recognised to be the most secure way of providing a defined pension and their closure is widely seen as worrying for employees.

All three Church of Scotland Pension Schemes provide a pension that is related to final earnings. As disclosed in the Actuarial Reports, all Schemes were fully funded as at December 2000. However, the continued financial health of the Schemes depends on investment performance and the life expectancy of members. This of course results in the employer having an open ended commitment.

2. The Church of Scotland Pension Schemes

The Church of Scotland has three Pension Schemes:

- The Church of Scotland Pension Scheme for Ministers and Overseas Missionaries,
- The Church of Scotland Pension Scheme for Staff and

- The Church of Scotland Pension Scheme for the Board of National Mission.

All Pension Schemes are "Contracted In" which means that Scheme members will also receive a State Earnings Related Pension (SERPS) up to 5 April 2002 and for service thereafter a State Second Pension, which replaces SERPS from that date.

The Pension Scheme for Ministers is the most complex with benefits coming from a number of different Funds, initially set up to supplement the Main Pension Fund which only commenced in 1978. A separate Joint Report to this General Assembly from the Board of Ministry and Pension Trustees proposes rationalisation of this Scheme linked to the introduction of the National Minimum Stipend Scale. Pensions would be based on 1/80th of Scale Stipend, and for service after January 2004, 1/80th of the value of a manse agreed with the Inland Revenue. Members would also contribute $2^{1}/_{2}\%$ of their stipend to the Main Pension Fund but compulsory contributions to the Insured Pension Fund by members would cease as would all contributions by congregations.

The pension formula of **The Pension Scheme for Staff**, with its two deductibles in respect of State benefits, leads to a pension which is a variable fraction of the member's final remuneration but generally not more than about 1/120th of earnings for each year of service. This is the only one of the Church of Scotland's Pension Schemes where employees are not required at present to contribute. The discussions to improve the benefits continued during the year. However, the two employers participating in this Scheme, the Board of Social Responsibility with its 1250 Scheme members and the Central Co-ordinating Committee (previously Personnel Committee) with its 240 Scheme members have not found, at the time of writing this Report, a basis for improvements which is acceptable and affordable to both employers, whilst also satisfying the prudency requirements necessary in the current economic climate.

The Pension Scheme for the Board of National Mission is the smallest of the three Schemes and provides a pension based on 1/80th of earnings with employees contributing at $2^{1}/_{2}\%$. This Scheme already provides what is considered the ultimate target pension for the two other Schemes with employees' contributions assisting the financing of the benefits.

3. Actuarial Valuations of the Pension Schemes

For all three Pension Schemes the Actuarial Valuations were carried out as at 31 December 2000. The Valuations resulted in the following employer contribution rates being recommended:

- **Main Pension Fund of the Pension Scheme for Ministers:** The contributions by the employer to remain at 20%.
- **The Church of Scotland Pension Scheme for Staff:** The employer's contribution payable by the Central Co-ordinating Committee and the Board of Social Responsibility to be increased from $10^{1}/_{2}\%$ to $13^{1}/_{2}\%$ on the existing benefit basis.
- **The Church of Scotland Pension Scheme for the Board of National Mission:** The employer's contribution rate to be increased from $10^{1}/_{2}\%$ to $12^{1}/_{2}\%$ with employees continuing to pay $2^{1}/_{2}\%$ as before.

4. Pension Increases

All pensions paid by the Pension Trustees under the three Pension Schemes were increased in line with inflation by 1.7% from 1 January 2002.

5. Annual Benefit Statements

This year the members of the Ministers' Scheme received for the first time an Annual Benefit Statement quoting their estimated pension from the Main Pension Fund at retiral. This statement is in the outline similar to the statements issued for the last three years to the members of the Schemes for Staff and the Board of National Mission.

6. Stakeholder Pensions

Stakeholder Pensions are a new type of pension scheme introduced by the government and available from April

2001. The Church arranged two Stakeholder Pension Schemes through Standard Life. These provide access to a Stakeholder Pension for any employee who is not eligible to join any of the three Pension Schemes. In addition, the Stakeholder Pensions are an alternative to AVCs for any Pension Scheme member earning less than £30,000.

7. Annual Report and Accounts

Copies of the Audited Report and Accounts for each Scheme for the year to 31 December 2001 are available from the Pensions Manager.

8. Trustees

In accordance with the Constitution of the Trustees approved by the General Assembly, Lisle Pattison and Roma Mary Hutchison Roy retire on 31 May 2002.

Mr Pattison is available for re-appointment and it is proposed that he be re-appointed.

Mrs Roy who has served as a Trustee for 13 years, first in the Retirement Scheme Committee and then from 1997 in its successor, the Pension Trustees, does not wish to stand for re-appointment. The Trustees would like to extend thanks and gratitude to her for the work undertaken during her service as a Trustee.

Arthur James Priestly is nominated for appointment by the General Assembly to fill the vacancy.

The Trustees would also like to thank Rev George M Philip who retired as a Member Trustee of the Pension Scheme for Ministers in October 2001 after having served for four years.

In accordance with the Scheme Rules, the Board of Ministry appointed Rev William J McMillan as a Member Trustee for the Ministers' Scheme to fill the vacancy. The Trustees extend a warm welcome Mr McMillan.

In the name of the Trustees

WILLIAM D B CAMERON, *Chairman*
W JOHN McCAFFERTY, *Vice-Chairman*
SIRKKA DENNISON, *Pensions Manager*

BOARD OF STEWARDSHIP AND FINANCE
MAY 2002

PROPOSED DELIVERANCE

The General Assembly:

1. Receive the Report.

2. Urge Kirk Sessions and Presbyteries to regard the teaching and promotion of Christian Stewardship as a priority in resourcing the Church for worship, mission and service.

3. Pass an Act amending Act V 1989 as set out in Appendix 1.

4. Approve the Regulations for Allocating the Mission and Aid Fund from 2004 as set out in Appendix 2.

5. Receive the 2001 Accounts of the Unincorporated Boards and Committees of the General Assembly.

6. Instruct the Unincorporated Boards and Committees of the General Assembly, via the Solicitor of the Church, to provide to the Board of Stewardship and Finance, on request from the General Treasurer, information about any pending property sales which may have a material effect on the financial position of the Boards and Committees concerned.

7. Approve the establishment of a Parish Development Fund in terms of the Regulations set out in Appendix 6.

REPORT

1. Stewardship

The Stewardship Department is a central resource for congregations and presbyteries. It exists to encourage people to think about the gifts of God and how they use these gifts. It exists to assist the Church in maximising the resources made available for worship, mission and service.

During 2001 the staff of the Stewardship Department worked with almost 100 congregations – presenting stewardship programmes to office-bearers, advising and supporting planning groups as they carried out a variety of such programmes in their congregations, and participating in Kirk Session conferences.

Some of the results of stewardship programmes can be quantified:

- More people giving their time to participate in worship;
- More involvement in the life of the congregation as more people offer their abilities and skills;
- Considerable increases in income from more generous giving of money.

This comment was made at the end of one programme:

> "The Family Meal created a positive atmosphere that has continued each week in worship. More people are attending regularly, more folk are involved, and our offerings have increased by more than we expected."

Other results are less tangible, but equally important. These might include more reflection on the use of resources, a clearer sense of direction, greater enthusiasm within the life of the congregation.

On some occasions stewardship programmes are not as successful as the Planning Group or the Stewardship Consultant would have hoped. Some of the reasons for limited success are:

- Lack of commitment and enthusiasm on the part of office-bearers;
- Minority of office-bearers actively undermining the programme;
- Choice of a programme about time, abilities and money or about time and abilities when the real need is to concentrate on money;
- Reluctance to talk about the giving of money.

In some congregations the result of a stewardship programme is the identification of one or more problems in the life of a congregation. At first sight such a result can appear negative, but the identification of problems can be the first step towards developing the mission of the Church in a particular parish.

In continuing to advocate the use of stewardship programmes, the Stewardship Department is conscious that Christian Stewardship should not be regarded as something in which congregations engage occasionally. The promotion of Christian Stewardship should be a fundamental part of the ongoing life of the Church. To help promote a stewardship culture within the Church the Stewardship Department has produced material for a four year stewardship cycle. This material encourages a focus on different aspects of Christian Stewardship over a four year period:

Year 1   —   Money
Year 2   —   Time
Year 3   —   Abilities and Skills
Year 4   —   Creation and the Environment

In years 1 and 3 there would be traditional stewardship programmes. The themes in years 2 and 4 would be considered through worship, study groups and practical projects.

2. Act anent Church Finance

Act V 1989 contains various regulations concerning Central Finance and Congregational Finance. This act was drafted before the era of church websites and takes no account of financial appeals which may be made by congregations through their websites.

The Board takes the view that financial appeals through congregational websites do not contravene section 3 of the Act as those who read the contents of these websites have made a conscious decision to do so. The Board does not wish to prevent congregations from making financial appeals in this way.

To avoid any confusion on this matter, the Board proposes the amendment to Act V 1989 set out in Appendix 1.

3. Allocating the Mission and Aid Fund

The Board has completed its review of the way in which the Mission and Aid Fund is allocated among congregations. The proposed regulations for the revised method of allocation are in Appendix 2 of this report.

The main features of the revised method of allocation are:

- Every congregation will receive an allocation. This will provide all congregations with an opportunity to contribute to the wider work of the Church;
- There will be a token allocation related to the first part of congregational income instead of an allowance for ministry costs. There will continue to be an allowance for the costs incurred in having approved additional members of a ministry team;
- Presbyteries will have the opportunity to reduce by a specified percentage the total allocated among congregations within their bounds. This will allow them to take account of financial pressures on particular congregations at any given time, and make reductions in the allocations of these congregations.

The proposed revised method of allocation is designed to be as simple as possible; to be fair to all congregations; and to be operative from 2004. It will be implemented each year in a manner that is consistent with the arrangements for collecting Ministry payments. While the Board of Stewardship and Finance and the Board of Ministry will be responsible for their own allocations, the two Boards will consult with each other and will endeavour to co-ordinate the process.

If the stipend proposals from the Board of Ministry are approved by the General Assembly, the Aid budget will be transferred from the Mission and Aid Fund to Ministry Funds. In these circumstances, the Board of Stewardship and Finance will propose to the General Assembly of 2003 a new name for the Fund from 2004.

4. Congregational Contributions

4.1 Ministry Funds (Appendix 4)

Because a minority of congregations are unable to remit their contributions in full during any one financial year, it is not possible to show the final allocation achievement until at least the end of the next financial year. By 31 December 2001, the net shortfall for 2000 had been reduced to 0.75%, continuing the excellent achievement of recent years.

At the end of 2001, the shortfall for that year was 2.45%, which was slightly higher than the equivalent figure of 2.07% a year previously. It is expected that the 2001 shortfall will be considerably reduced by late payments in 2002.

It is noted with appreciation that voluntary Aid repayments of £40,711 were made in 2001 by Aid Receiving congregations, which was higher than the equivalent figure of £38,919 in 2000.

4.2 Mission and Aid Fund (Appendix 5)
As with Ministry Funds, Mission and Aid Fund statistics are affected by late contributions. An additional, but welcome, factor is the receipt of voluntary extra contributions, which may be undesignated or may be restricted to a particular Board, Committee or project.

Since 1993, shortfalls have been carried forward and the effect of this has been dramatic. In 1991 and 1992 the net shortfalls were over 4.0%. For the period from 1993 to 2000, the net shortfalls for each year have been less than 1.0%.

The contributions position for 2001, at the end of 2001, was also encouraging, the shortfall at that date being 1.98% being the lowest ever (the equivalent figure a year earlier being 2.41%). With late contributions already received and still to be received in 2002, it is hoped that the shortfall for 2001 will be reduced to the low levels of previous years.

The Board expresses its gratitude to all congregations who met their allocations in full and to those who made additional voluntary contributions in 2001. As well as general undesignated extra contributions of £80,752 (2000 - £85,115), congregations gave extra contributions to specific areas of work within the Mission and Aid Fund of £193,338 in 2001. This was a decrease on the 2000 figure of £274,452 for designated extra contributions, which benefited from an exceptionally large contribution of £40,000 from one congregation. As in past years, the main beneficiaries of designated extra contributions in 2001 were the Board of World Mission (£141,871) and Christian Aid (£18,361).

5. Accounting Matters
5.1 Accounts and Financial Overview
As in previous years, separate sets of Accounts for 2001 have been produced for each of the following:

> The Church of Scotland Investors Trust
> The Church of Scotland General Trustees
> The Church of Scotland Trust
> The Church of Scotland Pension Trustees
> The Unincorporated Boards and Committees.

The first three of the above bodies are statutory corporations and the Pension Trustees are an unincorporated body, constituted by the General Assembly. All four bodies are responsible for producing and approving their own Accounts.

The Board of Stewardship and Finance is responsible for preparing and approving the Accounts of the Unincorporated Boards and Committees, which comprise Ministry Funds, Mission and Aid Funds, Miscellaneous Funds, Board of Communication and Board of Social Responsibility.

A Financial Overview, giving a summary of the main features of the Accounts of the Unincorporated Boards and Committees for 2001, has also been produced for Commissioners to the General Assembly.

5.2 External Audit Arrangements
The Board wishes to report to the General Assembly that Messrs Deloitte & Touche, who audited the 2001 Accounts of the Church, have been reappointed to audit the Accounts for 2002.

5.3 Attestation of Presbytery Accounts
In 1997 the General Assembly approved Regulations anent Presbytery Finance, which cover the content, audit and attestation of Presbytery Accounts. After the Accounts have been approved by the Presbytery, they have to be submitted for attestation to the Board of Stewardship and Finance, which then has to report to the Assembly. The Board is pleased to report that the

2000 Accounts of Presbyteries showed a further improvement in the standard of accounting presentation.

5.4 Presbytery Attestation of Congregational Accounts

The Law Reform (Miscellaneous Provisions) (Scotland) Act 1990 imposed on charities a new code of law, including specific requirements as to the keeping of Accounts. Section 3 of the Act made provision for the "designation" by the Secretary of State for Scotland of religious bodies which meet certain requirements. To obtain "designation", a religious body must have a tiered structure, with authorities exercising supervisory functions, particularly in respect of imposing requirements as to the keeping of accounting records and auditing of Accounts. The effect of "designation", which has been granted to the Church of Scotland, is to exempt the Church to a great extent from the provisions of the legislation.

As part of the central supervisory process, the General Assembly in 1994 approved Regulations anent Congregational Finance and instructed Presbyteries and Congregational Financial Boards to give effect to the Regulations. The Regulations lay down procedures to be followed by Presbyteries in attesting Accounts of all congregations within their bounds.

The reports from Presbyteries on the inspection of 2000 Congregational Accounts indicated continuing progress in achieving compliance with the Regulations anent Congregational Finance. The Board is conscious of the heavy demands placed on voluntary office-bearers but it is essential that Congregational Accounts comply with the Regulations and that this can be demonstrated to the regulatory authorities. In this, the Church is heavily dependent upon and appreciative of the diligence of presbyteries and their Accounts Inspection Committees.

The Board is awaiting the promotion of legislation by the Scottish Parliament, following on from the report of the independent commission on the Review of Scottish Charity Law, before bringing to the General Assembly new Presbytery and Congregational Accounting Regulations (see Section 6). It is unlikely that legislation will be produced until after the next Scottish Parliamentary Election in 2003.

6. Review of Scottish Charity Law

The Scottish Charity Law Review Commission, which was set up by the Scottish Parliament, published its Report in May 2001. The Commission recommended that a new body, called "CharityScotland", should be established in Scotland with powers to determine eligibility for status as a Scottish Charity. CharityScotland would have the dual role of protecting the public interest and providing an effective support and regulatory system for charities.

The Commission also recommended that "designated religious bodies", in the first instance, should be subject to the same registration, accounting and reporting requirements as other Scottish Charities (although CharityScotland should have a power to exempt, from reporting and accounting to it, any charities which appear to be sufficiently well regulated elsewhere). Subject to this exception in relation to registration, accounting and reporting requirements, the Commission has recommended that the current statutory arrangements applicable to "designated religious bodies" should be continued and, in addition, they should be exempted from CharityScotland's new investigatory powers and its powers of temporary management.

Comments on the Report were invited from charities and both the Church of Scotland Trust and the Board of Stewardship and Finance made submissions to the Scottish Executive. Particular concern was expressed at the recommendation to withdraw the exemptions from accounting and reporting requirements presently available to "designated religious bodies". A request has therefore been made that there should be consultation on this issue with the Scottish Churches Committee, which represents the principal religious denominations in Scotland.

7. Audit Management Letters

The Report of the Special Commission on St. Ninian's Centre, Crieff recommended that the Board of Stewardship and Finance should lay down guidelines in relation to acting upon Auditors' Management Letters. The Board is pleased to report that guidelines on this matter have been provided to all Boards, Committees and

Statutory Corporations. The Board has also established an Audit Committee to liaise with the Church's Auditors. The members of the Audit Committee will receive copies of all Management Letters issued by the Church's Auditors.

8. Property Purchases and Sales

Also arising from the Report of the Special Commission on St. Ninian's Centre, Crieff, the Board is now required to give approval to the proposed purchase of any heritable property or other asset valued in excess of £50,000 by a Board or Central Department of the Church. The Board has approved procedures for implementing this requirement and has issued details of these to the relevant Boards and Committees. (The approval procedures do not apply to proposed purchases by the Church of Scotland General Trustees, the Housing and Loan Fund for Retired Ministers and Widows and Widowers of Ministers and the Committee on New Charge Development).

The General Assembly of 1988 instructed "Boards and Committees that the amount of any sales or purchases of property should be reported to the Board of Stewardship and Finance and the Assembly Council". (In practice, the reports on sales and purchases are made by the Solicitor of the Church to the General Treasurer). The General Assembly of 1992 instructed "the Board of Stewardship and Finance to take such further necessary steps as will ensure that the revenue on the sale proceeds of properties is taken adequately into account when deciding allocations from the Mission and Aid Fund to Boards and Committees of the Church". Because Mission and Aid Fund budgets are drawn up some time in advance of the year in question, it is essential that the Board of Stewardship and Finance is made aware, not just of completed property sales, but also of pending sales. The Board is therefore asking the General Assembly to instruct Boards and Committees, through the Solicitor of the Church, to advise the Board of Stewardship and Finance, via the General Treasurer, of any pending property sales which are likely to have a material effect on the financial position of the Boards or Committees concerned.

9. Parish Development Fund

The Report of the Special Commission anent Review and Reform to the General Assembly of 2001 envisaged the establishment of a Community and Parish Development Fund to resource local initiatives. The Board of Stewardship and Finance was given the following instruction by the General Assembly:

"The General Assembly affirm the need to resource local initiatives, and instruct the Board of Stewardship and Finance, in consultation with the Co-ordinating Forum, to consider the Community and Parish Development Fund set out in terms of Appendix 8 and to bring proposals for appropriate implementation to the General Assembly of 2002."

In carrying out this instruction the Board of Stewardship and Finance was advised that its task was to bring forward a proposed scheme to implement a Community and Parish Development Fund and not to consider whether such a fund was a good idea or not. The Board consulted the Co-ordinating Forum at its meetings in September and December 2001. The Board also decided to consult Kirk Sessions.

A Community and Parish Development Fund, as envisaged in the Report of the Special Commission anent Review and Reform, would provide central funding for local mission initiatives. It is hoped that such central funding by the Church would attract further funding from outside agencies. Projects would primarily be concerned with the employment of people to engage in particular aspects of local mission. However, the Fund could assist in a minor way with related fabric needs of new projects.

Kirk Sessions were invited to comment on their interest in the establishment of a Community and Parish Development Fund. Despite the short timescale for responding to this brief questionnaire, 500 Kirk Sessions replied to this approach from the Board. 392 replies indicated an interest in submitting projects for funding. A substantial number of the replies were interested in employing someone to lead a youth or community project. Some replies indicated the possibility of joint projects by a number of congregations in an area.

On this basis the Board of Stewardship and Finance proposes the establishment of a Parish Development

Fund for a pilot period of five years. The word 'community' has been omitted from the proposed title to give the Fund a shorter, more succinct, title : this has been done on the understanding that the word 'parish' is understood in its traditional sense – the community which a congregation serves.

The main concern of some Boards was that this Fund might lead to unnecessary duplication of the Church's work. To avoid this, the Board is proposing that there be representation on the Committee administering the Fund from a number of Boards and the General Trustees. This Committee would report directly to the General Assembly. The staffing and administration required by the Fund would be located within the Department of National Mission.

While the Report of the Special Commission envisaged a Fund of £7.5 million, this was on the basis of contributions from the reserves of major Boards and the General Trustees. None of the Boards nor the General Trustees felt able to invest in the new Fund as this would have curtailed existing work at a time when deficits were already being incurred by some Boards. Over the five year period £3 million would be provided by grants from the Mission and Aid Fund - £1 million in the first year, and £0.5 million in each of the subsequent four years. This funding would cover both the grants made to support local mission projects and the staff support required to administer the Fund.

Proposed regulations for the establishment and administration of a Parish Development Fund are contained in Appendix 6.

By the authority of the Board

J COLIN CASKIE, *Convener*
VIVIENNE A DICKSON, *Vice-Convener*
DONALD F ROSS, *General Treasurer*
GORDON D JAMIESON, *Director of Stewardship*
FRED MARSH, *Administrative Secretary*

APPENDIX 1

Act amending Act V 1989 anent Church Finance

The General Assembly enact and ordain that Act V 1989 is amended as follows:

Amend section 3 by the addition of the following sentence:

For the purposes of this Act an appeal contained on a website belonging or pertaining wholly to a single congregation or linkage shall not constitute an appeal outwith the congregation or parish as defined above; upon request from any party the Presbytery shall determine whether any appeal for funds constitutes an exception of this type, subject to a right of appeal or dissent or complaint.

APPENDIX 2

Regulations for Allocating the Mission and Aid Fund

1. All congregations will receive a Mission and Aid Fund allocation.

2. To facilitate the process of calculating allocations, Financial Boards will be required to send annually by 31 March a copy of their audited Congregational Accounts for the previous financial year to the General Treasurer.

3. The allocation will be based on unrestricted income and will ignore expenditure (except as noted in paragraph 7 below) and transfers between funds.

4. The total unrestricted income of the congregation for the year will be calculated.

   In the terminology of the Statement of Recommended Practice – "Accounting and Reporting by Charities", the calculation will include the income from Unrestricted Funds (which includes Designated Funds) but will exclude the income from Restricted Funds. For allocation purposes, Fabric Funds will be treated as Designated Funds and their income will be included in the calculation.

5. Total unrestricted income will include:

   (a) General Fund income;

   (b) Ministry income (including glebe rents and stipend endowment income);

   (c) Fabric Fund and Reserve Fund income (including income in Fabric Funds held by the General Trustees);

   (d) A percentage of rental income and income from outside agencies in excess of a sum to be determined by the Board of Stewardship and Finance (initially £10,000).

6. Total unrestricted income will not include:

   (a) Legacies or capital receipts, e.g. the proceeds from the sale of property or investments (although unrestricted income from invested legacies and capital will be included);

   (b) Income in restricted funds, such as funds for Special Projects, e.g. the building of a new hall, the purchase or rebuilding of an organ.

7. Where a congregation incurs the cost (or part of the cost) of additional members of a ministry team, the appointment of whom has been approved by Presbytery and the Committee on Parish Reappraisal in terms of the Presbytery Plan as necessary for the work of the charge, this cost will be deducted from the total unrestricted income figure, to produce a net unrestricted income figure.

8. The average of the net unrestricted income figures for the latest three years, calculated as specified above in paragraphs 5, 6 and 7, will be the base figure for calculating the Mission and Aid Fund allocation, with the exception that only the average of the total unrestricted income figures for 2001 and 2002 will be used in calculating the base figure for the 2004 Mission and Aid Fund allocation.

For the purposes of the 2004 allocation, the following procedure will be followed:

   (a) Where the base figure is £15,000 or less, the allocation will be £100;

   (b) Where the base figure is between £15,001 and £30,000, the allocation will increase by £10 for every £1,000 above £15,000 : when the base figure is £30,000, the allocation will be £250;

   (c) Where the base figure is over £30,000, the allocation will be £250 plus a percentage of the base figure over £30,000 : the percentage will increase as the base figure increases.

The base figure bands £1 to £15,000 and £15,001 to £30,000, together with the allocations of £100 and £250 will be revised regularly by the Board of Stewardship and Finance.

9. Where a congregation is part of a linked charge, the base figures for each congregation in the linked charge will be added together. The Mission and Aid Fund allocation for the charge will then be calculated (as outlined in paragraph 8 above). This allocation will then be divided between/among the congregations in the linked charge in proportion to their individual base figures.

10. The Board of Stewardship and Finance will determine a percentage for annual maximum increases or decreases in proposed allocations for individual congregations issued to Presbyteries. In terms of paragraph 11 below, each Presbytery will have scope to decrease an allocation by more than the permitted maximum percentage of the previous year's allocation if it deems this to be appropriate. Presbytery will also have the right to increase an allocation by more than the maximum percentage permitted where a congregation received a reduced allocation in the previous year.

11. The Mission and Aid Fund total budget plus 6% will be the total proposed allocation to congregations. Presbyteries will have the opportunity to decrease the proposed allocations by up to 5% of the Presbytery total, on the basis of local knowledge of the financial situation of congregations within the bounds. This provision does not mean that any proposed allocation to a congregation may only be reduced by 5%. The percentages mentioned in this paragraph may be reviewed by the Board of Stewardship and Finance.

APPENDIX 3
Legacies to Central Funds of the Church

	2001 £	2000 £	1999 £	1998 £
Social Responsibility	1,250,720	1,224,931	1,202,920	2,250,148
New Charge Development	951,025	174,186	120	2,155
General Trustees	946,497	10,420	314,312	60,175
Ministry Support	405,782	25,739	310,685	190,894
The Church of Scotland (Unrestricted)	185,764	1,740,591	503,459	879,645
World Mission	148,361	646,183	661,754	296,505
National Mission	80,386	22,958	268,593	26,538
Housing and Loan Fund	57,946	225,693	327,619	42,419
Education for the Ministry	35,000	80,295	19,992	12,500
Pension Funds	32,745	42,052	487,196	97,744
Mission and Aid Fund	24,806	50,604	29,375	6,892
Christian Aid	1,722	26,974	7,747	125,368
Chaplains to HM Forces	5	1,388	75,351	—
Special Trusts	—	74,412	1,239,983	1,357,650
Parish Education	—	1,666	152,146	130,451
Miscellaneous	—	599	—	—
The Guild	—	—	5,120	—
Manse Auxiliary	—	—	425	22,381
Ecumenical Relations	—	—	418	6,892
Priority Areas Fund	—	—	—	100,000
Total Legacies to Central Funds	**4,120,759**	**4,348,691**	**5,607,215**	**5,608,357**

APPENDIX 4

Congregational Contributions to Ministry Funds

Year	Allocated £	Received by 31 Dec £	Shortfall in Year £	%	Contributions received in Later Years £	Net Shortfall £	%
1992	23,092,167	22,459,273	632,894	2.74	474,786	158,108	0.68
1993	24,191,147	23,391,116	800,031	3.31	583,258	216,773	0.90
1994	24,760,852	24,090,435	670,417	2.71	529,257	141,160	0.57
1995	26,288,881	25,600,603	688,278	2.62	543,600	144,678	0.55
1996	27,507,754	26,849,322	658,432	2.39	510,410	148,022	0.54
1997	28,168,983	27,594,122	574,861	2.04	414,153	160,708	0.57
1998	29,079,993	28,486,879	593,114	2.04	420,021	173,093	0.60
1999	30,025,114	29,445,071	580,043	1.93	350,302	229,741	0.77
2000	27,272,959	26,708,186	564,773	2.07	361,520	203,253	0.75
2001	27,718,809	27,040,077	678,732	2.45			

Note: The figures for 1992 to 1999 are inclusive of ministers' travelling expenses. The figures for 2000 and 2001 exclude ministers' travelling expenses, following operational changes implemented from 1 January 2000. Congregations no longer receive an annual requirement for ministerial travel (based on estimated mileage) but now are invoiced periodically (usually quarterly) in arrears, based on actual mileage returns from ministers.

Similarly, the figures for 2000 and 2001 differ from those of prior years in that they are exclusive of the voluntary contributions which congregations make to the Insured Pension Fund on behalf of their minister. This conforms with the treatment of such expenditure as a local, rather than, a central cost in the Co-ordinated Budget.

APPENDIX 5

Congregational Contributions to the Mission and Aid Fund

Year	Allocated £	Received by 31 Dec £	Shortfall in Year £	%	Contributions received in Later Years £	Net Shortfall £	%	Voluntary General Extra Contributions £	Designated Extra Contributions £
1992	8,513,391	7,936,862	576,529	6.77	224,115	352,414	4.14	91,263	180,240
1993	9,123,848	8,520,794	603,054	6.61	540,279	62,775	0.69	68,392	151,198
1994	9,512,064	9,040,541	471,523	4.96	420,168	51,355	0.54	81,464	167,660
1995	9,222,444	8,835,357	387,087	4.20	347,727	39,360	0.43	85,000	228,529
1996	9,493,627	9,208,986	284,641	3.00	250,022	34,619	0.36	151,207	446,832
1997	9,822,169	9,573,439	248,730	2.53	219,237	29,493	0.30	87,801	173,551
1998	10,170,417	9,923,349	247,068	2.43	217,108	29,960	0.29	95,319	201,829
1999	10,341,879	10,098,505	243,374	2.35	194,627	48,747	0.47	84,459	197,291
2000	10,550,936	10,296,433	254,503	2.41	189,225	65,278	0.62	85,115	274,452
2001	10,883,504	10,668,488	215,016	1.98				80,752	193,338

APPENDIX 6

Regulations for the Parish Development Fund

1. The Parish Development Fund will be established for a period of five years from 1 January 2003.

2. The Fund will provide all or part funding for local mission projects initiated by congregations.

3. The Board of Stewardship and Finance will provide grants from the Mission and Aid Fund - £1 million in the first year of the Fund's existence and £0.5 million in each of the subsequent four years of the Fund's existence. This money will cover grants to fund local mission projects and the cost of administering the Fund.

4. The Fund will be administered by the Parish Development Fund Committee, which will report directly to the General Assembly.

5. The Parish Development Fund Committee will have the following composition:
   Convener and Vice-Convener, each appointed by the General Assembly through the Nomination Committee;
   Seven members with appropriate skills and knowledge, appointed by the General Assembly through the Nomination Committee;
   One non voting representative from each of the Boards of Ministry, National Mission, Parish Education, Social Responsibility, Stewardship and Finance, and World Mission, and the General Trustees.

6. The Parish Development Fund Committee will have powers to co-opt, each for a period of three years, not more than three non-voting advisers who will represent public and voluntary agencies.

7. The Convener of the Parish Development Fund Committee will be a member of the Co-ordinating Forum.

8. Staff required to service the Parish Development Fund Committee and to act in its name will be located within the Department of National Mission and accountable to the General Secretary of the Board of National Mission.

CENTRAL CO-ORDINATING COMMITTEE
MAY 2002

PROPOSED DELIVERANCE

The General Assembly

1. Receive the Report.
2. Agree the proposed changes to the Central Co-ordinating Committee's Constitution. (Section 1.3)
3. Encourage the Committee in its consultative and advisory role to the General Assembly Boards, Statutory Corporations and Committees. (Section 7)

REPORT

1. Introduction

1.1 The General Assembly of 2001 received and approved the report of the Joint Working Party which was set up on the recommendation of the Special Commission on the Board of Communication. The Working Party's proposals related to the management of the Church's central administration through a new Central Co-ordinating Committee which would have a dual role:

- responsibility for matters previously within the remit of the Office Management Committee and the Personnel Committee, and oversight of the other central services, namely the functions performed by the General Treasurer's and Law Departments.
- operating as a sounding board in cases where any of the central bodies were planning substantial re-organisation or other changes with personnel implications.

1.2 The new Committee was established on 1st September 2001, at which time the former Personnel Committee and Office Management Committee were discharged and the ownership of the offices at 117-123 George Street was passed from the Board of Stewardship and Finance to the Committee. In accordance with the approved structure, the Committee appointed an Executive Committee, a Personnel Committee and an Internal Audit Committee.

1.3 In the light of the Committee's experience since its formation, it now seeks Assembly approval for a number of changes to the constitution. These relate to the Committee's structure and are outlined in bold text in Appendix I.

2. Personnel

2.1 Salaries
The voting members of the Committee, taking account of inflation and other relevant parameters, reviewed the salaries payable to all members of staff for which the Central Co-ordinating Committee is the Employing Agency. As a result the salary scales were increased by some 2.5 per cent which the Committee believes was a fair and reasonable review for its employees. The new salaries were implemented with effect from 1st January 2002.

2.2 Pensions
Following extensive consideration, the former Personnel Committee informed last year's General Assembly of its intention to improve scheme benefits for its staff to reflect more equitably those which apply in similar employment. These improvements included the removal of deductions in respect of basic pension and SERPS, but with a reduction from 1/60th to 1/80th of final pensionable salary accruing for every year of qualifying service. Despite the costly nature of these adjustments it was felt necessary to proceed with their implementation in order to correct a considerable anomaly that has been of concern for some

years. These changes would be subject to a ruling that would ensure no member could be worse off than provided for by the present scheme arrangements.

2.3 Maternity Pay
In accordance with the instruction of the General Assembly of 2001, the Committee reviewed its maternity provision. As a result, the Committee increased the provision for those employees with one year's service and over, with effect from 1st January 2002. The new rate payable is twelve weeks at full pay and six weeks at half pay instead of six weeks at 9/10ths of full pay followed by twelve weeks at £62.20 per week, i.e. the lower rate of statutory maternity pay (SMP).

2.4 Short-Term Contracts
As directed by the Central Co-ordinating Committee, the Personnel Committee considered the addendum to the deliverance of the Special Commission anent Review and Reform to give consideration to making certain appointments in the central organisation of the Church time-limited, but on renewable contract. Although recognising that such contracts could be of use in certain circumstances, having considered many factors including existing, and likely, changes in employment law, demographic trends and potential skill shortages, the Committee does not feel that it can recommend such a policy to the General Assembly.

2.5 St Ninian's Centre, Crieff
As required by the decision of the 2001 General Assembly relative to the Special Commission's recommendation regarding the St. Ninian's Centre, Crieff, all the necessary personnel procedures were completed in connection with the closure of the Centre on 30th September 2001.

2.6 Staff Development
A Staff Development Scheme has been introduced in the Church's offices and will be applied to all members of staff for whom the Central Co-ordinating Committee is the employing agency.

2.7 Review of Salary Scales
The Committee has appointed a working party to examine the current rates of remuneration in relevant external markets for similar posts to those that exist in the Church Offices, as well as to review the structure of the present salary scales.

2.8 Employee Statistics
Appendix II shows the number of employees under the remit of the Central Co-ordinating Committee as at 31st December 2001 and the previous two years, for each Board, Committee and department.

2.9 Consultation
As an ongoing process, both formal and informal, consultation has continued throughout the year with various Boards, Committees and departments of the Church as well as with representatives of both the former Office Management Committee and the Staff Association.

3. Internal Audit

3.1 The internal audit function is provided through the services of an independent firm of Chartered Accountants, Messrs Scott-Moncrieff, working in close co-operation with the Internal Audit Committee. The function covers all Boards and Committees of the Church, with the exception of the Board of Social Responsibility, which has its own internal audit function, using the same firm of accountants.

3.2 The Internal Audit Committee has undertaken a major exercise on risk assessment, through workshops run by Messrs Scott-Moncrieff for specific Boards and Committees of the Church and for the General Trustees. This exercise will facilitate compliance with the requirement of the Statement of Recommended Practice – "Accounting and Reporting by Charities" – that the Church's Annual Report and Financial Statements should confirm that major risks have been assessed and that systems are in place to mitigate exposure to them.

3.3 The Internal Audit Committee is entitled to report directly to the General Assembly, should it consider it appropriate and necessary. There are no issues at this time that the Committee wishes to report directly.

4. Centralised Insurance Service
In an attempt to co-ordinate insurance cover for risks

common to a number of Boards and Committees, the Central Co-ordinating Committee has formalised an arrangement whereby a member of staff in the General Treasurer's Department organises the cover required for risks such as public liability, employers' liability, personal accident, business travel, fidelity guarantee, computers, etc. This arrangement does not include the Board of Social Responsibility, nor car fleet requirements, nor policies relating solely to an individual Board or Committee. The common policies are taken out with the Church of Scotland Insurance Company, which continues to offer a good service.

5. Information Technology

5.1 The Information Technology Department is responsible for the provision, support and development of computer facilities in the George Street Offices and for approximately seventy-five sites throughout the country, primarily Presbytery Clerks and National Mission offices and staff, as well as the telephone service in George Street.

5.2 The Department has undergone major restructuring and development based on the report in Spring 2001 from the University of Strathclyde consultant. This provides the opportunity for further development of the technology and systems to meet the needs of Boards and departments. Alongside the restructuring, major developments have included the provision of a training programme in 'Office' products used extensively by staff; improved access to the Internet for George Street staff; the release of the Presbytery Information Management System (PIMS) to Presbytery Clerks and the introduction of a new non-subscription E-Mail and Internet provision for those working outwith George Street.

5.3 In 2002 the IT Department will continue to work alongside Boards and departments to plan and develop facilities. These will include the introduction of an upgraded financial application in conjunction with the General Treasurer's Department; improvements in document management software; further assessment of the validity of software licences; the introduction of enhanced anti-virus software; development and support

of the various in-house applications written to support the Department's work; the development of the George Street network to meet the increasing demands being placed upon it and a major upgrade to the core Microsoft software in use throughout the offices.

6. Office Management

6.1 Fairly Traded Tea and Coffee

In response to an instruction from last year's General Assembly, the Committee has taken forward the matter of providing fairly traded tea and coffee in the Church Offices. In consultation with the Staff Association, it has been agreed that there should continue to be a choice of tea and coffee products, including fairly traded varieties.

6.2 Sodexho

Last year's General Assembly encouraged the Office Management Committee to re-examine its catering contract with Sodexho, in the light of Sodexho's close involvement with the Voucher Scheme put into operation for asylum seekers. Having made contact with Sodexho, the Office Management Committee concluded that the matter was political and that the best route for seeking changes to the system would be through pressure on the Government. The Church and Nation Committee's Report provides the Assembly with an update on this matter.

6.3 Health and Safety Matters

Over the past year a number of improvements have been made in relation to bringing the George Street Offices up to date with current health and safety legislation. These include removal of all old lead pipework and water tanks; inspection of all electrical systems, with remedial works being carried out; new emergency lighting installed to the main staircase; safety features installed to both lifts; the undertaking of a Fire Risk Assessment; the training of first aiders; and regular statutory checks on portable appliances, fire alarms and extinguishers.

6.4 Disabled Access

The Committee has approved outline plans for disabled access to the George Street offices. The consultant architect is in the process of finalising drawings for further consideration. Additional advice has been sought from the Joint Mobility Unit. Final plans will be submitted for a Building Control Warrant in the Summer of 2002, tenders submitted by late Autumn and the work anticipated to commence in early 2003.

6.5 Security

The Committee is pleased to report that the new security system in the George Street offices was completed in April 2001 and fully operational by June 2001.

7. Consultative and Advisory Work

7.1 The Committee is pleased to report a greater sense of co-operation between departments and a desire to operate more efficiently. The Executive Committee has met with department heads to discuss a range of matters of shared interest, such as the web-site, office management issues and the Society, Religion and Technology Project. The Committee has concluded that at least two such meetings per annum will be necessary to ensure better co-ordination, and formally brings this matter to the Assembly under section 1.3.

7.2 The Committee wishes to remind Boards and Committees that any central body proposing to implement any substantial re-organisation, or other changes in the manner in which it undertakes its remit which have personnel implications, is bound, at the outset, to intimate such proposals to the Committee in order that the Committee may assess their impact on the work of the wider Church.

7.3 The Committee believes that while the Church might be moving towards devolving some decision making to local areas, a national Church will continue to require a central support structure.

In the name of the Committee,

LEON M MARSHALL, *Convener*
JOHN NEIL, *Vice-Convener*
PAULINE WILSON, *Administrative Secretary*

APPENDIX I

Proposed Changes to the Constitution of The Central Co-ordinating Committee

Structure

The Committee shall appoint an Executive Committee which shall comprise the Convener **and Vice-Convener** of the Committee together with the Convener(s) of the Personnel and Internal Audit Committees aftermentioned and of any other Sub-Committee established by the Committee and the *ex officio* members of the Committee.

The Convener of the Committee shall be the Convener of the Executive Committee.

The Executive Committee shall meet at least twice per annum with **the Staff Association and also with the departmental heads of the Central bodies.**

The Executive Committee shall in all matters be subject to the authority and direction of the Committee. Between meetings the Executive Committee shall act as the Committee in relation to all matters referred to it.

The Committee shall further appoint a Personnel Committee which shall comprise three of the Assembly appointed members together with the **Convener, Vice-Convener and** *ex-officiis* members of the Committee. One of the Assembly appointed members shall act as Convener of the Personnel Committee.

The Committee shall further appoint an Internal Audit Committee which shall comprise three of the Assembly appointed members together with **a representative of the Board of Stewardship and Finance *ex officio* and the Convener and Vice-Convener of the Committee**. One of the Assembly appointed members shall act as Convener of the Internal Audit Committee which shall be entitled to report directly to the General Assembly, should it consider it appropriate and necessary so to do.

The Committee shall be entitled to set up other Sub-Committees as it considers to be necessary to facilitate the implementation of its remit.

APPENDIX II
CENTRAL CO-ORDINATING COMMITTEE
Employees as at 31 December

Board/Committee/Department	2001 Full Time	Part Time	Total	2000 Full Time	Part Time	Total	1999 Full Time	Part Time	Total
Assembly Council	2		2		1	1		1	1
Central Co-ordinating Committee		1	1						
Church and Nation	1	2	3	1	2	3	1	2	3
Communication	27		27	31		31	27	1	28
Ecumenical Relations	2		2	2		2	2		2
Education	2		2	2		2	2		2
General Trustees	8	9	17	9	9	18	9	9	18
Information Technology	12		12	10		10	9		9
Law	9	6	15	12	3	15	11	3	14
Ministry	17	2	19	17	2	19	18	1	19
National Mission	22	10	32	34	17	51	36	15	51
New College		1	1		1	1		1	1
Office Management	5	5	10	5	5	10	5	2	7
Parish Education	31	5	36	31	8	39	22	12	34
Pensions	3	2	5	3	2	5	3	1	4
Personnel	4		4	4		4	4		4
Practice and Procedure	4	2	6	5	1	6	6	1	7
Scottish Parliamentary Office	2	1	3	2		2	2		2
Stewardship & Finance									
—Administration	2		2	2		2			
—General Treasurers	17	6	23	19	5	24	16	5	21
—Stewardship	6		6	7		7	7	1	8
The Guild	3	2	5	3	2	5	3	3	6
World Mission	19	3	22	18	2	20	19	2	21
Worship, Doctrine & Artistic Matters	1	3	4	1	3	4	2		2
Total Employees	**199**	**60**	**259**	**218**	**63**	**281**	**204**	**60**	**264**
National Mission Groups									
National Mission	13	1	14	13	2	15	12	2	14
Badenoch	1	2	3	1	1	2	1	2	3
St. Ninian's				11	4	15	13	2	15
Mission and Evangelism	1	4	5	2	5	7	2	5	7
Priority Areas Fund					2	2	1	1	2
Netherbow	6	3	9	6	3	9	6	3	9
Well	1		1	1		1	1		1
	22	10	32	34	17	51	36	15	51

THE GUILD

MAY 2002

PROPOSED DELIVERANCE

The General Assembly

1. Receive the report, thank the office bearers and staff and welcome Vivienne Macdonald and Moira Alexander as Convener and Vice Convener respectively for 2002–3.

2. Commend the Guild for its continuing support of the Church's mission through the current Project Scheme, "*Strength for Living*".

3. Welcome the setting up of the Initiative Fund and encourage local groups to explore the opportunities for community outreach which this affords.

4. Support the Guild in its participation in the UK anti-trafficking campaign and welcome HM government's intention to address the issue of trafficking of persons in forthcoming legislation.

5. Recognise the need for the Churches to increase their understanding of the issues underlying domestic violence and respond to them, and welcome the Guild's involvement in and support of forthcoming ecumenical initiatives, on this issue.

REPORT

"What is the church we need in these days? It is a society of redeemed men and women banded together to continue and extend Christ's redeeming work upon earth, bringing sight to the blind, freedom to the captive, the Gospel of God's love to the poor." (Prof. Archibald Charteris, the Baird Lectures 1887)

1   Introduction: "*Banded together*"

1.1   One of the perhaps less radical, but possibly more achievable, suggestions to be found in the "Church Without Walls" report was that the General Assembly might be restyled to fulfil a more inspirational role within the life of the Church, possibly including themed conference sessions. This kind of focus has certainly proved effective in the life of the Guild over recent years and we now find ourselves in year two of a three year programme, "Strength for Living". Support for six projects selected under that heading continues, while the current session's Discussion Topic, "Overcoming Violence", has provided challenge and stimulus for debate throughout the country. The theme for the 2001-2 session, which was launched at the Annual Meeting in September, has been "Strength Through God's Presence".

1.2   When guild members gathered in Glasgow for that Annual Meeting, the title adopted for the event was "Together 2001". Chosen partly for its neat alliteration, partly because it followed the pattern of recent years : Celebration '98, Discovery '99, Vision 2000, and partly because the Youth Assembly had already snapped up the obvious "Odyssey 2001", it has proved an apt label for the year's activities. In mutual support at difficult times, in joint meetings and events, in partnerships with parallel organisations and in local and national initiatives, guild members have shared *together* their hopes and concerns, their challenges and achievements, both personal and collective. The togetherness of the day itself was enhanced by the live webcast, which enabled members and friends to tune in to what was happening from their own homes, in places as far apart as Benbecula and Australia.

1.3   In her keynote address at "Together 2001", the writer and broadcaster, Elaine Storkey, said that "The perseverance of the real Christian is living, day by day, in the presence of God, who will renew us daily, giving us strength to cope".   If the Guild is to remain true to its initial purpose and fulfil its current aim of encouraging people to explore the Christian faith and commit their lives to Christ, then the issues of daily living are those with which it must continue to engage.   In pursuing its aim the Guild hopes to make a contribution to the national life of the Church, but this is most effectively achieved by its activities locally.   John Miller, Moderator, recognised the importance of this in his own address to the Annual Meeting, when he referred to his own experience of the nurturing role of the guild within the local congregation.

2   Concerned Together

2.1   When the Assembly Council consulted the Church's Boards and Committees through the Co-ordinating Forum, about a possible re-ordering of the Church's structures to reflect the core aims of the church, it was not readily apparent where the Guild might slot in. However, reflecting on what is reported here, it seems that the Guild's most natural contribution would be to the core function of faith nurturing, witnessing and evangelisation - its calling at local level.

2.2   There is also, however, a national strand to Guild involvement which might be accounted for under the heading of policy and engagement.   Responses to Consultative Documents, either to the Scottish Executive or, through its membership of the Women's National Commission, to Westminster, continue to be sought and delivered.   Links through networks of voluntary associations and of ecumenical groupings bring the Guild's voice to a wider audience, where its distinctive contribution on a range of issues, like parenting, education and justice, is valued.   Recent submissions to consultations include those on sectarianism and the treatment of witnesses in rape trials.   Always alive to issues of international concern, as far back as 1998 the Guild was inviting its members to support the WomenAid International campaign, "Living Shadows", against the treatment of women by the Taliban regime in Afghanistan. Another current concern is the trafficking of people, a major area of work for the Ecumenical Forum of European Christian Women, of which the Guild is a member organisation. The Guild has joined the UK Anti-Trafficking Network and has tried to raise awareness of this evil trade and welcomes the fact that measures to tackle it form part of the government's White Paper on Nationality, Immigration, and Asylum.

3   Learning Together

3.1   The resource material prepared by the Programmes and Resources Committee to help local groups address the Theme of "Strength through God's Presence", emphasises the peace of God as a gift derived from His presence in our lives.   This is not the peace which guarantees immunity from all that is painful and disturbing, but the peace which brings clarity of understanding and strength for living. As the related Discussion Topic for the year, the Projects and Topics Committee had selected "Overcoming Violence", a subject chosen partly in response to the World Council of Churches' call for a "Decade to Overcome Violence", and partly to explore further those issues of peace building with which the Guild had become involved in recent years : domestic violence in Scotland, the contribution of women to the peace process in Northern Ireland and the treatment of women by oppressive regimes worldwide.

3.2   In preparation for the 2001-2 session on these themes, ten local training days for group leaders were planned for March 2001.   These annual events are designed to deliver practical help with programme building and presentation at accessible venues throughout the country, led by experienced Council members, using material prepared by the national team.   The response, both in terms of numbers participating and as expressed in the evaluation process, is encouraging, but new approaches to expressed needs are always being sought. A further series of training days has been arranged in preparation for the 2002-3 session, on the theme of empowerment and its related discussion topic of globalisation.

4 Caring Together

4.1 In the event, only nine of the ten scheduled training days were held last year, the one planned for Annan being cancelled because of the effects of the Foot and Mouth epidemic in that area. A steady stream of phone calls and e-mail messages to Guild Office regarding cancellation and postponement of AGMs and Spring rallies painted a picture of the disruption to normal rural life and the painful reality of the consequences of the disease and the strategy for its eradication. There were many stories of individual distress amongst the membership and also of consistent generous mutual support in many practical ways. The sense that this was something in which we were all involved *together* was confirmed by the response of one of the Guildlink partners of a rural guild in this area. The correspondent of Middlebie Guild wrote : "Our link helped us a great deal when some of our members lost their sheep. The prayers, cards, letters and telephone calls from members of Kilbowie: St Andrew's Guild were a marvellous support." Lochmaben Guild were conscious too of the thoughts and prayers of Glasgow: North Kelvinside at that time.

4.2 The Guildlink scheme, setting up partnerships between guilds in different areas has now been in operation for ten years. The levels of contact vary according to circumstances. Some links are maintained by correspondents who exchange news and greetings regularly, some are able to arrange meetings and visits, while others have extended the friendship to congregational level, arranging pulpit exchanges, as happened recently between Larkhall: Trinity and Glasgow: Sherbrook St Gilbert's. Following their interest in a recent Guild project, the group at Skene in Aberdeenshire have begun exploring the possibility of a link with a guild in Malawi.

5 Working Together

5.1 Involvement in the Project Partnership Scheme has led many guilds to work collaboratively. The scheme continues to demonstrate that, working *together*, the Guild can achieve far more than individual members or groups might imagine possible. The extent of such possibilities was brought home most significantly through the visit of Fiona Lange, Information Officer, to Papua New Guinea in September at the invitation of one of our partners in project work, Mission Aviation Fellowship. The sum of £45,000, raised by guilds in support of the "With Wings as Eagles" project during its first year, had seemed substantial enough back in Scotland, but only on meeting the beneficiaries in PNG, did its real significance become apparent. The gratitude of patients and both hospital and flight staff was overwhelming as they explained to Fiona what this sum of money could pay for in terms of training, equipment and medical supplies. "...the Guild's money is the answer to prayer...it felt as if this money had fallen straight from heaven".

5.2 At the halfway point of the current "Strength for Living" project scheme, the amount raised by guilds is over £255,000. We are grateful to our partners for their willingness to visit guilds and speak about the work of their various departments and organisations. Sometimes they may find themselves addressing a large gathering at a Council Rally; at other times they may have travelled many miles to speak to a small rural group. This is much appreciated by our members who respond with interest and support which goes beyond what can be measured in monetary terms. The element of choice does, of course, mean that the individual projects do not each receive an equal proportion of the funds raised. At the time of writing this report the amounts donated are as follows :

With Wings as Eagles (Mission Aviation Fellowship)	£ 66,179
Forgotten Frontier (Scottish Bible Society)	£ 24,597
A Way of Life (Board of Communication)	£ 12,435
Rebuilding Lives (Lodging House Mission)	£ 77,800
Rainy Hospital (Board of World Mission)	£ 67,439
The Well (Board of National Mission)	£ 23,534
Total	£271,984

5.3 It is interesting to note that the backmarker is the "Way of Life" project supporting the Church of Scotland's own website. This may be a result of members feeling that it is better to give away money than to use it on one's own organisation, in this case the Church. At the time of the selection of the current set of projects, the members of the Projects and Topics committee were keen to include this one, not because they wished to show that the Guild was clued up about IT, but because of their conviction that the Church should be using every tool available to communicate the Gospel. However, this kind of diversity of response must be both expected and respected if the shift of decision-making and responsibility from the central to the local is to mean anything in the Church.

5.4   Reference was made in the 2001 Report to the successful conclusion of the Banners 2000 exhibition and tour. In August the Moderator joined Irene McGugan MSP in launching the commemorative book and video, which are now available through bookshops or direct from St Andrew Press and Guild Office. The banners themselves, the tour and the book and video are another demonstration of the value of working *together*, the resulting whole being considerably greater then the sum of its parts.

5.5   Projects of a more local dimension have been submitted by several guilds for consideration by the Finance and General Purposes Committee following the establishment of an Initiative Fund. This fund has been set up, using funds from the interest on invested legacy money, to enable local guilds or councils to undertake work of benefit to the community. Imaginative ideas of practical value, which require start up funding to make them a reality, have been put forward and the first grants will be made later this year.

5.6   The role of Project Co-ordinator at Council level, introduced in 1997, is proving to be one of great possibilities. The annual Day Conference for co-ordinators gives them a wealth of information and ideas on which to draw in visiting local groups and arranging events designed to stimulate interest in the projects.

6   Sharing Together

6.1   The Day Conference as a means of sharing ideas and expressing concerns is also valued by the Council Conveners. Their 2001 event looked at issues of homelessness, the future of the Church following the various reports on reform presented at the General Assembly, and continuing Christian education. This last concern has always been a major element of Guild life, implicit in its aim to enable people to explore and express their faith. The Council "Ed Reps" have a vital role here and are greatly helped in fulfilling it by the Board of Parish Education which services their support group. This group provides resource material and organises the annual overnight conference.

6.2   Beyond its own particular concerns and activities, the Guild has continued to play its part in the life of the Church of Scotland. Members have contributed at congregational and Presbytery level to the planning and decision making processes, responding to, and participating in, the various consultations and debates emanating from Boards, Commissions and the Assembly Council. Guild representatives have served on the Boards and Committees of the Church and support has been given for specific undertakings such as the Youth Assembly, the Year of the Child, the Conference on Weapons of War, the Gender Attitude Project and the Interfaith Forum.

6.3   The National Convener, Elspeth Kerr, and her team have represented the Guild at various conferences and at events held by our sister organisations in the Network of Ecumenical Women in Scotland. Janette Henderson, a former Committee Convener, has continued to serve the Guild by co-ordinating our involvement in issues relating to the WCC Decade to Overcome Violence. In this capacity she has attended several nationwide events, most significantly those mounted by Methodist Women's Network. September will see a major conference on domestic violence, planned in conjunction with the Catholic Council for Social Care and representatives from Network and the Salvation Army.

6.4   The close links which have resulted from the Guild's membership of NEWS were further strengthened by the opportunity to be part of the Scottish Ecumenical Assembly in September. The Convener, Vice-Convener and General Secretary were among the delegates from the Church of Scotland, along with several other Guild members attending in different capacities. The experience was both inspiring and exhausting. The contacts made in both informal and structured settings did indeed break new ground, and it is hoped that a new enthusiasm will be stimulated for ecumenical partnership and initiative. Guild Ecumenical Representatives at council level have sometimes found their role frustratingly vague, but personal contact within local communities can lead to opportunities for dialogue as a first step towards closer working relationships. The inclusion of these representatives in events organised by the Committee on Ecumenical Relations is much appreciated.

7   Serving Together

7.1   During her term of office, Elspeth Kerr has managed to meet a huge number of Guild members through visits to local groups and Councils. This task has been a real pleasure, not simply because of the warmth of the welcome from Corby to Forres but because of the level of interest in, and commitment to, the Guild's local and national activities and concerns. Other members of the national team, notably the Vice-Convener, Vivienne Macdonald, together with committee conveners, Moira Alexander, Eleanor Butters, Margaret Carey, Valerie Light and Sylvia Macfarlane, have shared in the work of visitation and representation and their support and teamwork has been of immense value to the movement.

7.2   Like other august bodies, the Guild is *semper reformanda* in the interest of growth and development. Five years after major changes to its structures, the Guild is undertaking a review of the Constitution to see whether any further amendments are necessary to improve the smooth running of the organisation. Although the process was always intended, the Review Group, under the chairmanship of former National Convener, Elva Carlisle, was kick started this session because of the need to respond to the pleas from several quarters, to be more inclusive in our language. Some local leaders felt uncomfortable with an Aim still expressed in terms of

women, when men at Guild meetings are no longer the startling oddity they once were. It is interesting to note that at an early meeting of the review group, the view was put forward that "she" might be taken to imply inclusion of "he" for all but the militantly masculinist. It is, however, more likely that the more generous amendment of "she or he" will prevail – our small contribution to gender attitude awareness.

7.3   The Guild's members, female and male, remain its greatest asset. All those who serve at local, presbytery and national level and all who contribute through this particular channel to the life of their congregation and community are valued. Statistics of membership and the details of financial donations are detailed in the Appendix below. The Newsletter, produced regularly by the Marketing and Publicity committee for every member, contained, in a recent issue, a monthly prayer calendar for personal use. Those who use this guide will be praying together for the mission of the Church, for the work of the Guild and for each other. In congregations where there is no affiliated Guild group there are some who join the organisation as individual members because they like to keep in touch with the work of the Guild. We are open to contact and partnership with all congregations whether or not a Guild group exists within their church and are very appreciative of the support received from individuals and congregations, particularly in respect of our current projects.

7.4   The staffing complement remains at 5, with General Secretary, Alison Twaddle and Information Officer, Fiona Lange, assisted by Ann Anderson, personal secretary to the General Secretary, Maureen Morrish, cashier, and Maureen Scoular, word processor operator and clerical assistant. All clerical staff have undertaken training in various computer programmes to improve their skills. Fiona Lange has successfully completed the first part of a course which will lead to full membership of the Institute of Public Relations and Alison Twaddle has benefited from membership of the Association of Chief Officers of Scottish Voluntary Organisations. The support of the National Executive Committee for all aspects of staff development is very much appreciated.

7.5   The General Secretary has had her busiest diary ever in terms of speaking engagements. Her visit to Bosnia and Croatia in March 2001 resulted in a great many invitations, most of which she has been able to accept. Although primarily undertaken at the invitation of the Reformed Church in Croatia to be present at the rededication of one of the Churches restored as a result of the project, "A Church for a Croatian Village" (1997–2000), the trip included a memorable visit to Bosnia. Fortuitous timetabling enabled the General Secretary to accompany the Moderator on part of his tour of the Balkans and to see some of the work being done by the Ecumenical Women's Solidarity Fund of the World Council of Churches.

7.6   These community-based projects, enabling women with professional skills to help individuals and communities rebuild their lives in the aftermath of war, were impressive and moving. Most of the project work visited was being done in a mainly Muslim area and the majority of the people involved, both as project workers and beneficiaries, and introduced to the visiting party by the co-ordinator, Carolyn Boyd, were Muslims. The funding, via the WCC, was mainly from the Christian churches. This proved, during the current session's tour of speaking engagements, to be a point of great interest and the start of many discussions on the relationship between faiths in our own and other cultures. The events of September 11 no doubt added to the realisation that there is a real need to increase our level of understanding of other faiths. Several members asked whether a seminar might be arranged to facilitate this. However, on exploring the issue with the Interfaith Forum members, it was discovered that the Churches' Agency for Interfaith Relations was already planning such an event at Dunblane in March, to which Guild members would be welcome.

8   Challenged Together

8.1   On September 11 the Guild's national committees were meeting together for their annual joint conference in the peaceful surroundings of Carberry. With our current discussion topic, "Overcoming Violence", in mind,

two external speakers had been invited to share in the programme. Mission partner, Margaret Fowler shared her experiences working with churches in Jamaica, encouraging them not to shrink from involvement in a culture, often violent because of the effects on people of alcohol and drugs. Janette Baird, of Castlemilk, spoke about the local project, Women Against Violent Environments, and challenged us to question our attitudes to women trapped in violent relationships, to understand their situation and their apparently incomprehensible choice to stay with a violent partner. These were disturbing talks - violence on our doorstep, violence in every kind of local and international community, involving every kind of person. All the while, reports were filtering in to our conference of the events, both distant and yet immediate, unfolding in the USA. On the second morning of the conference, September 12, a young American minister, currently serving in a Scottish congregation, led our communion service. It was emotional, it was poignant, it was full of questions and the questions have remained.

8.2   A few weeks later there was another day event for Guild members. This time the target audience was our younger members and the event was called "Time Out" - a day for quiet and reflection in the midst of demanding lifestyles. The emphasis here was on personal faith journeys, an opportunity much welcomed by those who were able to take part. A stimulating talk, informal conversations and guided meditation in a relaxed atmosphere were major ingredients and feedback indicates that all these elements added to the value of the day. In the final worship, however, the focus shifted and became more outward looking. Conscious that we were meeting on the International Day of Action on Violence against Women, and still very aware of the effects of violent terrorism, the organisers used worship material prepared especially for the International Day by members of the Methodist Network.

8.3   This material was based on the saying of Jesus: "I have come that they may have life and have it in all its fullness". The Guild is in the business of pointing people to that truth. We invite people to commit their lives to Christ, placing the individual at the heart of our aim. But we also exist to encourage and enable individuals to express their faith in worship, prayer and action, which brings into play the quality of relationships, the community of purpose and the collective effort in the service of others. It is in the exploration and expression of their faith *together* that we invite people to enjoy that promised fullness of life. In 1893, the fledgling Guild published its first Annual Report, the conclusion of which serves as well today as it did then and might be applied as much to our denomination as to the Guild. It reads : "Let our last and clearest thought be that organisation, reports, conferences are means to an end - and that end is not the extension of the Guild: it is the advancement of the kingdom of Christ. The Guild is not a motive power or a goal: it is an opportunity."

ELSPETH H KERR, National Convener
ALISON M TWADDLE, General Secretary

ADDENDUM

At the General Assembly of 2002, Elspeth Kerr completes her year as National Convener of the Guild. The outstanding feature of her term has been the personal contact she has had with so many of the Guild's members. Every opportunity has been taken gladly, no journey has seemed too far or too complicated. The reward for this energy and commitment has been the warmth of the response from those who met the Convener and found themselves affirmed and enthused by her. We now record our thanks to Elspeth, who had guided us gently and firmly, (only occasionally slipping into infant mistress mode). We now return her to the family who have so willingly supported her and whose interest has been an encouragement to us all.

VIVIENNE MACDONALD, National Convener
ALISON M TWADDLE, General Secretary

APPENDIX
Financial Contributions

Sums given by guilds were as follows :

Mission and Aid Fund	£189,486
Congregational Funds	£538,624
Work of the Church (including projects)	£275,585
Work outwith the Church	£ 97,249
TOTAL	£1,100,944

Membership: 40,396
Affiliated groups: 1,380

(Amounts based on most up-to-date information available at the time of preparation of this report.)

ASSEMBLY COUNCIL

MAY 2002

PROPOSED DELIVERANCE

The General Assembly:

1. Receive the Report.

2. Welcome the widespread discussion of the Report *Church Without Walls* and encourage all who are studying it to respond to the Council's consultation on the progress and development of the Report.

3. Instruct Presbyteries and Kirk Sessions and encourage congregations to undertake the consultation process outlined in sections 5.3.6-8 of the Report, with reference also to section 7(d) of the Report of the Board of Practice and Procedure and to send responses to the Assembly Council by 31 December 2002.

4. Invite the National Youth Assembly 2002 to study the issues outlined in sections 5.3.6-8 of the Report, with reference also to section 7(d) of the Report of the Board of Practice and Procedure and forward to the Principal Clerk an extract deliverance from its debate.

5. Instruct the Council and the Board of Practice and Procedure to consider whether elders might moderate Kirk Sessions, to take account of the relevant responses to the consultation on the eldership, and to report to the General Assembly of 2003.

REPORT

The Kingdom of Heaven is like a mustard seed ... though it is the smallest of all your seeds, yet when it grows, it is the largest of garden plants and becomes a tree, so that the birds of the air come and perch on its branches.

1. A significant Assembly? ...

1.1 <u>Friday 18 May 2001.</u> About 100 Assembly Commissioners and Youth Representatives gather in a central Edinburgh church hall for the first ever orientation evening for first-time commissioners, designed to provide helpful information, answer questions, most of all to make them feel welcome to the Assembly. Some are apprehensive, some are excited, some have never travelled so far from home before. The buzz of conversation rises as introductions are made, travel experiences exchanged, accommodation compared, questions asked and answered: 'Is there parking at the Hall?' 'What number of bus do I take?' 'Do I need the Blue Book with me every day?'

1.2 Donald Smith of the Storytelling Centre at the Netherbow has been asked to track the course of the week as the story of the Assembly develops. He quarters the room with his camera team looking for likely candidates to interview. 'What are your hopes for this Assembly?' 'What are you most looking forward to?' It quickly becomes clear that what has captured everyone's imagination is the Report of the Special Commission on Review and Reform – 'It puts into words a lot of what has been going on in my head for a long time'. More particularly, the phrase 'Church without walls' has struck a chord, provided a concept, conjured up an image to which everyone relates in his or her own way:

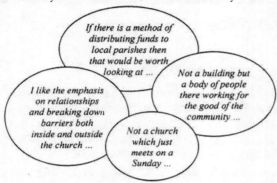

If there is a method of distributing funds to local parishes then that would be worth looking at ...

Not a building but a body of people there working for the good of the community ...

I like the emphasis on relationships and breaking down barriers both inside and outside the church ...

Not a church which just meets on a Sunday ...

1.3 On the Monday, the Special Commission Report is received with enthusiasm and with scarcely a dissenting voice. Was this the significant step forward which so many had hoped for? Why was it so appealing to so many? Was it because review and reform had been rooted so firmly in a return to the Word of God?

> We have discovered the primary purposes of the church by returning to the Gospels. The core calling of the church is to follow Jesus. We call the church to risk the way of Jesus. God's future begins with today's obedience. (Peter Neilson, Special Commission)

'This was the real story of the week' said Donald Smith, summing up all that he had heard in debate and conversation. 'Review and reform, yes, but walking in the way of Jesus, the way of obedience. This Assembly may have begun to change the Church because it changed people's sense of the Church and redirected lives.'

1.4 The parable of the mustard seed encourages us to reflect upon the hidden power of what is apparently small and insignificant. While we may instinctively look for significance in major reports or big events such as the General Assembly, the greatest influence of all may be exerted by men and women leading dedicated lives in their own places – lives which witness to the authenticity of the Gospel by their selflessness and integrity and love.

2. One year on ...

2.1 One year on, the phrase 'Church without walls' is everywhere, used freely in connection with many different ideas and concepts. But are these concepts making a real difference in the life of the Church? Did the enthusiasm of last year's commissioners survive the return to the reality of everyday congregational concerns? What is the impact of the Report on those who were not part of last year's experience and who have to pick up most of their information from the written word?

2.2 The Council is instructed by the Assembly *to monitor and evaluate developments through its ongoing consultations and assessments* ... and report to the General Assemblies of 2003 and 2005. That monitoring process has already begun and details are given later in this report.

2.3 At this early stage, what we have heard gives us cause for encouragement as we learn of imaginative developments, new thinking, and 'risk-taking' throughout the Church. In so many ways and in so many places the 'mood for change' is becoming a 'movement for change'. The Council believes that there are considerable grounds for hope and optimism.

2.4 However, the Council is also aware that the very word 'change' can raise considerable fears for some. There often seems to be a tension within the Church at large, within congregations and within individuals between a desire to see progress and a fear of the cost of change.

2.5 There may be a number of reasons for this: one is that reactions can take place on more than one level. We can all hear the logical argument and even sign up to it but at another level and at the same time can be resistant to it. We can see such a situation, for example, with proposals to reduce the number of buildings and with talk of team ministries and local co-operation. Almost everyone will sign up to these as good ideas but few as yet seem to want to make them a reality.

2.6 Another reason is that while there may be a longing for change, that longing may not be particularly focused and may remain comfortably hypothetical. The resistance then comes when real worked-out initiatives are presented, especially if they are seen as imposed from the 'top'. Loren Mead, in reflecting on the situation in the American churches says this:

Today we are experiencing obvious pain in the organisational structures that make up our denominations: relationships among congregations, between congregations and their regional bodies … between congregations and national bodies, and between regional and national bodies. … An assumption of suspicion has replaced the assumption of trust. Congregations are now predisposed to resist whatever initiatives those in the 'upper' structures propose, even when the proposals are first rate. This climate of distrust and suspicion severely handicaps communication and effective collaboration from the top down or from the bottom up. No matter how hard the 'upper' levels try to listen to the 'grass roots' they are not perceived as being very attentive. The assumption of distrust makes neither party willing to allow the other to change behaviour. Organisational paralysis can be the result.[1]

Perhaps we might fruitfully reflect on whether we can learn something from these observations. If there seemed to be some truth there for us, the task would be to take time to listen more patiently to each other and to work to restore trusting relationships in all areas of the Church's life.

2.7 One wise commissioner said last year:

The biggest thing the Church has to realise is not that change is coming, but how to manage change – to educate and allow congregations to participate within that change and not to coerce them.

The indications are that change is not to be imposed or hurried. The *Church without Walls* Report will take time to work through. The mustard seeds will take time to grow. The Special Commission recognised that this was the start of a journey which would be travelled for some years to come. It did not try to ensure that its proposals would be carried forward but handed over its reflections to the people of the Church where the trust and responsibility rests. It is important then that experiments are allowed to happen, pilot schemes organised, news of good practice circulated, helpful contacts made, opportunities given for exploring new thinking, thorough consultation carried out. As new ideas become less strange and more familiar they may be more readily accepted or at least given worthy consideration.

[1] Loren Mead, Five Challenges for the Once and Future Church, The Alban Institute, 1996, p 17f.

3. Passion, Patience and Perseverance

3.1 The beating heart at the core of the present movement of development within the Church is *passion:* a deep desire to be more fully the living Church of Jesus Christ in our nation and in our generation. This fire of passion is burning brightly in many places and people: warming and welcoming, renewing and reforming. But there is a need to keep that fire burning and to fan embers into flames. However, the Council is not unaware that in any process of change and development there is a degree of pain. A passion for ongoing renewal and reform must be accompanied by a deep sensitivity to those who regard talk of change as threatening or as an implied criticism of years of faithful service.

3.2 *Patience* is therefore essential as this journey of ongoing renewal and reformation continues. There is no 'quick fix', and no instant solution, and certainly no justification for riding roughshod over the genuine concerns of some. Change in the Church is not simply about organisation and structure. It is about people and relationships, and so demands a pastoral concern and a deep understanding of the fears that can arise. Our passion will find expression in patient and caring understanding.

3.3 This is not the patience of inactivity and resignation, but the patience of *perseverance*. This present time of transition and development in the church is a process more akin to a marathon than a sprint. It will take time to change perceptions and alter mindsets. 'Church without walls' is not a programme but a process.

4. ... though it is the smallest of your seeds ...

4.1 Wonderful things happen when people go forward and take risks in faith: large sums of money can be raised, major undertakings planned. But transformation and reform is not always measured in terms of big successful projects or major structural change. Equally potent is the impact of individuals who bring love, patience, kindness, cheerfulness, willing service and faithfulness into our lives.

4.2   Mustard seed stories

David and Carol:

David and Carol, a young couple, recently moved into the area. Both have a church background, though David had never become a member, drifting away when he left home to go to University. Attending the Church, they have gradually moved through the circles of commitment and belonging, from the fringes to nearer the centre. With the support of Carol, David has joined the Church in the traditional way. Carol joined a Lent discussion group and later the Board.

At the Annual Stated Meeting, their minister, hardly expecting a positive response, asked if they would consider running the Sunday morning Breakfast Club attended by 12-16 year olds. They joyfully accepted, explaining that they wanted to share with others their own good, positive experiences of youth fellowships.

Now, on Sundays, 14 young people attend, affirmed and enthused by the energy, warmth and imagination of David's and Carol's leadership. The

Allowing people to move into and share the fellowship at their own pace, yet not being afraid to ask them to share their own particular gifts.

'old hands' who help find themselves similarly energised. Where running it had been a source of worry and a burden to the minister, it seems to be a joy for David and Carol.

Marion:

Marion runs her own business. Her connection with the church helped her confidence and has, she says, changed her life for the better.

It began at a low point after her divorce. In the course of dropping her son off at Sunday School, she agreed to participate as a leader, and though lacking in confidence, soon found her niche.

Through the months and years she found companions for the journey of life with faith becoming an increasingly important compass for her own journey.

The more I have given, she says, *the more I have received.*

She experienced the encouragement and support of the church community when her dad died and her mum's health declined with dementia.

She found her voice through helping to lead services in her congregation and participating in congregational holidays. She brought to the congregation the gifts she learned in the business community, particularly the skill to train others, while honing her own skills and discovering new gifts in leadership.

Marion is now an elder, has written and led courses, and encouraged others along the path of life.

Mark:

Though Mark was not a committed or faithful member of the congregation, indeed it had been some time since he had been associated with any Church, he was invited to take on an important musical role. It was soon evident that this provided him with a welcome opportunity to re-engage with the Christian community and to take a significant step on the faith journey which, in his own thinking and reflecting, he had been hesitatingly pursuing.

Almost as soon as he took up his post, he began to engage enthusiastically with the Gospel. After attending an Alpha course, he reached a point of firm commitment to the Christian life, professed faith and was confirmed.

His enthusiasm and skill transformed the musical life of the congregation. His joy and warmth were infectious.

Soon several of his friends began attending worship,

involving themselves in the life of the congregation. This was not due to Mark engaging in personal evangelism in any traditional sense but because of the evident passion, love and joy he now unconsciously displays.

Lately, one of those who has started coming around church mainly through his contact with Mark, has begun to ask searching questions about what it might mean for him to follow Jesus more fully, and how he might find something of the joy of Christian living.

Perhaps the most telling observation is that he almost certainly does not recognise the effect he has had!

Although this might be the most open and explicit example of someone being affected by Mark's influence, it is far from unique. It would not be an exaggeration to say that the whole congregation has been positively affected by Mark's presence and contribution.

4.3 Walls and barriers disappear through the influence of such people. Likewise partnerships of all kinds break down the divisions which so often separate us: Presbyteries are more in touch with each other than ever before, Boards and Committees are co-operating in many new ways, congregations are increasingly working together.

4.4 Encouraging stories are coming in from different parts of the country. For example, in a rural area one congregation with three church buildings began to develop a common identity by holding services in each church in rotation, seeing the movement round the buildings as a kind of pilgrimage – 'walking in pilgrimage … united in faith'. When retaining three buildings became a burden they took the decision to sell two and develop the other as a flexible, multi-media worship area. In another small town, the largest and richest congregation accepted a minister on reviewable tenure to allow the three congregations in the town to work towards a union in the future, based on a seven year project to consider the buildings and ministry team which would be needed to serve the community.

4.5 These are stories of vision and also of sacrifice – sacrifice which breaks through barriers and encourages fruitful relationships for the future. Such progress is within the grasp of everyone – everyone can resolve to take a step, large or small, to work in partnership with others – with a nearby congregation, with one in an entirely different part of the country, with a partner denomination, with a project or congregation of the world church.

The Kingdom of Heaven is like a mustard seed … though it is the smallest of all your seeds, yet when it grows, it is the largest of garden plants and becomes a tree, so that the birds of the air come and perch on its branches.

---

5. The work of the year

5.1 Listening Group

… monitor and evaluate developments through its ongoing consultations and assessments … and report to the General Assemblies of 2003 and 2005.[2]

5.1.1 The Council's Listening Group was set up to fulfil the instruction given by the Assembly to monitor the progress of the *Church without Walls* Report and has been encouraged by the variety of initiatives which have been inspired by it.

5.1.2 The resource books – *Church without Walls* and the *Working it out together* study guide are now widely disseminated throughout the Church and a second print run will be necessary to meet demand. Further resources are in the pipeline, in particular a series of booklets produced by the Advisers in Mission and Evangelism on key themes in the report. There have been series of seminars and conferences to help people begin to address the issues involved, initiated both by Boards and by individuals.

5.1.3 The *Church without Walls* Report did not promise a blueprint for the church. The 'one size fits all' approach was never an option. Instead, the aim of the report was to offer a vision, a space to stop and reflect on the meaning of Christ's command 'Follow me' for each congregation, each Presbytery, indeed every aspect of the Church's life.

5.1.4 Throughout Scotland local congregations have begun discussing the Report in groups large and small: in Kirk Sessions, in Guilds, with neighbouring congregations of the Kirk and of other denominations. 'Living with a Gospel', the cycle of grace, the guiding principles and new ideas about worship are on the agenda of many congregations.

5.1.5 Presbyteries have also responded in different ways – by setting up groups to consider the report, by holding local conferences, by providing support to help congregations in the area to address the report. So far there are no specific resources to help Presbyteries address the particular instructions given to them but members of the Council have arranged to visit those who requested help with these matters and these meetings will hopefully generate resource material for the future.

5.1.6 The impact of the *Church without Walls* Report is also being felt in other areas of the Church as Boards and Committees explore its themes and absorb its thinking into their working structures. There is also evidence that beyond the Church of Scotland, the Report is being read and considered and that the concept of a 'Church without walls' is inspiring and encouraging many.

5.1.7 Of course less enthusiastic and more critical voices have been heard, too. The Urban Priority Areas Committee has written a detailed critique of the Report, commenting on its conservatism, its church-centredness and its too timid call for redistribution of financial resources. The *Church without Walls* website (http://www.churchwithoutwalls.org.uk) continues to receive comments, both positive and negative. Some have called for the movement for change to be slowed down; others have found the pace just too slow.

5.1.8 However, it is undoubtedly true that from the grass-roots to the Boards and Committees of the Church the vision of the *Church without Walls* Report is being debated and engaged with. In the coming year in preparation for reporting to the Assembly of 2003, the Listening Group will consult widely on its progress and will be grateful for feedback, both positive and negative, from all quarters.

5.2 Spirituality Group

5.2.1 The Group was established following the undertaking given to last year's Assembly that consideration would be given to a growing concern 'for a true spiritual renewal, a fresh understanding of God's grace, a focus on the spiritual life, and a recovery of prayer'. The Group also noted the relevant sections of the *Church without Walls* Report urging congregations and Kirk Sessions to 'form paths for the spiritual journey to help people become Christian disciples in today's world'; to 'identify the spiritual gifts of the people and grow the Church around the people'; and to 'identify ways of deepening the prayer life of congregations'.[3]

5.2.2 This has been a year of enquiry in the course of which the Group has met with a wide range of people concerned with a renewal of Christian spirituality and has familiarised itself with some of the literature on the subject, including papers provided by other denominations. It has begun to look at aspects of Reformed, Ignatian, Evangelical and Celtic spirituality. The Group has also considered the spirituality of those outwith the Church and looked at ways in which churches are experimenting with worship.[4]

5.2.3 The work undertaken has also included a consideration of spirituality in the workplace and in this connection, insights have been gained through reading relevant papers on Benedictine spirituality[5], and in talking with Peter Neilson, whose work has included connections with the Edinburgh business community. Representatives of the Department of Ministry met with the Group as they explored the place of spirituality in ministerial training, and there were wide-ranging discussions with John Drane, Professor of Practical Theology, University of Aberdeen, David Searle, Warden

> *Spirituality in life and at work is about space and pace, rythm and balance. God is encountered both in silent contemplation and in active engagement and each enriches the other.*

of Rutherford House, Edinburgh, Norman Shanks, Leader of the Iona Community, and Desmond Ryan, Senior Research Fellow, Department of Nursing Studies, University of Edinburgh. It has also been interesting to observe the lively way in which the topic is debated by Christians and non-Christians on internet discussion boards.

5.2.4 In the course of these enquiries the Group's vision of spirituality was broadened again and again so that while quickly realising that there is no possibility of a simple definition, a rich vision was built up through the many windows which were opened, some of which are in turn offered here.

Micah 6:8 is absolutely fundamental in the development of spirituality: What does God require of us? To do justice (engaging in the issues of the day), love mercy (engaging with other people); and walk humbly with God (engaging with God).

Life in all its fullness. (John 10:10)

Life in the world orientated towards God. (Martin Luther)

Knowledge of ourselves not only stimulates us to seek God, but, as it were, also leads us by the hand to find him. (John Calvin)

The practice of the presence of God.

All that we are, responding to all that God is.

Spirituality is part of being human.

Peace and justice as well as prayer and worship.

The call for spiritual renewal in the Church of Scotland is a call to build on that which already exists. It is a fundamental call to recognise Jesus Christ as the Son of God. It is a call to recognise and then complement that which already exists with resources and direction that can be sustained through life. It is a call that recognises that there is a spiritual hunger in everyone which will satisfy the soul in a way which the commodities of a consumer society apparently do not.

5.2.5 As the Group moves into its second year, the hope is to continue with:

- research into what is already happening in Scotland
- listening and responding to those involved in this work
- the desire to encourage a wide debate about nurturing spiritual renewal in the Church of Scotland.

5.2.6 The Group would welcome comments or contributions, which can be made through the Council pages on the Church website (http://www.churchofscotland.org.uk) or directly to the Council office at 121 George Street, Edinburgh. A bibliography and a list of resources is also available on request from the Council office.

5.3 Eldership Group

... undertake a review of the office of elder in the Church of Scotland ... with a view to enabling the whole church to rediscover the full significance of the eldership as a spiritual office ...

5.3.1 The work of the Eldership Group during the year has been carried out in response to the remit given by the General Assembly of 2001 and members of the Council have been greatly helped by the co-option of two members of the Eldership Working Party of the Board of Parish Education who have brought considerable experience and knowledge to the task.

5.3.2 The Group began by considering the content of the Panel on Doctrine Report *Ordination in the Church of Scotland*.[6] It was also grateful for the helpful historical background provided in the Panel's 1989 Report, *The Ministries of the Church*[7]. Among matters arising which prompted – and continue to stimulate – prolonged discussion, were the call to ministry (ie the ministry of the whole people), ordination, and the nature of the oversight and authority expected of and implemented by the eldership. But the question which most preoccupied the Group was what was meant by the description of the eldership as a 'spiritual office'. This issue in the continuing concern of the Group has become intimately tied up with the question of what it is that particularly distinguishes the office of eldership (from the minister, from the deacon, from the manager, from the committed member of the congregation).

5.3.3 Anxious to obtain the widest possible view on the eldership and in particular on these last matters, the Group decided to seek comment across the country from elders themselves. A brief questionnaire, with five questions framed to elicit opinion based on the experience of serving elders, was drawn up and distributed to one Kirk Session in each of the Church's Presbyteries. In most cases experienced Elder Trainers attended meetings of the chosen Kirk Sessions to guide discussions, gather responses and report back to the Group.

5.3.4 By January 2002 the majority of Sessions had returned the questionnaires. These were then collated and an analysis of the responses made (this appears as Appendix 1 to the report).

Key strands emerging were:
- a desire for a flexible and diverse use of individual gifts
- reflections on ordination and terms of office
- matters of training and support
- dissatisfaction with the format of Kirk Session meetings
- positive and negative aspects of the pastoral care of districts
- the possibility of the wide use of elders in leading worship
- a wide variety of interpretations of the phrase 'a spiritual office'
- different views about the nature of the office, either emphasising the leadership or the diaconal role.

5.3.5 It is perhaps important to note as an aside that many of the suggestions or ideas put forward by elders as desirable are already available or possible to implement by using local initiative. To take two examples, courses on many of the training topics requested are presently provided by Elder Trainers, and changes to the format of Kirk Session meetings are matters for the decision of the Sessions themselves.

5.3.6 It is now the Council's intention to extract the key trends of thought emerging from this survey, and, through a discussion leaflet, to invite the Church at large to comment upon them. A number of questions for discussion are included at the end of Appendix 1. What would an eldership be like which is founded on scriptural authority, respectful of the presbyterian tradition, and suited to the service of Christ in the twenty-first century? By promoting prayerful reflection about the role of the elder and provoking a creative reinterpretation of that role, it is to be hoped that the whole Church may be enabled 'to rediscover the full significance of the eldership as a spiritual office'. It will be important to hear the voices of members, adherents and young people as well as ministers and elders.

5.3.7 In the context of the *Church without Walls* Report, the Board of Practice and Procedure was instructed to examine whether the present 'model constitution' represents the best and most flexible way of managing a local congregation. Work has been carried out on this and proposals framed for comment by the Church. As there are obvious areas of overlap with the work of the Eldership Group, it is proposed that this be a joint consultation with comment invited both on the issues raised in the Council Report and on the proposals outlined in the Report of the Board of Practice and Procedure, section 7(d).

5.3.8 No particular proposals are being made by the Council at this time. However there is one issue which the Council feels could be profitably explored sooner rather than later. This is on the possibility of elders moderating Kirk Sessions. The Council understands that the Board of Ministry is bringing to the Assembly the matter of elders acting as Interim Moderators, but the Council feels that there is a wider issue and a matter of principle to be addressed. The Council asks the Assembly to instruct the Council and the Board of Practice and Procedure to consider whether elders might moderate Kirk Sessions, to take into account the responses coming through the Council's consultation in the coming year, and to report to the Assembly of 2003.

5.4 The Co-ordinating Forum

5.4.1 The supplementary report of the Assembly Council

to last year's Assembly indicated that the Co-ordinating Forum had started work on establishing priorities.

5.4.2 Following the acceptance of the report of the Special Commission anent Review and Reform, two sections of the deliverance of that Report are relevant to this work:

Urge the Co-ordinating Forum to develop its role of capturing the larger vision within which people are operating.[8]

Urge the Assembly Council, through the Co-ordinating Forum, to establish overall priorities for the work of the Church in the light of the emerging shape of the Church and to convey these to the Board of Stewardship and Finance, so that these priorities can be incorporated into the Co-ordinated Budget proposals which the Board will be bringing to the General Assembly in 2003 and subsequent years.[9]

5.4.3 With regard to the latter the Council has begun discussions in the Forum on the possibility of allocating available finance to areas of work rather than to individual Boards and Committees. These areas of work are based on the thinking which the Forum itself has done on establishing priorities related to the core business of the Church and reported to the Assembly last year.

5.4.4 The intention is to work eventually towards a slimmed-down central administration (whatever the outcome of the Presbytery Boundaries Report), but this is not a process which can be achieved overnight. It is hoped that the method referred to above may provide a framework within which changes can be made through departments co-operating with each other to deliver necessary services.

5.4.5 None of this can be done effectively without the goodwill and co-operation of the representatives of the Boards and Committees who constitute the membership of the Forum. The Council is greatly encouraged by the willingness of all of them to work together for the good of the Church as a whole and also by the many examples of collaboration which have already existed for some years. This year there has once more been a willingness on the part of the bigger fund-holding departments to contemplate budget cuts so that other work may be funded.

5.5 Other work

5.5.1 The Council has set up a group to consider issues relating to right of call and security of tenure. The Council has indicated in the past that there is a need for a re-examination of these principles and this was also said last year in the reports of both the Panel on Doctrine (section 5.1) and the Special Commission (section A.4.4). The Group consists of representatives of relevant boards and two Presbytery Clerks with a particular interest in these topics. At the time of writing the Group had just begun its work.

[2] Special Commission anent Review and Reform, General Assembly 2001 Deliverance, section 38.
[3] Special Commission anent Review and Reform, General Assembly 2001 Deliverance, sections 8, 14 and 26.
[4] Understanding the spirituality of people who don't go to church, David Hay and Kate Hunt; Alternative Worship in the United Kingdom, David Denniston.
[5] Benedict in the Boardroom, Dermot Tredget; Christian Spirituality: Work Wealth and Human Flourishing, Angela Tilby.
[6] General Assembly Reports 2001, 13/2ff, in particular the section on the Eldership, 13/7ff.'
[7] General Assembly Report 1989, p 191ff, in particular The Ministry of the Eldership, p 198f.
[8] Special Commission anent Review and Reform, General Assembly 2001 Deliverance, section 31.
[9] Special Commission anent Review and Reform, General Assembly 2001 Deliverance, section 34.

6. Conclusion

6.1 The vision conjured up by the Church without Walls theme is a rich and varied one. It is of a church which is hospitable, generous, transparent, truthful, flexible, inclusive, reaching out to the world, full of grace, trust and loving relationships. It is a vision of breaking down barriers wherever and however they occur. The Council's work this year has been concerned with this wider picture and also with the breaking down of barriers in more specific areas: in the co-operative work which the Boards and Committees are undertaking together in the Co-ordinating Forum; in thinking of how the exploration of spirituality together may cross barriers between those inside and outside the Church; in looking at ways which allow the gifts of the elders and people of the church to break through the traditional and sometimes stereotyped role of the eldership.

6.2 The *Church without Walls* Report is also about local congregational and personal reform. The Council chose the mustard seed as the theme of this year's report to emphasise the importance of the commitment and service of the people of the Church in their own local places; to encourage the seeds of reform however small; to offer the vision of a mighty tree, a shelter and a home for all who seek the love of God.

In the name of the Council

HELEN McLEOD, *Convener*
DAVID DENNISTON, *Vice-convener*
ELEANAR TODD, *Research and Development Officer*

Appendix 1

Analysis of eldership consultation

1. Methodology

1.1 The Council intends to spend two years consulting widely on the eldership. The first year has been spent in setting the agenda, by finding out what elders consider important to their office, and where they see areas of possible change. One Kirk Session was chosen in every Presbytery, and a two-part survey carried out. All the elders were sent a questionnaire to complete on their own, which asked the following five questions:

  1   What have you found most worthwhile about being an elder?

  2   What have you found least worthwhile about being an elder?

  3   How far and in what ways do you see your role as a spiritual one?

  4   What changes would you like to see in the role of the elder?

  5   How would you like to see the spiritual role of the elder developing?

1.2 Subsequently they held a discussion as a Session on the same questions. These were led, in most cases, by Presbytery Elder Trainers. This method meant both that every elder in the survey had a chance to express his or her own personal view in a questionnaire, and that more considered ideas and consensus opinions would emerge from the Group discussions. At the time of writing a total of 327 questionnaires had been received.

1.3 The resulting data was analysed using content analysis, a technique which worked well for the Council's consultation in 2000. The report consists mostly of elders' own words, chosen either because they are representative of a widely held view, or because they make a particularly creative or perceptive comment. There are indications of what proportions of those who responded held various views, but there is no statistical analysis.

1.4 The Council would like to thank those elders who contributed for their honesty, thoughtfulness, and openness, and the elder trainers for giving of their time to this exercise. Feedback on the discussions has been very positive, with several Kirk Sessions reporting plans to practise some of the ideas which had emerged from the consultation process. The result of the survey has been a large quantity of extremely rich data, which has been encouraging in its evidence of the dedication and commitment of elders. A very wide range of views were expressed on a very wide range of issues, which are summarised below. The aim of this paper is not to bring proposals, but to allow elders to raise questions and possibilities, which it is hoped will in turn stimulate the whole Church to consider and respond to this question of the future of eldership.

2.   A distinctive office

2.1 The two most distinctive characteristics which elders identified about their office were their position as a channel or connection between the congregation and the minister; and the fact that they work as a team. These offer opportunities of a particular kind of service to elders, and scope for development and exploration.

2.2 Elders who talked about their position as communicators felt that it was a positive one, for example, identifying serious pastoral concerns which can be passed on to the minister. An important task is to 'find ways of communicating what decisions had been made to the membership'. They could also 'ensure that members realise that the "powers that be" are human'. Attendance at Presbytery and the General Assembly gave them the opportunity to connect members with the wider work of the Church. Elders are frustrated when they are not consulted by ministers, or when members think that they are 'just a delivery system of Church information'.

2.3 Because they are a team of people, elders want to be able to exercise the talents they have, without being expected to be all-rounders. It is satisfying for elders to be able to use in God's service the skills they learned elsewhere, whether pastoral, financial, social, artistic, administrative, or managerial. More than a quarter of the respondents wished that elders' roles could be more flexible and diverse. 'There is a wealth of talent in a Kirk Session, much of it not used', and 'individual elders who have the time and talent should be encouraged, and provided support, to develop specific ministries within their congregations or the wider church'. Some elders, such as those who have retired, may work almost full-time for the Church, which is a tremendous resource; but other elders may be trying to juggle almost the same commitments with a job and family, and would more profitably do a few things thoroughly than rush through their duties. Flexibility might be introduced into posts such as that of Session Clerk, whose 'enormous workload' might sometimes be shared with 'a team of elders who could be called upon to undertake tasks on his/her behalf'.

2.4 Elders are effective servants of the Church when there is 'friendship of the other elders in the Session', and 'a shared vision for the Church', and they feel that they are 'part of the wider church'. They are frustrated when they feel that their colleagues are 'getting bogged down on things I don't think that important' or 'do not bother', or that they are having to do unsuitable jobs like 'serving on the Board with nothing to contribute', or feel that they are being taken for granted, or that their own spiritual life is neglected because of duties during Sunday morning worship.

2.5 There were a number of ideas about how teamwork could be encouraged. Some parishes might benefit from having larger districts, with visitors 'structured in teams to give support to each other', rather than one elder, one district. It was suggested that an 'experience sharing meeting from time to time would help confidence' amongst elders facing similar pastoral, practical and spiritual problems. There could be greater co-operation in visiting, so that, for example, 'members who are rarely seen at church services could be given to one more able to talk to them'.

3. Terms of office

3.1 For elders to develop their roles, it may be important first to encourage the development of more flexible patterns of service. At present, elders are ordained for life and in general expected to remain active in district visiting and attending the Kirk Session for most of their lives. Although it is possible for elders to take sabbaticals or to retire, those who do so often feel a sense of guilt, even if it is because they 'already make a major contribution to other areas of Church life, for example, to the work with young people or to the music of the congregation'.

3.2 There are various possibilities which were suggested by the respondents:

- Elders should not be ordained for life, especially because at present 'young people are frightened off' by the commitment. 'Being an elder for life is a scary business and if it were for fixed terms there would be more people involved'. They could be elected to serve on the Session for a few years at a time. This was not a widespread view: most elders felt ordination was 'meaningful', 'inspiring', 'humbling' and 'awesome', and gave them strength and conviction.

- Elders should be ordained for life, but that from this group 'a smaller executive group be elected to run the affairs of the Church' while 'other elders continue with districts and other duties'.
- There should be 'a way for elders to retire gracefully' at a given age. On the other hand, if the age were set too low or retirement made compulsory, the valuable time and talents of active retired people might be lost to the Church; and some Churches might struggle to find elders at all.
- Eldership should continue to be ordained and for life, but with regular sabbaticals, perhaps 'followed by a service of recommitment'. 'Life long commitment accepted, but need of support, sabbaticals, team working'.

3.3 A few elders suggested that there should be more flexibility in how elders serve in the wider Church. One respondent was concerned at 'the lack of inter-church relations between linked charges'; while another suggested that elders should play 'a broader role in the Church, for instance, in Urban Priority Areas: weaker Sessions should be helped by adjacent stronger ones'. At present, it is certainly possible for linked Sessions to have close relations, or for a large Session to help another by lending personnel or expertise, but judging by the responses, these do not seem to be widely practised.

4. Training and support

4.1 Very many respondents mentioned training, which may partly have been because the consultation was conducted by elder trainers, so the subject was raised simply by their presence. Several elders mentioned ways in which they had been personally enriched either through training, or more generally through their experiences as an elder: 'being encouraged to think about religion; learning to listen; learning about life and religion' as a Session, or learning through district visiting 'how everyone had different ideas about the church and things in life.'

4.2 On the other hand, many elders expressed frustration at feeling they lacked the skills to fulfil their role, especially in difficult pastoral situations. It is 'difficult to share faith'. It is difficult, for an elder brought up in the Church, to know how to deal with a district where 'there is a lot of non-marital cohabitation'. It is difficult to cope with bereavement.

4.3 About six per cent of the responses expressed reservations about having more training for elders, either because they felt elders are already overstretched, or because they feared that this would lead to more responsibility for matters which are currently left to the minister. Over a third, on the other hand, were of the opinion that more training in some form would be a great help to them in carrying out their role. There were various ideas, all of which could be combined:

- Pre-ordination training: this could range from a probationary year to a formal course, but would probably involve both. Several elders were unsure of what is expected of them, and felt 'thrust in to the deep end' when they are ordained.
- Compulsory in-service training, for example every three years: this could take all sorts of forms and subjects, but would mean that it was not up to the minister, or the individual elder, to initiate training.
- Training which is organised at Presbytery level: 'courses with elders of other churches to see what they do and get ideas from them' might be a good thing in itself regardless of the content of the training. It would also allow better resourced training than might be possible for the congregation to organise.
- More informal development in the Kirk Session: this might involve activities like 'informal discussions, team building, and retreat weekends', rather than 'training'. It would also have the advantage of being 'more local and at more convenient times'.

4.4 Topics for training were also suggested. These included:

- Pastoral training: 'how to get past the doorstep and how to bring a conversation round to a more spiritual content'; training 'for bereavement', how to pray with people, and so on.
- 'Training in conducting worship and preaching made available without the full Readership training being necessary'.
- Teaching on the Bible, and 'more engagement with ideas of spirituality, Celtic Christianity, Ignatian exercises etc'.

- Seminars on issues in the wider Church and the world.
- Seminars on mission, in many different forms: for example, how the Church might 'make plans to invade the week' to fit in better with modern lifestyles.

4.5 As well as giving training, there were other ways in which elders felt that the Church could support their work. The national structures of the Church were a source of some frustration: 'lack of communication' in one direction, and 'failure of the Church to listen to what elders are saying' in the other. On the one hand, 'responses to deliverances are to be returned within an impossibly short time', while on the other, 'everything takes too long because things have to be filtered through 121 George Street'. At the same time, some elders felt misunderstood by congregations, who 'did expect that a minister might pray in their homes but not an elder', and so 'insist on a visit from the minister'.

5. Leadership

5.1 A third of the elders who responded said that one of the things they found most worthwhile in being an elder was their part in planning, leading and observing the work of the Church. 'Taking part in activities to consider ways of taking the church into the new Millennium', 'leading some key groups and meetings', 'attending the General Assembly' were all mentioned as positive experiences.

5.2 However, Kirk Session meetings themselves tended to be a subject of complaint. There were meetings which are full of 'routine business'; which dealt with 'nothing of importance'; which were 'tedious and repetitive' or just 'too long' but on the other hand with not enough time for 'in-depth discussion and democratic decision making'; at worst they could be 'stressful' or 'fractious'. The best Kirk Session meetings go almost unnoticed: they were mentioned positively only by one respondent who had suffered long meetings at a previous church, and added gratefully that 'our meetings are suitably short and to the point'.

5.3 This assessment highlights the difficulty of the task facing ministers as Kirk Session moderators, who have to not only get through all the business, but also allow all voices to be heard in a proper debate. With the best moderator in the world, it may be that in large Kirk Sessions, 'forums of discussion are too large and unwieldy for effective management of the Church'. 'Better use of Committees; more delegated functions' can be a good way to delegate business, but when each one has to report at length to the Kirk Session and each decision must be approved, this can create huge amounts of routine business at the Session meeting.

5.4 The reduction of routine business at Kirk Session meetings was seen to be important not only because of the morale of the elders attending, but also because many elders would welcome more creative use of Kirk Session meetings which at present is precluded by the pressure of business. Suggestions included time to discuss 'issues of the day in our community, and national ones', and also 'matters of faith'; 'prayer and discussion on problems encountered'; 'in-house training'; and 'open prayer, for the items discussed in the Session meeting, at the end of the meeting'. It was felt that such activities would 'help elders to gain the confidence required to become more active', create 'acceptance that different views would be shared', remind elders that their office is 'a voyage of discovery and not about materialistic concerns', and that 'real changes in the role might come out of more opportunities for close fellowship'. Such activities 'might be led by elders', and might be built in to regular Session meetings, or given more leisurely treatment at special meetings or retreats. At the very least, 'a cup of tea after meetings might make space for elders to get to know one another better and offer an opportunity for them to discuss informally matters of common concern'.

6. Visiting and pastoral care

6.1 Almost eighty per cent of the respondents said that they found visiting one of the most worthwhile things they did as an elder. This was particularly the case when visiting the elderly or housebound, 'giving sympathy and support in times of illness and bereavement', or 'transporting people to church who would not otherwise manage to attend', or just 'letting them tell me all about themselves and how their family are getting on'. Elders had the advantage that people who 'don't want to waste the minister's time will open up to you if you make time for them'. Elders felt that they also benefited from visiting: they had 'gained good friends' and enjoyed 'a closer relationship with their neighbours'. Their minds were broadened through listening to older people talk of their life, which was always 'very interesting and a privilege and often a humbling experience'.

6.2 Many elders considered their pastoral role to be a spiritual one, a 'way of representing Christ', and a fulfilment of the instruction of James, 'to visit the orphans and widows in their affliction' (James 1:27). Some saw this as a 'spiritually inspired temporal role', in which the practical actions became spiritual because of the prayers and beliefs which inspired them. Others considered there to be 'a spiritual element in all our work – whether it is listening or getting to know people or giving practical help with transport'; and perhaps especially at crisis moments such as bereavement. Most elders who expressed a view felt uncomfortable about reading the Bible or praying on a visit, although several added that praying *for* the members they visited was important. Elders might find more agreement in the suggestion that their pastoral role is a deeply *Christian* one, in that it is a service of love: visiting is about 'loving and encouraging people'.

6.3 Against this very positive picture must be balanced the many respondents – almost forty per cent – who also expressed frustration with at least some aspects of their district visiting, especially at 'the doors where there is no response and never has been after 10 years', or members who 'open door – take card – say thank you and close the door'. In these cases, visiting becomes a frustrating 'meaningless ritual' and the elder feels 'awkward and perhaps even unwelcome'. There are also busy people for whom 'there may only be two hours of an evening available for visiting', who feel guilty that their members never get a proper visit, and find it a burden.

6.4 Several elders suggested ways in which the district system might be changed 'in the light of the needs and wants of the modern world'. Visiting 'should be concentrated on those who need'. This might mean only those members who are housebound or otherwise in need of particular pastoral care, and not active and busy church members or those who have no interest in the Church

and resent the intrusion of 'that biddy fae the Kirk'. Another option would be 'a change in the definitions of membership to generate more inclusive arrangements for adherents and newcomers.'

6.5 It might also be useful if visiting were not conducted only by elders, but by a 'pastoral care team of people who enjoy visiting and have the appropriate skills'. This would have the advantage of sharing the burden: 'smaller numbers in districts - more opportunities to visit'. It would also mean that elders who feel ill-equipped or too busy to serve in this way would not feel they had failed in their duty if they relinquished their district. On the other hand, the present system does mean that decisions made in the Kirk Session are rooted in personal knowledge of the people who will be affected by those decisions, and this is a very important connection. A few expressed concern at 'what else is there for us to do, if we do not visit?' which raises questions about what is distinctive about the eldership.

6.6 Another possibility is that 'districts should be rotated, say, every five or seven years', to broaden the elder's experience and ensure that they do not face the same problems for decades; although this would risk cutting off lasting relationships which link members to the Church. Another helpful policy might be to give elders 'a chance to discuss together some of the difficulties which they face', while bearing in mind that this is yet another demand on elders' time, and perhaps should take place only annually.

7. Worship, study, prayer

7.1 Much of the discussion of the spiritual office of eldership centred around the question of how much involvement elders should have in worship, and opinions varied widely. Around twelve per cent said that they enjoyed taking part in worship, whether serving communion, welcoming people, reading lessons, singing in the choir, or admitting new members or elders.

7.2 There was also considerable feeling that elders could increase this role. Some Kirk Sessions agreed that 'most were interested in taking an active part in the worship', and felt that 'this should not be the sole prerogative of the minister. The talents and spiritual development of elders should not be overlooked'. It might be no more than making 'a contribution to the Sunday worship, doing readings or even saying a prayer', or it might be taken much farther so that elders be given 'legal recognition within the church to preach and lead worship where God has clearly gifted and called them'. Apart from anything else, having to lead worship 'concentrates the mind and makes one appreciate the preparation and effort required'; but it would also be extremely practical in linked or vacant charges, if the church did not have to rely on the presence of an overstretched minister. Some thought that 'we could perhaps plan and conduct a 9.30am service or an evening service', and suggested that 'a Worship Committee should be set up' to do this. To carry this idea further, one might envisage a future church in which 'with fewer ministers available, elders if they are able should be prepared to teach, preach, lead prayers, whatever is needed'. Elders could be part of a ministry team, for example in a 'chaplaincy type role' in their places of work.

7.3 At the same time, there were many notes of caution sounded. Several elders, while agreeing with the principle, admitted that they did not 'feel competent or confident enough to take a service', but would 'admire those able to do it'. It would be counterproductive to expect elders suddenly to lead services, as 'there is nothing to be gained if the elder or congregation feel uncomfortable or embarrassed'. Leading worship 'requires a lot of time commitment and confidence' and perhaps could best 'be worked at gradually'. There was also a widespread feeling that 'the minister must be the spiritual leader of the church', and that elders should not take over this role. Others, however, felt that 'leadership should be shared', and 'ministers are not trained in this' (ie, sharing leadership). Far from trying to take over the minister's place, 'an elder should be a support to the minister eg probably be able to stand in if required to take a service'.

7.4 Less controversial was the use of elders to lead not Sunday worship, but smaller prayer, study and worship groups, which several elders already found rewarding. Elders could lead 'cell groups' of the members in their district: this sort of group often 'gives a greater sense of belonging and is "more spiritual"'. Elders may find a role

as spiritual leaders through 'a caring ministry of prayer' for the congregation, or, for the more confident, 'by the use of a Bible and prayer programme for district visitations'; through 'leading a prayer group' or leading 'young people in a Bible class'; or through 'home communion and small worship situations'.

8. Mission

8.1 Several elders said that they were glad of the opportunities eldership gave them for Christian witness and sharing their faith in the community. Some found visiting those members who do not attend church a positive experience for this reason, and others felt that their ordination had given them the confidence to speak about their faith. One of the most rewarding experiences was 'having regularly visited individuals on my district over a period of time, seeing them choosing to become members of Christ's church'. There was also regret at the declining influence of the Church, and fear that this is 'due to their failing as elders'.

8.2 Elders' contributions to mission might include organising 'social activities to help members, especially new ones, to meet others', or 'visiting in the community not just church members', or 'appointing ambassadors for the church in the community.' For the less outgoing, Christian witness might be 'leading by example in exercising their gifts'.

9. Spiritual role

9.1 The Council was asked by the General Assembly to consider the office of elder with a view to its rediscovery as a *spiritual office*, and this was put to the elders without any commentary. The result was a very wide range of meanings for the phrase and reactions to it. Half of those questioned had reservations about this description of the office, and their responses are described in the next three paragraphs; while the other half were favourable, as described in paragraphs 9.5 and 9.6.

9.2 A few respondents saw the elder as 'a recognised manager', an administrative, not spiritual role. More said that the role was 'not spiritual, more pastoral'. Often, the reason for this negative response was that 'a minister is trained for many years to be a spiritual leader, and people expect him to do the job, not an elder'. This was accompanied by a feeling that 'I am totally unfit to be a spiritual guide to anybody', and that elders do not 'know their way around the Bible well enough to be a spiritual guide and support for others'.

9.3 Many of the objections were more qualified. Several elders asked what was meant by 'spiritual', suggesting that the term is 'over-used and even vague or meaningless'. Does it mean 'religious', 'pastoral', 'helping others', 'following the teachings', 'Christian', 'more evangelical', 'conducting services', 'engagement in every aspect of life'? Others said that an elder had a spiritual role, but only insofar as every Christian does, and as an elder, 'my lifestyle should be at a certain standard and have a level of accountability to the Church'.

9.4 Several elders said that although their experience of the office was not spiritual, they felt that it ought to be. Often this was felt to be due to personal inadequacy, that 'I don't think I have been as outgoing in this sense as I think God would have wanted me to be', and in general, 'elders have more to offer if it can be coaxed from them'. Others felt this to be a widespread problem in the Church of Scotland, which displays 'too much "head" – not enough "heart"', and considered that 'we need to gain confidence in "administering" spirituality – it's an unfamiliar role!'. A more critical view was that 'it probably should be spiritual but in fact it is more pastoral and, it seems, mechanical'. Some felt there to be a need 'to change from the view that the spiritual role is only for the minister'.

9.5 On the other hand, just as many respondents said that their role was a spiritual one. Many saw their pastoral duties as a spiritual ones through love. 'Spiritual – is it the same as compassion?' asked one elder. Another said that it means 'relating in a real sense and feeling vulnerable'. The office is spiritual in that the elder's visit represents 'the friendly face of the Church'. Spiritual eldership is seen as being about 'loving – caring – care in action', 'love for my Lord and for his people', and 'believing that people are more important than the church buildings'.

9.6 Others regarded eldership as 'a completely spiritual role', 'including completing the tax return!' Even if the district visit was indistinguishable from a social call, 'this is the Church visiting at least four times a year and it is spiritual no matter what is talked about'. A spiritual eldership might involve 'leadership, commitment, enthusiasm, encouragement, humility and following Jesus'. The spiritual aspect of the role may be more one of attitude than action. In one Session, 'phrases like "we know that God is there" and "hope and trust" were used'.

10.   Visions for the future

10.1 Although almost all the responses concentrated on specific aspects of elders' work, and did not set these within a larger framework of the sort of office which eldership might become, the developments which respondents hoped for in the eldership tended to point in one of two directions. General visions of how the eldership might look emerged, although individuals did not necessarily choose between them.

10.2 The first vision is that of a much better resourced, better trained and perhaps smaller eldership, 'alongside the minister developing a joint team ministry to provide pastoral and preaching support not only to the congregation but as the beginnings of an outreach into the whole community'. They would be 'able to be Interim Moderator', and perhaps 'able to give communion'. Rather than appointing elders when they are needed, 'only to fill districts', elders would be ordained when suitable candidates were found, perhaps with some selection process, and with proper training – although different elders might well be chosen for their different skills and strengths. As well as having a greater leadership role in the congregation, they would have a 'bigger role in Presbytery' and in the wider Church. Rather than trying to do everything themselves, they would 'focus on leadership, seeking God's will for our fellowship so that all believers can exercise gifts to the benefit of the body of Christ.'

10.3 The second vision is of an eldership which is closer to the congregation, larger, more representative of the worshipping members, 'approachable not scary', and perhaps no longer called elders. A number of respondents indicated that they thought 'the formal roles, maybe even the title, should be dropped, because they are divisive between the congregation and Session'. This eldership would be 'ordinary members of the congregation working to develop the church in the community', perhaps called 'deacons', 'church friends', or different things depending on their roles. They would be 'elected by Church membership not simply by the Kirk Session', would 'invite the congregation to our meetings', and would be a 'friendly presence' whether at church or in the community.

10.4 However, given that around a third of respondents expressed concern about change, it is perhaps unlikely that one or other of these visions could be imposed. The eldership may continue to be diverse, between and within Sessions, with different functions depending on what was needed in a particular place, or according to the different talents of individual elders.

Starter questions for discussion

- Several New Testament passages refer to elders (eg Titus 1:5-9; Acts 14:23; 1 Peter 5:1-3; Acts 11:30; James 5:14-15; 1 Timothy 5:17; 1 Timothy 3:1-13). How should the biblical passages be applied to the eldership today?

- What makes the eldership distinctive? How could these characteristics be developed to allow the elders to be the best possible servants of the Church today?

- How far and in what ways is the elder's role a spiritual one? How would you like to see the spiritual role of the elder developing?

- Are the present arrangements, whereby elders are ordained and usually expected to serve for life, the best ones?

- What should training for elders be like?

- What are your views on elders moderating Kirk Session meetings?

- How might the elders, as part of the whole Church, best exercise pastoral care?

- Should elders be more involved in leading worship?

- Does the present 'model constitution' reflect the best and most flexible way of managing a local congregation?

- Are the two 'visions' in para 10.2 and 10.3 helpful for thinking about the future of the eldership? What would an eldership be like which is founded on scriptural authority, respectful of the presbyterian tradition, and suited to the service of Christ in the twenty-first century?

- How has your congregation experimented with ideas such as those outlined in the report? How do you plan to put into practice suggestions which have come up in your discussions?

CHURCH AND NATION
MAY 2001

PROPOSED DELIVERANCE

The General Assembly

1. Receive the Report and thank the Committee and those who by their support and shared concerns have helped in this work.

ACTION TAKEN BY THE COMMITTEE

2. Support the introduction of legislation to provide "secure status" for the Gaelic language.
3. Give thanks for the work of those who continue patiently to seek peace in Northern Ireland and who pursue it with care and imagination.
4. Encourage congregations to mark 21 September 2002 as the first Global Cease-Fire Day.

SECTARIANISM

5. Recognising that sectarianism is not someone else's problem, commend the Report to the Church for study and encourage congregations to set up local working groups to look at the issue within their own communities.
6. Instruct the Church and Nation Committee to set up the working group recommended in the Report, and to seek to do this in partnership with the Catholic Justice and Peace Commission.
7. Commend the Nil by Mouth Charter to congregations and individual Church members.
8. Commend all those who seek to combat sectarianism in Scotland today.

LAND REFORM

9. Encourage the Committee to continue to pursue the Church's concerns for land reform, as outlined in the Report.

FOOT & MOUTH DISEASE

10. Re-affirm the continuing prayerful and practical support of the Church for the communities and individuals still adversely affected by the outbreak of foot and mouth disease.
11. Urge HMG to allocate sufficient resources on risk assessment and disease control and prevention.
12. Support the Scottish Executive's ongoing concern for animal welfare issues in agriculture.
13. Recognise that the Common Agricultural Policy requires continuing review, in particular with respect to caring for the environment and moving towards encouraging farmers to adopt the principle of sustainable rather than maximum yields.
14. Urge the Scottish Executive to give priority to health promotion in its food policy.
15. Urge Church members to be thoughtful in shopping priorities whenever possible by: a) buying locally produced food and fairly traded goods and urging retailers to stock such items; and b) giving consideration when shopping to questions of animal welfare and to how far items have been transported

COMPENSATION CULTURE

16. Commend the contents of this report to congregations for study and reflection.
17. Recommend to Her Majesty's Government and the Scottish Executive the further study of no-fault compensation and of the implications of its introduction in this country.

ASYLUM

18. Commend the work of the UNHCR as it seeks to revise the UN convention in order to strengthen refugee protection; and commend to them the needs and rights of those who have been forced to leave their homes for economic or environmental reasons.
19. Call on HMG and those of other developed economies to recognise the influence of their economic policies and the destabilising conditions which force migration.
20. Support the European Commission in its positive approach to Immigration and Asylum policy and in its recognition that a welcoming society must be central to the formulation of such a policy.
21. Urge Her Majesty's Government, the other European Union governments and the European Commission, to adopt a common action plan covering migration, common standards for reception of asylum seekers and a specific programme to combat racism and xenophobia.
22. Urge Her Majesty's Government to take a positive stance on migration issues and tackle negativity concerning asylum seekers.
23. Welcome the efforts of local congregations in offering support to refugees and asylum seekers, and encourage others to develop awareness of these issues.
24. Regret that British asylum policies have led to injustice and to a denial of human dignity.

NUCLEAR SUBMARINES

25. Welcome the consultation programme on the future handling of nuclear waste and instruct the SRT Project, in co-operation with the Church and Nation Committee, to make responses as appropriate on behalf of the Church, and to keep this matter under review.

EUROPE WHOLE AND FREE

26. Affirm the principles of peace, freedom, justice and security as the primary goals of the European Union.
27. Support the enlargement of the European Union and urge HMG to explain the benefits of enlargement, both to member states and to candidate countries, and to the UK electorate.
28. Urge the European Commission and member states to proceed creatively with Common Agricultural Policy reform.
29. Urge HMG and the governments of other member states to adopt a spirit of generosity and co-operation in the allocation of funds for development in candidate countries.
30. Instruct the Committee on Church and Nation to monitor the work of the new "Convention on the Future of Europe", contribute to it where possible, and report to a future General Assembly.
31. Urge the European Union to implement policies with the rest of the world which are economically just.

THE TERRORIST ATTACKS ON THE UNITED STATES AND THE WAR IN AFGHANISTAN

32. Condemn the terrorist attacks on the United States of America on 11 September 2001.
33. Express profound sympathy for all those in America and in Afghanistan who have been injured, traumatised or bereaved as a result of the events of September 11 and the consequent military campaign.
34. Call on HMG to promote the use of international law in any response to international terrorism and, in particular, to urge upon the government of the United States the appropriate use of the Geneva Convention and support for the establishment of the International Criminal Court.
35. Affirm that the United Nations should have the central role in resolving international disputes and call on all member nations to support its work financially and to adhere fully to its resolutions.
36. In view of the death and injury caused to Afghan men, women and children, regret the disproportionate use of military force by the US-led coalition in response to the September 11 attacks.
37. Note with deep concern indications from members of the US administration that it wishes to extend military intervention to other states and strongly urge HMG to take the initiative in promoting the alternative strategies recommended in paragraph 6.5 of this Report.
38. Commend to the Church inter-faith dialogue and acts of solidarity which seek to overcome religious or racial intolerance.

IRAQ

39. In the light of the severe suffering being inflicted on the Iraqi people through economic sanctions and the failure of this policy to bring about real change in Iraq, call for the immediate suspension of sanctions.

NATIONAL MISSILE DEFENCE

40. Deplore the total waste and unethical use of resources and the serious threat to international stability represented by the proposals for National Missile Defence; and call for the cessation of the present testing process and for the abandonment of the proposals.
41. Recognising the importance of the 1972 Anti Ballistic Missile Treaty in maintaining arms control, a) express deep regret that the United States intends to withdraw from it; and b) urge HMG to reject any request from the United States to adapt the facilities at RAF Fylingdales and Menwith Hill to become part of the NMD system.

DISTRIBUTION

42. Instruct the Committee to send copies of the Report with the Deliverance to appropriate Government Ministers, Members of the Scottish Parliament, Scottish Members of the UK Parliament, Scottish Members of the European Parliament, and others involved in the issues addressed by the Report.

REPORT

ACTION TAKEN BY THE COMMITTEE

1. Introduction and Thanks

1.1 The Committee's work continues between meetings of the General Assembly. This introductory section of the Report seeks to bring to the Assembly a flavour of that work and to bring it up to date with the progress of matters raised and discussed in previous years.

1.2 In addition to the political visits mentioned below, the Committee has, since its last Report was written, visited the Presbytery of Ayr in a meeting held at Prestwick Airport. There we heard much of the employment and social worries and opportunities in the area. We have also visited the Presbyteries of Annandale and Eskdale and Dumfries and Kirkcudbright as part of our investigation into the effects of the Foot and Mouth epidemic. We would like to express our gratitude to all those who come to meet us on occasions such as these and put on record the debt we owe to the thoughtfulness with which they respond to our questions.

1.3 The Committee also this year asked members of the Church to send in their comments on Foot and Mouth and on Sectarianism. We take this opportunity also to thank those who responded for their time and effort.

1.4 The Committee restructured its work this year to the following five groups: International, Europe, Westminster, Holyrood and Social Issues.

2. Matters from the General Assembly

2.1 *Civilian Peace Service*

The Committee continues to work on the remit on this subject given by the 1998 General Assembly. Following several meetings and a conference held on September 8th 2001, the *Scottish Network for Civilian Peace Service* has been formed. Its aims include the publicising and advocacy of the concept and development of civilian peace services, the exchange of information about them, and the enlistment of appropriate support for these from individuals, organisations and Government. The Committee's Secretary currently convenes this network.

2.2 *Racial Justice*

In addition to the reports on Refugees and Asylum, which appear later, the Committee continues to be involved in discussions to take forward ecumenical work on racial justice along the lines reported to and supported by the General Assembly of 2001. The Committee will also continue to monitor and encourage work in this area by the Church of Scotland in all its parts.

2.3 *Decade to Overcome Violence*

The ecumenical "decade" began last year. The Committee has set itself the aim of producing a report relevant to this theme every year for the duration of the decade. Last year we reported on the *International Arms Trade*; this year our report covers *National Missile Defence*. How the decade is to be marked in an ecumenical context remains under discussion, with the Committee being represented in discussions at Scottish and UK level. The Lent Study material for 2004 will be on this theme. The General Secretary of the World Council of Churches, the Revd Dr Konrad Raiser, spoke of the aim of the decade at a meeting in London and said that, *we cannot expect at the end of the decade for violence to be over, but we can trust that the spirit of reconciliation will transform the churches and help them create a culture of peace for all.*

2.4 *Debt and Poverty*

2.4.1 The Committee continues to be part of the *Debt on our Doorstep* campaign, brought to the attention of the General Assembly in 2000, which aims to develop policy proposals to address irresponsible and extortionate lending, to campaign for reform of the Social Fund, to promote Credit Unions and socially responsible lending by banks, and to campaign for equitable and just forms of debt recovery.

2.4.2 This past year has seen two important

consultations - one from the Scottish Executive on debt recovery, *Striking the Balance*, and one from the Department of Trade and Industry, *Tackling Loan Sharks*. Both contained many measures to be welcomed, though both still fell short in significant respects. The most important issue requiring attention is that of "joined-up" thinking and action. For this reason the campaign is trying to promote the idea of a joint group comprising representatives from both the UK and the Scottish Parliament alongside people from the voluntary sector.

2.5 *Globalisation*

2.5.1 Following the report on this subject to the General Assembly of 2000, the Committee continues to be involved in promoting discussion of the issues involved. The Committee was a co-sponsor of a conference in Ushaw College, Durham in July 2001, entitled *Global Capitalism and the Gospel of Justice*. Following the success of this conference, attended by 250 people from a wide range of churches, places and backgrounds, it was agreed that another event be planned for 2003. The Committee is part of this planning.

2.5.2 We are also involved in promoting a CTBI study process entitled, *Poverty and Prosperity in the Context of Globalisation*. This project involves groups in England, Wales, Ireland and Scotland working on the theme. The work will bring together activists, academics and people from financial institutions with the aim of producing work available for discussion in the run-up to the next UK General Election.

2.6 *Rhu Consultation*

The same desire to bring people together lies behind the consultation in Rhu, first discussed by the General Assembly in 2000. At the time of writing this is planned for the beginning of May when for 24 hours, church people, military personnel and politicians will come together in a meeting chaired by the Moderator to discuss nuclear weapons and how best to work toward their elimination. Eminent speakers have agreed to be there.

2.7 *Human Rights*

Following the General Assembly's support for human rights legislation and also, in 2001, for the formation for Scotland of a Human Rights Commission, it is pleasing to report plans from the Scottish Executive for just such a Commission to be formed. The Committee's September conference was addressed by Professor Christine Bell of the Northern Ireland Human Rights Commission and we were much encouraged by her account of its work and by the thought that similar work could also be carried out in Scotland.

2.8 *Swords into Ploughshares*

Following the report last year on the International Arms Trade and the suggestion contained there that those employed in arms production in this country might be redeployed in other kinds of manufacture, the General Assembly asked the Committee to meet with the STUC to discuss these matters. This meeting took place on February 7th 2002. Thinking is still at an early stage and we anticipate further consultation.

2.9 *Gaelic*

The Committee reported to the General Assembly in 1999 on the status of Gaelic. In the past year we have been represented at the Scottish Executive's consultations on the future of the Gaelic language. The result of this consultation was that legislation should be introduced to provide "secure status" for the language. This would involve an action plan for recovery. The plan would include nationally and locally driven strategies, with targets for increasing the number of learners. The aim is the recovery of the use of Gaelic in everyday life. Following the 1999 Report, when the General Assembly *urged the Scottish Parliament to develop policies which give the Gaelic language practicable support and its appropriate status in the life of Scotland*, we believe that the Church can give its support to these moves.

2.10 *Northern Ireland*

2.10.1 The General Assembly has continually expressed its concern for the people of Northern Ireland. The Committee's contact with Northern Ireland has been maintained over the past year and, in particular, contact with the Presbyterian Church in Ireland has been, we believe, enhanced. Three representatives from the PCI took a full part in our September conference, both in a session in which they brought us up to date with developments in Northern Ireland and also in the conference as a whole. One of those representatives also accompanied our Europe Group in its visit to Brussels. In addition, plans are underway for a joint conference to be held in Belfast later this year.

2.10.2 We have been encouraged and, in our turn, encourage others to recognise the great strides which have been taken in recent years in Northern Ireland, to empathise with those for whom the future being offered seems like a betrayal of the past, and therefore to be patient with the continuing attempts at healing and progress. It is important that no community in Northern Ireland feels isolated or feels that there is nothing to lose - because down those roads lie disaster. Those who are working carefully, patiently, creatively and sensitively to bring about something new need our strong support and all the people need our prayers.

2.11 *Israel-Palestine*

2.11.1 The General Assembly has returned many times to discuss the issues of Israel and Palestine, most recently in 2001. That meeting set up the working group on *The Theology of Land and Covenant*, which has now been constituted and has begun its work under the convenership of the Very Rev Dr Robert Davidson. Meanwhile the situation on the ground has not improved and in many respects has deteriorated. The Committee continues to be dismayed by actions which can only exacerbate conflict. In particular, the Committee was outraged by the actions of the Israeli Defence Force in Bethlehem in the period leading up to Christmas. It appears that these actions were particularly aimed at Christianity.

2.11.2 The World Council of Churches has called upon its member churches to focus attention in 2002 *on intensive efforts to end the illegal occupation of Palestine*. To this end it has called for a boycott of goods produced in illegal settlements, participation in non-violent resistance to the destruction of Palestinian properties and international prayer vigils *to strengthen the chain of solidarity with the Palestinian people*. In addition the World Council is developing an accompaniment programme based on the experience of the Christian Peacemakers Team. Like the Board of World Mission, the Committee has expressed its support in principle for these measures, although it has expressed some doubt concerning the ability of consumers to identify what Israeli goods were produced in illegal settlements.

3. Political Contacts

3.1 *Visits to Political Institutions*

3.1.1 As in previous years the Committee paid a St Andrews-tide visit to Westminster and held meetings with MPs in party groups. These meetings were as usual very helpful, with views exchanged on a number of subjects, although the subject of September 11 and its aftermath inevitably dominated discussions on this occasion. Once again we were indebted to the Speaker, the Rt Hon Michael Martin MP, for his hospitality. As a result of this visit, the Minister of State at the Ministry of Defence, the Rt Hon Adam Ingram MP, asked for the opportunity to address the Committee, and this took place at the Committee's January meeting.

3.1.2 The newly formed Europe Group of the Committee used one of its meetings to visit Brussels. A full programme of meetings with representatives of the Parliament and the Commission, along with meetings with Scotland's representatives, meant that the visit contributed enormously to the understanding of the Group and eventually, we hope, of the entire Church concerning the European institutions. The thanks of the Committee go to Stewart Lamont of the Conference of European Churches and to Dermot Scott of the European Parliament's Scottish office.

3.1.3 As this report is written arrangements are being made with the Scottish Churches Parliamentary Office to institute an annual series of meetings at the Scottish Parliament. The intention is that when the Committee's report is published it will, as before, be circulated to MSPs but that with the report will go an invitation to come and discuss the contacts with representatives of the Committee. We believe that this will come to play as important a part in our annual programme as does the visit to Westminster.

3.2 *Relationships with Political Institutions*

The restructuring referred to in 1.4 was undertaken with the intention of giving more appropriate recognition to the institutions where decisions are made which affect the lives of the people of Scotland. This means that three of our groups engage with the issues covered in Holyrood, Westminster and the European institutions. We hope that this arrangement will enable new relationships to be built with each to the benefit of the work of the Committee and of the Church.

3.3 *Consultations and Responses*

The Committee has responded to the following consultations since the last General Assembly:

- Movement of sheep and cattle (May 2001)
- Freedom of Information (May 2001)
- Review of Common Fisheries Policy (June 2001)
- Human Rights Commission for Scotland (June 2001)
- Consultative Panel on Land Use (June 2001)
- *Striking the Balance* - debt management and recovery (October 2001)
- Media Ownership (January 2002)
- Reform of the House of Lords (January 2002)
- Sectarianism Bill (January 2002)
- Local Government Bill (February 2002)
- The Size of the Scottish Parliament (March 2002)
- Opencast Mining (March 2002).

3.4 *Representation and Constituency Boundaries*

At the time of writing, there are discussions concerning boundary changes both for Westminster and for Holyrood elections. These come as a result of the provisions of the Scotland Act. Included as an appendix to this report is the contribution from an ad hoc group put together to consider the issues in the light of the principles laid down by the Consultative Steering Group. The Committee is in support of the conclusions of this paper.

4. Other Matters

4.1 *Scottish Ecumenical Assembly*

Representatives of the Committee were pleased to be among the Church of Scotland delegation at the Scottish Ecumenical Assembly. As reported elsewhere, the Assembly spent an intensive few days discussing many matters which have concerned the Committee and the General Assembly for many years. We believe that it will be important that the emphases of that Assembly are carried forward with imagination in the years to come. For us, this will mean a continuing and ecumenical focus on issues of poverty, taxation, globalisation, racism, migration and sectarianism.

4.2 *Peace One Day*

The United Nations with the support of many national governments including, prominently, that of the United Kingdom, is promoting the introduction of an annual Global Cease-Fire Day. This is to be marked for the first time on September 21st 2002. The churches have been asked to give this initiative their support and the Committee believes that it would be right for the Church of Scotland to do so. We do not propose to make any suggestions about how this might be done, but we believe that local groups and congregations will find ways of marking the day in appropriate ways. For those who wish to find out more, this can be done at www.peaceoneday.org.

4.3 *Contributions*

In the past year the Committee has given financial assistance to the following organisations:

- Centre for Theology and Public Issues
- Scottish Centre for Nonviolence
- Refugee Survival Trust
- Churches Commission for Migrants in Europe
- CCADD.

The Committee has also received special assistance from the Board of Stewardship and Finance for the Rhu Consultation and for the Theology of Land and Covenant visit to the Holy Land, and from the Church of Scotland Guild for the Rhu Consultation, for which our thanks.

APPENDIX

THE SIZE OF THE SCOTTISH PARLIAMENT: A RESPONSE TO THE SCOTLAND OFFICE'S CONSULTATION DOCUMENT

A Consensual Approach

1. Following the publication of the consultation paper by the Scotland Office on the size of the Scottish Parliament, the Centre for Scottish Public Policy convened a meeting bringing together a group of interested individuals and organisations to seek a consensus view on this important issue. Membership of the Group was drawn from a wide range of Scottish civic society and included members and representatives of:

Centre for Scottish Public Policy (CSPP)
Institute of Governance, University of Edinburgh
Scottish Trades Union Congress (STUC)
Scottish Civic Forum
Scottish Council for Voluntary Organisations (SCVO)
Action of Churches Together in Scotland (ACTS)
UNISON
Educational Institute of Scotland (EIS)
Scottish Council for Development and Industry (SCDI)
Convention of Scottish Local Authorities (COSLA)
individual members of the Consultative Steering Group (CSG)

The Group met under the convenership of Neil McIntosh, head of the recent Commission on Local Government and the Scottish Parliament.

2. The Group welcomes the consultation and the opportunity to comment on this important issue. We support the sentiments expressed in the consultation document, and note the Government's intention to press ahead with the reduction in the number of Scottish Westminster MPs. We endorse the position expressed in the document that the electoral system of the Scottish Parliament should not be altered at this time. Our comments below reflect the sentiments of the consultation paper and reflect also unanimity among the Group as to the response to this important issue.

A Young Parliament

3. The Scottish Parliament is a young institution. It was established less than three years ago as the product of an overwhelming constitutional consensus among the people of Scotland that a devolved legislature was needed. That consensus found political expression in a 74% vote in favour of establishing the Parliament in the 1997 Referendum.

4. The establishment of the Parliament arose from a broad consensus that a democratic deficit existed in Scotland. The original proposals of the Scottish Constitutional Convention sought to address that deficit and were again based on a broad consensus across Scottish civic society. That spirit was carried into the key guidance for the Parliament developed in the CSG Report, and the final current size, electoral basis and operation of the Parliament arose from that spirit of consensus and reflect those principles.

A Framework of Principles

5. The CSG Report of 1998 outlined a framework of principles that have guided the establishment and early years of the Parliament. The Report was widely endorsed, including by all political parties in Scotland. The CSG principles are power sharing, accountability, access to and participation in the Parliament by civic society and a commitment to equal opportunities. These principles should continue to be applied in the future work of the Parliament and be central to consideration of the question of the size and operation of the Parliament.

6. Experience of the operation of the Parliament so far has been that Parliamentary structures and individual MSPs are fully employed and busy. The Parliament recognised the need to monitor and review its procedures and arrangements, and to act to improve these when necessary. This has already seen changes to the make up and structure of committees to ensure better scrutiny and more effective use of time for MSPs. The Procedures Committee of the Parliament is presently engaged in a major review of its operation, and early findings in this review indicate that it would be difficult to operate with

fewer MSPs and that there is little support for change at this time.

7. The Parliament should continue to monitor and review its operation and be prepared for change, but such a process must be based on the considered experience of its work. The relationship between Holyrood and Westminster will develop naturally over the years, and must reflect the needs of both legislatures rather than be based on a formulaic approach. Certainly, change should not be forced upon the Scottish Parliament through the mechanical application of a formula, and driven by changes in another legislature. At this stage in its development the Parliament needs a stable environment in which to grow.

Applying Consensus and Principle

Power sharing

8. The history of the establishment of the Scottish Parliament shows the important and distinctive role of consensus across a broad range of Scottish civic and political life and the development of important guiding principles supported by that consensus. These principles, which we have outlined above, should continue to guide the work of the Parliament, and when we apply them to the questions before us, it is clear that the current size and electoral basis of the Parliament should not be reduced or changed at this time. We offer the following reasons in support of this view.

9. First among these reasons is proportionality and a commitment that the political balance of the Parliament should broadly reflect the votes cast by the people of Scotland in electing that Parliament. This is intrinsically linked to the sharing of power between layers of governance in Scotland. This reassurance that their vote matters is a fundamental strength for the Parliament and is essential to the process of building confidence in the legislature among the electorate.

Equality and representation

10. A second reason is the need to ensure that the Parliament reflects the whole population of Scotland in all its diversity. From the outset, the size and make up of the Parliament have tried to reflect the varied geography and demography of Scotland, to offer opportunities for our rich ethnic base and, in particular, to maximise the participation of women in the Parliament. Scotland's legislature has been praised internationally for its early commitment to family friendly working practices and for the high number of women MSPs - at 37% among the top five in the world. We need to build on this success. It is a source of confidence and strength for the Parliament among its electorate and a reassurance that the Parliament speaks for them.

Access, Participation and Accountability

11. A third area of importance is that the Parliament is accessible and accountable to the people and transparent in its operation. Its powerful committee structure and impressive number of cross-party groups emphasise the involvement of civic society in its work, offering and facilitating contact and dialogue between the legislature and the people it represents. Much Parliamentary time is devoted to this process, and the Parliament has already changed its committee structure to ensure that MSPs have the ability to participate fully in this important scrutinising and legislative role of the committees. It is again a feature that reassures the electorate that the Parliament is working for their interest.

Problems of Reducing the Size of the Parliament

Working with Fewer MSPs

12. If the terms of the Scotland Act were applied, the number of MSPs would automatically be reduced, following the reduction in the number of Scottish Westminster MPs. A reduction in the size of the Scottish Parliament would fundamentally undermine the principles on which it was established and has been operating. It would undermine the committee structure and other accessibility mechanisms of the Parliament. It would undermine the ability to promote the adoption of women candidates and would introduce working time pressures that would in turn act to reverse the family friendly operation of the Parliament that encourages wider participation. It would also reduce the

representation and participation of regional diversity, and make representation of ethnic minorities more difficult.

13. A smaller Parliament would mean less MSP time available to carry out the busy schedule currently undertaken by MSPs. Less available time would undermine current commitments to extended consultation, to decentralising the operation of Parliament and to encouraging proper working hours. The result of these pressures could be changes in the electoral procedures or practice that would in turn put at risk the ability of proportionality to operate.

14. The ongoing review of the operation of the Parliament being carried out by the Procedures Committee has indicated that many of the functions currently carried out by the Parliament would be extremely difficult to achieve with fewer MSPs. Moreover, there is strong evidence from that review that there is no consensus for fundamental change to the Parliament at this early stage in its existence.

Coterminous Boundaries of Constituencies

15. If the Scotland Act as it currently stands were not applied, a situation would arise where the boundaries of electoral constituencies for the Scottish Parliament were not coterminous with those for Westminster elections. We do not see this as a fundamental problem.

16. Scotland has a sophisticated and politically aware electorate. This electorate has long accepted that constituencies vary with the character of elections. At the present moment, an elector is faced with a different size of constituency for local authority elections, Westminster elections, Scottish Parliament list elections and European elections. This has become an accepted fact of political life. The electorate has shown a sophisticated understanding of these differences, creating varying voting patterns in order to achieve a variety of political outcomes. Changes in the size of the Westminster constituencies will change this landscape once again, but there is no evidence to suggest that this will have an adverse effect on the electorate.

17. Crude application of the Scotland Act as it stands might address the issue of non-coterminous boundaries. However, it would do so at the expense of the fundamental principles and practices which have come to characterise the Scottish Parliament, at a stage in its existence where the Parliament itself has had little opportunity to review its operation and arrangements.

18. In addition, there is considerable evidence from elsewhere that non-coterminous constituencies are not a problem. The consultation document itself states that "in England ... there is in practice less coterminosity between Westminster and local government boundaries". Similarly, in Germany, one of the most developed devolved governments in Europe, the Bundestag and Landtag constituencies diverge considerably in many Länder - for example, in Baden-Württemberg and in Bavaria. If we look further afield, Newfoundland and Labrador in Canada is divided into seven federal ridings in order to elect seven representatives to the 301-strong Canadian Parliament, but split into 48 provincial ridings for the election of the provincial parliament. A similar situation exists in the other Canadian Provinces.

Conclusion

19. We believe that the Scotland Act should be amended to allow the proposed reduction in the number of Scottish MPs at Westminster to go ahead, while at the same time maintaining the size and basis of representation at Holyrood.

20. Review and change are inevitable, but should come through the considered experience of the Scottish Parliament, not the application of a mechanical rule so early in the life of the Parliament.

21. We have sought in this submission to present both the practical reasons and the fundamental principles which support our view that the Scottish Parliament must continue at its current size, retain its current proportional system of representation and continue to adopt accessible and family friendly procedures in its operation. This is a view which is unanimous in our Group and, we believe, commands considerable support across Scotland.

SECTARIANISM

Instruct the Church and Nation Committee to carry out a study of the adverse effects of sectarianism within Scottish society and report to the General Assembly of 2002 and encourage all who work throughout the Church to work to overcome sectarian barriers. (General Assembly 2001)

1. Introduction

1.1 The format of this report reflects the process undertaken by the Committee. We realised at an early stage that it would not be wise to rush to conclusions about what is a large and complex subject. We have instead approached the topic in a spirit of humility and with an attitude of listening. The style and content reflect what we have learnt from the conversations we have had, the reading we have done and the research we have carried out. We offer our recommendations, not as "experts" but as those that have participated in and seek to reflect Scottish society as experienced in 2001-2002.

1.2 Although the report is limited to sectarianism between Protestant and Catholic, it is our contention that much of what has been learned is readily applicable to other forms of bigotry and intolerance, evident in Scottish society today.

Sectarianism in Scotland today ...

- is seen and heard in the small asides which say little and reveal much
- is most publicly evident in behaviour associated with football matches but is by no means confined to this.
- is, thanks to recent legislation and changing patterns in society, less blatant than before in employment and recruitment practices but continues to generate claims of prejudice in the work situation.
- is still, in its most extreme form, ugly, intimidating and murderous, including a series of attacks on a priest in Easterhouse and the murders of eleven Rangers and Celtic football fans since 1995;
- is still very much in the public eye, generating extensive media coverage and comment

- is capable of demonstrating itself throughout Scotland. It is not limited to cities and urban communities
- is pervasive and will continue to be so unless we are willing to search our own consciences and to review our own language, attitudes and actions.

Sectarianism is not someone else's problem. It is an issue for all of us.

2. We have researched our past

2.1 We have researched our past as the Church of Scotland and we have learned that our Church's record on this issue in times past is far from blameless.

2.2 In the years around the Great Depression of the early thirties of last century, the Church and Nation Committee campaigned intemperately against Irish immigration into Scotland.

2.3 The reports and letters of the Committee from 1926 to 1934 on this issue make disturbing reading today. Let one quotation from a letter written by the Committee to the Secretary of State for Scotland in 1926 stand as one example. On the subject of Irish Immigration the Committee writes:

A law-abiding, thrifty and industrious race (the Scots) is being supplanted by immigrants whose presence tends to lower the social conditions, and to undermine that spirit of independence which has so long been a characteristic of the Scottish people, and we are of opinion that, in justice to our own people, steps should be taken to prevent the situation becoming any worse.

2.4 This is racism akin to the "rivers of blood" speech of Enoch Powell in the 1960s. The Irish immigrants are shown in the worst possible light. No attempt is made at understanding the social and economic conditions both in Ireland and Scotland, which produced the immigration and shaped the character and life-style of the immigrants. Of course, the great majority of the immigrants were

Roman Catholic and the sectarian implications are clear.

From a current perspective, it is a matter of regret that the Committee and the Church could have taken such a position.

2.5 Reflecting on this, it is worth making two comments:

2.5.1. First, it is cautionary to note the prejudice that so recently infected churchmen and a committee, which in general were generous and socially concerned. It ought to raise for us the question as to where our blind spots and prejudices are today. We may consider ourselves enlightened nowadays, but unless we are prepared to put ourselves under the spotlight we may also be judged, in hindsight, to have turned a blind eye to sectarian attitudes which still remain on and under the surface of the Church of Scotland of today.

2.5.2 Second, while the issue of continuing sectarian attitudes and practices must be pursued with sensitivity and vigour, we do have to recognise that a demon in our society has been acknowledged and brought into the open. Much progress in breaking down barriers across Scottish society has been made since the days of the 1930s. Ecumenical relations, friendship and co-operation between the Church of Scotland and the Roman Catholic Church have improved greatly at both official and local parish levels in the last fifty years.

3.   We have listened

We have met and listened to many individuals and groups, both secular and church-based, who recognise the effects of sectarianism in Scottish society and are working in different ways to counter it. These include:

3.1   *Cara Henderson, founder of Nil by Mouth*

Cara Henderson was a school friend of Mark Scott, the Glasgow schoolboy who was brutally murdered on his way home from a Celtic v Rangers football match in 1995. She was moved to act, however, by Donald Findlay's singing of sectarian songs at a Rangers Supporters function in 1999. Her letter to *The Herald* about this event evoked a huge response – much very supportive, some very abusive. This in turn encouraged Cara to "do something", which became Nil by Mouth.

Nil by Mouth acts as a catalyst by asking the awkward questions and raising awareness of the issues. In 2001, Nil by Mouth launched its Social Charter, inviting people to sign up to a code which challenges sectarian attitudes, language and behaviour (see Appendix 1). They believe that language is a key factor and that, by fostering attitudes of tolerance and respect, a positive change is possible in Scottish society.

It is through the work of this very small group and its dedicated founder that much has happened in the West of Scotland.

3.2   *Celtic Football Club has developed its own social charter*

Celtic F.C. and Rangers F.C. are working together with Glasgow City Council to develop educational materials for incorporation into the school curriculum.

Celtic FC and Rangers FC, along with Glasgow City Council, Glasgow Presbytery and the Archdiocese of Glasgow, have come together to promote the Millennium Awards, which will be granted to individuals working against sectarianism in local situations (see below).

3.3   *Glasgow City Council*

On 22 February 2001, Glasgow City Council formally recognised that sectarianism continues to be a major problem facing Glasgow and the West of Scotland and instructed the Chief Executive to identify current policy and how that might be developed. The report from the Executive argued that in the absence of a coherent assessment of the scale, nature, causes and impact of sectarianism, future policy might not be as well informed as it might be, and therefore policy made from a flawed basis. Research has been commissioned and is at present being undertaken. It will attempt to describe the features of sectarianism in Glasgow today, who is affected, and how and what the scale of the problem is. The findings of this report will be key to future work for churches in Glasgow and it is hoped will provide baseline data for other academic work.

3.4 *Sense over Sectarianism*

A joint initiative between Glasgow City Council, Rangers FC, Celtic FC, Glasgow Presbytery and Glasgow Archdiocese has been set up. Each organisation has two representatives (in theory, one policy maker and one practitioner). The mere fact of their getting together in this way is a significant breakthrough. The initiative has received over £500,000 from the Millennium Awards to distribute to individuals who are tackling sectarianism locally. A co-ordinator has been appointed who will promote the scheme, support applications and facilitate the assessment process. Several innovative applications have already been received and the Church and Nation Committee learned how seriously the issue is being taken.

3.5 *Celtic and Rangers Football Clubs*

Football, and what goes on around football, provides the context for the most overt expression of sectarianism in Scottish society and as such defines us quite differently from expressions of sectarianism in Northern Ireland. The Committee met with representatives from both Rangers and Celtic Football Clubs. We were impressed by their commitment to tackling the issue, firstly by education (both have packs for schools) and secondly by monitoring behaviour. Celtic now has a social charter (code of behaviour) which they use in educating youth supporters, and which anyone who has caused trouble at a match must sign. A further breach of the code means dismissal from the ground and being barred from attendance at games. Both Celtic and Rangers have been working with Glasgow City Council in the production of a film and study pack, which will be sent to every school in Glasgow, and both are willing participants in the Millennium Awards scheme (see above).

A key issue for both clubs and teams is behaviour at away games, where they have much less control over the fans. They are also concerned about the material offered by street vendors at their home games, who sell goods which are blatantly sectarian and divisive. The clubs have no control over these vendors, whose licences are granted by the local authority. Both clubs are arguing for a mile-wide vendor-free zone around the grounds to diminish the sale of this material. We believe that both clubs are committed to co-operation, but that they are ahead of many of their fans in their way of thinking.

3.6 *The Orange Order*

The meeting with Jack Ramsay, General Secretary of the Order, highlighted our very different understandings of sectarianism. The Orange Order believes that by our very church membership we are sectarian, and Mr Ramsay's description of the Orange Order was of something primarily "tribal". This is at odds with our understanding, which emphasises the destructive patterns of relational behaviour. It does not sit easily with our belief that our identity comes primarily from Christ and not from our culture. Although we must all be free to enjoy our separate cultural/religious identities, this liberty cannot be at the expense of others or, indeed, the sole basis of our faith.

We were told that the marching bands so widely associated with the Order are in fact quite separate from it, be it the Grade A, the Accordion or the Blood and Thunder bands. Members of the Order see these as distorting their image and giving them a bad press. Mr Ramsay described these as the *bêtes noir* of the Order and also made adverse comments about some fringe supporters.

The Order clearly see themselves as a law-abiding group which promotes civil and religious liberty in Scotland. This attitude led us to reflect on the difference in emphasis we might place between law and grace, or on upholding the letter of the law rather than the spirit.

Whatever the statements made to us in all sincerity, we are aware that the Orange Order is widely perceived to be a sectarian organisation. The Order is not alone in being viewed in this way, but in its case there is a sharper focus which results in the perception becoming, for many people, the reality. We believe that those within the Church of Scotland who associate themselves with the Order should reflect upon this and take this to heart.

3.7 *Dr Elinor Kelly*

Dr Elinor Kelly, Research Fellow in Race and Ethnic Issues at Glasgow University, spoke with us about her research into serious crime committed within the context of Old Firm hatred, and also shared her submission to Holyrood in response to Donald Gorrie's proposed bill.

Dr Kelly has documented a disturbing sequence of football-related incidents resulting in death or serious injury in recent years. The Committee found this a chilling catalogue of repeated violence sparked by a mixture of football and sectarian division. One incident feeds off another and assumed sectarian labels provide a focal point (occasionally mixed with a racist dimension) for regular life-threatening violence on our streets. We forbear from recording them in detail because the Committee does not focus on individual cases, but would not wish anyone to underestimate what it repeatedly means. We are also sympathetic to Dr Kelly's concern about the unwillingness of certain members of the judiciary to take seriously the issue of "sectarian aggravation" in the trial and subsequent sentencing in these cases.

We would commend two of her proposals for the Assembly's consideration. In relation to the serious crime issue, we note that the Anti-Terrorism, Crime and Security Act (ACTSA), December 2001, introduced in the wake of September 11 brought into law measures relating to "religiously aggravated" crime. We commend Dr Kelly's submission that there is a need for the introduction of similar measures relating to "sectarian aggravation", to deal with crimes which arise from divisions within faith communities.

Such measures would go some way in dealing with the most serious and obvious injuries caused by sectarianism in Scotland. In the longer term we have argued for the need for a persistent and sustained approach, geared towards changing societal attitudes. In this context, Dr Kelly draws attention to the measures introduced in Scotland by the Race Relations (Amendment) Act 2000 (RRAA), which both places a duty on all public authorities to promote racial equality and requires them to follow a Statutory Code of Practice that challenges custom and practice and requires new standards of professionalism within institutions. The RRAA could well serve as a template for equivalent measures relating to sectarianism.

4. We have taken a view from Northern Ireland

4.1 We met with Joseph Liechty of the Irish School of

Ecumenics, who with his colleague, Cecelia Clegg, has led the Moving Beyond Sectarianism project on examining the rôle of the churches in contributing to, nurturing and ultimately tackling sectarianism in Northern Ireland. The project has run for five years and had two distinct phases:

- A consultation with focus groups and a wide range of interviews, which led to the design and piloting of a new model for group work. This phase ended with two major conferences, one a Northern Ireland conversation and the second applying international insights to the situation.
- Phase two focused on training and dissemination of findings.

4.2 We found his definition of sectarianism helpful and would wish to commend it:

Sectarianism is…a complex set of attitudes, actions, beliefs and structures at personal, communal and institutional levels, which involves religion and typically involves a negative mixing of religion and politics. It arises as a distorted expression of human needs, especially for belonging, identity and the freedom of expression of difference, and is expressed in destructive patterns of relating.

4.3 The core of this Northern Irish project focused on helping people understand how sectarianism works, as a system of which they are part. Those who found this most difficult to accept were (a) those who work ecumenically and (b) those who see themselves as victims of sectarianism rather than contributors to it. While there are gradations within sectarianism, as experienced in Northern Ireland, Dr Liechty found a continuum from comparatively innocuous, subtle and polite forms to the overt violence on the streets, and argues that all are complicit to some degree. However, long-term endemic sectarianism breeds a culture of blame when what is needed is a culture of responsibility, in which we start from our own part in sectarianism and what we can do to change that. Rejecting the common feeling that "if we were all secular the problem would disappear", the project aimed at redeeming the parts of identities/institutions/

communities that have been distorted by sectarianism. This redemption nurtures hope where other approaches are perceived as threatening. As one person had put it, "Whatever you do, don't take our communities away from us."

4.4 The study found that issues of power and its imbalances are important, and must be correctly named in their various forms in different communities. Sensitivity of approach is also needed when initiatives claim the moral high ground. We all find it easier to deal with the "safely other" (the groups with whom we don't expect to find common ground) than with the groups in which we see something of ourselves but which speak with a different voice.

4.5 While the churches (in Ireland) can find reasons to exonerate themselves from blame (for example, that many of the sharpest instances occur where churches have least impact), the study recognises that no-one else has a comparable "socialising" influence. Churches are found to have a tendency to evade responsibility and miss opportunities when they say that the problems are political rather than religious. While there are examples of co-operation among churches (as well as contradictory stories), churches could do more to spread examples of good practice and give clear, authoritative "permission" for grass-roots working together. Church leaders run the risk of becoming too focused on one model of reconciliation work and thereby becoming alienated from their base, but still have the responsibility of "speaking with a voice that cannot be duplicated to a community that cannot otherwise be reached". Perhaps the most widespread and damaging contribution of churches is to reinforce segregation. To counteract this has led the Church of Ireland to look at reconfiguring its whole understanding and practice of ministry.

4.6 While noting that these observations are made from a Northern Ireland perspective, they cannot be dismissed as being only relevant to that context. The wide spectrum of sectarian behaviour is worthy of note. Although we may perceive our own attitudes to be on the "comparatively innocuous, polite and subtle" end of the scale, we must recognise our complicity in the system as a whole. Furthermore, however sectarianism is expressed within our own country, the notion of a redemptive and transformative approach to tackling it must be a challenge to the Church in Scotland today.

5. We have witnessed

We have witnessed local and national initiatives including joint work by churches and community organisations, which can act as a source of hope and encouragement, addressing sectarianism at its roots.

5.1 *Bridging the Gap*

Bridging the Gap is an initiative in Gorbals, Glasgow where Gorbals Parish (Church of Scotland) and Blessed John Duns Scotus (Roman Catholic), have come together to work on ways of breaking down barriers, whatever they might be. Their aim is "to work across the divides which are apparent in the community" and to provide opportunities for people to discover their "common ground".

Their statement of mission for the new Millennium reads:

As we enter the year 2000, the year which closes the Second Millennium of the Christian era, we are moved by the Holy Spirit to make this statement of common ground on which we stand.

As the Church of Jesus Christ in Gorbals, we recognise that we serve one Lord Jesus Christ; that we worship one God, the Father Almighty; that we enjoy one baptism in the Holy Spirit, through the grace of God revealed in Holy Scripture.

Grateful for opportunities we have already found to grow in faith, we undertake to work together in the service of God, in whatever ways are found to be appropriate. We celebrate our common work in the church and community project "Bridging the Gap" through which we aim to extend the work of the church in serving all God's people in this place.

We pray that the church will find, in joyful obedience, the path by which God will bring us to fuller unity, now that we acknowledge that all are one in Jesus Christ, to whom with the father and the Holy Spirit be all glory and praise now and for ever, Amen.

Blessed John Duns Scotus   *Gorbals Parish Church*
Fr Brian McGrath   *Rev Ian Galloway*

This statement hangs in the foyer of each church as a sign of their commitment to the work and as symbol of their commitment to working together.

Bridging the Gap employs two project workers, part funded by the Board of National Mission, and they are working in many creative ways, including through music and art, to bridge the gaps as they find them in Gorbals society. They registered their delight at a recent remark about the "Christian community " in Gorbals, and by working together on gaps between primary and secondary school, between young and old, between incomer and resident, they provide a model of good practice for the national church to follow.

5.2 *The Scottish Centre for Nonviolence*

Based in Dunblane, the Scottish Centre for Nonviolence has a good track record of working on reconciliation and conflict resolution, and is now looking at transferring those skills to understanding the hurt and violence associated with sectarianism. They have begun work with a group in Livingston (Women in West Lothian for Peace) and are planning to develop a "tool kit" for the training of trainers, including teachers and community workers.

5.3 *Donald Gorrie's Private Member's Bill*

The Committee was represented at a gathering of Scottish churches to discuss the proposed Bill with Donald Gorrie, and subsequently made our comments on the Consultation document (Appendix 2).

6. We are aware of the limits of this study

6.1 We are aware that, within the time and resources which were available to us, we have been unable to carry out in-depth studies across the length and breadth of Scotland and that our contacts have centred primarily in West/Central Scotland. We are conscious that while sectarianism may be more overt in that area, it would be wrong to ignore its presence in other communities across Scotland. We hope that churches and congregations will give earnest consideration to their own local circumstances.

6.2 We are also aware that we have not included the issue of Education and separate schooling in our study. Nevertheless we have been conscious of the depth of this issue and we have learned of the hurt and mistrust experienced by people working in education. This burning issue has been considered as recently as 1999 by the General Assembly which reached the conclusion that *"Separate schooling, while not necessarily causing sectarian attitudes, and indeed there is no real evidence to show that denominational schools, in themselves, lead to prejudicial attitudes, may nevertheless help reinforce the prejudices and stereotyping which are passed on by society."* We have heard that, for some, this statement itself has been perceived as sectarian. **We believe that it is right to acknowledge this perception and, in the spirit of our report, to reflect upon its significance**.

7. We have learned

7.1 We have learned that:

- we each have a personal responsibility to tackle sectarianism in Scotland today. We are not guiltless in our own behaviour and, as in addressing other areas of discrimination such as gender and racism, we must be very cautious and remember that "we will be called to account for every useless word" (Matthew 12:36).
- while we must be part of the solution, we should recognise that we may also be part of the problem.
- our silence often renders us complicit in sectarianism and that an awareness of the consequences of our behaviour and language is the first step towards change.
- much can be achieved by committed individuals, even when tackling a belief system which goes deep in our society.

7.2 We have learned that:

- as a church we have a rôle to play in countering sectarianism.
- what might honestly be expressed and intended as a positive statement of our faith may be heard and experienced by others as sectarianism.
- although there is common consensus that sectarianism is not the blight it has once been in Scottish society, local media reporting suggests that it is still a live issue which we need to be aware of as a church, both nationally and locally.
- although sectarianism in Scotland is at its sharpest outside the church, nevertheless, the church can have an impact in a local situation which could be transformative.

7.3 *We have learned from the Irish School of Ecumenics:*

- that while there are significant cultural and other differences between our experience and that of Northern Ireland, in some ways the situations in both countries can feed off one another.
- about starting from an acceptance of our own part in a culture of sectarianism and discerning what we can do to change things.
- about the need for an honest analysis of power imbalances.
- that we must move from a culture of blame to a culture of responsibility.

7.4 We have learned that much good work has been initiated by many individuals and organisations in society and that there is a need to document these and to share good practice. What we have learned has reinforced our awareness that a positive embracing of diversity can and does enrich human life and society (and does not diminish it).

8. We recommend

In the light of all that we have learned we recommend:

8.1 That the Church of Scotland signifies the seriousness of its role in eliminating sectarianism by initiating the setting up of a working group along with the Roman Catholic Justice and Peace Commission to:

- research, document and communicate good models of practice;
- act as a point of contact for those seeking resources, human and material;
- offer creative additions to the established patterns of ecumenical activity.

8.2 That all congregations in Scotland commit their full support to those who are working to combat sectarianism and dissociate themselves from any who would seek to undermine this work.

8.3 That congregations set up working groups to consider the issue of sectarianism in the circumstances of their own community. We recommend that they give specific consideration to the Nil by Mouth Charter as a way of encouraging each member to fulfil their personal responsibility to tackle sectarianism and feed back their findings to the working group outlined in para.8.1. (Resources which might provide a starting point for this consideration are listed in Appendix 3.)

8.4 That we must each search our own conscience and examine any reluctance to embrace the diversity of faiths and cultures which enrich Scottish society today.

Appendix 1

The Nil by Mouth Social Charter

This charter is a non-political, non-religious document and is inclusive of all sections of Scottish society, regardless of creed, colour, sexuality or religion. Although its principles are formed in response to the particular issue of sectarianism in Scotland, such principles can and should be applied to other forms of prejudice and pejorative stereotypes that influence our society.

(a) The Nil by Mouth Social Charter calls upon members of society to examine their own attitudes and language and not to view bigotry simply as an external problem.

(b) The Nil by Mouth Social Charter calls upon individuals to see that his language, actions and behaviour do make a difference in his society and have determining influence in the shaping of it.

(c) The Nil by Mouth Social Charter calls upon the individual to accept that his rôle in society carries with it a personal responsibility for the effects of his behaviour.

(d) The Nil by Mouth Social Charter calls upon the individual who sings sectarian songs, who tells and laughs at bigoted jokes, simply because those around him do so, to stop and think about the meaning of the words, even for a few seconds.

(e) The Nil by Mouth Social Charter calls upon the individual to see that he has a choice to collude or not with a bigoted code of behaviour. In recognising this choice, the individual can no longer claim to be acting out of habit and thereby not see the implications of his actions.

(f) The Nil by Mouth Charter calls upon all members of society to work towards a genuine pluralism which respects all people and resists bigotry, intolerance and racism in any shape or form.

(g) The Nil by Mouth Charter subscribes to the philosophy that if we are to go forward as a society we need to look at our own individual attitudes and the language we use to express these attitudes.

Nil by Mouth Charter for Change

Nil by Mouth calls on:

(a) The Scottish executive and local authorities to promote anti-sectarianism throughout the education system

(b) Rangers and Celtic to agree on and announce measurable targets for reducing sectarian behaviour among their supporters.

(c) Employers to make clear in their recruitment and employment processes that they do not tolerate any form of sectarianism or bigotry.

(d) Voluntary organisations, sports clubs, public bodies and businesses to include a commitment to non-sectarianism in their constitution or mission statements and application/registration forms.

(e) The Scottish parliament to change the law so sentences can be increased for anyone convicted of an offence aggravated by sectarian behaviour

(f) Churches to convey a strong anti-sectarian message and to work in partnership across the diversity of faiths followed in Scotland.

Appendix 2

Comments submitted to Protection from Sectarianism Consultation (Donald Gorrie)

Question 1
Do you have any views on the deterrent effect of making sectarian behaviour an aggravating factor which the courts can take account of in sentencing?

This does seem to be a more practical means of addressing those aspects of sectarianism which can be dealt with in the Courts than by introducing new criminal offences. It would be important to monitor its effect and to ensure that police and court record systems were developed to provide the necessary statistical information.

Question 2
Do you think the Bill should require all relevant organisations to draw up their own Code of Conduct?

Yes – this would ensure public commitment to the principles underlying the Bill by these bodies.

Question 3
Should the following be required to draw up their own Codes? The relevant organisations could include all public bodies- Councils, schools, Health authorities, universities and colleges, quangos, the Executive Departments and Parliament- and all major employers, voluntary organisations, churches, football and other sports clubs, and housing associations. Are there any other bodies that should be included?

It is considered that youth organisations might have been included as specific category as might media organisations. Otherwise the broad categories of public bodies, voluntary organisations and major employers would appear to cover all eventualities.

Question 4
Would it be appropriate to define major employers as those who employ say 15 or more people?

This could be considered too small a number for a definition of a "major" employer. Could this not be defined as 100 employees or more with an added proviso that smaller employers would be expected to conform to a recommended code of practice set out in the legislation?

Question 5.
Should the Bill specify points that each Code must include?

Yes – in terms of key headings for areas of conduct, which could be expected to appear in all Codes.

Question 6
Do you think that the Bill should provide a sample Code that organisations could adopt if they wish?

Yes – as a reference point for smaller organisations.

Question 7
Who should be responsible for overseeing the system of Codes and dealing with appeals?

These could be considered as separate issues. Firstly it could be a requirement that all codes should contain details of arrangements for internal appeals. (Employing bodies, for instance, might deal use existing employee grievance procedures.) Appeals beyond the individual organisation open up a more difficult issue in terms of powers to intervene. It may be preferable, instead, to look for an Ombudsman type rôle exercised by an Equal Rights Commission.

Additional Point
A field, which is not covered, is that of employment issues – because it is a reserved matter. Would it not be possible, nevertheless, to stipulate that the code should include reference to employment practices?

Appendix 3

1. We recommend the following for study:

Moving Beyond Sectarianism, Cecelia Clegg and Joe Leichty, Irish School of Ecumenics (Columba Press 2001) This book is written as a result of a five-year project and outlines the findings of the research. The task was to help the churches understand better their contribution to sectarianism and offer resources for moving beyond it. From the beginning they tried to get alongside people and work co-operatively with them; materials were developed and piloted extensively; these have resulted in two handbook, which would be useful tools for local congregations to use.

Moving beyond Sectarianism; A Resource for Adult Education
Moving Beyond Sectarianism: A resource for Young Adults (youth and school)

Available from Irish School of Ecumenics (Trinity College Dublin), 48 Elmwood Avenue, Belfast BT9 6AZ, Tel (028) 90 382 750.

2. The following addresses may also offer support:

The Centre for Nonviolence
Scottish Churches House
Kirk Street
Dunblane
FK15 0AJ
Tel: 01786 824730

Corrymeela Community
8 Upper Crescent
Belfast
BT7 1NT
Tel: 02890 508080

Community Relations Council
6 Murray Street
Belfast
BT1 6DN
Tel: 02890 227500

LAND REFORM

The campaign for land reform is driven by ideals; by a desire to curtail the powerful and to empower the disempowered; by a concern for stewardship and community; by a passion for freedom and justice. (Professor Donald MacLeod)

1. The General Assembly of 1998, after receiving a major report from the Church and Nation Committee on *Land Tenure and Use*, gave support to the urgent need for land reform and to the formation of a Scottish Land Reform Convention to draw up proposals for that reform. This brief report updates the position in terms of activity since 1998 and the debate on the current Land Reform Bill. The churches were founder members of the Scottish Land Reform Convention, and have continued to contribute to the debate on land reform; the Committee is represented on the Scottish Churches Land Reform Reference Group, which includes different strands of the churches' engagement with land reform issues (such as the General Trustees) and has responded to recent consultations from a perspective rooted in the pastoral experience of the churches and in a theological understanding of the earth as belonging to God.

2. Land is not a product or a commodity, but given in trust; a finite resource to be enjoyed, and cared for in responsible, shared stewardship, or the commitment to sustainable development that is built into the structures of the Scottish Parliament. This Biblical vision - reflected in the covenant that brings God, land and people together in partnership - repeatedly recognises the dangers of the gathering of land into large estates which give disproportionate power to those who control the land. Biblically, that understanding of the relationship of land and power prompted the corrective justice of the jubilee, restoring land rights to those who have lost them over the years - not because all large landowners are bad but because the concentration of power over land and therefore over people's lives is fraught with danger. That then underlies a recognition of the need for intervention in the operation of a land market to safeguard the interests of the community as a whole and especially the most vulnerable.

3. In the light of that vision, we find ourselves very much in sympathy with the stated objectives of the Land Reform (Scotland) Bill: "to remove the land-based barriers to the sustainable development of rural communities" through:

- increased diversity in the way land is owned and used: in other words, more variety in ownership and management arrangements (private, public, partnership, community, not-for-profit) which will decrease the concentration of ownership and management in a limited number of hands, particularly at local level, as the best way of encouraging sustainable rural development; and

- increased community involvement in the way land is owned and used, so that local people are not excluded from decisions which affect their lives and the lives of their communities.

4. The Bill has three main sections, dealing with rights of responsible access, the community right to buy, and a specific crofting community right to buy. While a great deal of public interest has focussed on the provisions for rights of access, comments from the churches have mainly been confined to the proposals for a community right to buy, reflecting the 1998 Report as well as reports from other churches.

5. We are not persuaded that the mechanisms within the Bill for enabling communities to buy their land provide an effective means of achieving that. The proposed procedure requires a community body to be constituted in specific ways, to register every five years its interest in a particular piece of land and to meet a range of criteria, while only being able to purchase land (at market value) when it comes on the market. Since most privately owned rural land has not come on the market for over 100 years, the procedure does not seem realistically empowering. In fact, we believe that the current proposals would have frustrated rather than encouraged notable successes of recent years such as the Isle of Eigg Trust, by imposing rigid requirements which may not fit local need.

6. The Churches' Land Reform Reference Group has called for the Bill to be amended:

- to recognise explicitly the public interest in land
- to give greater flexibility in the legal form which community bodies may take, and a presumption of continuity in renewing a registration of interest
- to allow for partnership between community bodies and non-governmental organisations in land ownership and management
- to include other forms of land transfer as occasions which give rise to the right to buy
- to promote better integration with local planning, and
- to provide for a clear commitment to ensuring that ownership of land cannot be concealed, and further consideration of restrictions on which bodies can own land.

7. Though taking some steps in the right direction, the current proposals do not represent a serious effort to change the most concentrated pattern of land ownership in the world, with half of rural Scotland owned by 343 landowners. What is needed for that is a more radical and far-reaching agenda addressing inheritance law, the land market and land values, absentee land ownership and taxation issues. Within the parameters of the present Bill, the proposals are, we believe, unlikely to enable many communities to gain control over their land; indeed the financial memorandum to the Bill itself anticipates only two non-crofting community purchases per year. We therefore do not believe that the provisions of the Bill can achieve the stated aims of increased diversity in the way land is owned and used, and increased community involvement in issues crucial to their future.

8. Although the Bill is expected to complete its passage through the Scottish Parliament by the summer of 2002, we are encouraged that it is only the latest stage in the Scottish Executive's programme of land reform. We would therefore hope that the General Assembly will encourage the Committee to continue to pursue the Church's concerns as outlined above.

FOOT AND MOUTH DISEASE

1. Introduction and background

1.1 In May 2001, at the time of the General Assembly, Foot and Mouth Disease (FMD) in the United Kingdom was three months old. Of course, there had been previous outbreaks and older generations of farmers, veterinary surgeons and others have spoken of the methods used then to tackle the disease and of their consequences. That was over a generation ago and at a time, in 1967, when farming was in a very different state. The immediate impact has been concentrated in Dumfries and Galloway and the Borders but there can be no doubt that FMD has affected not just the farming community but the country as a whole.

1.2 A decision was taken in advance of the General Assembly of 2001 to hold a special meeting, an evening meeting open to the public to which farmers and others particularly severely affected were specifically invited. Over 200 attended. At that meeting at the General Assembly, we heard from representatives of the Board of National Mission, the Church and Nation Committee, from ministers from the four presbyteries in which culls had taken place and, most importantly, from those who had had direct experience of the loss of livestock. From that meeting emerged an instruction from the General Assembly to the Church and Nation Committee to "set up a working party to explore the implications of foot and mouth disease for the rural community, and all the issues it raises for agriculture and to report to the next General Assembly". A small working party was established and has been engaged on that task.

1.3 The task is, on any view, enormous. The implications of the foot and mouth crisis are extremely wide ranging and the situation is still developing. A complete investigation would require an examination of all of the factors - political, economic, nutritional and social, among others - which affect agriculture in the United Kingdom. Several commissions have been appointed by the Government and others to examine many of these factors. The working group has focused on addressing those issues which appeared to it to be of particular importance, including the impact on our rural communities and concerns about the future of farming. In our investigations and considerations, we have attempted not only to look back to the intense difficulties of the past year, but also to give thought to what lies ahead. Future years may prove that FMD in 2001 was only one of many factors helping to shape agriculture, or it may be that it proves to be a turning point. There will be other reports to write on specific areas affecting agriculture. This report cannot be seen in isolation. Rather, it forms a part of the continuing concern of the Church for agriculture, for those who depend on it for their livelihood and for the welfare of our society which relies on its produce. These questions will continue to concern this Committee and the Church as a whole. The SRT Project has produced this year a report on *Sustainable Agriculture*, which is another contribution to the Church's discussions on these matters.

1.4 An important part of the work of the working group was the gathering of information and evidence. This was not work done in the abstract but relied on the willingness of many individuals to assist. We have spoken to experts and we have heard from those who have been directly affected. Perhaps the most significant meetings were in Dumfries and Lockerbie when we had the opportunity to meet a wide range of people able to speak from direct experience of foot and mouth disease. The group met not only farmers, but representatives of the local authority and of the business community. The Committee is indebted to all those who took the time and the trouble to speak to the group. We are, in addition, most grateful to all those who have written to us with their accounts and views.

1.5 Although we have had the benefit of being able to draw from scientific and other forms of expertise, the Committee does not make scientific judgements in this report. We are not in a position, in particular, to support or condemn the overall decision to cull rather than to vaccinate on scientific grounds. However, there are moral questions that we would want to draw to the Assembly's attention. There are serious questions about the use of mass culling of animals as the means to eradicate a non-

fatal disease in livestock. This was an unusually virulent strain which was very difficult to detect in sheep, but even so the extent of the disease's spread raises the question of whether we had a regulatory and veterinary system with sufficient resources to meet such an eventuality. In addition the growth in animal movement seen in recent years, has contributed to this calamity. On these issues, we have heard numerous arguments and have read much evidence. We appreciate the complexity of these and many other associated issues and acknowledge their importance. Our contribution has been to reflect from a Christian and Church perspective on the impact of a devastating disease on our country and on the ways in which we produce food.

2. The scale and the impact of the outbreak and the economic impact on farming

2.1 In Scotland, there were 183 confirmed cases of FMD. This does not include farms where animals were slaughtered on suspicion or because of the contiguous cull policy. Across Scotland, 89,000 cattle and 655,000 sheep were slaughtered in the foot and mouth cull, representing 4.4% and 7% of the national herd and flock respectively. The scale of the slaughter in the UK was unprecedented as a response to an outbreak of FMD. The numbers themselves are as thought-provoking as the images of burning carcasses, but the sense of shock and loss felt by individual farmers is of a different type.

2.2 It is not known for certain how Foot and Mouth Disease started in the UK. One theory is that the disease entered the UK from imported contaminated meat. The scale of the outbreak can be attributed at least in part to the way in which food is produced. It has been estimated that there were more than a million sheep movements in the UK in the three weeks prior to the imposition of a ban on animal sales and movements at the start of the outbreak.

2.3 The far-reaching economic effect of the crisis combined with the long term nature of the problem means that Foot and Mouth cannot be regarded purely as a rural problem. It has implications for the whole country. The costs are not restricted to money spent on the slaughter policy, the compensation programme and the value of lost exports. There are other less obvious economic costs of the crisis.

2.4 The foot and mouth crisis must be understood in the context of the pre-existing economic problems in agriculture. In 1995 the total farm income in Scotland was £694 million; in 2000 it was only £228 million. Incomes fell by almost £500 million during that time.

2.5 During the outbreak, 371 farms and other locations were infected with FMD. There were 1,122 other premises which were either contiguous to the infected sites and where animals were culled, or were within the three kilometre area within which all sheep were culled. Compensation for the cull of the cattle and sheep exceeded £162 million. Factors other than agricultural played a part in the crisis. The media were a powerful influence. To what extent they manipulated and to what extent they were manipulated are difficult to say. Its importance either way cannot be underestimated. In the first few months of the crisis some parts of the media created or perpetuated an idealised image of the rural farmer which was combined with a sentimental view of animals. Tourism is arguably more important to the balance of trade than farming. What was decisive was that the image of an empty hotel is less emotive than the image of burning sheep or cattle. Therefore the impression given to the general public was that this was a disaster which affected the farming community in a narrow sense and not the wider rural economy in all of its complexity and diversity. The effect of this kind of reporting is that the predominately urban public can easily believe that FMD problems are over.

2.6 The tourist industry in both affected and unaffected areas was badly hit. To many potential US and other visitors the UK was effectively closed with airlines reporting loss of income even before September 11. VisitScotland carried out a survey of the economic impact of FMD on the Scottish tourism industry. The survey found that 44% of tourism business surveyed had been adversely affected by the epidemic with about 11% saying

that they had reduced the number of their permanent staff. A few of those who were surveyed (6%) felt that they had gained business. In Dumfries and Galloway the impact was extended to all businesses with 52% losing trade as a consequence of the outbreak. In response the Scottish Executive together with VisitScotland put in place a £6.5 million marketing and recovery plan and in Dumfries and Galloway an Economic Recovery Plan was promoted.

2.7 Tourist movement within the UK to and from Foot and Mouth affected regions was limited. Whether or not the resulting drop in income was due to ignorance of the facts does not matter. The reason was Foot and Mouth, and the Government and others responded by discouraging people from visiting the countryside. Hill walking, climbing, field sports, sheep dog trials - even rugby and football matches - were stopped or were cancelled.

2.8 The knock on economic effect on hotels, the retail trade, the transport industry and related service industries was in many areas dramatic. The loss of exports and the long term effect on affected parts of the industry of supermarkets and others having found new suppliers of meat and other products is significant. Whether this will prove permanent is impossible to predict with any accuracy.

2.9 Some of the greatest costs were less easy to define. The loss of hefted flocks, where, over generations, sheep (especially hill sheep) become familiar with their local environment, cannot be easily expressed in monetary terms. The significance and lasting effect of the destruction of important blood lines and pedigree cattle and sheep is difficult to understand for those who work outside the farming community. What does not appear in any of the statistics is the loss to the economy of skills which will not be replaced, experience which will not be utilised and a fundamental sense of despair.

2.10 Also difficult to quantify are the costs of the clean-up operation. The costs borne by the NHS are in the same category, as are the investment in time and other resources by the Royal Scottish Agricultural Benevolent Institution, Samaritans, churches and other organisations in the voluntary sector who were responding to the effect on those who had lost not only animals but a way of life. These illustrate the extent of the crisis while telling only a small part of the story of a social, economic, political and historical disaster. These costs are increased once the army personnel who were traumatised, the vets, and others involved in the slaughter operation, the distressed children of farmers, shopkeepers, people employed in the tourist trade are added to the list.

2.11 FMD was not the first crisis to hit British agriculture. BSE, swine fever, fears over salmonella in eggs and other products, listeria in dairy products, the effect of implementing regulations in respect to slaughterhouses, to list some of the main crises, had left many British farmers doubtful about the future of farming as a viable means of making a living. FMD and the Government's chosen means of eradicating it dealt a blow to farming at a time when it was already suffering. It may well be that the public interest and financial investment in farming will leave the industry more buoyant than it would have been had there been no FMD epidemic.

3. A pastoral view

3.1 *Bereavement*

3.1.1 In its visits to rural communities, the Committee found evidence not only of economic hardship but also of disruption to a way of life, trauma following the culling of herds and flocks, and anxiety in contemplating an uncertain future. All this recalled pastoral encounters of a kind familiar to every parish minister, only this time involving the suffering of entire communities. The grieving experience of shock, anger, loss and painful recognition were apparent. We were forcibly reminded of the need for the Church, particularly one conscious of exercising a territorial ministry throughout all the land, to stand alongside and to listen to those who are suffering. And we were impressed by the struggles of local ministers and congregations to fulfil this incarnational ministry in

difficult circumstances, even when it was never more than partially successful. The remit of the Committee was thus firmly set within the Church's pastoral ministry to the country.

3.1.2 The impact of the foot and mouth crisis on both individuals and on whole communities can be described in terms of multiple bereavement. Bereavement often appears to be about the loss of the past, but it is in fact the loss of a future or the anticipation of a very different future. It has been experienced in varying degrees of intensity for different communities.

3.1.3 Throughout this process the churches have been at work. Clergy of all denominations offered what help they could. Pastoral visiting in the normal way was not possible in relation to many farms and differing forms of contact had to be found. Some ministers kept up regular contact with some farms and farmers by making regular telephone calls. Some used e-mail. The churches' Rural Officer organised a regular and much appreciated Farm Crisis Newsletter. Not long after the FMD outbreak, this Committee wrote to Ministers in the first affected areas to express our prayerful concern. In some cases where personal movement was not forbidden, some farmers and their spouses came to church from time to time, disinfecting themselves before and after and making complete changes of clothing, doing all this because the need to come to worship was so great. Following the Moderator's visit to Dumfries in April 2001, the Church of Scotland raised £150,000 for the Royal Scottish Agricultural Benevolent Institution. This amount was subsequently doubled by the Scottish Executive. It is nevertheless true that some farming families found the Church unable to meet their needs, which has meant sadness to all concerned.

3.2 *Shock*

3.2.1 Perhaps the primary loss was that of the herd or flock. Where it was a pedigree herd or flock, the loss was of blood-stock carefully built up over generations which cannot simply be replaced by going to market six months or a year later. For farmers, there was loss of freedom of movement, the physical isolation experienced by many intensifying the misery. That there has been loss of income is obvious. In many cases, money was cut off at a stroke, followed by no income in real terms for months (especially for those farmers living on a financial knife edge in the normal way of things). Then there was the loss of all the physical tasks which go to make up the routine of the average day, followed by the consequent loss of the rhythm of the farming year. For many, the sense of emptiness which accompanies many a bereavement was so overwhelming that men and women alike were reduced to tears. Where there were young families there was an added difficulty of helping them to come to terms with what had happened – sometimes hard when they were present or able to observe the slaughter or the fires. In one case, slaughter was begun in the field adjacent to a primary school during school hours.

3.2.2 For many communities in areas adjacent to outbreaks the tension was ever present. They also experienced many of the factors we associate with bereavement. There was a clear loss of freedom to carry out normal work. There were animals 'caught' in the wrong place, for example, part of a herd over-wintering anything up to 50 miles away, or sheep in the wrong place for lambing. Even for those with all the stock intact, there was a denial of the normal routines of good husbandry. There was such a fear, understandably, of infection that most farmers did not leave their farms for many months being virtually imprisoned and without normal human contact until the worst of the outbreak was over.

3.2.3 Many of those loss factors were also present for farmers who had in fact diversified in recent years. We met people who had responded to Government exhortations to diversify and had invested their savings in other businesses on the farm. Severe access restrictions killed off those businesses and, in the worst cases, whole new enterprises were lost at a stroke, with no possibility of any kind of compensation being available now or in the future. That particular sense of loss was intensified by the fact that they had moved out of livestock, as they had been encouraged to do.

3.3 *Control and coping*

3.3.1 Fortunately, in some areas at least, a service which is available in conventional bereavement situations came into operation. In the Dumfries area, telephone counselling similar to that offered by CRUSE and the Samaritans was set up for those who needed it. In Dumfries and Galloway, the local authority's emergency planning strategy provided an immediate framework within which support agencies operated. This was heavily used and much appreciated. We had the opportunity to speak both to those who had been involved in providing counselling, in professional and voluntary capacities, and to those who had used those services. In most areas, the local branch of the NFUS provided support, as did the Royal Scottish Agricultural Benevolent Institution. In Dumfries and Galloway an advisory service was set up almost immediately.

3.3.2 In addition to the help that was offered in emotional and spiritual fields, there was much ingenious practical help offered by the community by way of shopping, mail collection and delivery. In some cases, one member of a group of farming communities dealt with the above for a whole group. Some supermarkets facilitated telephone ordering and pick-up facilities, which was felt by many recipients to be a hand held out in friendship. One should not underestimate the sense of isolation felt even by those in the 'at risk areas', some of whom were unable or felt unable to leave their farms for weeks on end. In some cases there were lengthy separations of parents from children.

3.4 *Despair, depression and anger*

3.4.1 For many, the sense of loss is still powerfully present. Some farmers found and still find it hard to accept what happened to them. A few said that while they would begin again, the restocking this autumn was emotionally beyond them. Some still feel anger, at the disease, the cause, Government policies, and other farmers. We heard anger expressed at situations where the official handling was considered clumsy, where there was inadequate or conflicting information or where the need to cull was disputed. We heard of one case in which it was claimed that 1,856 animals were slaughtered by mistake. In some cases, resentment has built up where some people appeared to have profited from being involved in the cull to the distress of their neighbours.

3.4.2   For some, professional help will be useful, but so too will the understanding of the communities within which they live and work. The support between some farmers, especially breeders, has been considerable, some offering bloodlines for restocking. But it can never be as if the tragedy had not happened. All those who were involved have been changed in some measure by events.

3.4.3   Particular anger and criticism have been directed at the Government and the official handling of the disease. This is not, typically, a blanket condemnation. Many have acknowledged that Dumfries and Galloway Council, in particular, has been efficient and helpful. Some have taken care to distinguish the actions of the Scottish Executive from those of the UK Government. It was important to many in Dumfries and Galloway that operations were, by and large, handled locally.

3.4.4   Confusion and unhappiness have surrounded the making of compensation payments. Some do not regard these as compensation at all, but as payments for compulsorily purchased stock subsequently killed. The criticism that was expressed when some of the compensation payments were leaked to the press was unhelpful, and most of it ill-informed. Of course, in some cases, compensation payments represented an opportunity to leave the industry.

3.5   *Acceptance and moving on*

3.5.1   The Committee was asked to look to what the future might be for the farming industry in the wake of Foot and Mouth. In looking to the future, it is necessary to consider both the reasons for food related agriculture and the economic context in which it exists.

3.5.2 The European Union (EU) Common Agricultural Policy (CAP) is an essential source of farm income in Scotland. The £500 million in direct support received by Scottish farmers from subsidies in 2001 was about twice the estimated £273 million net income from farming in Scotland in the same year.

The CAP is in the process of review and change and the Scottish Executive recognises in its Forward Strategy for Scottish Farming that as the EU enlarges there will be pressures to reduce current agricultural support levels. It also recognises that there will be pressures during the current round of World Trade Organisation negotiations to reduce direct subsidies to farmers.

The Report of the Policy Commission on the Future of Farming and Food appointed by the Government to advise the Government on the future of farming in England is very forthright in its criticism of the CAP. Its view is that production subsidies have discouraged farmers from taking their business in new directions by dividing the producer from the market, distorting price signals and masking inefficiency.

There are other critics of the CAP in its current form. Christian Aid is concerned because the subsidy and protection systems in developed countries, including the EU, act against the interests of farmers in developing countries. The Consumers Association claims that the CAP adds £16 a week in taxes and high food prices to the average British family.

3.5.3   However, farming is not simply about producing and marketing a commodity. If the shop or the factory becomes unprofitable, at worst, it can be shut down and one can walk away from the site. In addition to the production of a marketable commodity, farming is also about the stewardship of the land - the major resource after its people, of any nation. We have a responsibility to tend, nurture and maintain the land for present and future generations. There is a proper place for "wilderness", but where an ecology has been cultivated and managed over many generations, it may need continuing human management rather than just "leaving it to nature". Whatever course the future of the farming industry steers, this must be taken into account. All sectors of society will have to be partners co-operating in the change that lies ahead.

3.5.4   It is difficult to predict the degree to which

confidence in the UK agricultural industry will or will not be restored. Legislation may permit the export and import of UK animals - dead or alive. The confidence of the markets will ultimately decide whether or not the trade will revive. To what extent the British agricultural industry itself will be able to recover is - at the moment - an unanswerable question because it is too early to be able to estimate the extent to which it has been damaged. The loss to the economy of farmers who are willing to farm, and to farming of men and women with the necessary skills and capital will have a lasting effect and will be an important factor in determining both the long term economic effects of FMD and the future of farming itself.

3.5.5 Much of the responsibility for what happens next rests with a weighty combination of the Government, the industry, and other agencies and land interest groups. That should not allow the rest of us to sit back. As a nation, we may need to change our expectations of how our food is produced, priced and delivered. If we ignore the needs of the land itself, future generations may rue the attitudes we have taken. If we fail to support the various forms diversification will take, many more farmers will have to leave the land. We need to take an active political interest in the workings of the parliaments in Edinburgh, London and Brussels and to use our votes.

3.5.6 Farmers, too, have serious responsibilities and can ignore neither the market nor political and social developments. Responsiveness to demand, and to new initiatives, is essential. We have heard, for example, a great deal of evidence about the numbers of sheep in Scotland. There is a view that sheep numbers in Scotland will have to drop by about 30% to enable a viable industry to emerge. The Forward Plan for Scottish Agriculture, produced by the Scottish Executive, notes the current mismatch between the demand and the supply for lamb. The Executive is exploring opportunities to introduce a voluntary buy out of sheep quota by the Government. Subsidy-driven stocking decisions cannot continue. The Scottish Agricultural College and local enterprise companies, among others, are involved in programmes providing education and assistance to farmers seeking

ways to develop and improve. Co-operation and an openness to change are vital.

3.5.7 The National Farmers' Union also has an important role. We heard a variety of reactions to the part played by the NFU in the past year and concerns expressed about how representative a union it is. The tension in both representing the interests of small scale farmers and participating in the wider national and international arguments about their future is real and will need careful handling.

4. Agriculture and food – our priorities

4.1 FMD in livestock generally has no effect on humans, nor is meat from infected animals unfit for consumption, but the impact of an outbreak of the disease does have implications for the food chain. Consumer confidence in British meat was shaken yet again just as the industry was recovering from BSE. The export trade and marketing of livestock was suspended, jeopardising the viability of many farm and related businesses. In addition, there has been an increase in the public debate about animal welfare, the movement of animals to markets and live animal exports. Many people have also expressed their horror at the wholesale slaughter during FMD of animals that were healthy, but slaughtered on suspicion. Others have questioned the waste involved in killing even infected animals when their meat was still fit for consumption. What drove the policy was the real risk that endemic foot and mouth disease would kill off an industry that currently depends so heavily on exports.

4.2 FMD comes in the aftermath of a succession of food scares and significant structural changes in the industry, such as the closure of local abattoirs and the continuing growth in the global market for an increasing range of foodstuffs. When treated as an industry there is a risk of seeing agriculture as a purely economic matter. The Scottish Executive declared in its recently published Forward Strategy for Scottish Agriculture that it expects the industry to provide a secure supply of safe and wholesome food, that it wants farmers to sustain a well-tended and beautiful countryside, caring for biodiversity and wild flora and fauna. It wants husbandry systems that allow animals to express their own character and live well and they want vigorous rural communities, where a mix of people can continue to earn a living off the land.

4.3   We question whether all these objectives can be achieved whilst at the same time encouraging farmers to compete in a global market in which regulatory systems, environmental controls, animal welfare standards and labour costs are not the same. Forcing farmers to maintain high standards at home whilst competing in a global market puts them in a very difficult situation.

4.4   People increasingly demand fast, convenience and cheap food. Pre-prepared foods and "complete meal solutions" are an increasing part of the market. Eating out is also increasing and many people do not cook and possibly cannot cook. This poses a significant challenge for the livestock industry. It is not so easy for the local butcher to supply that demand from locally sourced meat. Ready meals tend to be produced with ingredients sourced from around the world at the cheapest cost. Convenience food is food from anywhere. Whilst the consumer may demand that it is flavoursome and cheap, it is questionable whether people ask whether the food is of sound nutritional value and has been produced to the highest possible animal welfare and environmental standards.

4.5   Globalisation casts a long shadow over the future of agriculture in Scotland. Our geology and our climate mean there are relatively few sectors which can expect to compete at global market prices. The Dohar ministerial summit of the World Trade Organisation (WTO) in November 2001 marked the opening of formal negotiations to bring agriculture under the agreements brokered by the WTO. This is proving highly controversial, with many different alliances of nations each arguing conflicting corners. Many Christians and those involved in fair trade, development and environmental issues are expressing deep concerns about how agriculture would be handled in the WTO fold. They fear that trade

rules will push key factors such as environment, animal welfare and employment to the margins, and drive an inevitable pressure towards reducing standards to a lowest common denominator. Instead of seeing such factors as foundational to agriculture, the free market philosophy tends to view these as externalities to trade, which indeed represent trade barriers under the guise of standards. There is also a fear that these trends will continue to place agriculture in the hands of a few very large producers, and lose the sensitivities to the needs of the local rural economy. There is a widespread feeling that the present WTO rules are not flexible and sensitive enough to cope justly with such deep ethical issues. There are also profound concerns expressed, not least through constant protests at WTO gatherings, that there are inequities of power there. The perception is widely held that the WTO has become more a tool of commerce than a mechanism to promote equality of rights across the globe.

4.6   The nutritional health of the people of Scotland remains a cause for concern. Ever since the nineteenth century, attempts have been made by governments to improve nutritional health through the provision of wholesome food in schools and through the teaching of home economics. However, rates of coronary heart disease and obesity are unnecessarily high. The success of other smaller nations (particularly the Scandinavian countries) in tackling these issues should be an inspiration to policy makers in the Scottish Parliament. It is the view of this Committee that good nutrition and health promotion should be among the main goals of the entire food chain in Scotland from the farm and the supermarket to the home and the school dinner hall. The Food Standards Agency, the Health Education Board for Scotland and the Scottish Executive all have their parts to play in this.

4.7   The globalisation of the food chain is a serious cause for concern. For example, powerful seed companies' interests in intellectual property rights, and the implications for agriculture across the world, are the subject of continuing controversy. The Government's stated support for trade liberalisation at times threatens to contradict other stated aims such as sustainability, improved animal welfare standards, food safety, maintaining a healthy environment and a vigorous rural workforce employed in agriculture and related industries. A highly competitive global market makes it very difficult to fulfil all these expectations and compete effectively. In the case of FMD it is clear that the unprecedented spread of the disease throughout large parts of the United Kingdom can be attributed at least in part to large-scale animal movements.

4.7.1 The global market in food is subsidised by the availability of cheap fossil fuels, allowing food to be transported thousands of miles. In some cases, food from the other side of the world is available more cheaply than the same product grown locally. The true cost of food must be taken into account. This includes the cost to the environment caused by transport.

4.7.2 The proportion of the pound that goes to the farmer for the food produced has declined in recent years. This situation is partly attributable to the increasing concentration of purchasing power amongst a few large players, such as the big supermarkets and global food producers who can search globally for the keenest price for commodities. The solution does not seem to be the application of subsidy to help the British farmer remain competitive as that uses tax payer's money to give the big producers an unfair advantage (80% of annual subsidy goes to 20% of the farmers in the UK). The application of subsidy has been shown also to encourage over production, which is bad for the environment and surplus food dumped on the global market undermines producers elsewhere. There is a commonly held assumption that farmers chase subsidy rather than produce for a known market. The Scottish Executive's *Forward Strategy for Scottish Agriculture* refers to possible options for the future of financial support, including land management contracts. There are similar proposals in *The Report of the Policy Commission on the Future of Farming and Food*. The Report recommends that the amount of subsidy given in direct payments should be reduced and payments for environmental and other public goods increased. The change should start now, throughout the UK. For the future, they consider that all subsidy should

be through stewardship payments made to farmers for the positive management of the environment.

4.7.3 When production moves around the world in a volatile and price sensitive global market, basic farming skills can be lost and are hard to recover. It is reported that many thousands of farmers in poorer non-subsidised farming countries around the world that have gone out of business because they cannot compete with cheap imports of subsidised food from the EU and the US. When they leave the land and abandon farming there is a risk of not passing on farming skills to future generations and abandoning land that can be difficult to recover for agricultural use later on. The consequent dependency culture of many of the world's poorest countries, even though their land might be fertile and productive, is a worrying trend. In lean years when basic produce may be scarce food flows towards the rich countries and away from the poorest. The risk is that in a global market for food, the poorest will suffer the most if for any reason global commodities become scarce or more expensive. These issues are dealt with in more depth in *Trade for Life*, published by Christian Aid.

4.8 Experience suggests that there are benefits which have been built up over the years from small scale local farming which utilises ancient know how, local knowledge and selection of appropriate seed or livestock for a particular area. There is a serious risk of these benefits being swept aside when farming and food production move towards standardisation and large-scale production.

5. Thoughts for the future

5.1 For most city dwellers the only regular contact with farm animals is at meal times—we eat them. This makes it difficult for many people to comprehend the grief felt by farmers in losing their animals. After all, some might say, are not these same animals being bred for slaughter to be sold as meat for human consumption? To ask such a question betrays an ignorance of the bond between farmers and their livestock. The breeding of cattle and sheep over generations with daily attention to their welfare reveals a companionship between human and non-human creatures. Even where animals are bred for consumption and economic profit, concern for their welfare should remain paramount. In our farming communities, it frequently does. One woman spoke to us of her sense of grief each morning when confronted by the chilling silence of the farmyard. All her working life she had wakened to the sound of her animals, but now the silence testified to their absence. Others spoke of their deep distress in witnessing the final separation of ewes from their new-born lambs.

5.2   Although beyond the immediate experience of many, all this recalls long-standing Biblical themes about the setting of human beings alongside the other animals, those things we share in common with non-human creatures, and the responsibility placed upon us of compassionate stewardship. The providential ordering of creation, celebrated in Genesis and the Psalms, is a sign of the harmony that God wills. It embraces not only human beings but all living creatures. Though that harmony may never be perfectly achieved before the end of time, we are called to seek and to celebrate it wherever we can in the way we live. In using parables and other images of shepherding, Jesus recalls this Old Testament awareness of our creaturely solidarity. And we should not forget that images of a transformed creation in Isaiah include not only redeemed persons but other animals.

5.3   The strength of these natural bonds to the land and other animals has been apparent in the dedication of some farmers to the task of re-stocking, even when the economic prospects are uncertain. We might even speak of a vocation to farm, reaffirming the Reformation insight that our service and call of God is exercised as much within the world of work and household affairs as in the life of the religious community. This is powerfully felt amongst many in our rural communities where farming is an entire way of life practised for generations. Our concern, therefore, must not only relate to pastoral solidarity but find expression in supporting efforts to ensure the future viability of Scottish agriculture and rural communities.

5.4   The Church of Scotland is at present trying to move forward by giving consideration to its report *Church Without Walls*. That report argues that members are "walled in" by those things with which we are comfortable and familiar, and are therefore unable to develop the life, witness, and growth of the congregation. We are afraid of stepping into the outside world, afraid of the demands change will make, afraid of what is new, sticking with tradition - in part simply because we know where we are. The same may be said in some measure of the farming world. There are radical farmers in the same way there are radicals within the church, but just as most of us need help to step outside the walls, many farmers will find the future a challenge they hardly want to face.

5.5   Any retailer will agree that their business will not last long if they do not listen to what the consumer demands. As consumers Christians should perhaps begin to become far more thoughtful in our shopping priorities. We should consider that cheapness is not always the best thing to look for. Frequently the producer, in the UK or across the world, is being played off against the other in order to drive down the price. This is not good for the farmer, the environment or the stability of the food chain. Organic produce is often deemed attractive, but is sometimes flown or hauled huge distances to the supermarket, with consequences for clogged roads and consequent pollution. The Committee's view is that the consumer should be urged to look for wholesome food from sustainable systems and, where possible, grown locally. The membership of the church constitutes a very significant consumer base. Mobilised in these directions we could begin to witness a difference and perhaps even see a brighter future for the Scottish farming industry.

Appendix

Groups and others consulted:
Dumfries and Galloway Council
Ross Finnie MSP, Minister for Rural Development
Scottish Agricultural College
National Farmers' Union Scotland
Royal College of Veterinary Surgeons
Royal Scottish Agricultural Benevolent Institution
Representatives of organic farming interests
Representatives of farmers from Dumfries & Galloway and the Borders

COMPENSATION CULTURE

Come to terms quickly with your accuser while you are on the way to court with him, or your accuser may hand you over to the judge. (Matthew 5:25,NRSV)

Can it be that there is no one among you wise enough to decide between one believer and another, but a believer goes to court against a believer? ... to have lawsuits at all with one another is already a defeat for you. Why not rather be wronged? (1 Corinthians 6:5-7, NRSV)

1. Introduction

1.1 Might you be entitled to compensation? The question in the television advertisement, addressed to us by the "no win, no fee" company, is perhaps the most immediately obvious indication of what has come to be known as "the compensation culture". Accidents, which at one time would have been taken as regrettable facts of life, or even ridiculous results of carelessness, are now to be taken as occasions on which to claim monetary compensation. The impression we are given is that, before we hit the ground, we should be thinking of suing whoever mislaid the paving stone.

1.2 Highly publicised claims for babies who were not expected to be born or even lives that have lasted longer than anticipated bring protestations and incredulity. The easily dented and highly expensive reputations of the rich and famous on occasion seem to be protected rather more by deep pockets than by "the sword of truth". Every injury, we begin to suspect, has been exaggerated, every trauma deepened in order to extract as much money as possible from misfortune. Even those meeting situations common to their line of work are encouraged to seek compensation for having to face them.

1.3 But if you have been wronged or injured by the action or negligence of another should there not indeed be some form of redress? Should we not be held accountable for our mistakes? Otherwise what is there to ensure that carelessness does not become commonplace, its results met simply with a shrug of the shoulders and the statement, "that's life"? Surely

employers, for example, should not with impunity place their employees in danger of injury - and, if injury results, surely they should have a responsibility to care for the victim of their disregard for safety.

1.4 The modern history of compensation really begins in 1932, with the watershed case of Donoghue v Stevenson, in which the House of Lords opened wide the doors by asking who is our neighbour to whom we owe a duty of care. Since then, and particularly in the last ten or fifteen years, the incidence of claims for compensation has grown inexorably. In the year 2000 the United Kingdom saw 750,000 claims and it is anticipated that by 2005 the "million-a-year" mark will have been reached. The cost of claims against the National Health Service would build a new hospital every year. A professional medical insurance can cost £24,000 per annum.

1.5 The largest growth in claims recently is to be found in three main areas - professional negligence, property loss and pension funds. For some pursuers the process of quantifying their suffering may take them a long way from their original intent. Many do not seek money but simply an apology. Unfortunately the system with which we live seems to make it easier to receive the former than the latter.

1.6 In Scotland there are various mechanisms in place which seek to limit the worst excesses of compensation claims. It has, however, to be borne in mind that a substantial part of very large sums awarded from time to time by the courts goes to compensate a victim for loss of wages and/or the cost of long-term nursing care. The courts do not award punitive damages (except, perhaps, in cases of defamation); no "ballpark" figures are used in cases of injury, with all potential problems being explored before a figure is reached and there is often an attempt to reach agreement before a case reaches court.

2. Standards and Expectations

2.1 Along with a rising standard of living and of health and life expectancy has come a rising expectation of ourselves, of our security and of those with whom we come in contact. Although there is a biblical anticipation of rising to perfection, there is no expectation that this is a state associated with earthly life. However, there is a danger that our expectations of one another presume some kind of state of perfection. Thus, any mistake is regarded by some as a reason to call for dismissal and certainly a case for compensation. It is important that we resist this demand for perfection. While we are all, quite rightly, expected to do our best and not to cut corners or put people in jeopardy, to suggest that anyone is incapable of error or that risk can or should be entirely removed from human life is to deny the nature of our existence. Any examination of that nature must conclude that risk is inherent in the human condition; it is part of our inheritance and the only way by which we make progress. Supremely, the life of Jesus of Nazareth is a life of total risk lived entirely at the mercy of others.

2.2   The consequence of a life in which we think risk can be avoided is that we hesitate before taking the risky step of helping others. If those others are going to expect from our help a perfection which we know to be beyond us, we are likely to fail to give help of any kind. It is already known for doctors in the USA not to offer their assistance in cases of emergency where they are not personally involved for fear of being sued if something goes wrong. In this country, even schools and churches have been known to cease certain activities because of fear of litigation. The expectation of perfection - in ourselves as well as in others can mean either self-delusion (born of a mistaken confidence in our own abilities) or self-loathing (born of our awareness of all the ways in which we fall short), the complete antithesis of the gospel of Jesus Christ. Our existence in, with and for one another can be torn apart by fear of risk.

3.   Blame and Responsibility

3.1   Very often the term "compensation culture" is actually a cover for a "blame culture". If something goes wrong, it must be someone's fault, there must be somebody to blame. Perhaps in previous ages it would

be God who would take the blame, but now we blame one another. The way of establishing who is to blame is to find someone to sue - and if the case is successful we have proof positive that the blame has been allocated, the responsible body identified. And, what is most important, it should not be us. One of the great "benefits" of compensation is that responsibility is apportioned elsewhere.

3.2   Must there always be someone to blame? Last year, in its report on the problems of the Scottish Qualifications Authority, the Committee discussed accountability. That discussion recognised the need to acknowledge wrongdoing and then to overcome it. It suggested that fear needs to be overcome by love and that the responsibility of love is to be part of a solution to, rather than the continuation of, a problem. This places our present discussion firmly within the field of human rather than monetary exchange. We question if money, in certain circumstances, can ever truly be compensation. Money can compensate for loss of earnings, but not for loss of life or even of reputation. The human exchange of apology, forgiveness and reconciliation holds out a true hope of newness and a fresh start for human beings who seek wholeness.

4.   Rights and Duties

4.1   It is held by some that our modern emphasis on human rights has exacerbated our tendency to exalt rights over duties. The Committee has commended various pieces of human rights legislation in the past and has supported calls for a Human Rights Commission for Scotland. We still see these as important. We believe, however, that to see such developments simply as part of an individualistic "me" generation is to misunderstand their potential. It seems to us that they are much better viewed as a framework within which we each recognise the rights of the other - and thus recognise our duty to uphold these. As Amnesty International put it, "there are very few absolute rights. In most cases there must be a balance between the right of an individual and the rights of the community." Once we recognise the responsibility we each have put on us by the rights of those around us, we acknowledge the duty we owe to one another.

4.2   Such duties, however, are not simply to be invoked negatively when something goes wrong, but positively as an integral part of human flourishing. Duties of care apply to those to whom we turn for assistance, but they also apply to each member of a society. That society cannot long survive in which people only relate to one another through monetary exchange, where fear holds people apart and where blame rather than a future is sought.

4.3   While we have certain reservations about "Good Samaritan" laws (for example, in France), which lay a legal duty on people to aid a person in trouble so long as their own safety is not thereby put at risk, we nevertheless believe that steps need to be taken to safeguard the position of someone who does go to the aid of someone else.

5.   Recommendations

5.1   *No-fault Compensation*

5.1.1   A substantial part of the time and cost involved in compensation cases at present is caused by the need to prove the fault of the defender. In spite of serious loss, injury and damage, pursuers can find that this is a hurdle they are unable to surmount - often because of circumstances outwith their control. A no-fault compensation scheme could avoid such problems.

5.1.2   The example of New Zealand where the government operates an Accident Compensation Corporation could be a useful model for our society to examine further. This provides comprehensive, compulsory, no-fault insurance cover for people with accident-related injuries and disabilities. Its operation removes the right to sue for damages in return for support for injured people, no matter who was at fault - if anyone. It is funded by income tax, by a levy on the annual registration fee for motor vehicles, and by a levy of two cents per litre on all fuel sales for vehicles. The

Committee believes that such a scheme is worthy of further research in this country.

5.1.3   In this regard we have been heartened to read the recommendations of the Kennedy Report, produced in response to a situation in an NHS hospital where babies were damaged at birth. This report makes it clear that Health Service Staff owe patients:

> *A duty of candour, meaning a duty to tell a patient if adverse events have occurred..* (Recommendation 33)

It also addresses the issue of apology to which reference was made earlier:

> *When things go wrong, patients are entitled to receive an acknowledgement, an explanation and an apology.* (Recommendation 34)

The report then importantly suggests a system of no-fault compensation. It recommends:

> *The introduction of an administrative system for responding promptly to patients' needs in place of the current system of clinical negligence.* (Recommendation 37)

It goes on to say that:

> *The criminal negligence system ... should be abolished. It should be replaced by an alternative system for compensating those patients who suffer harm arising out of treatment from the NHS. An expert group should be established to advise on the appropriate method of compensation to be adopted.* (Recommendation 119)

A White Paper in response to this Report is expected soon. We hope that the Government will take Professor Kennedy's suggestions very seriously.

5.2   *Mediation*

Although attempts are currently made, as mentioned earlier, to bring parties to an agreement before court, we understand that as matters presently stand there is considerable incentive not to settle - there being the chance of greater sums available after a court case. We believe that it should be possible to introduce an additional and alternative system based on mediated settlements, thus reducing the chances of the largest sums involved being the fees charged.

6. Conclusion

There are fundamental issues at stake here - issues to do with how we regard human life, issues than can tell us about ourselves and about the society in which we live. We believe that there needs to be a much more widespread and public debate about these matters and these reflections are one small contribution to that debate.

REFUGEES AND MIGRATION

The Committee has undertaken a three-fold examination of issues concerning refugees and migration. We ask firstly if our definition of a refugee is adequate to the world of today; we then look at how the search for a common European policy raises questions of common European identity; and finally we examine current developments in Britain concerning the treatment of those who come to live among us.

1. The International Situation: Who is a Refugee?

Stories from Keith and Lai Fun Russell, Church of Scotland Mission Partners in Cairo working with Sudanese refugees:

Our refugees are fleeing Sudan mainly because of the chaotic war going on in the south of the country. It began as probably a religious war (Christian south v Islamic north) but it's degraded into an inter-tribal mess, with very few people able to explain its causes to the outside world. Fundamentally it is to do with personal identity - whether you feel you are an African (the southerners) or an Arab (the northerners). Now that oil has been found the government is ethnically cleansing whole areas to allow for drilling/extraction of the oil - and it cares little which ethnic group gets in the way of its plans. It recently cleared an area of its Muslims by firing ground-launched missiles into their villages.

Our people are urban refugees, scattered round this vast city. They are extremely poor and seriously discriminated against. They pay exorbitant rents for their accommodation. They cannot educate their children, and they have no quality health care. Most hate living here and want to move on. Every year about 5,000 are resettled to other countries - Australia, Canada and the USA. The UNHCR (who determines whether or not they fit the criteria of refugee under the 1951 convention) is overwhelmed. Over 9,000 new people have arrived this year. It now takes 30 months just to get your first UN interview! The churches try to do what they can to help - but we too feel overwhelmed with the level of need/ demand we see.

1.1 The Scale of the Global Problem

1.1.1 The last decade since the fall of communism, inaugurated with predictions of a "new world order", has seen the biggest global increase in the number of refugees in fifty years. When the United Nations Convention Relating to Refugees was agreed in 1951, there were approximately 2.1 million refugees; in 2001 there were over 27 million, with a significant increase since 1990 of those seeking refuge from war, persecution or famine.[1]

1.1.2 Given the current concern frequently expressed in the UK about the number of refugees seeking asylum here, we need to be reminded that it is the poorer countries of the world that open their borders to most of the world's refugees. The overwhelming mass of refugees are to be found in host countries in Africa and Asia, though the largest refugee group remains the Palestinians, estimated at 3.7 million,[2] some of whom have lived in refugee camps for over fifty years. In the past decade, over three million Afghan refugees have been accepted by Pakistan, and that was before the present war in Afghanistan. Iran has catered for nearly 2 million Afghans and Iraqis with very little outside help; Thailand took one million refugees from Vietnam, Laos and Cambodia. Malawi, with a per capita income of $170 per annum, and a population of nine million in the early 1990s, accepted one million refugees from Mozambique in the war years. Guinea, which has a population of less than 7 million, supports 500,000 refugees from Sierra Leone and Liberia - a ratio 50 times that of the UK. Some of the poorest countries in the world support the largest numbers of refugees. The twenty countries with the highest percentage of refugees have an annual per capita income of US$700. These figures put in perspective the approximately 80,000 UK applications for asylum in the year 2000.[3]

1.2 *The 1951 UN Convention*

1.2.1 The word *refugee* was precisely defined in the 1951 United Nations Convention Relating to Refugees as a person who:

owing to well-founded fear of being persecuted for reasons of race, religion, nationality, membership of a particular social group or political opinion, is outside the country of his nationality and is unable, or owing to such fear, is unwilling to return to it.

1.2.2 The 1951 Convention applied only to European nationals. In 1967 a UN Protocol applied the terms of the Convention to any person in the world. The UK, along with over 130 other countries, is a signatory to the Convention and its protocol. The Convention and Protocol are the foundation of current international refugee law.

1.2.3 The Convention has been criticised for failing to deal with all the issues relating to refugees.

- It confers no right of assistance on refugees unless and until they reach a signatory country.
- It confers no right of assistance at all on "internally displaced persons". Millions of people have left their homes for fear of persecution, or because their homes are destroyed, but they have not left their homeland. The UN Convention offers no safeguard for them.
- It imposes no obligation on governments not to persecute their citizens, or to guarantee their safe return.
- It imposes no mechanism for preventing mass outflows, for burden sharing between states, for ensuring speedy assistance for those most in need,

or for maximising the effectiveness of international resources.

- It takes no account of the capacity of receiving states to cope with numbers of refugees. As stated above, most refugees in the world are in the countries least able economically to support them.

1.2.4 The UN Convention no longer addresses the economic and political world of the 21st Century. It was drafted in the specific context of Europe in the aftermath of a war that had redefined national boundaries and had created millions of homeless people. The drafters of the Convention could not have foreseen the major changes in the management of the global economy, in world politics, and in the fragile global environment, that have taken place over the past fifty years, and particularly in the last decade.

1.3 *A wider definition of refugees?*

1.3.1 The UN Convention did not address environmental factors in the creation of refugees; it is estimated that today there are approximately 25 million "environmental" refugees who have been forced to leave their homeland through the breakdown of some aspect of the environment. One stark example, the impending death of the Aral Sea, bordering the Central Asian Republics of Kazakhstan and Uzbekistan, illustrates the way intensive economic development can destroy an environment once capable of sustaining a human population. For over forty years, water has been diverted from the Amu-Darya and the Syr-Darya Rivers feeding the Aral, to irrigate millions of acres of land for cotton and rice production in Central Asia. This has caused a loss of more than 60% of the lake's water., exposing large areas of the lake bed. The once thriving seaport of Muynak is now fifty miles from the sea. As the water retreated, salty soil remained on the exposed lakebed. Karakalpakia, on the southern edge of the sea, with a population of over one million, has seen its land rendered barren by the salt borne by dust storms and even by the water used to irrigate the fields. Scientists in Karakalpakia predict a life for the region round the Aral Sea of less than ten years before it is turned into a desert. The point of this example for a report on refugees is stated by a doctor in Nukus, the state capital: *Since 99% of the Karakalpac nation lives within the boundaries of the Aral Sea, we may very well be witnessing the death of a nation as the result of human folly.*[4]

1.3.2　The Convention does not mention the need for economic improvement as a factor in the definition of a refugee. In recent years, however, the terms "migrant", "economic migrant", and "asylum seeker" are frequently used interchangeably with "refugee". The loose use of the words is confusing. The confusion may sometimes be deliberate. If the intention is to hold back refugees from entry to the UK, it can be implied that most of those who seek asylum are not "genuine" refugees but "bogus" economic migrants. But this distinction is inadequate in the face of the world tide of people on the move because their personal "economy", *ie* their ability to survive, has been threatened.

1.3.3　People may flee their homeland fearing persecution for reasons of "race, religion, nationality, membership of a particular social group or political opinion", but they may also flee their homeland because the physical environment or the economy has declined to the point where their survival is threatened. The argument of those who wish to restrict even further the entry of refugees to the UK can be turned round. Far from suggesting that many refugees are in fact economic migrants who are simply seeking a better life beyond their homeland, it can be argued that many who are called "economic migrants" should be considered as "refugees" who are forced to leave their homeland because they will starve if they stay at home. Most importantly, the West and North are not neutral observers of their plight but bear part of the responsibility for their plight. In that case, the question of why people become refugees leads us into questions of the global causes for people moving from more adverse circumstances to more favourable ones. We cannot answer the question of why people become refugees simply in terms of internal politics and discrimination within a country, while ignoring international responsibility for the environment, and the effects of a globalised economy and politics on the poorest of the world.

1.4　　*Political refugees, economic migrants and global responsibility*

1.4.1　Economic migration has always existed, as people have always been driven by the urge to find a better life. Over 50 million Europeans migrated in the 19th Century, mostly to the Americas. But two factors over the past forty years have brought about an escalation of migration.

1.4.2　The first factor is the increasing and gross inequality between the economies of rich and poor countries, with hundreds of millions of people in conditions where life is almost unsustainable. But even within a poor country, those with resources can survive and move, while those who are the poorest are unable to move. It is those with a desirable skill who are able to move and who may be recruited in Western countries with a skill shortage. The West does not need, as it did in the 1950s, a migration of unskilled workers. *The West is quite happy to take in economic migrants if they are … professionals, or technologically skilled. It welcomes the computer wizards of … Bangalore but does not want the persecuted peoples of Sri Lanka or the Punjab. And it is these it terms "economic migrants" with all its connotations of scrounging.*[5]

1.4.3　The distinction between "economic migrants" and "political refugees" is one that has, over the fifty years of the UN Convention, been used in different ways by UK Governments as economic and political conditions have changed in the West. In the 1950s and 1960s when there was a labour shortage, both skilled and unskilled, in the UK, it did not matter whether immigrants were fleeing the effects of Partition in the Punjab or seeking a better life in the west. Immigrants were a pool of labour. But by 1968, when Asians with British passports were expelled from Kenya and sought refuge in the UK, they were refused automatic right of entry. Four years later, *British Asians from Uganda were deemed acceptable as political refugees because they, unlike the Kenyan Asians, belonged by-and-large to the entrepreneurial class and could contribute to Britain's coffers. "British", "alien", "political", "economic", "bogus", "bona fide" —*

governments choose their terminology as suits their large economic or political purpose.[6]

1.4.4 The second factor is that in both the Soviet Bloc and in countries controlled by the colonial powers, the ruling powers had failed to respect divisions based on local allegiance, nationality, ethnic difference and often historical and geographical boundaries. They had done this for reasons of administration and economic exploitation. In the Soviet Bloc, communist policies of centralism suppressed minority cultures and ethnic differences. With the fall of communism, the eruption of ancient divisions that had been held down for two generations is one of the tragic stories of the past decade. In the case of former Western colonies in Africa, the European powers swept aside the boundaries of established nations in order to create their own administrative territories. Eventually, resistance to the colonial powers by Africans awakened a sense of nationalism, drawing people together and to some extent transcending their differences. The former colonial powers could have nurtured that fragile post-independence sense of nationhood. Instead, all too often they undermined it - as they continued their policy of "divide and rule", favouring members of one group over another, and as they provided massive loans which tied the new nations to a new financial dependency. While the world economy supported the servicing of these huge debts national cohesion held but, with the collapse of African economies over the past twenty years, violence has erupted on an appalling scale. It seems that at least some of that violence is generated by the perception that one or another group has been favoured economically over decades.

1.5   *A New Convention?*

1.5.1 The UN Convention relating to refugees needs to be revised. The plight of a refugee as defined by the 1951 UN Convention and the plight of a person, whose life is unsustainable economically through external factors, should not be held apart. People who are poor also have the right to protection that was granted to refugees as defined in the Convention and Protocol.

1.5.2 The United Nations High Commission on Refugees (UNHCR) is aware of the need for reform in its founding text. UNHCR has throughout 2001 conducted Global Consultations, culminating in a meeting in Geneva in December 2001 of the 141 States that have signed the 1951 Convention and/or 1967 Protocol. After the international community overwhelmingly reaffirmed its commitment to the 1951 Refugee Convention, UNHCR's Global Consultations process will move forward on an Agenda for Protection, a series of activities which will serve as a guide to humanitarian organisations and governments in strengthening refugee protection. The Agenda for Protection will cover five main objectives:

- Strengthening the implementation of the 1951 instrument and its 1967 Protocol
- Ensuring better protection of refugees within broader migration movements
- Sharing the burden and responsibilities for refugees and asylum seekers more equitably among states
- Handling security-related concerns more effectively
- Increasing efforts to find long-lasting solutions for refugees.

1.5.3 What is not stated in the objectives is the need for the "developed" economies of the world to recognise the relationship between their economic policies and the destabilised conditions that generate economic migration and refugee situations in other parts of the world. UNHCR High Commissioner, Ruud Lubbers, recognises that refugee issues cannot be addressed simply in terms of response to crises, but that the West must recognise the part it plays in creating conditions for these crises to happen:

[With] the end of the cold war we really thought we would go to a more prosperous world with less violence and less conflicts but that's not true. We see many "failing states" and we see in quite a number of countries politics based on ethnicity and sometimes leading even to ethnic cleansing. These things together bring us a world with a lot of refugees and internally displaced persons. The strange thing is, that although we have prosperous market economies in the West and the North, at the very same time we allow "warlords" in these conflicts to export

illegally their diamonds and other mineral resources, we provide them illegally with arms and provide safe bank accounts. We talk a lot about democracy and human rights but set the conditions for on-going violence.[7]

2. The European Union: Who is My Neighbour?

2.1 *Migration and Identity*

2.1.1 In recent years the Church and Nation Committee has addressed issues relating both to Asylum and Immigration (largely in the domestic context) and to the development of the European Union (EU). The forming of a Europe Group enables more focussed attention to be given to the vital question of Asylum and Immigration within the broader, and increasingly important, EU context.

2.1.2 We live in an era of intensifying international migration, with 2.5% of the world's population now estimated to be international migrants. The International Organisation for Migration (IOM) divides international migrants into two major groups: those who migrate of their own free choice for the purposes of work, study or family reunion and those who flee to escape persecution, conflict, repression or natural disasters. The flow of migrants is always from the poorest to the richer countries where there is the possibility of obtaining some kind of employment.

2.1.3 The EU is one of the four main centres of attraction for migrants – together with the United States, the oil-rich Middle East and, increasingly, Asia/Pacific, including Australia and New Zealand. The challenges for the EU, as for others, of managing international migration are both complex and urgent. According to Kasasa, they include "harmonizing and improving refugee reception policies that regulate the legal entry of migrants, while discouraging illegal immigration, and taking a more active part in the development policies of the migrants' country of origin". The EU is currently seeking to address these challenges. The urgency of the task is increased by the present international situation in the wake of 11 September which will increase further the numbers of those seeking refuge and asylum (from countries like Afghanistan) and also increase pressure for even tighter controls on immigration in receiving countries.

2.1.4 It is part of the faith and tradition of the Christian church to care for the poor and oppressed and to uphold the dignity of the individual. In this regard, rich biblical resources are available, not least in addressing the issue of immigration and asylum policy. For example, the issue of sanctuary was discussed in the Committee's report to the General Assembly in 1997.

2.1.5 Burnside argues that the New Testament highlights a number of issues relating to the treatment of immigrants. Jesus' attitude towards immigrants and foreigners (as expressed, for example, in the parable of the Good Samaritan and in his statement, "I was a stranger and you invited me in") cannot be dismissed as of relevance only to the church. The latter reference occurs in the context of Jesus' teaching on the judgement of the nations. In any case, there is a sense in which "the church is intended to challenge and influence the national (and international) position".

2.1.6 Of potential significance as a resource is the place given to the foreigner in biblical law. This sought to balance love for vulnerable people (in light of Israel's own experience of oppression) with the need to preserve a distinct identity in terms of her covenantal relationship with God. The concern of biblical law to uphold national identity without becoming xenophobic and to discriminate between different categories of foreigners (depending on the degree to which they assimilated) can be particularly instructive in the current debate.

2.1.7 Biblical law suggests a number of duties in relation to the immigrant, the economic migrant, the refugee and the asylum seeker (the modern equivalents of the *ger*, *nokri* and *zar* of biblical times). They include, broadly:

- to protect such persons from abuse, including protection from racially motivated violence and harassment;
- to protect them from unfair treatment in the courts;

- to offer varying degrees of social inclusion, depending on the foreigner's wish to assimilate;
- most radically, to love the alien.

2.2 The European Union's developing asylum and immigration policies

2.2.1 Since the early years of the European Community and the European Union, international migration has been on the agenda of European institutions. The European Union was created at a time when migration for employment was considered of benefit for all parties concerned and therefore encouraged. Increasingly, however, member states responded to migratory pressures by seeking to control the movements of migrants and asylum seekers.

2.2.2 The single market's demand for the removal of physical barriers on the free movement of persons, as well as of goods within it, compelled the EU to give close attention to the issue of the movement of persons across its external borders also. An informal intergovernmental body, the ad hoc Working Group on Immigration (AWGI), was established in 1986 and as a consequence, the EU governments agreed two conventions in the area of immigration policy: the Dublin Convention on Asylum (in 1990) and the External Frontiers Convention (in 1991). The Dublin Convention has in view the prevention of multiple asylum applications by means of a number of provisions, while the External Frontiers Convention "provides for the mutual recognition of visas for non-EU nationals, and abolishes the need for third-country nationals who are legal residents in one member state to obtain a visa to travel to another EU state for a period of less than three months" (Hix p.314). These Conventions met with varying responses within member states, with several initially refusing to ratify the Dublin Convention (ratification in all member states was not achieved till September 1997). Britain and Spain refused to sign the External Frontiers Convention because of the ongoing disagreement over Gibraltar (dating back to the 1713 Treaty of Utrecht which ended the War of the Spanish Succession).

2.2.3 The Treaty on European Union (better known as the Maastricht Treaty, 1992) took the significant step of formalising co-operation on immigration and asylum policy. By bringing the work of the AWGI into the framework of the EU, co-operation between member states would henceforth be within the intergovernmental "third pillar" of the newly created EU – that of justice and home affairs. The Maastricht Treaty recognises as areas of common interest:

- asylum policy
- rules governing the crossing by persons of the external borders of the member states
- immigration policy and policy regarding third country nationals.

The weaknesses of Maastricht in developing agreed European policies on asylum and immigration were several: the basis of decision-making was confirmed as unanimity in the Council of Ministers; the Commission still had no right of initiative, and although one article stated that matters of common interest would be dealt with in compliance with the European Convention on Human Rights and the Geneva Convention, the absence of any rôle for the European Parliament and the European Court of Justice made compliance impossible to enforce. Moreover, the linking together by Maastricht of immigration policies with police and judicial co-operation ensured that immigration issues continued to be viewed largely as "security" matters rather than issues of citizens' rights and freedoms.

2.2.4 The need for clearer definition of the relationship between free movement, immigration and asylum was central in the discussions leading up to the Amsterdam Treaty, negotiated in June 1997. Under the Amsterdam Treaty, immigration and asylum issues were moved from the area of intergovernmental co-operation into the section of the EU Treaty which concerns action by the Community as such. In this way they were combined with the provisions for the removal of internal borders and separated from that section of the Treaty which deals with intergovernmental co-operation in criminal matters.

2.2.5 The meeting of the Tampere European Council in October 1999 addressed the need to carry forward the

Treaty of Amsterdam's call for the development of a common asylum and immigration policy over a five-year period. In the "Tampere Conclusions", the European Council affirmed that, in principle:

freedom should not…be regarded as the exclusive preserve of the Union's own citizens…It would be in contradiction with Europe's traditions to deny such freedom to those whose circumstances lead them justifiably to seek access to Union territory. This in turn requires the Union to develop common policies on asylum…The aim is an open and secure EU, fully committed to the obligations of the Geneva Refugee Convention and other relevant human rights instruments, and able to respond to humanitarian needs on the basis of solidarity….

In pursuance of this objective, the Council set out its strategy in terms of short and long-term goals. The former include:

* a clear and workable determination of the state responsible for the examination of an asylum application;
* common standards for a fair and efficient asylum provision;
* common minimum conditions of reception of asylum seekers;
* the approximation of rules on the recognition and content of the refugee status;
* subsidiary forms of protection and an appropriate status to any person in need of such protection.

In the longer term, "Community rules should lead to a common asylum procedure and a uniform status for those who are granted asylum throughout the Union." Tampere clearly establishes that the EU recognises the applicability of human rights treaties to refugees, asylum seekers and migrants.

2.3   *The present situation and challenge*

2.3.1   EU commitment, in terms of Amsterdam, to the creation of an area of "freedom, security and justice" is clearly of fundamental importance. It is equally important that the sense in which these terms is understood be pinned down. Pieter Boeles, a leading specialist in immigration law, has argued convincingly that, in this

context, *freedom* must be understood as encompassing "fundamental freedoms, freedom of movement and, as far as it is within the power of governments to provide such, freedom from worry and fear". *Security* should mean not only "safety from external threat and from criminal acts but also protection against persecution, torture and inhuman or degrading treatment or punishment". *Justice*, while certainly referring to a system of law enforcement, refers "above all to a system in which injustice is fought by respecting the rule of law, fundamental rights and the principle of non-discrimination". As Harlow (p.310) points out (following Boeles):

freedom may, in the context of Title IV EC,* simply mean "crime-free", while justice may be equated with criminal justice and law enforcement, in which case the area of freedom, security and justice might degenerate into an open prison…We have come down to earth with a vengeance, landing abruptly on the familiar land of Fortress Europe.

2.3.2   It is clearly of great importance that the EU chooses the correct model in adopting its immigration policy. Steve Peers has identified various possible models for which the EU can opt, with the entry into force of the Treaty of Amsterdam. He argues that the EU should aspire to what he calls the "human model", based on a strongly positive interpretation of the concept of "freedom, security and justice". This position holds that the protections of the area of freedom, security and justice should extend to all within EU boundaries, whatever their origin. This arguably follows from the (central) notion of liberty in western political philosophy where rights of self-determination are regarded as fundamental. As Harlow (p.309f) puts it:

Liberty should be curtailed and limited to the least possible extent. Similar reasoning must be applicable to the core Treaty principles of liberty, democracy, respect for human

---

*This is Title IV of the "Treaty establishing the European Community" and is called "Visas, asylum, immigration and other policies relating to free movement of persons". See the Treaty of Amsterdam, Cm 3780, pp. 150-53.

rights and fundamental freedoms, and the rule of law for, if liberty is equated with freedom, then the rule of law must be synonymous with justice.

2.3.3 In seeking to develop a common approach to immigration in the EU in terms of an area of "freedom, security and justice", the following are among issues requiring careful consideration:

2.3.3.1 There is a need to address causes before symptoms. Effective steps need to be taken to deal with the conditions which cause migration and refugee flow. Given the scale and complexity of the problem, both the EU and the wider international community must take responsibility for attempting to avert refugee flow by making policies in areas such as defence, aid, trade, arms sales and debt contribute to that goal. After all, the preamble to the Treaty of Rome (1957) declared that the six signatory states intended "to confirm the solidarity which binds Europe and the overseas countries and [desired] to ensure the development of their prosperity, in accordance with the principles of the Charter of the United Nations".

2.3.3.2 International human rights standards must form a cornerstone of EU immigration and asylum policy. All measures which infringe human rights should be proportional to the harm they are intended to redress. A monitoring body should be established to review immigration and asylum law and its administration to ensure that it conforms to human rights standards.

2.3.3.3 The likely consequences of immigration law for race relations need to be studied in depth. "Firm" immigration control has been argued to be good for race relations but does not appear, hitherto, to have had this effect. For example, has discrimination against (non-white) African and Asian people at the point of entry contributed to discrimination against them internally? Governments should take a lead in changing people's attitudes towards migrants and refugees.

2.3.3.4 Further study of the economic impact of immigration needs to be undertaken. For example, has the economic potential for the European Union of many of those who enter certain member states under humanitarian categories been adequately recognised?

2.3.3.5 In the post 11 September world situation, close consideration must be given to the way in which the imperative of preventing terrorists from finding a "safe haven" in Europe should take account of the need for a common approach to immigration policy.

2.3.3.6 Cultural pluralism should be encouraged in Europe in which social order is increasingly cemented by identity rather than simply "toleration". In this connection Siedentop has identified two pluralistic visions. The first, which he argues has its origins in the Christian culture of Europe, is that of "individuals choosing to pursue different values within a framework of law which protects individual freedom but also sets clear limits to such freedom." The second form of pluralism involves "a vision of social groups or cultures, each defined by and expressing its own values." The first form, with its presupposition of both moral universalism and the principle of equal liberty, "makes it possible to protect individuals from arbitrary interference and social pressures." The second form of pluralism "provides no such guarantees." The challenge of plurality within a common European identity can be seen to be as important in the context of immigration as it is in the context of the nations who come together to form the EU.

2.4 *Recent developments*

2.4.1 Many issues affecting a common European policy have been addressed in two recent Communications of the Commission, which recommend steps towards the implementing of the "Tampere Conclusions".

2.4.2 The Communication, *Towards a common asylum procedure and a uniform Status, valid throughout the Union, for persons granted asylum* (COM [2000] 755 final), expresses the Commission's thinking on issues relating to such procedure and status. A detailed response to the Communication by an informal consortium of

Brussels-based church organisations in general welcomed the Commission's analysis of the situation as "an important step towards harmonisation of asylum policy". It applauded the Commission's recognition that asylum and immigration are separate although related issues and welcomed the opportunity "to address some of the main flaws in the current national asylum systems, in particular: the problem of access to the territory, reception conditions that amount to a de facto barrier to seeking asylum in some Member States, and national discrepancies in recognition rates and statuses granted, which raise serious concerns about protection gaps" (p.2). A detailed commentary on the text of the Communication concludes with a welcome for the involvement of civil society and states that the churches represented are "ready to take part in the preparatory work necessary for the creation of a harmonised European asylum system" (p.7).

2.4.3   Another Communication of the Commission in response to Tampere, *On a Community Immigration Policy* (COM [2000] 757 final), seeks to develop an "open approach" to "an overall policy for the EU for the admission of new migrants", recognising that "effective migration management must be based on partnership" (p.21). The Committee strongly endorses the welcome given by the above-mentioned consortium to this "policy shift towards a pro-active immigration policy" reflected in the Commission's new approach, with a "welcoming society" as an essential element in that policy (p.2). The response calls for a common European approach regarding admission criteria, recognition of equal rights and free movement as a necessary contribution towards an area of freedom, security and justice (p.6). It also argues the need for better integration into society of migrants (p.7). Among its conclusions, the Response urges the need for much better information to be provided for the public in European societies (p.9) and supports the idea of setting up a "European Monitoring Centre for Migration" which would be "competent for monitoring regular and irregular migration as well as advising on legal immigration and integration policies" (p.10). Despite the good intentions embodied in the Communication, the Committee recognises that difficulties exist in achieving bilateral agreement between member countries as, for

example, between France and Britain regarding the Sangatte camp.

2.4.4   While the European summit in the Belgian town of Laeken in December 2001 was unable, in view of events following 11 September, to give as much attention to issues of asylum and immigration as would have been desirable, it did represent some progress in this area. The summit called for the adoption of a common European policy as soon as possible; for an action plan on illegal immigration; for urgent action on common standards for reception of asylum seekers and family reunification and for a specific programme to combat racism and xenophobia. The Committee welcomes these developments. During a recent visit of the Europe Group to Brussels, the Group was encouraged by the clear aspiration of various politicians and officials from whom we heard who advocated best practice for the EU in the area of immigration and asylum policy. We strongly encourage EU countries to implement best practice in this area, particularly those countries which have not been exercising their responsibility at the first port of entry.

2.4.5   As the aforementioned consortium's response suggests, it is important that we, together with other Christian churches, seek to create mechanisms to monitor and influence developments in the ongoing debate on common European asylum and immigration policies, "in a spirit of constructive dialogue". This will be with a view to the shaping of the Union as a place where freedom, justice and security provide a common identity.

2.5 *Bibliography for this section*

Boeles, P. (2001), "Introduction: Freedom, Security and Justice for All," Guild, E. and Harlow, C. (2001), pp.1-12

Burnside, J.P. (2001), *The Status and Welfare of Immigrants. The place of the foreigner in Biblical law and its relevance to contemporary society* (Cambridge: The Jubilee Centre)

Communications from the Commission to the Council and the European Parliament, "Towards a common asylum procedure and a uniform status, valid throughout the Union, for persons granted asylum," (COM [2000]

755 final); and "On a community immigration policy," (COM [2000] 757 final)

"For I was a stranger and you welcomed me". Comments on the above Communications, prepared by an informal consortium of Brussels-based church organisations (May 2001)

Geddes, A. (2000), *Immigration and European Integration: Towards Fortress Europe?* (Manchester: Manchester University Press)

Guild, E. and Harlow, C. (eds.) (2001), *Implementing Amsterdam. Immigration and Asylum Rights in EC Law* (Oxford: Hart Publishing)

Harlow, C. (2001), "Endpiece," Guild, E. and Harrow, C. (2001), pp.309-18

Hix, S. (1999), *The Political System of the European Union* (Basingstoke: MacMillan Press)

Kasasa, A. (2001), "Asylum and immigration – Europe's search for a common policy," *The Courier* (the magazine of the ACP – EU development co-operation), Issue 187, July – August 2001

Peers, S. (2001), "Aliens, Workers, Citizens or Humans? Models for Community Immigration Law," Guild, E. and Harlow, C. (2001), pp. 291-308

Siedentop, L. (2000), *Democracy in Europe* (London: Penguin Books)

Spencer, S. (ed.) (1994) *Strangers and Citizens. A Positive Approach to Migrants and Refugees* (London: Rivers Oram Press)

3. British Asylum Policy: Improving the System?

3.1 *Background*

3.1.1 Immigration Policy, including dealing with refugees seeking asylum, is a reserved function under charge of the Home Office, which has allocated responsibility to two departments:

- The Immigration and Nationality Directorate (IND), which processes applications;

- The National Asylum Support Service (NASS), which looks after the physical and housing needs of refugees, including their dispersal.

The system is also buttressed by a substantial body of asylum law interpreting the 1951 Geneva Convention in respect of Home Office decisions, hearings by Adjudicators, and references to the Immigration Appeal Tribunal, all overseen by the national courts. Since October 2000, human rights law has also been applied.

3.1.2 Among states in Europe in 2000, only Germany (95,000) has exceeded the UK total of 80,000. Although in world terms this is not a high figure, admissions have mounted dramatically in recent years and governments have found it difficult to cope.

3.1.3 Initial processing is not the sole problem. At the end of 2000, in addition to the 89,100 cases awaiting decision by the Home Office there were 46,000 appeals outstanding as the system was able to deal with only 19,395 appeals. Since then, hearings have been speeded up as new resources were introduced. All in all, the Directorate processed 109,205 cases in 2000 but the limited success rate of 11% for asylum and 12% by the administrative device of granting exceptional leave to remain means that many disappointed refugees will appeal further.

3.2 *The Situation in Scotland*

3.2.1 Scotland has hitherto received only a small proportion of asylum seekers coming to the UK since most of the asylum seekers are admitted from the Channel ports and London airports. In 1999, there were only 400 Scottish based applications for admission and 500 in 2000. Estimates suggest that around 1,500 to 2,000 people were in residence.

3.2.2 This changed suddenly as a result of a new Government policy for dispersal of asylum seekers from southern England to Glasgow. Glasgow Council had entered into a contract with the Home Office to provide 2,000 family homes, 500 single person homes and other local authorities are also addressing the matter. There are now 6,000 refugees in Scotland, with an 80% success rate in claiming asylum. The Scottish Refugee Council reckons that 40% have graduate qualifications.

3.2.3   The speed and impact of the arrival of bus loads of refugees decanted into low amenity housing schemes with limited support and without adequate preparation of local communities, combined with the perceived injustice of upgrading of accommodation not available to locals, led to unrest and racial harassment until the problem was highlighted by the tragic murder of Kurdish refugee, Firsat Dag in the summer of 2001.

3.3   *Government Reforms*

3.3.1   The Glasgow example was evidence that the rushed programme of dispersal of reluctant asylum seekers from existing cultural communities or language clusters in the South of England was at best not working and at worst inhumane. Additionally, the capacity of the UK Government to keep track of the arrivals and to process their cases had been taxed to breaking point.

3.3.2   On 29 October 2001, Home Secretary David Blunkett announced that he did not intend "to tinker with the existing system but to bring about a radical and fundamental reform of our asylum and immigration policy". He announced that he would introduce short stay induction, semi-compulsory accommodation and deportation centres. The much-criticised vouchers would be replaced with smart cards, which would also serve as electronic identity cards. There were to be restrictions on rights of appeal.

3.3.3   It was against this background that the Committee interviewed welfare officers in The Well (an Asian advice centre in Queen's Park, Glasgow operated by the Church of Scotland) and Bridging the Gap (a welfare agency in the Gorbals, Glasgow, run by the Church of Scotland and the Catholic Church), the Director of Corporate Policy of Glasgow City Council, and the Scottish Refugee Council. We also had the benefit of a report of a meeting on 6 November 2001 that the Moderator and a member of the Church and Nation Executive Committee had on these issues with Lord

Rooker, Minister of State at the Home Office, at the request of the Refugee Survival Trust.

3.3.4   From this evidence the Committee came to the following assessment of the Blunkett reforms:

- *Induction Centres* are intended to be for reception of newly landed asylum seekers where there will be assessment of support needs and orientation including initial legal advice. The Committee believes that if these are indeed used only for a short period they will be a great improvement on the chaotic arrangements now prevailing.

- *Accommodation Centres* will be developed on a pilot basis to house asylum seekers during the time when their applications are being processed and to reduce the need for dispersal. They are not called detention centres but as there will be a residence requirement, the difference may be semantic only. While these centres will have initial capacity limited to 3000 places, there is a danger that they could develop into institutional asylum seekers camps if refugees are kept there too long. Although none are in Scotland, the Committee believes that the operation of these centres should be closely monitored.

- *Reporting Centres* will record holding places where asylum seekers will report for tracking purposes. If used efficiently and sensitively they could be a welcome improvement on the current arrangements. In Scotland, reporting is presently to the police.

- *Vouchers* will be replaced by "smart" cards but there was initial doubt as to whether these were to be purely electronic versions of the vouchers, widely regarded as humiliating and degrading, with only £14 to be available in cash. The Home Secretary has stated that cash will replace vouchers. The General Assembly will recall its Deliverance last year calling for such a replacement of vouchers. The Moderator made this a key request at his meeting with Lord Rooker, and the Church should be pleased that its voice has been heard. The Moderator and the Convener of the Committee on Church and Nation had earlier discussions with the Bank of Scotland regarding accounts for asylum seekers.

- *Deportation Centres* will be used for detention of those whose appeal process runs out. The UK has deported very few of the failed applicants but it can be assumed that the new regime will be tougher. Dungavel, a former prison, will be re-designated as Scotland's deportation centre. Issues about time held and outside contact should be monitored.

- *Refugee Resettlement* policies are being introduced to welcome refugees recognised by UNHCR to the UK and EU. On a broader front, the Government is considering changing the immigration rules to allow entry to economic migrants with special skills.

- *People trafficking* by criminals is an international problem that has led to inhumanity and insufferable conditions as people are herded across continents. The Committee approves of the proposals from Mr Blunkett to co-operate with other EU countries in an attempt to reduce the exploitation of asylum seekers, but also warns that such police action should not be directed towards eliminating asylum claims by closing frontiers.

- *Dispersal* will continue, but hopefully on a more sensitive basis, with attention being paid to language and cultural clusters so that isolation of asylum seekers is reduced. The Committee heard evidence of bewildered asylum seekers being placed on buses to Glasgow without fully realising where they were being sent. Many were unwilling to come given the bad reputation that Glasgow had gained. The Committee accepts that there is an obligation on Scotland to take a larger share of refugees but believes that this should be on a voluntary basis with Scotland being a welcoming destination.

- In Scotland, the *Scottish Refugee Integration Forum*, with church and other faith representation, has been set up. As an attempt to bring an integrated approach to bear on the task of making people arriving here feel welcome and involved in our society, this is greatly to be welcomed.

3.4 *Welfare Concerns*

3.4.1 The welfare of asylum seekers dispersed in Scotland has been an area of grave concern for Scottish Christians and one where churches have been most closely involved. Without the support of the voluntary sector the arrangements for asylum seekers would have collapsed. Key players in this response have been the congregations located in areas where asylum seekers have been housed. Congregations in difficult circumstances themselves are the ones looked to for support, echoing the global situation described in 1.1.

3.4.2 Asylum seekers face huge welfare difficulties. Owing to the inefficiency of NASS, the Government sponsoring agency, it is common for a dispersed person to arrive before the paperwork they need to get into the housing and voucher system. As a result, many asylum seekers find themselves housed in bed and breakfast accommodation with emergency vouchers supplied by the Refugee Council. In some cases, this temporary accommodation becomes home for several months where there is no suitable alternative accommodation. In some places, this can create difficulties for children who cannot be allocated a school place until they have a permanent address. In one case, a family of five with another child expected have been living in one room in a bed and breakfast place for more than four months since NASS have not been able to find them suitable accommodation.

3.4.3 The voucher system, set at 70% of income support - itself recognised to be marginal for subsistence - does not provide the means to buy more than the most basic food and toiletry items. Often people arrive in the UK with only the clothes they are wearing and they are not usually designed for the rigours of Scottish weather. The churches have opened their doors to new arrivals and provided clothing cooking pots, kitchen utensils, prams, shoes and bedding. One such project that we visited in the Gorbals is run jointly by the Church of Scotland and the Catholic Church. Another imaginative scheme in Castlemilk lends bicycles to asylum seekers so that they can get around without using precious cash on bus fares.

3.4.4 The churches, often in partnership with other agencies, have been able to identify further needs. There are now regular surgeries in church premises to enable asylum seekers to access health and legal information, English classes and the services of community police officers. Perhaps more importantly, these drop-in centres have provided a safe space for long-term and new residents to get to know each other. Such activities have placed huge pressures on congregations, many of which were already small and vulnerable. However, all would say that the experience has been overwhelmingly positive. Despite what the papers say, there are dozens of stories of good neighbourliness and lives enriched by new friendships forged between indigenous and new Scots.

3.4.5 Many Christians who have taken on asylum-seeker posts with a sense of vocation have told of the tension between their faith and the stringencies of the system in which they have to work. Many go beyond the extra mile in their care of asylum seekers. Christians are amongst those who have raised concerns about the lack of support for torture victims and are campaigning for the establishment of a Scottish Centre for Victims of Torture.

3.5 *Decision Making and Appeals*

3.5.1 The Committee expresses utmost concern about the proposals of the Home Secretary to "streamline and simplify" the appeals process. We welcome the intention to increase resources to expand capacity of the adjudication service and to speed up the hearing of cases, since it is not in the interests of both the appellants and the State to have cases under consideration for years. However, the system must be fair and just, since the mistaken refusal of an application could lead to an asylum seeker being deported with the risk of imprisonment, torture and death on return to their country of origin. The Committee has therefore taken evidence from an experienced practitioner of asylum law and also consulted the Scottish Legal Aid Board, since the Home Secretary's announcements are driven by English arrangements. Our comments are based on the evidence taken.

3.5.2 As a first step in the process, asylum seekers are required to complete a Statement of Evidence Form

(SEF) - issued within days or months of the application, but more usually immediately on making the application. Sometimes, the SEF and an interview date arrive together. The SEF must normally be returned within fourteen days and refugees who may not have a proper grasp of English, and may be still disoriented, find these ten page forms difficult to complete. The IND uses these forms to reject or accept appeals and an appeal can be imperilled by any flaws or lack of detail. Applicants should be given legal representation right at the outset. With up to one third of appeals failing because of failure to complete the forms properly or turning up for interview, early legal advice is essential.

3.5.3 As a second step, applicants may be requested to attend for interview at Croydon or Liverpool, sometimes at very short notice. There is no interview centre in Scotland. Interviews took place at Glasgow Airport previous to dispersal but have been discontinued since dispersal. At the meeting with the Moderator, Lord Rooker said that there were technical legal reasons why interviews should be in England but that a centre may be established in Carlisle. The Committee can see no technical, legal or practical reason why there should not be a centre in Glasgow.

3.5.4 Current time limits are stringent, with seven days being given for appeal against first refusal and five days in respect of a second refusal. The Committee is concerned that the Home Secretary, in "streamlining" the appeals process, has in mind restrictions on the right to appeal. The problem for asylum seekers in dispersed areas is that their papers are usually with London solicitors and asylum seekers do not always receive notice with the change of address.

3.5.5 The Committee is very concerned that following new procedure introduced by Her Majesty's Government in January 2002, the majority of asylum seekers will not be informed of the results of their appeals against refusal of asylum. In practice, they will find out only when immigration officials come to arrest and remove them from the UK. This procedure denies them the chance to apply to the Court of Session for a judicial review.

3.5.6 There is a critical shortage of interpreters for all stages of the appeals process. In Glasgow, asylum seekers represent some 34 language areas, with dialects taking the number up further. The shortage of interpreters can be a source of injustice and the Committee believes that it is essential to seek more, perhaps from the ranks of the asylum seekers themselves.

3.5.7 There is also a shortage of solicitors willing to do asylum work on legal aid with consequent almost unmanageable pressure on those who do. Some solicitors are reluctant to take up this work as, unlike in England, they have to carry substantial outlays from their own funds of the fees payable to interpreters, which run from £25 to £35 per hour. The Scottish Legal Aid Board is aware of the problem and is discussing solutions with the Scottish Executive. The Committee draws attention to the need for urgency. Between 1999 and 2000, legal aid applications increased by 50% and since then the flood of asylum seekers has risen. There is also a great need to simplify the present system to eliminate the requirement to seek approval of work, although the Board normally grants this.

3.5.8 The Committee also expresses surprise that with the higher number of Scottish appeals since dispersal, the Immigration Appeals Tribunal has become London based although it hears cases by video link. The Committee can see no reason why it should not also meet within Scottish jurisdiction.

3.6 *Conclusions and Recommendations*

3.6.1 The United Kingdom consists of nations comprising immigrants who have settled here successively over thousands of years. Scotland has also provided migrants to many other lands and now, with a declining birth rate, needs more people, especially younger ones, to keep a balance in our population. Continued immigration is something that must be managed but should be welcomed as giving hope. Negative language about asylum seekers and ethnic minorities needs to be tackled, and the Government should give a lead.

3.6.2 The Government, public bodies, communities and churches must do all they can to welcome and ease the suffering of those fleeing oppression, danger and persecution in their country of nationality. We welcome the contribution of the churches in Glasgow which have provided "drop in" and other services for asylum seekers.

3.6.3 There should be no coerced dispersal, but efforts should be made to make other parts of the UK more attractive to asylum seekers. Support systems must be improved to help those already dispersed and to assist those who are still to come. Interviews being held at short notice in Liverpool and London are not acceptable. Interviews should be conducted as close to the place of residence as possible.

3.6.4 At the General Assembly in May 2001, the Church called upon the Government to abandon the Voucher Scheme. We therefore welcome its abolition.

3.6.5 While we welcome the speeding up of decisions, the proposed compression of process and elimination of appeals causes concern that the UK will fall short of human rights standards and the requirements of justice. In particular, with one third of applications failing because applications are incorrectly completed or the applicants fail to turn up, immediate access to legal representation is needed to help those in the former category.

---

1. United Nations High Commission for Refugees (UNHCR) estimates 2001
2. United Nations Relief and Works Agency (UNRWA) figure for mid 2000
3. Refugee Council and UNHCR statistics
4. Dr Ataniyazova, quoted in Requiem for a Dying Sea, People and the Planet, www.oneworld.org/patp/pap_aral.html
5. Ambalavaner Sivandandan, Director of the Institute of Race Relations, writing in The Guardian 8th August 2000.
6. Ibid
7. BBC World Service, The Road to Refuge
8. This is Title IV of the "Treaty establishing the European Community" and is called "Visas, asylum, immigration and other policies relating to free movement of persons". See the Treaty of Amsterdam, Cm 3780, pp. 150-53.

A FUTURE FOR NUCLEAR SUBMARINES?

1.1　At the General Assembly 2001 the following Deliverance was approved:

Urge HMG to look at ways of disposing of decommissioned submarines, while the necessary trade skills are still available.

Behind this lay the fact that Rosyth Dockyard, which for many years had been the site for maintenance and refitting of the UK Nuclear Submarine fleet, had lost out to Devonport in its bid to do the same for the Trident Fleet. By the time of this year's Assembly the last of the present submarines to be refitted will have left Rosyth. The Ministry of Defence had for some time been considering the problem of dismantling decommissioned submarines and on 30th August 2000 Babcock Rosyth Defence Ltd. submitted an application to be allowed to dismantle HMS Renown as a pilot scheme.

1.2　Although the Deliverance was directed to Her Majesty's Government, the Church and Nation Committee has followed up the General Assembly deliverance by visiting Rosyth, discussing the matter with those both in Rosyth and elsewhere in the nuclear industry, and considering several current Government and other reports on the matter. The appendix to this section provides a brief summary of the theory of decommissioning, not only for military but also for civil nuclear installations.

2.1　At present there are 14 submarines "laid up", both Polaris and Hunter Killer, at Rosyth and Devonport. (7 at Rosyth afloat in the basin) It is estimated that by 2012 there will be no further space to store such submarines afloat at Rosyth or Devonport. The Swiftsure Class is due to be replaced from 2005 and 7 Trafalgar Class are due to be decommissioned from 2010. In these "laid up" submarines the weapons systems and the fuel have been removed; the vessels have been drained of all oil, water *etc.* (to reduce fire risk); all openings have been sealed so that no water can enter; a fire protection system installed; and the ship is checked once a month.

2.3　The MoD announced on 28.11.01 that it was not prepared at present to proceed with the proposal to dismantle HMS Renown which means that the submarines will remain where and as they are until further consultations and consideration of ultimate disposal are complete.

3.1　There are several possible solutions, none without problems:
- Storage afloat, in dockyard or loch;
- Deep Sea disposal;
- Cutting out of reactor area, with separate disposal/storage of reactor area, the remainder of the submarine going to the breaker's yard.

**Typical Nuclear Submarine
With Reactor Compartment Identified**

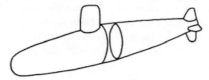

3.2　A Polaris submarine is 425 feet long. The hazardous section is about 60 feet long; viz. the sealed reactor compartment containing core and cooling system and steam generating system. The USA has experimented by cutting out this section and storing it in the desert until the means of its dismantling becomes available. In the UK, however, this position is not favoured not least because we have no convenient deserts! If the submarines are to be moved, where do we move them to? The management at Rosyth is not simply wishing to preserve employment. The submarines occupy potentially usable dock space, and their continued presence may impede attempts to develop the former Naval Dockyard as a centre for tourist travel, eg the new Rosyth–Zeebrugge ferry and the attempt to attract more of the lucrative cruise liner business. But "NIMBY" also applies to the residents nearby a remote Highland Sea loch who may not have the political clout of Rosyth. The attempt by the Oil Industry to seek deep-sea disposal of redundant oilrigs demonstrated that there is considerable opposition to this option.

3.3 This brings us to the heart of the matter. The moment work begins to deconstruct the reactor area of a submarine we must ask where the waste is to be stored. Given the sound structure of the submarine it could be argued that this is a safer and equally permanent storage until an alternative repository is available. The submarine was designed as an excellent "containment vessel". Before beginning to dismantle the active area you need to be clear on ultimate disposal of resultant waste. A submarine has a much stronger and more water tight hull than surface vessels and can be expected to remain sound for a further 30 years or so. The submarine will be taken to dry dock and the hulls checked from time to time.

3.4 Given that the Navy's preferred option for propulsion is nuclear, the number of such vessels being laid up will increase. Given that civilian reactors are also past or approaching the end of their life, the problem of decommissioning is now a major problem facing not just the nuclear industry or the Government, but all of us. Any decision on how the submarines are to be decommissioned will depend on the question of long-term storage of waste being addressed. It could be argued, therefore, that the present situation is not unreasonable; it is in accord with the perceived public demand for safe, on-site, above-ground storage of nuclear waste.

4.1 As mentioned in the appendix, almost all low-level nuclear waste is stored on a long-term basis at Drigg, in Cumbria. At present there is no proposal, let alone a site, for the long-term storage of either intermediate or high-level waste. Dounreay is presently building "temporary" storage facilities for intermediate waste designed to have a service life of 100 years. "Temporary" in this case clearly does not mean "short-term".

4.2 Far from being a declining task, decommissioning will be an ever-increasing one. Yet sadly there is now only one training reactor in the UK - at Imperial College, London; and only one dedicated Nuclear Engineering degree course - at Birmingham University. So where are the experts to come from? The Nuclear Installations Inspectorate is already trying to put pressure on the nuclear industry to fund research and training, and we would support them in this. The Government needs to see this matter as both urgent and in need of both investigation and funding. The RWMAC's (Radioactive Waste Management Advisory Committee) recent annual report to Ministers is critical of the present impasse.

4.3 In the autumn of 2001, the Department for Environment, Food & Rural Affairs (DEFRA) issued a consultation document Managing Radioactive Waste Safely, and we welcome its appearance. This document points out that there are at present more than 10,000 tonnes of radioactive waste safely stored in the UK which "await(s) a decision on their long term future." This is expected to increase to 250,000 tonnes when nuclear material currently in use is requiring storage. The DEFRA document continues:

Even if no new nuclear power plants are built … about another 250,000 tonnes of waste will arise during the clean up of those plants over the next century … some of the substances involved will be radioactive and potentially dangerous for hundreds of years.

The DEFRA document sets out the timetable for decision-making:

- 2001-2002: the consultation on the programme outlined in the document, and planning the next stage;
- 2002-2004: research and public debate to examine the different options and to recommend the best option or combination.

4.4 We are sure that the Church will wish to be involved in this consultation process. The SRT Project is already considering the whole matter of energy policy, of which the handling of nuclear waste is an important part. One thing we can say at this stage: it is important that both military and civil nuclear matters are considered in tandem. There may well have been good historic reasons for keeping defence and electricity industries separate.

But we are saddened to see that the DEFRA document makes no mention of the ISOLUS document (interim storage of laid up submarines) or vice versa. If a solution is to be found, it has to be worked out by both civil and military acting in concert.

5. A review of energy policy conducted by the Cabinet Office Performance and Innovation Unit has now been published. It recommends a considerable increase in renewable energy capacity in the UK but leaves open for the time being the question of whether further nuclear power stations should be constructed to replace those which are nearing the end of the working life. Whatever decision was taken, this would not substantially change the existing waste disposal questions, which have to be solved regardless. There are many complex issues involved in this and the associated question of the disposal options for civil and military nuclear waste. The Society, Religion and Technology Project is proposing to review these issues during the next year.

APPENDIX
DECOMMISSIONING OF REACTOR

A. At the end of a nuclear reactor's active life, the fuel is removed and decommissioning takes place in three stages:

1. *Post Operative Clean Up or POCU*
   Like a spring cleaning POCU uses mechanical and chemical means to remove surface radiation and other contamination, removing debris and any soluble waste. Produces only low level waste.

2. *Removing non-radioactive bits eg the rest of the submarine, or turbine hall etc.*
   This should produce only ordinary waste.

3. *Dismantling of reactor core and structure*
   At a much later stage the remaining structures would be dismantled. This involves removal of core (the area which contained the fuel) and transferring this to a purpose built cell where it will be cut up. This

will produce in the main intermediate level waste assuming fuel has already been totally removed.

B. Nuclear Waste is traditionally classified as follows:

1. *Low Level* eg discarded protective clothing, wrapping material.

2. *Intermediate Level* eg irradiated fuel cladding, reactor components, and chemical residues. Emits little heat.

3. *High Level* Spent and fuel removed from the reactor area, and the main concentrated waste arising from fuel reprocessing. Emits considerable heat as well as radiation.

C. Liquid HLW is vitrified for storage, solids in drums or cementation
Low level Waste is either stored on site for a period or transferred to the only National Low Level Waste Repository at Drigg, operated by BNFL. All Scottish waste except from Dounreay goes to Drigg. At present, there is neither an Intermediate nor High National Repository. Attempts to resolve this unsatisfactory situation have been frustrated by both political and technical problems. Finland and Sweden are well advanced in planning such repositories. Dounreay is presently building "temporary" ILW stores with a service life of 100 years, for use until such time as National Storage facilities become available.

D. At present, ILW waste is stored in internationally agreed form; either 500 litre stainless steel drums, or 3 metre cube boxes. The process when a store is eventually established would be:

WASTE-DRUM-FLASK-TRANSPORT-DRUM REMOVED-FLASK RETURNED FOR NEXT LOAD

E. NIREX, the existing body charged with the responsibility of examining options for the disposal of nuclear waste, is owned directly by the nuclear industry. (UKAEA 15%; BNFL Magnum Group 75%; British

Energy 10%). It is understood that NIREX is to be replaced by an independent group.

The nuclear liabilities of UKAEA and BNFL are to be taken over by a new Nuclear Liabilities Management Authority at the end of 2003.

EUROPE WHOLE AND FREE

1. The Origins of the European Union

1.1 In the aftermath of World War 2, with much of Western Europe brought to its knees, a European Recovery Plan was launched on 5 June 1947 by US Secretary of State George Marshall in these terms:

Our policy is directed against hunger, poverty, desperation and chaos. Its purpose should be the revival of a working economy in the world so as to permit the emergence of political and social conditions in which free institutions can exist. Such assistance must not be on a piecemeal basis as various crises develop .... there must be some agreement among the countries of Europe as to the requirements of the situation and the part those countries themselves will take. The programme should be a joint one, agreed to by a number, if not all, European nations.

The Soviet Union rejected this offer but, in May 1948, the first sign of progress was announced; the Organisation for European Economic Co-operation was formed consisting of sixteen states who between them received grants and loans for reconstruction of the basic infrastructure of their countries amounting to some $13,150 million.

1.2 It is fair to say that the European states which had largely dominated the globe in political and economic terms prior to 1939 now had to adjust to their loss of world standing and power of decision on a global scale. The two existing super-powers, USA and USSR, rapidly began to fill this vacuum and to actively promote their opposing ideologies on the world stage for the first time. It became clear that only the emergence of a united Europe could begin to rebalance this equation or mount a challenge to the overall hegemony of the super-powers. Despite their acceptance of the generous spirit of the Marshall Plan, there was also a wider concern amongst European states that they would gradually drift into even greater dependency on the USA or become overwhelmed by the power of American technology, inward investment and the growing influence of large US financial, commercial and industrial corporations.

1.3 The next important steps were taken by Jean Monnet, the First Commissioner of the French National Economic Plan, and also by Robert Schuman, the French Foreign Minister. It was Schuman who, having accepted Monnet's idea, actually launched the European Coal and Steel Community on 9 May 1950 with the following declaration:

Europe will not be made all at once, or according to a single plan. It will be built through concrete achievements that first create a de facto solidarity ... [the French Government] proposes that Franco-German production of coal and steel as a whole be placed under a common High Authority, within the framework of an organisation open to the participation of the other countries of Europe .... a first step in the federation of Europe ... The solidarity in production thus established will make it plain that any war between France and Germany becomes not merely unthinkable, but materially impossible.

Acceptance of this proposal thus represented the first essential building block for the new post-war Europe as it arose from the ashes of conflict.

1.4 At this stage, the working structure which resulting from inter-governmental negotiations later in 1950 could be summarised as follows:

High Authority + Special European Council of Ministers + Common Assembly + European Court of Justice.

This structure was then subsequently adopted as the first institutional pattern for the European Economic Community and the European Atomic Energy Community that followed from the two Treaties of Rome in March 1957. Belgium, France, Italy, Luxembourg, the Netherlands and West Germany were the six initial member states of the EEC; all of the Six ratified both treaties and the two new Communities came into being in January 1958. The United Kingdom decided to wait it out on the sidelines, and remained there for the next fifteen years.

1.5 One of the primary tasks of the European Economic Community (the Six) in July 1958 was to negotiate and agree the basic principles of a Common Agricultural Policy which would embrace:

- A single market (allowing free movement of agricultural goods)
- Joint financial responsibility for an agricultural budget
- Community preference over imported produce
- A secure system of financial support for the agricultural industry

This policy was adopted in July 1962, although full implementation of the Common Agricultural Policy throughout the Six was not achieved until 1968. It is also worth noting that funding of the Common Agricultural Policy was a significant factor in one of the most difficult crises the European Economic Community ever encountered in 1965-66.

1.6 It is clear that during the early years of formation and development, the European economic Community was able to record substantial progress on many fronts, including:

- Expansion of trade and investment
- Progress in dismantling trade barriers and tariffs
- Development of the CAP
- Agreement on a VAT system
- Beginnings of free movement of people
- Start of a competition policy
- Influence on the world economy

There were, of course, many diversions along the way, several off-stage. De Gaulle (President of France 1958-69) removed France from NATO in March 1966 using the argument that France could not become beholden or subordinate to any other entity, whether this was another state or a European organisation. This brought into focus the very real possibility of national sovereignty being used as a potential fracture plane for the European ideal. Then, when the UK applied for membership of the EEC (on 31 July 1961), de Gaulle stepped into the ring and exercised a veto over the application on 14 January 1963 on the grounds that the British were not ready to accept the conditions of EEC membership, having maintained a dependence on and allegiance to the USA.

1.7 It was clear that the French, led by de Gaulle, had alternative views on how the various member states of the EEC should be expected to co-operate in pursuit of both economic and political ends. In February 1961, for example, the French had introduced the idea of a "Union of *States* not of *People*" which drew considerable hostility from the other states; this was subsequently withdrawn. The French government were adamant that individual member states of the EEC should retain the power to veto all matters that they consider to be essential to their own national interest. The economic significance of the French farmer and the continuing rural way of life throughout much of France was the real issue at that time. The political recognition that a major state of the EEC could not have a policy imposed on that state to which it objected became a reality. The other states caved in and accepted the French demands over the CAP in order to maintain the solidarity of the EEC itself.

1.8 When de Gaulle resigned in April 1969, there was an immediate opportunity for the EEC to consider both "widening and deepening" of the Community. Widening corresponded to enlargement – as it does to this day – and this is the point at which the UK signed up, "to accept the Treaties and their political aims, and the decisions taken since the entry into force of the Treaties and the options adopted in the sphere of development."

By June 1971, the mains sticking points in the British negotiations – the scale of the UK Budgetary contribution, the length of the transitional phase, the Commonwealth's access to the British sugar market, and future prices for New Zealand lamb and dairy produce were all settled. Parliamentary approval was obtained and Britain signed the Treaty of Accession to the EEC on 22 January 1972.

The new Community of Nine, which included the UK, Ireland and Denmark, came into being on 1 January 1973. Only Norway rejected the terms on offer in a referendum held in September 1972. Subsequently, in June 1975, a referendum was held in the UK on continuing membership with 67.2% voting in favour.

1.9 In October 1972 at a Paris conference, the new Community of Nine set out an ambitious programme for the years ahead which included:

- A commitment to economic and monetary union.
- A capacity to address regional imbalances through a Regional Development Fund
- Improvements to the quality of life through renewed emphasis on social policy and a Social Fund
- Harmonisation of industrial policy in key areas
- Evolution of environmental and energy policies
- Co-operation on foreign policies and engagement with the wider world community
- Strengthening of European institutions, in particular, the European Parliament

1.10 A great deal of the optimism was dented by the world energy crisis in late 1973 and the quadrupling of the posted price of crude oil in the international petroleum market. Progress in the development of the Community was held back by these momentous political and economic events. Then, not a great deal happened until the election of a new Government in Britain in 1979 led by Mrs Thatcher.

1.11 The road to the Single European Act of 1986 was long and hard. Mrs Thatcher proved second to none in her defence of the sovereignty of the nation state, the appropriate roles of national governments within the European Economic Community, and in her assault on the bureaucracy of the European Commission and the Presidency itself in the person of Jacques Delors. She also insisted, with undoubtedly great determination and resolve, in getting some of Britain's money back. In fact the Prime Minister obtained a considerable reduction in the UK financial contribution to the running of the Community.

1.12 At the same time, for better or worse, M. Delors

and Lord Cockfield (who had been nominated by Mrs Thatcher as one of the two British Commissioners) pushed through 300 measures by the target date of 1992 against a considerable degree of opposition and outright resistance to remove frontier controls on the movement of goods, services, capital and people. This laid the foundations for the Single Market and was the next great leap forward for Europe. It is worth noting that prior to the signing of the Single European Act, the accession of Greece to the Community was followed by Spain and Portugal. Twelve states now made up the Community.

1.13 The stage was set for the push towards economic and monetary union. In June 1989, the European Council of Ministers agreed to begin preparations for the second and third stages, the first being the completion of the single market. The second stage was envisaged as the foundation of the European Central Bank, and the third and final stage would be the introduction of a single currency throughout all member states. Britain, still led by Mrs Thatcher, did not dissent but entered a caveat to the effect that there was nothing automatic about the third and final stage. At the same time Britain also laid down some conditions on entry to the European Exchange Rate Mechanism; in October 1990, with John Major as Chancellor of the Exchequer, it was decided that the 'time was right' and Britain joined the Exchange Rate Mechanism.

1.14 The Treaty on European Union 1992 (the Maastricht Treaty), with John Major now leading the British negotiating team as Prime Minister, covered the following:

- The creation of the European Union
- The timetable and criteria for EMU
- A new structure consisting of the European Council surmounting two pillars
- The innovation of the Common Foreign and Security Policy pillar and the Justice and Home Affairs pillar
- Statements of competence in consumer protection, public health, visa policy, the establishment of trans-European networks, development co-operation, industrial policy, social cohesion, education, culture, environmental protection, and social policy

1.15 Various crises had to be overcome within several member states before the Maastricht Treaty was finally ratified in 1993. Britain was not alone in this. In September 1992, a sterling crisis overtook the Major Government, and after a sustained run on the pound, Britain withdrew rather ignominiously from the ERM. However, at the Edinburgh Inter-Governmental Conference in December 1992, with Britain holding the Presidency, the European Council of Ministers resolved many of the difficulties, including the disagreement over the future financing of the Community. Britain also managed to secure a substantial statement on subsidiarity:

the Community should only act where given the power to do so .....,

the Community should only take action where an objective can be better attained at the level of the Community than at the level of the individual Member State ....;

the means to be employed by the Community should be proportional to the objective pursued .....

1.16 Austria, Finland and Sweden became members of the European Union on 1 January 1995. The membership of the European Union therefore currently stands at fifteen states.

1.17 The Treaty of Amsterdam 1997 achieved a number of different objectives

- Introduced a new Title on Employment, which says that the Member States will seek to co-ordinate their strategies for employment, particularly the areas of promoting a skilled, trained and adaptable workforce; and that they will seek to achieve a high level of employment throughout the Union.
- Incorporated the Social Chapter into the main body of the EC Treaty, following the abandonment of the British opt-out.
- Reflected the need to bring Europe closer to the citizens by laying a foundation for "freedom, security and justice"; providing for common rules on immigration, asylum and visa policy; transforming Justice and Home Affairs into "Provisions on Police and Judicial Co-operation in criminal matters".

However, certain matters remained largely unresolved which revealed that the Union remained unprepared for a planned enlargement to twenty-one Member States.

1.18 Even as the 1995 enlargement was being negotiated, Poland and Hungary both applied for membership. They were followed by Romania, Bulgaria, the Czech Republic, Slovenia, and Slovakia; the Baltic States (Estonia, Latvia and Lithuania) also joined the list, applications having been already received from Malta, Cyprus and Turkey. In most of these states, negotiations for European Union membership are still progressing.

1.19 The idea of the European Union having a "federal vocation" has been supplemented by the notion of subsidiarity which advocates that people should become closely involved in decisions that affect them, and the bodies that take these decisions should be close to them. This means that, in principle, decisions should be taken as low in the political hierarchy as possible. Given the nature of European Union institutions, their location and methods of working, it is difficult to see how subsidiarity can be taken forward in practical terms over the years ahead. But this is undoubtedly one of the real challenges facing the European Union over the years ahead, and one requiring a great deal of attention at every level of our national political life. It is highlighted by the need to establish clear communicating links between the Scottish Parliament in Edinburgh and the European Commission in Brussels!

1.20 The major factors driving towards greater integration – the so-called "ever closer union" – within Europe no longer seem to prevail with the same power of argument. Much has been achieved under the Six (1951-73), the Nine (1973-81), the Ten (1981-86), the Twelve (1986-95) and the Fifteen (1995-), mainly in the economic reconstruction of the member states following the Second World War. However, the building of consensus is no longer so straightforward and the prospects for enlargement could very easily introduce further constraining factors.

1.21 The advent of the single European currency -

the euro - on 1 January 2002 - may or may not determine the pattern of future changes. Britain has yet to decide where it stands on this matter but a decision could be made within the term of the present Parliament. Public opinion appears to remain divided on this issue – as indeed it does over the whole relationship of Britain to its partners in the European Union. This is not a healthy state of affairs and politicians seem to be perpetually avoiding the real issue of where Britain's future really lies at the start of a new century. Current political and military events only serve to complicate matters further as the true nature of the globalisation process throws up fresh and potentially unresolvable problems.

1.22 This short history of the European Union can only illustrate the merit of building European institutions carefully and methodically, while retaining "flexibility" as the simple watchword in all future negotiations which may seek to "widen and deepen" the working relationships and means of co-existence between the Member States.

1.23 Finally, it is worth recalling the objectives that the European Union set itself in the "Common Provisions" of the Treaty as signed in Maastricht on 7 February 1992:

- To promote economic and social progress which is balanced and sustainable, in particular through the creation of an area without internal frontiers, through the strengthening of economic and social cohesion and through the establishment of economic and monetary union, ultimately including a single currency in accordance with the provisions of this Treaty.
- To assert its identity on the international scene, in particular through the implementation of a common foreign and security policy including the eventual framing of a common defence policy, which might in time lead to a common defence.
- To strengthen the protection of the rights and interests of the nationals of its Member States through the introduction of a citizenship of the Union.
- To develop close co-operation on justice and home affairs.

2. Enlargement of the European Union

2.1 The European Union stands on the threshold of one of the most dramatic and challenging enlargements in its history. Negotiations between the European Union and a number of its neighbours in central and eastern Europe are underway regarding enlargement of the Union by incorporating new member states and are nearing completion with ten states. Accession will have far reaching consequences for all the current member states, as well as for those seeking membership.

2.2 At the end of the Intergovernmental Conference held in Nice in December, 2000, a statement was issued by the European Commission calling for a wide ranging debate within member states about the future shape and direction of the European Union. It explicitly asked that this debate should be conducted not just in political circles but throughout civil society. The Committee offers this report in the hope that it will form part of the Church of Scotland's contribution to this debate.

2.3 *The Vision for Enlargement*

2.3.1 The vision which inspired the founding of what was to become the European Union was that the constituent states of Europe and their citizens should be able to live peacefully together without the threat or the reality of warfare. It was envisaged that such peaceful coexistence of people of different languages and cultures, both secular and religious, would lead to and be supported by growing prosperity within the continent of Europe. It is this same vision which makes enlargement of the Union to include those states of the continent still outside the Union, and which desire to join, not only desirable but morally imperative. It must be remembered that those who laid the foundations of the Union had first hand experience of the evil that tore the continent apart in the 1930s and 40s. Those who do not remember those times, those who do not live on land and in cities which were fought over, field by field, street by street, those who have had no direct, personal experience of war in Europe should never lose sight of their vision. European union, and enlargement, are fundamentally about securing peace.

2.3.2 In many ways, to withhold the opportunity to others to join in this quest for peace, supported by enhanced prosperity, would be morally indefensible. Hoarding riches in the comparatively affluent North and West of the continent would only, in the longer term, lead to instability. As a church, we advocate radical acts of sharing resources, offering support and solidarity with all people. Enlargement is about extending prosperity, tackling poverty, increasing stability and security and building a society across the continent of Europe in which people can trust one another and live in freedom, free from fear, and able to realise their full potential.

2.3.3 The Europe Group, meeting in Brussels with politicians and officials dealing with the process of enlargement, was impressed, not only by that quality of the presentations which were made to us but also by their evident passion and belief in the project of uniting Europe. The Group is grateful to all those who met, spoke and debated with us.

2.3.4 The representatives of the Committee were struck by the force of the moral imperatives of enlargement. Many arguments were made including promotion of respect for human rights, the extension of the rule of law, the support of democracy, the protection of the environment and the building up of prosperity. But perhaps the most significant argument for enlarging the European Union was summed up best in the phrase, "If we don't export stability now, we will surely import instability in years to come." This is not self interest; it is interest on behalf of all the people of Europe.

2.4 *Candidate Countries*

2.4.1 The candidate countries are Bulgaria, Cyprus, The Czech Republic, Estonia, Hungary, Latvia, Lithuania, Malta, Poland, Romania, The Slovak Republic, Slovenia and Turkey.

2.4.2 In 1993, the European Council declared that "the associated countries of Central and Eastern Europe that so desire shall become members of the Union" and the process towards enlargement was launched in 1997.

Accession negotiations started in stages between 1998 and 2000 and are expected to be completed with ten candidate countries by the end of 2002. Ratification procedures in the parliaments of member states and candidate countries should be completed in time for the European Parliament elections in June 2004. Bulgaria, Romania and Turkey are not expected to be ready within that time scale.

2.5 *Overview of previous enlargements*

2.5.1 As described elsewhere in this report, the European Union has enlarged itself on a number of occasions, growing from six original members to fifteen at present. Each enlargement has brought benefits and opportunities and has enriched Europe as a whole. Different factors have enabled each of these enlargements to take place.

2.5.2 In the history of the European Union, the unification of Germany following the fall of the Berlin Wall in 1989/90 in part provides a case study for the accession of the Central and Eastern European candidate countries. The problems faced by Germany as a whole in the last decade give some indication of what the European Union may face when new members from the old Soviet bloc join. Massive investment has been required to modernise East German industry. There have been problems caused by insensitive acquisition of land and other resources by buyers from the west, eager to exploit new resources. Prices have risen as a result which has put a considerable financial strain on residents and businesses in eastern Germany. The structures of civil society and the culture of democratic government, denied under communism, have had to be developed rapidly. These sorts of problems should be seen as challenges to be overcome, not as insuperable obstacles to the accession of new candidate countries.

2.5.3 Lessons may also be learned from the accession of Greece, Spain and Portugal, which were joining from a lower economic base. The current enlargement will bring in countries with more extensive levels of social and economic deprivation than those of southern Europe. Further redistribution of resources within the EU will be necessary.

2.5.4 Each previous enlargement (with the exception of the accession of Sweden, Finland and Austria) has taken place within the context of a politically, ideologically and militarily divided Europe. There is now a historic opportunity to unite the continent.

2.6 Motives for Accession and enlargement

2.6.1 Candidate countries see membership of the European Union as offering the prospect of peace and stability by joining an area of freedom, justice and security. As members of the European Union, protection of individual human rights is enhanced. The importance of the freedom to live without fear of oppression and to trust others in countries which have experienced oppression and persecution by the state cannot be overstated.

2.6.2 Also, on a more pragmatic level, membership of the European Union is seen as offering:

- Consolidation of recently emerging democratic systems of government
- Access to wealthy markets
- Access to investment and economic and developmental assistance
- Political influence beyond their own borders
- Boost to economy and job creation
- Drawing rights on available EU funds
- Better quality of life

2.6.3 Member states see enlargement as offering:

- An extended area of peace, security in defence, and prosperity through political stability and democratic participation
- New investment opportunities
- The strengthening and support of representative democracy
- The enhancement of strategic relationships
- Economic growth and job creation
- Strengthened role for the European Union in world affairs

2.6.4 All current member states accept the principle of enlargement.

2.7 Criteria for membership

2.7.1 The European Union has declared that all candidates for membership must meet certain criteria to bring their own national rules and practices in line with those of the European Union (Copenhagen European Council, 1993). These are:

- A stable democracy
- Respect for human rights
- Legal protection of minorities
- Rule of law
- Competitive market economy
- The "capacity to cope with competitive pressure and market forces within the Union, [and] the ability to take on the obligations of membership including adherence to the aims of political, economic and monetary union". This means that candidate countries must apply all existing European Union legislation to their domestic law and must also be able to implement it effectively through appropriate administrative and judicial structures.

2.7.2 The Union has imposed upon itself the condition that it must have the capacity to absorb new members while maintaining the momentum of integration.

2.7.3 In general, the negotiation process is asymmetrical, the power being concentrated on the Union's side. The Union's members have determined and are enforcing the entry criteria and this is resulting in a considerable degree of European Union supervision of the internal affairs of the applicant states. A further difficulty is the fact that the European Union is continuing to develop itself and candidates are being forced to comply with ever more legislation over which they have had no say. However, the need to comply with and implement European Union rules in preparation for membership has been helpful to reformers within the parliaments of candidate countries.

2.7.4 The rules of the European Union are known as the *acquis communautaire* and are not negotiable. The candidate countries must commit themselves to adopt the *acquis* in its entirety, though transitional arrangements have been agreed in some areas such as environmental policy. These are divided into thirty-one chapters covering all the political, economic and social policy areas in which the European Union has competence. With most candidate countries, twenty-five of the thirty-one chapters have been completed with only those chapters relating to regional policy, aspects of the Common Agricultural Policy, financial and budgetary provisions and the institutions of the Union still to be negotiated. Despite the fact that these are arguably the chapters with most possibility for contention, reaching the current stage in negotiation represents a considerable achievement.

2.8 Summary of Candidates

2.8.1 In general terms, a number of factors are found in common across the candidate countries which set them apart from the current member states of the European Union. Many have experienced communist rule and this has made them significantly different from those countries which did not. In particular, they have relatively poor economies and are often very dependent on agriculture. Some have weak civil societies and the stability of their new democratic institutions is uncertain. Many areas have major environmental problems.

2.8.2 *The Czech Republic, Hungary and Poland*
These countries are among the largest applicants and are making the best progress towards meeting the criteria for entry. They also offer some of the greatest opportunities to existing member states in terms of new markets. Some of the particular problems faced are poor records on the treatment of minorities, outstanding property disputes with Germany and heavy economic dependence on labour intensive agriculture. The accession of Poland would double the European Union's farming population with obvious and serious consequences for the Common Agricultural Policy as it is currently formulated.

2.8.3 *The Baltic Republics*
Estonia, Lithuania and Latvia have large Russian minorities and strong relationships with Russia which present problems. Estonia has however developed strong and stable political institutions.

2.8.4 *Slovenia*
Slovenia is the only former Yugoslav republic currently seeking admission but it has unresolved problems with Italy.

2.8.5 *Bulgaria and Romania*
Both their economic and political systems present major difficulties but their strategic importance in relation to stabilising the Balkans may help their case in the longer term.

2.8.6 *Cyprus*
Cyprus's case is complicated by its partition and the tension between Turkey and Greece. However, at the time of writing (January 2002) negotiations between the two sides have resumed, at least in part as a result of impending European Union membership.

2.8.7 *Malta*
Frequently alternating governments have supported and opposed membership resulting in difficulties in proceeding with accession negotiations.

2.8.8 *Turkey*
The size of the population (64.8 million) might threaten to unbalance the Union. The involvement of the military in government and a poor human rights record, especially with regard to the Kurds, mean that accession is unlikely in the near future.

2.8.9 *General*
Economic problems abound. If all applicants, less Bulgaria, Romania and Turkey were to join, the population would rise by 19.94% but the Gross Domestic Product by only 4.1%.[1] Much of the European Union budget for grants and investment in basic infrastructure, for example, will have to be redirected and this may lead to popular discontent in regions of the current Union which have been net beneficiaries. On the other hand, the experience of the peripheral regions, such as parts of Portugal, Ireland and Scotland, has shown that prosperity has increased and the elimination of poverty, while by no means complete, has been advanced.

2.9 *Attitudes within the Union*

2.9.1 The fifteen current member states also have much to gain, but the negotiation process has been hard given the difficulty of negotiating with fifteen different states, each of which have their own particular interests and concerns. For example, Germany, perhaps in part because of its own enlargement, has been the country most keen on promoting enlargement. It stands to gain in terms of access to large markets on its eastern borders and its own security would be enhanced by greater stability among its eastern neighbours. It also has historic interests towards the east going back several centuries, while its more recent history may be leading it to seek to make amends for its past rôle in Eastern Europe. On the other side, France has been reluctant to see the Union expand so dramatically. It fears that Germany will become the dominant player in the European Union and that France will lose influence as the French/German partnership weakens. Southern European countries, especially Spain are fearful that resources and grants will switched to supporting the new member states. Greece, for strategic and political reasons, wants Cyprus to join and Sweden and Finland likewise are keen to see the Baltic States accede. The United Kingdom's attitude has been pragmatic rather than strategic. With relatively little trade with Central and Eastern Europe, the UK's interest in enlargement has extended little beyond general security and stability.

2.9.2 Outside government circles, public opinion has focussed on anxieties about cuts in funding of development projects, the perceived threat of the spread of organised crime as border controls are relaxed, the threat to jobs in current member states as people migrate from new member countries, and the loss of distinct cultural identity. Not all of these anxieties are justified but the debate needs to be engaged. Already, as part of the pre-accession arrangements, the Union's trade surplus with candidate countries has grown and this generates employment and growth in the member states.[2] As the new member countries prosper, so will their people be encouraged to remain at home to share in and contribute to that prosperity. The European Union has increased co-operation on policing and criminal matters, in particular on combating terrorism and the trafficking in people. The protection and development of cultural identity remains a priority for the Union.

2.10 *Institutional reforms required*

2.10.1 Enlargement has provided the impetus for much needed institutional reform, recognition having been given to the fact that existing structures and methods will not work with a much larger Union.

2.10.2 Meeting in Berlin in March 1999, the European Council agreed to a restructuring of the budget of the European Union. Up to +3.12 billion (£1.95 billion) has been set aside annually between 2002 and 2006 for pre-accession expenditure in candidate countries and a total of +58 billion (£36.25 billion)[3] has been allocated to finance Structural Fund programmes, internal policies, administration and agriculture in the newly acceding states.[4]

2.10.3 Although it is widely felt that the Treaty of Nice (December 2000) did not go far enough, progress was made in a number of areas, including:

- Extension of majority voting
  More decisions will be taken by Qualified Majority Voting, a system which seeks to balance the power of larger and smaller member countries. The number of matters which may be subject to a veto from any one country is also being reduced. However, no progress has yet been made on voting reform on Immigration and Asylum matters which remain subject to unanimity.
- Composition of the European Commission
- Simplification of Treaties
- Review of the size and powers of the European Parliament
- Security and defence policy
- Enhanced co-operation
- The powers of the European Court of Justice
- The Single Currency (minimally)
- Social policies

Many of these matters were brought under review at the Laeken meeting of the European Council (December

2001) and a Convention on the Future of Europe was set up to make concrete proposals for reform in the fields of making a distinction between the powers of the European Union and those of the member states; of incorporating the Charter of Fundamental Rights into European law; and, most importantly, of re-awakening public understanding of, and support for, the aims and policies of the European Union. The Committee will be examining the work of the Convention and reporting on it to a future General Assembly.

2.10.4 Decisions on other matters, including the rotation of the presidency around member states, reform of the Common Agricultural Policy and reform of the Regional and Structural Funds have still to be taken but should be addressed at the 2004 Intergovernmental Conference.

2.11   *Unresolved Issues*

2.11.1 Some of the transitional problems associated with enlargement are in fact challenges which the European Union as a whole faces. The impending accession of candidate countries may place an intolerable strain on the institutions of the Union but more especially on the ethos of the European Union. As modifications are made to the political processes to make a greatly enlarged European Union workable, there is a threat to the traditions of liberalism and moderation which characterise the best of what the European Union stands for. Institutional reform must not come at the cost of democratic accountability. Cultural diversity, which the European Union explicitly promotes, must not, in the rush to convergence, be sacrificed.

2.11.2 Specifically, there is a danger that powers may become more and more centralised, contrary to the spirit of subsidiarity. The speed at which monetary union has been achieved has given the impression that the political elites who make the decisions have left public opinion behind. The Danish "No" vote on the euro and the Irish referendum rejection of the Treaty of Nice can be interpreted as a public backlash not only against too rapid

integration but also against perceived lack of public consultation and democratic accountability. A particularly good example is provided by France and Germany, where there has been no opposition to monetary union from any of the main political parties and consequently there has been little debate about it. Opinion polls have shown that, in both countries, politicians are not representing the majority of public opinion.

2.11.3 This demonstrates that more time and effort must be put into bringing public opinion along with the direction in which the Union is going. The European Union must encourage the governments of existing member states to explain fully the reasons for enlargement – its likely impact, the challenges to be faced and the advantages to be reaped.

2.11.4 Decision making in Brussels must not come to be seen as being done by and on behalf of others. The citizens of the European Union must feel ownership of both the institutions and their work. The principle of subsidiarity needs to be seen in practice. The process of deepening (*ie* more openness and clarity, simpler decision making, a stronger European Parliament, a more accountable Commission, Council of Ministers and European Council, and more involvement of the public) must now catch up with the rapid progress made in widening since 2000.

2.11.5 The public case for Europe, and to some extent for enlargement, has been made almost exclusively in economic terms. But it also has major political implications and yet this is not reflected in public debate on the subject. This illustrates the regrettable fact that the political values of dispersal of power and democratic accountability upon which the project of Europe should consciously be built are being relegated to secondary importance behind economic growth.

2.12   **Benefits of Enlargement**

2.12.1 *Promotion of Peace within Europe*
In a continent which has been fought over for centuries,

the importance of peace cannot be overstated. Both candidate countries and existing members will gain by rolling out the area in which countries are so bound together by trade, economics and shared political aims that warfare becomes "not only unthinkable but materially impossible". The growing awareness of European Citizenship engendered most obviously by a common currency and also in documents such as passports and driving licences is also contributing to a sense of a common purpose and destiny for all people across the Union.

2.12.2 *Extension of respect for human rights*

Many of the candidate countries have recently suffered under régimes which have paid scant attention to human rights, particularly the rights of minorities. The freedom and protection afforded to individuals under the European Convention on Human Rights and the European Union will thereby be extended.

2.12.3 *Economic justice and the tackling of poverty*

It is morally inconceivable that the existing member states of the European Union should exclude their immediate neighbours from the benefits of what they already have. At the very least, to do so would be likely to lead to instability, hostility and further European wars.

2.12.4 *Promotion of prosperity*

Stability which allows the flourishing of human potential mitigates against the build up of tension within and between nations. This stability can only be built upon a sound economy in which everybody has access to an

2.12.5 *Promotion of stable, just government and society in all countries of Europe*

This requires not only democratically elected and accountable local and national government and an impartial judiciary but also a flourishing civil society to promote dialogue and debate on matters of public policy. Such civil society can only exist where people are free to express and promote opinions and beliefs. The churches are an essential part of civil society as was demonstrated by their role in the recent history of east and Central

Europe which was instrumental in the collapse of communism.

2.12.6 *Environment*

The application of European environmental legislation should promote and enforce high standards of environmental protection across the Union as illustrated by air and water quality standards already in existence under EU Directives.

2.12.7 *Reform of the Common Agricultural Policy*

Enlargement is providing an impetus for reform of the Common Agricultural Policy. This should aim to promote sustainable agricultural practices, production of wholesome food and good stewardship of land. The future of farming itself also depends on farmers having a fair and reasonable level of income to maintain good farming practice and livelihood.

2.12.8 *Resolution of existing disputes*

Enlargement may provide the impetus to sort our several longstanding disputes such as those between the two parts of Cyprus, Germany and Poland, and Italy and Slovenia.

2.12.9 *Reduction in crime*

Co-operation in tackling crime is developing between member states and will be extended to new members, particularly in relation to terrorism, trafficking in people (a large contributor to illegal immigration) and the trade in illegal drugs.

2.12.10 *Strengthened role in international affairs*

As the progressive coming together of the peoples of Europe advances, it brings forward the possibility of a more unified voice speaking for Europe in the international community on matters such as development aid and humanitarian assistance, global environmental issues and international trade.

3. Conclusion

3.1 The Church of Scotland has consistently stood for the principles of peace, justice and equality. The opportunity which now faces the Continent of Europe to unite as never before is one that must be taken for the good of people who inhabit this part of the world. If we are serious about unity in faith, believing that God calls all people into union with him through Jesus Christ, then the same qualities of mutual respect, sharing of resources, and living together in peace which should characterise our church life ought also to characterise our political life.

3.2 While there are undoubtedly problems of a practical nature which need to be overcome, the potential gains for the people of Europe mean that enlargement of the European Union is a goal which must be supported.

3.3 Enlargement will involve sacrifices being made by those countries and regions which have already benefited from investment by the European Union as levels of further grants and are reduced to facilitate redistribution towards the new members. We would argue that this is no basis for opposing enlargement and would run contrary to the spirit of generosity which we are called to display. The Gospel teaches that wealth must not be hoarded but used and shared. What is true for individuals must be true for states also.

3.4 Much has been made in this report of the principles and benefits which we would argue must underlie and drive the process of enlargement. It must be acknowledged that in no part of the current European Union are these principles universally observed or these benefits universally felt. Poverty has not been eradicated, human rights are compromised, minorities are still disadvantaged and the environment is still despoiled. Enlargement must not be seen solely as a process whereby candidate countries are brought up to the standards of the existing members. Rather, it should be seen as a means of sharing the task of realising these ideals and of working towards them in partnership.

3.5 The question remains as to whether the European Union is nearing its final size. Even with the probable accession of Bulgaria, Romania and Turkey, gaps will still exist notably in the Balkans and elsewhere in Central and Eastern Europe. The goals of peace, justice and prosperity through developing strong democracies in the remaining countries of Central and Eastern Europe must be pursued just as rigorously as they have been pursued with the current candidate countries. The European Union must not close itself to the possibility of further enlargement.

3.6 Ultimately, the success of European Union enlargement must not be judged solely on its effect within the Union. While a strong economy is needed to generate wealth which may be applied in this way, aid is, however, not a long term solution to the problems of the South. What is needed is economic justice, not just within Europe, but in Europe's dealings with all those with whom it trades. The pressures of enlargement must not be allowed to become an excuse for ignoring this need. As it extends freedom to trade eastwards into Central and Eastern Europe, the European Union must also remove its protectionist policies in relation to the South. An enlarged, strengthened and potentially more inward looking European Union may very well cause dismay in developing countries.

3.7 The success of enlargement should be judged, at least in part, by the generosity and justice displayed by the European Union towards those countries not of its number and, in the long term, by the part it plays in instituting the principles of peace, justice, respect for human rights and the rule of law, and the promotion of democracy and prosperity both within its borders and in the wider international context.

Appendix 1

Candidate Countries

Candidate countries (all thirteen including Bulgaria, Romania and Turkey) represent 45% of the European Union population and 7% of its Gross Domestic Product. GDP per capita varies between 24% of the European Union average in Bulgaria and 82% in Cyprus.

	Population on 1 January 2000 (1000)	Area in km²	GDP in 2000 (bn euro)	GDP per head in 2000 in PPS+
Bulgaria	*8 191*	*110 971*	*13.0*	*5 400*
Cyprus	755	9 251	9.5	18 500
Czech Republic	10 278	78 866	55.0	13 500
Estonia	1 439	45 227	5.5	8 500
Hungary	10 043	93 030	49.5	11 700
Latvia	2 424	64 589	7.7	6 600
Lithuania	3 699	65 300	12.2	6 600
Malta	388	316	3.9	11 900
Poland	38 654	312 685	171.0	8 700
Romania	*22 456*	*238 391*	*40.0*	*6 000*
Slovakia	5 399	49 035	20.9	10 800
Slovenia	1 988	20 273	19.5	16 100
Turkey	*64 818*	*769 604*	*217.4*	*6 400*
European Union	**376 455**	**3 191 000**	**8 526.0**	**22 530**

PPS (purchasing power standards) is an artificial currency that allows for variations between the national price levels not taken into account by exchange rates. This unit improves data comparability.

Issued by: Eurostat Press Office
Eurostat news releases on the Internet: http://europa.eu.int/comm/eurostat/

Appendix 2:

The Institutions of the European Union

1. Introduction

1.1 The institutions of the European Union (EU) are:

- The European Council
- The Council of Ministers
- The Committee of Permanent Representatives
- The European Commission
- The European Parliament
- The European Court of Justice
- The Economic and Social Committee
- The Committee of the Regions
- The Court of Auditors
- The European Investment Bank
- The European Central Bank

1.2 The Union has a considerable measure of institutional autonomy and is not merely an instrument of nation states:

The European Union is a polity or system of governance, in its own right. It has its own will, agenda and institutional prerogatives.[5]

2. The European Council

2.1 Created in 1975 at the behest of the French President, Giscard d'Estaing, the European Council only became a formal institution in 1986. It is composed of Heads of State (*ie* the French President) and of Government, *ie* the Prime Ministers, and the Foreign Ministers of the Member States. Its main functions are to take final decisions on issues which the Council of Ministers have failed to decide (*eg* agricultural commodity prices) and to act as the primary decision-maker on the Common Foreign and Security Policy .

2.2 As from 2000, one meeting of the European Council will take place during each six-month Presidency in Brussels; any other meeting will usually be held in the Member State holding the Presidency.

2.3 The European Council also discusses initiatives in any policy sector of the European Union and is thus able to agree at times on "decision packages" which balance at one time the interest of Member States in various policy areas. A latecomer to the array of European institutions, the European Council, with few Treaty provisions to constrain it, is often the scene of nationalistic clashes between Prime Ministers, to the detriment of coherent decision-making. After each meeting the Prime Minister of the state holding the six-month presidency of the Union, who presides over the European Council, makes an oral report to the European Parliament, which is followed by a debate. This is one of the rare occasions on which the European Council is in any way accountable to the other institutions. The latest European Council was held at Laeken, near Brussels, in December 2001; the Presidency passed to Spain on 1st January 2002.

3. The Council of Ministers

3.1 The Council is legally designated by the Treaties as the decision-making institution – a function it shares increasingly with the European Parliament. It is composed of the General Council, which now has only time to discuss foreign affairs, and is where the Foreign Ministers sit, and numerous sectoral Councils, such as the Agriculture, Environment or Overseas Development Councils. Since the Treaty of Maastricht 1992, the increasing predominance of economic and monetary questions has given new importance to the Economic and Finance Council; this is incidentally the only forum where the three Member States outside the single currency area (Denmark, Sweden and the UK) can discuss economic and monetary issues with the states within it.

3.2 The Amsterdam Treaty 1998 made the Secretary-General of the Council the High Representative of the Member States for the Common Foreign and Security Policy. The Deputy Secretary-General now runs the Council secretariat. The Presidency of the Council has gained power recently through the extension of the "co-decision procedure" by which Council decisions are taken by qualified majority voting, and which involves detailed negotiations between the Presidency and the Parliament. Under qualified majority voting, each Member State disposes of votes very roughly related to its population. For example, France, Germany, Italy and the UK each have ten, Denmark, Ireland and Finland three each and Luxembourg two. To obtain a qualified majority, 62 votes have to be recorded on one side; if 26 votes are recorded on the contrary side, however, this constitutes a "blocking minority", and no majority decision is possible. This provision is designed to protect the position of the smaller Member States.

3.3 The co-decision procedure, introduced by the Maastricht Treaty, obliges the Council of Ministers to examine the amendments proposed by the European Parliament to the text of a legislative proposal made by the Commission. If the Council disagrees with some or all of the amendments, the Parliament can insist on making the case for its amendments to Council representatives in a conciliation committee. If the conciliation committee reaches agreement, and the amended proposal is formally adopted by both Council and Parliament, it becomes law. If either institution, however, rejects the agreement reached in the conciliation committee, the amended proposal is lost.

3.4 If, on the other hand, the conciliation committee cannot reach an agreement on Parliament's amendments, a new situation is created. The Council may, by qualified majority, adopt its own version, with or without some of Parliament's amendments. If this happens, Parliament has to muster an absolute majority to reject Council's version. Should it fail to do so, Parliament has amended its Rules of Procedure to ensure that, after its President has tried to win the agreement of both the Commission and the Council to Parliament's point of view and has failed, Parliament can still reject the proposal. This rather complicated procedure leaves Parliament, in the event of disagreement in the conciliation committee, with the last word. It must be said, however, that the two institutions usually have sufficient interest in the Commission proposal being adopted in one form or another to seek agreement on some text at some earlier stage of the procedure.

4. The Committee of Permanent Representatives

4.1 Each Member State appoints an Ambassador to the European Union, or Permanent Representative, and a Deputy Ambassador to the European Union. The former sit in Part II of the Committee, and prepare meetings of the European Council, and the General Affairs, Economic and Financial, Budget and Development Councils. The latter sit in Part I of the Committee, responsible for the internal market and other technical Councils such as those concerned with the environment, agriculture and social policy.

4.2 Much of the detailed work of decision-making falls to the Council working groups, about 150 in number. About 70% of the Union's legislative output is decided by the groups, which are composed of a majority of national civil servants, briefed by national government ministers to defend the national interest. The totality of this complex decision-making procedure on legislation is conducted in private, a matter which has attracted sustained criticism from the European Parliament for many years.

5. The European Commission

5.1 The Commission is perhaps the most generally misunderstood institution, yet its functions include the sole power to make policy proposals, the implementation of such proposals and their enforcement and, increasingly, foreign trade and policy responsibilities. It can be described as "a political civil service". It is not generally realised how few proposals for legislation originate from the Commission itself.[6]

The Origins of Commission Proposals (data collected in 1998)

International obligations	35%
Amendment to or codification of existing law	25-30%
Response to requests from other EU institutions, Member States or interest groups	20%
Required by Treaty	10%
Pure, spontaneous, Commission initiatives	5-10%

5.2   At present there are twenty Commissioners, two from each of France, Germany, Italy, Spain and the UK, and one from the other Member States. The "Big Five" have, on enlargement, agreed to surrender their second Commissioner. Since the mid-1980s more than two-thirds of Commission members have had previous ministerial experience. Although Commissioners are by Treaty required to act independently, most have over the years tended to espouse the causes of "their" government. The Commission must agree to every policy proposal, if necessary by a vote, and is bound by collective responsibility to support the decision thereafter.

5.3   Controversy has raged for years on the method of appointment of the Commission.   At present, a candidate for the Presidency of the European Commission is nominated by the governments of the Member States. The person nominated is then subject to a vote in the European Parliament, and may be approved or not, as the case may be.   The governments then, by common accord with the candidate approved by the Parliament (Article 214, *Treaty on European Union*), nominate the other members of the Commission. All the members so nominated are then subject as a body to a vote by the Parliament, *ie* the Parliament, having approved the President as an individual, cannot vote on the other candidates individually. Thus is the accountability of the Commission to Parliament constrained.

5.4   Various suggestions have been advanced to "democratise" the election/selection of the Commission. One proposes that national candidates for the Commission would stand for election to the Parliament. It would then elect the President from among them and, "in common accord" with him or her, would elect from MEPs one Commissioner per Member State. National governments might be expected to resist this loss of their influence, however.   Another suggestion for rendering the Commission more accountable would be to have each candidate nominated by the governments voted on individually by the Parliament.

6.   The European Parliament

6.1   The European Parliament is the only directly-elected, representative and democratic institution of the European Union. It thus gives the Union an important measure of democratic credibility.

6.2   The European Parliament numbers at present 626 Members, all elected by different systems of proportional representation. Until the next election in 2004 a majority of members hails from the European People's Party (centre-right) and the European Liberals, Democrats and Reformists (centre).   Other major "political groups" or parliamentary parties are the Party of European Socialists, the Greens and European Free Alliance group, and the European United Left group (left-wing).

6.3   Since 1973 the European Parliament has consistently fought to increase its powers. Its first victory was to win the right to be directly elected, the first such election being in 1979. The Parliament then devised the policy of increasing its powers by persuading the Commission to back Parliament's proposals for a series of treaties amending the Treaty of Rome. Thus the Single European Act 1986, the Maastricht Treaty 1992 and the Amsterdam Treaty 1998 all advanced the European Parliament's powers considerably, although the Treaty of Nice 2000 did not do so. This "ratchet effect" has seen the "co-decision procedure" between Council of Ministers and the Parliament on Commission proposals extended to some 80% of policy areas. The Parliament also has power to sack the entire Commission, which it did in March 1999.

6.4   Since 1975 the European Parliament has exercised a type of "co-decision" with the Council on the Community Budget, and has deployed this leverage skilfully on occasion to win further powers from the Council. But the Parliament still has no power over the 50% of the Budget devoted to the Common Agriculture & Fisheries policies, which undermines its credibility with many European citizens.

7.   The European Court of Justice

7.1   European Union law can be said to constitute an autonomous legal system, imposing obligations upon, and creating rights for, both individual Union citizens and Member States, and limiting the sovereignty of Member States. European Union law does not range as widely as national law; for instance, it is not directly concerned with family law, and has little to do with policy areas such as education or health. On the other hand, in many areas Union law co-exists with national law, examples being in competition policy and environment policy. And the range of European Union law has broadened considerably over the years, in areas such as the single market, and the environment.

7.2 During most of its existence since 1958 the European Court has tended to give judgements which served to buttress and extend Community law and (in the 1970s and 1980s) the powers of the Parliament. It has been attacked as a federalist body for so doing, but in fact it can be argued that in interpreting the Treaties the Court is bound by their provisions, particularly those relating to the powers of the Commission and, increasingly, of the Parliament.

7.3 The Court sits in Luxembourg and is divided into the main Court and the Court of First Instance, which deals with competition, personal, and other technical cases. Judges are appointed by national governments and since 1973 there has always been a Scottish judge, denoting the origins of Scots law in the Continental Roman-Dutch system. One of the Advocates-General has always been an English barrister.

8. The Economic and Social Committee

8.1 As complements to the six principal institutions, the European Community (now Union) has established two advisory and consultative bodies and three financial bodies.

8.2 The Economic and Social Committee was created by the Treaty of Rome 1958 to enable sectoral interests, *eg* employers, employees and socio-economic organisations (such as the all-Europe bodies representing business and farmers) to express their standpoints and opinions to the Community institutions. Similar bodies

exist in many Member States but not in the UK. The increase in the powers of the EP has reduced what influence the Committee may once have had.

9. The Committee of the Regions

9.1 This advisory body consists of "representatives of regional and local bodies", nominated by the national governments. The Council and the Commission are obliged by Treaty to consult the Committee of the Regions which can, in turn, adopt opinions on its own initiative (and frequently does).

9.2 Membership ranges from the Prime Ministers of major German Laender to councillors from local authorities. The Scottish Executive is currently proposing to nominate Scottish ministers to the Committee, a move hotly contested by Scottish councillors. There is further competition for representation between large cities such as Barcelona, Marseille and Milan and rural areas in Spain, France and Italy. The Committee has not yet lived up to the hopes nurtured by its creation, despite its serious input to the institutions.

10. The Court of Auditors

10.1 A Parliament resolution of 1975 led to the creation in 1977 of the Court, whose task is to examine and report upon the accounts of all revenue and expenditure by the Communities and the Communities' Budget. These reports are closely examined by the Parliament which can refuse to give a discharge (or authorisation to proceed) to the Commission until its criticisms have been met.

11. The European Investment Bank

11.1 Created by the Treaty of Rome in 1958, the Bank has the task of contributing on a non-profit-making basis to the "balanced and steady development of the common market in the interest of the Community" (Art. 267 Treaty of Rome). By granting loans, the Bank finances projects for less developed regions (*eg* the Portobello sewage works, Edinburgh), projects for modernising firms and projects of common interest to Member States (*eg* power lines from France to Spain). The members of the Bank are the Member States' governments.

12. The European Central Bank

12.1 The Treaty of Maastricht 1992 provided for the establishment of the European Central Bank as an institution of the Economic and Monetary Union. The Bank is headed by a Governing Council, comprising the governors of the Central Banks of the participating states and an Executive Board which includes the President, and five other members appointed by the governments of these states. The European Central Bank operats through the European System of Central Banks, which unites it with the Central Banks of the participating states.

12.2 The tasks of the European System of Central Banks are to:

- define and implement the monetary policy of the European Union;
- conduct foreign exchange operations;
- hold and manage the official foreign reserves of the participating Member States;
- promote the smooth operation of payments systems.

At present only Britain, Denmark and Sweden are not members of the European System of Central Banks, which runs the single currency.

---

1. Calculated from figures issued by Eurostat Press Office based on population on 1 January 2000 and GDP in 2000.
2. Enlargement of the European Union: an historic opportunity, European Commission, 2001, p 5.
3. Approximate exchange rate of £1 = +1.6
4. Enlargement of the European Union *op.cit.* p.26
5. *Decision Making in the European Union,* by J. Peterson and E. Bomberg, 1999, Basingstoke, McMillan, pp32-33
6. Extract from *Decision Making in the European Union op.cit*

THE TERRORIST ATTACKS ON THE UNITED STATES OF AMERICA AND THE WAR IN AFGHANISTAN

1.11 September 2001

1.1 In the United States of America on Tuesday 11 September 2001, a group of terrorists boarded four passenger planes and set in motion a chain of events, which was later described by some commentators as having changed the world. By hijacking the planes, the terrorists turned them into weapons and flew them into both towers of the World Trade Centre in New York, into the Pentagon in Washington; the fourth plane crashed in Pennsylvania due to the intervention of passengers. The sheer scale of the loss of life and the horrific manner in which innocent people died led to a deep and widespread sense of insecurity and uncertainty about the future. This was exacerbated by the ease with which the terrorists undertook the attacks, in using small knives and box cutters, creating a sense that everyone was at risk.

1.2 The fact that the attacks on the twin tower blocks of the World Trade Centre were televised live across the world brought the horror home to viewers in a vivid and dramatic way. It was possible to witness and to identify with ordinary people, beginning just another working day, in the busiest office complex in the world. These were people of every background from 86 different countries, whose lives were cruelly ended, either instantly with a crashing violence or with unimaginable pain and terror. It was also possible to identify with the passengers on the planes, whose final phone messages to loved ones were made in the knowledge that they were going to die and would never see them again. The sheer horror of what happened to so many innocent people, and the pain and anguish of the bereaved families, could barely be imagined.

1.3 The shock for the American people themselves was profound, shattering their perceived immunity from attack by forces outwith the United States. The fact that the terrorists targeted the centre of the financial capital of the largest economy on the planet and also the military headquarters of the world's most powerful nation struck at the very heart of the social, political and economic structures of the United States and its place in the world.

1.4 The response by the United States Government to these attacks has had a major global impact. This has clearly been felt most severely by the people of Afghanistan, but many other world trouble spots have been affected. Relations between the United States and a number of other nations, such as Pakistan, have been radically altered. The rôle of the United Nations has been tested and the importance of bringing the perpetrators of the atrocities to justice has demonstrated the need for an International Court of Law. The economic consequences have also been significant, particularly in regard to the airline industry. The financial cost of the "war against terrorism", including the need for increased security, has been very high at a time when the world economy is already experiencing a significant downturn. There has been a further impact in regard to the world's religions, in particular in relation to the dangers of religious extremism.

1.5 The events of September 11 were so shocking that they almost defied belief and their impact on global politics, the world economy and the lives of millions of people will continue to be felt for a long time to come.

2.   Committee statements and their context

2.1 The Church and Nation Committee has a long tradition of speaking out on major international issues involving justice and peace and the resolution of conflict.

2.2 On 12th September, the Committee sent a letter to the American Ambassador in which profound sympathy for those injured and for the families of those who had died was expressed. The letter also said that those who planned the outrage and financed, trained and equipped those who put it into operation should and must be brought to justice. However, it also stated that the Committee did not believe that any retaliation which killed thousands more people would provide an answer.

2.3 At a time of worry and waiting, on 4th October, the Committee issued a statement in regard to the ongoing crisis. At this time, America had been praised for not retaliating immediately, but all the indications were pointing to the commencement of military action. The main points of this statement were as follows:

- The Committee had yet to be convinced that the use of military force in Afghanistan could be justified and stated that any military response would have to be proportionate, accurate and have a reasonable expectation of success;
- Strong concern was expressed that military action would worsen the already serious humanitarian crisis in Afghanistan, that a bombing campaign would risk the lives of innocent Afghan civilians and that it could lead to a new generation of "martyrs" rising up;
- The importance of the rule of law was expressed, as well as the need for the United Nations to play a central rôle;
- Efforts to oppose terrorism, including financial, security and diplomatic measures, were all supported;
- The moral argument being brought to bear on any government which supports terrorism or harbours terrorists must be unending;
- The underlying causes of the crisis were highlighted, including the large and growing divide between the rich and the poor in the world;
- Church members were called upon to be to be neighbours in word and deed to those made vulnerable by the crisis;
- Support was expressed for our armed forces, their chaplains and the families of service personnel; the Committee indicated that they were all in our prayers.

2.4 At a time of considerable confusion and uncertainty, the Committee issued a further statement on 1st November. At this stage, the bombing of targets in Afghanistan had been ongoing since 7th October, with the loss of life of many Afghan civilians being one of the consequences. The refugee crisis was now critical. The main points of the second statement were as follows:

- Raising questions about the situation was vital and any attempt to stifle debate was wrong;

- The questions about military action were thrown into sharp relief not only by the dangers faced by the civilian population of Afghanistan, but also by the dangers in which our armed forces were being placed and our thoughts and prayers continued to be with them, their families and their chaplains;
- The campaign was doing more harm than good, further dividing humanity and widening the gulf between the world faiths;
- The bringing to justice of those behind the attacks was reaffirmed, but concern was expressed about the lack of clear aims in the campaign and the fact that the bombing was going on long after all the targets had been hit, with the consequent loss of innocent lives;
- Deep regret was expressed in regard to the lack of willingness by the US and the UK to accede to pleas for a pause in the bombing to allow humanitarian aid to get through;
- Any true political solution would have to examine the running sores of the world, particularly in the Middle East;
- Support was again expressed for our armed forces, their families and their chaplains;
- The statement concluded by calling for the bombing to cease immediately.

3. Committee actions

3.1 There was considerable interest in the media and the wider community about the Committee's stance in regard to the crisis. The Convener fulfilled a number of media engagements on radio and television, undertook newspaper interviews and contributed articles to the national press. The Convener, Vice Convener and other Committee members also took part in rallies in a number of towns and cities in Scotland, organised by the anti-war coalition. The majority of letters received by the Committee were in support of its stance; what critical response there was came mainly from people in the US. The general reaction from the wider community was supportive, with many accepting the Committee's right to speak out, while not necessarily agreeing with every aspect of its position. The second Committee statement was sent to every minister in the Church, with congregations being encouraged to write to their MPs to stress the need for clarity in the campaign and to be aware of the damage to the civilian Afghan population. Throughout this period, the Convener was in regular contact with the Convener of the General Assembly's Committee on Chaplains to HM Forces.

3.2 On 26 November 2001, representatives of the Committee met with Scottish backbench Members of Parliament. With the Labour Group and the Liberal Democrats the discussion centred entirely on the international situation. Most Labour MPs were highly critical of the Committee's stance and a key question asked of us was what alternative there was to military action. It was noted that some of those present did not appear to be averse to widening the campaign to attack other states alleged to be supporting terrorists.

3.3 The Committee held a meeting with Mr Adam Ingram MP, the Armed Services Minister, at Scottish Churches House, Dunblane. Mr Ingram had received an early draft of this report and offered a critical analysis of it. His main argument was that the Committee had failed to offer a realistic alternative to military action and that it was only by attacking the Taliban and destroying the al-Qaeda terrorist network that the threat posed by international terrorism could be overcome. The Committee listened to Mr Ingram's arguments with interest and found it very useful to be able to engage in a discussion with him afterwards. The fact that the Minister took the time to attend this meeting, and discuss the issues with us, was much appreciated.

4. The origins of the crisis

4.1 The origins of the attacks on America on September 11 and the subsequent international crisis are complex. The following appraisal is a brief summary of some of the reasons which can be put forward to explain why the events took place.

4.1.1 When the Soviet Union attacked Afghanistan in

December 1979, the initial prognosis in the West was that the various ethnic groups in the country would never unify enough to drive out the communists. However, a solution came in the form of the Mujahadeen, who were fighters from across the Muslim world prepared to take up arms in the name of a "holy war". They were supported by the US Central Intelligence Agency and played a critical role in ending Soviet occupation. The ground was therefore laid which allowed the al-Qaeda terrorist network, headed by Osama bin Laden, to develop. Founded about ten years ago, it was able to base itself in Afghanistan when the Taliban took control in 1996. A number of terrorist training camps were established and the network spread throughout other countries, including many in the West. During this period, Western governments effectively turned their backs on Afghanistan.

4.1.2   The rise of Islamic fundamentalism undoubtedly created circumstances in which terrorism was seen as the most effective means of achieving certain goals. Many fundamentalists chose to practice extreme forms of the Islamic faith, such as Wahhabism, which was developed in the 18th century in the Arabian Peninsula. It is the militant form of Islam practised today in Saudi Arabia and probably influenced Osama bin Laden.

4.1.3   In many Arab nations, there has been a growing sense of hostility towards the West, its values, culture and politics, particularly among the younger male generation. At the heart of this hostility is a set of specific discontents that have created a feeling of powerlessness and alienation. It is a discontent being driven by a myriad of social, demographic, political and economic problems. Specific reasons for this anger and sense of injustice include the support given by America to Israel against the Palestinians, the continued sanctions and ongoing bombing campaign against Iraq, the presence of US troops in Saudi Arabia, and what is perceived to be the corrupt nature of US backed Gulf governments.

4.1.4   The role of Saudi Arabia is particularly significant in relation to the causes of September 11. It was Saudi Arabia which helped to finance the Mujahadeen and is believed to have allowed Saudi-based charities to channel

money to al-Qaeda. However, the presence of so many US troops stationed in Saudi Arabia also played a vital role in inciting the fury of Osama bin Laden and his associates; Saudi Arabia is America's closest ally in the Gulf.

4.1.5   Finally, a failure in Western intelligence, security measures and insufficient financial sanctions against terrorists were serious weaknesses exploited by those who carried out the September 11 attacks. For example, in 2000, 628 million trips were taken on US planes[1]. Achieving this level of business required the airlines to keep security to a minimum with delays being seen as totally unacceptable by the travelling public.

5.   Points of agreement

5.1   The Committee is in agreement with the actions of the United States-led coalition of countries opposed to terrorism in regard to the financial action which was taken. The freezing of terrorist assets across the world was a vital and necessary step, although it was regrettable that such actions had never been undertaken to the same extent prior to September 11. Improvements in security, particularly at major airports, were also a necessary and welcome step.

5.2   We fully support diplomatic action to overcome the running sores which have created an understandable sense of injustice and anger among people in Muslim communities across the world. This particularly applies to the Israel-Palestine conflict where the need to restart the peace process is of vital importance. The General Assembly's previous statements on this conflict have recognised that a negotiated and just settlement is the only realistic way forward. The recognition among many governments that such disputes have been an underlying cause of global terrorism is to be welcomed.

5.3   Global poverty is a major factor in encouraging resentment in developing nations against the West, which a minority of extremists are able to exploit. There are 6 billion people in the world today of whom 4.8 billion live in developing countries - 80% of the world, with 20% of the income. Again, it is encouraging that there is recognition of the seriousness of the situation among world leaders and figures, such as by James D. Wolfensohn, President of the World Bank, Gordon Brown MP, the UK Chancellor of the Exchequer, and the Prime Minister, Tony Blair.

5.3.1　In a speech a few weeks after September 11, Mr Wolfensohn expressed the view that the two worlds, developed and developing, no longer exist and that "poverty in one place is poverty everywhere." He went on:

......if anybody believed that there was a wall around the two worlds surely they must now believe, both symbolically and really, that that wall has come down. For me that is a huge change in terms of the issue of interdependence, globalisation and the role of my own institution, but beyond that the way in which we all think about questions of development. The two worlds are gone. There is one world. We need to understand indigenous people and the cultures in which they live. We need to reach out and look behind the people that we're dealing with, to try and be more open. We also need to deal with people in poverty. People in poverty are no different from any of us here. If we don't reach out to people in poverty and create a better sense of equity, there won't be peace. It's very simple.[2]

5.3.2　Gordon Brown has argued strongly for debt relief for developing nations and increased aid. He called for the creation of an International Development Trust Fund, which would create a fund totalling £50 billion to help alleviate world poverty. He also echoed the comments by James D. Wolfensohn in the following remarks:

The alliance we have forged against terrorism since September 11th, an alliance across thousands of miles, across boundaries of nationality, faith and race, across all conditions and stages of economic development, confirms a profound and pervasive truth: that in the new global economy we are, all of us, the richest countries and the poorest countries, inextricably bound to one another

by common interests, shared needs and linked destinies; that what happens to the poorest citizen in the poorest country can directly affect the richest citizen in the richest country; and that not only do we have inescapable obligations beyond our front doors and garden gates, responsibilities beyond the city wall and duties beyond our national boundaries, but that this generation has it in our power - if it so chooses - to abolish all forms of human poverty.[3]

5.3.3　In February 2002, Tony Blair embarked on a tour of West Africa. We warmly welcome the motivation behind this tour and the fact that Prime Minister clearly recognises that global poverty, an unjust world trading system and international debt relief should all be issues requiring urgent action by the world's richest nations. We note that the Prime Minister acknowledged the work of the Jubilee Coalition for the cancellation of international debt. We also welcome his understanding that these global issues can all be contributory factors to encouraging a deep sense of injustice and the growth of international terrorism among a minority of extremists.

5.4　While these views and initiatives are all to be welcomed, it is vital that they do not amount merely to fine speeches and clever sound bites. Action is required, such as the UK and other rich nations bringing the amount they give in international aid from the present average of 0.24% to 0.7% of annual income,[4] thus creating a further $100 billion a year. It is deplorable that international development aid to LDCs (Least Developed Countries) has dropped by 45% in real terms since 1990.[5]

5.5　Their attempts at reform notwithstanding, institutions like the International Monetary Fund and the World Trade Organisation still perpetuate the economic and political hegemony of the rich. Until these institutions are fundamentally restructured, for example to foster fairer trade arrangements, people in poorer nations will continue to be marginalized and denied justice.

5.6　The gulf between rich and poor nations does not only apply to the poverty gap. There is a clear need for major efforts to be made to build a greater understanding and consensus between different nations in regard to culture, religion and politics. The UK Prime Minister, Tony Blair, has proposed that rich states embark on a mission to bring "greater understanding between nations and between faiths, and above all, justice and prosperity for the poor and dispossessed."[6]

5.7 It is encouraging to note that there is some recognition from the UK Government that lessons have to be learned from the past and that a foreign policy which broadly ignored what was happening in Afghanistan from the early 1990s onwards was mistaken. In a BBC interview on 9 October 2001, Tony Blair said:

But I think there is a very real sense that I have, and I know that this is shared by President Bush and other leaders, that at the end of the 1980s and early 1990s, we in a sense walked away from people in Afghanistan. The Russians had left Afghanistan. We really should have, at that point in time, put together a proper plan, a rescue plan for the country, to help it get back on its feet again, and we didn't. And one of the things that I want to say is that this time round we must not repeat that mistake.[7]

6. Unresolved issues

6.1 *Defining terrorism*
While the methods used by today's terrorists have changed significantly in recent times, the actual concept of terrorism or insurgency is nothing new: it has existed for centuries. A good example of this was the attempt to blow up the Houses of Parliament in 1605 by a group of men whom we would now term terrorists and who were, like many of today's terrorists, viewed as religious extremists. But what do we mean by terrorism today? It is beyond the scope of this report to fully explore this question; we simply wish to draw attention to the fact that, as the US State Department has pointed out, "no one definition of terrorism has gained universal acceptance."[8] One example of this is the debate over the words *terrorist* and *freedom fighter*. When the Mujahadeen undertook attacks on the Soviet Union in Afghanistan in the 1980s, or when the Contras sought to undermine the Nicaragua government in the same period,

they were described as freedom fighters by the United States. When Palestinian extremists commit atrocities against Israel, Western governments describe them as terrorist attacks, but Israeli retaliation (which may involve assassinations) is not defined in the same way. The US State Department believes that terrorism can never be inflicted by a state, which is why it always accuses "rogue states" of sponsoring terrorism, but not actually carrying it out.

6.1.1 At a conference of the Islamic Fiqh (jurisprudence) Academy of the Muslim World League, the scholars put forward their definition of terrorism and called for a distinction to be made between acts of violence and legitimate self-defence by people under occupation. They described acts by the Palestinians against the Israeli occupation as a form of *Jihad* and legitimate self-defence. In other words, neither side in the Israeli-Palestinian conflict views their own actions as acts of terrorism.

6.1.2 The UK Government has defined terrorism in law as the use or threat of action which involves serious violence against a person, serious damage to property, endangers a person's life (other than that of the person committing the action) creates a serious risk to the health or safety of the public or a section of the public, or is designed seriously to interfere with or seriously to disrupt an electronic system. It also includes the use or threat of action to influence the Government or to intimidate the public or a section of the public, including where the use or threat is made for the purpose of advancing a political, religious or ideological cause.[9] The September 11 attacks clearly fall within the terms of this definition.

6.1.3 In undertaking aerial bombing in Afghanistan, the US air force undoubtedly created terror among many civilians. However, the US government argues that unlike those who carried out the September 11 atrocity, it did not deliberately target civilians and their deaths and injuries were unintended. We would point out that the terror experienced by Afghan civilians was not somehow lessened because their village happened to be an unintended target of a bomb, but we fully accept the argument that the motivation behind inflicting such terror was fundamentally different in nature from those who undertook the attacks of September 11. Nevertheless, we would draw attention to the fact that there can be a thin dividing line between acts of terrorism and the military response carried out by states.

6.2 *International law*

An important question to be addressed is whether or not the United States has acted in accordance with international law in regard to Afghanistan. The situation in regard to international law is complex and the following is a brief summary of some of the main issues involved.

6.2.1 The United Nations Charter requires UN member states to settle their international disputes by peaceful means. The Charter preserves states' inherent right of individual or collective self-defence if an armed attack occurs[10] and the UN Security Council has the power to take any action it considers necessary to maintain or restore international peace and security.

6.2.2 Given the sheer scale of the September 11 attacks many experts have argued that it amounts to an armed attack on the US, giving rise to the right of self-defence. However, the question of self-defence is complicated by the fact that the US was attacked by an organisation harboured by another nation and not directly by a nation in its own right.

6.2.3 The UN Security Council passed resolution 1368, in which it categorises the September 11 attacks as a threat to international peace and security. The Security Council's resolution refers to "taking all necessary steps" in response to the situation, but this is a reference to the Council as a collective body and not the sanctioning of individual states taking all necessary steps.

6.2.4 When military force is used, there must be compliance with the law of armed conflict. That is a substantial body of law, found in numerous international treaties, including the Geneva Conventions of 1949, which requires discrimination in targeting, the avoidance of collateral damage, and the protection and humane treatment of civilians, victims of armed conflict and prisoners of war. The manner in which the US conducted the campaign was not, in our view, compliant with these important principles.

6.2.5 While it may be the case that the US did not deliberately target civilians, its policy was such that it chose to risk the lives of many innocent people by bombing targets where they were liable to be. The use of cluster bombs with the subsequent risk to civilian life from unexploded ordinance was indefensible. It must have quickly become apparent to the US military that there were very few targets to aim for in the first place. As Jason Burke, an expert on Afghanistan wrote, "We are told that the Americans have knocked out the Taliban "command and control centres". I have seen many of these. They largely consist of a man sitting on a rug with a radio, an ancient, unconnected telephone and the mother of all teapots."[11] The part America played in the deaths of hundreds of prisoners at a fort near Mazar-e-Sharif left many unanswered questions and appeared to have been in breach of the Geneva Convention. The refusal to have an inquiry into this incident is regrettable. The bombing campaign continued after the fall of the Taliban, with unconfirmed reports of over 100 civilian casualties in one particular strike. There was no legal, military or moral justification for this policy, which received the acquiescence of America's coalition partners and little media coverage.

6.3 *Putting suspected terrorists on trial*

6.3.1 On 13 November 2001, President Bush authorised secret trials under military commissions, with the possibility of prisoners being executed by firing squad. In January 2002, the US began transporting alleged al-Qaeda members and Taliban fighters to territory it has leased from Cuba at Guantanamo Bay. It refused to call them prisoners of war, a decision which caused widespread disquiet among human rights groups, the International Red Cross and within the United Nations. Instead, it called them "illegal combatants", a term not recognised in international humanitarian law. The decision meant that those captured were denied their rights under the Geneva Convention, although the US argued that they were treating the prisoners humanely and in accordance with the principles of the Convention. The Convention states clearly that "any member of the armed forces of a Party to a conflict is a combatant and any combatant captured by the adverse Party is a prisoner of war."[12] The US has stated that their status is unclear, partly because they were not in uniform when captured. However, the Geneva Convention also states, "any person taking part in hostilities and captured is presumed to be a prisoner of war and is treated as a prisoner of war, even in case of doubt as to his status. In the latter case, the question must be decided by a tribunal at a later date".[13] Furthermore, if these prisoners are recognised as prisoners of war under the Geneva Convention, Taliban fighters recognised as defending their country should be returned home and only suspected terrorists should be tried. On 7 February 2002, the US appeared to recognise this distinction when it stated that Taliban prisoners would now be treated under the terms of the Geneva Convention. Since this did not include calling them prisoners of war, it did not amount to a significant change in their status.

6.3.2 By denying them prisoners of war status, the US is able to try the prisoners before secret military tribunals and by holding them on Cuban territory, they have no recourse to appeal to a higher US court. This form of justice would lack all the essential guarantees for independence and impartiality. The only exception to this has been in regard to an American prisoner suspected of supporting the Taliban, who will be tried under normal US legal procedures, thus displaying double standards on the part of the US government.

6.3.3 We share the concerns expressed about the treatment of these prisoners and we communicated these to the American Ambassador to the UK in January 2002. We would argue that if America chooses to fight against terrorism in the interest of upholding freedom and human rights, then it must be seen to fully uphold these same principles.

6.3.4 The formation of the International Criminal Court (ICC) would have been the right forum in which to put the alleged terrorists on trial. The Rome Statute to establish the ICC was adopted in July 1998 by the votes of 120 countries over the opposition of seven nations, including the United States. The Court will come into existence when 60 countries have ratified the Statute. It will try only the most serious perpetrators of future mass crimes against humanity, war crimes and genocide and only if national courts cannot or will not do so. Unfortunately, the formation of the ICC will probably come too late to try alleged terrorists and it is unlikely to be able to do so retrospectively. The alternative could be an *ad hoc* tribunal created by the UN Security Council and patterned on the international tribunals for former Yugoslavia and Rwanda. Another would be an international panel created by all or some of the various states whose citizens were victims of the attack. This would have the advantage of drawing upon the expertise of justices, lawyers, and legal staff trained in the application of international law. It will however be necessary to secure a venue that is both neutral and accessible.

6.4 *Military action as a last resort*

6.4.1 World leaders have argued strongly that the military action taken against the Taliban was a last resort. In an article by the Foreign Secretary, Jack Straw, he wrote:

No one wanted to take military action. It always has to be the policy of last resort, proportionate and targeted. But there can be no peace for the Afghan people - just as there will be a continued threat to the rest of the international community - until the terrorist network which has taken root in Afghanistan is defeated. Long before Osama bin Laden's henchmen hijacked the aeroplanes which flew into the World Trade Centre and the Pentagon, they hijacked Afghanistan. And the people who have suffered most from the terrorists and their Taliban supporters are the Afghan people[14]

6.4.2 While we agree that the Afghan people are the ones who have suffered most at the hands of the Taliban, we would disagree with the view that the military action was a last resort as other means of overcoming international terrorism had not been given sufficient time to work through. The historian Sir Michael Howard has written that:

The use of force is no longer seen as a last resort, to be avoided if humanly possible, but as the first, and the sooner it is used the better. The press demands immediate stories of daring-do, filling their pages with pictures of weapons, ingenious graphics, and contributions from service officers long, and probably deservedly, retired. Any suggestion that the best strategy is not to use military force at all, but more subtle if less heroic means of destroying the adversary are dismissed as "appeasement" by ministers.[15]

6.4.3   Treating terrorists as criminals to be hunted down across nations does not meet the demands of the press and public for immediate and obvious action. The elements required are secrecy, intelligence, covert actions that remain covert, and above all infinite patience. All of these are forgotten or overridden in a media-stoked frenzy for immediate results.

6.5   *What was the alternative?*

6.5.1   Strong arguments were put forward by the US and many other nations that there was no realistic, viable alternative to military action. They argued that a military response was the most effective means by which terrorist atrocities could be quickly prevented in the future and that there was no other effective means of destroying the al-Qaeda network in Afghanistan. We understand the thinking behind these arguments, but we would strongly question whether such a policy offers a lasting solution. We accept that there can be some international situations in which a military response can be justified. We pointed out in our statement of 4 October 2001 that if military action was to take place in Afghanistan, then it should be proportionate, accurate and have a reasonable expectation of success. In view of the scale of the bombing campaign and the large number of civilian casualties, our contention is that these criteria were not met. We accept that determining casualty figures is difficult. While some estimates have been as high as three thousand, one of the most cautious estimates from a US source is provided

by the Boston-based Project on Defense Alternatives. PDA, drawing on western media reports, concluded that over one thousand Afghan civilians were killed by the bombing and several thousand more have died or will die from hunger, disease or exposure as an indirect result of the war.

Military action alone has no prospect of eliminating international terrorism and in this case has probably strengthened the resolve of terrorists to strike back. An FBI assessment at the end of 2001 concluded that the al-Qaeda network had had its capabilities diminished by no more than 30%. Even by the beginning of February, it was reported that 16 of the top 22 al-Qaeda leaders were still free. Furthermore, while the fall of the Taliban is to be welcomed, it is far too early to know whether the new Afghan Government will be able to stabilise the country in the long term. The past history of Afghanistan indicates that creating such stability will be an extremely difficult task. According to Paul Rogers, Professor of Peace Studies at Bradford University:

...lawlessness and disorder are affecting much of the country. The UN special envoy, Lakhdar Brahimi, has urged a major expansion of peacekeeping operations. Brahimi is widely regarded as one of the most able diplomats in UN service, with a long record of work in Afghanistan. His conformation of the need for a level of peacekeeping that far exceeds the work of the small ... force in Kabul indicates the extent of the problem facing the interim administration.[16]

6.5.2   The American led international coalition could have treated the atrocity of September 11 as a criminal act and used their extensive intelligence resources to bring those behind the attacks to justice. Such an approach was followed in regard to the bombing of a Pan Am flight over Lockerbie in 1989. When America declared "war" on terrorism, it should have been in the same sense as a war against crime or drugs, *ie* the use of all available resources against a dangerous activity which can never be completely eliminated, but which must be contained to ensure stability in society.

6.5.3   The coalition could have sought to co-operate

on a global scale to undermine and isolate terrorist activity by treating the perpetrators as criminals, greatly enhancing the resources of the intelligence services, ensuring that terrorists cannot obtain funds to resource their activities, taking all necessary steps to prevent them obtaining weapons of mass destruction and isolating countries suspected of harbouring terrorists diplomatically.

6.5.4 To have undertaken such an alternative approach would have been a huge political risk for Western governments and it would have been deeply unpopular among the American people in particular. The strong need for politicians to be seen to act was fuelled by the understandable public anger against those who carried out the terrorist attacks. Undoubtedly, politicians will have been advised by the security services that they had to be seen to act quickly and decisively in the face of such an assault. Nevertheless, it is necessary to ask whether responding to the public and media's thirst for action is the right way to form policy in today's world.

6.6 Extending the "war"

6.6.1 There have been some indications that the US is planning to extend its war on terrorism to other nations considered to be harbouring terrorists. The clearest indication came from President Bush in his State of the Union address in January 2002. Mr Bush termed Iraq, Iran and North Korea as an axis of evil, despite the fact that they have little in common with each other and pose different dangers. Any attempts to intervene in these and other nations would be extremely dangerous and would almost certainly break apart the international coalition against terrorism and cause a major backlash from Arab nations. It would be very hard to justify any such moves under international law, particularly in regard to the argument of self-defence.

6.6.2 At a White House Press Briefing on 5 December 2001, a journalist asked President Bush's spokesman on what authority the President could go into other nations and bomb them. He replied, "The right as the Commander-in-Chief to protect and defend the American

people".[17] This statement is effectively saying that America can intervene in any country if it believes US security and interests are threatened. Such a policy will encourage other nations to argue that they too have the right to attack other countries in the war against terrorism. This has already happened in regard to Israel's military actions against the Palestinians and in the crisis between India and Pakistan over Kashmir.

7. The role of the United Kingdom

7.1 The UK Government was among the first to offer unreserved support to the United States in the "war" against terrorism. This policy met with almost total support in Parliament and opinion polls indicated that the general public strongly supported the Government's stance. With some exceptions, most notably the Daily Mirror, the press were also behind the policy. Strong efforts were made by the Government to reassure members of the Muslim community that this was not a war against them, but against terrorists. There was an anti-war coalition, but this did not appear to have any direct influence on Government policy.

7.2 The UK offered logistical support in the refuelling of planes early on in the conflict, although no British planes were involved in direct attacks. Despite large numbers of British troops being kept on 48-hour stand-by, America made it clear that they were not required, although some special forces were deployed. The UK also played an important leadership rôle in regard to the international peacekeeping force, which entered Afghanistan in late December 2001.

7.3 The Prime Minister, Tony Blair, played a significant role in helping to strengthen the international coalition against terrorism and in successfully arguing against a swift American response in the early days after September 11. While we acknowledge that other world leaders undertook similar diplomatic activity, there is little doubt that the good relationship enjoyed between the US and the UK put the British Government in a stronger position to argue for restraint and the importance of countries acting together.

7.3 We note with concern that the United States began to adopt an increasingly unilateralist stance, particularly after the fall of the Taliban. The "international coalition" became an increasingly meaningless phrase, because the military operation was almost entirely implemented by America and the overall US strategy appeared to centre solely on serving America's interests. It was regrettable that the British Government did not offer stronger criticism of the treatment of prisoners held by the US in Cuba or seek publicly to warn against the dangers of the US intervening in other nations.

8. The role of the United Nations

8.1 During our visit to Westminster, one MP said to us, "after September 11th the world is going to be run differently."[18] This leads on to the question of who "runs the world?" On the surface, it appears to be America with its strong economy and military might, supported to varying degrees by other Western governments. This would be unacceptable, since international affairs cannot be governed by one state acting unilaterally. However, our world today is a complex place and globalisation now means that the world order can no longer be conceived as purely state-centric or even primarily state governed, as authority has become increasingly diffused among public and private agencies at the local, national and global levels. Nation states are no longer the sole centres or the principal forms of governance or authority in the world. Regional organisations such as the European Union and the Association of South-East Asian Nations now play a major role, and large corporations and financial institutions have seen their power and influence grow enormously. Institutions such as the International Monetary Fund, the World Bank and the World Trade Organisation also yield considerable influence. Amidst this complex situation, it is important to stress that the rôle of the United Nations in international affairs must be central. It is not a world government and certainly does not "run the world", but its role in resolving international conflicts and maintaining peace and international security is of considerable importance.

8.2 Following the September 11 attacks, both the UN

Security Council and the General Assembly adopted strong resolutions condemning the attacks and calling on all countries to co-operate in bringing the perpetrators to justice. As stated in section 6 of this report, the Security Council expressed its determination to combat, by all means, threats to international peace and security caused by terrorist acts. The Council also reaffirmed the inherent right of individual or collective self-defence in accordance with the Charter of the United Nations. According to the UN General Secretary, Kofi Annan, the countries concerned have set their current military action in Afghanistan in that context.[19] The Security Council also adopted resolution 1373, aimed at targeting terrorists and those who harbour, aid or support them. It requires member countries to co-operate in suppressing the financing of terrorism, co-operating in criminal investigations, and exchanging information on possible terrorist acts. The UN General Assembly has already adopted a total of twelve conventions and protocols on combating terrorism and it is hoped that this will provide a common legal framework for international co-operation in the fight against terrorism. The UN played a significant role in brokering the peace between the various factions in Afghanistan following the fall of the Taliban.

8.3 All of the resolutions and protocols adopted by the UN are to be applauded. However, the reality is that the United Nations has been sidelined in the campaign against terrorism by the United States. Its role, as is the case in many other international conflict situations, seems to be viewed as one of picking up the pieces when the fighting is over and providing humanitarian assistance.

8.4 The UN Secretary General, Kofi Annan, called on "all parties to take all possible precautions to minimise civilian casualties. As the world unites in the fight against international terrorism, we must, at the same time, do everything possible to protect innocent civilian populations."[20] However, the UN did not protest about any specific aspects of the conduct of the military campaign, nor did it question whether the US stretched Article 51 beyond its limits. It has been silent in regard to the targeting of sites close to civilians in Afghanistan and the conduct of US forces in their operations against

Taliban prisoners. Our concern is that the UN seems to have no real authority in dealing with conflict situations and simply has to abide by whatever the United States and its allies choose to do.

8.5 The United Nations must be given greater authority over the conduct of military campaigns in ensuring that they are conducted in accordance with international law. It also requires greater authority and powers in its rôle of providing political solutions to conflict situations and in its role of preventing conflicts from arising in the first place. At present, the UN is suffering from financial restraints, bureaucratic problems and is over- burdened in its humanitarian and peace keeping roles. It requires greater resources, and the fact that the United States owes substantial amounts towards the UN budget is a situation which must be resolved. The UN also requires to be more robust in speaking out about the conduct of its more powerful members, but this will not happen without radical reform of the Security Council.

9. The role of the Church

9.1 Faiths throughout the world responded to the events of September 11 by initially issuing statements expressing shock at what had happened, deep concern for the victims and their families and condemnation of those who were behind the attacks.

9.2 The Church played an important role in allowing people to express their grief and horror at what had happened and to pray for the victims. Many special services were held, and some members of the clergy noted that church attendances had increased. Churches were also involved in raising money for charities involved in helping the victims of hunger and homelessness in Afghanistan and the families who lost loved ones in New York, including the many fire-fighters who sacrificed their lives.

9.3 There was a much more varied response from churches to the stance which the US should take in response to what had happened. Many churches called for restraint, with the central point made being the fact that violence should not be answered with violence. The Christian Conference of Asia, for example, expressed concern about the risk of America inciting communal violence in many Asian countries. A US Interfaith Statement covered a broad spectrum of the US religious community, including Christian, Jewish, Muslim, and Buddhist leaders. The statement urged that "those responsible for these utterly evil acts be found and brought to justice," but cautions that "we must not, out of anger and vengeance, indiscriminately retaliate in ways that bring on even more loss of human life. Let us deny them [the terrorists] their victory by refusing to submit to a world created in their image."[21] Shortly after September 11, we contacted the Presbyterian Church (USA) to express our concerns and reassure them of our prayers. They issued a pastoral letter on the day of the attacks which included the following words, "As they [the US government] seek to find effective and appropriate responses to this terror, it is our prayer that these responses may be of the kind that will contribute to a future of peace and not serve in any way to escalate the cycle of violence and counter-violence to a higher level. Further, we call our leaders and all people of good will to resist the stereotyping of enemies that so often occurs in these types of situations."[22]

9.4 The World Council of Churches have stated that Inter-faith dialogue has become more difficult in some countries as a result of the 11 September attacks and the aftermath. In both South Africa and Kenya, there has been an apparent reluctance by Islamic groups to join in inter-faith events on issues such as domestic violence since the attacks. In other countries, interest in inter-faith dialogue has increased.

9.5 There were a number of incidents of physical attacks on members of the Muslim community and those perceived to be Muslims. It should be noted that attacks also took place against Christians, with the worst example occurring against worshippers in Pakistan. We commend political and religious leaders who sought to calm this tension.

9.6 There is a role for Churches to play in seeking to overcome the lack of understanding and ignorance which exists among many people about different world faiths. The Quran is often presented within western society in a distorted way in order to give the impression that it sanctions acts of violence. An example of the misunderstandings which exist is in regard to the interpretation of the word *Jihad*, which the majority of Muslims understand as meaning a struggle or effort. The defining of *Jihad* by Islamic extremists as meaning "Holy War" has been widely accepted by many in the West. Efforts by churches and interfaith groups to engage in dialogue and increase our understanding of different faiths are greatly to be welcomed. The need to demonstrate what the world's religions have in common, and that religious extremism applies to a minority of people within them, is vitally important.

10.   An eye for an eye leaves everyone blind

10.1 The phrase "the world will never be the same again" has been used repeatedly by many commentators in regard to the events of September 11. Why should this be so, when so many other appalling atrocities have been committed in recent times? For example, such sentiments were never uttered when 800,000 people were massacred in Rwanda in just 100 days as the rest of the world looked the other way. What this statement could mean is that the Western world will never be the same again. As the BBC journalist George Alagiah has pointed out:

This easy conflation of the fate of the rich world with the fate of all mankind is part of the arrogance that so many in the poor world railed against, and still do. In the majority world, among the wretched billions, life had not changed much at all. It was as precarious and cruel as it had always been.[23]

The probability is that when viewed over time, the events of September 11 will be seen as part of a pattern in which extremists used ever more violent and devastating methods to achieve their aims. The response by the United States may also be viewed in the future by historians as yet another example of the human race answering violence with violence, which fails in the long run to resolve the world's ongoing problems. In a sense, nothing has changed, and no lessons have been learned.

10.2 Did the response to September 11 take the form it did because it happened in the world's richest and most powerful nation? Would there have been such a strong reaction if it had taken place in the Sudan, or Russia or Chile, and not covered live on television? The answer is probably not. This is not to imply that the horror, shock and outrage expressed about what happened went too far. In fact, it affirms all that is good and positive about human beings that people reacted in the way that they did. However, it is to say that a terrorist act taking place anywhere in the world, whether in the world's richest nation or poorest, whether it was filmed happening or not, whether there was one death or a thousand, merits the same level of outrage, shock and expressions of condemnation. It is to say that every human being is of equal value. It became obvious during this crisis that the lives of Afghan civilians were considered by some in the West to be of less value than those killed or injured on September 11. For example, the loss of civilian lives through the bombing campaign gradually received less attention in the media, particularly when the bombing continued after the Taliban had fallen. Jesus Christ treated all human beings with equal value and respect and this forms a central teaching of Christianity. To view the lives of innocent civilians as expendable is entirely contrary to the teachings of Christianity.

10.3 We all have a part to play in working towards a fairer world. One body with a major role to play is the United Nations. Fundamental reform of the UN and its various agencies should be undertaken and all member countries which have failed to contribute their full share financially to the UN's work must seek to do urgently.

10.4 In an interview shortly after the Taliban fell, Tony Blair stated that he believed that the world was now a safer place.[24] However, it will take more than the fall of one evil regime to achieve this. To do that requires much more fundamental changes in human affairs. For example, the world will be a safer place when the obscene trade in arms across the planet has come to an end and when we eliminate nuclear weapons altogether. It will be a safer place when far more effective means of overcoming the injustices prevalent in the world's poorest nations are pursued. It will not be any safer when governments believe that going to war is the only viable means of resolving the problems which face our world today.

10.5 Mahatma Gandhi said, "An eye for an eye leaves everyone blind". It is our sincere hope and prayer that world leaders will have their eyes opened to the fact that in our world today responding to evil with more violence is rarely the answer. It is equally our prayer that they will come to understand that the most effective way of eliminating international terrorism is to overcome the running sores which exist in so many parts of the world, as well as in seeking ways to enhance greater understanding between nations, races and religions. Our world leaders must recognise that religious and cultural intolerance and economic and social inequality require to be overcome so that they will not act as a breeding ground for potential terrorists of the future.

10.6 We affirm the following words of Konrad Raiser, General Secretary of the World Council of Churches, who said:

The answer to terrorism cannot be to respond in kind, for this can lead only to more violence and terror…. As long as the cries of those humiliated by unremitting injustice, by the systematic deprivation of their rights, and by the arrogance of power of those who possess unchallenged military might are ignored or neglected by a seemingly uncaring world, terrorism will not be overcome. The answer to terrorism must be found in redressing these wrongs that breed violence between and within nations.[25]

[1] Article by Gregg Easterbrook in *How Did This Happen, Terrorism and the New War*, edited by James F. 2. Hodge Jr, and Gideon Rose, page 164

[2] Speech at the Inter American Press Association 57th General Assembly, Washington, 13 October 2001

[3] Speech to the Federal Reserve Bank in New York, 16 November 2001

[4] Organisation for Economic Co-operation and Development recommendation

[5] The United Nations Conference on Trade and Development (UNCTAD) Report, 12 October 2000

[6] Labour Party conference, 2 October 2001

[7] BBC World Service, 9 October 2001

[8] US State Department Report: *Patterns of Global Terrorism, 2000*, section 3

[9] The Terrorism Act 2000

[10] UN Charter, article No. 51

[11] *The Observer*, 21 October 2001

[12] Article III, 4; protocol I, 43, 44

[13] Article III, 5, Protocol I, 45

[14] *The Guardian*, 26 October 2001

[15] Speech at Royal United Service Institute, 30 October 2001

[16] article of opendemocracy website, 14 February 2002

[17] White House Press Conference, 5 December 2001

[18] See Section 3.2

[19] Press Conference in Geneva, 1st November 2001

[20] UN Press Release, 15 October 2001

[21] US Inter-Faith Statement, 21 September 2001

[22] Pastoral Letter issued on behalf of the Presbyterian Church (USA), from the Moderator, Stated Clerk and Executive Director of the General Assembly, 11 September 2001.

[23] *The Day That Shook the World*, BBC News, page 39.

[24] Interview, Foreign and Commonwealth Office web site, 7 December 2001.

[25] WCC Consultation, Geneva, 29 November–1st December 2001

SANCTIONS AGAINST IRAQ

The General Assembly call upon Her Majesty's Government, through its membership of the Security Council of the UN, for a clear plan to be produced for the reduction of sanctions against Iraq in order to bring speedy benefit to the health and welfare of its people and the return of Iraq to normal international relations. (General Assembly, 1995).

1. When the General Assembly declared its mind on Iraq in 1995, economic sanctions had been in place for four years. Seven years later they are still in place and, despite their devastating effect, there seems little hope of them being lifted.

2. As recently as 30 November 2001, UK Foreign Secretary Jack Straw was unequivocal:

Iraq holds the key to its re-integration into the international community - compliance with UN Security Council Resolution 1284. There must be independently verified compliance with the international community's insistence that Iraq give up its weapons of mass destruction. In the meantime, we will continue to fulfil our obligation to contain the threat that Saddam Hussein still poses to the International community.

3. With the exception of the UK and US governments, virtually the entire international community, including Kuwait, is now urging the lifting of economic sanctions, the regeneration of Iraq's economy and the ending of Iraq's isolation. If the aim of economic sanctions was to bring a dictator to his knees they clearly haven't; instead they have brought 23 million civilians to their knees. The UN has stated that:

Infant Mortality rates are the highest in the world, chronic malnutrition affects every fourth child under five, only 41% of the population have regular access to clean water, 83% of all schools need substantial repairs and the Iraqi health care system is in a decrepit state[1]

In August of the same year, UNICEF reported:

If the substantial reduction in child mortality during the 1980s had continued through the 1990s there would have been half a million fewer deaths of children.

In February 2000, following a visit to Iraq to assess the impact of sanctions, the Catholic Agency for Overseas Development summed up the wider consequences as follows:

The damage, which has been inflicted on every sector of society, has resulted in a complex of problems, which are mutually reinforcing. Inadequate diet and dietary deficiencies, particularly of protein and vitamins, makes people more vulnerable to opportunistic diseases. Hyperinflation means that people routinely have two jobs. At the same time, the unemployment rate is estimated at 50%. Yet people still cannot afford to go to hospitals/clinics and medicines, when available, are beyond their reach. Young people are taken out of school to look after their siblings. Crime rates have soared. Prostitution has emerged as young women try to help their families. All this has led to a breakdown in normal family life, has undermined moral values and is slowly eating away - like a biblical plague of locusts - at the very fabric of society.

4. To alleviate some of the worst excesses, a UN/Iraq *Oil for Food* programme was launched in December 1996, with 72% of oil revenue held in a UN account in New York for basic needs. Although the UK and US governments insist this is adequate, the UN's own Humanitarian Panel conceded, "There are some things that Oil for Food simply cannot do".

5. After eleven years, the UK Government is proposing to introduce various changes to the sanctions regime (sometimes referred to as "smart sanctions"). The changes would lift most "holds" on civilian goods, but the "dual use" category would still prevent essential components getting through; oil would be the only permitted export, undermining all other economic activity; no foreign investment would be allowed, and the Iraqi Government would not be permitted to use oil revenue to reconstruct society.

6. Even "smarter" sanctions are envisaged with zero holds but stricter controls, but these will still be based on the premise that Iraq continues to constitute a military threat. However, Scott Ritter, former head of the UN weapons inspection (concealment) unit stresses, "it was possible as early as 1997 to determine that, from a strictly qualitative standpoint, Iraq has been disarmed".

7. On 4 February 2002, Iraq informed UN Secretary General Kofi Annan that it was ready to hold talks "without preconditions". US Secretary of State Colin Powell insisted that any discussion with Iraq would be "very short" and repeated his demand that UN Weapons Inspectors be allowed to return to the country. The reinstatement of the inspection team's powers could indeed be a factor in the negotiations which might lead to the lifting of sanctions, but Colin Powell added that changing the Iraqi régime is something the United States "might have to do alone."

8. The people of Iraq face many problems already, and following President George Bush's State of the Union address on 29 January 2002, in which he singled out Iraq as part of an "axis of evil", they would appear to be facing more. There are no quick solutions to the oppressiveness of the Iraqi government, the enormous foreign debt, the internal tension and political uncertainty, the legacy of more than a decade of deterioration in social services, physical and mental health, and under-investment in its infrastructure. The brutal nature of the Iraqi government has not been lessened through the sanctions policy and this policy has led to even greater suffering being inflicted on the people of Iraq. Sanctions have not achieved their original objective and the time has come for them to cease.

[1.]Report of the UN Humanitarian Panel, March 1999.

THE UNITED STATES NATIONAL MISSILE DEFENCE SYSTEM

1. Introduction

1.2 At the 2000 General Assembly, the Committee was encouraged to initiate a new study of the issues surrounding nuclear and other weapons in the wider context of modern warfare. It was decided to respond by examining different issues relating to this subject each year. A report was presented to the 2001 General Assembly on the Arms Trade. This year, we have undertaken a study of the United States proposed National Missile Defence system.

1.3 The General Assembly has been consistent in its opposition to nuclear weapons and, in particular, the Trident Missile System. It is therefore appropriate that the Committee should also express its view on one of the most significant nuclear arms developments of recent years.

2. The Race between the Sword and the Shield

If you look at world history, ever since men began waging war, you will see that there's a permanent race between sword and shield. The sword always wins. The more improvements that are made to the shield, the more improvements are made to the sword. We think that with these [anti-missile] systems, we are just going to spur sword makers to intensify their efforts.[1]

French President Jacques Chirac sums up a fundamental concern about National Missile Defence (NMD), which is that it will lead to an escalation in the nuclear arms race because other countries will seek to enhance their nuclear capabilities in order to circumvent the United States defensive shield. Other concerns about the proposed system include:

- The questionable logic to such a proposal following the terrorist attacks on the United States on 11 September, 2001;
- The decision by the US to withdraw from the 1972 Anti Ballistic Missile Treaty between Russia and America, which has been seen as a cornerstone of

ensuring stability between the nuclear powers, but is now viewed as a Cold War relic by the US;

- The potential to damage the relationships which the United States has with Russia and China;
- The potential of environmental damage caused by installation and operation of the system, particularly with regard to Alaska;
- The possibility of the UK becoming a "sitting target" because of the United States utilising the facilities at RAF Fylingdales as part of the proposed system.
- The question of the morality of spending billions of dollars on a technologically risky system when there are well over a billion people on the planet living in severe poverty.

3.   What is NMD?

3.1   The primary function of the proposed NMD system is the defence of US territory against a threat of a limited strategic ballistic missile attack by a "rogue" state. The system is also intended to provide some capability against a small accidental or unauthorised launch of ballistic missiles by other states with nuclear weapons. The latter particularly applies to Russia and the Ukraine in view of the deteriorating condition of their nuclear arsenals. The US insists that the system is not intended to protect against Russia and China and that Moscow should recognise that it also faces threats from rogue states.

3.2   The proposals comprise radar and satellite systems optimised to detect and track a missile attack, ground-based interceptor missiles designed to destroy warheads by colliding with them as they fly through space at huge speeds so that both will completely disintegrate on impact. It also includes supporting battle management, command, control and communications facilities on the ground to co-ordinate the operation of the defence. It is envisaged that the system will be deployed in three main stages by 2011 and the total cost has been estimated at $60 billion. The tests which have taken place to date have demonstrated that the technological hurdles to be overcome are considerable. Five tests of a planned nineteen have taken place (at a cost of £71 million each) in which two were successful, two failed and another was

only a partial success. Even the tests which are deemed to be successful have taken place in very strict conditions, with one being postponed due to poor weather.

3.3   It should be emphasised that the term "Son of Star Wars" in regard to the proposals is misleading. At present, the proposed system is much less extensive and does not envisage putting defensive weapons into space.

4.   An Assessment of the Threats

4.1   On 7 July 2000, the American Federation of Scientists wrote to President Bill Clinton urging him not to deploy the NMD system. They stated, "North Korea has taken dramatic steps towards reconciliation with South Korea. Other dangerous states will arise. But what would such a state gain by attacking the United States except its own destruction?" There are many others who argue that the perceived threat from rogue states is unrealistic and that what really lies behind the proposed system is a defence against Russia and China. Many experts also believe that the policy is being driven, not by objective strategic assessment, but by political and commercial interests. A National Intelligence Estimate Report, issued by the CIA, insists however that:

Emerging ballistic missile states continue to increase the range, reliability, and accuracy of the missile systems in their inventories - posing ever greater risks to US forces, interests, and allies throughout the world. Proliferation of ballistic missile-related technologies, materials, and expertise - especially by Russian, Chinese, and North Korean entities - has enabled emerging missile states to accelerate missile development, acquire new capabilities, and potentially develop even more capable and longer range future systems.[2]

4.2   Iran, North Korea and Iraq are the three main "rogue states" which the US views as potential threats.[3]

4.3   North Korea has hundreds of No Dong and Scud missiles and continues to develop the longer range Taepo Dong-2, which will enable the North to target the United States. In May 2001, however, President Kim Chong-il unilaterally extended the North's voluntary flight-test moratorium until 2003, provided negotiations with the United States proceeded.

4.4 Iran is a party to the Nuclear Non-Proliferation Treaty and has not been proven to have contravened the terms of the treaty, despite suspicions about its civil nuclear programme (which benefits from Russian assistance). It is also party to the Chemical Weapons Convention and to the Biological and Toxin Weapons Convention although, again, there are strong suspicions that Iran may possess illegal stocks of chemical weapons. The US intelligence agencies agree that Tehran "does not yet have a nuclear weapon . . . [but] could have one by the end of the decade".[4]

4.5 Iraq has used ballistic missiles against Iran, Israel and Saudi Arabia. It has initiated two major wars in the Middle East during the past twenty years, it has broken the terms of the Nuclear Non-Proliferation Treaty to which it is a State Party, and it has refused to comply with consequent UN Security Council Resolutions. Some US intelligence agencies believe that President Saddam Hussein "could test different ICBM concepts before 2015 if UN prohibitions were eliminated in the next few years."[5]

4.6 Most experts believe that the threat from these states is low. However, even if the risk was high, we do not believe that a missile defence system is the right answer. One alternative means of action would be to improve diplomatic relations with so-called rogue states because isolating these countries tends to enhance their pariah status and can therefore be counterproductive. Examples of a diplomatic approach include the attempt by President Clinton to open a dialogue with North Korea. The European Union has now restored diplomatic ties with Iran, with the UK's Foreign Secretary undertaking a controversial visit there.

5. 11 September 2001

5.1 The events of September 11 have caused many to question whether NMD makes any sense in a world in which terrorists can hijack planes and use them as weapons to kill thousands of innocent people. The CIA appears to be moving toward the view that the US is more likely to suffer a nuclear, chemical or biological attack from terrorists using ships, trucks or aeroplanes than one by a foreign country using long-range missiles. According to the *Washington Post*, "the new estimate could affect the debate over the Bush administration's $8 billion increase this year in spending on missile defence research to meet what it has argued is the growing threat of an intercontinental ballistic missile attack from North Korea, Iran, Iraq or other "rogue" states."[6] This is a significant development, which has arisen as a direct result of the events of September 11.

5.2 It would appear that the Bush Administration is still determined to continue with the programme and that the events of September 11 have even caused Democrats to back away from opposing NMD in the interests of national unity. The argument being put forward is that the September 11 attacks demonstrated the ruthlessness and expertise of terrorists supported by rogue states, and so the US has to be prepared for every conceivable threat. However, it is highly unlikely that a terrorist organisation could achieve the technology or finances required to launch a missile attack and even if they could, they have shown that there are much easier and less expensive ways of creating terror.

5.3 Joe Volk, Executive Secretary of a US Quaker lobby group, sums up the situation well when he writes, "Do the attacks [of September 11] signal the need to move more quickly to develop a working shield, or does the catastrophe of September 11 make missile defence a gold-plated Maginot Line in the sky which terrorists can bypass at will?"[7]

6. The ABM Treaty and Russia and China

6.1 The proposed NMD system fails to comply with the 1972 US-Russian Anti-Ballistic Missile (ABM) Treaty which, among other provisions, commits each party "not to deploy ABM systems for a defence of the territory of its country". In May 2000, the 187 members of the Non-Proliferation Treaty, including both the US and Russia, issued a statement reiterating the necessity of "preserving and strengthening the ABM Treaty as a cornerstone of strategic stability." The Clinton Administration argued that the best way to preserve and strengthen the treaty was to modify it to permit NMD deployment. However, the Bush administration has now made it clear that it intends to withdraw from the treaty altogether.

6.2 In an Adjournment Debate on NMD in the House of Commons on 17 May 2000, Mike Gapes MP (a member of the Defence Select Committee) argued that amending Article I of the ABM Treaty (which forbids the deployment of missile defence to defend the territory of a country) "would break the very principle on which the treaty is based". Saying that US plans were "fundamentally at odds with the entire purpose of the treaty", Gapes suggested that if the treaty was amended "to permit rather than prohibit national missile defence ... at some point it will cease to be an arms control treaty; it will become an arms expansion treaty".[8] In response, Keith Vaz, who was then Minister of State at the Foreign Office, said, "We have stressed consistently at the highest level that if the US decides to proceed with the deployment of a national missile defence system, we strongly hope that it will be in a context of agreement with Russia. We have made clear to both sides the importance that we continue to attach to the ABM treaty, and our wish to see it preserved. Neither we nor the United States are about to give our long-standing policy of deterrence." [9] The Convener of the All Party Group on Global Security and Non-Proliferation, Malcolm Savidge MP, warned , "Not only may it [NMD] not reduce danger - it could increase danger. If the ABM Treaty is torn up, both Russia and China are likely to increase their weapons. It could also destroy reliance on all other treaties."[10]

6.3 Russia and China, as the world's other main nuclear powers, are deeply concerned about the plans for NMD because it runs the risk of creating a fundamental imbalance between the nuclear powers, with the US having a military advantage over the rest.

6.4 In July 2000, China's President Jiang Zemin and Russia's President Vladimir Putin, issued a joint statement:

The nature of the [American missile defence] plan is to seek unilateral military and security advantages. Implementing this plan will have the most grave adverse consequences not only for the security of Russia, China and other countries, but also for the security of the United States and global strategic stability. . . . Therefore China and Russia are firmly opposed to such a system.

6.5 Russian concerns were tempered by the proposal, agreed by Presidents George Bush and Vladimir Putin during the latter's visit to the US in November 2001, that sweeping cuts would be made in nuclear arsenals. Mr Bush said the US would cut back over the next ten years from its current total of some 7,000 warheads to about 2,000. Mr Putin said that if the US were to do this, Russia would follow suit, cutting down from some 6,000 to about 1,500. However, these plans have now been thrown into jeopardy with the decision by the US to put some of its nuclear weapons into storage rather than destroy them. It has said it needed to keep weapons in reserve in case of "unforeseen international events". If the Americans are not scrapping the warheads, the Russian military may see unilateral destruction of their nuclear weapons as a sign of weakness. This is therefore a deplorable move by the US in regard to the general issue of nuclear disarmament, as well as specifically in relation to Missile Defence.

6.6 The first step in the Bush administration's missile defence system is the building of a small missile site at Fort Greely, in central Alaska near Fairbanks. Most arms control experts believe that pouring concrete for the five missiles required there will be the point at which the US breaks the ABM Treaty. Clearing of trees has already begun at the Alaskan site.

7. The Environmental Impact

7.1 A coalition of environmental groups in the United States took legal action last August to delay preliminary work on NMD on the grounds that the US Defence

Department has not completed the necessary environmental impact statement for the sites involved. The case brought by six Alaska-based groups claimed that the department failed to complete the federally required environmental impact statement for building facilities at Fort Greely, near Fairbanks, Alaska, and other planned sites in Alaska, Hawaii and the Marshall Islands. The Pentagon responded by saying that environmental impact studies had been carried out under the Clinton administration, when it was considering a plan to place 100 missile interceptors at Fort Greely. Environmental groups stated that the US military had already left a toxic and radioactive legacy at Fort Greely and throughout Alaska, endangering workers and the public and that the military should concentrate on cleaning up their messes rather than creating new ones.

7.2 The building of the facilities required for National Missile Defence will inevitably impact on the local environment wherever sites are situated. The Pentagon, under the Clinton administration, undertook a Draft Environmental Impact Study reviewing the "potential impacts of deployment and operation of the land-based NMD system" at the proposed US X-band radar site. This huge study shows the proposed X-band radar, similar to the one that could be deployed at RAF Fylingdales in the UK, encompassing an area of approximately seven hectares (17 acres). The site would require a complex of security structures, as well as the establishment of an airspace blackout zone of about 6.7 kilometres (4.2 miles) around the radar unit, to protect pilots from potential electromagnetic interference hazards. Other steps would be required to prevent local exposure to electromagnetic radiation.

8. The UK Government's position

8.1 While other European governments have been clear in their opposition to NMD, the British Government's position has been more ambivalent. Ministers, anxious to avoid offending their key ally, have been sticking closely to the line that "it is for the United States to decide whether or not to proceed with deployment", but backbench MPs from all sides of the House of Commons have expressed concern both about the possible impact of NMD on international stability and security and about the Government's unwillingness to adopt a more outspoken stance.

8.2 On 25 July 2000, the Foreign Affairs Select Committee issued its report on Weapons of Mass Destruction, which included a section on NMD. It recommended that, "the Government articulate the very strong concerns that have been expressed about NMD within the UK. We are not convinced that the US plans to deploy NMD represent an appropriate response to the proliferation problems faced by the international community. We recommend that the Government encourage the USA to seek other ways of reducing the threats it perceives."[11] The Committee also called for "the Government, as one of the five nuclear weapon states and as a close ally of the US, to make an early public statement on its analysis of NMD's likely impact on strategic stability and its assessment of whether this would be in the overall security interests of this country."[12]

8.3 On 24 October 2001, the Prime Minister stated in the House of Commons:

I do not agree with those who are opposed to [NMD]. During the summit with President Bush in February, we made it clear that we were prepared to look at defensive as well as offensive systems. We have not as yet, however, had a specific proposal from the United States. I think that it is better to declare our position finally when we do have such a proposal. I take this opportunity of welcoming greatly the dialogue between Russia and the United States, which I think offers a way forward for the future.[13]

8.4 The UK Government has repeatedly refused to be drawn on its stance on the ABM Treaty. Its position is set out in a joint memorandum from the Ministry of Defence and the Foreign Office which states, "As with any other international treaty, the interpretation of the ABM Treaty is a matter for the parties. It is not for non-parties, such as the United Kingdom, to offer their own interpretations of its provisions." Although the

Government wishes to see the ABM Treaty "preserved", the Joint Memorandum highlights the fact that since 1972, the US and Russia have reached "other agreements which have had the effect of modifying or further clarifying the Treaty's provisions". It also notes that Article XV "gives each party the right to withdraw from the treaty 'if it decides that extraordinary events related to the subject matter of this Treaty have jeopardized its supreme interests.'"

9. The Fylingdales dilemma

9.1 The Government has so far been careful to avoid stating whether they will approve the controversial integration of RAF Fylingdales into a possible NMD system. Concern is mounting in Westminster that the inclusion of the facility will make the UK a "sitting target" and that the Yorkshire base may attract protest on a scale not seen since Greenham Common in the 1980s. As the Foreign Affairs Committee notes, in the event of a unilateral US withdrawal from the ABM Treaty, the position of Fylingdales and also the Menwith Hill base would present the Government with "an acute dilemma", as a UK refusal "would have profound consequences for UK/US relations".[14]

9.2 If the UK Government does agree to the US use of Fylingdales for the NMD system, then it would be party to the breaking of the ABM Treaty. Article IX of the Treaty prohibits deploying ABM components in other countries. The UK Government has to face up to the dilemma of co-operating in a system which breaks an international arms treaty and is opposed by other European states, while not wishing to take the unprecedented step of refusing assistance to its closest ally. The impression from the Bush administration to date has been a lack of understanding of this dilemma and an expectation that the UK will follow past precedent and fully co-operate.

10. Conclusions

10.1 The US policy of deploying a National Missile Defence system is fundamentally wrong and presents a serious threat to world peace. There are considerable doubts as to whether it will ever be technologically effective. It will almost certainly herald the end of the 1972 Anti Ballistic Missile Treaty. It has the potential to encourage other nations to enhance their nuclear capability in order to respond to what will be perceived to be America's improved defence capability.

10.2 While the UK Government's position has remained unclear, it is likely that it will support NMD by allowing the US to utilise the Fylingdales and Menwith Hill facilities. The fact that the UK is unlikely to benefit from NMD makes the Government's stance even more extraordinary. The UK will become a "sitting target", be party to the breaking of an international arms treaty and contribute to a probable escalation in the arms race.

10.3 A large number of defence experts, The American Federation of Scientists, many European governments, Russia and China, many UK Members of Parliament and (prior to September 11) many Democrats in the United States, have all expressed strong reservations or complete opposition to National Missile Defence. Despite this, the Bush Administration seems determined to go ahead.

10.4 The spending of $60 billion by one nation in order to protect itself against unlikely threats using technology which may not actually work, is morally indefensible. Rather than seeking this dubious form of defence against a remote threat, the United States should be putting far more resources into nuclear arms reduction and the prevention of rogue states obtaining nuclear weapons in the first place. The ultimate solution against the threat of a ballistic missile attack is the elimination of nuclear weapons and the arms trade in general. This may seem impossible, but there is little hope of beginning to go down this road when the US has a policy of implementing NMD, which has the potential actually to increase the number of nuclear weapons in the world.

10.5 A major flaw in the thinking behind NMD is that it assesses security by the military supremacy of one nation over others. For the United States, as the most powerful nation in the world, a major threat is uncertainty. Since equality implies uncertainty, the task is to maintain supremacy at all costs, which simply creates greater insecurity for the international community.

10.6 The Church of Scotland's consistent stance against nuclear weapons must lead it to call on the United States not to implement the NMD system. The human race must seek to resolve disputes peacefully and it must ultimately rid itself of all weapons of mass destruction. NMD is a backward step which can only make our world an even more dangerous place. In the interests of world peace and security, it should not go ahead.

---

[1] *New York Times*, 17 December 2000;

[2] National Intelligence Estimate: *Foreign Missile Developments and the Ballistic Missile Threat, Through 2015*, section 3, 10 January 2002;

[3] Ibid;

[4] Ibid, section 9;

[5] Ibid;

[6] *Washington Post*, 10 January 2002;

[7] Quakers' Publication, *New Agenda for Defence No: 5*, October 2001.

[8] Hansard, 17 May 2000: Column 106WH.

[9] Hansard, 17 May 2000: Column 110WH.

[10] Hansard, 7 June 2000: Column 378

[11] Select Committee on Foreign Affairs Eighth Report, Weapons of Mass Destruction

[12] Ibid

[13] Hansard, 24 October 2001: Column 273

[14] Ibid

In the name of and by the authority of the Committee

ALAN D. McDONALD, *Convener*
MORAG ROSS, *Vice-Convener*
DAVID SINCLAIR, *Secretary*

PANEL ON DOCTRINE

MAY 2002

PROPOSED DELIVERANCE

The General Assembly:

1. Receive the Report.

2. Welcome the Panel's reflection on *The Nature and Purpose of the Church* in relation to emerging patterns of mission and outreach in urban priority areas.

3. Note the Panel's intention to produce a statement on the Doctrine of Baptism.

4. Note the Panel's intention to produce a report on the nature of Church membership.

REPORT

The Nature and Purpose of the Church

1. THE PURPOSE OF THE STUDY

One of the responsibilities of the Panel is to be available for consultation by other Boards and Committees of the General Assembly. During 1999, two approaches received seemed to overlap. One, from the Committee on Ecumenical Relations, was an invitation to participate with others in the forming of a Church of Scotland response to the World Council of Churches' recent Faith and Order paper (no.181) on *The Nature and Purpose of the Church*. The other was from the Priority Areas Fund (now part of the Scottish Churches Community Trust) which, working under the Board of National Mission, had enabled the establishment of a variety of projects within local communities[1] and whose officers believed that something could be learned from these projects for the benefit of the Church in general concerning future patterns of witness and service.

The Panel decided that it could be instructive to bring these two "statements" into dialogue with each other. The Faith and Order paper, itself a staging post on the way to an agreed common statement, sought an understanding of the Church by listening to the experience and reflection upon it of different world churches. On the other hand, the Priority Areas Fund projects could be seen as being in themselves individual statements of belief as to how the Church should embody the Gospel in the present day. Both were at the cutting edge of current reflection and practice. Would they agree with each other, and thus offer an unmistakable way ahead in a time of uncertainty for the Church? Would they contradict each other, and thus reveal a confusion in the Church's thinking about its future? At any rate, it was hoped that they would shed light on each other and thus lead to deeper understandings of the directions in which God was calling his people.

The projects enabled by the Fund were wide ranging, geographically as well as in structure and goal. From the "street level" youth project in the Central Belt to a children's ecumenical initiative on a northern island, from a knitting co-operative amongst destitute mothers and children in Harare to a breakfast club for children in an urban priority area in an eastern Scottish city, support and seed money has been provided for local church and people to identify and respond to the most pressing needs in their particular community. Many of these are ecumenical, or become so.

A working group from the Panel, therefore, was set up to describe and attempt to analyse the patterns that were

---

[1] The earliest of these were described in *Good News for a Change* (Boards of National Mission, Social Responsibility, World Mission, 1998).

emerging as local churches responded to the challenges and opportunities which were characteristic of the districts in which they worked, and to study the WCC document in that lively context. The group felt it important not to intrude upon the projects or disturb them in any way, and help was sought from the Fund's staff in preventing this. It was also deemed important to try and understand the situation as it was seen by the participants and not allow our expectations to distort our perceptions. Five out of the many possible projects were chosen: a rent deposit scheme, a support network for families in which there was drug abuse, a drama initiative for young people, a community flat in an "unchurched" area, and a community-building project. Members of the working group would "adopt" one project and over a period build up their appreciation of what was taking place in it and through it. With other members of the group, they would reflect on theological themes which were suggested as the project developed, explicit or implicit.

The Panel is grateful to members of the working party, two of whom gave their time generously in spite of not being members of the Panel: the Rev. Ian Barcroft of St. Mary's Episcopal Church in Hamilton and the Rev. John Harvey. In the closing stages, the group had the benefit of consulting with the Rev. Kathy Galloway, who had recently been engaged in a similar theological reflection. Gratitude is due in particular to a number of people involved in the planning and pursuit of the projects who welcomed the members of the working party and willingly discussed with them aims and outcomes.

2.   THE PROJECTS

The criteria which resulted in the selection of the five projects were that such initiatives should have been established long enough for emerging patterns to be detectable, and that they should together represent the variety of project assisted by the Fund. It had been intended that one of the projects selected should be a rural one, situated away from the Central Belt, but for various reasons this could not be followed up in the same way as the others. The projects in question are now briefly summarised. Further information and reflection is included in later sections of the report. The use of the past tense does not mean that these initiatives are now over but indicates that a particular period in their history was being observed.

2.1 The West End Churches Key Fund (Glasgow)

The Woodlands area of Central Glasgow is bounded by St. George's Road, Woodlands Road, the River Kelvin, and the Great Western Road. The area has changed socially and physically in the last thirty years as large dwellings were converted into multiple occupancy flats to provide housing for a numerous transient population. Two thirds of the area is populated by young professional people and students with an average age of under forty, and one third of the area has the second largest group of ethnic minority communities in Glasgow. Young families have particular difficulty in finding affordable and suitable accommodation.

The proposal for this project arose from the observation that many people were held back by not having the deposit invariably required by landlords when wishing to rent a property. If this initial hurdle could be removed, so much else could follow as families and single people, independent and more in control of their own lives, became established and secure. The aim was not just the funding of deposits but to help with start-up furnishings and provide ongoing support for people moving off the streets into a permanent home.

Quite early on in the history of this initiative, as contacts developed with professional bodies and with other interested parties, the base broadened considerably to include such groups as the Simon Community, Barnardo's and the YMCA. The Scottish Executive became involved as the greater potential of the scheme became obvious and additional sources of funding were sought. As the project expanded, those who participated found that new skills were required – in financial management, in the handling of interpersonal relations, in the matter of employing personnel. In time, the staff grew to include a project manager, two development workers, and a finance worker.

The churches welcomed this broadening of the base of the scheme but found their own role changing. From being a "major player" in the initial stages, with the increasing involvement of professionals, church representatives found themselves being channeled towards the "human" side of the enterprise and given a "befriending" role towards beneficiaries of the scheme.

2.2 The Abigail Project (Possilpark, Glasgow).

Possilpark lies on the north side of Glasgow, a mixture of century-old tenements, inter-war council property and thirty-year-old high-rise flats. It is often described as an area of multiple deprivation, but a wide-ranging regeneration programme is now under way. The project was initiated by Possilpark Parish Church to support young drug users and their families. It centred round a café/drop-in centre and an evening support group, run by a group of women who had first hand experience of the problems which could arise from the abuse of drugs. The fact that these leaders were local and non-professional, working from within, was a significant factor. The café acted as a safe haven in that it was understood that members of the police force could not enter to make an arrest. At the same time, drug dealing and drug taking in the café were outlawed. An unexpected bonus was that members of the public who had come to use the café (tradespeople working in the area, for example) mixed well with those whom they had regarded as "druggies", and people were learning to relate to each other.

In the Constitution of the project, reference is made to the local Kirk Session, which supplied the premises in the church complex free. Their willingness to do this arose from their understanding that the women were able to do what they could not directly do themselves. While not being members of the church, the leaders welcomed the participation of the Session, seeing this as in effect protecting them from any outside manipulation or interference. Members of the congregation helped with supplies for the café, such as home baking. The local deacon had played a large part in the establishing and support of the project. The importance of the church's supportive role was proven by the way that, on the departure of minister and deacon together to another charge, the pressure from drug dealers on the volunteers increased sufficiently to cause the closure of the café, although the evening support group continued to meet.

2.3 The Star Project (Paisley)

The area generally referred to as the "north end" of Paisley combines the three districts known as Shortroods, Mossvale and Gockston. Originally providing the homes for thread mill workers and later for workers in the car industry, the housing stock is both pre- and post-war, much of which is currently being demolished, with the inevitable effect on the landscape. There are few local shops, and only one community hall. There are two good primary schools, but the secondary school is shortly to be closed. Now with unemployment high and facilities limited, plans are being laid for the much needed regeneration of the district.

The initiative in question was taken as the result of the Presbytery's request to the two congregations of St. James' and Wallneuk North to work together in the area, which was distanced from both churches. A joint service was established but attracted mainly people from the congregations rather than from the immediate community. This prompted the ministers involved to make their own survey of the district, which they found to be an area in which there was considerable community-building activity but one also in which there were many problems. A function of the church could be to offer support for the activists as well as for those experiencing problems. Rather than try to establish an institutional presence, it was decided to find a form which allowed maximum identification with the place and its people. The idea of a community flat was proposed and accepted, a deacon was given oversight, working in association with two Roman Catholic sisters.

The project began in 1998, with two adjacent ground floor flats being secured in 1999. The project was managed by a committee made up of representatives from the local churches and from the community. A training programme was developed through the Scottish Churches Open College and the Scottish Qualifications Authority. In time, facilities included an advice centre, a meeting room, a payphone, toilets, a quiet room, a drop-in café, and a playroom. The aim of the project was stated as being "to provide services and facilities in accordance with the identified needs of the residents of the North End of Paisley, thus promoting education, social welfare, religious awareness and an enhanced quality of life".

2.4 The Colston Milton Drama Project (Colston, Glasgow)

Milton is a post war housing scheme, situated on the north side of Glasgow, typical of many in the city with all the associated social and economic problems. The project had a threefold base: in Colston Milton Church of Scotland, St. Andrew's Methodist Church and the local community itself. The focus was on young people, both in existing organisations (the Church of Scotland had Girls' and Boys' Brigade companies) and at large, with the worker contributing to and supporting individual groups as well as promoting co-operative ventures.

The worker appointed was trained in drama and dance, and these media were used in the "Wanderers" youth club to explore issues such as drug use. In these settings, preparations were also made for the staging of musicals, of which three in total were produced: *Joseph and his Amazing Technicolour Dreamcoat*, *Godspell* and a new work from a Methodist source designed to encourage church and community groups to work together, *Hopes and Dreams*. These musicals both helped build confidence and identify talent in the participants, one of whom now works through drama with disadvantaged children, as well as to raise the profile of the churches. Many participants had had no church connection but some as a result were to be found more "round the church".

The project led to the establishment of a church youth club and youth fellowship, but a shortage of people with the necessary combination of confidence and experience has meant that these have not continued. However, a fourth musical is now planned, which is likely to bring together those who had participated in the others. The local churches have accepted that, because of the nature of urban priority areas, short term projects and programmes are an appropriate way to proceed. It is not always possible to make firm future plans and the best solution is to make the most of what is currently running and working.

2.5 The Ripple Project (Restalrig and Lochend, Edinburgh)

The parish of St. Margaret's in Edinburgh is set in an urban priority area made up almost entirely of a mix of council housing totalling 4,000 units, with now only 1,950 units in council ownership. These range from cottages to (four) tower blocks. Most of this is Wheatley Act housing, begun in 1925 and finished, in the main, about 1938, with some post-war housing. The parish has a population of around 8,000 in the area of a square mile, has the second lowest car ownership and the highest number of single households where the occupant is sixty-five plus in Edinburgh. Male unemployment runs at about 7% in a city where the average is less than 2%. Over 300 households need home help care, most receiving more than three hours per day.

The Ripple Project was inaugurated in 1996. The purpose was "to improve the quality of life for all sections of the community by providing a range of services and support which help people help themselves". It began with *The Information Place*, intended to make people aware of where support might be found in problems they were experiencing and to assist users to access such support. While this was no longer part of the portfolio, what was seen as the crucial function of providing information about facilities and services, welfare and legal rights, and the giving of help in communicating with statutory agencies and local government, was carried on in the context of other projects. A community newspaper was also planned, with the aim of assisting in the development of a greater sense of community in the district.

The project grew to embrace some dozen initiatives, which together provided "wrap round" care for all age groups. In addition to groups for children, young people, the elderly etc., an interesting initiative was the surgery project, where volunteers staffed a room in the local surgery during hours, offering a listening ear for users. Doctors, as part of the treatment given, "referred" patients to this facility. Elsewhere, *The Listening Place* provided a similar confidential listening service, where users were offered up to six hour-long sessions per week. A *Referral Group* offered support for children with behavioural problems. There was strong involvement on the part of the local churches. The project was launched at morning worship in St. Margaret's, as was each new initiative thereafter.

3. QUESTIONS FROM THE DOCUMENT TO THE CHURCH

The Faith and Order document which was the group's companion during the study of these five projects is divided into six sections: I The Church of the Triune God, II The Church in History, III The Church as *Koinonia*, IV Life in Communion, V Service in and for the World, VI Following our Calling: From Converging Understandings to Mutual Recognition. The exercise which follows could have been applied to all six sections but, for reasons of space, a selection has been made from those most germane to the matter in hand. The main thrust of sections I, III, and IV is now recalled, with the addition, in italics, of corresponding challenges which might be put to the Church in Scotland today. Later, the projects under discussion will be examined for the challenges they, for their part, might be interpreted as making, with cross references.

3.1 "The Church of the Triune God"

3.1.1 The Church is the creation of God's Word and Holy Spirit. It cannot exist by and for itself.

Do we have the sense of being brought into being and sustained by God rather than by our own planning? How open are we to being re-created by an agency other than our own?

3.1.2 It is not primarily the sum of individual believers in communion with each other but their common partaking in God's own life, a divine and human reality.

Do we act, in worship, governing, serving as if we were merely individuals who have to find the way of working which suits us best? How do we attain to a lively appreciation of sharing in the life of God and of allowing that to pervade the human dimension?

3.1.3 We are the PEOPLE OF GOD, a prophetic sign of the fulfilment God will bring in Christ by the power of the Holy Spirit.

How strong is the sense – and evidence – of gathering others together with us towards such a more complete community?

3.1.4 We are the BODY OF CHRIST, participating by the exercise of the gifts we have been given.

Gifts are discovered and come into play when they are needed most; do we often enough risk circumstances which would demand more of our giftedness?

3.1.5 We are the TEMPLE OF THE HOLY SPIRIT, a driving force which overflows into prayer, love, work, service.

How far do we allow ourselves to be "swept" into action? Or do we rather undertake our tasks as out of Christian duty?

3.1.6 Other images characterise the Church – vine, flock, bridge, wedding party.

Do we give the latter image enough rein? What would happen if we looked on ourselves less as an organisation, more as a group of people on the way to a party?

3.1.7 The purpose of the Church is to gather all creation under the Lordship of Christ; mission belongs to its very being.

Do we tend to want to gather everyone to ourselves rather than gather with others under Christ?

3.1.8 The Church shares in the world's suffering by advocacy, care for the marginalised, critically analysing and exposing unjust structures and working for their transformation.

How can those at the "grass roots" of the Church participate in this rather than "leave it to the professionals" or specialist agencies?

3.2 "The Church as *Koinonia*"

3.2.1 *Koinonia* is a strong concept meaning to "be in contractual relationship involving mutual accountability". This embraces all of creation and all people as it reaches forward to the new community in the new heaven and the new earth.

Does our more common concept of "fellowship" adequately translate this powerful biblical term?

3.2.2 This is only possible by gift.

Do we tend to see the quality of our church life as something achieved rather than given? What difference would it make if we saw it as gift?

3.2.3 Divisions hinder the mission of the Church.

Do we tend to meet more easily in sharing outside the Church than within it?

3.2.4 This communion derives its fullness in part from being in lively touch with those (the saints) who have gone before.

How aware are we of our forebears, national, in our congregation, those who have helped form the wider community in which we live?

3.2.5 Community remains broken as long as we are within history, necessitating repentance, mutual forgiveness, restoration.

Do we sometimes see a livelier expression of this dynamic of repentance, forgiveness and restoration in groups and agencies who come face to face with human life, experience and need rather than in the life of the congregation?

3.2.6 The Gospel has to take flesh authentically in every place.

Do we prefer to establish a uniformity throughout the country, as providing a measure for our effectiveness or success, or even as a convenience for our administration, than to encourage each local church to seek its own best shape even when it looks very different from the norm?

3.2.7 There is a place for legitimate diversity, but when unity becomes uniformity, diversity can become division.

Can we sometimes fear diversity so much that it divides us from each other in the Church, if not the Church from other parts of society?

3.2.8 The local church is fully the Church, but it also is part of the one, holy, catholic and apostolic Church.

Might a fuller awareness of this allow us to embrace fellow Christians from other branches of the Church and help us also to appreciate that people at different "levels" of society also belong together?

3.3 "Life in Communion"

3.3.1 We are to make the apostolic faith relevant and alive in our particular cultural, social, political and religious context, not as a formula but expressed in the living tradition.

How well does the local church know its own context, allowing this to shape and nuance the way it worships and witnesses?

3.3.2 Baptism, in bringing Christians into union with Christ, also places them in solidarity with others in joy and suffering, and thus face to face with Christ who identifies with victim and outcast.

Do we allow generosity towards the poor to become a substitute for engagement with the conditions which marginalise and exclude?

3.3.3 In Holy Communion, whatever distorts human community is challenged and reconciliation is brought within reach.

Do we see and feel our celebrations as having an actual impact on the life of Church and world?

3.3.4 The whole Church are "ministers of the Gospel", in words, in love for each other, in the quality of service to those in need.

Have we limited the opportunities for ministry to certain clerical tasks within the community of the Church rather than embracing the many opportunities for diaconal service in the life of the world?

4. LESSONS FOR A LISTENING CHURCH

How far are these challenges reflected in the projects under study? In pursuing this enquiry, it seemed important to find a method of working that did not allow either projects or document to "lead". Neither should set the agenda for the other. The document having been scrutinised, the projects would be allowed to speak for themselves as themes emerged which were characteristic of the approaches followed. In the correspondences or discordances between document and projects hints of the future shape of the Church might be seen and guidance extracted on the all important and topical question of the prioritisation of resources. What emerged was not a coherent theological *schema*, but a random cluster of concepts. In setting these out below, cross references are made to the previous section (3) to show where there is common ground between the WCC document and the local initiatives.

4.1 Community

The theme which presented itself most immediately was that of *community*. All five projects had as their goal the healing or restoration of human community; where the needs of individuals were targeted, the aim was also that these be restored in their relationship to the community. The West End key fund provided many who were "outside the system" with the means towards acquiring a physical place within the community of home dwellers. The Abigail Project sought to restore the relationships, family and community, disrupted by drug abuse. The Star Project offered through its community flat a symbol of community and had as one of its aims the enhancement of the quality of life of the people of the district. In Colston, as well as other provision, there was an emphasis on developing the artistic skills of young people with the result that they were given value by those amongst whom they lived. In the Ripple project, by being listened to in a disciplined way individuals were reconnected to the care of fellow human beings, channels of communication were cleared and made to run fresh, and lonely people brought together.

The concept of community is particularly close to the Church's understanding of its own nature and purpose, never more so than today when it has been given a high profile in ecumenical discussion. In the WCC document examined above, we have noted the substantial treatment given to *koinonia*, a word usually translated as "community". To appreciate the meaning of *koinonia*, more needs to be done than simply interpret in its biblical context each individual use of the word, for it is a concept which has a rich hinterland of meaning, in both the Old and New Testaments. Behind the Decalogue, for example, is the actual experience of a community called to live in responsible freedom under God. The Gospels themselves are a rich illustration of the meaning of *koinonia*, with their account of the disciples' life with Christ. There, they are shown not only as growing in understanding through their sharing in the life and actions of Jesus but also in being called to account by him and by each other. Further, this was not a community apart but one embedded in the wider community, interacting with its need, its relationships, its religion. In the subsequent history of the Church, it is noteworthy that at times of notable renewal, new forms of community life have often arisen out of the current nature and needs of the human communities in which they were set, their members finding patterns of accountability to God and to each other.

Projects and document both recall the Church to its true nature as standing in judgement and protest against the broken, unequal and uncaring substitutes for community that so often prevail. Human community must be inclusive and not "select out" certain groups of people (3.2.1 above). It is not enough for the Church to address an imagined human community (stereotyped as "sinners", "unbelievers" etc.); the Church's prophetic voice is to be heard in the actual local community in which it is set, which means getting to know and love the place we are in (3.3.1), and being vigilant in identifying those things which distort human community (3.3.3). Our response to our community, however, must not be palliative only. We are to be careful not to adopt policies or programmes which simply prolong injustice and keep people victims (3.3.2).

"Community" in the local church is often translated as "fellowship". The initiatives under study often sat in unwitting judgement on the quality of fellowship in the Church, particularly in the quality of the interaction between project volunteer workers. Their own awareness of the demands of the work could force them to create a "counter community" through which their own balance could be kept and their goals kept fresh. The Abigail volunteers developed this aspect by withdrawing to the MacLeod Centre on Iona and by working at the relationships within the group. Other projects had the same experience, that genuine encounter with others requires repentance and mutual forgiveness (3.2.5).

It is this quality of interaction that Jürgen Moltmann seeks when he writes[2] of the congregation as "a new kind of living together for human beings that affirms:

—that no one is alone with his or her problems,
—that no one has to conceal his or her disabilities,
—that there are not some who have the say and others who have nothing to say,
—that neither the old nor the little ones are isolated,
—that one bears the other even when it is unpleasant and there is no agreement, and
—that, finally, the one can also at times leave the other in peace when the other needs it".

Within the Church we can rightly affirm that our baptism, our celebrations of Holy Communion, and our life together in Christ model and enable true *koinonia* in the face of the breakdown of trust and the absence of peace endemic in life in society. We should not, however, assume that we are the only models. The experience of the projects serves to remind us that there are people who, although not formally within the church, have a vision of what true *koinonia* might mean and in their work and relationships make this real for people. These also can be signs of God's *koinonia* in the world even though they may not satisfy the criteria for belonging to the household of God.

The challenge to the Church is to examine the quality of its fellowship. Are members enabled to be open to each other, able to give mutual account of their attempts to live out the Christian life, willing to share doubts as well as conviction (3.2.1)? Is ours a fellowship in which repentance is true and forgiveness really experienced (3.2.5)? Is there a fear or distrust of those who seem different, or is diversity welcomed as a gift to the Church (3.2.7)? Is our fellowship genuinely open, or is it marred by an exclusiveness which does not readily accept newcomers (3.2.1)? Are we prepared to venture into the "open ground", seeking encounters with wider forms of human community in all their need, perhaps to find

our own community deepened as prayer becomes more urgent, gifts are recognised and used, as members share more with each other – their flaws as well as their strengths (3.2.5)?

4.2 Advocacy

A common strand in the projects studied was the desire to open lines of communication, between residents in a neighbourhood where some were stigmatized, between people in need and the agencies which existed to help them, between whole communities and government, between people in domestic conflict, between body and mind, between church and community. A strong image in the Gospel of St. John is the Holy Spirit as Advocate (chapters 14-16). It is a concept which the *Nature and Purpose* text itself develops when it speaks of the way the church must share in the world's suffering by advocacy, "critically analysing and exposing unjust structures" (3.1.8).

This vigorous role was embraced by more than one of the projects. The Key Fund was placing its support with those who were weakened by their lack of money or possessions. The Abigail project affirmed those who had been labouring under the stigma of drug usage and offered a safe haven. The Ripple project had successfully argued for social inclusion money to be available not just to the bigger areas where it might be more easily administered but to smaller centres of population with equal need. Within its own programme too, there was a strong advocacy component as those who were troubled or felt marginalised were "listened into speech". There were examples also in the Colston Milton project in that the foundation of the work done was not through the building of structures but of relationships. The Wanderers Club was a safe space for young people, where they could be themselves. The arts project gave young people their voice by building confidence and identifying the talent within, thus contributing to their sense of identity.

Here was a question not just of interpretation but also of the redress of the balance of power. Those who could

---

[2]Jürgen Moltmann, *The Open Church* (SCM Press, 1978), p.33.

express themselves easily had greater control; such control could be increased by creating an "officialspeak" which kept people at a distance. The Church had the role of "writing on the sand", being eloquent on behalf of those who were silent, or silenced.

The challenge to the Church is not to fall into the trap of keeping people in their place, or of placing at a distance those who do not conform to certain expectations. It is also to make the effort of imagination necessary to see things through the eyes of those who are differently placed. In acting as their advocates, we do not fear disturbance to the *status quo* and are to be ready to make appropriate challenges to those who hold power and patiently urge that injustices be acknowledged and tackled.

4.3 Spirituality

One of the greatest "growth industries" in our day has been in personal development when philosophies or programmes which promise inner peace and a sense of purpose have flourished. Since a great many people have seemed to find solutions outside its historic provision, the Church has been struggling to make better known its conviction that true spirituality is not about individual fulfilment alone. Not only is it best undertaken along with others, enriched by their insights, but it is also developed in service and love towards others. Self-help and self-fulfilment requires also self-giving and corporate commitment. Nor does the Church define spirituality only in religious terms. The home of the Ripple project was beside the ancient St. Triduana's Well and the image was a reminder that the "living water" of Jesus Christ was not just for the "soul" but for the whole person.

Nor is a person's "spiritual side" solely about prayer and meditation. One of the projects studied related to the arts and their place in assisting people towards a sense of their personal identity, and there have been many other examples of this in Scottish communities in recent decades. A feature of such community arts projects has been a realisation that a gifted person can also contribute to a recreated community. What is more, the discovery has so often been that to be "gifted" – while many more people than is often assumed do have artistic gifts of different kinds – it is not necessarily to be able to play,

sing, paint or act. They may have other kinds of beauty and grace in their characters, even if at the time they are deeply hidden because of the need to cope with adverse circumstances. The *Nature and Purpose* text reminds of the way the Body is given "flesh" in each place through the giftedness of its members. Volunteers in the Abigail project recognised that all were potentially gifted, that the situation was compelling them to draw on these gifts, and that steps would need to be taken to develop them. It is often in extremity that one recognises gifts one did not know one had (3.1.4).

The matter of spirituality did not only arise in relation to the rationale or results of the projects. Of equal interest was what prompted the volunteers who initiated and supported them. It was recognised that people may be responding to profound spiritual values, even if they did not have the language to make these public, or even if they would not be expressed in overtly religious terms.

Reference was made above to the experience that the discovery of personal gifts could lead to a recreated community, but what about a recreated church? A question raised in relation to the Colston Milton project was relevant also to some of the others: how do moments of "spiritual" insight – in preparing for performance, in the deepening of relationships – relate to that gathering of "seekers after spirituality", the public worship of the Church? Many would come through the projects to a respect for the Church, if this was not already present, but the feeling among them seemed often to remain that worship was not "for them", that it was for the "holy ones". They might feel they belonged in the cast of a religious musical but did not feel equally at home in the "strangeness" of Sunday worship.

The challenge to the Church is to enable people to move from the impersonal to the personal, to help members and others develop patterns of prayer, meditation, conduct, study and service which make for growth of spirit. It is to value the rich variety of the giftedness of its people, encouraging individual gifts to be recognised and developed. It is to accept that each person is potentially creative and to nurture this. Such a realisation would add the dimension of gratitude to our experience of being in the Church, where the doggedness of duty might be overtaken by a greater spontaneity, an impulse to respond more creatively to life and faith, similar to the experience of those who participated in the community arts project (3.1.5). In developing such patterns, it will draw on its own traditions but may also find hints and directions in the experience of other religions and cultures. In this way, it will be better prepared to be a resource for the many who seek guidance in these matters today but often do not look to the Church. It will also be more able to recognise and welcome a greater variety of "spiritual" experience in those who cannot as yet recognise themselves as part of the Church.

Recognising also that many of our number are exploring patterns of spirituality but do not find enough connection with public worship, the challenge is to develop the link between the "inner room and the upper room", reviewing our often too crowded and busy services of worship. We also need to design worship whose raw material is the very stuff of ordinary life and which give people insights, experiences and symbols which they can carry away with them into their daily life and prayer, a continual aim of the St. Margaret's congregation who cradled the Ripple Project (3.3.3). People's "own stories" should be acknowledged and related to the narratives of salvation in Scripture and in the lives of the saints and forebears in the faith (3.2.4). The challenge to the Church is also to see itself as a gift given to humanity rather than as human creation which serves its participants, and to welcome new forms, such as emerged during the Star Project, which follow life lived in faith (3.2.2).

4.4 Hospitality

It was noteworthy how many of the projects centred round cafés, lunches or drop-in centres: several of the Ripple projects centred around meals, the Star flat set out to be a "home from home", the Abigail project was focused on a café. This latter project indeed was named after an Old Testament character whose welcoming of strangers in defiance of her husband is seen by many as a model of hospitality. The Abigail centre leaflet speaks of the move from hostility to hospitality, a concept developed by Henri Nouwen when he speaks of reconciliation as being "to convert the *hostis* into a *hospes*, the enemy into a guest and to create the free and fearless space where

brotherhood and sisterhood can be formed and fully experienced". Hospitality is not to change people but to offer them space where change can take place. "It is not to bring men and women over to our side, but to offer freedom not to be disturbed by dividing lines". It is an active and vigorous task – like a patrolman trying to create some space in the middle of a mob of panic-stricken people for an ambulance to reach the centre of an accident.[3] This kind of hospitality gives something up at the same time as it offers. It does not dictate how a person might use one's hospitality ("you sing our hymns and we'll give you our soup"), set parameters, lay the ground rules. The pattern that it takes will be as much dictated by the guests as the hosts.

The dimension of hospitality is by no means only discovered in the obviously hospitable contexts of café or centre. Actions and strategies can be such as "make room" or clear space in ways other than physical. Thus the Kirk Session of Possilpark were seen by the leaders as creating a safe space by their role in the structuring of the project, where the danger of interference was lessened. The role of befriending which was allocated to the church representatives participating in the Key Project was one of hospitality, the hospitality of relationship rather than of place. Ripple offered a hospitable "listening place" to visitors to the surgery and to others who had been walled in by their own fears or external forces.

It is not enough simply to declare oneself hospitable by stating that "all are welcome". It may be necessary to make alterations so that the inaccessible (as seen by those on the outside) can be made accessible. It is difficult for members of the Church to grasp the idea that many see them as being somehow alien, "on another planet", when this is so far from their intention. This is not to say that these others are estranged; they may wish the Church well. Perhaps there is need for interim "places of belonging", common ground where all may meet on an equal basis.

In terms of structural change, although some congregations have made bold experiments, in general the Church holds to certain unalterable practices. Our

---

[3] Henri J.M. Nouwen, *Reaching Out* (Fount, 1986), p.69.

focus is weekly and generally on Sunday morning. Yet it is increasingly common for other duties or pursuits to claim people on that day. Young people may be shackled by homework; men and women may need to work to service the increasing demands on public facilities; young people may seek to keep their place in the teenage market by taking Sunday jobs; football leagues meet on a Sunday morning; leisure pursuits have developed to claim more of the weekend. Need Sunday be the only main focus of Church life? Might a six week rather than a weekly cycle be tried? Might energies be channeled to a large scale weekend event once in a while? Might Saturday evening have more possibilities for some?

The challenge to the Church is to work to create hospitable space so that imprisoned people are given freedom in their lives, and to do so "without strings". But the challenge is also to create a genuinely open Church so that those in the process of finding their freedom may also be enabled to encounter the Son's freedom "which is freedom indeed" (John 8:36). The idea of hospitality is at the very heart of the Gospel, just as the eucharistic meal is at the heart of the Church's life. The meal provides the most vivid image, also, of humanity and creation fulfilled in complete community with God, that of the "banquet of rich fare for all the peoples" (Isaiah 25, REB). There is a challenge here for a Church which limits points of access to its life, and to the faith of which it is custodian. The "open church" will be one which considers those not of its number as potential partners and feel incomplete as long as this goes unrealised. It will also be challenged to discover what it means to be not "the sum of individual believers in communion with each other" but to have a lively appreciation of sharing in the hospitable life of God (3.1.2), to be a people "on the way to a party" (3.1.6).

4.5 Service

In a previous Report, the Panel noted how proclamation and service were not only at the heart of the Gospel but were inextricable each from the other.[4] *Diakonia* is of the very being of the church rather than an implication or outcome of the life of faith. The *Nature and Purpose* document speaks of baptism as inevitably placing us, with Christ, alongside those experiencing any lack or adversity (3.3.2). In *Diakonia: Reinterpreting the Ancient Sources*

(Oxford, 1990), John Collins attacks a stereotype of Christian service when he writes:

> In the world in which the early church lived, *diakonia* seems to have referred to the service of a "go-between" or agent who carries out activities for another. In the letters of Paul, it also appears that *diakonia* is used to describe Paul and some of his associates as the "go-between" who carries the gospel from God or Christ to those who are to hear the message of salvation. *Diakonia* seems more concerned with apostleship than with our present understanding of the diaconate.[5]

This theme was one of the most obvious to emerge from our study, and prompted the question as to how far these initiatives should be seen as of the essence of local Church life and how far they were "additional" to it. We noted the prevalence of the "project culture" which can grow up in the churches where service is given "in parallel" with the church structures. Great generosity of mind and purse can be shown, but this can be a substitute for allowing this diaconal ministry to arise from and to feed back into the life of the Church (3.3.2). Without being specific, since we are dealing here with projects that are developing all the time, we found that the closeness of project to local church varied.

It is often the case, speaking generally, that tensions can arise between the "home church" and an initiative of community service or outreach. One approach may see the community as having the problems while the Church has the answers. Another approach may vigorously, and effectively, address the symptoms of breakdown but fail to tackle the causes. Another church may engage in a critique of the causes of the problem and become so closely involved with those it seeks to serve that it finds itself at loggerheads with its own networks. From the perspective of the community, the church can be looked upon as mere do-gooders or as people with an ulterior

---

[4] *General Assembly 2000*, 13/14.

[5] Quoted in *The Diaconate as Ecumenical Opportunity* (the 'Hanover Report' of the Anglican-Lutheran International Commission, 1996), p.7.

motive, which was the experience of the churches involved in the Key Fund at first.

A continual pitfall for the diaconal Church is to lay down conditions for the service it offers, not just in how far it is prepared to go but what sort of activities and initiatives represent the sort of service a church might be expected to engage in. There is the great temptation to tread well worn paths, feeling more secure with patterns of service which have become established, happy with initiatives which deliver "church-assured things".

The challenge to the church is to be open to being led by Christ the Servant into tasks and areas of activity which are not necessarily part of our "repertory". Being able to hear where we are being led means being sensitive to the context in which we are placed (3.3.1). We will not be satisfied with a survey or a cursory analysis or with the gathering of statistics. There will be a need for "active listening", involving patience, courage and cost. The challenge is also to question our habit of seeing ministry as a series of clerical tasks and to value equally the ministry whose starting point is diaconal (3.3.4).

4.6 Proclamation

How far were these projects "message bearers"? Where there was suspicion on the part of "receivers", found to be the case in at least one situation (the Key Fund), the church initiators realised that they would have to disarm before they could deliver. In the case of the Abigail project, the support of the Kirk Session and the form it took was welcomed and valued; realising that the leaders were in a position that they themselves could not be, the Session saw them as "acting in their place"; in turn the project appreciated the security from other outside interference that this gave them; the message in this case was eloquent. It is often assumed that the effectiveness of such projects should be measured by how many of those helped "came to church". It was the Ripple project's experience, however, that it was those who became involved as volunteers that were more likely to become part of the church. In what they had been asked to do they had seen a version of the Church that seemed to have a point and a place, and they wished to be associated with it.

The matter of how much is said and how much "merely" done is a sensitive one. There is a temptation not to leave the Gospel to find its own way. There is also the perennial anxiety about building up the Church and increasing its operational numbers. The Church does not always realise the effect that its evangelisation can have. The Panel is very aware that even in engaging in the present exercise there was a risk of "speaking over" those with whom we had been meeting. It sought to learn from another group which visited one of the projects and subsequently (and rightly) used biblical "tools" to achieve closer understanding of the significance of what was happening. Those who worked locally, however, felt "removed" from the resulting analysis.

Steven G. Mackie, in analysing contemporary approaches to mission, has identified three (with sometimes more than one operating together). The "Church for others" approach in which "the world provides the agenda" was derived from a dynamic view of the Church and shared an activist strategy. The "Church and Kingdom" approach was one in which the Church remained "intact" as it were and provided for individual Christians the security, fellowship and spiritual resources to participate in the work of the Kingdom. Finally, the "Christian presence" model saw the world as an alien milieu where Christ is present; the Church's task was to be with him and point to him through practical deeds, personal obedience, silent testimony and dialogue as much as through verbal proclamation.[F]

The challenge to the Church is to examine its approach to proclamation. It has to ask how far it derives from patterns which once served well but are not so applicable today. Are the opportunities being offered today being taken? How well does the local church know those with whom it wishes to share the Gospel (3.3.1)? How much does it love them? The challenge also is to face any guilt we may have over not working hard enough at the missionary task, as a Church and as individual Christians. Have we allowed this guilt to affect our practice? What this report is not suggesting is that the Church should not proclaim. This is of its very being. There should be no embarrassment at inviting people to become of our number. We are happy to say, "This is who we are". We also say, "It matters to us who you are".

[F]Paper to Committee of Forty

PROPOSED DELIVERANCE

The General Assembly:

1. Receive the Report.
2. Welcome the Panel's willingness to be invited by Presbyteries and congregations to give assistance in the development of worship.
3. Welcome the intended provision of printed material to give guidance in the planning of worship for all ages.
4. Receive the Report of the Church Hymnary Trustees.

REPORT

1. All-age worship

The General Assembly of 1994 asked the Panel to "examine the merits of all-age worship, and report on its findings to the next General Assembly". The following year, it was reported that work was in progress and in 1996, in the hope of addressing more particularly the needs of the Church, the Assembly invited members, Kirk Sessions and Presbyteries to communicate with the Panel by the end of that year. Many helpful submissions were received, indicating considerable exploration in this area. The same Assembly added another task, which the Panel saw as closely associated with the original remit: namely, "in response to the rediscovery [of] and interest in storytelling, to give guidance in its usage in services of worship and to provide the Church with the resources and skills to develop this form of communication". All are now aware of the significant developments in this area in the work of the Netherbow Centre. The Panel warmly commends the new book by the Centre's Director, Dr. Donald Smith, *Storytelling Scotland: a Nation in Narrative*[1], and in paricular the second in the Netherbow's 'Art of the Parish' series, *Shaping Stories*.

In 1998 the Panel expressed its regret that other projects (the preparation of *Common Ground* was one) had delayed work on all-age worship. The unfolding of plans, however, for the Year of the Child, now in progress, was its cue for returning to this important issue. In taking the discussion forward, the Panel affirms that any discussion of all-age worship should take place in the context of the need continually to renew worship generally and to plan each act of worship both in relation to its contemporary context and to those who are to share in it. It keeps in mind the main thrusts of its Reports to recent General Assemblies which variously called for worship which was well made and prepared with imagination (1995), which was "an adventure in beauty, an exploration of truth, an encounter with the living God" tested not on the cleverness of its ideas but "whether or not it makes the presence of Christ more real" (1996), which both welcomed attractive features of modern culture but also rested in the abiding traditions of the Church (1997), and which drew upon the treasures of the whole ecumenical sea and not just "the loch of our Presbyterian heritage" (1998).

However, with many congregations actively seeking to plan worship which is appropriate as much to those who come with the familiarity of years as to those in younger age groups, there is much that can be said both to encourage the best and to help avoid blind alleys. It is some time since the Panel published *New Ways to Worship* (1980) which gathered together, with

---

[1] Polygon, ISBN 074866310X.

commentary, many of the ideas which were then in use. The Appendix to this Report sets out some of the results of the considerable experience of renewal in worship which has continued since then and some of the lessons learned. This is one part only of the Panel's response to the remit, since it also intends to make available a printed resource to assist congregations in advancing their own explorations in these matters. Such material could also encompass the question of multimedia worship, which is raised in the Report of the Board of Communication, a discussion to which the Panel has been party.

2. Ongoing work

The Prayer and Devotion Committee's principal work of producing the daily devotional resource *Pray Now* continued with this year's volume (and accompanying tape) based on the Psalms. The cover designs were derived from the Dupplin Cross, now in the National Museum of Scotland, which bears a detail of David seated with harp, bardic-style. *Pray Now 2003* will centre round significant places referred to in the biblical narrative. The Saint Andrew Press has been generous with its help in developing the appearance and layout of this publication. Some users have commented on the size of the print and this has been noted for future editions. The Committee is currently working on a devotional resource for young people aged 16-25.

During the year, a *Common Ground Part-Book* was published, edited by Susan Wilson of the Panel's office. In it some three dozen songs and hymns are arranged for a comprehensive range of instruments, aimed at both beginners and those of more advanced skills. The Panel is grateful to the musicians who provided these arrangements and it is hoped that the volume will enable greater participation in worship by those who wish to contribute by their skill in playing. Most arrangements are set out clearly across double A4 facing pages and it is intended that sufficient photocopies be produced locally for the number of participants. However, individual parts in larger print can be supplied for single items on demand, albeit more expensively. The Part-Book is available from the Office for Worship only.

The increasing use of praise bands and other consorts of instruments in worship has been the focus of two consultations and is being explored further. Topics will include the widening of repertoire, the improvement of skills and the appropriate handling of this resource in the context of worship. Members of the Music Committee continue to visit congregations to introduce *Common Ground* but it is hoped that in due course their services will be placed at the disposal of the Hymn Book Revision Committee for a similar purpose.

The Panel continues to welcome comments on the *Interim Ordinal* before going forward to produce an expanded and more permanent publication to replace that of 1962. It also continues work on the invitation of the General Assembly of 2001 to investigate the possibility of providing worship resources through electronic media. Already, material from *Pray Now* appears on the Church's website, altered each day, while on occasion special prayers are provided in response to the events of the day.

In the name of the Panel

GILLEASBUIG MACMILLAN, *Convener*
IAN McCRORIE, *Vice-Convener*
DOUGLAS GALBRAITH, *Secretary*

APPENDIX A

ALL-AGE WORSHIP

1. Why all-age worship?

In the kitchen, Gran is listening to the Archers on Radio 4. Fourteen-year-old Pauline in the front room is glued to the latest exploits of a waif-like American teenager who has a powerful way with vampires. In a corner of the sofa Andrew, aged seven, is engrossed in his Play Station 2. Suzanne, just started high school, communes with text messages on her mobile. Upstairs, fifth former Alison scans the web for material for a school project. Outside in the drive Peter, their father, pores over the electronic navigational equipment in their latest car. His wife Gayle has taken her exhausted self to the local Odeon, and is now transported to Middle Earth. Tomorrow being Sunday they will all go to church where they will listen to one person praying on their behalf and addressing them for twenty minutes, interspersed with which they will sing five similar-sounding hymns.

Today, when different generations make use of a great variety of media through which to relate to others and the world in general, it can often seem that our worship is limited and monochrome by comparison. Technology has changed the way we communicate and receive information. There has been a sea-change in the way that people are educated. Gone are the inflexible authority of the teacher and of rote learning procedures. Instead, greater participation offers the chance for people to engage at their own pace and level; you are even allowed to enjoy it! Materials to assist learning are more plentiful, from school trips to electronic media. Relationships are less formal; value is placed on the individual; intellectual IQ is not the only or the principal measure of someone's ability; the senses are given their place.

These have had their echoes in the Church. The Liturgical Movement, Tell Scotland with its "Kirk Weeks", and the writings of such as Ralph Morton and Hendrik Kraemer have accompanied the heightening of the profile of the non-clerical majority of the Church, recognized as having their own gifts and life experience to bring. Study throughout the world Church on the image of the "Body of Christ" has brought home the truth that God gives gifts to Church and world through gifted people brought into unity in Christ. There has been a recovery of procedures in worship that involve greater participation, not just of the voices of the congregation but in the appeal to senses other than hearing, and where people's feelings are seen as important as their understanding. Materials and resources which many are finding useful, however, like the *Whole People of God* (now to be called *Seasons of the Spirit*) or *Salt* programmes, have another dimension also – they tend to be planned so that adults, teenagers and children can participate together. This new emphasis requires consideration.

What is this "all-age worship", or intergenerational worship as many call it? Has our worship not always been "for all ages"? A large number of those in our churches (and in our pulpits) today will attest to the sense of belonging in the church of their youth and in which they continue. Many young people find in the full grandeur, dignity and indeed intimacy of worship enough for them to grasp and the promise of more to discover. Evelyn Waugh in his autobiography captures the effect that the normal "adult" service had on him, albeit in a different tradition from our own, when he writes: "I rejoiced in my nearness to the sacred symbols and in the bright early-morning stillness and in a sense of intimacy with what was being enacted".[2]

However, there are many others who fear that one reason at least for people falling away from church attendance, especially in their teenage and early adult years, is that they do not feel worship is "for them". Both in style and content, worship as it is generally encountered in our churches seems best suited to those who have long experience in the Church and understand its ways. Children are "seen and not heard" in that worship seems to be designed for those with mature understanding. Yet the week by week experience of the structure of worship is in itself important for younger members of the congregation. The modelling and witness of the constancy of older members is a powerful source of instruction to the younger. Worship is as much caught as taught. It could be argued that there have been disadvantages in our practice of segregating children by removing them to Sunday School and that as a result we now have a generation or two who have never learned how to worship. However, if there are to be more occasions when children experience "full length" worship, consideration may need to be given to style and content.

Such an analysis has led many congregations either to redesign their morning service, or to establish an earlier service each Sunday characterised by more active participation on the part of worshippers and more variety of "input", although the use of the term "family services" to refer to these is now less frequent because of negative reactions from many who do not themselves belong to an immediate family.

---

[2] Evelyn Waugh, *A Little Learning* (Chapman and Hall 1964, Penguin Books 1983), p.93.

2. What is all-age worship?

How is all-age worship to be defined? It is important to affirm at the outset that all occasions of public worship be fully "inclusive", and not just in terms of age. This is given further consideration in the next paragraph. Yet we acknowledge that there are times when it is important to make a special effort to see that the youngest as well as the oldest are enabled to connect with what is going on. Children will relate best when they feel personally involved, when there is activity; teenagers, with their predilection for testing the conventions, may respond best to that aspect of worship which challenges social norms; young adults look for acknowledgement of the pressures they experience in career and in family life; the middle aged look for refreshment, in ideas and in their spiritual lives; the older age group seek hope and reassurance, for themselves, the world, their children and grandchildren. It is significant that having made such a list – and any number of parallel lists would have been possible – no one group mentioned has the monopoly on the characteristic beside their name. *All* age groups hope to be involved not as an onlooker but as an intimate, *all* may be enlivened in spirit through the action of the body, *all* to a certain extent wish to break free of the conventions, *all* long for refreshment, *all* wish to know hope. That is why it is possible to talk at all of "all-age" worship, for we are speaking of dimensions which are common to all.

Yet it would be a mistake to think that if we have satisfied the needs of each age group in this general way, we shall have achieved truly inclusive worship. For within these groups there is even greater variety. There are many whose experiences of life and living are different from the majority of church goers. They may be particularly well read and expect a similar quality of ideas and insights in their worship; they may serve professionally in a situation where there is particular suffering which saps their own energies; they may be sceptical about the Christian claims and yet acknowledge themselves as seekers after the truth; they may have served the Church overseas and approach domestic matters from a broader perspective; they may feel unsure of their reception because of marital failure, or the inability to have children, or sexual orientation, or other perceived "difference"; they may be physically or mentally challenged – the list is as

wide as humanity itself. Our more limited quest for all-age worship reminds us that our goal is wider than generations, that the inclusiveness we seek is not confined to age brackets, but that we seek refreshment for all worship.

3. The planning of all-age worship

One way of including all persons may be achieved by including the whole person. That is why explorations of this issue generally involve an appeal to the senses. Words are not just used for statements but used for questions and dramatic sequences; participative activity carries meaning; the visual speaks to the eye of faith; paint and puppetry, storytelling and singing all have their part. We do not leave these things to "the professionals". Created in the image of a Creator God, each person is a potential resource. Nevertheless, you do not make for inclusive worship merely by including certain procedures. There are principles which underlie the use of *any* medium in worship. Applying these in the case of all-age worship, we might say –

3.1 All-age worship should genuinely *be* worship. What we hope to introduce children into is the special activity which is worship, and the challenge is to create acts of worship which are continuous with the children's world as well as the adult's. It should be remembered that children are as capable as adults of responding to the solemnity of an occasion, of being overtaken by awe or beauty, of responding to and with love. As well as developing forms which children in particular can relate to, we should offer children a chance in "ordinary" worship to take on "adult" tasks – leading the psalm, contributing a bidding to a prayer of intercession, reading a lesson, taking up the offering, welcoming at the door, playing an instrument or singing in a choir.

3.2 All-age worship will potentially engage all generations and not be worship for children with adults present. This is not to say that there may not be "positive discrimination" in favour of children. Thus, as well as making sure that the atmosphere and content of the service as a whole does not alienate the attention of children (the length of individual sections, the use of responsive material, the way that people sit in relation to each other, the use of the visual), parts of the service may be quite specifically geared to the children present. Care should be taken to make sure that the ideas or insights which provide the starting point for these sections are of a quality which also challenge the adults present – not to mention the children, for children as well as adults can be embarrassed by being "talked down to". Care should also be taken not simply to replace words with more words. There is the temptation sometimes in our Protestant tradition to be didactic and "tell people what to think and feel". In services involving children we may be particularly prone to this. A single good idea, which appeals to people other than at a purely cerebral level, can greatly alter the "feel" of a service and unite all ages and stages in one act.

3.3 Even if much in a service of all-age worship is geared to the children present, that act of worship is part of the worship of the whole Church in all places and in all ages. There should therefore be elements in it which help those present to grow into the whole worshipping body "on earth and in heaven". Some of the material used could be universal worship material – a repeated collect (even if all the words are not in the everyday vocabulary of all present), one of the standard hymns of the Church (children often respond to the images in hymns without accessing the doctrines), the sharing of the Peace, the singing or saying of a doxology, joining in the Lord's Prayer.

3.4 All-age worship should be well made. Worship as it has been practised for generations has not only developed a content, albeit variable, but principles of construction. *Common Order* is compiled as much to offer models and make available the Church's long experience in designing worship as to provide texts. In exploring new forms of worship, it is incumbent on us to bring the same integrity to their design. We may often expend all our effort in tracking down new ideas and not have time left over to make them work in our context. The result can be that people are alienated not because of the medium but by the out-of-tune guitar, the inaudible reader, the drama enactment that is comical rather than adding insight. A commentator has written: "Liturgical celebration can be friendly and marked by spontaneity without being sloppy and devoid of physically manifest reverence. It can be warm and free without being anarchic and chaotic. It can embrace poverty and simplicity without being squalid and ugly" (Robert Hovda, *Dry Bones* 1973). That being said, the give and take in a congregation should mean that people are accepting of each other and give each other leeway, even when things don't work out.

4. Music

Music can be a particular asset, being no respecter of age or background. Attention is drawn to the Panel's most recent music pamphlet, *Assist our Song*, which pays particular attention to the choice of music where children are involved and offers examples and sources. It is important not to underestimate children's ability and confine our choice to "simple tunes to simple words expressing simple ideas. Good children's songs don't have to be couched in kidspeak" (p.11). Nor do we need to select only the most familiar melodies. There are other dimensions to music. Children enjoy participating in "eventful" music – where there is interaction between groups of singers, or cantor and congregation; the repetitiveness of short chants, meaningfully placed, is as attractive to them as adults; canons and rounds, itself an ancient form, are fun because of the alertness required to know when to come in; rhythm is as important as melody in engendering a feeling of participation, and many of the hymns and songs from Africa and other countries come into their own when sung by children with adults together.

Again, congregations could with profit make far more use of their young musicians. More and more are getting the opportunity of learning an instrument at school. It means a great deal to a child or a teenager to be able to contribute directly to worship in this way. The Panel provides a part-book (main report 2) to contribute to the formation of groups of local instrumentalists. Another significant contribution children can make is through children's choirs. A number of Church of Scotland congregations now have established such choirs, which either are responsible for a regular second service or share duties with an adult choir. Some follow the Royal School of Church Music's *Voice for Life* scheme which combines a religious education component with a programme to develop musical talent. The Panel's office can give information about this.

All in all, the Church does not take sufficiently seriously the potential for its music (and for its future health generally) that resides in its younger members. Even when such choirs are formed, they are sometimes seen as a separate activity for children and are not enabled or allowed to contribute to the music of the local church. In this, as when children are sequestered in the Sunday School and not given their place in the worshipping community, the Church jeopardises not just its future but the quality of its present life.

5.   The other six days

In exploring the issues connected with all-age worship, while attention is rightly paid to the focus of the Church's life, its Sunday worship, it is important to consider the overall pattern of the congregation's life. The renewal in worship that we seek is not just about "new scripts". The quality of interaction within the congregation and its own openness to the community in which it is set are important factors. For example, children may not feel at home in a service simply because the ethos of that church is not particularly welcoming in other ways. Restrictions may be placed on the uses of the building that young people, or groups in the community whose members potentially might link up with the church, find irksome. There can be "us" and "them" divisions in a congregation – with adults and young people seen as categories, or "non-church" groups which use the halls considered as "outsiders". The question to be asked is how good is the interaction between groups in our church *anyway*, let alone in Sunday worship.

Returning to worship, our assumption has been that this properly takes place on Sunday, and that it will look as much as possible like the services of worship that we know. It might be worth asking whether there is room for other events of a celebratory nature which could be spread throughout the local church's life. Might the weekend be used more imaginatively? Could there be gatherings which have a worshipful intent but where there is genuine participation by all age groups, outwith the constraints and expectations of the Sunday service? Might there be room for such events on week nights, or on special festivals of local significance – or even relating to a saint's day. (This may be a surprising suggestion for the Church of Scotland, but a great many of our churches are named after saints and many more localities have saints associated with them; it is a good opportunity to use story telling.)   An example might be the Saturday night Festivals of Faith that were popular in recent years, where workshops were offered according to Christian experience and the age range of worshippers could be from five to eighty-five. No one came with expectations and this freed people for new experiences. In addition, a body of people were created who had experienced something different who would be a leaven in established worshipping communities. The same would obtain for Wild Goose's "Big Night Out" or its current *Holy City* series in Glasgow.

6.   "Traditional" or "contemporary"?

It is the custom in a few churches to approach the matter of more inclusive worship by offering a choice between "traditional" or "contemporary" worship. The fact that these may be at different times is not an issue (see section 8 below) but the Panel believes that the implied distinction is misleading if it is being suggested that received practices are inimical to the renewal of worship. "Tradition" in this interpretation is read as a surviving outward manner whose original power has been lost. Yet what our traditions hand on is not "the remains of the day" so much as a constantly unfolding and living encounter with God in worship, to which people have brought the best of their gifts, and of which we today are an evolving part. Our task is constantly to "renew this tradition" and any questions about creating worship for all ages needs to be addressed to the way we approach the practices of worship we have received. Even if providing parallel experiences of "all-age" worship, the Church is not absolved from the responsibility Sunday by Sunday of approaching "regular" public worship creatively. What opening words will raise the expectations and awareness of the worshipper as to what is now to happen? How should the reading from Scripture be announced so that hearers are made ready to assimilate the full import of what follows? What stance or tone of voice will best awaken the appreciation that this act of worship is a corporate one? How does one avoid prayer being a recital of topics and help it to become a shared expression of longing for healing and justice or an outpouring of gratitude? Very often it is steps in this direction which "open" worship to those who have felt excluded.

Indeed, it is often when we "search our traditions" that we find the best ideas for the more inclusive worship that we seek! The following list is eclectic and each item is best considered in the context from which it came; the purpose here is more to encourage than to prescribe. In various periods, deacon, people and presiding minister would spread the prayer throughout the congregation; brief but vivid enactments of key moments in the Gospels brought home their meaning and import, sometimes with humour; processions gathered everyone up as they moved around the church or along the streets, bringing offerings, carrying crosses; lighted candles given to the baptised were a vivid reminder of their new status; ceremonies of the washing of feet spoke not only of the servanthood of Christ but of the nature of the Christian life; there was the ringing of bells (or their absence on Good Friday and Saturday), the smell of incense, the sprinkling of water on the congregation, the changing colours of the hangings and coverings, stained glass which told a story, the warmth of the sharing of the Peace. In our own more immediate tradition, coming forward to sit round the Table could emphasize the communal nature of the Sacrament, while "skailing" during the closing psalm reminded worshippers of the opportunities of praise in daily life. Movement, gesture, visual images, sound, smell, taste, touch, silence – all may have something today to contribute to the uniting of all generations in worship.

7. The minister and all-age worship

Those who have made forays in any of the above directions know that to "produce" such services can be more demanding than usual. The more people participate, the more careful planning and rehearsing is required. Using media other than the tried and tested spoken words and their accustomed forms means time spent in gauging the effect of what you want to do, given the building you are in, the persons who are delivering the material, and the people who are going to be watching or listening. Rather than feel the burden of always needing to find new ideas, building and improving on what we have done before can be most effective. Too often, we desperately seek "something new and different". The quest for renewal in worship is too often interpreted as to make every one as different as possible from the last. Strangely, this can lead to a kind of "sameness" as the techniques predominate and block entry to the underlying "true" worship which is the goal of our words, rituals and music. Many congregations approach these matters through groups and committees which share in the planning of worship with the minister.

However, it cannot be denied that a considerable burden is put upon the minister and any others who are particularly associated in the leading of worship. Upon them is placed the responsibility of releasing their own imaginations so that they can both help others to articulate ideas and be able to respond positively to the suggestions of others. A minister's creativity is often to be hard won, and may mean keeping in touch with creative people in the secular field, at first hand or through what they make. It will certainly involve the obligation to be aware of movements and trends in communication, electronic or not. The minister will acknowledge also that there are people in the congregation who are at home with creative processes, with enabling participation, with using technological resources – whether as parents, teachers or youth workers. Working as a team will free the minister to bring his/her best gifts to the worship and liberate others to bring theirs. Care needs to be taken that such a group does not become too firmly established and create another hierarchy or "in group" in the congregation. Those who work this way have often built into their recruitment a continuing change of composition – weekly in one case, monthly in another, or in another case an element of constancy coupled with variety.

Also, since the true test of worship is whether it "connects" with those who worship, he or she will be a student of human events and human nature. Renewal in worship is not just about media but about *content*. We often concentrate on the former to the detriment of the latter. Above all, the minister will expend considerable effort in learning about the people of the congregation and community (and recording this for later retrieval). Only then may the gifts and talents that someone could bring be discovered, and expertise which might contribute both form and content be accessed.

The Panel has been interested to learn of ministers who have elected to spend study leave on worship-related projects and has been most grateful to those who have made available their findings. It has appreciated being invited to offer comment, in some cases before as well as after, and has found this most helpful in its own work.

8. A cause of division?

Many fear that the establishment of different occasions for worship will cause physical division in the congregation. However, the provision of such a varied "menu" of worship opportunities is not new. Today, churches may variously offer an evening service particularly geared towards young people; an early Sunday or week day service of Holy Communion; a service which features a substantial teaching component; a mission service designed with enquirers in mind; a meditative hour of live music; week day services, say at lunch time, for those working in the parish; acts of worship in a particular style – charismatic, or featuring Taizé chants, or multimedia. As well as variety in opportunities, people themselves make choices from what is available: some may only attend at Communions, others only at services of healing, others only at the principal festivals, others may deliberately avoid any ecumenical occasion. At no time have worshippers always attended the same services, nor has this caused division. There is plenty of room, and reason, for what the "Church without Walls" report calls "a variety of menu and variety of venue" that allow people different points of access to worship, rather than to try to squeeze everybody through the same doorway.

There is often a concern that two congregations have emerged, and talk of being divided. In fact, there has usually been a more serious division between those who previously came to the one option on offer and those who stayed away. The issue of maintaining a unity of spirit is nonetheless a real issue for a Gospel community that is to offer a sign of a healed and reconciled humanity. For some, that is encouraged by a coffee break between services where the two worshipping communities can meet each week. Others work a pattern of weekly segregation with regular joint celebration services around the Festivals when a variety of styles can be integrated. Others again have worked to bring the separate strands together, beginning with worship, followed by separate teaching times in which adults move as well as children, and then ending with a time of shared worship for all. In a Church which lives with the image of being the Body of Christ, we will recognise the importance of celebrating diversity while expressing a spirit of unity. The worship of the God and Father of our Lord Jesus Christ must not become the battleground for power struggles and worship wars. We are to "maintain the spirit of unity in the bonds of peace". That is about humility, patience and mutual respect, where the strong help the weak, whether the "weak" be the children or those of immovable convictions about minor issues! Grace is the key.

There are many examples in practice of a separate "all-age worship" service. Often at an earlier time, this has been found to attract people other than children and their parents. Many elderly people may enjoy the different atmosphere and the energy of the children. Some of these may be in the round with a carpet where the toddlers can play. Some meet in a transept or a less formal hall where the building works for them rather than against them. Some involve families in the planning and the leading of the worship so that they are encouraged to think and pray at home about the worship. Some have a group of people of all ages sharing in the preparation, with a rolling membership to ensure that all voices and viewpoints are included.

The separate service allows space for new patterns to emerge and new people to find confidence without undue disruption to the normal pattern of worship. In some cases these early services have become more popular than the later service. They also provide an opportunity to develop fresh approaches to the sacraments. Some see such separate services as transitional on behalf of all members, hoping they will lead to new "official" patterns – just as a diversion can allow the building of a more permanent roadway while not interrupting the normal flow of traffic (too much!).

9. Taking the first steps

Many are now "seasoned travellers" in these areas. Some have still to take the first step. Many initiatives for more inclusive, or specifically "all-age" worship, can falter or fail because of the way change is managed. Every worshipper has a set of expectations about what happens on Sunday morning at the prescribed hour. Moving ourselves on to a new mental carriageway is not easy. Sometimes there may be a feeling in a congregation that change is in the air but no one is sure what kind of change, if any, is appropriate for their situation. Changes of this kind involve much care, and often a great deal of patience. The following suggestions are derived from what some seasoned travellers have found helpful:

9.1 Congregation and Kirk Session are invited to discuss with the minister their views on worship as it is or as they would like to see it. The local Children's Forum (set up under the now running Year of the Child) should be encouraged to contribute. Advice could be sought from the Panel on Worship and the Board of Parish Education. Existing patterns of Christian education in the congregation would be taken into account.

9.2 A team of "explorers" could be asked to visit congregations who have been making significant changes in their worship practices. They might report to a day conference at the church or a day away in a retreat centre to which interested members of the congregation are invited.

9.3 A strategy for development over a period of three years could be mapped out, with a review after one year. This would give time for the process to mature. The cost implications for equipment and materials should not be overlooked.

9.4 The minister might invite a worship team to share in the oversight of these developments, with the condition that they continually invite the participation of others. Those who already take leadership roles in worship, such as the organist, should be closely involved from the beginning.

10. Further material

The pack or booklet to be provided will offer further guidelines and report on 'examples of good practice' already developed in congregations. It will also contain a comprehensive description and assessment of material from sources within and outwith the Church of Scotland, as well as a list of useful websites.

APPENDIX B

RECOMMENDED SALARY SCALES FOR ORGANISTS

The revised form of contract for the employment of an Organist now available from the Law Department leaves the figures for the salary scale blank. From time to time, the Scottish Federation of Organists offers a recommended salary scale which the Panel is pleased to endorse and include in its Report. It is recognised that it is not possible to lay down a figure that will be right for every church which employs an organist. It is also recognised that many posts will not fit exactly into any one of the undernoted categories, but it is hoped that those whose responsibility it is to determine a church musician's remuneration will be guided by these figures.

Section A – Organists, Organists and Choirmasters, Directors of Music.

1	Churches without choirs	£1,100-£1,700
2	Churches with choirs making an occasional individual contribution to worship	£1,700-£2,675
3	Churches with choirs making a substantial contribution to worship	£2,675-£3,575
4	Churches with complete and competent choirs singing full choral services	£3,575-£5,350
5	Churches employing a full or part-time professional director of music with extensive responsibilities are recommended to consider salary scales higher than scale 4.	

Section B – Additional Services

It is recommended that additional services such as weddings and funerals should have a fee in the range £35-£80. In cases where such a service is being commercially recorded, the fee should be increased by 50% in respect of a sound recording, and 100% in respect of a video recording.

Section C – Deputies

The minimum rate for a deputy should be £35 per service. Where the incumbent organist receives a remuneration above the minimum recommended level, the deputy's fee will normally be increased proportionately.

It is recommended that the above salary scales should remain valid for a period of two years from May 2002.

Copies of the above may be obtained from the Office for Worship.

COMMITTEE TO REVISE THE HYMNARY
MAY 2002

PROPOSED DELIVERANCE

The General Assembly:

1. Receive the Report and the Supplementary Report.
2. Thank the Committee, especially the Convener, and Secretary.
3. Approve the Final List of Contents.

REPORT

1. Introduction

The past year's work of the Revision Committee has been largely concerned with editing material already selected for inclusion in the new hymnary, and in scrutinising new materials sent to the Committee or published in the most recent collections of Christian hymns and songs in the English-speaking nations.

This should mean that the book, when produced, will be as up to date as possible as regards proven texts and tunes available elsewhere, and as inclusive as possible of work produced by new authors and tune-writers in the British Isles. The Committee acknowledges that it will not be possible to publish every original hymn submitted, but thanks the many people who, since the Committee was set up, have sent manuscript and recorded music, thus helping to ensure that the final selection is made from as large a source-pool as possible.

2. Summary of Returns

The Committee is most grateful to the 25 presbyteries, 9 kirk sessions, 1 choir, and the 41 individuals who responded to the Draft List, often in great detail. As might be expected, the views expressed represented a wide range of opinions, from outright rejection on the one hand - 'Why do we need a new hymn book anyway?' - to warm welcome on the other. The Committee was gratified by the overwhelming support of the majority of respondents for its proposals. Of the individuals who

sent in returns, 15 were ministers, 4 were organists, and the remaining 22 were not identified further than by their names.

A total of 461 complete hymns (text and tune) was suggested for inclusion in the hymn book, some of them appearing in more than one submission, and 20 separate tunes. The Committee had previously considered most if not all of these, and many of them were in fact already in the list. Those not in the list were considered afresh. Among those re-instated are:

> A little child the Saviour came
> By cool Siloam's shady rill
> Jesus loves me
> O breath of life, come sweeping through us
> Summer suns are glowing
> What a friend we have in Jesus

Among the tunes now included in the list are *Sagina* for *And can it be* and Lowell Mason's music for the *Aaronic Blessing (The Lord bless thee and keep thee).*

Representations were also made for 13 hymns to be excluded from the list, and these, too, were considered carefully. There was particular objection to the hymn *God, our Mother caring* and it no longer appears on the list.

3. Work to be done

The next year's work, leading up to publication, the main work will involve:

a   further editing and proofing of all texts;
b   music editing and arranging;
c   work on copyright, indexing, and proof-reading;
d   preparation of promotional materials.

4. The new book

Already the following aspects of the publication can be clearly discerned, each helping to make the book stand worthily in succession to its predecessors but also to be significantly different:

a   standard edition will have a melody line, and chords (where appropriate);
b   almost 50% of texts written in second half of 20th century;
c   substantial representation of Scottish texts and tunes;
d   re-publication of some hymns which have an iconic value for Scottish presbyterians;
e   increased provision of material in such sections as the Life and Ministry of Jesus, the Ministry of Healing, Personal Devotion;
f   over 100 Psalms represented in a variety of styles;
g   inclusion of contemporary worship songs;
h   hymns for such occasions as communion, weddings, and funerals set to known tunes;
i   a wider selection of children's hymns;
j   easily singable material from the world-wide church.

5. Historical sketch

Most people in our churches have grown up knowing two hymnals, *The Revised Church Hymnary* of 1927 and *The Church Hymnary: Third Edition*, 1973, and many of them may be unacquainted either with the history of hymn books in Presbyterian Scotland or with the hymnody of other traditions. They may assume, therefore, that it is only when a new book is announced that a people's repertoire is increased or that new material is written. It was interesting in this context to meet the comment of a member of one of the Scottish Organists' Societies who, on hearing of the proposed hymnary, exclaimed in sincere puzzlement, 'But who is going to write the new hymns?' It was even more distressing for the questioner to be told

that many of them had already been written - by Baptists, Methodists, Catholics, Anglicans, and Presbyterians all over the world. Our 'new' hymns have always come from these other sources as well as from within our own tradition. And what was true of the past is true now.

Before the 1650 Psalter was produced (the one from which our metrical psalms come), there had been a string of both authorised and unofficial publications stretching all the way back to the early attempts at psalmody by the Wedderburn brothers in mid-16th century Dundee.

Before the Paraphrases were authorised in 1781, there had been numerous popular versifications of scripture in metre circulating in different parts of the country. Robert Burns was one notable layman who experimented with metrical versions, and his verses on Psalms 1 and 96 were published in his collected works.

Before the first Church Hymnary was produced in 1896, there had been a *Scottish Hymnal* published by authority of the General Assembly, and during the life of both the 1896 and the 1927 books, there was a number of popular supplements (all unauthorised) including the famous book of 1200 *Sacred Songs and Solos* compiled by Ira D Sankey.

Between 1896 and 1927, there appeared, again by authority of the General Assembly of the Church of Scotland, the *Scottish Mission Hymn Book*. And between 1927 and 1973, there was a variety of publications used in different areas of church life, including books primarily for use in youth work and by Gaelic speaking congregations. Few people over the age of 50 will not share some indebtedness to Carey Bonar whose collections of music for children enabled thousands of Sunday School scholars to 'hear the pennies dropping' well into the 1960s.

Between 1973 and today, the tradition of having supplementary material has continued with both authorised and unofficial volumes of song. *Songs for the Seventies* was devised as a contemporary supplement to the recently published *CH3*, but fell short of Assembly approval. *Hymns For A Day* followed. Then in 1988, *Songs of God's People* attempted to offer a sample of several styles of contemporary hymnody and, over the next decade, sold a quarter of a million copies. *Common Ground*, the first wholly ecumenical book of its kind in

Europe, followed in 1998. And throughout that whole period, congregations were also free to supplement their diet of praise in CH3 by volumes such as *Mission Praise* and *Songs of Fellowship.*

What this indicates is that there has always been a to and fro movement between the core hymnary produced, on average, every 30 years, and supplementary books which have a shorter life span because they represent current material which has still to prove its longevity.

It would therefore be unusual if the forthcoming Church Hymnary did not pick up on what had been tried and tested in a variety of volumes since 1973 as well as including hitherto unpublished material which the compilers believe is valuable for broadening and deepening congregational singing.

In this respect, when the final edited contents of the fourth Church Hymnary appears, it will be seen that while the fine icons of congregational singing from the past have been retained, almost half of the material will have been written in the second half of the twentieth century.

6. Two caveats

However, with the 20th century have come two tendencies in congregational song which have to be seriously considered.

The first one might be called liturgical or musical hedonism - in other words, a desire to sing only that which makes the singers feel good. This has undoubtedly always been an aspect of church musical life, evident in 'favourites' evenings, when the sanctuary can sound almost like a bingo hall as numbers are called out by people keen to have a hymn important to them sung by the whole congregation. It would be foolhardy to dispute the enjoyment and value of such occasions. But, just as it would be wrong to believe that the musical and theological predilections of the minister, organist, or worship leader were alone sufficient to guarantee a balanced diet of praise for the congregation, so it would be wrong to confine congregational song to nothing but praise and personal devotion. The Book of Psalms with its range of poetic styles and emotional registers is a timely reminder that there is a need and a time to ponder, regret, and bemoan as well as shout for joy. While we pray that

God may spare us from any repetition of tragedies such as that of September 11th, the Church must have in its armoury of song material which speaks to and of the human condition in all its aspects, and provides for expression of grief as well as gladness, loss as well as love.

The second reality we have to face is the understandable tendency of the Church to emulate popular musical styles. Again, this has a long pedigree. The Wedderburn brothers employed Scottish ballad tunes, Luther wrote texts to be sung to melodies more associated with the tavern than with the House of Prayer. And, were we to have walked through Leeds at the end of the 19th century, it might have been possible to catch snatches of 'Wide, wide as the ocean' intermingled with 'Come, come, come and make eyes at me' sallying forth from very different establishments, but possibly both being accompanied by accordion bands. Come the 1960's, writers like Sydney Carter were employing folk or folk-like melodies for gritty texts, while Graham Kendrick in the 1980's began to popularise songs which were avowedly based on the Beatles genre of a good verse and singable chorus. There is nothing intrinsically new or wrong with such tendencies. Indeed one could claim that a faith which is predicated on the incarnation of God requires human cultures to cradle the Gospel rather than keep it in an other-worldly or antiseptic time capsule.

What is a more disquieting phenomenon, however, is the tendency - much more evident in North America and the South of England - to have the communal song of the Church supplanted by performance music. Of course, this has happened before. The annals of Church history give testimony to how little over a hundred years ago a prestigious congregation was brought to the bar of the presbytery to answer to allegations that rather than sing, the congregation simply listened to the virtuoso choir. Indeed, many parish records give testimony as to how, when the choir movement was developing at the end of the 19th century, Kirk Sessions made stipulation about the size and purpose of the choir precisely to prevent a performance mentality being foisted on a tradition which was founded on the belief that God called *all* the people to sing a new song.

Just as it is disrespectful to the Body of Christ to have an organist and choir manage the music to suit themselves and turn the congregation into an audience, so it is also a mistake for a 21st century praise band to try to make public worship the forum where its musicians take centre stage and expect the congregation to be passive consumers. In the Church we should have no hesitation in both affirming the musical giftedness of performers and in ensuring that their self-esteem or desire to play does not sideline the music-making of the whole congregation.

It is with this in mind that, as well as gathering fine texts and tunes from writers such as Carl Daw, Ruth Duck, Timothy Dudley-Smith, Christopher Idle, Fred Kaan, Shirley Erena Murray, Brian Wren (authors), and from Colin Gibson, Al Fedak, David Hurd, James MacMillan, Sally-Anne Morris, and Richard Proulx (composers), the Revision Committee has also included contemporary worship songs suitable for congregational use from singer-songwriters such as David J Evans, Bernadette Farrell, Marty Haugen, Graham Kendrick, Dan Schutte, and Stuart Townsend.

7. The complete list

Around the world, new books of hymns continue to be published and the stream of new material seems to be endless. But the task of selection must come to an end sometime, and the Committee feels that that time has now come. The final list of the contents for the new book, both text and tunes, will be produced as a Supplementary Report and be presented to the General Assemblies in May. If the list be approved, the Committee will proceed with all due diligence to prepare text, music, and indexes with a view to publication of the new book in 2003.

The Committee is greatly indebted to the Church Hymnary Trust for its financing of the Committee's work and is glad of this opportunity to express its thanks.

In the name of the Committee

JOHN L BELL, *Convener*
CHARLES ROBERTSON, *Secretary*

COMMITTEE ON ARTISTIC MATTERS
MAY 2002

PROPOSED DELIVERANCE

1. Receive the Report.

2. Encourage congregations to consult with the Committee before making approaches to artists or craftspersons regarding the design of stained glass windows or furnishings for churches.

3. Acknowledge the balance to be kept between the conservation of fabric and the re-ordering of churches to meet contemporary needs.

REPORT

COMMISSIONING STAINED GLASS WINDOWS

1. New works of art

During the year 2001, the Committee was in discussion with over 300 congregations concerning alterations to their buildings and the commissioning of new works to enhance their sanctuaries. Members are grateful for the growing acceptance by congregations that the Committee is not simply a hurdle to be overcome but a body which, valuing their buildings as much as they do, is able to offer advice, both from the professional skills of members but also from a growing experience of working with many churches to help ensure that their buildings are such in design, arrangement and condition as to point to the 'Magestie of God' as well 'as unto the ease and commodity of the people' in their relation to the word of God and the sacraments.[1]   Sometimes the solution was straightforward and the Committee could encourage the congregation to proceed without modification. Sometimes it took time to clarify goals, as when the immediate aim concealed other needs, and find the most effective solution. Sometimes conversation had to be lengthy and visits numerous, as when congregations were custodians of buildings or furnishings or internal layouts of special historical value or aesthetic beauty, and a compromise had to be found.

It is often when commissioning new works that the most protracted conversations take place and where there is most potential for misunderstanding. Of no medium is this more true than stained glass windows. Like music, visual art communicates on many levels depending on the recipient. While a tune or a representation in glass may fill our own soul, when commissioning a new window (as in producing a new hymn book) we have to plan not only for posterity but for those also whose ear or eye - or whose life of the spirit - is more experienced or more developed than our own. Much that is said below about stained glass windows - the most frequent example of new commission to come before the Committee - may be applied to the commissioning of any work of art or furnishing.

2. Making the colours sing

Scotland's record of stained glass is a fine one, as is demonstrated in Michael Donnelly's book, *Scotland's Stained Glass*.[2]   It is true, as he says, that the dramatic change of direction at the Reformation resulted in the loss of glass from the earliest period, although this was often an indirect result of changed practice or policies rather than of deliberate destruction. Lack of maintenance was often a culprit, and there was also the loss of the skills which the former monastic communities had nurtured. Of direct destruction there was undoubtedly some, even a fair amount, but this seemed far from being official policy. A letter issued in 1560 to the 'purifiers' of Dunkeld Cathedral warns them to 'tak guid heyd that neither the dasks, windocks, nor durris, be ony ways hurt or broken - either glassin wark or iron wark'.[3]

After several centuries of little activity in the making of stained glass, Scotland in the nineteenth century seemed intent on making up for lost time. With the growth of the middle classes and with increased prosperity, coupled with the upsurge in church building following the Disruption, a demand for stained glass in churches, public buildings and in the houses of the well-to-do began to grow, and there was no lack of glass companies and artists to satisfy this. The quality of work was high and the techniques innovative. Artists were receptive to and built on current Europe-wide movements in artistic sensibility. Teaching in the Schools of Art was encouraging and imaginative.

One of the earliest studios to produce successful designs, mid nineteenth century, was that of James Ballantine of Edinburgh (d.1877) who finally broke through Presbyterian reserve about pictorial glass with commissions in the present Sandyford Henderson building in Glasgow, Ibrox Parish Church, St. Giles' Cathedral and Dunfermline Abbey, among others. Worthy of particular mention are his firm's nine windows in Greyfriars' Kirk in Edinburgh, commemorating notable ministers of that church. One of the most distinctive of the earlier artists was Daniel Cottier (d.1891), known as much for his richly polychromatic decorative schemes for the interiors of churches as for his colourful geometric windows (such as those in Pilrig St. Paul's Church in Edinburgh; there are examples of his work also in St. Machar's Cathedral, Aberdeen, Paisley Abbey, Largs St. Columba's and St. Michael's Linlithgow, among others).

Cottier, who ultimately took his skills to Australia, was as notable for the apprentices he encouraged. These included Stephen Adam (d.1910), in whose work is seen the stylistic influence of Japanese art (e.g. Pollokshields; Clark Memorial, Largs; New Kilpatrick, Bearsden). The combination of the talents of draughtsman, designer, and glass stainer, all brought to a high technical level, took Alf Webster (d.1915, aged 31), one of Adam's assistants, into the 'category of genius'. In Lansdowne Church in Glasgow, his 'great north and south transept windows are among the crowning achievements of Scottish stained glass'.[4] Oscar Paterson's (d.1934) innovative techniques,

unusual colour schemes and the dominant role of leadlines contributed to the development of the 'Glasgow style' (an expression of the movement known as Art Deco); although arguably his best work was found in domestic settings and ocean-going liners, he produced windows for a large number of churches, including St. Magnus' Cathedral in Kirkwall and Crichton Memorial Chapel in Dumfries. On the east coast, Douglas Strachan (d.1950) produced powerful multi-themed windows in remarkable colour (many examples, including St. Andrews Holy Trinity, Kirkcaldy St. Brycedale, Hyndland in Glasgow). Distinctive also was William Wilson (d.1972) whose vigorous designs are widely to be found, significantly in the series of windows in Brechin Cathedral and in the recently recorded series of fourteen windows at Craigiebuckler.

These eminent Scottish artists have their contemporary counterparts. Examples of Sadie McLellan's (1912 -) powerful and imaginative designs, some of which used the new technique of *dalles de verre*, can be seen in Alloa, Netherlee, Glasgow Cardonald, the Robin Chapel in Edinburgh and Glasgow Cathedral. Crear McCartney, who weaves into his designs not just colour but sound, deriving inspiration from the works of different composers ranging from Carver to Elgar, has windows in St. Michael's Linlithgow, Dornoch Cathedral and the Auld Kirk of Ayr, and many others. There are several other artists who could have been mentioned, like Carrick Whallen and Sax Shaw, and a proper account can be found in Michael Donnelly's readily available publications. The next generation includes such artists as John Clark, Douglas Hogg and Christian Shaw, while a younger generation continues the tradition of breaking new ground which has distinguished Scottish stained glass makers since James Ballantine. With our churches so full of striking and well made windows, it would seem important that when we add to this legacy today we should take similar trouble to provide works of art which will be similarly valued by those who follow us.

It is also worth recording that the Committee is able to examine buildings which are to be closed to see if there are windows - or other artifacts - of particular significance that ought to be saved. It has been party to the conservation of such windows and their re-instatement in other locations. It is not always easy to fit a redundant window into another building, although it is sometimes achievable, and the other option, of mounting the window in a screen or on a wall, backlit, has been selected.

3. The importance of good design

In our information leaflet *Church Windows*, we discuss the matter of design in the following way. In beginning a design, a stained glass artist will have in mind the architecture of the building and the other windows already in place, since all the features of a building must add up.

A good design will have something new about it. This does not necessarily mean that it must be abstract, but it will contain the unexpected, even when traditional themes are used. This means that the attention will be caught, and mind and imagination stimulated. A weak or derivative design will simply, in turn, weary those who live with the window - a missed opportunity, or worse.

A good design wears well - so that both we ourselves and future generations find something fresh and refreshing in it rather than cease to notice it because it has too soon reached its sell by date. It should not be the kind of 'unexpected' that will only be a seven day wonder and then become a spent force, nor should it slavishly follow styles of yesteryear, resulting in a window which may be pleasant to look at but does not arrest us and address us in quite the same way.

The reason that good design matters so much is that the finished window has so much to do. The preface to a book about the glass in York Minster speaks of its windows as being 'to greet, instruct and inspire the medieval pilgrim'.[5] Windows still have this function. To people as they enter, they may be the friendly face of an austere building, the medium of a dialogue between visitor/worshipper and God, enabled by the artist. Of course, a window may as much send people out as welcome them in; in one aspect, looking towards pulpit and table, a window may invite tranquillity, but the window they face while leaving the church may be designed to uplift and encourage. As far as instruction is concerned, as they image events in the biblical narrative, or the history of Church and nation, windows can remind and teach of the foundation of the faith. They also inspire, in that the creativity of the artist, drawing on his/her imagination to explore the subject matter, can draw an answering creativity in the spectator in such a way that the beauty in the subject and in the person can mediate the beauty that is God. What Angela Ashwin claims for the words and music of worship is true also for stained glass: 'When we reach out to God corporately in the poetry and music of liturgy and hymn, our desire for God meets his desire for us. The channels are open for him to reclaim and remake us, not only individually but also as the Body of Christ, the place of his indwelling'.[6]

For many people, money spent on stained glass windows or other artifacts is wasted, an indulgence when a church is having difficulty in meeting running costs. Sensitive choices *do* have to be made, but we cannot ignore the observable fact that, in a Church so leery of art works as ours has been in the past, there is today an increasing number of commissions. This would have delighted Millar Patrick, the first Convener of the Artistic Matters Committee, who in the 1930s spoke of the 'divining rod of the imagination', which he rated as much an essential instrument of thought as reason itself. 'If you are to teach the truth of Scripture you must maintain a constant play of the imagination over the symbolic language it uses'.[7] Window, mural, mosaic, the colours and designs of pulpit falls or table frontals, tapestry, organ case, carving, the light holders above pulpit or table, these and other artifacts can be part of the hearing of the gospel and offer to lodge it more securely in the mind.

A recent Art and Christian Enquiry leaflet suggests that such works of art have an influence even if we are not aware of it:

> Worship calls out all our sensibilities. We expect words and music to engage us. We are worked upon, often unconsciously, by architecture. Painting and sculpture each in their different ways also have the power to draw us deep into the understanding and the believing which belong to worship. The church building has therefore been a vital and critical setting for works of art created specially for it.[8]

4. Before commissioning a window

The Committee has found that the commissioning of new stained glass windows has been one of the most difficult areas to handle. This has arisen mainly because in many cases matters have advanced too far before the Committee has become involved. Even a decision locally to instal a new window can be a 'decision too far'. Considerations at this early stage include:

4.1 Function. Why do we wish to put in a window? Is it to help people focus during a time of worship? Is it to declare the faith, or teach about the Bible, to those who visit the church during the week? Is it to commemorate someone's notable Christian witness (see 6.3 below)? Is it to celebrate an event? Is it to remind worshippers of the scope of their task of Christian witness and service in the world? Is it simply practical - to soften the light in a problematic window, for example? The answer to this question about function helps subsequent planning to get off on the right foot.

4.2 Clear glass. In some buildings clear glass has been part of the original architect's inspiration and to disturb this with stained glass will noticeably change the quality of the building. Although the intention may be to create what is felt to be a more suitably 'religious' environment, this can often blur the religious statements already being made by the building - about light, about clarity, about the fact that our worship takes place within, and not apart from, the natural or the human world framed through clear windows.

4.3 Decorated glass. Some buildings have matching windows which while not pictorial are attractively patterned and coloured and give a unity to the building. To many worshippers these may seem unremarkable and 'not saying anything' in the way that pictorial windows do. Familiarity has caused people not to see them for what they are, and it is therefore hardly surprising that they wish to replace them with 'real' stained glass windows.

4.4 Light source. The addition of pictorial windows over a period may have darkened the interior of the church unacceptably. Even though it may seem that precedent has given permission to continue the practice,

in that some stained glass windows have already been installed, the point may have come at which further windows may lower the light level too far, especially when it may mean starting to fill in a part of the building which is as yet untouched by stained glass. On the other hand, there may be very positive reasons for placing a window in a particular place. It could be that in inserting such a window a forgotten corner of the church can be 're-instated', connecting that part with the church as a whole.

5. Creating a better brief

The importance of a full briefing and exchange of views with the artist, when he/she visits the church or at another time, cannot be overstated. The desired window is not a disembodied work of the sort that can be displayed in a gallery but is to be part of a particular building which houses a particular people and which stands as witness in a particular situation. This particularity will be conveyed to the artist, who requires this as part of the inspiration of the design. This is not always a straightforward task because of the difference in vocabulary between the world of the Church and world of the artist, with their very different 'raw materials' (doctrinal, ecclesial on the one hand; colour, texture and form on the other). Sometimes it is difficult to know where to begin! The Committee is willing to assist in this process. The following should be borne in mind.

5.1 Choosing an artist. It is important to approach an artist with proven ability in designing and making windows for churches. The Committee has included in its *Church Windows* pamphlet a list of such artists, but it is one that is continually being added to as younger artists become established. The list is to assist congregations and not to limit choice; the Committee is willing to consider designs from any stained glass artist, studio or company. It is worth while travelling to churches to look at examples of work by, say, two or three chosen artists before approaching one. The alternative course of action, inviting a similar number of artists to submit designs (a fee is usually paid), can also be helpful to congregations but has the possible disadvantage in that the design does not issue from a developing dialogue between congregation and artist.

5.2 Who briefs? Rather than the donor(s), the congregation, through a representative group, should have the main role in the planning of the window. As users of the building, it is their prayers and praise it will enrich. The group briefing the artist should contain someone with theological awareness and a knowledge of worship from both the point of view of conducting and participation. This is not to suggest that the donors be bypassed. Their knowledge of the person commemorated, or of any information relating to the reason for the window being commissioned, is important. Even if they are not members of the congregation, their contribution should be made.

5.3 Choosing the theme. The theme should be thoughtfully chosen. Given our immediate tradition, with the content of our worship rooted in Scripture, a biblical starting point is appropriate. Given the nature of our Scriptures, this is also a most varied and endlessly renewable resource, with rich content of imagery, sayings and stories. However, care should be taken not automatically to pick on the most popular images or stories, already the theme of many windows. The Bible needs to be 'interrogated' from the point of view of the congregation's own situation, or from the particular witness of the person being commemorated. It is a task which calls for both prayer and study.

5.4 The contemporary context. Our understanding of Scripture, however, is that through its pages the living Word of God is proclaimed in our own time. Scripture has to be interpreted in terms of the life we know and the challenges we face. This leads to a consideration of the times we are in and the situation in which the particular congregation witnesses and serves. The setting of a church may be rural or urban, farming or fishing, industrial or technological. There may be particular features of the landscape or particular challenges in the life of the local community. Both church and community will have their own history. The chosen scriptural theme may be reflected in the witness of the person commemorated.

5.5 From the specific to the general. That being said, we do not offer the artist a list of specific items or images that we want included. The aim is a design which has a universality about it. Too literal a treatment will not achieve this. The finished window should not be 'about' a family or person or situation but speak through these of the God who is both within and beyond, and speak in such a way that those who look upon the window will be able to recognise that God as one who speaks to them also.

5.6 Leaving it to the artist. The purpose of briefing the artist is not to establish a hard and fast content which now simply has to be realised. The designer will have his/her own sources of inspiration - mentors, music, the colours of the natural world. The aim is to establish a dialogue, which continues until the design proposal is completed and the final cartoon made.

6. Avoiding pitfalls

6.1 When approaching a local artist. The intention might be to approach a local artist, perhaps a member of the congregation, whose talents are well known and valued. However, where the artist is not conversant with the craft of making windows, this can give rise to problems later. The artists to which we have referred above (2), if they did not make the glass to their own designs, knew the process inside out. There is a fundamental difference between creating a well-composed painting and preparing a cartoon for construction as a stained glass window. However, the Committee affirms the importance of tapping into the imagination and creativity of persons and groups in or related to a particular congregation, and has been involved in encouraging and working with projects involving local schools or other groups, in murals, mosaics, and even in the creation of new windows. Of great importance is the necessary step between idea and execution. The design of a stained glass window needs to be made in close consultation with a skilled stained glass artist, who may indeed welcome starting points from local designers.

6.2 Glass companies. Again, it is sometimes the case that a congregation has approached one of the several companies who produce decorative glass for both public and domestic situations, and who may advertise widely. However, often the designs provided by these companies may not be suitable for church windows. The Committee has begun to take a proactive approach and is in touch with such companies (both in glass and in other furnishings) to discuss with them designs acceptable in churches today.

6.3 Memorials. Often it is assumed that the most appropriate way to commemorate someone is to commission a stained glass window. The Committee's pamphlet *Gifts and Memorials* reminds the Church that the best way to remember someone who has made an active contribution to a congregation's life and witness may be to make a gift which enables this contribution to be continued. In the case of a choir member, for example, the commissioning of a new piece of music, special to that congregation, would have particular point; in the case of someone whose talent was for friendship, the redesigning of the vestibule as a place of greater welcome might be undertaken.

7. An example

With so many fine windows in Scottish churches, it would be difficult to select one. One example furth of Scotland clearly shows how artist and those commissioning worked together on the design for the window. It is in the cloister of Worcester Cathedral, marking the millennium, and is in etched glass. The artist was Mark Cazalet. It gathers up many local references but also contains images which show the relevance of the faith to the opening of a new era. There can be found the translating of the Worcester Antiphoner, St. Wulfstan, William Langland's vision of Piers Plowman, Richard Baxter composing hymns in prison, the burning of the monastic books on the Green, Woodbine Willie and the troops, Elgar conducting the "Dream" at the Three Choirs Festival. There is a mediaeval pilgrim, but also a humorous portrayal of a modern counterpart - a tourist complete with camcorder, his hat on backwards. To earth this in the promise of the Gospel, there has been selected four healing incidents and four of Jesus' most famous sayings.

OTHER MATTERS

8. Disabled access

The year 2004 marks the final stage of implementation of the Disability Discrimination Act which requires 'reasonable adjustments' to be made to the physical features of buildings, including churches. The Committee has by now dealt with a large number of applications in this regard. It reminds the Church that access ramps and other modifications should be appropriate for the people going to use them and should not detract from their dignity by being merely an expedient structure to satisfy a law. Where possible, such arrangements should not look like something added on to a building but integral to its design. In the Introduction to the Committee's publication, *Open Church*, which gathers together practical advice on the matter, and is available free to all who request it, we stated that this information pamphlet was

> as much about our continuing attempt to fulfil a much older duty of the Church, the provision of a ready welcome for 'all sorts and conditions' of people. Jesus' ease with people who made others uncomfortable, embarrassed or threatened - because of accident of birth, health, or social status - is a pattern for the hospitality which is part of the declaration of the Gospel. For us, therefore, the Act is not simply a piece of legislation to be conformed to but an opportunity to lead the local community into a fuller acceptance of those who for various reasons are, or feel, excluded.

The Committee is happy to be of help to congregations considering the matter of disabled access.

9. Conservation

The Committee greatly values its continuing contact with agencies whose concern is the conservation and recording of the heritage of our country and welcomes these as regular observers at its meetings. Neither at the establishment of the Committee in 1934 nor at any time subsequently has there been published a definition of the work of the Committee as such, although there have been many statements about goals and responsibilities in the course of which conservation has been referred to.

The Committee would like at this time, when arrangements are being explored with the Department of Culture, Media and Sport on the matter of jurisdiction over listed Church of Scotland buildings in England, to place on record its understanding of its role in conservation. The Committee believes that the duty of conservation is implicit in its remit in respect of alterations to churches in that any re-ordering of an interior or change to an exterior of a church building must be appropriately continuous with what is presently the case. By the same token, the Committee acts to assist local churches who wish to modify their buildings so as to be more effective in the Church's witness and worship in the present day, when appropriate changes and developments may be hindered by buildings designed for a different era. The Committee allows neither consideration to dictate the outcome but seeks solutions by which the historical and theological record that the building itself enshrines can contribute positively to the desired contemporary outcome. Material is currently being prepared by the Committee to help congregations become more aware of what they themselves have inherited in their buildings, both for their own enrichment and to ensure an evenly balanced dialogue with the Committee when alterations are envisaged.

10. *Scottish Life and Society*

The Committee is pleased that six of its members or consultants have contributed articles for the forthcoming thirteen volume reference work, *Scottish Life and Society: A Compendium of Scottish Ethnology* being prepared by the European Ethnological Research Centre under the general editorship of Professor Alexander Fenton. Professor James A. Whyte provides a history of church architecture and explores the influence of other Christian groups in Scotland; Professor John Hume records

industrial monuments in a number of contexts; Dr. Donald Smith surveys the developments in literature and drama and their relationship to religion; David Maxwell charts the variety of uses which have been made of redundant churches; Dr. Henry Sefton contributes material on church furnishings, church occasions and, more generally, on Presbyterianism; the Secretary explores relationships between music in church and in society.

DOUGLAS LAIRD, *Convener*
RICHARD FRAZER, *Vice Convener*
DOUGLAS GALBRAITH, *Secretary*

---

[1] J.K.Cameron (ed.), *The First Book of Discipline* (Saint Andrew Press, 1972), p.202.

[2] Michael Donnelly, *Scotland's Stained Glass* (The Stationery Office, 1997).

[3] George Hay, *The Architecture of Scottish Post-Reformation Churches* (Oxford, 1957), p.13.

[4] Donnelly, pp.41,43. See also his *Glasgow Stained Glass* (Glasgow Museums and Art Galleries, 1981).

[5] Sarah Brown, *Stained Glass at York Minster* (Scala, 1999); preface by the Dean of York.

[6] Angela Ashwin, "Spirituality and Corporate Worship", in *Worship* Vol.75, No.2, p.126.

[7] Millar Patrick, "Pulpit and Communion Table", *Church Service Society Annual*, 1932-33, p.8.

[8] *New Art for Church Buildings* (London: Church House Publishing), short pamphlet.

BOARD OF MINISTRY

MAY 2002

PROPOSED DELIVERANCE

The General Assembly

1. Receive the report.
2. Note the interim report on the Auxiliary Ministry and look forward to receiving a final report in 2003, produced in collaboration with other boards and committees, on new models of stipendiary and non stipendiary ministry to meet the Church's ministry and mission priorities. (Section 2)
3. Encourage Presbyteries to participate in the Board of Ministry's planned consultation on future models of ministry. (Section 2.6.4)
4. Note with approval the intention of the Board of Ministry to inform all current and new enquirers, applicants and candidates for the Auxiliary Ministry concerning possible changes arising from the Board's report of 2003. (Section 2.6.6)
5. Express gratitude for the significant contribution of retired ministers serving as locums in vacant charges. (Section 3.2.3)
6. Instruct the Board to investigate compiling a national database of ministers willing to undertake locum work. (Section 3.4.2)
7. Approve the recommended level of remuneration for locums. (Section 3.4.2)
8. Adopt the Overture anent Act V 1984 as amended, as set out in Appendix 3, concerning interim moderators and transmit the same to Presbyteries under the Barrier Act, directing that replies be sent in to the Principal Clerk by 31 December 2002. (Section 3.5.2 – 3.5.3)
9. Note with approval the encouraging response to the new Enquiry, Appraisal and Assessment Scheme and thank Presbytery representatives and local coordinators for their contributions and valued participation in the scheme. (Section 4.1)
10. Approve the alteration to the closing date for applicants to section 4 of Act V 1998. (Section 4.6 and Appendix 4)
11. Express gratitude to the retiring Director and assessors for their work and service in the Church's Assessment Process. (Section 4.8.3 and 4.10.2)
12. Express gratitude to Tom and Barbara Carruthers for their exceptional service to the Church as psychologist assessors. (Section 4.8.4)
13. Approve the adjustment to the delegation of duties in terms of section 6(a) of Act V 1998. (Section 4.13.2)
14. Approve the change to the process of reconsideration as set out in section 6(d) of Act V 1998. (Section 4.13.3 and Appendix 4)
15. Encourage the Board in its continuing review and evaluation of the new Enquiry, Appraisal and Assessment Scheme. (Section 4.17)
16. Encourage the Board in its support for all candidates for the Ministry of Word and Sacrament and the Diaconate and express appreciation to those involved in supervision. (Section 4.20.3.1)
17. Note that the Board will make an interim report to the General Assembly of 2003 on the continuation of candidature. (Section 4.20.4)

18. Approve the new stipend scheme, authorise the Board to implement the new scheme from 2004 to 2006 and instruct the Board of Stewardship and Finance in consultation with the Coordinating Forum, to amend the share of the Co-ordinated Budget Income Disposition available to Ministry Funds as necessary. (Section 5.2)
19. Instruct the Board of Ministry to work with the Board of Stewardship and Finance in providing information to presbyteries and congregations on the implementation of the new stipend scheme. (Section 5.2.8)
20. Note the Minimum Stipend and other related allowances declared for 2002. (Section 5.3 and Appendix 6)
21. Note the levels of Travel Expenses in 2002 for cars, motor cycles and pedal cycles. (Section 5.4 and Appendix 7)
22. Note the revised limits and conditions for investments in Further Endowment and amend the regulations accordingly. (Section 5.7)
23. Note and commend the uptake of the Study Leave Programme for ministers. (Section 5.10.3 and Appendix 10)
24. Note and commend the developmental work on Interim Ministry. (Section 5.11)
25. Note the Board's commitment to ongoing review of the Pastoral Support Scheme and encourage presbyteries in their responsibility for ongoing implementation. (Section 5.13.6)
26. Pass an act amending the Act X (2000) anent Long-Term Illness of Ministers in Charge. (Section 5.14 and Appendix 11)
27. Approve the appointment of the President and Vice President of the Diaconate Council for three year terms, serving throughout as members of the Board of Ministry. (Section 6.)
28. Thank all the Board's staff and express particular gratitude to the Very Rev Dr Alexander McDonald for his distinguished service to the Board and the wider Church as General Secretary and latterly as Senior Pastoral Adviser.

REPORT

1. INTRODUCTION

1.1 The Board of Ministry is responsible to the General Assembly for the recruitment, education, development and support of the ministers and deacons of the Church of Scotland. It seeks to carry out this remit in the light of the Ministers of the Gospel and Deacons of the Gospel reports. In this year's report, the Board wishes to highlight the following encouraging developments in the life and ministry of the Church supported through the work of the Board in fulfilling its remit:

- The growing numbers taking part in the Enquiry, Appraisal and Assessment Scheme for ministry and other forms of church service. (Section 4.4.1)
- The recognition of the need for fresh thinking on new patterns of non-stipendiary ministry. (Section 2)
- Affirming the contribution of the parish ministry through a new National Stipend scheme. (Section 5.2)
- An integrated approach to pastoral care for ministers, deacons and their families through the partnership between presbyteries, the Board of Ministry and other agencies. (Section 5.13)

1.2 The Board recognises and shares the growing concern in the Church about the following issues in ministry and understands that the focus of its work in future years will be in addressing these issues in collaboration with other boards and committees of the General Assembly, and presbyteries:

- The increasing number of vacant charges and the consequences of this for congregations, ministers and presbyteries.

- The need for new forms of ministry including team ministries.
- The need for effective development, support and pastoral care of ministers and deacons.
- The need to respond to the vision of the "Church Without Walls" report in growing collaboration among the boards and committees in serving the local church in its ministry and mission.

1.3   The Board has now put in place its senior staffing team to lead the implementation of the Board's work and to serve the pastoral needs of the ministry in partnership with the Presbytery schemes for pastoral care. The new General Secretary, Ruth Moir and the Senior Pastoral Adviser, Sandy McDonald have established an effective partnership in the context of the Board's new way of working. Since September 2001, Dr McDonald has been investigating the effectiveness of the provision of pastoral care across the Church and has been advising the Board on its future arrangements. The Board has ensured the continuity and future development of pastoral care services provided through its senior staff team by restructuring within the department and making efficient use of the skills and experience offered through its existing staff team. Through this restructuring, the Rev John Chalmers has been appointed by the Board to undertake the role of Senior Pastoral Adviser.

The Board records its appreciation and gratitude for the time, commitment and contributions of each of its members and all of its staff.

1.4   The Board is also developing its collaboration with other boards and committees in formulating joint strategies for serving the wider ministry and mission of the Church. In particular, responding to the deliverances of last year's General Assembly, the Board is developing a coordinated process of recruiting and training people with missionary gifts through its shared work with the Board of National Mission and the Board of Parish Education in a joint enquiry conference programme. The Board's Working Group on Ministry is also collaborating with representatives of these boards and the Panel on Doctrine to develop new patterns of locally recognised ministry and to equip the whole people of God for

Christian service. The Board looks forward to reporting in future years on the growing benefit to the wider Church of such collaborative work.

2.   WORKING GROUP ON MINISTRY

2.1   Remit

The Working Group on Ministry[1] produced a report on the education, training and development of the diaconate for the 2001 General Assembly. Since then it has turned its attention to address the second part of its remit regarding the status of the auxiliary ministry. The terms of the remit were as follows:

"To consider how the Board's theological understanding and vocational profile of the ordained ministry of Word and Sacrament could operate in new models of deployment in stipendiary and non-stipendiary ministry that meet the ministry and mission priorities of the Church of Scotland."

2.2   Process to Date

2.2.1   This preliminary report is set within the context of the Board of Ministry's report entitled *Ministers of the Gospel*, presented to and approved by the General Assembly in 2000. Mindful of the social, economic and cultural changes in Church and society highlighted in that report, this present report on auxiliary ministry has been prepared following consultation with the Board of National Mission, the Panel on Doctrine (including the Panel's Report to the General Assembly 2001[2]), the Senior Director of Selection Conferences and Presbytery Clerks.[3] A survey was also conducted of practising auxiliary ministers[4] and an extensive consultation process with auxiliary ministers and candidates for the auxiliary ministry commenced in June 2001 at their annual conference.

---

[1] see Appendix 1, section 1
[2] General Assembly [2001], 13/1-13/24
[3] see Appendix 1, section 2
[4] see Appendix 1, section 3

2.2.2 Considerable attention has also been paid to the 1970's Assembly Reports of the Committee of Forty out of which the concept of the auxiliary ministry was first proposed for the Church of Scotland. The Working Group has found that re-reading these and subsequent reports on the development of auxiliary ministry in the Church has shed considerable light on the present situation[5]

2.3   Present Situation

2.3.1 As part of its research, the Working Group issued a questionnaire to the Church's auxiliary ministers. As well as providing a great deal of helpful information, the questionnaire produced a private correspondence. With the permission of the original authors, three case studies have been prepared. Although they have been disguised to protect the identity of the sources, the Assembly can be assured that what follows is the actual experience of some of the Church's auxiliary ministers. The case studies do not make for pleasant reading but they do illustrate many of the present difficulties. Having presented the case studies the report will explore the background that has led to the present situation and then present the Working Group's proposals on what should happen next.

2.3.2   Case Study 1

2.3.2.1 An auxiliary was appointed to a congregation where there were certain strains on the finances. There was a freeze on the salaries of church employees. The Finance Committee was informed that, while the appointment of an auxiliary would save on pulpit supply fees, there would be the additional cost to the congregation of the auxiliary's travel costs.

2.3.2.2 It was suggested that the auxiliary's expected three visits to the parish per week, involving a round trip of some thirty miles, in addition to the Sunday service to undertake parish visits to the housebound elderly, be curtailed to two, with one of these being of a full day's duration (morning and afternoon). No meal arrangement was proposed nor was access to church premises available. The auxiliary was obliged, therefore, to provide and eat lunch in the car.

2.3.2.3 In placement, the auxiliary was expected to purchase at least two tickets for every congregational function; the auxiliary also had to provide full clerical dress as she/he was expected to wear this in worship; the auxiliary was truly giving of her/his time and at a real financial cost to the family budget, as he/she did not receive a stipend and was expected to spend money in accomplishing the task of an auxiliary minister.

2.3.2.4 It has been remarked often to auxiliaries that what people do not pay for they do not value. They do not appreciate it if it comes cheap; often churches appear to value auxiliary ministry as worth less than nothing.

2.3.3   Case Study 2

2.3.3.1 An auxiliary minister was appointed to be part of a parish of a large industrial town. The appointment came as a result of a two-minute conversation at the end of a Business Committee meeting of a Presbytery. The minister welcomed the appointment, but the Kirk Session did not want to pay the expenses of the auxiliary; only at the insistence of the Convener of the quinquennial visitation and the Presbytery Clerk was this rectified.

2.3.3.2 The area allocated to the auxiliary was one of high deprivation in a large Urban Priority Area population; the responsibilities given to the auxiliary were for pastoral and worship leadership in the area and also participation in the chaplaincy in the local high school. During the first Christmas period, in the two weeks beforehand, there were seven funerals, the extra Christmas services and the school service.

2.3.3.3 During this appointment, there were many funerals. Many were difficult relating to alcohol, drugs, suicides and children including a very complex family funeral with a number of relatives dying at the one time.

2.3.3.4 An invitation to conduct a wedding in another Presbytery was given and appropriate permission sought from the other Presbytery and the wedding conducted. The Presbytery expected a proper check to be made and this was done. The Presbytery, in which the wedding

---

[5] see Appendix 1, section 4

took place, did not expect such courtesy. The auxiliary minister was not allowed to become an Interim Moderator, but instead was made Convener of the Advisory Committee in the same vacancy. It was also expected that the auxiliary minister convened quinquennial visitations which was done without any reference to experience or the difficulty of carrying this out in an auxiliary role.

2.3.4 Case Study 3

2.3.4.1 This auxiliary minister would like to ensure that parity be insisted upon across the Church – for the good of all who volunteer their services in this way. He/she also pointed out that auxiliary ministers are required to offer a minimum of ten hours per week in parish service plus a Sunday. Ten hours was suggested as a reasonable input, but in practice, for a person in full-time employment, this is a huge commitment. After a day's work, it means at least two hours each evening Monday to Friday, with Sunday on top. Also pointed out is the fact that this envisaged position does not work out in practice and many auxiliary ministers are no longer in full-time employment. Most are either retired or not in full-time paid work. The church gets more than it ever expected.

2.3.4.2 Some other Presbyteries, unlike her/his own, had allowed auxiliary ministers to become Interim Moderators. The current legislation does not permit this. There are real problems in country areas regarding long term vacancies or ongoing vacancies where the post of auxiliary minister may be an ideal means of addressing the pastoral and worship needs of the community.

2.3.4.3 This auxiliary minister pointed out that readers can be appointed as locums and be paid; most readers are in receipt of honorariums for their services for doing pulpit supply. A reader could be appointed as a paid locum, while an ordained auxiliary minister is classed as someone who could not undertake such a responsibility. This auxiliary minister has over six years' experience and has worked in vacancies in an unpaid capacity in an almost full-time manner. Preaching every week, sometimes doing two services, chaplain in five primary schools and

pastoral cover for three parishes. Often the auxiliary minister is expected to work even five, six and seven days and conduct many funerals in this wide area. This auxiliary minister wished to have the freedom to act as the Presbytery might determine in meeting the needs of the Presbytery in its various parishes, as this particular situation and the pastoral needs required rather than any regulation dictated.

2.3.5 Comment on the Case Studies

Without claiming to offer a comprehensive view of the experience of auxiliary ministers, these case studies illustrate the confusion that exists in the Church regarding the role and practice of auxiliary ministry. It is evident that this confusion is found at all levels of the Church, Presbytery, Kirk Sessions, congregations and among ministers themselves. Different Presbyteries interpret the guidelines in different ways and this has led to auxiliary ministers fulfilling certain roles in one Presbytery (eg Interim Moderator, hospital chaplain) but being barred from doing so in another. There is confusion in terms of the relationship between the auxiliary ministry and the other agents of the church e.g. readers. There is also a variety of practice regarding remuneration and expenses.

2.4 Other Issues

2.4.1 Selection Process

Although it is not highlighted in the case studies, the Working Group also learned that there is confusion in terms of the assessment and selection process. At present assessors have to apply the same tests, exercises and standard in marking to those applying for both the full-time ministry and the auxiliary ministry but they have to recognise that there are differences between the two forms of ministry. This raises the question of whether the Church proposed a separate doctrine of the ministry of Word and Sacrament for auxiliary ministers. The Working Group also learned that anyone wishing to transfer from full-time to auxiliary ministry or vice versa is required to re-enter the selection process from the very beginning.

2.4.2 4th Major Review

The very fact that this present report marks the fourth time that the Assembly has instructed a major review of the auxiliary ministry is indicative that something is wrong. It is evident that the Church has never owned the concept of auxiliary ministry. In the course of its twenty year history thirteen Presbyteries have no experience of auxiliary ministry while a further eight have only had one auxiliary minister working in their bounds. It is also evident that the concept of auxiliary ministry never developed as first proposed. In order to understand more fully how the present situation has developed, it is to these Committee of Forty proposals that this report now turns.

2.4.3   Committee of Forty Proposals

2.4.3.1   The concept of an auxiliary ministry originated in the Committee of Forty Reports to the General Assembly in the 1970s. As part of its planning for the life and witness of the Church in what it perceived to be a time of change, the Committee of Forty believed that an affirmation of the ministry of all the people of God was essential. In doing so, it looked to the development of particular ministries and forms of service which would enrich and enable the diverse gifts of the membership of the Church to be utilised efficiently for the witness to the Gospel. In making its proposals for what eventually became the auxiliary ministry, the Committee of Forty was also attempting to address the decline in numbers of candidates for full-time ministry. In proposing the concept of the auxiliary ministry, the Committee recognised the need for adaptable and suitably trained personnel to meet creatively the parochial and non-parochial developments in the Church.

2.4.3.2   While much may be said in support of the Committee of Forty's work, it is evident that some of the conclusions drawn and forecasts made proved inaccurate.

2.4.3.3   The Committee of Forty believed that this new development of non-stipendiary ministry would be attractive to the Church and recruit many potential ministers, initially, at least, from the readership. The popularity of the model was not confirmed by the early responses from Presbyteries and recruitment to auxiliary ministry has never been as high as expected by the Committee of Forty or the General Assemblies which received its reports so enthusiastically. In its twenty-year

history some sixty auxiliary ministers have been ordained.

2.4.3.4   The Committee had visualised a local ministry, ordained for service, calling for the individual to serve where the need arose in his or her particular congregation. This is not the model that has been adopted by the Church. In fact, the legislation framed debarred an auxiliary minister from serving in his or her own congregation.

2.4.3.5   The Committee of Forty expected that an auxiliary minister would be able to exercise ministry only under the direct supervision of a full-time minister. In practice auxiliary ministers have been appointed to positions without such direct supervision.

2.4.3.6   The Committee of Forty proposed that an auxiliary minister's membership of Presbytery would be suspended when the person was no longer authorised to exercise that ministry in a particular appointment. This was clearly contrary to the doctrine of ordination outlined by the Panel on Doctrine. It has proved pastorally hurtful to individuals concerned. The practice resulted in one Presbytery appointing an auxiliary minister as a corresponding member of Presbytery, so that the person could continue their Convenership of a Presbytery Committee despite the fact that their post as an auxiliary minister had ended.

2.4.3.7   The Committee originally perceived auxiliary ministry as a part-time appointment. In practice each Presbytery is free to draw up its own terms and conditions of appointment and many have done. The case studies reveal some of the difficulties surrounding the time commitment.

2.4.3.8   The Committee of Forty envisaged that auxiliary ministers would be in paid employment. In fact the majority of serving auxiliary ministers are retired from full-time paid employment.

2.4.3.9   The Committee of Forty envisaged a ministry different in certain aspects from the full-time ministry, but not one of a secondary nature. It emphasised the need for a rigorous selection and training process for ordination. In practice the lack of clarity regarding the distinctive nature of this ministry has created difficulties in the selection and recruitment process.

2.5 Development of Auxiliary Ministry since its Inception

2.5.1 The Committee of Forty recommended the development of auxiliary ministry and, while the General Assembly approved its proposals in broad outline, it was left to the Education for the Ministry Committee to develop a regular scheme that included the following:

- nomination of candidates by Presbytery;
- central selection procedures;
- a uniform scheme of training;
- a definition of the area in which the powers conferred by ordination would be exercised;
- service under an Interim Moderator or other minister authorised by the Presbytery; and
- termination of the exercise of powers conferred by ordination.

2.5.2 1981

In 1981, the Education for the Ministry Committee reported to the General Assembly on the development of its plans for the training of an auxiliary ministry. The report mentioned the contact with Presbyteries, the development of the selection process and the way in which candidates for this ministry would be nurtured and supported in their formation. The Committee highlighted certain matters which appeared to be of great importance, but were not specifically in the remit of the Education for the Ministry Committee. In particular the Committee asked three questions:

1. Is the ordination of the auxiliary minister a general one, as in the case of regular ministers, or is there a limitation connected to a presbyterial area and designation?
2. What is the relationship between the ordained auxiliary minister and the full-time lay agents of the Church, eg, lay missionaries and deaconesses?
3. Does the concept of the auxiliary ministry extend only to assistance in a regular ministerial parish or is it

envisaged that it should be associated with other forms of ministry, e.g., industrial chaplaincy?

These questions were deferred to the General Administration Committee in consultation with the Assembly Council in the hope that procedures would be established to address them. **It is the view of the Working Group that the failure to address these questions is critical to understanding the present situation of the auxiliary ministry.**

2.5.3 1982

In the General Assembly Report of the Education for the Ministry Committee of 1982, the need was emphasised once again to answer these fundamental questions to allow the development of auxiliary ministry. The reports in subsequent years emphasised the quality of the candidates who had offered themselves for training and their diligence in fulfilling the demands of the General Assembly, a point which the present Working Group is glad to reiterate. The reports also noted the small numbers of people responding to this challenge throughout the Church.

2.5.4 1986

In 1986, a report to the General Assembly suggested a special Committee be appointed to review the auxiliary ministry. This was established and reported in 1987. This report emphasised the need for the Church to take the notion of auxiliary ministry more seriously, to promote it more widely and to utilise it effectively. It also considered the whole process whereby a minister, who was ordained as an auxiliary, might become a full-time minister and how the selection and recruitment process needed to take account of the particular issues of auxiliary ministry as distinct from those of full-time ministry. In this report, the question of payment was raised, but no firm recommendations were made.

2.5.5 1992

2.5.5.1 The subsequent reports to the General Assembly noted the small numbers being accepted as auxiliary ministers, alongside a proportionally small number of those offering themselves to the selection process. In 1992, a Working Group reported on issues relating to the readership and auxiliary ministry. This group attempted to address the problems of the almost competing and overlapping nature of the readership alongside the auxiliary ministry. It also noted that almost all Presbyteries had readers within their bounds, but less than one-half of Presbyteries had auxiliary ministers.

2.5.5.2 The report further noted a lack of interest and support in the Presbyteries for auxiliary ministry, as well as a dearth of applicants. There appeared to be a lack of understanding of the nature of auxiliary ministry. Neither were auxiliary ministers featured in any strategy of ministry and mission in Presbyteries. The report emphasised the need for the readership to have a more rigorous form of training, which the Committee believed would be achieved through the use of the T.L.S. programme, available through St Colm's and Parish Education. The report highlighted the issue of selection for the readership which it believed was highly inappropriate and needed to be changed. While the way in which readers were selected was to change, the process remained Presbytery based.

2.5.5.3 The issue of payment was discussed in this report, namely that readers were eligible for payment but auxiliary ministers were not. The report also emphasised that auxiliary ministers were likely to be financially poorer after training, while having made enormous sacrifices to be trained for this important service within the Church. The report did not recommend payment of an honorarium, believing it was undesirable. This was based on the belief that there was no demand for payment from the auxiliary ministers themselves and that the non-stipendiary nature of the auxiliary minister was inherent in the original conception of the office. As is seen from the case studies, questions of remuneration and expenses continued to be an issue yet to be resolved. The current Working Group has found that there is a wide range of opinion on the issue of remuneration and expenses within the present group of auxiliary ministers.

2.5.6   1996
The reports in the 1990s emphasised yet again the very

small number of candidates coming forward for training. They also include reference to the change in the training programme, with new candidates from 1996 being involved in the Certificate and Diploma in Christian Studies, available at Aberdeen and Glasgow Universities.

2.6   Conclusions
2.6.1   Based on its research of Assembly reports, its consultations with other boards and committees and Presbytery clerks and, in particular, the consultations, correspondence and conversations with auxiliary ministers themselves, the Working Group has reached the conclusion that the present situation regarding auxiliary ministry in the Church of Scotland is unsustainable. In terms of selection and assessment, deployment, employment, remuneration and expenses, expectation and current practice, it is no exaggeration to say that confusion reigns throughout. While the Working Group expresses its admiration for the work of auxiliary ministers in the midst of this confusion, the restrictive nature of the legislation, piecemeal development, the failure to promote and a lack of ownership by the whole Church mean that the status quo is not an option.

The question is what to do next?

2.6.2   In seeking to discharge its remit, the Working Group will address the following questions:-

- Does the concept of an auxiliary or non-stipendiary ministry have a meaningful role in the future ministry and mission of the Church?
- How is that role to be determined?
- What will be the relationship between such an auxiliary ministry and the other agents of the Church?
- How will any new model of auxiliary ministry relate to the readership?
- On what basis will candidates for this role be assessed and selected?
- How will they be deployed?
- The issue of reimbursement will be addressed.
- What will be the status of auxiliary ministers within Presbytery?

2.6.3 If these indicate some of the questions which the Working Group is addressing, the Assembly should know that it will do so in terms of its remit of developing *'new models of stipendiary and non-stipendiary ministry to meet the ministry and mission priorities of the Church.'*

2.6.4 The Working Group is pleased to report that extensive consultations have already taken place with the Board of National Mission, the Board of Parish Education and the Panel on Doctrine in order to address the issues identified and it looks forward to bringing a further report to the General Assembly 2003. Further consultations will also be held with Presbyteries and with auxiliary ministers themselves. The Working Group is in touch with partner churches to learn from their experience of non-stipendiary ministry. The Working Group is also mindful of the Board of Ministry's work on stipend arrangements and recognises that this will impinge on the viability of any proposals it brings forwards.

2.6.5 The Working Group is committed to bring to the Assembly and the wider Church a proposal regarding the future practice of the ordained ministry of Word and Sacrament consistent with the theological understanding and vocational profile articulated in the Board's *Ministers of the Gospel Report* and responsive to the mission opportunities and challenges facing our Church.

2.6.6 In the light of this ongoing work, the Working Group wishes to propose that all current and new enquirers, applicants and candidates for the Auxiliary Ministry should be informed about the Board's intention to report to the General Assembly of 2003 on proposals regarding the future of Auxiliary Ministry and arrangements for non-stipendiary ministry that may affect their training and deployment.

3. PROJECTED MINISTERIAL SHORTAGE AND RELATED ISSUES: AN INTERIM RESPONSE

3.1 Introduction
The General Assembly of 2001 instructed the Board to prepare a report which addressed the projected shortage of ministers in a realistic and pastoral way. A number of related matters were also remitted for consideration and the Board is now in a position to present a report on progress to date.

3.2 Projections of Ministerial Supply
3.2.1 The Board presents statistics in the table in Appendix 2 which show a five year projection of the number of vacancies based on the trends over the last five years and on the current number of charges. These figures are not precise, but they are indicative of a serious trend leading to a major shortfall in the number of ministers available to fill vacancies over the next five years.

3.2.2 The challenge to the Church is quite clear; a range of imaginative measures must be taken to deploy and support existing ministers in different ways and to find ways of building up the ministry of the whole people of God.

3.2.3 However, the immediate task of the Board of Ministry is to assure the Church that it is examining the matter of this projected shortfall very seriously and that it is concerned about the burden of demand that this shortage is placing on the whole ministry pool. In this connection a number of points are worth noting:

- That more and more ministers are having to serve as Interim Moderators for prolonged periods of time, and that the level of work being asked of many ministers results in frustration, low morale and even illness.
- That the demands of Presbyteries and of the boards and committees of the General Assembly are being shared by fewer and fewer ministers and consideration has to be given to how this work can be better delegated or, indeed, how this burden can be reduced.
- That presently, without the contribution of retired ministers, the Church would have an even greater crisis on its hands, and the Board is anxious to recognise their ongoing contribution to ministry in the Church
- The Board's resources and many of its recent developments are aimed at supporting ministers who are facing an ever more complex set of demands, i.e. providing opportunities for personal development,

developing a positive Ministry Review Process, offering quality Occupational Health Care and underpinning the ministry with a variety of pastoral support arrangements

3.3   Specific Matters under Review
3.3.1   Last year's Assembly noted the following concerns which it asked the Board to examine:

- The role and remuneration of locums
- The possibility of the appointment of non-ministerial Interim Moderators
- Pension and other rights of ministers who accept reviewable/terminable tenure.
- Age of entry, [and by extension age of retirement]
- Entitlement to Study Leave for ministers within five years of retirement
- The rights of ministers who come into the Church of Scotland from other denominations in respect of such matters as study leave, stipend, recruitment etc
- The possible introduction of shorter or part-time courses for mature candidates, deacons and auxiliary ministers

3.3.2   The Board is now able to make recommendations on some of these issues, while others are being considered at greater length and will be the subject of future reports to the General Assembly.

3.4   The Role and Remuneration of Locums
3.4.1   Retired ministers do the bulk of this work and the Board is anxious to affirm this vital contribution to the Ministry of the Church of Scotland. However, it is clear from recent experience that Presbyteries and Kirk Sessions are struggling to find enough locums to provide adequate cover, particularly in more remote settings. Many retired ministers are prepared to do pulpit supply on a regular basis, but are reluctant to commit to working in longer-term locum positions. Furthermore, it is often difficult for remote Presbyteries to identify and engage appropriate personnel.

3.4.2   As one of the short-term solutions to these problems, the Board proposes the following two changes in the appointment locums.

- The Board proposes investigating compiling a national database of ministers willing to undertake this kind of work. With the new Presbytery internet communication system in place it would be easy for local parties to access the names of available personnel. However, after due consideration and consultation with the Board of National Mission and the Board of Parish Education, the Board does not consider it practical or cost effective at this time to develop a database with the current curricula vitae of all ministers, auxiliary ministers, deacons, readers and paid youth workers, particularly in the context of the stringent requirements of the new Data Protection Act.
- The Board also proposes a significant increase in the level of remuneration paid to those who carry out locum work. At the moment the locum fee is paid at the rate of £510 per month which includes the weekly pulpit supply fee. This amount is well below a pro rata payment of the minimum stipend. Instead the Board proposes that in future the Pulpit Supply Fee and the day-rate for locum work should be separated, and recommends that locum work should be paid at the level of £300 per month for every day worked per week. This would, in effect, allow a locum carrying out the present level of duties to earn (including Pulpit Supply Fee) up to a £800 per month. This rate of remuneration would also be available to ministers from overseas and others who are interested in providing short-term cover. The Board hopes that this will go some way to encouraging a greater pool of people to become involved in this type of work, and recommends that these changes in remuneration should take affect from 1st January 2003.

3.5   The Appointment of non-ministerial Interim Moderators
3.5.1   The Kirk Session is now the only body that cannot be moderated by anyone other than a minister. The Board believes that there are many deacons, elders, readers and others with a recognised pastoral role, who would be more than capable of carrying out this vital role, and this in itself could take some of the strain that is falling on the ministers of the Church. The Board of Ministry would

provide advice and support for such non-ministerial Interim Moderators and, from time to time, will provide opportunities for appropriate training.

3.5.2 Accordingly, the Board brings forward an Overture, recommending that legislation be introduced that would allow for the appointment of non-ministerial Interim Moderators. In doing so, the Board is fully aware of the fact that this would lead to a fundamental change in the make up of one of the Courts of the Church, namely that a Kirk Session could be constituted entirely of Ruling Elders. It is also noted that the advent of non-ministerial Interim Moderators could lead to the inference that the Church ceases to provide a territorial ministry throughout Scotland.

3.5.3 The Board is not persuaded that either of these arguments is powerful enough to stand in the way of a proposal that seeks to address the realities of the local church situation. It is the Board's view that it is proposing an optional interim arrangement during vacancies, and this does not alter the normal membership of the Kirk Session. Furthermore, the "Church Without Walls" report calls for courageous solutions to the challenges we face and it further calls on the Church to find imaginative new ways to use the gifts of the whole people of God. This proposal would not only relieve the workload being asked of already busy ministers, it would provide the Church with a more honest and viable way of fulfilling its obligation to provide Scotland with complete ministerial cover. The tenor of this Overture is set out in Appendix 3 of this report, and the Board encourages the General Assembly to transmit this to Presbyteries for consideration under the Barrier Act.

3.6 Pension and other Rights
3.6.1 The General Assembly of 2001 expressed some concerns about the rights of ministers made vulnerable as a result of accepting Reviewable and Terminable Tenure appointments. The sudden ending of an appointment can lead to an involuntary break in service which has implications on entitlement to 'Death in Service' benefit and on a minister's pension rights.

3.6.2 However, the pension issue has to some extent been addressed, in that earlier periods of broken service are now being preserved at a better rate of annuity and a factor for inflation has been built into a person's entitlement. Otherwise, the question of further examining the issue of Tenure is a much bigger and longer-term matter. The Board continues to be involved in discussions with the Assembly Council and other boards and committees about this perennial concern, and will continue to contribute to the debate.

3.7 Age Limits and Retirement Policy
3.7.1 The 1998 General Assembly, which approved the new Act Anent Education and Training for the Ministry, approved the present age limit for entry into the Ministry of the Church of Scotland. The Board argued that the cost of training justifies the right to expect a reasonable number of years of service from those trained and prepared for Ministry, and it also argued that there had to be adequate time for formation in Ministry during the period of active service.

3.7.2 Ten years ago the average length of a Church of Scotland ministry was twenty eight years. Working back from a retirement age of sixty five, fourteen years was chosen because it represented the timescale required to give half of the average length of ministry and also allowed a minister to give two, seven year cycles of ministry to the Church.

3.7.3 However, the Board is conscious that every organisation is under obligation to reconsider age limits in the light of pending European legislation, and has begun a detailed consideration of these matters in consultation with the Law Department. The Board will report on this matter to the General Assembly of 2003.

3.8 Study Leave Entitlement
The Board has already modified the detail of the Study Leave Scheme, so that ministers within five years of retirement, have one further year in which to use any Study Leave entitlement which has accumulated.

3.9 The Rights of Ministers from Other Denominations

3.9.1 In terms of qualification for Study Leave, the Church of Scotland currently recognises the length of service from the date of ordination of ministers entering the Church of Scotland from other denominations. However, only certain categories of ministers have qualifying years of service which are recognised in respect of payment of the Service Supplement. This means that, for instance, ministers who come from other denominations and ministers who have previously served as School Chaplains do not have their years of service recognised.

3.9.2 The Board recognises this anomaly and has planned the new National Stipend Scheme in such a way as to recognise all years of ordained service which have entitled a minister to a seat in Presbytery in terms of the Act III 2000 or the equivalent body in the denomination from which they have been admitted. It is proposed that the new scheme, recommended to the General Assembly in section 5.2 of this report, should be introduced in 2004. The Board does not propose any alteration to the current regulations governing the Service Supplement Fund.

3.10 Shorter or Part-Time Courses

This is a major policy question and it has been remitted, as a matter of urgency, to the appropriate working groups and Committees of the Board for consideration.

3.11 In presenting these interim comments and proposals in response to the present shortage, the Board also notes the encouraging number of candidates in training for ministry in proportion to the annual number of new communicant members.

4. VOCATIONAL GUIDANCE EDUCATION AND TRAINING

4.1 Progress in Implementing the Enquiry, Appraisal and Assessment Scheme

Few ventures in the life of the Church have been as well received as the Enquirers' Conferences. They are meeting a real need, allowing church people to explore the variety of ways in which they might understand their sense of vocation and develop their service in the Church.

4.2 The Enquirers' Conference

Enquirers' Conferences are twenty-four hour events that are funded from the resources of the Board of Ministry. As such, they are now an integral part of the process of application for candidature. However, while the Board of Ministry takes a lead role, these events have been a model of collaboration between the Boards of Ministry, National Mission, Parish Education, Social Responsibility and World Mission, all of whom play a major role in setting out the variety of areas of service that can be pursued within the scope of the Church of Scotland.

4.3 The Enquirers' Conference Programme

The Conference Programme has been very well received. Participants have almost universally affirmed the positive nature of the event and the programme that has been slowly developing now contains the following vital elements:

- A Keynote Address on the "Call to Service Today"
- Five presentations showing the variety of areas of service being developed through the work of the Boards referred to above and a sixth presentation on the vital calling to service in the local congregation.
- An address on Integrity of Faith and Life and
- A series of workshops setting out the detail of taking Enquiries to a further stage.

4.4 Encouraging Response

4.4.1 In the last eighteen months some 300 people have attended the three Enquirers' Conferences and another 100 are expected to attend the Conference in March 2002. For many, it has been a developmental experience in itself, and they have returned to their congregations excited by the challenge of engaging in some vital aspect of the ministry of the whole people of God. For others it has been the beginning of a further journey of exploration and discovery. The most common affirmation is that of people who have been grateful to the Church for making this journey of exploration possible.

4.4.2   The Board of Ministry can report that as a result of these Conferences, more than 118 people have continued the process of Enquiry into a period of Accompanied Appraisal and, of that number, forty seven are currently undergoing a period of Field Assessment leading to a Local Review. Six are still engaged in a period of extended enquiry. While it is too early to report the detail of one complete cycle of this new process, nonetheless, the Board is encouraged both by the progress made in implementation and by the general level of acceptance of the scheme by the Church. The other Boards, which have been involved in setting up this process, have also been encouraged by the level of enquiry and interest that has ensued.

4.5   Evaluation of the Scheme
4.5.1   Putting the scheme into practice has already allowed the Assessment Scheme Committee to begin to fine-tune its processes. The Committee will establish a continual evaluation process in order to ensure a proper and efficient delivery of this scheme that is crucial to the work of recruiting ministers and deacons of the Gospel. The Board will continue to keep the General Assembly informed of significant changes as and when they occur.

4.5.2   One of the first changes identified that would allow for the better organisation of the scheme is the need to establish a proper rhythm of the Enquirers' Conference cycle in the mind of the Church. It should be noted, therefore, that the main Enquirers' Conference will be held in March each year. This will be followed by a second conference in late August or early September. In attending one of these two conferences, Enquirers will have ample time to complete a period of Appraisal, Field Assessment and Local Review in time attend a National Assessment Conference in the first half of the following year.

4.6   Closing Date for Applications to begin a Period of Enquiry
To allow for the best use of an Enquirer's time and to ensure the fullest consideration of an application it is necessary, therefore, to move the closing date for applications to 30th September each year. Appendix 4 of

this report sets out the alteration which is required to section 4 of Act V 1998.

4.7   Recruitment and Training of Presbytery Representatives and Co-ordinators
4.7.1   The Church's assessment and selection process has undergone more change in the last year than in the previous thirty years. A major responsibility now rests on the shoulders of a variety of individuals who contribute to the Field Assessment and Local Review process. It has been necessary, therefore, to provide training and support for all those who have such a vital role at local level.

4.7.2   Following last year's General Assembly, when the agreement was reached on the shape of the new scheme, every Presbytery was invited to submit the names of those who might be considered for selection and training in the various roles required to operate the process. Those names submitted, together with others, who had already been nominated by Presbyteries and trained as supervisors, became the first to be invited for training.

4.7.3   More than 180 ministers, deacons and elders took part in a series of regional Information and Training days. From this group, the Board was able to identify the necessary number of personnel required to take the first set of enquirers and applicants through the local process. Presbytery Representatives and Co-ordinators are committed to three days of training which cover such aspects of the scheme as confidentiality, keeping a reflective journal, giving feedback and report writing in an open system. These have been valuable days in themselves with many of the participants speaking of the benefit they have derived from the input provided. In particular, these training days have attempted to offer an experience of reflective self-appraisal and spiritual direction. These have been in line with the aspirations of the reports *Ministers of the Gospel* and *Deacons of the Gospel*, and as a result the Board is confident that it has laid good foundations for best practice in Field Assessment and Local Review.

4.7.4   The Board records its sincere thanks to all of those Presbytery Representatives and Local Co-ordinators who have been so willing to give of their time and energy to this important work. It is a measure of how seriously this matter is being taken throughout the Church that there have been few problems in finding the personnel needed to operate the process. The Board also records its thanks for the contribution of its staff in the implementation of the new scheme. Their knowledge of the scheme and its fundamental requirements has helped to shape an excellent process of training and induction. In addition, it has been their energy and gift in administration that has enabled the Board to achieve so much in such a short space of time.

4.8   The Role of Assessors

4.8.1   Alongside the training of new personnel, there has been a parallel process of preparing the departmental staff, existing church and psychologist assessors and directors for their part in both the Local Reviews and the new National Assessment Conferences. The Board has never before committed itself to such a thorough training schedule. However, it believes that the highest possible standards have to be applied at the point of examining the Call and suitability of applicants. Personnel who have not attended the requisite training programme as set out by the Assessment Scheme Committee will not be used in the scheme until they have participated in what will be an ongoing process of recruitment, selection, training and retraining.

4.8.2   New Assessors

The Board through its Assessment Scheme Committee has also continued to exercise its responsibility for the recruitment and selection of new assessors. It is pleased to report the appointment of 16 new assessors who have been brought through an intensive selection and training programme to prepare them for participation in all parts of the new scheme. They are: Rev. Dr Iain Barclay, Mrs Eileen Brown, Rev. Peter Dickson, Rev. Suzanne Dunleavy, Mrs Dorothy Ferguson, Rev. Graham Finch, Mrs Sandra Holt, Rev. Marjorie Macaskill, Rev. Donald McLeod, Rev. Colin Renwick, Rev. Lindsay Schluter, Mr Charles Shepherd, Rev. Elisabeth Spence, Rev. Alan Ward, Rev. Isabel Whyte, and Rev. Evelyn Young. Having been selected for this important work they will be used

in the assessment process in accordance with the standards and conditions agreed by the Board. The Board is also pleased to welcome the appointment of three new psychologist assessors. They are: Mrs Janet Allan, Ms Hazel Bech and Mr Ralston McKay.

4.8.3   Retiring Assessors

The Board also wishes record its thanks to the Rev. Kenneth Borthwick, Rev. Neil Campbell, Rev. Arthur Kent, Rev. William McLaren and Mr John Muir who are retiring at this time.

4.8.4   Retiring Psychologist Assessors

4.8.4.1   Over the years since the inception of a national selection process the Church has been well served by a succession of psychologist assessors who have given their professional services to the Church. The current team continues to give invaluable service and the Committee continues to recruit psychologists in order to maintain a proper balance of assessors. However, during this past year both Tom and Barbara Carruthers have retired from the team and their going should not pass without a special mention.

4.8.4.2   Barbara Carruthers has served as a psychologist assessor over several periods during the last three decades. She has made a valuable contribution to our development and training processes and many in the Church will remember her with appreciation. The contribution of Tom Carruthers, over a period of thirty years, has been of an exceptional order. Much of the shape and integrity of the present Assessment and Selection process has been influenced by Tom's thinking. He has also been a vital contributor to the development of the new process of Enquiry, Appraisal and Assessment. We wish Barbara and Tom well in their retirement.

4.9   Ongoing Recruitment and Selection of Assessors

4.9.1   The Enquiry, Appraisal and Assessment Scheme requires some degree of expansion of the assessing team and the Board through its Assessment Scheme Committee will almost certainly be involved in a continuous process of adding to the pool of both church and psychologist assessors. In fulfilling this most important responsibility the Committee will continue to apply the highest of standards. Clear steps are taken by the Board to describe to the Presbyteries the skills and criteria required for this demanding task.

4.9.2 In accordance with accepted practice, the Committee continues to collect the names of potential assessors from members of the Board, from other members of the assessing team and principally from lists submitted by Presbyteries. It is made clear from the beginning that the demands of being an assessor are arduous and that the selection process itself is thorough and demanding.

4.9.3 In correspondence with Presbyteries the process for selection of assessors is fully explained, and Presbyteries are invited to put forward the names of those considered to have experience in the practice of interviewing, assessment, selection and report writing. It is pointed out that a certain level of existing competence and a willingness to make this work a priority will be required in those who are selected for this important task. Nominees must be committed to dedicating a significant amount of time and energy both to training and participating in the scheme, and it is pointed out that Presbyteries should look beyond their own membership for suitable people. The Board would stress the need for Presbyteries and their Committees to apply rigorous standards to the way in which they compile lists of potential assessors. From the outset the fullest possible information should be conveyed to those whose names are submitted to the Board, in this way the disappointment of non-acceptance might be reduced to a minimum.

4.9.4 The responsibility for the now well-established method of selection and induction, whereby members of the Committee together with the Selection Conference Directors run a training and assessment process, now passes to the Assessment Scheme Committee. This process includes:
- A presentation on the reports *Ministers of the Gospel* and *Deacons of the Gospel*
- A detailed synopsis of the Assessment Scheme

- Participation in mock interviews
- Examination and analysis of application and reference material
- Preparation and writing of reports

Following this, the names of potential assessors are removed from their submissions and their work is evaluated anonymously by the appointed group. At the end of this process a shortlist is brought before the Committee to be recommended for appointment by the Board. In due course these names are brought before the General Assembly for information.

4.10 Directors
4.10.1 The Board through its Assessment Scheme Committee is also responsible for the appointment of Assessment Conference Directors. The Director's role is to ensure consistency of standards and assessment criteria throughout an Assessment Conference, to chair the Final Conference and to furnish the Assessment Scheme Committee with a report of the Conference decisions. Like assessors, Directors are appointed for a period of six years. Presently, the system operates with three Directors. Each Director normally presides at one conference a year.

4.10.2 In the last year, the Committee received with regret the resignation of Mrs Liz Kemp who had served as a Director since 1998. Both as an assessor and a Director, Liz was thorough in all of her work and served the assessment process with distinction. Presently, the Committee is taking steps to appoint a new Director. Following the appropriate procedure, the Committee will, in due course, appoint a person with considerable experience of the assessment process.

4.11 Re-shaping the National Assessment Conference
As a result of the introduction of Field Assessment and Local Review (see General Assembly Report 2001, 17/13), it has been necessary to review the structure and content of the National Assessment Conference. A number of major issues had to be taken into consideration in the context of this review. Namely:

- Ensuring that the assessment criteria were consistent with the reports *Ministers of the Gospel* and *Deacons of the Gospel*
- Developing a process around the areas of assessment already agreed by the General Assembly (2001 sec 6.4.3.1.4)
- Avoiding duplication of that which had already been assessed in the field
- Taking account of new material available from Local Reviews
- Developing a process that took full account of changes in Human Rights, Data Protection and Freedom of Information legislation.

4.12   Working Group on Assessment Conference Structure

4.12.1   The Working Group

A small working group that achieved a remarkable amount during its short life, completed the task of carrying out this review and making recommendations to the Board.

4.12.2   Consultation Process

The Working Group consulted with a variety of other bodies that were also directly involved in similar sorts of selection procedures. These included: the Civil Service (Associate Director, FastStream), Christian Aid (Scotland), Standard Life (Senior Recruitment Officer), the Methodist Church, the Church of England, the Baptist Union of Great Britain and the United Reformed Church. In addition, representatives of Presbyteries were invited to participate in a consultation day and two major meetings were held with Directors, church assessors and psychologist assessors. This gave an opportunity both to contribute to the discussion and to help develop a process that could fully be owned by those who would operate it.

4.12.3   Content of New Assessment Conference

As a result of this process the Board, at its December meeting, resolved to replace the traditional exercises and adopt, in principle, a new style Assessment Conference containing the following major elements:

- An exercise in which pastoral skills were assessed in a particular situation

- An exercise in which applicants demonstrate an ability to work together collaboratively
- A presentation exercise
- Two face-to-face interviews, one with two church assessors and one with a psychologist
- A Director's interview (not part of the assessment)

4.12.4   Context of the New Assessment Conference

4.12.4.1   Since the patterns of ministry outlined in reports *Ministers of the Gospel* and *Deacons of the Gospel* require specific skills and aptitudes in the area of interpersonal and reflective skills, the emphasis in these exercises will be to observe carefully the applicant's awareness of the effect of their behaviour on others, and to see their response to other people's attitude to them. Since collaboration is to be such an important part of ministry in the future, it is intended that ministers and deacons will be assessed together in the context of the same Assessment Conferences.

4.12.4.2   In addition to concentrating on exercises that require a high degree of self-awareness and interpersonal/ group skills, the Assessment Conference will also focus on:

- A continuing examination of the articulation of 'call' to Christian ministry
- Indications of a positive motivation towards ministry
- Leadership potential
- Balance and resilience in terms of commitment and lifestyle and
- Willingness to work on areas of limitation

4.12.4.3   With these matters being of such importance it was decided, as a result of the consultation process, to add a sixth main heading to the five that had already been approved by the Assembly, namely, 'Preparation, Call and Leadership Skill'.

The six headings are:

- Integrity of Faith and Life
- Preparation, Call and Leadership Skill
- Openness to Learning

- Interpersonal Skills
- Reflective Skills
- Coping with Change

4.13 Other Main Proposals for Change

4.13.1 Open Reporting

4.13.1.1 The entire process of assessment now belongs in a climate of openness and transparency. Reports in the period of Field Assessment will have been openly available to applicants and this practice will continue into the new Assessment Conference. The Board in taking this decision has taken full account of the changing legislation in Data Protection, Freedom of Information and Human Rights.

4.13.1.2 This will also address a variety of concerns that have been expressed regarding the process of offering feedback to non-accepted applicants. In future the Director will still give structured feedback in the context of a face-to-face interview, however, this will also include the hand-over of the Assessment Conference Report which will now be shared in full. Accepted applicants will also receive their report in the context of such a feedback session. In their case the feedback may highlight issues that will have to be addressed during the period of training.

4.13.1.3 However, changing legislation not only means that all reports on applicants (whether written within the Assessment Process or by a Presbytery) must be written to be seen by applicants, it also means that the Assessment Scheme Committee must take on a different role in relation to the Assessment Conference.

4.13.2 Decision-making Powers of Final Conference

4.13.2.1 The current practice of the Board is to exercise its duty under Act V 1998 (sec 6a), by inviting the Assessment Conference to make recommendations to the Assessment Scheme Committee. The Committee reviews these recommendations and makes final decisions on whether or not to accept applicants as Candidates in Training. This has the advantage of ensuring that the Board, acting on behalf of the General Assembly, is clearly seen to be directly exercising its responsibility for making the decision on whether or not to accept an applicant. However, this process has the overwhelming disadvantage of meaning that final decisions about applicants are made by a group that never meets them.

4.13.2.2 The practice of the Civil Service, upon which the Church of Scotland based its current procedure, has now changed, and those who have had direct contact with the applicants make decisions on acceptance at Final Conference. This is the procedure that is now commended for future practice in Assessment Conferences.

4.13.2.3 Accordingly, assessors will make decisions at Final Conference, acting under powers delegated by the General Assembly. Assessors will make their decisions within the policies and criteria set by the Board and will in all matters continue to be subject to the Board through its Assessment Scheme Committee. The Board through its Assessment Scheme Committee will continue to be accountable to the General Assembly for all assessment matters and to the Commission of Assembly in the case of individual appeals. In this respect the Act V 1998 (sec 6a), remains unaltered.

4.13.3 Reconsideration of Decisions

4.13.3.1 This change in relationship between the Committee and the Final Conference, however, does lead to a necessary change in respect of the process for reconsideration as described in Act V 1998 (sec 6d).

4.13.3.2 Presently, a non-accepted applicant (prior to any process of appeal) has the right to appear before the Committee to ask for a reconsideration of the decision. It is intended that this right should continue for the time being, but the procedure will have to be modified so that the Director of the Assessment Conference shall also appear before the Committee to present the case for the decision that was made at Final Conference. Accordingly Appendix 4 of this report sets out the amendment to the Act that allows for this particular change.

4.14 The Committee's Role in Monitoring and Developing the Process

4.14.1 In order to exercise its constitutional responsibility to the full the Assessment Scheme Committee will continue to hear reports on each conference from the Conference Director. In so doing the Committee will be responsible for reading all conference reports, bringing quality control to the process, ensuring that the decisions are being made in accordance with delegated authority and checking that report writing and decision making meet the highest standards.

4.14.2 Furthermore, the Board through its Assessment Scheme Committee will continue to develop such matters as assessor recruitment, training and appraisal and the ongoing development of the Assessment Scheme. It will, of course, do this important work in collaboration with the assessors, directors and psychologists themselves.

4.15 Streamlined Assessment Conference

4.15.1 The General Assembly will appreciate that a good deal of investment and energy has been made in the early stages of Enquiry, Appraisal and Field Assessment. The Board is completely committed to this change in emphasis, and is hopeful that this will prove to a valuable tool in the process of recruitment and formation of ministers and deacons. It is pleased that as a result it is now possible to reduce the length of the National Assessment Conference so that much of the initial investment is paid for by a considerable reduction in the costs involved at the national assessment level.

4.15.2 The new style Assessment Conference will mean that applicants will be present for twenty-four hours with assessors present for forty-eight hours. The Board however, is at pains to underline that the development of the new National Conference was not driven by cost considerations. There is major financial commitment to training and development and the underlying theme has been that of developing a system that encourages and develops the kind of people that the Church requires in some of its key leadership positions.

4.15.3 This change (together with a final decision being made at the Conference itself) leads to a streamlining of the process, without omitting consideration of the necessary issues. It has also meant that it will be possible to run some of the Assessment Conferences over the period of a weekend, which will suit many of our applicants and many of our assessing team.

4.16 Appeals

The above change in the process of reconsideration of assessment decisions is a modest, interim amendment to take account of the change in the way the Assessment Scheme Committee relates to the Final Conference of the Assessment Conference. However, a more major issue is that of the Appeals Procedure itself. It is a matter of concern that more and more requests for reconsideration are based only on an individual's dislike of the substance of the decision. Currently the Committee is actively pursuing a discussion that proposes the introduction of "Grounds for Appeal". This discussion is ongoing and the Board will report further on this matter to the General Assembly in 2003.

4.17 Continuing Review

The Board is aware that such changes will require review and thorough appraisal after one year of operation. The Board will ensure that the details of the Assessment Process are regularly examined in the light of practice.

4.18 Selection Conference Statistics

Acceptance statistics for Full-time Ministry, Auxiliary Ministry and the Diaconate are as listed in Appendix 5.

4.19 Admission and Readmission of Ministers

4.19.1 Certificates of Eligibility

The Committee on Admission and Readmission reports the issue of the following Certificate of Eligibility:

Rev. James Sloan   Presbyterian Church Canada

4.19.2 Petitions

The Committee has interviewed seven people who had indicated their intention to petition the General Assembly for admission or readmission as a minister in the Church of Scotland.

4.19.3 Completion of Course

The petitioners, Rev. Dr Martin Scott and Rev. James Cook have now satisfactorily completed the courses stipulated by the General Assembly in 2001 and have been duly admitted by their respective Presbyteries.

4.19.4 Transference of a Deacon to the Church of Scotland

Currently, there is no formal process by which deacons are admitted into the Church of Scotland from other denominations. Due to this, the Committee on Admission and Readmission agreed to consider and make a recommendation on the application of Mrs Sandra Bell, a deacon in the Presbyterian Church in Ireland, for recognition as a Deacon in the Church of Scotland. Following interview, the Committee was pleased to recommend to the Presbytery of Glasgow that she should be admitted as a Deacon.

4.20 Candidate Supervision

4.20.1 The Committee has continued to maintain the work undertaken by the previous Committee on Education and Training in relation to the oversight, care and development for the Ministry of Word and Sacrament, auxiliary and diaconal ministries. The Committee has adopted, at all levels of its work, the principles approved by the General Assembly in the reports entitled *Ministers of the Gospel* and *Deacons of the Gospel*.

4.20.2 Development of Ministerial and Diaconal Formation and Education

4.20.2.1 This scheme of academic training linked with placements and candidates' conferences has now been extended to include all diaconal candidates. The auxiliary ministry candidates who commenced training in 2001 attended the first weekend of the five-day conference in St Andrews. All candidates for the auxiliary ministry will continue to be participants in these conferences. They also will have regular contact with those who are already serving as auxiliary ministers though participation in their conferences on a regular basis.

4.20.2.2 During 2001–2002 the final group of Probationers who started training before the present scheme of education and training was instituted will complete their periods alongside those who are in their fourth placement of fifteen months. A large number of candidates undertook a summer placement in a variety of town, country, city and institutional settings in the summer of 2001. These have provided the type of experience visualised in the Assembly Report of the Board of Ministry in 1999. Candidates have been able, while freed from the demands of academic studies, to engage, on a full time basis, in a wide variety of ministry opportunities. These placements have raised issues and provoked theological reflection on the nature of ministry for the candidates. The Committee believes these experiences are vital for their future growth and understanding

4.20.2.3 The processes of reflection and integration of theology and practice of ministry have been encouraged through the preparation by the candidates of essays, experience reports and statements of theological understanding on the nature of ministry in the Church of Scotland. These have demonstrated, on the whole, a capacity for theological thinking and questioning that is appropriate and compatible with the *Ministers of the Gospel* report.

4.20.2.4 In the light of the feed back from the candidates and a determination to provide the best quality conference opportunities for candidates, the conference programme is now arranged in a cycle of five conferences. Each conference lasts five days, and is held in September (Friday to Wednesday) and April (Monday to Friday) of each year to fit in with the different terms of the four academic institutions. These have been designed in collaboration with the candidates themselves to ensure that peer development and appropriate topics and issues are addressed in sequence.

4.20.2.5 The Board's Education and Development Officers have continued to work closely with the university faculties of divinity and supervising ministers. They have also been able to keep contact with Presbyteries, when necessary, to ensure appropriate support, assistance and encouragement is given to candidates during their training and whilst serving in placements.

4.20.2.6 The Education and Development Officers have visited the candidates regularly during their academic studies, and have also made contact with the candidates and supervisors as in placements when appropriate. Meetings with the candidates have also involved the Committee members who read reports and approve the reports on progress of each candidate. These yearly reports are sent with academic progress reports from the Colleges to the Presbyteries to enable the appropriate Committee of each Presbytery to undertake their annual review of their particular candidates.

4.20.2.7 Through the generosity of the Session of Kilmacolm Old Church, the Committee is now able to make available to candidates, full time summer ten week placements, in countries in the developing world at no cost to the host churches. The Committee is most grateful to the Session for their thoughtfulness and looks forward to the contribution this will make to the development of the candidates who avail themselves of this opportunity.

4.20.3   Supervision
4.20.3.1 The Committee once again would like to extend its gratitude to those ministers who act as supervisors to candidates, giving the gifts of their time and energy to this vital task. Their expertise and diligence in ensuring good supervision is supported by the Committee through ensuring that all supervisors are given the opportunity of attending a course in basic supervision. The Committee is determined to use supervisors who are willing to be trained in supervision who are committed to engaging in ongoing training. The Board expresses its gratitude to all those who have undertaken training and those who continue to provide such a wealth of experience for the benefit of our candidates.

4.20.3.2 The Committee is therefore anxious to ensure that the recommendations of the working group on supervision are implemented as soon as may be practical and within the budget of the Board. During the next year, the Committee aims to organise a programme of selection and training of facilitators for local cluster groups of Supervisors. It will draft a Supervisor's handbook and consider the production of material to facilitate theological reflection by Supervisor and Candidate. Greater attention will be given to the integration of the training of Co-ordinators for the Enquiry, Appraisal and Assessment Scheme and the Supervisors of Candidates.

4.20.4   Candidature
4.20.4.1 The Board undertook to explore the issues relating to candidature at the 2000 General Assembly. This is an issue of complexity and the Committee and Board are keen to ensure that the rights and responsibilities of Presbyteries in relations to candidates are preserved. The Committee has therefore continued its essential policy of holding extensive consultation with Presbyteries whenever difficulties or problems regarding the training of individual candidates occur.

4.20.4.2 The Committee will prepare a report and recommendations regarding the continuation of candidature after a wide consultation process. The legal issues, human rights legislation and implications for the good of individuals and the Church as a whole all need to be carefully and thoughtfully explored and included. Progress on this work will be reported to next year's General Assembly.

4.20.5   Bible Examinations
The Committee's decision to insist that all candidates undertake the Bible examinations in the correct order and at the earliest opportunity in their candidature has proved helpful to all concerned. The Board, through the Policy Committee, will consider how best to ensure that the General Assembly's regulations regarding the candidates' knowledge of the Bible may be fulfilled.

4.20.6   Probationers
The Committee has maintained its conference programme for probationers who commenced their

period of probation in 2000. The Committee has noted with pleasure, in their reports, how many of the probationers have found this experience helpful and useful in their development and growth. The following table indicates the progress as at February 2002 of those candidates who began in 2000 and have had their placements sustained:

Parish Ministry	18
Associate/Assistant Ministry	1
Community Ministry/Chaplaincy/Alternative Form of Ministry	0
Seeking a Call	4

4.20.7   Visit/Placements in Israel and Palestine
The Board was instructed by the General Assembly in 2001 to consider including a visit to Israel and Palestine in the training of probationers. Due to the current political climate, it has been agreed not to proceed with this but that the situation will be kept under review.

4.20.8   Auxiliary Ministers
4.20.8.1 The Committee has maintained its work with auxiliary ministers in training, providing support of their academic and placement work and involving them in the Candidates Annual Conference. There are at present twenty auxiliary ministers in training, two of whom are probationers.

4.20.8.2 The Working Group on Ministry (section 2) has consulted with the practising auxiliary ministers and the candidates in training as part of their review and research. The future shape and pattern of this ministry will determine the training required for candidates for the auxiliary ministry. Meanwhile the Committee continues to operate the previously agreed course with candidates studying as external students in the Certificate and Diploma in Christian Studies programme. In the light of the changes that are being instituted in Glasgow University with the introduction of a new distance learning degree programme, the Committee has resolved to enable students to continue studies at Aberdeen University until

the working group's report with its recommendations regarding training are agreed by the Assembly in 2003.

4.20.9   Deacons
The recruitment of deacons recommenced immediately after the Assembly of 2001, following the endorsement of the report *Deacons of the Gospel*. The five candidates for diaconal ministry undertaking academic studies have been involved in the conference programme for other candidates for ministry. The two probationer deacons have likewise been participants in the fourth placement conferences.

5.   MINISTRY SUPPORT AND DEVELOPMENT

5.1   Introduction

5.1.1 The policy Committee on Ministry Support and Development has as its prime objective the overall support of the ordained and commissioned ministry and this is reflected in the following report. A very important aspect of the work since the last General Assembly has been to develop a future stipend policy, and this is included in the report at section 5.2 below. The new Stipend Scheme is proposed for introduction in 2004 and, in the meantime, the Committee will endeavour to maintain the value of ministerial income at least at its present level.

5.1.2 Pastoral care has also been high on the agenda and a process of reviewing progress in the implementation of the Presbytery Pastoral Advisors and Pastoral Colleagues Schemes for ministers and deacons has begun (see section 5.13.6). Following an instruction from the General Assembly of 2001, we have consulted with the Board of Practice and Procedure in order to bring forward a more effective revised Act anent Long-Term Illness of Ministers in Charge (section 5.14 and Appendix 11).

5.2   Proposal for a New Stipend for Parish Ministers.
5.2.1   The Historical Background.
5.2.1.1 It has been a long held principle of the Church that first the Maintenance of the Ministry Committee and now the Board of Ministry has held the responsibility for

the annual declaration of the minimum stipend. In pursuance of that responsibility the General Assembly has, over many years, urged the Board to do all that it could to increase the minimum stipend to a level in keeping with the demands and responsibilities of a modern ministry.

5.2.1.2   Over the last two years, the Board of Ministry has alerted the Church to the fact that the present stipend structure would need to be replaced. The current service supplement scheme is full of anomalies, is difficult to understand and implement and the Board has recognised the need to provide the Church with a scheme that is easy to understand and interpret both at Presbytery and local Congregational level, and is easier to administer centrally. There is a need to bring together the best principles of the minimum stipend, which has served the Church well over many years, and the more recent concept of an incremental scale, which recognises the years of service that a minister has given to the Church.

5.2.2   Principles of the New Stipend Scheme

There are two main principles that we believe will benefit the Church in this scheme:

1. A scheme which attains the highest minimum stipend the whole Church can afford.
2. The categories of *aid-receiving* and *aid-giving* will be abolished, in favour of a scheme that asks for an appropriate contribution from every congregation towards the total costs of ministry in Scotland.

In addition, the scheme will produce the following additional benefits:

- Simplification of the completion of Vacancy Schedules
- Significant reduction in the need for Revision Schedules
- Significant reduction in the number of different stipend (from c.1000 to 40).
- A scheme which allows for the opportunity for congregations to pay their ministers more than the minimum, but only at one of three different levels: minimum plus five per cent, minimum plus ten percent, minimum plus fifteen per cent.

- That when the new scheme is introduced no minister will receive a stipend that is less than the stipend they received under the old system in the previous year
- That in future years a minister would be guaranteed the National Minimum Stipend Scale figure according to years of service

5.2.3   "Ministers of the Gospel"

5.2.3.1   In presenting this new scheme, the Board of Ministry is aware that in the past the Church has tried to benchmark stipends against the income levels of other groups or professions. The Board now believes that it has not been helpful or appropriate to draw such parallels. This new scheme, therefore, does not draw on comparisons with other salaries or professional groups, instead it stands in the context of the report *Ministers of the Gospel* which affirms the contribution of the ordained ministry, "seeing it in its context within our Biblical, Reformed and ecumenical understanding of the Church and its mission in the world."

5.2.3.2   Within that context of the ministry of the whole people of God, the role of Ordained Ministry is placed at the heart of the Church. The Board recognises that the responsibilities and challenges of Parish Ministry brings with it a commitment and responsibility that is laid on every Minister of the Gospel at his or her Ordination that can never be acknowledged simply by financial remuneration. However, the Board believes that the Church must strive to pay ministers a stipend that reflects the requirement placed on our ministers and manse families to engage in life, work and recreation in the real world.

5.2.3.3   In presenting this new scheme the Board of Ministry seeks the support and commitment of the General Assembly to place the ordained ministry at the very heart and core of the work of the Church in Scotland

5.2.4   A National Minimum Stipend Scale

5.2.4.1   The Board recommends to the General Assembly the introduction of a National Minimum Stipend Scale. The National Minimum Stipend Scale meets all the guiding principles laid out in the last year's

General Assembly Report. It provides a scheme which is consistent with the expressed views of the General Assembly. This scale would be a ten year scale, which would pay the minimum stipend at ten different levels corresponding to years of service in the Ordained Ministry of Word and Sacrament.

5.2.4.2 The new scale increases the national minimum stipend for a minister with ten years qualifying service to a level equivalent to the stipend and service supplement of the highest paid minister in the Church as at 2002. The Board believes that such an increase goes some way to meeting the increased demands and responsibilities that are made on ministers and manse families today.

5.2.4.3 In the future, the national minimum stipend for a minister with ten years service will be equivalent (in today's terms) to the present minimum stipend plus fifteen per cent plus today's Service Supplement, i.e. £25,713.

5.2.5 Incremental Stipend Scale at 2002 figures
5.2.5.1 For the purpose of illustration only the following table shows the stipend levels if these proposals were to be implemented against the levels of stipend for 2002:

Year 1	£18,737
Year 2	£19,512
Year 3	£20,287
Year 4	£21,063
Year 5	£21,838
Year 6	£22,613
Year 7	£23,388
Year 8	£24,163
Year 9	£24,938
Year 10	£25,713

5.2.5.2 Providing a congregation can meet all of its appropriate requirements they will be encouraged to pay their minister at one of three other specific appropriate levels; at National Minimum Stipend Scale plus five percent, National Minimum Stipend Scale plus ten percent or National Minimum Stipend Scale plus fifteen percent. The Board of Ministry will set base allocation scales from year to year in relation to the plus five/ten/

fifteen per cent levels. This will allow a charge, with the agreement of Presbytery, to pay stipends above the National Minimum Scale provided all ministry and Mission and Aid requirements for the previous three years have been met.

5.2.6 A National Stipend Fund
5.2.6.1 The Board proposes that every congregation, according to its means, will be responsible for making an appropriate ministry payment to a National Stipend Fund. By this means, all Stipend and Employer's National Insurance Payments and Pension Contributions will be covered; and The Housing and Loan Fund's two per cent of Stipend Levy will be ingathered. The ministry allocation will be based on congregational income and will take account of all unrestricted income and endowment and glebe income (please refer to the Report of the Board of Stewardship and Finance regarding the regulations for allocations to the Mission and Aid Fund). The ministry base figure will be the same as the base figure for the calculation of the Mission and Aid allocation.

5.2.6.2 At this stage it is not possible to give specific examples of what this will mean for individual congregations. However, the Board of Stewardship and Finance and the Board of Ministry will jointly limit the allocation figures (Mission and Aid and Ministry respectively) to a maximum and minimum percentage for annual increases or decreases declared. In conjunction with this scheme, congregations will cease voluntary contributions to the insured pension fund. Any payments already made into the insured pension fund will be protected and details of the proposed changes to the Ministers' Pension Scheme are described in the Joint Report of the Board of Ministry and the Pension Trustees. (see section 5.9 of this report.)

5.2.6.3 The Board believes that using the revised method of allocation will provide a fairer and simpler standard calculation for both ministry and Mission and Aid payments and that this is a more just and fair approach to the allocation and payment of ministry costs. In particular, the removal of the status of *"aid-receiving"* will establish a system of support and communal effort which will enhance the unity of the Church. It is hoped that *"aid receiving"* charges will be better off through this scheme and that there will be more money available to them for local mission.

5.2.6.4 Under the new stipend scheme, congregations within a vacant charge would pay a discounted sum into the National Stipend Fund for the period of the vacancy. The amount of the discount will be determined by the Board according to its available funds. This vacancy allowance has been built into the cost projections to help congregations normally cover the costs of pulpit supply from their own resources.

5.2.7 Implementation and Cost of the Scheme

5.2.7.1 The Board is keen to implement such a scheme as early as possible but is conscious of the fact that any new structure, which brings about significant improvement in the stipend of ministers, is likely to impact on the work of the other boards and committees of the Church. Immediate and full implementation of the proposed scheme (at present numbers in ministry) would mean a substantial increase in the income disposition given to the Board of Ministry to fund stipend. However, following a process of consultation with other boards and committees through the Co-ordinating Forum, the Board has sought to respond to views and concerns about the impact of immediate implementation of this scheme. Following discussions with the Board of Stewardship and Finance, the Board is proposing that the new scheme be phased in over a period of three years, starting from January 2004 in order to reduce to a minimum the impact on other work.

5.2.7.2 Appendix 2 of section 3 of this report shows a projection of the number of parish ministers based on trends over the past five years. The Board has deep concerns about this situation and the impact this has on ministers and the Church. In planning the new stipend scheme, the Board has based its costings on a realistic assessment of the projected number of ministers plus a substantial contingency so that the scheme could be paid for at the current levels of ministers if required. However,

it is anticipated that the actual costs of the implementation of the new stipend scheme will be lower than those forecast. On the basis of costings including the contingency, it is anticipated that the annual increased cost of the new scheme during the first three years will be:

Estimated figures of:	2004	2005	2006
Actual increase in allocation of funding (from 2002 level)	£680, 000	£329,000	£21,000
% Change in Income Disposition from 2002 base	0.98%	0.48%	0.03%

5.2.8 Dissemination of Information

The Board acknowledges that these are major and complex changes that are being placed before the Church. However, there is a significant lead-time before the proposed date of implementation. Therefore, in keeping promises made at last year's General Assembly, the Board will engage in a series of roadshow presentations, explaining the details of this new scheme to the relevant representatives of the whole Church. Because this scheme also depends on a fundamental change in the assessment and collection requirements of Mission and Aid, these roadshows will be carried out in partnership with the Board of Stewardship and Finance. It is planned that these will take place early in 2003.

5.3 Stipend and Service Supplement

The level of minimum stipend for 2002 has been declared at £18,737 and a manse, with the real value of ministerial remuneration being maintained through the increase in the minimum stipend as detailed in Appendix 6.

5.4 Ministers' Travel

5.4.1 Travelling Expenses

The principles of this scheme remain unchanged for 2002 and the Committee endeavours to maintain the real value of travelling expenses. The Inland Revenue has, from April 2002, declared the authorised mileage rates to be forty pence per mile for the first 10,000 miles travelled in connection with an individual's work and twenty five pence for any miles in excess of 10,000. The Committee has increased the mileage rates to the Inland Revenue levels for 2002 but has not changed the lump sum. (see Appendix 7).

5.4.2 Car Loans

Car loans are still in considerable demand and the Committee will continue to offer these to all serving ministers. Once again, it has not been possible to increase the level of loans as previously planned, due to changes in fiscal policy. The Committee will, however, increase loans when it is appropriate to do so.

5.4.3 Car Leasing Scheme

The Board continues to make available to ministers, deacons and church staff information regarding various leasing offers. It is important that all those considering this method of car provision should do their homework carefully since the contracts are between the company chosen and the minister, deacon or member of staff. The experience to date is that this alternative is of considerable benefit to those using one of the schemes.

5.5 Pulpit Supply

There has been an increase recommended to Pulpit Supply fees but otherwise there was no alteration to arrangements and the detailed regulations are contained in Appendix 8.

5.6 Maintenance Allowances

Two Maintenance Allowances were provided in 2001.

5.7. Further Endowment

During 2001, the following grants were set aside:

| Congregations | 10 |
| Consolidated Stipend Fund Shares | 7,242 |

The Committee submits the following amendments to the Regulations for Further Endowment so that a grant may be given:

The limits for investment in Further Endowment for stipend to be as follows:

a. Following the approval of the grant, the average of the charge's contribution to stipend over the previous three years, together with the current year's endowments, must be not more than £17,900 and the endowments must be raised to not more than £4,300.

b. Further Endowment capital will be brought directly into the Consolidated Stipend Fund and the relevant grant allocated every quarter. The pre-determined price will be the previous quarter's price, any movement in price being met by the Committee. Dividends are payable from the date of entry into the fund at the rate of return quoted from the Consolidated Stipend Fund.

5.8 Endowments for Stipend Purposes

In terms of Act XXVII 1953 and of the Regulations governing the Consolidated Stipend Endowment Fund, the Committee considered every vacancy involving the use of endowments and reported that agreement was reached with the Presbytery in every case.

5.9 Ministers' Pension Scheme

5.9.1 In 2001, the General Assembly noted that the Pension Trustees would begin discussions with the Board of Ministry regarding contributions to the Insured Pension Fund under the Church of Scotland Pension Scheme for Ministers. Following an actuarial valuation of the Scheme on the 31st December 2000, and after consultation with the Pension Trustees, improvements are proposed in a joint report of the Board of Ministry and the Pension Trustees.

5.10 Ministry Development
5.10.1 Aims

- To provide and evaluate appropriate post-ordinationtraining for ministers at key stages in their ministry
- To offer opportunities for further study to update existing knowledge or to develop new areas of expertise relevant to the minister's work

- To facilitate exchange of experience among ministers
- To assist ministers in evaluation of their ministry
- To direct all activities towards fulfilment of the aspirations of the Board's policy document, *"Ministers of the Gospel"*

5.10.2 Programme of Courses and Conferences

5.10.2.1 The Committee has been reviewing the relevance of the standard programme of courses and its cost-effectiveness. While the current programme will run until January 2003, it is likely that significant alterations will be introduced thereafter, since the bases on which the present pattern was established have now been superseded. One possibility under consideration is an invitation-only conference for those with, say, ten or fifteen years left to serve and other service-based conferences may be replaced

5.10.2.2 Unfortunately, a proposed conference on Congregational Management had to be cancelled (June 2001) owing to lack of numbers. In response to the popular demand of ministers attending recent conferences, the Committee is now planning a Reflective Event, with a restricted number of participants. There is also a feeling that such thematic conferences, open to all, will be more successful than the standard programme which potential participants often miss through circumstances pertaining at the time of their invitation. The number attending conferences is shown in Appendix 9.

5.10.3 Study Leave Programme (see Appendix 10)

5.10.3.1 Study Leave continues to be a popular option with ministers, many of whom have now taken advantage of the scheme several times. The Committee has published an anthology (*"Study Leaves"*) featuring selected participants' reports which illustrate the wide variety of uses to which study leave is put. It is, however, a matter of concern that a few Presbyteries have, as yet, produced few or no applications and letters were sent to all session clerks to familiarise elders with the scheme and to encourage their support for ministers wishing to apply. Ministers who have been accumulating study leave will be eligible for periods of leave up to twelve weeks from January 2003.

5.10.3.2 The Committee carefully monitors the cost of the scheme and the effect on congregations and Presbyteries as longer periods of leave become available. There is encouraging evidence that ministers are becoming aware of the necessity for longer periods of forward planning to facilitate their leave. Also, the greater flexibility granted by the Committee, through extension of the number of closing dates, has met with approval. A review of the cash available to individual applicants (£250 for each year of service) is ongoing, with a view to increasing to £300 at the earliest opportunity

5.10.3.3 The Committee continues to attempt to counteract the difficulties faced by ministers in remote areas, a further concession being the agreement to pay accommodation expenses of locums where manse location is impracticable

5.10.4 Personal Ministerial Review

5.10.4.1 Since 2000, the Board has been operating a pilot Personal Ministerial Review scheme that began with almost fifty volunteers, mainly parish ministers, participating. The scheme takes the form of an accompanied self-appraisal with each of the reviewees being allocated a reviewer for this purpose. Reviewers underwent a course of appropriate training and undertook to be reviewed before carrying out reviews with others. The pilot, which concluded towards the end of 2001, was evaluated at a meeting of reviewers early in 2002. Decisions are now being taken about continuation of the scheme for the original cohort of volunteers and further expansion to other ministers who have been expressing an interest.

5.10.4.2 Any minister wishing to be kept informed of further developments with a view to possible participation, should contact the Board and ask to have that interest noted

5.10.5 Links with Princeton Theological Seminary

There was an encouraging response by Scottish ministers to the 2001 Joint Institute in St. Andrews that greatly enhanced the experience for the American visitors. Indications are that the 2002 Institute in Princeton will attract significant numbers from Scotland – many using study leave entitlement to support their attendance. Some will form links with congregations in the United States by extending their stay after the Institute. St. Andrews looks forward to hosting again in 2003.

5.10.6 International Ministry Exchange (IME)
The Board has formally linked the Church of Scotland with I.M.E. that organises exchanges between ministers in the four home countries, along with Canada, the United States, Australia and New Zealand. South Africa is another new addition to the list. These exchanges would be suitable for ministers with the maximum period of study leave due to them but others prepared to resource themselves will, of course, be eligible to apply. Further information is available from the Department.

5.10.7 Directory of Ministry Development Opportunities
The improved directory continues to provide ministers with information about the full range of opportunities available, including a calendar of activities planned for the following year. Departmental staff are always ready and willing to offer advice on development-related matters.

5.11 Interim Ministry

5.11.1 Aims of the Committee

- To consider and develop appropriate initial and in-service training for interim ministers.
- To create a structure of salary and expenses for interim ministers.
- To encourage and support interim ministers by regular contact and active participation in monitoring groups.
- To develop clear guidelines for the roles of Presbyteries and congregations in monitoring groups.
- To raise awareness throughout the Church of the potential role of interim ministry in a variety of situations.
- To establish a process whereby Presbyteries, the Committee and Board staff can effectively engage with congregations in assessing the value, relevance and appropriateness of interim ministry in their situations.
- To review and investigate future development of interim ministry within the Church.

5.11.2 Interim Minister Placements
The Board is pleased to report that there is continuing positive work being done by the interim ministry team. There are at present six interim ministers serving in widely differing situations. During the past year periods of interim ministry have been completed on Islay and in Greenock. Interim ministries are continuing in Rosyth and Ballingry and Lochcraig and others have begun in Law, Paisley, Corstorphine, and Aberdeen.

5.11.3 Interim Ministry Training
The Committee, in consultation with the team of interim ministers, have been working on plans for training particularly geared to the challenges of this specialised form of ministry. A period of initial training undertaken by new interim ministers has been found helpful and relevant. It is hoped that arrangements will shortly be finalised for all present interim ministers to take part in in-service training.

5.11.4 Interim Ministers' Salary and Expenses
The Committee has reviewed the arrangements initially put in place for the interim ministry pilot study. It is now appropriate for salary and expenses to be regularised. Interim ministers are currently contracted to a salary comprising minimum stipend, plus maximum service supplement and an interim ministry allowance. A new four year scale, with annual increases each of one quarter of the total interim ministry allowance was introduced from the 1st January 2002. This scale will be restated, in the same manner as the minimum stipend, in January each year to reflect inflation. Thus each interim minister will receive an annual inflation-linked increase. As implemented, this scale has accommodated all current salaries with no interim minister being disadvantaged. This structure also facilitates the integration of the interim ministry salaries into the proposed new stipend structure at a future date.

5.11.5 Monitoring Groups

The Committee recognises the importance of supporting interim ministers in their placements by active participation in the Monitoring Groups. New guidelines on the roles of Monitoring Groups are being developed for the assistance of Presbyteries.

5.11.6 Development

5.11.6.1 The Committee is developing a procedure to provide information, assistance and evaluation for Presbyteries enquiring about interim ministry. The Board wishes to emphasise the opportunities which interim ministry can provide to congregations and Presbyteries in many differing situations to conduct a meaningful review of the vision of a worshipping community under specialist guidance. Consideration is also being given to further development of the interim ministry network possibly on a regional basis.

5.11.6.2 The Board recognises the challenges and often difficult decisions faced by many congregations at times of vacancy. Interim ministry can be an opportunity at a time of transition to resolve problems, to reassess priorities and to renew vision and enthusiasm as congregations seek to share the gospel and grow in faith.

5.11.6.3 The Board believes that interim ministry is a positive and creative option which may be appropriate in a wide variety of situations, and would encourage Presbyteries to consider wider use of this valuable resource.

5.12 Protection of Children and Young People

The Board is aware of changing legislation in this area and will monitor and respond to these changes through its ongoing work in conjunction with the Joint Board Group on Child Protection and the Child Protection Unit.

5.13 Pastoral Support

The Board is committed to the provision, review and development of a range of confidential services in conjunction with, and in support of, the developing Pastoral Adviser and Colleagues schemes provided at Presbytery level. The support of Ministers and Deacons has provided much of the insight into Ministry that has informed the Board's Ministry Development Programme and the expansion of its various Ministry Support systems.

5.13.1 "Ministers of the Gospel"

The theological underpinning to the Board's work is expressed in its "Ministers of the Gospel" report. This emphasises the crucial role of *"integrity of person and practice"* in ministry, as well as affirming an approach to ministry which is *"collaborative"*, *"reflective"* and committed to ongoing *"personal formation and development"*. The Board recognises that ministers need to be supported and valued by a church which truly cares for them. The support and development programmes offered by the Board over recent years have helped in the formation of ministers who increasingly understand when to ask for help. Needing the help, advice and support of others is thankfully no longer seen as weakness.

5.13.2 Board and Staff Support

All members of staff play their part in providing support for ministers and manse families. Some of that support is of a very practical nature and staff provide a range of information and guidance in response to the wide range of queries raised. The continual telephone assistance on matters of stipend, expenses, car provision and loans, pensions etc all provides support for busy people and their families. Staff support is also required for a range of highly sensitive issues which are dealt with by the Department's senior staff and in particular by the Senior Pastoral Adviser.

5.13.3 Occupational Health Scheme

The Board, on the advice of the Medical Panel, continues to use the services of Salus Occupational Health and will continue to keep this under review.

5.13.4 Manse Family Counselling

There has only been a small take-up in the Face-to Face Counselling Service, but it remains an important service in the overall pattern of pastoral care being provided.

5.13.5   24 Hour Help Line

The 24-hour telephone counselling service provided by First Assist is still proving to be of great help to a small number of ministers and manse families and the Board feels fully justified in continuing to provide this service.

5.13.6   Overview of New Presbytery Pastoral Support Scheme

5.13.6.1 The Presbytery based Pastoral Adviser and Pastoral Colleague Scheme was described in the Board of Ministry's report to the General Assembly in 2001. The Assembly agreed to "instruct Presbyteries to work cooperatively in the effective implementation" of the scheme. Under the revised scheme, Pastoral Advisers would be appointed by Presbyteries and allocated to Ministers in their first three years and Pastoral Colleagues for the provision of an ongoing support network.

5.13.6.2 Since September, the Senior Pastoral Adviser has been visiting Presbyteries and meeting with Presbytery representatives to review the Pastoral Care Schemes in place and to assess how these are being developed in relation to the General Assembly's instruction. The new scheme of Pastoral Advisers and Colleagues proposed in 2001 is in its infancy and is emerging from present schemes rather than being implemented as something totally new. However, most presbyteries take their responsibility for pastoral care very seriously and, although there is little uniformity and a range of schemes are in place, many see that as a strength since these schemes have evolved to meet local need and particular circumstances.

5.13.6.3 The important message to report at this time is that the pastoral care of ministers, deacons and their families within presbyteries is being taken very seriously and is being dealt with sensitively.

5.13.6.4 Whilst the majority of presbyteries have not implemented the new Pastoral Colleague Scheme as laid down, most have endeavoured to make some provision for those beyond the first three years. There is clearly a very real attempt to provide Pastoral Advisers based on the original five year scheme and this is now being adapted to take account of the new three year instruction. At the moment most feel the schemes they have in place or are working on must have time to settle in and are not anxious to change too soon.

5.13.6.5 Unfortunately, some presbyteries have been unable to establish any formal scheme other than goodwill among colleagues which can be effective. However the lack of structure and clear guidelines can lead to some feeling left out or abandoned if and when trouble comes. In the very small Presbyteries which sometimes face real difficulties, encouragement and support is being offered to facilitate the setting up of a more regular and easily accessed system of pastoral care support.

5.13.6.6 Clearly the smaller Presbyteries have to tackle things in a different way and with many vacancies and ministers and deacons off ill any scheme can be difficult. Some smaller Presbyteries have the benefit of considerable numbers of retired ministers in their midst while others have none at all. It is important to note that the Church continues to value the pastoral help of retired colleagues but must not make excessive demands on them for what are essential and important responsibilities for the Presbytery.

5.13.6.7 The Board will continue to monitor the implementation and effectiveness of the Pastoral Adviser and Colleague Schemes in co-operation with presbyteries and will continue to report to the General Assembly on progress being made. It is likely that this will be an evolving and ongoing process since circumstances are continually changing.

5.14   Act X (2000) anent Long-Term Illness of Ministers in Charge

In 2001, the General Assembly instructed the Board of Ministry to consult with the Board of Practice and Procedure and to produce a revision of the Act anent Long-Term Illness of Ministers in Charge in order to bring forward a more effective revised Act for the future. The revised Act is detailed in Appendix 11 to this report.

6. MEMBERSHIP OF THE BOARD

6.1 Diaconate Council

The Diaconate Council is represented on the Board of Ministry by the President and Vice President of the Council. In order to give continuity and enable a full contribution of these members to both the Diaconate Council and the Board of Ministry, the Diaconate Council have unanimously requested that both President and Vice President be appointed for three year terms. The Board of Ministry is happy to support this proposal.

ADDENDUM

The Very Rev Dr Alexander McDonald

The Board of Ministry is profoundly grateful for the service of Dr McDonald both as General Secretary and latterly as Senior Adviser for Pastoral Care, a post he took up in September 2001.

Dr McDonald was appointed as Joint Secretary of the Board of Ministry and Mission in 1988 and General Secretary of the new Board of Ministry when it was established in 1990. Since then, Dr McDonald has overseen changes in the Board's work with an increasing emphasis on the pastoral care of ministers and the delivery of a programme for ministry development. Following the instruction of the General Assembly in 1997, the Board of Ministry and the Department of Education were brought together combining the education and developmental training of the ministry under the auspices of the Board. Dr McDonald has played a key leadership role in enabling the Board and its staff to fulfill their wider responsibilities for the recruitment, formation and support of the ministers and deacons of the Church of Scotland. Known affectionately to all as Sandy, his pastoral gifts have been a source of strength and comfort to many ministers and their families over the years. With them, the Board gives thanks to God for Sandy's pastoral ministry.

Dr McDonald was elected Moderator of the General Assembly of 1997, reflecting the high regard in which he is held throughout the Church. Sandy has made a major and unique contribution to the work of the Board and continues to provide invaluable insights and guidance in a period of change within the Church and society.

Rev Dr Christine Goldie

Rev Dr Christine Goldie has served the new Board of Ministry since its inception in 1998 and for the past 3 years as Vice Convener. During the past year, Christine has been joint Convener of the Board's new Policy Committee on Vocational Guidance Education and Training. Christine has played a leading role in the development of the new Assessment Scheme incorporating local enquiry and assessment and a new national assessment conference. The Board is very grateful for Christine's time and energy and the special contributions and personal qualities she has brought to its work.

Mr William Greenock

Bill Greenock joined the Committee on the Maintenance of the Ministry in 1997 and the Board of Ministry in 1998. He has served as a Vice Convener of the Board for the past three years. During this time, Bill has convened the Board's Committee on Ministry Development and has played a major role in the planning and delivery of Ministry Development conferences working closely with the staff of the department. The Board is very grateful for the time and commitment shown by Bill and for the particular contributions he has made to the Board's work bringing a valuable perspective and distinctive insights from his professional background and role as an Elder of the Church.

In the name of the Board,

WILLIAM F STORRAR, *Convener*
R DOUGLAS CRANSTON, *Vice Convener*
CHRISTINE M GOLDIE, *Vice Convener*
WILLIAM GREENOCK, *Vice Convener*
IAN TAYLOR, *Vice Convener*
RUTH MOIR, *General Secretary*
ALEXANDER MCDONALD, *Senior Adviser for Pastoral Care*
JOHN CHALMERS, *Depute General Secretary*

APPENDIX 1

WORKING GROUP ON MINISTRY

1. Members of the Working Group on Ministry

Convener: Rev. Dr Russell Barr
Secretary: Rev. Nigel J Robb

Rev. Arthur Barrie, Rev. Fergus Buchanan, Dr Liz Hare, Rev. Lorna Hood, Miss Pat Munro DCS, Rev. Douglas Nicol, Rev. Dr John Oswald, Rev. Tom Riddell

2. Collation of Results from Questionnaire to Presbyteries

2.1 Statistics

Never have had an AM	13
Presbyteries that currently have AM's in training	8
Presbyteries that currently have or had AM's	32

2.2 Deployment

The current use of the auxiliary ministers includes leadership of worship, including preaching, working in vacancies, and assisting in the duties of Presbyteries. The location of auxiliary ministers ranges from rural linkages, to groups of churches in one area, and in large town churches.

2.3 Impressions of Auxiliary Ministry

2.3.1 The Presbyteries which have had and currently have auxiliary ministers working within their bounds commented positively on the contribution that these ministers make to the congregations and Presbyteries. Some expressed a desire for this form of service to be extended and developed, particularly in the light of the changes anticipated in the pattern of stipendiary ministry in the years ahead.

2.3.2 Comments were also made by Presbyteries on the confusion and difficulty created by the use of readers in roles which were similar to those of the deployment of auxiliary ministers. Other comments drew attention to the vast amount of confusion over the restrictions on

auxiliary ministers, and the need for better understanding of their unique contributions. While there was no desire for the auxiliary ministers to be a substitute for the full time stipendiary minister, the Presbyteries indicated that some other important areas of Church life, e.g., youth work, could benefit from the extension and development. It was also recognised that the limited time available for service naturally imposed limitations on the use of auxiliary ministers. Presbyteries also expressed disquiet about how the auxiliary ministers were treated or misunderstood.

3. Questionnaire on Auxiliary Ministry to Auxiliary Ministers - General Information

3.1 Family Circumstances

Married	23
Single	3
Widowed	2

3.2 Enter to training before or after retirement?

Before	19
After	6

3.3 Transferable skills

The present group of auxiliary ministers bring a vast range of skills and experience to the service of the Church, ranging from teaching, civil service, nursing, social work, counselling and business management, and include representatives of many who might be found occupying the pews on any given Sunday. Most of the present serving auxiliaries had a background in the Church as elders, Board members, Sunday School Teachers, and involvement in many leadership roles in church organisations

3.4 Hours of work

The number of hours worked in paid employment range from sixty hours per week to seven hours, indicating the enormous differences in occupation of the serving auxiliary ministers. One consequence of this is the difficulty of establishing a standard time commitment to be made by auxiliary ministers.

3.5   Pre retirement Occupations

As in the case of those who are still in employment, the serving auxiliary ministers who are retired from full time employment come from many professional and vocational backgrounds, including teaching, engineering, social work, hospital service, and clerical occupations

3.6   Deployment

AM's deployed outwith home congregation	21
AM's deployed in home congregation	6

3.7   Age at ordination.

Average age at ordination	54

4.   Current Patterns

4.1   Worship Leadership

The survey suggested that the vast majority of auxiliary ministers conduct public worship and preach at least once per month. They are also participants in funerals, chaplaincy in hospitals and schools, and a number of other pastoral tasks. The infrequency of involvement in the celebration of the sacraments by the serving auxiliary ministers was noted. It is often less than once per month or even less often, and suggests that the ministry itself is less crucially involved in this aspect of service than the conduct of other aspects of the Church's life and witness.

4.2   Areas of Deployment

Rural	10
Town	10
UPA/SIP	7
Suburban	4
Housing Scheme	4
City Centre	3

4.3   Is the parish a linkage?

Yes	8
No	16

4.4   Support of Ministry

While the majority of the serving auxiliary ministers reported that they had been offered helpful and useful supervision, a significant number raised questions regarding the nature of the guidance and help offered to them in accomplishing their ministries. Many would appreciate a more definite and clear statement regarding the type of supervision which ought to be offered to all who serve as auxiliary ministers. Auxiliary ministers depend on a wide group of agencies and persons to support and encourage them in their work.

4.5   Hours worked in parish and in preparation for services

Avg. hrs/week in parish	8
Avg. hrs/week in preparation	7

4.6   Moderators of any Kirk Session meetings?

Yes	18
No	8

4.7   Wider Work

It was noted that the present auxiliary ministers undertake a wide variety of tasks, like moderating a Kirk Session, which was not in the vision of the regulations and the expectations of the origins of this order of ministry. Several undertake the duties of locums in vacancies, and provide a number of important types of services never anticipated by the Committee of Forty or the General Assemblies which approved the regulations. At times this has led to misunderstanding and hurt among those which serve as auxiliary ministers as practice has varied from one Presbytery to another.

4.8 Home Congregation

The auxiliary ministers reported the following reactions when they applied from their home congregations

Encouragement	25
Welcome	6
Showed little interest	2
Showed no awareness	1

4.9 Presbytery

When asked about the Presbytery's response to their expression of interest, the following reactions were noted

Encourage	25
Show no interest/contact	5
Have supportive individual ministers	1
Show signs of division	1

4.10 Did you foresee your ministry for what it now is?

Yes	10
No	14

Those who indicated a negative response to this question expressed frustration about their gifts not being fully utilised, restrictions laid upon them by inappropriate regulations, lack of understanding in the Church about their role, misapprehensions in congregations and among the members of the stipendiary ministers, and lack of clarity about the whole basis and practice of auxiliary ministry.

APPENDIX 2

MINISTERIAL SUPPLY PROJECTIONS

		2002	2003	2004	2005	2006	Cumul-ative Totals
1.	**Projected annual reductions in the number of parish ministers:**						
	Deaths in Service	5	5	5	5	5	**25**
	Ministers reaching 65 + (a factor for those retiring on the grounds of ill-health)	54	43	60	45	57	**259**
	Leaving to take up extra-parochial appointments and join other denominations	5	5	5	5	5	**25**
	Leaving Ministry	4	4	4	4	4	**20**
	Total Projected annual reduction in number of parish ministers	**68**	**57**	**74**	**59**	**71**	329
2.	**Projected annual intake of parish ministers**						
	Graduates likely to be available for Ordination	20	14	23	24	24	**105**
	Entering the Church of Scotland from other denominations	10	11	7	3	6	**37**
	Ministers in service after reaching the age of 65 (average of the last five years)	3	3	3	3	3	**15**
	Projected annual intake of parish ministers	**33**	**28**	**33**	**30**	**33**	157
3.	**Projected net annual loss**	**35**	**29**	**41**	**29**	**38**	172
4.	**Projected number of Vacancies (Total vacancies of 169 at April 2001)(Not allowing for readjustment)**	**204**	**233**	**274**	**303**	**341**	

APPENDIX 3

OVERTURE ANENT ACT V 1984 AS AMENDED

The General Assembly adopt the Overture the tenor whereof follows, and transmit the same to Presbyteries for their consideration under the Barrier Act, directing that returns be sent to the Principal Clerk not later than the 31st December 2002.

The General Assembly, with the consent of a majority of Presbyteries, hereby enact and ordain as follows:

1. Act V 1984 anent Settlement of Ministers is hereby further amended as follows:

by the deleting in section 1 of the phrase 'a ministerial member of the Presbytery' and substituting ' a member of the Presbytery in terms of Act III 2000 or Act V 2001' and by deleting the phrase 'of the vacant congregation' and substituting 'in the vacant charge'.

2. Act II 2000 anent ministry, as amended, is hereby further amended as follows:

By the insertion in section 19(2) after the words 'Interim Moderator', of the words ', if an ordained minister,'

APPENDIX 4

ACT V 1998 ANENT SELECTION AND TRAINING FOR THE FULL-TIME MINISTRY AND ELIGIBILITY FOR ORDINATION (SECTIONS 4 AND 6d)

The General Assembly enact and ordain as follows:

4 An Enquirer who submits an application for Assessment by the 30th September will have his/her application fully considered by the 30th June of the following calendar year.

6d An applicant who has not been accepted as a Prospective Candidate by the Board of Ministry (acting through its Assessment Scheme Committee) may request the Committee to reconsider its decision. The applicant shall be required to lodge a written submission within three months of receiving the Committee's decision, and shall be entitled subsequently to appear in person before the Committee. An Observer, who shall not be entitled to speak, may accompany the applicant. The Assessment Conference Director will also appear before the Committee to present the case made for the decision reached at the Final Conference. All parties will be in possession of the reports from both the Local Review and the National Assessment Conference. If after such reconsideration, the applicant wishes to appeal against the decision of the Committee, a formal appeals procedure shall be invoked.

APPENDIX 5

SELECTION CONFERENCE STATISTICS

Acceptance Statistics for the Full-time Ministry, Auxiliary Ministry and Diaconate for 1997-2001 are as follows:

	1997	1998	1999	2000			2001		
				Male	Female	Total	Male	Female	Total
Full-time Ministry (Applicants)	57	45	47	39	25	64	22	23	45
Full-time Ministry Accepted	20	18	17	14	12	26	9	7	16
First time Applicants	37	31	29	28	14	42	18	16	4
Accepted	16	7	15	11	7	18	8	5	13
Returning Applicants	20	14	18	11	11	22	4	7	11
Accepted	4	11	2	3	5	8	1	2	3
Auxiliary Ministry (Applicants)	7	7	9	6	10	16	8	5	13
Auxiliary Ministry (Accepted)	3	4	3	4	5	9	5	3	8
Deacons (Applicants)	N/A	N/A	13	Moratorium			4	9	13
Deacons (Accepted)	N/A	N/A	4	Moratorium			0	4	4

APPENDIX 6

STIPEND AND SERVICE SUPPLEMENT

1.   Level of Minimum Stipend in 2002

The Committee has declared the minimum stipend for 2002 at £18,737, an increase of four per cent, and a manse. In making this declaration, the Committee recognised the need to maintain the real value of the stipend plus service supplement and, taking this into account, the increase for ministers is in the range of 3.5% to 4%.

2.   The Service Supplement

The Service Supplement now fully implemented is not being increased.

3.   Island Allowances

The Committee has declared the Inner and Outer Island Allowances to be increased by three per cent to the following levels:

Inner Island Allowance	£541
Outer Island Allowance	£1,354

4.   Manse Disturbance Allowance

The Committee has declared the Manse Disturbance Allowance to be £1,500.

APPENDIX 7

MINISTERS' TRAVEL

1.   Cars

The Board has declared travelling expenses for 2002 from April as follows:

A capital Allowance of £960 will be paid in twelve equal payments with the necessary Tax and National Insurance being deducted at source. Travelling expenses will then be paid at the Inland Revenue levels which do not incur further Tax and National Insurance irrespective of the miles travelled:

- 40p per mile for the first 10,000 miles
- 25p for all additional mileage
- 22p per mile for Pulpit Supply.

2.   Motorcycles

In the case of those who use motorcycles, their Travelling Expenses are

- 24p per mile travelled per annum

3.   Pedal Cycles

In the case of those who use pedal cycles, the level of travelling expenses in 2002 will be twelve pence per mile which relates directly to the rates supplied by the Inland Revenue. Ministers claiming travelling expenses for pedal cycles should do so from local treasurers and not from the Board. It is not proposed to set up a centralised scheme for the payment of travelling expenses for pedal cycle users.

APPENDIX 8

PULPIT SUPPLY 2002

1. In charges where there is only one diet of worship the Pulpit Supply Fee shall be a Standard Fee of £47 (or as from time to time agreed by the Board of Ministry).

2. In charges where there are additional diets of worship on a Sunday, the person fulfilling the Supply will be paid £10 for each additional service (or as from time to time agreed by the Board of Ministry).

3. Where the person is unwilling to conduct more than one diet of worship on a given Sunday, s/he will receive pro rata payment based on the total available fee shared on the basis of the number of services conducted.

4. The fee thus calculated shall be payable in the case of all persons permitted to conduct services under Act II 1986.

5. In all cases, necessary travelling expenses shall be paid. Where there is no convenient public conveyance, the use of a private car shall be paid at twenty two pence per mile and updated from time to time by the Board of Ministry. In exceptional circumstances, to be approved in advance, the cost of hiring may be met.

6. Where weekend board and lodging are agreed as necessary, these may be claimed for the weekend at a maximum rate of that allowed when attending the General Assembly. The fee and expenses should be paid to the person providing the supply before s/he leaves on the Sunday.

APPENDIX 9

CONFERENCE ATTENDANCE (2001-2002)

Conference	Date	Invited	Attending	Percentage
8-Year	29-31 Oct 2001	55	31	56%
5-Year	21-23 Jan 2002	44	29	66%
15-Year	23-25 Jan 2002	36	22	61%
Recently Ordained	29-31 Jan 2002	41	32	78%

APPENDIX 10

STUDY LEAVE

Approved Study Leave Applications- 2001

1. By Male or Female

	TOTAL
Male	120
Female	25
	145

2. By Age Group (2001 only)

	TOTAL
30-34	3
35-39	17
40-44	26
45-49	31
50-54	29
55-59	34
60+	5
	145

3. By Year of Ordination (2001 only)

	TOTAL
1950s	1
1960s	1
1970s	39
1980s	61
1990s	43
	145

4. By Presbytery

		TOTAL
1	Edinburgh	15
2	West Lothian	0
3	Lothian	8
4	Melrose & Peebles	2
5	Duns	4
6	Jedburgh	1
7	Annandale & Eskdale	1
8	Dumfries and Kirkcudbright	2
9	Wigton & Stranraer	3
10	Ayr	2
11	Irvine & Kilmarnock	4
12	Ardrossan	1
13	Lanark	1
14	Paisley	5
16	Glasgow	11
17	Hamilton	10
18	Dumbarton	4
19	South Argyll	1
20	Dunoon	0
21	Lorne & Mull	1
22	Falkirk	7
23	Stirling	5
24	Dunfermline	3

		TOTAL
25	Kirkcaldy	3
26	St Andrew's	6
27	Dunkeld & Meigle	1
28	Perth	5
29	Dundee	3
30	Angus	6
31	Aberdeen	6
32	Kincardine & Deeside	1
33	Gordon	3
34	Buchan	5
35	Moray	2
36	Abernethy	1
37	Inverness	1
38	Lochaber	3
39	Ross	3
40	Sutherland	0
41	Caithness	2
42	Lochcarron & Skye	0
43	Uist	0
44	Lewis	1
45	Orkney	2
46	Shetland	0
47	England	0
		145

APPENDIX 11

ACT ANENT LONG TERM ILLNESS OF MINISTERS IN CHARGE

The General Assembly hereby enact and ordain:

Definitions

1. For the purposes of this Act and the Schedule attached hereto:

(a) 'the Board' shall be the Board of Ministry

(b) a 'minister' shall be a minister inducted to a charge

(c) 'absence' shall be absence from duties through illness; absence for any other reason, including compassionate leave or study leave, shall be notified to the Presbytery and, in all cases except where this is not reasonably practicable, shall be subject to the permission of the Presbytery, but shall not be otherwise subject to the provisions of this Act.

(d) the 'Consultative Committee of the Presbytery' shall be a committee of three presbyters, who on behalf of the Presbytery shall have sole and confidential access through the Board of Ministry to the opinion of the Medical Adviser for the purposes of this Act, and shall advise the Presbytery with regard to its responsibilities.

Procedure in the case of illness

2. (1) Whenever the minister of a charge is absent due to illness, he or she shall inform the Board of Ministry in terms of the Regulations appended as Schedule A to this Act.

(2) Failure to fulfil the requirements of Schedule A shall be intimated to the Presbytery, which may consider whether the minister is in desertion of his or her charge or whether any other matter of discipline has arisen.

3. (1) Whenever the Clerk of the Presbytery is notified in terms of Schedule A, he or she shall record the dates of commencement and expiry of absence in a record apart.

(2) The Presbytery shall be informed by its Clerk of the minister's absence (a) if an Interim Moderator is to be appointed or (b) if the Presbytery requires to take any action in support or superintendence of the congregation or congregations or (c) for the appointment of a Consultative Committee of Presbytery if the terms of section 4 may require to be fulfilled before the next ordinary meeting of the Presbytery.

Long-term illness

4. (1) Following the date ("the section 4 date") on which a minister's absence has extended to nine calendar months continuously, or has totalled 450 days out of any thirty-three month period:

(a) the Board shall immediately remind the minister of the requirements of this section;

(b) the minister shall consult with the Medical Adviser appointed by the Board and give the Medical Adviser permission to consult with any medical practitioner or consultant whose opinion the Medical Adviser requires in order to prepare his or her own opinion on the likely duration of the minister's absence;

(c) the minister shall make available to the Consultative Committee of the Presbytery, through the Board of Ministry, the opinion of the Medical Adviser in terms of subsection (b) above, and shall meet with the said Committee;

(d) the Consultative Committee shall inform the Board of the recommendation it intends to bring to the Presbytery, and shall receive within seven days of such intimation any comments and advice from, or on the authority of, the General Secretary of the Board;

(e) the Consultative Committee shall inform the Presbytery, at an ordinary meeting of the Presbytery of (i) the likelihood of the minister's returning to work within a further three months after the section 4 date and (ii) the comments received in terms of section 4(1)(d) from the Board of Ministry;

(f) for the avoidance of doubt, the Consultative Committee shall retain in confidence all medical information received and shall not divulge any of it to the Presbytery;

(g) the Presbytery shall take such further pastoral or superintendence measures as may be required, and the Board shall offer the minister such assistance and advice as it deems appropriate in all the circumstances.

(2) In the event of failure by the minister to fulfil the requirements of section 4(1) within a reasonable period of time in accordance with medical advice, the Presbytery may consider whether the minister is in desertion of his or her charge or whether any other matter of discipline has arisen.

Dissolution of the Pastoral Tie
5. If, in terms of section 4(1), the Presbytery has been advised that there is no prospect of the minister's return to duties on or before a day three months after the section 4 date ("the section 5 date"), it shall take account of the comments received in terms of section 4(1)(d) and shall either:

(a) inform the minister that, if he or she has not resumed duties by the section 5 date, his or her pastoral tie shall be dissolved by the Presbytery[1], or

(b) declare that exceptional circumstances exist that justify a decision not to dissolve the pastoral tie in terms of section 5(a), and record its reasons in its Record Apart, along with a note of the comments received from the Board.

6. (1) If, in terms of section 4(1), the Presbytery has been advised that there is a prospect of the minister's return to duties on or before the section 5 date, but the minister does not return to duties by that date, the requirements of section 4(1)(a)-(d) above shall again be fulfilled, and the provisions of section 4(2) shall apply.

(2) The Presbytery shall meet as soon as possible thereafter, shall take account of the advice of its Consultative Committee and the comments received in terms of section 4(1)(d), and shall either:

(a) inform the minister that his or her pastoral tie shall be dissolved, on a date that is (i) determined by the Presbytery with due regard to all the circumstances and (ii) within three calendar months of the section 5 date, or

(b) declare that exceptional circumstances exist that justify a decision not to dissolve the pastoral tie in terms of

section 6(2)(a), and record its reasons in the Record Apart, along with a note of the comments received from the Board.

7. In the event of the Presbytery making a decision in terms of section 6(2)(b) above, the requirements of sections 4(1)(a)-(d) and 6(2) shall be fulfilled at intervals of three calendar months for the whole duration of the minister's absence.

8. Before dissolving a pastoral tie in terms of this Act, the Presbytery shall be satisfied that the minister and his or her family have received advice from the Board.

9. For the avoidance of doubt, it is hereby declared that in cases of dissolution of the pastoral tie in terms of this Act, it shall not be necessary for the minister to make formal application to demit in terms of Act V 1984 section 27.

Confidentiality
10. (1) In the interests of confidentiality, all procedure under this Act shall be taken in private, and no information shall be shared except as required above.

(2) Notwithstanding the foregoing generality, and in the event of a dissent-and-complaint being taken against a decision in terms of section 5(b) or section 6(2)(b), the reasons of the Presbytery, as recorded in the Record Apart, and the comments of the Board shall be available to the Commission of Assembly

Repeal
11. Act X 2000 anent Long-term Illness of Ministers in Charge is hereby repealed.

---

[1] The Board shall provide information on any application to retire from active ministry on grounds of ill-health, but the dissolution of a pastoral tie in terms of this Act does not necessarily constitute demission on grounds of ill-health for e.g. pension purposes.

Schedule A

Regulations anent Illness of Ministers of Charges

1. (1) A minister absent through illness, or his or her appointed nominee, shall inform a designated staff member of the Board as soon as practicable.

(2) The minister shall submit pro-forma notification of absence (in such form as the Board of Ministry or the General Treasurer's Board shall from time to time provide) upon return to duties or after seven days' absence, whichever is sooner.

(3) Where an absence continues for more than seven days, the minister shall as soon as possible provide a medical certificate to the Board, and shall continue to provide such certificates, covering the whole period of absence, and a final certificate showing the date of return to work.

2. Whenever the Board is initially informed by a minister of his or her absence due to illness, it shall notify both the Clerk to the Presbytery of the bounds and the Payroll Unit of the General Treasurers' Department.

3. A minister absent in terms of this Act shall receive full stipend appropriate to the charge and years of service, subject to tax and National Insurance contributions and subject to allowance made for state benefits received in respect of the illness.

4. When a minister has been absent from work for six months the payroll unit will make appropriate arrangements for the payment of stipend in terms of regulation 3. At the same time the Board of Ministry will make contact with the minister to ensure that appropriate pastoral support and advice are in place.

CHAPLAINS TO HER MAJESTY'S FORCES

MAY 2002

PROPOSED DELIVERANCE

The General Assembly:

1. Receive the Report of the Committee.
2. Reaffirm the commitment and support of the church to the chaplains whom it sends to the Armed Forces.
3. Encourage the church to uphold in prayer those who face tension, separation, danger, and demanding pastoral responsibilities as they serve their nation.
4. Welcome the supportive dialogue and exchange of advice with the Committee on Church and Nation since the General Assembly of 2001.
5. Note the urgent and continuing need to recruit imaginative and reasonably fit men and women to serve as chaplains in the Armed Forces.
6. Welcome the re-establishment of the Royal Navy Reserve Chaplaincy; commend it to the Church, and encourage suitable ministers to apply.
7. Amend Regulations VI, 2000 by the addition of the words 'AND RNR CHAPLAINS' in the title of the regulations; and the addition of the words 'or a Royal Navy Reserve Chaplain' to the first line of the first regulation, after the words 'Territorial Army Chaplain'.
8. Note that a formal report on the satisfactory nature of the reorganisation of the RAF Chaplains' Branch in 1999 has not yet been submitted.
9. Welcome the Committee's involvement in the planning of the Board of National Mission's Conference on Chaplaincy.
10. Endorse planning for the first tri-service conference for Church of Scotland chaplains, and encourage the role of the Armed Forces Chaplaincy Centre in constructing policy and vision for the future.
11. Welcome the appointment of the Reverend Leslie Bryan as Assistant Chaplain General at HQ 2 Division in Edinburgh, and the Reverend Peter Mills as Principal Chaplain Church of Scotland and Free Churches, RAF.
12. Thank the Venerable Peter Bishop CB, the Reverend Roger Bayliss, and the Venerable Simon Golding CBE for service and leadership in the RAF and RN, and welcome the Venerable Barry Hammett QHC as the new Chaplain of the Fleet.
13. Thank the Reverend Professor Iain R Torrance for his distinguished convenership of the Committee over the past four years and thank the Vice Convener, Secretary and Committee members for their work.

REPORT

1. Delineating the prophetic voice of Chaplains to the Forces

The issue

In February 2001, the then Moderator of the General Assembly, along with a number of other Christian people, and at least one bishop, demonstrated at Faslane against this country's possession of a nuclear deterrent. Serious discussion followed. One uneasiness with the Moderator's presence at Faslane was a sense that this was the projection of a single perspective, whereas, in fact, there is now a multiplicity of voices. A consequent anxiety was felt – possibly a false one – that the Moderator, if representing the entire Church, might thereby call in question the credibility of the Chaplains whom the Church sends to the Royal Navy. The drama of the demonstration attracted press coverage, and in the heat of the debate, perspectives were absolutised and sides were taken. At one point, it was even suggested that a chaplain to the Royal Navy might be an appropriate spokesman to defend the nuclear deterrent. This was surely a sign that a false polarisation had set in, and the Committee undertook to examine part of the dilemma underlying this dispute.

All ministry involves conflicts of role, and chaplaincy to the armed forces involves more than most. A traditional solution has been to find some way of reducing the conflict between being a Christian minister and a member of a combatant unit. For some this meant adopting a largely pastoral role; for some it has meant disruption-patterned pyjamas and heavy investment in just war thinking. The skilful have always attempted to walk along the ridge, without stumbling down either slope. The report attempts to address these issues, seeking especially to delineate an appropriate prophetic role. We hope, thereby, in certain senses, to re-establish the relationship between the proper activities of this Committee and those of the Committee on Church and Nation.

Setting the agenda
Historically, not least because of various types of Church-State relationships, chaplaincy in the Armed Forces has tended to be accommodating, at worst docile. An issue is the extent to which we will continue to collaborate in the construction of non-prophet chaplaincy. We would like, in a cautious way, recognising the constitutional constraints and privileges of the position, to reformulate a notion of prophecy. Thus, we will suggest that chaplaincy – even in the Armed Forces – has a prophetic role. This is rooted in the fact that all chaplains are the accredited representatives of sending churches or religious communities. We live in a time when spiritual values – and that includes specifically religious values – are highly esteemed. We suggest that prophets are perfectly used to being in a minority and contradicted or ignored. Contradiction is healthy, unless the prophet happens to be in a situation of establishment of such a kind that contradiction would undermine the activity of prophecy. Paradoxically, in a world of competing voices, we suspect we risk marginalisation more from prophetic self-denial than from disagreement. It may be that Christianity has

drunk too deeply from the waters of establishment to retain a useful spiritual independence. It may be that there can be a recovery of perspective from those who have never drunk from those wells.

The legacy of the past
Contemporary historians[1] suggest that current understandings of Army chaplaincy, at least in Britain, were forged during the First World War. The social context was that society was broadly Christian and church leaders were respected public figures. The enlargement of the war led to conscription, and with raw soldiers, not yet battle hardened, morale was seen to be an issue. Contemporary study, for instance of the relationship between Field Marshall Haig and his chaplain, shows that morale-building and pastoral work were seen as the chaplain's primary task. He was not a prophet, nor was he there to provide an independent moral voice. There were, of course, luminous figures of self-sacrificial goodness: Theodore Bailey Hardy, the most decorated British non-combatant of the First World War, would be an example[2]. Studdert Kennedy would be another, but his very nickname of 'Woodbine Willie' is suggestive[3].

---

[1] An example is Dr Michael Snape, of Birmingham University, England. See his forthcoming book: *Religion in the British Army, 1707-1945* (Routledge, 2002).
[2] See Alan Wilkinson: *The Church of England and the First World War* (1978) for other examples.
[3] Note Studdert Kennedy's own reflection: 'For the men to whom I owed God's Peace / I put off with a cigarette' (cited in Alan Wilkinson, 'The Paradox of the Military Chaplain', in *Theology*, 1981 (vol 84), p.254). Yet General Plumer stormed out of one of Studdert Kennedy's sermons and demanded his removal from the chaplaincy (see David Raw, *'It's Only Me: A Life of the Reverend Theodore Bailey Hardy VC, DSO, MC* [Frank Peters, Gatebeck, 1988]. After Hardy's death, Studdert Kennedy wrote to Mary Hardy, Hardy's sister-in-law, telling of their meeting. He wrote that he advised, 'Our first job is to go beyond the men in self-sacrifice and reckless devotion … There is very little purely spiritual work, it is all muddled and mixed – but it is all spiritual. Take a box of fags in your haversack and a great deal of love in your heart, and go up to them, laugh with them, joke with them; you can pray with them sometimes, but pray for them always' (from Mary Hardy: *Hardy V.C.* (Skeffington, 1919), pp.24-7).

Thus, the long association of the chaplain with concert parties, chocolates and cigarettes was born. It is now increasingly clear that the highly controversial First World War courts martial and executions of British soldiers for cowardice and desertion were attempts to bolster morale. It seems equally plain, though it is the object of current research, that chaplains accepted what was being done and provided no concerted protest.[4] This has to be placed in the context of the time.

At the end of the First World War there was a significant reappraisal of Army chaplaincy. This was conducted not by a soldier, but a civil servant, H. J. Creedy[5]. The Creedy Report addressed issues of management, for instance the role of principal denominational chaplains in a united department and how they might relate to each other. Constitutionally, it provided that each Church represented in the Royal Army Chaplains' Department would appoint an accredited representative to act as a nexus between it and the War Office with regard to Chaplaincy Services. It noted that prior to the War, chaplains had not been permitted to wear uniform. This created an impression that they were not 'an organic part of the Army' and 'limited the scope of their usefulness'. The Report noted that 'given a suitable personnel and adequate opportunity, the Royal Army Chaplains' Department can make a very much more effective contribution to the well being and moral [sic] of the Army than had been realised'.

The effects of this were far reaching and complex. A unique relationship of both belonging and independence was given constitutional form. Clergymen (at that stage there were only men) could only be appointed Army chaplains if they were nominated by an accredited representative of their Church, who served on an Interdenominational Advisory Committee. This meant that chaplains had to be and remained fully accredited priests and ministers of a participating Church. It meant that they had a continuing spiritual oversight for their beliefs and conduct of the sacraments from beyond the military world. At the same time, so as to be an organic part of the Army, they wore uniform, carried badges of relative rank, and had organised structures for pay and promotion. The independence was and remained very important. It meant that chaplains, not being part of a normal chain of command, could receive and retain confidentialities. They were not to be involved in matters of discipline. It was an extraordinary privilege. Potentially, it provided for a continuation of the dialogue between Church and State, at a micro-level, within the Armed Forces themselves.

However, it is doubtful if this potentiality was ever fully exercised. Modern historians believe that it was practically impossible for a chaplain at that time to exercise a genuine moral independence. Published memoirs show that an expectation existed for there to be a mutually supportive relationship between commanders and chaplains. In the First World War at least, there was friction between regular and volunteer chaplains. Walking the ridge between being a churchman and soldier, the temptation was for chaplains to 'go native' on the military side. A social construct was formed, and with it, there were encoded all the conflicts of role every chaplain has subsequently had to face: How to represent Jesus in a military institution? How to belong in a combatant unit and hold a non-combatant role? How to symbolise catholicity, while serving a national cause? How to be both a priest and an officer? How to exercise a prophetic role?[6]

---

4 Service chaplaincy was not alone in this. For a non-military example, see the French Bishops' Declaration of Repentance of 30 Sept 1997, near a Jewish deportation camp on the edge of Paris. 'The bishops declared that their predecessors in the Vichy era had been too "caught up in a loyalism and docility" towards civil authorities', and had done too little to spare French Jews from deportation and death. The declaration acknowledged that there had been 'too little indignation'. Quoted from footnote 10, page 55, in Nigel Biggar (ed): *Burying the Past* (Georgetown University Press, Washington, DC, 2001).

5 *Précis for the Army Council, Number 1026: Future Administration of the Royal Army Chaplains' Department*, by J. H. Creedy (May, 1920)

6 See Alan Wilkinson: 'The Paradox of the Military Chaplain' in *Theology*, vol 84 (1981), pp 249-57. See also Gordon Zahn: *Chaplains in the RAF* (1969); and W.W.Burchard: 'Role Conflicts of Military Chaplains' in *American Sociological Review*, vol 19 (1954).

This is where the moral ambiguity of the military chaplain is located, not in pretending to have at hand knock-down resolutions to a series of dilemmas in combat or policy.

Pieces of the jigsaw

Over the last decade, the British Armed Forces have more than once found themselves wrong footed or embarrassed by appearing out of touch with the times. The most obvious public issue was over the rights of gay people. Such issues highlighted the diminishing credibility afforded by the traditional reliance on the certainties of the established Church and the consequent muffling of independent prophetic voices. Indeed, certain issues were directly related to constructions of gender, power and purity which had ecclesial roots. There are current issues to do with the status of partners. For a period, chaplains who divorced and remarried tended to leave; for a period there was reluctance to accept woman ministers of the non-episcopal churches. In the context of the social changes of the early to mid 1990s, and a sharply declining ability to recruit, British Armed Forces had to respond to accusations of hypocrisy, classism and of being out of step with European legislation.

The response was vigorous and well thought out. Certain absolutes were called in question. Ethos became more spoken of than tradition, so there was a turn to anthropology and a qualified acceptance of postmodernism. The military community came to be seen as a moral community. New codes of conduct were drafted, in which characteristics which contributed in an exemplary way to maintenance of ethos or function were seen as paradigm virtues. By speaking of disciplined activities rather than abstracts, the Armed Forces were able to show that the virtues of their practices – fitness, cohesion, honesty – could only be fully appreciated by insiders. This gave at least partial cogency to the late 1990s claim of the Armed Forces that they had a 'Right to be Different'. But further reflection and hindsight show a downside to a communitarian derivation of value. The military community is too small and too diverse to generate genuinely distinctive virtues. For example, it is simply not true to maintain that all military people are different because ultimately they have an obligation 'to

close with the enemy at short range, face to face and kill them or be killed'[7]. More importantly, a telling criticism is that 'communitarianism runs the risk of giving individual members of a particular tribe or community no critical distance [from] their own situatedness'[8]. Thus, if one were a slave and one's entire identity, role and duties were defined by one's community, then one would have no moral vocabulary left with which to object to one's status. Similarly, if a soldier's identity and virtues were defined *purely* in terms of the military community (military communitarianism, or even military efficiency), and he or she were ordered to commit an atrocity, they would be left without a vocabulary of moral disobedience. What is missed out is the role of the prophet, the visionary or the genuine leader (rather than the facilitator). This is the aspect of the chaplain's role upon which the Committee wishes to place its finger. It may be called 'critical solidarity' (a phrase used by James Harkness, a former Chaplain General), or likened to the notion of 'Her Majesty's Loyal Opposition' in the constitution of Parliament, but without a firm delineation of this independence, the chaplain's role is fatally diluted.

The late 1990s saw a renewed seriousness with which spiritual values were taken[9]. A British example is the *Spiritual Needs Study* of 1999 by Brigadier Ian McGill[10]. This excellent report acknowledged that the United Kingdom is now a multi-ethnic society and that the recruiting and equal opportunities factors cannot be ignored. An individual has a right to belong to any religion or none; it expected that the ratio between Non-Christians and Christians in the Army would rise; and it

---

7   This striking phrase is a quotation from an Army Human Resource Strategy document of the mid 1990s.

8   Frank G. Kirkpatrick, 'Public and Private: The Search for a Political Philosophy that Does Justice to Both Without Excluding Love'. A paper given to the conference on John Macmurray at the University of Aberdeen in April 1998, which will be published in 2002 by the publisher Peter Lang Inc (Berne and Baltimore).

9   This seriousness was certainly encouraged by the careful attention given to the moral component in fighting force earlier in the 1990s.

10   *Spiritual Needs Study: An Investigation into the Need for Spiritual Values in the Army* (May 1999) by Brigadier I D T McGill CBE, late RE

acknowledged that all soldiers of whatever faith have a need for spiritual values. It suggested that these issues are wider than chaplaincy and introduced a new Army Training Directive, 'Moral Understanding'[11]. Again with the benefit of hindsight, one might suggest that the *Spiritual Needs Study* partially, no doubt, because of its proper attempt to be broad, separated spiritual *values* from *practice* or worship. That led to a new abstraction, not unlike the old abstractions about tradition. How may such values be embedded? The training package was imaginative and thorough, but such packages are more usually complied with than welcomed as agents of transformation. The report was unintentionally, but most significantly, an anti-establishment move, in that it acknowledged that Christianity does not have a monopoly of spiritual values.

The 1990s also, not least as a result of the end of the Cold War, saw Christianity formulate more clearly its ambivalence about war. The shape of the traditional just war argument is very familiar. Just war required a legal authority, a just cause and a just intent. The just cause was punitive or restorative. Just intent enjoined that combatants be peaceful, not cruel or greedy. From these roots, the principles of proportionality and discrimination grew. According to this version, the notion of just war is neither an argument nor a test of the rightfulness of actions, but a genuinely Christian doctrine, an evangelical praxis[12] – that is, an injunction rooted in the command of Jesus that we love our neighbours. Love lay behind restraint. Even punitive war was based on love, as it aimed to restore relations between neighbours. The opposite of this, pacifism, was an evangelical counter-praxis, which is martyrdom, not passivity. All of that is familiar ground. However, a series of Papal statements over the last four decades has consistently unfolded a different vision.

James Turner Johnson traces the beginning of this shift in perspective to 1870 when a *Postulatum* was presented to the First Vatican Council. The purpose of this was to challenge 'the justice of the form of war practised by modern states'[13]. The objection was rooted in reaction to the Franco-Prussian War, and possibly the American Civil War. It pointed to the nationalistic ambitions of various states, the militarism of national armies, and 'hideous massacres' which the Church could not accept as just.

The *Postulatum* dismissed the idea that a first use of force could be just, though it allowed the justice of a second use of force in defence[14]. That was a first step. Following the carnage of the First World War, the Conventus of Fribourg in 1931 distinguished between defence, which was lawful, and the argument for war from national 'necessity', which was judged illicit. These documents changed the agenda, setting in motion a 'presumption against war', which provided an alternative starting point to the thesis that the just prosecution of war is rooted in the command to love our neighbour.

This trend was carried forward implicitly in a Christmas message of 1956 by Pope Pius XII, and explicitly in the 1963 encyclical *Pacem in Terris* of Pope John XXIII. Here the Pope said: '[I]n this age which boasts of its atomic power, it no longer makes sense to maintain that war is a fit instrument with which to repair the violation of justice'. What the Pope intended is still disputed, but one interpretation is that this was an outright rejection of all just war theory, not simply a condemnation of first strike. The same trend was continued by Pope Paul VI in his 1965 address to the United Nations General Assembly: '[N]ever again war, war never again!', and in the 1983 pastoral letter of the American Catholic bishops, *The Challenge of Peace*.

These Papal statements have been immensely influential. There is now a genuine pluralism in Christian

---

[11] ITD 11: Moral Understanding (1999).

[12] I am borrowing this term from Oliver O'Donovan, who, in turn, borrows it from John Milbank.

[13] For this discussion, see James Turner Johnson: 'Just War: A Broken Tradition' in *The National Interest*, Denville, New Jersey. Number 45, Fall 1996, pp.27-36. Turner argues, very importantly, that some current versions of the just war arguments form a 'broken tradition' as they have shifted in recent Catholic thought **from** their foundation in the duty of love protecting the innocent **to** a Christian presumption against doing harm. For the quotation, see James Turner Johnson, *op.cit.*, p. 30.

[14] Johnson sees this, the undercutting of the first use of force, along with the acceptance of the second use (defined as defence) as being a factor not only in Catholic thought, but also in twentieth century international law (*op.cit.*, p.31).

thinking, ranging, for example, from the cautious endorsement of humanitarian intervention, including the use of armed force, from the World Council of Churches in February 2001, to their statement of 8th October 2001: 'We do not believe that war, particularly in today's highly technologised world, can ever be regarded as an effective response to the equally abhorrent sin of terrorism ... Nor do we believe that war can be described as an act of humanitarianism or that the practice of war can be legitimately linked to the promise of humanitarian assistance'. This is echoed by the 1st of November 2001 statement of the Church and Nation Committee of the Church of Scotland, which called for an end to the bombing in Afghanistan, and questioned the use of force (ever) as a means of resolving international disputes.

Such statements are uncomfortable for governments, and mark a further stage in the ending of the accommodationism between the Christian Church and the State, which marked much of the last century. The Christian churches, though now much more pluralist, are beginning to recover a prophetic voice.

Drawing the threads together

It is evident that there is now clear water between 'the moral view' (whatever that is) and the Christian one. There is clear water between 'spiritual values' and 'Christian values', and, increasingly, there will be more than one Christian perspective. The pluralism and vigour of contemporary Christianity sit uneasily with the traditional construction of a Chaplain to the Forces, especially where there has been an elision of 'moral' and 'morale'.

How serious is this? We believe the recovery of a prophetic role would be of the greatest benefit to Chaplaincy. We believe a relationship which is forthright is also of benefit to government. But how easily may this be achieved? How may one be a prophet within the constraints of the double citizenship described at the beginning?

A genuine valuing of the contributions of the other-than-Christian religions is helpful. They come to Chaplaincy without the same historical baggage in terms of Church-State relations and are unused to muzzling their prophetic voices. This enables Christianity also to

recover expression of what it believes to be distinctive. It may be feared that a dilution of the Church-State relationship may permit discordant or maverick voices to be heard. However, the exercise of that independence of voice is still within certain constraints. These are not different in kind from those under which an industrial or prison chaplain may work. Integrity of practice in all ministry involves negotiating such paradoxes.

Finally, we offer a model whereby that which is distinctively religious and prophetic is aligned to the restraints of political responsibility. The example is the process of political forgiveness in South Africa, drawing from a paper on 'Politics and Forgiveness' by Jean Bethke Elshtain[15]. Elshtain refers to Hannah Arendt, who called forgiveness the greatest contribution of Jesus of Nazareth to politics. Her intention by this striking remark was to indicate the need for repetitive cycles of vengeance to be broken by some unexpected act which allowed something else to begin. Our embedded sense of order requires us to keep count of the past. However, too much past overwhelms the future and limits the possibility of transformation. Elshtain coins the phrase 'knowing forgetting' to indicate a recollection of the past, but not one of such a kind that one's identity is entirely defined by it. There are circumstances, Elshtain suggests, where the ingrained thirst for retributive justice is out of place, and yet compensatory justice is prudentially impossible. An example is the South African Truth and Reconciliation Commission, created by the post-apartheid democratic parliament in 1995. Here, as a minimum, full disclosure of politically motivated crimes was required. To the objection, What about justice?, the South Africans could reply that they were challenging the prevalent models of justice (which are, in fact, the very notions upon which our understanding of Just War depend). They were deliberately trying to create a *politically restorative* justice, which was neither cheap forgiveness nor the prevalent mode of retributive or punitive justice. There was a

---

[15] 'Politics and Forgiveness', chapter 3 (pp 40-56) in *Burying the Past: Making Peace and Doing Justice after Civil Conflict*, edited by Nigel Biggar (Georgetown University Press, Washington, DC, 2001).

compromise here, but one made so as to create a moral space: a deliberate setting aside of what had hitherto been seen as strict justice, so as to enable a new beginning, within which justice might flower again.

This provides an example of *the kind* of prophecy which we suggest needs to be reconstructed: a prophecy which is genuine, yet responsibly within constraints; constructive and future-looking rather than merely score-keeping. We suggest that retention of such a voice is crucial for the moral integrity of military chaplains, if they are not to reduce themselves to being merely the guardians of other peoples' protocols, failing thereby to remain true representatives of their sending Churches and faith communities.

2. Co-operation with the Church and Nation Committee

Following discussions initiated at the General Assembly of 2001, the Conveners of the Committees on Chaplains to Her Majesty's Forces, and on Church and Nation, consulted regularly during the year and exchanged information and advice. The Committee on Chaplains to Her Majesty's Forces uses the occasion of its annual report to thank the Committee on Church and Nation, and to record appreciation for their interest, prayers and concern for chaplains during the conflict in Afghanistan and its aftermath.

3. Recruitment

The Army has now endorsed most of the recommendations made in the 'Spiritual Needs Study' conducted by Brigadier Ian McGill in May 1999, and has agreed to fund six additional chaplains' posts for the coming financial year. This will require the Chaplain-General to recruit a total of sixteen chaplains between April 2002 and March 2003 in order to replace those due to retire and to achieve the new target. This is an area of mission and it remains as crucial as ever to encourage imaginative and reasonably fit men and women to respond to its challenges. There are vacancies in all three Services.

4. Re-establishment of the RNR Chaplains' Branch

Royal Naval Reserve Chaplaincy is being resurrected after a period of nearly 10 years. The intention is to recruit up to 18 chaplains from all denominations, to provide surge capability to release additional Royal Navy Chaplains for front line service in times of crisis or war. Applications are welcome from ministers who have been ordained for at least 3 years, are aged under 50, and are in good health. It is hoped to recruit the first tranche of RNR Chaplains by the end of September 2002.

5. RAF Chaplains' Branch

The RAF Chaplains' Branch was due to report to the Inter-denominational Advisory Panel, and thence to the General Assembly of May 2002, about the satisfactory nature of its reorganisation in 1999. Changes of personnel have delayed a formal report which will be submitted subsequently. However, every indication suggests that the new arrangements have been most successful.

6. Conference on Chaplaincy

The Board of National Mission is planning to organise and fund a Conference on Chaplaincy in the Spring of 2003. The conference will address both the isolation felt by chaplains of different kinds (hospital, prison, industrial, school), and the increasing realisation of the absolutely crucial role of such agents who navigate between different structures and institutions. The Committee on Chaplains to Her Majesty's Forces is delighted to be included and Senior Chaplains from all three Services will be involved in planning the conference.

7. Joint ventures

Servicepeople are increasingly involved in Joint Ventures, which require tri-service attitudes to training (see the Report from the Royal Navy). This affects chaplains as well as all others, and it is planned to bring together Church of Scotland chaplains of all three Services to a single annual conference, so that they may share common approaches, institute best practice and get to know each other better. Such a conference, now agreed, is a major step forward as service chaplaincy evolves in the twenty-first century. Such evolution in policy and vision must be informed by a wider range of conversation partners. The dialogue with National Mission and Church and Nation, referred to above, is an instance of this. The newly formed Armed Forces Chaplaincy Centre at Amport has a pivotal role to play here, reflecting on the specific opportunities and challenges of chaplaincy in a military environment (towards which this Report is a contribution). The generous endowment of the annual W G A Wright Memorial Lecture is another resource (delivered in 2001 by Professor Oliver O'Donovan FBA, Regius Professor of Moral Theology at Oxford), and the annual Military Chiefs of Chaplains Conference provides a further range of conversation partners and a unique international forum. We cannot afford to be blinkered by the past.

8. Changes in senior posts

The Committee records its gratefulness to the Reverend Roger Bayliss, a Methodist minister, who retired in 2001 from the post of Principal Chaplain Church of Scotland and Free Churches, RAF, and welcomes the Reverend Peter Mills QHC, a minister of the Church of Scotland, in his place. It thanks the Venerable Peter Bishop CB, the now retired Chaplain-in-Chief, RAF, and welcomes the Venerable R D Hesketh QHC who succeeds him. It bids farewell to the Venerable Simon Golding CBE, who retires from his post as Chaplain of the Fleet on the 30th of May, and thanks him for his consistently gracious support for the Church of Scotland. It welcomes the Venerable Barry Hammett QHC, who takes his place. Finally, the Committee welcomes most warmly the Reverend Leslie Bryan, who is the new Assistant Chaplain General at HQ 2 Division in Edinburgh.

In the name of the Committee

IAIN R TORRANCE, *Convener*
HERBERT A KERRIGAN, QC, *Vice Convener*
DOUGLAS M HUNTER, WS, *Secretary*

ADDENDUM

Iain Torrance will retire as Convener at the conclusion of this year's Assembly, following four years during which he has not only unfailingly served this committee but has also accepted a Personal Chair in Patristics and Christian Ethics at Aberdeen University, only to be followed by his appointment in 2001 as Dean of the Faculty of Arts and Divinity. The Committee was also pleased to note the honour done him by his appointment as a Chaplain-in-Ordinary to Her Majesty The Queen. As a former TA chaplain, Iain well understood the implications that Full Time Reserve Service – voluntary mobilisation – would have in order to meet the escalating peacekeeping requirements particularly in Bosnia. The regulations put before the General Assembly in May 2000 were the result of Iain's meticulous planning and negotiating skills including a fact-finding visit to Bosnia. He has also dealt with recurring problems among the sending churches at meetings of the Inter Denominational Advisory Board at which the respect for the Church of Scotland has been further enhanced. He has also tackled the distinction between Christian chaplaincy and spiritual needs within the Army whereby foresight is required to see that at a future date it will surely be necessary for religious representatives from different faiths to become fully integrated into the armed forces on equal terms with Christian chaplains as witnessed in the detail of our report. Without doubt this committee will require to seek Iain's wise counsel from time to time in the future but we say thank you for the moment for a sterling contribution.

In the name of the Committee

HERBERT A KERRIGAN, QC, Vice Convener
DOUGLAS M HUNTER, WS, Secretary

APPENDIX 1

REPORT ON CHAPLAINCY IN THE ROYAL NAVY

The year 2001 has seen many changes within the Naval Service. The reorganisation of the operational aspect of the Navy, Fleet First, has moved forward swiftly. Already many sections of the Fleet organisation have moved from Northwood in London to Portsmouth and are much more directly involved in running naval operations. Chaplaincy has been affected in that the posts of Staff Chaplains to Commander in Chief Fleet and Flag Officer Surface Flotilla have merged and are now located in Portsmouth.

The single most important factor in the Naval Service remains the service person. Increasing concern has been shown in the demands being put upon our service persons, especially those who deploy with ships and submarines. The concern centres around the ability to give these sailors an adequate amount of quality time at home with their families. The increasing number of operations involving the Royal Navy and the shortage of manpower are putting an increasing pressure on those who serve. To answer this is the 'Tomorrow's Personnel Manpower System' (ToPMaSt). ToPMaSt will enable the manpower planners to use the Navy's well trained sailors to the best advantage while guaranteeing them a sensible amount of time with their families.

Several factors point to the changing attitude to life in the Royal Navy. While it is recognised that young men and women join the Navy to see the world they do not wish to spend every day at sea. A greater proportion than ever marry young and have families and, as a result, want a reasonable amount of time at home. Another factor is their expectation of a career in uniform. Ten years ago most of those who joined up did so expecting to make it their career. Now the majority join for a shorter period, to do something different, before settling into a career job. This presents the Navy with the difficulty of developing the future leader and senior service person.

The three services are conscious that an increasing amount of our activity is Joint. As a result the Heads of Chaplaincies have set up four working groups to look into the tri-service aspects of training, appointing, operations and inter-faith issues. By way of example, the Defence Training Review, which reported in 2001 and is in the process of being implemented, has identified Defence Training Establishments or Schools, where, for example, all heavy engineering for all three services will be centred in one location. Likewise Air Training, Communications, Policing, etc.

Last year it was reported that Naval Chaplaincy Service was at full strength. Unfortunately since then, as a result of a block of retirements, there is a shortage of Chaplains. It is vital that there is a return to full strength as soon as possible and all enquiries will be welcomed.

It is reported with pleasure that approval has been given for the reintroduction of Royal Naval Reserve Chaplains. When selected they will be linked to specific shore establishments where they will be able to support the Chaplaincy team and, should a situation require it, replace the commissioned Chaplain if he or she were to be appointed to sea duty in a time of crisis. There could also be the possibility of a short period, say one year, of Full Time Reserve Service (although any such secondment could only be managed under the Regulations passed by the General Assembly in May 2000).

Like so many organisations, the NCS has adopted a Child Protection policy. Initially this may seem to apply only to Chaplains with Congregations and a Sunday School or youth club, but Child Protection legislation covers all minors, ie those up to the age of 18. Procedures are now in place should incidents be reported and a Chaplain has been appointed as Child Protection officer for the NCS.

Teaching remains an important part of the Naval Chaplain's remit. All trainees have periods with a Chaplain during their initial and career training courses and the Spiritual and Personal Development syllabus has been developed specially for these classes. The syllabus continues to be developed and now covers new entry officers, ratings and marines. Several Chaplains have reported an increased interest in issues like the ethics of war and the cultural and religious issues that have arisen as a consequence of the terrorist attacks on the USA.

During the 2002 Assembly, the Venerable Simon Golding CBE QHC will retire as Director General Naval Chaplaincy Service and Chaplain of the Fleet. He will be replaced by the Venerable Barry Hammett QHC MA. We wish Simon well as he returns to parish life.

The NCS is very grateful for the help and support given by the Chaplains' Committee during the year. That support is very important to us and we are very grateful for it.

Chaplains' locations:

Retirement:

The Reverend Donald Keith MA BD Royal Navy (Presbytery of Angus) (May 2002)

Serving Royal Navy Chaplains:

The Reverend Donald Keith MA BD Royal Navy
Continues to serve with the Fleet Protection Group Royal Marines and the Clyde Naval Base. During May 2001, FPGRM moved from Arbroath to Faslane. Moving with the group and continuing to minister to FPGRM and their families, Donald has joined the ecumenical Chaplaincy team within the Clyde Naval Base. He also continues to act as Chaplain to HMS CALEDONIA in Rosyth and to provide spiritual and pastoral support to personnel on ships in refit. He retires from the Royal Navy in May 2002.

The Reverend Scott Rae MBE BD CPS Royal Navy
Continues to serve as Naval Director at the Armed Forces Chaplaincy Centre at Amport House, Andover, where he is Programme Director. This multi-denominational, tri-service team of Chaplains at Amport has continued to develop courses and conferences in support of Chaplaincy throughout the Armed Forces. This year the House has responded to short notice requirements for briefing and meetings related to world-wide operational deployments and exercises. Scott expects to move to a new appointment at HMS NEPTUNE in May 2002.

The Reverend Alison Britchfield MA BD Royal Navy
Moved from HMS FEARLESS in June 2001 and is now serving as Church of Scotland & Free Churches Chaplain and Establishment Co-ordinating Chaplain at Britannia Royal Naval College. The College has a high proportion of overseas students which adds an extra dimension in what is essentially a multi-faith community. In addition, large numbers of recruits from the British Isles have rejected any spiritual allegiance. With her two colleagues at the College, Alison is closely involved in the spiritual and ethical development of all Officers joining the Royal Navy, as well as providing for their pastoral and spiritual requirements.

The Reverend Scott Shackleton BA BD Royal Navy
Continues to serve as Staff Chaplain to Commandant General Royal Marines, based with 3 Commando Brigade in Plymouth. During the year, Scott completed his six-month tour of duty in Kosovo as the Multi-National Brigade Senior Chaplain. Following leave, he returned to his home location with the Royal Marines at Stonehouse Barracks, Plymouth. Two specific highlights of a busy year were the Presentation of new Colours to 40, 42 and 45 Commandos by HRH the Duke of Edinburgh and involvement in the international exercise Saif Sareea II in Oman.

The Reverend Scott Brown BD Royal Navy
Continues to serve at HMS SULTAN, the Royal Navy's largest training establishment, meeting the spiritual and pastoral needs of trainees and staff. At Assembly time Scott will be on a 4 month exchange with the Royal Australian Navy at their Defence Academy near Canberra. Having served at SULTAN for 2½ years, he will begin a sea-going appointment on his return from Australia in September 02

The Reverend Rory MacLeod BA BD MBA Royal Navy
Continues to serve at the Commando Training Centre Royal Marines, at Lympstone, Devon. This has been a crucial year for the Chaplaincy team at CTCRM as the Chaplains bed-in and develop the initiatives begun in their first year together. Two world events affected that stability – Foot and Mouth, which resulted in Marine training being moved to the USA, with Rory accompanying as Chaplain – and September 11, with the tension and disruption the events brought. A significant consequence of this tragedy has been the sharpened interest taken by recruits in cultural and religious awareness and the ethical issues surrounding armed conflict. Rory moves to RM Poole in 2002.

The Reverend Iain McFadzean MA BD Royal Navy
Continues to serve at the Clyde Naval Base at Faslane

Helensburgh. Iain is presently approaching the end of his appointment at Faslane. In this appointment he has been involved in the development of increased co-operation with local churches and the initiation of new church and welfare provision particularly in relation to families and young people. The creation of a new charity and drop-in café, working specifically with teenagers, has been very satisfying. Iain's next appointment will be to serve at sea.

The Reverend Stan Kennon MA BD Royal Navy
Continues to serve at RNAS Culdrose in Cornwall as Church of Scotland and Free Churches Chaplain. This vast and complex Royal Naval Air Station provides helicopter squadrons to meet the requirements of the naval fleet and employs almost 3000 service and civilian personnel. The first frontline squadron of the Navy's new Merlin helicopter was created at the end of last year marking a milestone in the life of the establishment.

Presbyterian Church in Ireland

The Reverend Terry Maze QHC BSc Royal Navy
Continues to serve as Principal Church of Scotland and Free Churches Chaplain and as Director (Training and Programmes) for the Naval Chaplaincy Service. In addition to his pastoral care for the CSFC Chaplains, he has overall responsibility for the training given to all Naval Chaplains and the training delivered by them to naval personnel, including the Spiritual and Personal Development syllabus.

APPENDIX 2

CHAPLAINCY IN THE ARMY

Church of Scotland Chaplains serving in the Royal Army Chaplains Department, as Regular Army Chaplains, are currently serving in Germany, Cyprus, England and Scotland. During this past year The Reverend Alan Cobain in Northern Ireland and The Reverend Alen McCulloch in Kosovo have served operational tours.

Territorial Army Chaplains have seen training in Germany and Gibraltar and have been involved in annual camps and various activities in Scotland in what is part of the wider work of the Church.

Army Cadet Force Chaplains continue their rewarding and invaluable work with young people on weekend training and Annual Camp.

Recruiting must always have an eye to the future, and though the Church of Scotland Regular Army Chaplains are at full strength at present we are always inviting Ministers to make inquiry into this exacting ministry. Those who do are normally invited along with their spouse to make a three-day 'acquaint' visit to an Army location. There they have the opportunity to discuss in depth with Chaplains the nature of Military Ministry, meet those who lead the various formations and most importantly meet with soldiers and their families.

We are always seeking new ways to encourage Trainee Ministers to develop an interest in Chaplaincy in the Army and in this past year we have had three students undertake some of their practical training for Ministry with Regular Army Chaplains at Catterick and Fort George.

In the Territorial Army one new Chaplain has been Commissioned, The Reverend Sean Swindells who serves with 225 (Highland) Field Ambulance (Volunteers). Previously he was Chaplain with 2Bn Highlanders, ACF in Aberdeen. There is at present only one vacancy in the Territorial Army with another occurring before the next General Assembly. These appointments are spiritually, physically and intellectually challenging and Ministers are encouraged to make inquiry about this type of Chaplaincy to the Convener or Secretary

In the Army Cadet Force one new Chaplain has been Commissioned, The Reverend Joyce Keyes who serves with the Orkney [Independent] Cadet Battery. This however still leaves five vacancies. These vacancies are with 2Bn Highlanders, ACF [centered in Aberdeen and including the North East of Scotland], Angus & Dundee, ACF, [centered on Dundee and including the Forfar, Brechin, Montrose and Arbroath areas], Glasgow & Lanarkshire, ACF, Lothian & Borders ACF [covering an area from West Lothian east and to the south] and the Argyll & Sutherland Highlanders, ACF [covering an area from Falkirk, west through Stirling to Argyll]. Each situation presents a most worthwhile opportunity for Ministers to engage in the wider work of the Church and the Committee is most interested to receive inquiries.

This year the Moderator, The Right Reverend John D Millar, paid visits to Army units in Northern Ireland and Germany.

In November 2001, the Army Chaplains serving within the 2nd Division [the area from Shetland to the Wirral in the west and the Humber in the east] had the pleasure of welcoming to the Headquarters in Edinburgh, The Reverend Leslie H Bryan, CF as the new Assistant Chaplain General. He assumed his appointment vice The Reverend John P Whitton, CF who has moved south to become the Assistant Chaplain General of the 4th Division.

Location of Regular Army Chaplains

Rev B J A Abeledo	1Bn Highlanders *Redford Barracks* Edinburgh EH13 0PP
Rev J W Aitchison	HQ BRITCON UNFICYP British Forces Post Office 567
Rev R N Cameron	Church Center British Forces Post Office 40
Rev A R Cobain	1Bn Kings Own Scottish Borderers Somme Barracks Catterick Garrison N Yorks DL9 4LD
Rev D Connolly	2 CS Regt Royal Logistic Corps British Forces Post Office 47
Rev Dr D G Coulter	Royal Military College of Science Shrivenham Swindon Wilts SN6 8HD
Rev J R Dailly	Deputy Assistant Chaplain General Headquarters 15 (North East) Brigade Imphal Barracks Fulford Road York YO10 4AU
Rev J C Duncan	35 Regt Royal Engineers British Forces Post Office 31
Rev D V F Kingston	Senior Chaplain Headquarters 20 Armoured Brigade British Forces Post Office 31
Rev A J R McCulloch	3 Regt Royal Horse Artillery British Forces Post Office 38
Rev S L Mackenzie	1Bn Royal Scots British Forces Post Office 802
Rev C A MacLeod	Royal Military Academy Camberley Surrey GU15 4PQ
Rev R N MacLeod	101 Logistic Brigade Buller Barracks Aldershot Hants GU11 2BX
Rev P L Majcher	HQ ARRC Joint Headquarters British Forces Post Office 404
Rev Dr A M Martin	16 Regt Royal Corps of Signals British Forces Post Office 40
Rev D K Prentice	1Bn Royal Highland Fusiliers Fort George Arderseir Inverness IV2 7TE

Rev J P Whitton	Assistant Chaplain General Headquarters 4th Division Steele's Road Aldershot GU11 2DP

Location of Regular Army Chaplains serving from the Presbyterian Church in Ireland

Rev N G McDowell	1Bn The Black Watch British Forces Post Office 38
Rev P W Paterson	1Bn Argyll & Sutherland Highlanders British Forces Post Office 806

Location of Territorial Army Chaplains

HQ 2nd Division	Rev Dr I C Barclay, TD
Lowland Volunteers	*vacancy*
Highland Volunteers	Rev I C Warwick
105 Regt Royal Artillery (V)	Rev J M A Thomson, TD
32 (Sc) Signal Regiment (V)	Rev S A Blakey
71 Regt Royal Engineers (V)	Rev A R Forsyth, TD
225 (H) Field Ambulance (V)	Rev S Swindells
205 (Sc) Field Hospital (V)	Rev L Kinsey
205 (Sc) Field Hospital (V)	Rev J M Gibson, TD

Location of Army Cadet Force Chaplains

Angus & Dundee	*vacancy*
Argyll & Sutherland	Rev I M Homewood
Highlanders Bn	Rev R D M Campbell, TD *vacancy*
Black Watch Bn	Rev Dr I C Barclay, TD Rev E A Fisk

Glasgow & Lanark Bn	Rev M A Whyte
Highlanders 1Bn	Rev J L Goskirk Rev G N Wilson
Highlanders 2Bn	Rev I A Sutherland *vacancy*
Lothian & Borders	Rev J E Andrews *vacancy*
Orkney [Indep] Bty	Rev J Keyes
Shetland [Indep] Bty	Rev I A Charlton
West Lowland	Rev D M Almond Rev A Sherratt

APPENDIX 3

CHAPLAINCY IN THE ROYAL AIR FORCE

Since the publication of the Strategic Defence Review White Paper in July 1998 there has been a shift towards an expeditionary Air Force, a shift which has gathered momentum since the dramatic events of September 11th. Gone are the days when the number of chaplains in the Branch was in direct proportion to the number of Service personnel. Chaplaincy establishment is now linked to the Crisis Manpower Requirement and, put crudely, means that we can only justify the existence of a chaplain if there is a role for him or her to play in an operational theatre or in direct support of operations. Consequently we have more chaplains than ever serving in remote locations. Duncan Shaw recently completed a very successful 4 month detachment to Ali Al Salam in Kuwait. Chaplaincy in such Theatres of Operation are much appreciated as, contrary to the popular view, the conditions under which our personnel live and work are less than ideal.

Further development is taking place in the training world. The old 'Padre's Hour' was replaced with a very sophisticated Beliefs and Values Programme some years ago. That Programme is now under major revision and will make a substantial contribution both to what the Military call the Moral Component of Fighting Power and to the Core Values and Service ethos.

Chaplains are more than ever an integral part of both the operational environment and the training of Service personnel. Their contribution is not just welcome, but is seen as an essential part of the RAF's ability to carry out its Military Task. A very positive aspect of this is that Commanders are asking both for more chaplains and for more from their chaplains. The negative aspect is that there are simply not enough chaplains to go round. The bottom line, however, is that there are greater opportunities for chaplaincy than ever before, if only we can seize the moment and if we are prepared to adapt to the needs and opportunities presented to us by a modern and expeditionary Air Force.

Location of Royal Air Force Chaplains:

The Reverend G T Craig
College Staff Chaplain
Room 34
Whittle Hall
RAF Cranwell
Sleaford
NG34 8HB

The Reverend A J Jolly
CSFC Chaplain
Chaplains' Centre
RAF Halton
Aylesbury
HP22 5PG

The Reverend C Kellock
CSFC Chaplain
Church Centre
RAF Marham
King's Lynn
PE33 9NP

The Reverend P W Mills
Principal Chaplain
Chaplaincy Services
HQPTC
RAF Innsworth
Gloucester
GL3 1EZ

The Reverend D Shaw
Senior Chaplain
Chaplains' Office
RAF Leuchars
St Andrews
KY16 0XJ

Report on the Air Training Corps

The Chaplaincy Service to the Air Training Corps continues to serve Cadets, Officers and Adult Instructors, making the most of the opportunities provided both by special Church Parades and ordinary meetings of the Squadrons. More and more use is being made of informal contacts and talks, rather than set periods of religious instruction. In this way links are formed with many who would otherwise have little contact with the Church. It is the responsibility of the Squadron Commanding Officer to encourage Cadets to pursue the religious faith to which they belong and 'to further this purpose the CO is to secure the services and the appointment of a suitable Chaplain'.

ATC Chaplains are honorary appointments – they are not commissioned and therefore they neither wear uniform, nor do they receive pay – but they are eligible to receive certain allowances. For administrative purposes within the Corps, Scotland is linked with Northern Ireland. There are 117 Squadrons within this Region. In Scotland there are a number of vacancies, and the Chaplains' Committee of the Corps would appeal to parish ministers to consider the claims of this service, with the opportunities it offers as an extension of their parish work, not only among the young people but also with their officers and instructors. The five geographical areas of Scotland are served by experienced Wing Chaplains and the Regional Chaplain for Scotland and Northern Ireland is the Reverend T W Tait, who can be contacted through Air Cadets Regional HQ at 25 Learmonth Terrace, Edinburgh, EH4 1 NZ.

TRUSTEES OF THE CHURCH OF SCOTLAND HOUSING AND LOAN FUND FOR RETIRED MINISTERS AND WIDOWS AND WIDOWERS OF MINISTERS

MAY 2002

PROPOSED DELIVERANCE

The General Assembly:

1. Receive and approve the Report and thank the Chairman, the Trustees and Staff.
2. Re-appoint the Rev. H J W Findlay as a Trustee.

REPORT

1. Aim of the Fund

1.1 The Fund exists to support retired ministers and widows and widowers of ministers in need of help with their housing. The Trustees endeavour to provide assistance by way of either a house to rent or a house purchase loan.

1.2 The Trustees own and regularly acquire additional houses for leasing at concessionary rents to those retired ministers and widows and widowers of ministers with insufficient resources available for house purchase. Alternatively, loans at very favourable rates of interest are granted up to seventy per cent of the house purchase price, but with overriding normal maximums of £25,000 for Standard Loans and £66,500 for Shared Appreciation Loans.

2. Houses

2.1 The Trustees own 202 houses. Eleven houses were purchased during 2001 at a cost to the Fund of £935,094, and eight houses were sold in the year for £632,022.

2.2 Currently Rents are chargeable to ministers at forty per cent of Market Rent and for pre-1989 leases seventy per cent of Fair Rent; and to widows and widowers of Ministers at twenty per cent of Market Rent or thirty-five per cent where Fair Rent is still the basis.

3. Loans

3.1 Seven Standard Loans, four Shared Appreciation Loans and three additional advances were made in 2001. These amounted in all to £346,000. Fourteen Loans (including one part-repayment) were repaid totalling £255,000.

3.2 The Fund provided Short Term Bridging support in eight instances to the extent of £268,000.

3.3 Interest only Standard Loans continue to be granted up to a normal maximum limit of £25,000. Current rates of interest are five per cent in the case of a minister, and two and a half per cent in the case of a loan granted or passing to a minister's surviving widow or widower.

3.4 Shared Appreciation Loans, which link loan values over their term to the value of the property concerned over the same period, can be granted up to a normal maximum limit of £66,500. Current rates of interest for these loans are three per cent for ministers, and one and a half per cent on loans granted or passing to a minister's surviving widow or widower.

4. Donations, Bequests etc

4.1 The Trustees are gratified to acknowledge the receipt of £2,900 during the year from donations, grants and income from trusts, and of £57,946 from bequests.

5.   Accumulated Funds

5.1 Net incoming resources for the year to 31st December 2001 amounted to £654,838. Realised and unrealised investment losses reduced the net movement in Funds to £460,038.

5.2 Long Term Loan advances at the year end numbered 158 which, together with four outstanding Short Term Bridging Loans of £142,000, amounted to £3,303,215.

5.3 Investments at Market Value and deposit balances at 31st December 2001 amounted to £ 4,823,185.

5.4 Commitments for further house purchases and loans approved by the year end, but still to be met from Funds, amounted to £1,773,500.

6.   Two Per Cent Levy on Stipend from Congregations

6.1 The Trustees have initiated a detailed review of the present rate of Congregational Contribution to the Fund. Provided this review indicates scope for a drop in the contribution level, without inhibiting the future work of the Fund, the Trustees will ask next year's Assembly to approve an appropriate reduction in the current rate.

7.   Further Information

7.1 Application forms and further information and guidance may be had from The Secretary, Mr Ronald C Mather, at the Church Offices.

In the name of the Trustees

WILLIAM McVICAR, *Chairman*
RONALD C MATHER, *Secretary*

BOARD OF NATIONAL MISSION
MAY 2002

BOARD OF NATIONAL MISSION

MAY 2002

PROPOSED DELIVERANCE

The General Assembly:

1. Receive the Report and thank the Conveners and members of the Board and Constituent Committees and Sub-Committees.
2. Thank all staff, especially those who retired in 2001, and commend the work of the staff to the prayerful support of the whole Church.
3. Welcome the response of the Board to the "Church without Walls" Report and instruct the Board to develop its strategy in responding to change. (Sec 1)
4. Endorse the immediate steps taken by the Board to control mounting deficits and instruct the Board to establish a task force for change involving the Board of Ministry and other Boards and Committees to develop a coherent strategy for Ministry and Mission, with subsequent implications for funding, and report by the 2004 General Assembly. (Sec 1.8)
5. Amend the Constitution of the Board of National Mission as detailed in Appendix I. (Sec 2.3)
6. Warmly encourage the proposed appointment by the Board of a Rural Adviser. (Sec 2.6)
7. Welcome the support given by the Board to the Scottish Church Census 2002. (Sec 2.9)

"Sharing the Pain – Holding the Hope" (Sec 2.2)

8. Affirm, in the light of the "Sharing the Pain – Holding the Hope" Report, that the whole Church must recognise that to be committed to the poorest and most vulnerable is the Gospel imperative facing us all.
9. Urge all Kirk Sessions and Presbyteries to consider, in particular, Section 5 of the "Sharing the Pain – Holding the Hope" Report, and to submit views to the General Secretary of the Board of National Mission by 31st December 2002.
10. Instruct the Boards of Ministry, Stewardship and Finance, Social Responsibility, Parish Education, National Mission and Practice and Procedure, the Committees on Church and Nation, Ecumenical Relations, and Artistic Matters, the General Trustees and Assembly Council, in partnership with representatives of the UPA Committee of the Board of National Mission, to consider the implications of the Report "Sharing the Pain – Holding the Hope" for their sphere of work.
11. Instruct the appropriate Boards and Committees to report to the General Assembly of 2003 on any changes made to their policy and practice as a result of these considerations.

Committee on Parish Reappraisal

12. Adopt the Overture anent Appraisal and Adjustment as set out in Appendix II and transmit the same to Presbyteries under the Barrier Act, directing that replies be sent in to the Principal Clerk by 31st December 2002. (Sec 2.4 and Appendix II)
13. Adopt the Overture anent Vacancy Procedure as set out in Appendix III and transmit the same to Presbyteries under the Barrier Act, directing that replies be sent in to the Principal Clerk by 31st December 2002. (Sec 2.4 and Appendix III)

14. Welcome the initiative of the Committee on Parish Reappraisal to work with Presbyteries to develop existing Plans to permit the early introduction of the "fast-tracking" scheme if approved by the General Assembly of 2003. (Sec 2.5)

Committee on New Charge Development

15. Welcome the completion of two new buildings in Kilwinning and Perth. (Sec 3.2.3)
16. Note the Committee's support of mission in New Charge Developments. (Sec 3.2.4)
17. Thank those who serve on New Charge Commissions and commend to the prayers of the Church all those engaged in this vital area of mission. (Sec 3.2.6)

Committee on Chaplaincies

18. Welcome the positive approach of the Scottish Executive Health Department to the provision of spiritual and religious care in the National Health Service. (Sec 3.4.2.4)
19. Instruct Presbyteries to review part-time Healthcare Chaplaincy appointments every three years and to terminate the appointments when chaplains reach the age of 70; and to review appointments within the next twelve months where chaplains in post already exceed the age of 70. (Sec 2.7)
20. Invite Ministers and Deacons to give consideration to entering the challenging and rewarding ministry of partnership or full-time chaplaincy in prisons. (Sec 2.8)

Scottish Churches Industrial Mission (Appendix VII)

21. Recognise the important contribution the Churches make to the life of Scotland's workplaces through the faithful and regular visitation by chaplains of all denominations.
22. Give thanks to God for the insight, vision and commitment of the Board of National Mission to the work of Industrial Mission.
23. Pray God's blessing on the continuing work of Scottish Churches Industrial Mission and commend to the prayers of the Church the work of chaplains and the worth of the prophetic word, challenged and tested in this incarnational ministry.
24. Give thanks for the increasing support of commerce and industry through their contributions to the Industrial Mission Trust.

Scottish Churches Community Trust (Appendix IX)

25. Commend the Scottish Churches Community Trust for its support of congregations seeking to use their resources to bring about change in areas of deprivation.
26. Draw the attention of congregations to the availability of funds from the Scottish Churches Community Trust for interchurch projects aimed at the relief of poverty.
27. Appoint Rev Ian Moir as the Church of Scotland representative on the Board of the Scottish Churches Community Trust for a further year.

Society, Religion and Technology Project (Appendix X)

28. Call upon the European Union to accept the proposals on GM foods, labelling and traceability in the current draft EC Directives, to ensure that the costs of such measures are not borne by conventional foods, and resist pressures to allow the import of GMO products unless they are duly labelled and segregated from the relevant non-GMO produce.

29. Call upon HM Government to investigate further the causes of animal welfare problems associated with nuclear transfer cloning.

30. Call upon HM Government that animal-human hybrid nuclear transfer is explicitly forbidden in law.

31. Encourage congregations to consider holding services and debates on themes to be discussed at the World Summit on Sustainable Development which will be held in Johannesburg, South Africa, in August/September 2002.

32. Urge congregations which have received introductory material for the Eco-Congregation Programme to register and formally adopt the programme and encourage other congregations to join the scheme.

33. Urge that an environmental and energy audit be performed on the activities of 121 George Street and other office premises of the Church of Scotland, with a view to identifying areas in which their environmental impact could be reduced.

34. Affirm the importance of moving to more sustainable forms of agriculture, including both integrated and organic farming systems, and urge HMG to provide more incentives and assistance for farmers to do so.

35. Urge HMG to submit the health and nutritional claims of organic agriculture to independent scientific research and evaluation.

36. Encourage members to adopt more sustainable food purchasing practices, as far as they are able, emphasising food which is grown locally, which is seasonal, and using more environmentally sustainable methods.

REPORT

1. Responding to Change

Following the Report to the 2001 General Assembly of the Special Commission anent Review and Reform the Board of National Mission offers the following response not only in the work undertaken in 2001, but also in offering a vision for the future mission of the Kirk.

1.1 Responding to Change...the Board of National Mission has been listening

From ministers and congregations in the Outer Isles to the Borders, from the urban to the rural, in city and in village the Board is aware of a growing clamour for change within the structures and strategies of the Church.

1.1.2 *The Changing Nature of Scotland*: Within a society besieged by change, the Church in Scotland finds itself on uncertain ground. Respected for its social work,

ministers are still expected to perform rites of passage. However, as an institutional force once central within Scottish society, the Church has been eased to the margins, no longer receiving the automatic right to be heard that once it had. Indeed, many people are now so far removed from the Church that several generations have passed without any family member every having seen the inside of a church building far less having taken part in Christian worship. This presents the Church with huge challenges and great opportunities for the fulfilment of its Calling.

Faced with such a dire situation, and encouraged by the desire for change fostered since the last Assembly by the Report anent Review and Reform, the Board of National Mission has determined to offer the Church of Scotland a new strategy for mission and evangelism that is relevant to the needs of congregations struggling against a lack of confidence and declining membership. While it has always been the task of the Board to support local ministry and outreach, it is believed that the situation confronting the Church is now so critical that strategies which are innovative, imaginative and courageous need to be developed and shared.

Listening to the real needs of ministers and congregations, chaplains and deacons within parishes and at the workplace is essential. Only then will we be able to respond in ways that are practical in their encouragement, and effective in their work, if the Board is ever to help each church be a community of Christ's People that lives and speaks, acts and presents the Christian Message. A community that stands at one with the oppressed and the poor; whose heartbeat is prayer and whose actions are at one with its worship. A community of hope and of faith: of mission and of outreach.

1.1.3 *The Changing Nature of Church Membership*: In 1930 the newly united Church claimed as members 26% of the total population of Scotland. This rose over the years reaching a peak of 27% in 1942's and gradually fell from this point over the next twenty years to 24%. From 1966 the slow decline speeded up and over the next twenty years until 1966 the percentage of the population retaining membership had dropped to 13%. Over this period the decline has been within the range of 15,000 to19,000 members per year and it is projected that if this continues the Church of Scotland, as we know it today, will have ceased to exist by the year 2050. Many reasons can be given for these trends – the declining population of Scotland and a reduction in the birth rate with a consequent reduction in baptisms and requests for Church membership – but the principle reason most often recorded in surveys is the lack of relevance of the Church in peoples' lives.

1.1.4 *The Changing Nature of Ministerial Retirements*: It is the Board's understanding that over the five-year period from 2000-2004 it is estimated that 211 ministers will retire from full-time ministry. This trend continues with a further 220 ministers due to retire from 2005-2009; another 201 from 2010-2014, and from 2015-2019 a further 184, making a total of 816 over the period of the

next twenty years.

Recorded figures indicate that in the five years from 2000-2004 the number of candidates training for the ministry totals 96 and this assumes that all 96 will actually enter the Church of Scotland Ministry rather than religious education teaching, chaplaincy or other careers. The resultant gap is deeply disturbing and gives the indication that many churches will not be able to secure a minister of their own.

These are not good reasons for changing the mission of the Church but they are good reasons to prepare the Church for what are inevitable consequences. A more positive way of looking at why we need to change is in order to live up to the claims of our reformed theology of affirming 'the priesthood of all believers' which sees an equal place for the ministry of all God's people.

Over the last forty years commissions such as the Anderson Commission, The Committee of Forty, and most recently, the Commission anent Review and Reform, all encouraged the Church to look to the ministry of all God's people and the formation of Community Parishes as better ways of being the Church than the 'minister-centred' structure we have at present. These changes are being recommended because it is a better way, rather than a second-best method of dealing with the decline in the number of ministers. Sadly the Church often decides to do the right thing for the wrong reason!

1.1.5 *The Changing Nature of Vacancies*: At the time of writing there are 187 vacancies within the Church of Scotland giving a huge headache for Presbyteries, both large and small, as well as individual congregations. It is, however, an opportunity for dynamic change within the Church. If there were no vacancies, ministers, office-bearers, congregations, and indeed the Church as a whole, would have little appetite for change. But there is an appetite for change – and we must satisfy it with creative and imaginative plans for the future.

1.2 Responding to Change…we have heard a Church looking for leadership
The Church in Scotland has been speaking in all sorts of ways. In last year's General Assembly, the 'Church Without Walls' Report, and also to the Board's representatives as they have met with congregations

throughout the country, in engagement with Presbyteries, and in chaplaincy work, and in the many ways the Board has sought to respond to the 'Church Without Walls' Report.

Declining membership, fewer ministers – and commensurate with this general shrinkage – increased vacancies, give the Church its biggest opportunity for change in a generation. In hearing of all these things the Board of National Mission wants to offer new ways of being the Church.

Vacancies are the time of greatest vulnerability for any congregation and they fall into various categories. Stronger congregations sensing increasing demands – both financial and on their Minister to serve as an Interim Moderator - want the Church to speed up the process; more fragile congregations want help to find a Minister, and an increasing number of congregations are courageously trying to maintain their membership struggling with vision with few ideas of how to grow. If we imagine these categories like a paint manufacturer's shade card – graded from light to deepening colour – the variation from one congregational vacancy to another goes from the straightforward to the complex and therefore requires different approaches. As at present, each vacancy needs to be examined individually and the suggested solutions negotiated and agreed with each congregation. We suggest a new way of meeting the ever-growing number of complex vacancies. (Section 1.4)

1.3 Responding to change...we have heard a Church on the brink

Over the past year the Board has been listening to the voices of the churches in some of our poorest urban communities. Their stories – full of pain and hope – present us with a series of challenges that we cannot afford to ignore.

One minister shared how he had shared a great deal of time with local drug addicts and had seen a number of them come to faith in Jesus. However, none had come to the local church as a result. Going by the numbers at worship on a Sunday it looked like a failure – yet he believed that these years had been the most significant of his entire ministry in terms of kingdom-building.

One congregation shared how a new building 15 years ago had given people the opportunity to stop worrying about their building and begin to concern themselves instead with the needs of their parish and the calling of the Church to announce good news to the poor. But another shared, with a righteous sense of anger, how they had been promised a new building for some twenty years – and were still waiting.

One congregation shared how they had been able to work with others to welcome asylum seekers and refugees into their community – and spoke of the immense privilege of working alongside some of the poorest people in our country.

There was anger expressed at a national gathering of UPA congregations that the wider Church often seems to offer platitudes, or sympathy, but the majority of the Church's resources continue to be spent in more prosperous communities.

There was a clear sense that some fundamental things need to change – not just in poor communities but even more critically in rich communities – if the Church in our poorest communities is to survive the next few years. This is the challenge – to affirm that the whole Church must recognise that to be committed to the poorest and most vulnerable is the Gospel imperative facing us all. Prophetically, the churches in the housing schemes and inner cities are calling the whole church *"to share our pain, but also to hold our hope."*

1.4 Responding to change...we have heard a Church looking for change

1.4.1 *Existing Charge Development* (ECD). There are many congregations where the whole vision of the congregation, office-bearers and Minister has been "lost". The possibility is being explored of developing Existing Charge Development (ECD) as a parallel model lying alongside New Charge Development (NCD), its purpose being to help congregations rediscover their vision using existing – if modified – buildings. In many congregations ECD would bring new life and vision and be a tool for mission. Ideally, a ECD would be used in conjunction with Interim Ministry. The Board already has a commitment to such work through the Team of Advisers in Mission and Evangelism but sees great scope for development.

1.4.2 *Developing Interim Ministry*: Building on the strategic work already undertaken by the Board of Ministry, the Board looks forward to co-operating with the Board of Ministry in the development of Interim Ministry. The reasoning, which lies behind this suggestion, is that there are a growing number of vacancies where the matter of calling a Minister is anything but straightforward. Where it is straightforward the Committee on Parish Reappraisal has little difficulty in appraising the situation and allowing vacancy matters to proceed accordingly. Less than straight-forward situations are in every Presbytery - in peripheral housing schemes, inner city UPAs, rural charges, city churches. Many of these congregations are still self-supporting – but office-bearers and Ministers need to reflect on their vision of what it means to be a Church in their particular parish. It is not the responsibility of the Board of National Mission, or the Presbytery, to tell congregations what they need to do in order to be the Church for their area. This is the task of the Minister and office-bearers. What many of these situations require could be provided in an expanded Interim Ministry.

The Board envisages an Interim Ministry that is specifically developed and structured in such a way as to be free-standing in its own right. Designed to enable experienced ministers demit their charge and offer themselves for a specific situation that they would explore and investigate before committing themselves. This system is used to great effect in the Uniting Church of Australia where there is provision for Presbyteries to have 'conversations' with ministers in post with a view to taking up Interim Ministry in situations that require their maturity and experience.

1.4.3 *Existing Buildings*: Given the age of many of our buildings, maintenance is a worrying problem and will continue to be so for the foreseeable future. A more imaginative approach to existing buildings is required. This would be part of the responsibility of the Existing Charge Development (ECD) since congregations with loss of vision would have buildings as part of their problem. Many of these buildings will be in poor state of repair, and this contributes to clouding the vision and adding to the burdens of the Minister, office-bearers and

congregation as to what their purpose was in that particular parish. Part of ECD's remit would be to facilitate thinking about how a building might be better used for the congregation and as a means of reaching out and engaging as a tool for mission with the immediate community. For some the solution would be moving out of the building and back into the Hall Church. For others it could involve the complete refurbishment of the building to be something other than a sanctuary. Existing expertise could be made available and the Board would work very closely with the General Trustees and others to guide congregations through the potentially complex legal implications. Funding help and advice would be required to put finance together for refurbishment programmes and this would complement the valuable support already given to congregations by the staff of the Board of Stewardship and Finance.

1.4.4 *Church and Community Involvement*: Many of these congregations serve communities that have over the years lost many facilities such as community halls and places to meet. The church often finds itself as one of the few remaining agencies with buildings in the centre of the community. It is possible that local authority and other funding may well be available for such proposals. All of this has the added benefit of showing the church in a new light, creating goodwill in the community and also drawing the congregation into much closer contact with the community of the unchurched.

1.5   Responding to Change…we have heard a Church asking for help

1.5.1 *Presbytery Facilitators*: The Presbyteries of Glasgow, Hamilton and Angus have already applied successfully to the Board for the appointment of Presbytery Facilitators and at the time of writing appointments are being made as Pilot Projects. Each is undertaking a different role responding to local needs. In one Presbytery, for example, a Facilitator will work closely with clusters of congregations who have 'signed-up' for Team Ministry in a wider geographical area comprising a number of parishes. The Facilitator will in effect be 'a walking tool box for mission'. The person appointed will be expected to be familiar with all the mission resources available within the Church and have the ability to 'hand-hold' congregations into working with each other, with other denominations ecumenically, and to engage with the non-Church community within the 'Community Parish'.

1.5.2 _Specialist Workers_: The Church is moving towards the development of Team Ministry in which many specialist workers will have a part to play. Youth, Development, Adult Workers, Community, Music and Drama Workers, etc. are going to be much more part of Team Ministry. There is already a need for a multi-disciplinary approach to ministry, and the need will be made greater by fewer Ministers of Word and Sacrament available for parish service. More attention will require to be paid to those who are in vocational Christian Service forming the team. Increasingly the Church will require to move from generic to specialist training.

1.5.3 _Gap Students_: We need to mirror and look more carefully at the potential of 'gap' or 'year-out' students as part of our personnel offering to Teams and congregations. A number of organisations such as Scripture Union and Careforce have successfully over the years drawn together a pool of young people who after interview are available to meet the needs of local congregations at the start of the church year in September. We need to give serious thought to the hundreds of young people who increasingly want to offer themselves to a year of full-time Christian service, either before they go to University, or (the much more favoured option from our point of view) having completed their degree, taking a year out before beginning secular employment. One of the additional unquantifiable benefits would be how many of these young people would have their appetite whetted for full-time service in the Church of Scotland. It is not unreasonable to believe that, having been placed within local congregations and teams within the Church of Scotland, and enjoyed the stretching, rewarding and meaningful life for a year might turn them into potential candidates for the Ministry.

1.5.4 _Fundraiser/Negotiator_: There is a need to have a full-time Fundraiser and skilled Negotiator to help congregations and Teams to fundraise for all kinds of projects and fabric work . As has already been stressed such an appointment would complement the existing work of the Board of Stewardship and Finance.

1.5.5 _Parish Development Fund_: The Board welcomes the proposed establishment of the Parish Development Fund and warmly offers it an administrative home within the Department. The provision of this financial resource will assist many congregations to rise to the challenge of serving changing communities.

1.6 Responding to Change...we have heard a Church seeking to work together

1.6.1 _Five Boards Group_: The Board is already committed to collaborative working and a clear indication is the role it has played over recent years in the formation and work of the Five Boards Group. The Group – bringing together the Conveners and General Secretaries of the Boards of Ministry, National Mission, Parish Education, Social Responsibility and World Mission – is undertaking imaginative work in team ministry development.

1.6.2 _Developing Team Ministry_: The term 'Team Ministry' is used frequently today. It is for example spoken of as a solution to 'difficult-to-fill' vacancies where finding Ministers of Word and Sacrament has become problematic. The Board's hope is that the concept will be expanded to embrace multi-disciplinary, inter-Board teams serving the parishes of Scotland.

It is notoriously difficult to take existing ministers within a geographical area and try to make them operate as teams. We can encourage them, we can appoint consultants to help them, but in most situations there is usually too much theological and personality baggage to be able to form a true team situation. It makes greater sense to appoint team leaders – where circumstances permit – and allow them, in conjunction with others, to build up a 'team' which will sign up for the vision of the congregation for that particular area.

1.6.3 _Exploring Community Parishes_: The structure of parish ministry as we know it today does not lend itself easily to this model of team ministry unless we allow 'cross-parish' activity. If we agree to cross-parish activity then we are agreeing to Community Parishes. In order to justify the financial cost of supporting this theological model of team ministry we need to see a number of parishes group themselves into geographical 'clusters'. Such thinking is reflected in the work of the Inter-Board Group on Presbytery Boundaries with the introduction of 'districts'; and 'parish groupings' will become a legal possibility if the proposed new Act Anent Appraisal and Adjustment is accepted.

The Board's thinking is as follows:-

A group of parishes could be brought together within the same geographical area thus forming a larger 'community parish' under the appointed 'team leader' who may or may not be a Minister. The vision for, and needs of, the whole community parish could be explored and brought together in a mission Plan. Apostleship in a modern setting could see the team leader as someone who would be spiritually mature, theologically balanced, with a good reputation in dealing with people, creative, and with vision.

Under such team leadership individuals could be appointed with various skills and ministries commensurate with the needs of the parish in the areas: work with children, young people, families; among adults, Bible Study Groups, Cell Groups, Christian Education, Elder's Training, Visitor's Training, Mission Resources.

Team Ministry and Community Parishes could give greater opportunity for the gifts of God's people to be used, thus breaking away from the traditional role model of everything that is considered to be important being done by 'the Minister'.

1.7 Responding to Change…we have heard a Church wanting change to continue

In offering this Report, the Board is not seeking to propose all the answers nor spell out the definitive way ahead. What it is offering is an immediate response to the 'Church Without Walls' Report and a direction for the future.

The Board records appreciation to the Co-ordinating Forum and the Assembly Council for the way they are participating in the listening process and, according to the Board's present understanding, are seeking to take forward the general direction offered in this Report.

In taking these issues forward the Board seeks to continue to work collaboratively with others and for this reason is proposing the establishment of a Task Force to take forward the ministry and mission of the Church in the early decades of the 21st Century, (Section 1.8.6)

The challenges before the Church are immense – not least in the area of finance as highlighted in the next Section of this Report. But the Board believes that the Church in our generation has to effect a radical and fundamental change in resourcing recognising that the Church is not merely an institution in the land but rather the living Body of Christ. The ultimate challenge before us today is to be open to God's call to change in ways that facilitate, rather than hinder, the emerging Church of tomorrow.

1.8 Responding to Change … we have heard a Church calling for new financial priorities.

1.8.1 Over recent years there has been an alarming reduction in the capital of the Board – from £31,273,694 on 31st December 1999 to £24,937,600 on 31st December 2001. Recognising the seriousness of this decline led the Board at its meeting on 6th September 2001 to appoint a Finance and Future Strategy Group which reported at the meeting of the Board on 5th December 2001. At that same meeting the Board unanimously approved the recommendations of the group and these are reported now.

1.8.2 By way of background the Board offers the following facts:

(a) The spend of the Board in 2001 was £5,663,745 and this income was derived from the following five sources
- Contribution from Mission
  and Aid Funds   £1,714,513   (30%)
- Income from Board's
  capital   £1,091,602   (19%)
- Use of capital to fund deficit   £951,741   (17%)
- Contribution from bodies
  outwith the Church   £1,649,473   (29%)
- Other   £256,416   (5%)

These figures do not include expenditure on the work of the Committee on New Charge Development which has its own budget.

(b) There are essentially three main cost centres in the Board:

Parish Staffing   36% of 2001 spend
Chaplaincies   34% of 2001 spend
Mission and Evangelism
  Resourcing   8% of 2001 spend

Over the last decade the Board has sought to maintain the existing level of staff working in parishes while financial prudence has been exercised in the other two areas. 86% of chaplaincies expenditure is funded by bodies outwith the Church

Expenditure on parish staffing supports strategic appointments largely in urban priority area and highlands and islands parishes – though it has to be said that demand for these appointments of deacons, parish assistants and project workers always exceeds supply. Such appointments have been increasingly required to support united congregations serving parishes with a large population; and where the readjustment has led to a reduction in the Aid required but a call on National Mission resources to fund an additional appointment such as a Deacon or Project Worker. There is no other source of funding within the Church for such appointments since the funds of the Board of Ministry are restricted or earmarked only for the payment of stipends for Parish Ministers and Interim Ministers.

The stark reality of the Board's position is that even eliminating the other two cost centres of mission and evangelism resourcing and chaplaincies there would still be a deficit in the Board's budgeting due to the amount now being spent on parish staffing. The Board believes that the General Assembly would never accept withdrawal from either of these vital areas of work.

(c) As reported to successive General Assemblies over

recent years the demand for expenditure particularly in the area of parish staffing has outstripped the Board's ability to pay. Increases in the minimum stipend and in the salaries of deacons and other staff have been consistently greater than the inflation related increases awarded to the Board through the Mission and Aid Fund. Each year planned deficit budgeting has resulted in further sums being taken from capital. In the following year this means the income available from the capital is less and consequently a larger sum has to be withdrawn from the capital. In everyday terms the Board has been living "beyond its means" and, added to a weaker stock market, is part of the reason that the capital of the Board has reduced so dramatically over the period. Over the period 2000 to 2001 the reduction in capital through a weaker stock market has been £4,834,701 and through the use of capital to fund work £1,501,393.

In 2001 the Board entered into discussions with the Church of Scotland Investors Trust to discuss the dilemma and the reality reported to the Board by the Investors Trust is that if the Board continues to fund its present level of work the Board's capital may last not more than ten years. If the capital is exhausted in that period either the central funds of the Church would require to find several millions of pounds annually to ensure the costs of Associate and Community Ministers, Deacons and others – or there would require to be considerable redundancies, the funding of which would mean that there were even less than ten years left.

The Board believes that this is not a direction which should be taken and that until there is a long-term assurance of funding that no further parish staff, other than for Ministers, and Deacons currently in training, should be recruited. Apart from the financial concerns, the Board has recognised a moral irresponsibility in entering into contracts of employment knowing full well that the income to pay these members of staff is guaranteed only for a relatively short time.

1.8.3 Strategy:

In order to determine future strategy the Board considered again its remit. This is defined in the Constitution of the Board as: "the responsibility for planning and co-ordinating the Church's strategy and provision for the fulfilment of its mission as the National Church". This is often abbreviated to "planning and resourcing the Mission of the Church in Scotland".

The present definition of the Board's strategy as approved by General Assemblies is "the development of strong congregations, adequately staffed and resourced, with a missionary concern for the parishes they are called to served – and all this work at congregational level backed by an interface with strategic areas in Scottish life". The Board believes that this should be strengthened with the addition of a sentence "the Board encourages the staffing of parishes through team ministry where appropriate and resourcing through the development of partnership opportunities".

1.8.4 Key tasks for the Board of National Mission:

The Board has identified the following key tasks for the Board:

- Agreeing with Presbyteries the deployment of Ministers, Deacons, and other parish staff throughout Scotland and in the Presbytery of England.
- The facilitation of congregations in making the transition from 'maintenance' to 'mission'.
- The development of 'Statistics for Mission' work in informing congregations about the nature of their parishes.
- Within available budget the appointment of staff – not Ministers or Deacons – to support New Charge Developments, specific mission projects (such as the Shopping Mall strategy), and in situations where a team ministry requires a specialist worker.
- The recruitment and deployment of a limited number of Summer Student Appointments with the specific need for such an appointment in Foula.
- The support and development of Ministry among Deaf People in Scotland.
- The appointment of a worker who can assist both the Board and local congregations and projects in 'partnership working' and who has skills in negotiation and fundraising.
- The development of a scheme – possibly built on the present work of the Missions Co-ordinator – of recruiting and supporting 'gap year' students to be placed with congregations and projects.
- The support and development of 'The Well', the John Knox House and Netherbow Centre, and the Society, Religion and Technology Project.
- The creation and support of the Scottish Mission Studies Project which through research and analysis should inform the Board in developing the mission of the Church in Scotland.
- The support of specialist Committees as appropriate such as the present ones on Apologetics, Projects in Evangelism, Urban Issues and Rural Issues with appropriate staffing, though the relationship of at least some of these to the Scottish Mission Studies Project will require consideration.
- The facilitation of Chaplaincy in Healthcare, Prison, University and Industry with the bulk of the financial resource coming from outwith the Church. Funding would be required for administration and for support and 'seed money'; though in the area of Industrial Mission more money should be sought from commerce and industry.
- The co-ordination of the production of quality materials to publicise the work of the Board.
- The production of quality resources to support missionary congregations in the fulfilment of their work.

1.8.5 Immediate steps:

Recognising the financial challenge lying ahead, the Board agreed the following immediate steps:

- That expenditure be controlled in as many ways as possible and specifically by exploring the future of the Badenoch Christian Centre, by containing expenditure on Summer Student Appointments, and by making all fresh National Mission Appointments other than of Ministers, and Deacons currently in training, over an interim period from existing staff.
- That the Board resolves that in future no housing owned by the Board is offered with posts for which the Board is the "employing agent".

- That the Scottish Mission Studies Project be established as a core element of the Board's work, and that the Board continues to view positively the proposed developments at the Netherbow, on the clear understanding that both will be funded primarily from the sale of properties.
- That the Board begins now to identify areas of overlap in the work of Constituent Committees with a view to revising the Constitution of the Board.

The Board believes it only prudent to take these steps at this time. The Board invites the General Assembly to endorse its stand.

1.8.6 Future Steps:

The implementation of these immediate steps is a short-term measure and not a long-term solution to the critical situation placed before the General Assembly.

A long-term solution will only be forged in collaboration with other Boards and Committees and will require decisive steps to be taken throughout the whole Church.

The Board recognises the good relationship that exists between the Board of Ministry and itself and would like to build upon that relationship by seeking an instruction from the General Assembly for the establishment of a Taskforce for Change drawn from the two Boards and other Boards and Committees to develop a coherent strategy for ministry and mission in the early decades of the 21st century. Such a Taskforce for Change would consider matters such as deployment, including team ministry, and funding for parish staffing and would offer a progress report to the General Assembly of 2003 in the hope that a final Report could be presented to the General Assembly of 2004.

2. Background to Deliverance

2.1 Introduction

This second section gives detailed background to the Deliverance of the Board.

2.2 "Sharing the Pain – Holding the Hope"

2.2.1 Introduction

2.2.1.1 "The whole Church must recognise that to be committed to the poorest and most vulnerable is the gospel imperative facing us all, not just the churches in urban priority areas (UPAs)." This was the central statement of the 2001 National UPA Consultation and is the primary challenge of this report.

2.2.1.2 'He grew up before him like a young plant, like a root out of dry ground'. (Isaiah 53:2) With these words the prophet Isaiah introduces a man whose sufferings are a horror and an embarrassment to the beholder, yet whose struggle had great significance in the eyes of God. This report challenges the whole Church to consider that the same might be said of the church in UPAs. As she seeks to worship and serve God in the poorest housing schemes and inner city parishes in Scotland, these deeply vulnerable communities of faith are of great importance to God.

2.2.1.3 The UPA congregations of Scotland's towns and cities draw deeply from the Church of Scotland's resources. Many of the 330 UPA congregations require assistance towards the stipend of their minister; central funds provide an additional parish worker; and in recent years a great many have applied for assistance, receiving grants towards the repair and refurbishment of their buildings.

2.2.1.4 In many parishes that have exhibited these features, there has also been a decline in church membership, a rise in the average age of the congregation, and serious erosion of the energies of those in positions of responsibility.

2.2.1.5 A group of people striving to be the Church in one of Scotland's poorest communities described their task as "Sharing the Pain and Holding the Hope." It is in this spirit that this report is written. The Church in the UPA calls upon the wider Church to share our pain and to hold our hope.

2.2.1.6 Without action and a critical realignment of resources over the next five years many of the churches in Scotland's poorest communities will die. If these congregations are allowed to perish through

a lack of resources, the whole Church of Scotland will be critically, and perhaps irredeemably damaged. If we cannot announce "good news to the poor," who can we announce good news to?

2.2.2 Urban Priority Areas

2.2.2.1 Urban Priority Areas (UPAs) is the Church of Scotland's term for describing poor urban communities, following the pattern laid down by the Church of England in its 1985 Faith in the City Report. It describes parishes where at least 10% of the parish population (under the 1991 Census) is in the poorest 20% of Scotland's population. There are currently 330 UPA parishes, 118 of which have over 50% of their parish designated as UPA. These communities are characterised by high levels of unemployment, poor housing and few public facilities, along with the related problems of poor health, and high levels of addiction and crime. They were largely by-passed by the growing prosperity experienced by many in Scotland during the 80s and 90s. During those years the gap between the richest and poorest in Scotland grew for the first time in over 500 years! In real terms many people in UPAs have become poorer over the last 20 years, and according to the 1999 Scottish Affairs Committee 25% of Scotland's population are living in poverty, and some of its communities are the most deprived in Europe.

2.2.2.2 Although there are pockets and areas of deprivation throughout Scotland, the greatest levels of poverty are in the former industrial communities of west central Scotland, from Inverclyde to Lanarkshire. Three-quarters of the poorest 1% of people in Scotland live in Glasgow. Considerable past public investment has often failed to improve things. In part, this is because investment has been short-term and insufficient (given the scale of deprivation) and partly because a great deal of the investment has leaked out of poor communities in the salaries of professionals, contractors and consultants who have worked in UPAs but lived somewhere else.

2.2.2.3 UPAs are changing, and in some cases, changing very rapidly. Although there has been considerable investment in many Social Inclusion Partnership Areas (SIPs), poverty remains deep-rooted. Despite limited

improvements in recent years, over 30% of Scotland's children are still growing up in poverty. In the midst of the majority's prosperity, the poor minority are becoming almost invisible and ever more marginalized.

2.2.2.4 Churches are changing in UPAs also. The days of full churches on a Sunday morning have become, largely, a distant memory. Often as a result of spiralling repair bills or structural faults, some congregations have found it necessary to demolish church accommodation and to relocate all of their activities back in the original hall church. Many UPA congregations now have less than 100 members, with often less than half that number attending worship regularly.

2.2.2.5 The picture, of course, is not universally bleak. In the midst of real adversity and human suffering, many UPA congregations are reaching their communities in powerful and innovative ways. The church remains an important part of community life in many poor communities. Worship is often fresh and relevant. Christians in UPAs are often successfully being the Church as opposed to simply going to the Church. Faith is very much alive, both among those who are committed to their local church in a plethora of different ways and also among many who sense that God walks with them, even if the institutional church has become largely irrelevant.

2.2.3 Why a Report on UPAs?

2.2.3.1 In recent years the wider church has often looked to the church in the UPA, admiring her perseverance in the face of adversity, her commitment to the local community and her ability to be innovative and creative in worship and mission. Some have even suggested that the models of church that have been emerging in the UPAs will, in some way, pre-figure the future patterns of the Church of Scotland more generally. Certainly, as a number of recent reports to the General Assembly have highlighted, some of the most innovative work going on in the Church today is happening in UPA parishes.

2.2.3.2 The overall picture, however, is far from

optimistic. The Board of National Mission reported to the General Assembly in 1999 that –

Perhaps 60 of the 330 UPA parishes live on the brink of a financial abyss. Without central funding for ministry costs and building repairs they will lose their buildings and the Church of Scotland may withdraw from the area completely.

Even among many of those congregations that have summoned up the necessary energy to embrace change, these changes have not necessarily brought an increase in membership or financial security. Christians in UPAs are learning that faithfulness to Jesus may well not lead to a numerical growth in the institutional church.

2.2.3.3 It was in the context of the crisis facing churches in UPAs that the 1999 General Assembly instructed –
… the Board of National Mission, working with other relevant Boards and Committees of the Church, in partnership with local congregations, to investigate the building and wider needs of congregations in UPAs, to consider possible solutions to the problems found, and to report to a future General Assembly.

2.2.3.4 From the outset, the Board of National Mission recognised the importance of this task and committed itself to listening. It was aware that local congregations are likely to be the real experts in this process, not only in identifying the key problems but also in presenting workable solutions. It recognised that its own practice, and that of other Boards and Committees, would be challenged by what it heard. This has indeed been the case and there are aspects of this report that make uncomfortable reading for the Board of National Mission. The Board also acknowledges that listening is not enough. **People in poor communities are tired of apparently constant consultations, which seem to change nothing. The effectiveness of this process will be determined by whether things improve for churches in Scotland's poorest communities.**

2.2.3.5 The Board has sought to listen to the voices from UPAs in three main ways –

A Postal Survey of all 330 UPA congregations, asking them to identify key needs and problems they are facing and, where appropriate, to share how they have met these needs or overcome their problems.

A series of four Regional Hearings (held in Glasgow [x2], Edinburgh and Dundee) where 18 UPA congregations shared their stories with representatives of many of the National Boards and Committees of the Church.

A National UPA Consultation (held at Carberry Tower in November 2001) attended by over 110 people, representing 39 congregations, at which a draft report was presented, amended and added to over the 48-hour meeting.

This Final Report has, as such, been subject to very close scrutiny by a large number of church members from UPA congregations, who have shaped and informed its core messages. Perhaps unusually for such reports, significant numbers of local people have been involved at all stages of its development.

2.2.3.6 In both the Regional Hearings and the National Consultation, attention was focused on churches within Scotland's poorest 118 UPA parishes (i.e. those with over 50% of their parish designated as urban priority area under the 1991 Census data). It is largely in these parishes that the struggles facing congregations and communities are most severe.

2.2.3.7 The problems facing the Church in Scotland's poorest urban communities are not just the concern of the Board of National Mission, but of the whole church. The Boards of Ministry, Stewardship and Finance, Social Responsibility, Parish Education and Practice & Procedure, the Committees on Church and Nation, Ecumenical Relations and Artistic Matters, the General Trustees, the Special Commission anent Review and Reform, and the Presbyteries of Edinburgh, Glasgow, Hamilton and Dundee were all represented at the Regional Hearings. The Board of National Mission not only thanks these Boards and Committees for their involvement in this process, but also acknowledges their existing major commitment to many of the poorest communities in Scotland. It also acknowledges the generous contributions of many congregations, and of individual Christians, to the witness of the Church in poor urban communities. UPA congregations are also very grateful for this current support, without which many would already have ceased to exist.

2.2.4 'Sharing the Pain – Holding the Hope': Regional Hearings and National Consultation

2.2.4.1 The Regional Hearings gave a number of people with little or no knowledge of UPAs the chance to get a flavour of life there. The local churches laid on visits to local people's homes, the schools, community projects, a credit union and the local shopping centre as well as simply walking the streets and the opportunity to meet local residents.

2.2.4.2 The diversity of UPAs struck many of those who were able to attend all four Hearings. Others noticed the bleakness and open spaces caused by demolition, young people hanging about on the streets and the lack of community facilities. While some saw little or no obvious signs of deprivation, others expressed a sense of embarrassment between where they themselves lived and what they saw in their visit. People were impressed by the projects they visited and by the commitment of the staff in the local schools. The voices of local people were challenging: their passionate commitment to the local area and yet a sense of having been constantly let down by outside authorities; their sense of the irrelevance of barriers between different churches and between church and the wider community; and the way that people supported each other.

2.2.4.3 People could not fail to be impressed with the range of innovative ways in which church buildings were being used – credit unions, cafes, food co-operatives, lunch clubs, day care, childcare, daily worship centres – nor by the extraordinary drive and energy of small numbers of people, seeking to live out their lives in faithful commitment to Jesus. The focus upon discipleship as opposed to membership is already a characteristic of a great many Christians in UPA congregations.

2.2.4.4 There was a recognition that UPA congregations have required to be very resourceful; that their size has

enabled people to feel more genuinely part of a Christian fellowship; that they relate more naturally and fully with the wider community; and that they are all round more 'people-centred church communities.' One person attending the Hearing in Edinburgh, where one of the visits was to a café run in a local church, shared her sense that "that café is the church." Certainly many commented on the fact that the Church in the UPA often seems to be a seven-day a week experience rather than being limited to an hour on a Sunday morning, with one other weeknight activity for the most committed.

2.2.4.5 Over 110 people from many of Scotland's most deprived communities attended the National UPA Consultation. It was an exhilarating, challenging and exhausting 48 hours, which had a profound impact on all who attended. In the context of awe-inspiring worship, participants shared one another's stories of pain and hope, frustration and delight, hope and anger.

2.2.4.6 If the people attending the National Consultation are representative of the wider leadership of UPA congregations then the Church is indeed fortunate to have such outstanding members in our poorest urban communities. But the energy, creativity and passion of many people are being constantly weakened by having to grapple with problems of resources, which are the responsibility of the whole Church. People grappled with how best to share this with others. Some felt that the time for words and gentle diplomacy is running out. A march on '121' was suggested. Others felt that it might be necessary to picket the General Assembly, or to hold an open-air fiesta to share the struggles and aspirations of many UPA congregations. It was clear that people were passionate that the Church must hear and hear soon.

2.2.4.7 The primary purpose of the National Consultation was to inform this report. This was done primarily through the work of 18 small groups where everyone present was able to participate fully. The main conclusions of these groups were agreed in a plenary session on the final morning.

2.2.4.8 Amid all the information that has been

gathered, the stories shared, and the sheer diversity of experience within UPAs make it difficult to draw out general conclusions. Nonetheless, over the last two years and particularly through the Hearings and National Consultation, a number of themes have continually re-emerged.

2.2.5 The Wider Church Does Not Seem to Understand

2.2.5.1 Throughout this entire consultation process representatives from congregations have continually expressed their frustration, and, on occasions, anger, that they felt that their needs had often not been heard. There was a sense that there are two churches within the Church of Scotland: a resource rich church, which can afford to make decisions for herself, and a resource poor church, which is dependent upon others and often senses that it is given the scraps left over from the rich person's table. The call to be one Church, and to put an end to the current two-tier system, was a recurring plea from people at the National Consultation.

2.2.5.2 This has been a constant theme of UPA reports to the General Assembly. As far back as 1990, the Urban Priority Areas Working Group Party stated.

The church in UPAs would like to make two basic pleas to the wider church:

That the church as a whole should try to deepen its understanding of what poverty does to people.

That the church should look at, listen to, and learn from the church in UPAs.

2.2.5.3 Last year's Report of the Special Commission anent Review and Reform also highlighted this issue and called for the development of friendships between rich and poor congregations. A number of such relationships already exist, often initially based on the friendship of ministers or a few influential office-bearers. These friendships are to be celebrated and encouraged. However, friendship cannot exist without justice and many in UPA congregations feel that they and their communities have been unjustly treated by both Church and wider society. A spirit of Christian friendship is desirable and possible. However, for this to flourish, steps need to be taken to ensure that the voices of those who are announcing "good news to the poor" are more adequately heard and understood by the wider Church.

2.2.5.4 There was a feeling that UPA congregations were failing to get their message across to the wider Church and that their stories were simply not being heard. This was either because they were failing to communicate their message of pain and hope effectively or because congregations in other, wealthier communities were not listening.

2.2.5.5 **One practical suggestion from the National Consultation was a gathering, which would bring together representatives of the financially poorest and richest 50 congregations in the Church of Scotland. Through this event there would be the opportunity for misconceptions to be broken down, solidarity across the Church to be increased and new friendships formed.**

2.2.6 A Buildings Crisis

2.2.6.1 In 1990 the Urban Priority Areas Working Party Report to the General Assembly identified buildings as a major problem facing UPA congregations. At the time they wrote:

The average UPA congregation is fully committed to worship, mission and service and there are many examples of a level of dedication that is a privilege to witness. But all too often, their energy and enthusiasm, so necessary for making any headway in their situation is totally absorbed in keeping up a set of buildings that is way beyond their means to maintain. The problems they face are:

—Buildings which, although built with the best advice of their generation, have not stood the test of time.
—Heavy wear and tear from heavy usage due to the lack of other premises locally.
—The ravages of persistent vandalism and frequent break-ins.
—Inadequate funds locally for timeous repairs resulting in greater long-term costs.

—Often little professional expertise to detect problems or to deal with them as they arise.

As a result, UPA church buildings all too often reflect the despair and desolation of the surrounding areas instead of being a sign of hope.

It is clear that in the subsequent 12 years these problems have only got worse. Action is now imperative.

2.2.6.2 A number of church buildings in UPAs are, quite literally, falling down. It has to be clearly stated that this has not been the result of neglect on the part of local congregations, many of which have struggled against the odds to keep their buildings wind and watertight. In some cases the buildings were structurally faulty from the outset. In others, the building materials have reached the end of their shelf life. The houses round about the Church have been demolished because they were falling down – the same now needs to happen to the church buildings.

2.2.6.3 It was the impending building crisis facing up to 60 UPA congregations that was the impetus for this consultation exercise, and without doubt, fabric issues have been a dominant theme throughout the entire process. Although many expressed their considerable thanks to the General Trustees, the Committee on New Charge Development, the generosity of individual well-off congregations and local Presbytery Committees, it was clear that this support is now insufficient.

2.2.6.4 Throughout the consultation process there was a constant appeal from UPA congregations that fabric management and costs should not be the burden of the local congregation. In the initial survey of UPA congregations (carried out in autumn 1999) many congregations shared problems caused by a range of problems including: poor structural design, wear and tear over 40 years, inadequate funding to carry out even the most basic repairs, lack of local professional expertise and skills, and vandalism. This picture was subsequently fully reinforced at the Hearings and National Consultation.

2.2.6.5 One congregation shared how its building had

had to be re-roofed twice within 2 years, because of bad workmanship, poor advice and the lack of local expertise. The saga of its roof had lasted 7 years and had placed a heavy strain on the minister and congregation during that time. Another congregation shared that it was currently paying back a low interest loan after re-roofing its church building, although such a requirement prevented it from carrying out other important work. It pointed out that the local congregation did not own the building in any case but by the General Trustees (to whom the loan repayments were being paid). A third congregation shared, with a real sense of righteous anger that they had been waiting for over 20 years for a promised new building and were continuing to worship in a condemned hall.

2.2.6.6 The picture is not universally bleak. At one of the Regional Hearings, representatives from a Glasgow congregation in one of the poorest areas in the city, shared how a new building 15 years ago had given a new lease of life to the congregation, enabling it to refocus its energy on mission. The problem is that this is the experience of only a tiny number of UPA congregations.

2.2.6.7 It is clear that many church buildings in UPAs are now in such a poor state of repair that they require either major expenditure to refurbish them, or in a number of cases, they should be demolished and new facilities built. These new buildings must be shaped by the needs of local communities and of other denominations as well as our own. There is considerable potential to work in partnership with others but this requires greater energy, innovation and resources from the wider church. **If the Church of Scotland wants to have church buildings in the poorest communities in urban Scotland then she must find the ways to maintain and build them. Responsibility for the maintenance and development of church buildings in the poorest 60-100 UPA parishes (identified initially through the 2001 Census data) should be transferred either to the General Trustees or to a newly established body with specific responsibility for UPA parishes.**

2.2.6.8 The problems of insurance have been an

ongoing theme within many UPA reports to the General Assembly. As early as 1990, the Working Party Report called for action. The ongoing problems of vandalism mean that insurance premiums are often disproportionately high in UPAs and materials most likely to be subject to vandalism (e.g. glass) are often excluded from any policy agreement. The excess clause on virtually all policies means that UPA congregations, which are likely to make a number of small insurance claims to cover vandalism, are particularly disadvantaged. A more effective sharing of this burden across the whole Church would do a great deal to ease the plight of the Church's poorest urban congregations. It would be possible to replace windows and repair toilets.

2.2.6.9 It is clear that church buildings in UPAs are amongst the most used in the country. When many church extension buildings were erected in the 1950s and '60s – in what was the most ambitious building project in the history of the Church of Scotland – they were among the first major community buildings in the new peripheral housing schemes. With a pattern of closure of many community facilities in recent years, these buildings are often the last remaining large enough to serve the needs of local communities. Many churches are open 7 days a week, addressing the social, economic and spiritual needs of people in the name of Christ.

2.2.6.10 A number of congregations have succeeded in securing substantial public and voluntary sector funding to enable them to refurbish their facilities to more adequately address the needs of the local congregation and community. It is clear that in the current climate of partnership there are opportunities for others to do the same. Nonetheless, it is clear that without substantial investment of energy and money on the part of the national church, a substantial number of church buildings will become virtually unusable over the next five years. The 1999 report to the General Assembly asked:

> 'Will these 60 UPA parishes, one by one, go to the wall? Is the Church simply going to mirror the gulf between the prospering and the "socially excluded," which is part of the structure of British society? Or is the Church going to illustrate a new pattern of economic relationships?'

To date, the Church has not answered that question. The longer she puts off, the higher the cost will be.

2.2.6.11 If the Church is to address the building needs of UPAs, it will take a programme of vision and commitment on the part of the whole Church akin to the spirit, which ignited the establishment of approximately 200 church extension charges in the 1950s.

2.2.7   Impossible Financial Demands

2.2.7.1 Throughout the entire consultation process it was clear that UPA congregations have succeeded in achieving an enormous amount of work with very limited resources. This achievement should rightly be celebrated as an example to the wider Church of what is possible through faith, prayer, careful budgeting, creativity and hard work.

2.2.7.2 It is clear that many congregations, in all parts of the country, are feeling an ever-increasing financial burden. This is particularly true within many UPAs where people are living in poverty, communities are shrinking and congregations are small. Many members of UPA congregations, nonetheless, give sacrificially of their time, talents and money. One congregation shared how it had for a number of years been the highest per-capita giving congregation in Presbytery. It is a fact that many church members in UPAs give proportionately significantly more to the work of the Church than their counterparts in wealthier congregations. This makes the complaints of rich congregations that they are being asked to pay for poor ones all the more galling.

2.2.7.3 The task of trying to "make ends meet" and of fulfilling their commitment "to Edinburgh" is increasingly impossible for many UPA congregations and a number are building up a sizeable debt in their Ministry and Mission and Aid allocations, as well as loan repayments to the General Trustees. For some, it is difficult to see how they will manage to pay off this debt. The Church has been at the forefront of the Jubilee 2000 campaign, calling upon the richest governments of the world to cancel the debt owed by the poorest countries. **The**

Church ought to do what it calls others to do – is it not time for the Church of Scotland to hold its own "jubilee," a time when the debt, which cannot be repaid by the poorest congregations, is cancelled?

2.2.7.4   Fundraising is a way of life for many UPAs, but this fundraising is not for the extras they would like, but essential simply to remain solvent. Such fundraising, while it may promote closer fellowship, often diverts the energy of congregations away from its primary task of mission. Existing stewardship campaigns seem to have relatively little impact in congregations where many are already giving as much as they possibly can and where family incomes often fall (with unemployment and pensions) rather than increase.

2.2.7.5   One self-supporting congregation shared how their contributions had altered over a ten-year period. While their overall expenditure had increased by 43%, including an increase of 163% in their contributions to the wider work of the Church (primarily their Mission & Aid allocation) the amount that they were able to spend on local mission work had increased by only 3%. Over the same period they had required to spend over £143,000 on their building.

2.2.7.6   The vast majority of UPA congregations are keen to make as full a financial commitment to the wider work of the Church as they can. Many are also aware of their dependency upon others who help to meet local ministry and mission costs. However, there is a deep sense of anger that while poor churches are often reminded that they need the rich congregations in order to survive, there is little recognition that rich churches also need poor ones.

2.2.7.7   While many congregations, from all parts of the country, are finding it increasingly difficult to survive, there are still a significant number of congregations in the Church of Scotland, which have vast reserves as a result of legacies, or the sale of property. The churches in the housing schemes, where the needs are greatest, are unlikely to be recipients of such legacies or to have significant reserves. **A Church that takes the challenges of the Jesus seriously must make the redistribution of her own wealth a priority. This is not simply an economic argument. It is a call upon churches to live by the liberating faith of the Gospel.**

2.2.7.8   Much has been written over the last few years about the level of the reserves of the national Boards and Committees of the Church. There is an obvious need for sound financial management. However, from the perspective of communities living in poverty it is clear to many in UPAs that the Church is rich beyond the imagining of many. She can no longer afford simply to keep her considerable reserves for the future. Unless money is spent in some of our poorest parishes soon, there will be no future.

2.2.7.9   It is clear to many within UPAs that the current budget-setting processes of the Church have in the past failed to recognise priorities and that the money, which is available, has not always been spent as prudently as it could have been. **One suggestion that emerged from the National Consultation is that the Church should consider establishing a Priority Areas Department, with its own dedicated budget and staffing with responsibilities for resourcing all aspects of the work and witness of congregations in Scotland's poorest communities.** Such a department might well have responsibility for supporting poor rural as well as urban communities, and could also focus on specific vulnerable groups, e.g. the homeless. In this way the Church would seek to ensure that whatever her changing priorities, the needs of the most vulnerable would remain central.

2.2.8   Inappropriate Structures
2.2.8.1   The Church, like any institution, needs structures in order to operate effectively. However, it is clear that the central structures of the Church often seem remote and inappropriate to many local congregations, particularly in UPAs. More critically, they appear to serve the needs of the central structures as opposed to the local Church. It is clear that new structures are needed and that these must be determined by the local needs. As a first step, there must be a major rationalisation of the administrative systems of the central Church so that only

essential information is requested from local congregations.

2.2.8.2   At the Regional Hearings and the National Consultation a number of Assembly Boards and Committees were sharply criticised for what was seen as inconsistent or poor decision-making. Perhaps this is because relatively few people from UPAs are involved in these committees – but why is that the case? – and therefore are unaware of the complexity of the decisions which have to be made. Or it may indeed be that poor decisions have been made in the past because there have been insufficient people involved who understand the particular circumstances facing the Church in UPAs. Until people from UPA congregations are more adequately represented in the decision-making bodies of the Church, there remains the danger that the priorities set will not reflect the particular issues of churches and communities living in poverty. Changing this places a responsibility on all parts of the Church.

2.2.8.3   There is also a strong feeling that decisions need to be more transparent, open to external scrutiny and to fully involve local people wherever possible. **Committee structures have to be adapted to ensure that those who are not used to meetings are included and their insights valued.**

2.2.8.4   Last year's report of the Special Commission anent Review and Reform highlighted that the Model Constitution on occasions placed an unnecessary management burden upon congregations, leading to a duplication of meetings. This issue is acutely felt within UPAs where the culture of meetings is often inappropriate and where office-bearers have many other commitments within the wider community.

2.2.8.5   Representatives at both the Regional Hearings and the National Consultation consistently stated that many of the present structures serve the needs of the central Church rather than the needs of local congregations. For example, over the last number of years, as different Boards and Committees of the Church have sought to improve their communications' strategies, they have developed link personnel within local congregations. As a central strategy, this makes good sense. However, the result is that there are an increasingly small number of people within congregations seeking to undertake an apparently ever-expanding number of roles. In some congregations, individuals are being required to take on three, four or even five different responsibilities, none of which necessarily enable the Church to be more effective at a local level but all of which help to justify the spending of some of the Assembly's Boards and Committees.

2.2.9   False Measurement of Effectiveness

2.2.9.1   Those who participated in the different Regional Hearings were in no doubt that, amidst the fragility and vulnerability of the UPA congregations that shared their stories, there was real evidence that the Kingdom of God was growing. Some went as far as to say that the churches they had heard about seemed more alive than those in more affluent communities. "How can we think of these churches as failures?" asked one participant.

2.2.9.2   There were examples of innovation and creativity told at every Hearing. Representatives from congregations shared how they had developed new, more participative and contextual models of worship, and an impressive array of new facilities and services to address the needs of local communities. A number of congregations had started to operate community cafés, while one congregation shared how, in response to changing needs, they had closed their café and developed, in its place, a growing Parents and Toddlers Group. Work with young people, older people and across many of the traditional barriers of age, race and sectarianism were also described.

2.2.9.3   A great deal of work occurring in UPAs is happening on an ecumenical basis, as congregations naturally come together to announce a common gospel in the face of enormous social, economic and spiritual need. A number of congregations highlighted the importance of the Priority Areas Fund (now part of the Scottish Churches Community Trust) as an important catalyst for innovation.

2.2.9.4 It is also clear that many individuals within UPA congregations are inspired by their faith to play a major positive role in the life of the wider community. Through her members the Church plays an active part in many tenants' associations, credit unions and voluntary management committees undertaking vital work in their local communities even when the Church is not technically represented. This role is often overlooked by others, who equate commitment to Christ as commitment to the Church. In UPAs Christian discipleship leads to people being involved in a wide range of activities, only one of which is the Church.

2.2.9.5 A number of congregations are working not only with other denominations but also with a wide range of other partners from the public and voluntary sector to tackle the results of poverty and to campaign for it eradication. This is clearly not just the Church doing the job of the Social Work Department, but rather her faithful following of Jesus' example and instruction.

2.2.9.6 This picture of creativity and faithfulness was frequently reinforced by the many stories shared at the National Consultation. **Many churches in UPAs rightly deserve their reputation as among the most innovative in the Church of Scotland. However, the Church's traditional measures of success and effectiveness often fail to count much of what Christians in UPAs are doing in the name of Jesus.**

2.2.9.7 It is clear, also, that while this work may well be an effective and appropriate way of sharing God's love in UPAs, it has not necessarily led to a growth in church membership or attendance at Sunday worship. This is a challenge to the Church if she assumes that such work will inevitably lead to the numerical growth of congregations. One minister who shared how much of his ministry in the past ten years had been with drug users most graphically made the point. He stated his conviction that, by God's grace, he believed that he had helped a number to make a strong commitment to Christ but none of those had ended up in the local church, the membership of which had haemorrhaged over the same period. (A number had in fact become involved in the

local pentecostal fellowship.) Nonetheless he was clear that, in terms of kingdom building, these years had been the most productive of his entire ministry.

2.2.9.8 Success and failure have never been appropriate terms to describe the effectiveness of churches striving to announce the good news and to participate with God in the building up of the Kingdom. The reality is, however, that if success and failure are still measured in terms of financial security and membership, then the majority of UPA congregations will be seen as "failures". Although there is increasing agreement that finance and membership are inappropriate measurements of church life, it remains unfortunately the case that these are very often the central criteria when a congregation's viability is being measured.

2.2.9.9 There is an increasing array of ways of measuring effectiveness against agreed and realistic outcomes using models of qualitative as well as quantitative analysis. **Local congregations need to be involved in setting their own targets, because they are most likely to know what can be achieved and what is most necessary. The wider community also has a role to play in the evaluation of churches – how do people who do not attend regularly the Church view it? What message does it convey about the Christian understanding of God?**

2.2.9.10 We cannot all succeed all of the time. One participant at the National Consultation spoke for many when she pointed out: 'We all fail at times. We must learn from these failures and support those who have been hurt by them.' Too often the Church treats those who have failed without the grace and mercy that we all need.

2.2.10 Mission in UPAs
2.2.10.1 It would be false to claim that a single missionary model for being the Church in the UPA emerged during the course of the consultation process. Different emphases were evident in different places, depending upon the theological traditions of the congregation and minister, available resources and upon the local context. At the same time, however, there was

overwhelming support for an incarnational model of mission, where local congregations have immersed themselves fully in the wider life of the community. On numerous occasions, participants spoke of emerging models of "churches without walls."

2.2.10.2 This consensus is in line with the 1992 National Mission Report to the General Assembly:

It is worth noting that though there is a breadth of theological opinion across the UPAs, there is a remarkable degree of unity over the agenda for UPA churches. Perhaps there is a sign here for the wider Church. The practical response to the reality of multiple deprivation unites us in our commitment to Church and community. In UPAs, we find ourselves questioning theologically and socially "What is Church?"

2.2.10.3 It is clear that for many UPA congregations mission is about involvement with the pain and struggle of suffering people and communities in the name of Jesus as well as calling people to become His disciples. Powerful and inspiring stories were told of the Church working with others to improve the local quality of life as well as testimonies of how faith has transformed the lives of individuals.

2.2.10.4 There was a regularly repeated sense that, although the problems facing the Church in UPAs are enormous, the context of poverty makes these communities special for the whole Church as she seeks to serve the poor Christ. Without a clear focus on poor and vulnerable communities in her missionary strategy, the Church of Scotland is in constant danger of losing her true calling. This has been a regular theme of the UPA Committee's reports to the General Assembly over the last 12 years and was again much in evidence during the consultation process. **The Church in the UPAs calls the wider Church to join us because we have had the awesome privilege of meeting the poor Jesus in our communities and want others to do the same.**

2.2.11 A Staffing Crisis.
2.2.11.1 If buildings were one of the constant themes of the Postal Survey, Regional Hearings and National Consultation, then staffing needs was the other. Over many years UPA congregations, serving large parishes, have had the privilege of ministry teams, nearly always paid for by the wider church. In recent years, as a result of changing priorities and the overall financial pressure within the Church of Scotland, there has been a reduction in the numbers of staff the Church has been able to employ in UPAs. In terms of congregational size, UPA churches remain proportionally higher served by staffing than other parts of the Church. However, as a result of the often large, poor and increasingly complex parishes that UPA congregations are serving, as well as the lack of other professional expertise within the congregation, it is clear that many staff and churches are close to breaking point. The experience of one community, where staffing levels have been reduced from 7.5 to 4 in the last five years, is not uncommon.

2.2.11.2 Although the population of many UPAs has fallen in recent years, as a direct result of government housing policies, parish populations remain large and there is likely to be a period of sustained growth in the coming years. It is vital that local churches are more adequately staffed to enable them to meet future challenges and opportunities when this regeneration begins.

2.2.11.3 Many UPA congregations are very grateful for all the assistance that they do receive from the wider Church, and recognise that in changing circumstances, such assistance cannot be taken for granted. However, there is a sense among some that they are made to feel "beholden for it" and are viewed as second rate because they cannot meet their own needs. There was a strong sense that this culture, where it still exists within the Church, needs to be challenged.

2.2.11.4 It was in the field of decisions over staffing that there was the greatest level of criticism of the employing Boards and Committees of the Assembly. Some called for a more informed assessment of local needs as a basis for decision-making and for the greater involvement of local parties in any revised process. Others complained that there was a lack of clarity about how decisions were reached and no clear system for how decisions were made.

2.2.11.5 At the National Consultation participants became aware of the current funding crisis within the Board of National Mission, which has led to a subsequent freezing on the numbers of National Mission appointments. UPA congregations are likely to suffer most as a result of this.

2.2.11.6 A number of congregations have succeeded in securing funding for development work and new staff posts from the public and charitable sectors, while other non-UPA congregations have generously supported others. A number of congregations shared how they were increasingly involved with other funders and agencies in partnership. For some this was as basic as sharing office and administration facilities, while for others they had become major local employers and were responsible for a range of activities.

2.2.11.7 It is clear that there are there are new opportunities for partnership between the local church and other funding bodies and agencies. Again the Priority Areas Fund has been influential in promoting this culture within rural and urban priority area churches. If the full potential for these partnership opportunities are to be realised, there is need for a growing flexibility in how nationally appointed staff are deployed. In the future an increasing number may be part-funded with the local church (or partnership) rather than National Boards being the employing agent.

2.2.11.8 Numerous stories were shared of how churches were working collaboratively with other local Church of Scotland congregations and other denominations to work more effectively together. Such joint working needs to be encouraged. However, there is a sense that it is viewed as a problem by the employing Boards of the Church, particularly when congregations are seeking to work ecumenically or in new partnerships.

2.2.11.9 The task of developing often complicated funding packages, upon which an increasingly number of UPA congregations depends for staffing, is a heavy and difficult burden. **Many congregations would benefit greatly from a national or regional team of trained staff with skills in community development,** **community auditing, project development and funding generation to work alongside them in advancing their local plans.**

2.2.11.10 At the same time as opportunities for joint working are growing, it is clear that there are some communities where the Church must continue long-term to resource the work, simply because it is a gospel priority to be committed to the poorest and most vulnerable. There are also posts which others are unlikely to be willing to fund. On a number of occasions, UPA congregations have asked not only for greater support of project or development workers, but of those who will be evangelists, living and sharing the Gospel in deeply incarnated ways.

2.2.12 A Constantly Changing Picture

2.2.12.1 The picture in UPAs is changing constantly and there is a need for the Church to remain constantly aware of these changes. Over 60 years one inner-city area has gone from a population of 90,000 to 10,000, and from 27 churches to 3 (only one of which is a Church of Scotland). However, a major rebuilding process is underway and it is anticipated that the population will have risen to 16,000 by the end of the decade. Other communities have been similarly affected and large open spaces (where tenements once stood) and entire streets of derelict housing with one or two homes still occupied are graphic evidence of some of the changes which are occurring in UPAs at this time. One person described her community as full of derelict ground and boarded up windows, still hoping that better days are coming.

2.2.12.2 The 1998 National Mission Report to the General Assembly painted a graphic picture of the changing nature of UPAs. It stated:-

Spurred on by central government legislation on housing, the redevelopment of the housing schemes continues. A long and wearying process is undertaken: decanting the current population from its current housing and re-housing them in temporary accommodation; demolition of some existing housing stock and the building of new; the refurbishment of other existing housing. Many housing schemes find that 90% of their population has moved house in the past ten years.

2.2.12.3 Since 1998 the pace of change has increased still further and UPA congregations are facing the challenge of being the Church in areas, which have been physically transformed, even if many of the old problems of high unemployment, poor health and high levels of crime and drug misuse remain. They are also having to do so at a time when many of their most active members have been forced to move, and where it is often the old and most vulnerable who currently remain. One minister asked how the local congregation ministered to the new private housing being built in the parish while holding on to the need to care for the poorest who remained. Another asked what happened when the population of the parish was halved in seven years and 4 of the 6 remaining elders were long-term sick.

2.2.12.4 The UPA Committee helped to pioneer the use of the 1991 National Census data to build a profile of UPA parishes. It was through the census materials that the list of 330 UPA parishes was identified. The proposal from the Board of National Mission to carry out a similar exercise on behalf of all parishes in Scotland using data from the 2001 Census as data becomes available is very welcome. This information will help the churches in Scotland to plot the changing nature of poverty in this country. However, given the rapid transitional position of many UPAs at this time additional information will be necessary to ensure that an accurate picture of UPAs is maintained over the coming years. Such information is becoming increasingly available through the Scottish Executive's Central Research Unit and through its annual Social Justice Report.

2.2.12.5 The ongoing impact of local government reorganisation, the advent of a Scottish Parliament, and the plethora of new policy initiatives at area, regional, national and European levels all add to the complexity of change which UPA parishes are experiencing at this time.

2.2.12.6 The situation in the Church is changing also. This may now be the time to reduce the number of parishes which are designated as UPAs to the poorest 60-100 (using the 2001 Census and updating over the next ten years with other data as available) where the problems of poverty are all pervasive and to challenge the whole Church to place the needs of these communities and congregations at the very heart of her life. This is not to ignore the needs of others, where different strategies will have to be developed to ensure that the poor are not forgotten in the midst of relative affluence, but to recognise the critical needs of a smaller number.

2.2.13 Conclusion

2.2.13.1 Listening to the needs and problems being faced by UPA congregations over the last three years – years of change in those local communities and in the wider vision of the Church – has been humbling and challenging. Many who have been involved have both shared the pain but also held the hope. The real test of this process, however, is whether it will make a difference for churches and communities at the point of delivery. For that to happen the major problems, which have been highlighted, will have to be addressed.

2.2.13.2 It is vital for the whole Church that the voices within this report – from people and churches at the margins of our society – are heard and that urgent steps are taken to address their concerns. There are challenges within it to every part of the Church, from the UPA to wealthy suburbia, from the local to the central. As the next step within this process the appropriate Assembly Boards and Committees are invited to consider the report, and with representatives from UPAs, to determine whether, and if so how, they will change their policies and practices in the light of it, and to report to the General Assembly of 2003. Congregations and presbyteries are urged to consider ways in which they can become more aware of each other's needs and to build new and genuine relationships with congregations struggling to witness faithfully to God's love in Scotland's poorest communities.

2.2.13.3 As was stated at the outset of this report, the challenge facing the Church in all her parts is that: **"The**

whole Church must recognise that to be committed to the poorest and most vulnerable is the gospel imperative facing us all."

2.3 Proposed Changes to Constitution:
2.3.1 The Board brings to the General Assembly the three amendments to its Constitution.

2.3.2 The first amendment involves deleting reference to "a regular National Mission Conference". When the first such conference was organised it cost £39,470 and, given that any future conference would be more expensive, the Board believes that it cannot at this time of financial stringency justify the cost. It is the intention of the Board to replace regular National Mission Conferences with "roadshows" to encourage two-way communication with Presbyteries. It is also planned to hold smaller conferences on specific areas of work and arrangements are in hand for a conference on Chaplaincies to be held in March 2003.

2.3.3 The second amendment is the deletion of the appointment of a representative of the Board of Parish Education on the Committee on Parish Assistance. Such an appointment was appropriate when the Committee was responsible for training staff but is now no longer necessary.

2.4 Background to Overtures anent Appraisal and Adjustment of Charges and anent Vacancy Procedure:
2.4.1 Acts IV (1984) and V (1984) have served the Church well as the basis for vacancy and reappraisal legislation for almost two decades. Over recent years however there has been a growing realisation that a revision of this legislation would be of value to meet the needs of a changing Church in a changing Scotland.

2.4.2 At the General Assembly of 2001 the Committee reported its intention to revise the legislation and in particular offered three areas where significant changes might be included in the revision. The Committee places on record its appreciation to all Presbyteries who responded to the remit from the 2001

General Assembly to give consideration to these three changes.

The first possible change, to allow Presbyteries the possibility of fast-tracking vacancies when decisions taken are in accordance with an agreed five year Plan, met with substantial support.

The second, to give the possibility for Presbyteries and congregations to fast-track each vacancy, met with substantial support.

The third, to give consideration to a variety of matters surrounding the role and membership of the Vacancy Committee, met with very little support.

2.4.3 Taking these views into consideration and following considerable further work with the Depute Secretary of the Board of Practice and Procedure, Rev Marjory A. Maclean, and representatives of the Board of Ministry, the Committee now offers to the Church the revised legislation contained in Appendix II and III.

2.4.4 In adopting the Overture anent Appraisal and Adjustment the Committee recognises there are two specific issues on which there might require to be further consideration. The first is section 12(2)(d) relating to "Demission in the Interests of Readjustment" and the second section 15 on "Members of Ministry Teams". It is the hope of the Committee that Presbyteries should feel able to support the Overture while expressing opposition to these two items and likewise the Committee on Classification of Returns to Overtures will not regard these as essential to the approval of the Overture.

2.4.5 Replacing Act IV 1984
2.4.5.1 The controlling idea behind the new draft is the taking of Presbytery planning, appraisal and adjustment away from the time of a vacancy and putting it instead into a systematic process of regular review.

2.4.5.2 The Board proposes the use of the neater terminology of 'appraisal' and 'adjustment' instead of "reappraisal" and "readjustment" in the hope that such a change will avoid confusion and inaccuracy. Where a plan produces a need for adjustment, concurrence by the

Assembly's Committee is required only for forms of adjustment (e.g. unions) that alter the characteristics of a charge. It is not required for the kinds of tools (e.g. transference, demission in the interests of readjustment) that are ancillary to the parishes themselves. Once Presbyteries have the concurrence of the Assembly's Committee to a Plan they have freedom to implement that Plan with no further reference to the Assembly's Committee other than reporting on actions taken.

2.4.5.3 The congregation's rights have been affirmed in the delicate circumstance where a union or linkage involves an incumbent in one part of the proposed charge. The vacant congregation will have a discreet opportunity to decide not to call the incumbent of the other part of the charge, and a deferral of planned adjustment will be the required alternative.

2.4.5.4 On the other hand where appraisal produces no need for adjustment, it will be possible (subject to the other requirements of vacancy procedure) for the search for a new minister to be completely unhindered by appraisal formalities.

2.4.5.5 Appeals against decisions under this Act will normally be dealt with when adjustment falls to be implemented. If taken immediately, much time and effort might be spent appealing decisions that might in any event be reversed because of future developments in Presbytery planning. A slight change of terminology removes the previous use of the term 'Reference' in this context, as it was a highly specialised use of the term.

2.4.6   Replacing Act V 1984
2.4.6.1 The principal idea behind the new draft is the removal of all current delays of vacancy procedure between full Presbytery meetings. The Committee whole-heartedly agrees that the immediate filling of a vacancy may be unhelpful in certain situations, and the legislation makes it possible for Presbyteries to create delays for important pastoral or other reasons. But a system like the current one, which builds such delays into every case, creates frustration more often than it does good, and the new suggestions enable Presbyteries and

their members to determine the appropriate pace of any vacancy.

2.4.6.2 A new standing committee of Presbytery is proposed (the Vacancy Procedure Committee) with authority to advance all stages of vacancy in simple cases. Conceivably, a very straightforward vacancy may be completed without ever being delayed by the wait for a Presbytery meeting to take place. In certain circumstances, or by request of parties in the congregation or the Presbytery itself, it will always be possible to ensure that the whole court debates and decides any difficult matter, and the Presbytery will be kept abreast of all the decisions of the committee.

2.4.6.3 Two innovations affect applicants for charges. The first removes all the complex of qualifications for eligibility to apply, contained in Act V 1984. The Overture anent Admission and Re-admission of Ministers and Others, which returns to this year's Assembly after its consideration under the Barrier Act, provides eligibility for all cases and simplifies the system completely. Applicants for charges simply require to be *either* Church of Scotland ministers, graduate candidates etc, *or* holders of a Certificate of Eligibility.

2.4.6.4 The second innovation is the departure from the system of short leets, which is very little used and not commended by the Committee. The consequence of this is that the successful applicant no longer requires to be distinguished as a 'sole nominee', and the term 'nominee' is used instead.

2.5   Presbytery Planning
2.5.1 Presbytery Planning, a responsibility of the Committee on Parish Reappraisal, was strengthened by the Act of the 1998 General Assembly instructing all Presbyteries to prepare a Presbytery Plan. The General Assembly of that year agreed the following section to the Deliverance of the Board of National Mission:

"Presbytery Plans

Presbyteries, in consultation with the Committee on Parish Reappraisal of the Board of National

Mission of the General Assembly or any successor body designated by the General Assembly, shall prepare Plans for the future deployment of staff within their bounds. Such Plans shall be statements of intent and proposals contained therein shall be subject to appeal or dissent and complaint at the point of actual readjustment in terms of Act IV (1984) as amended and on no other occasion.

Plans should be drawn up according to the following guidelines:

(a) The period of time for which the Plan is made should be specified, with this period being no less than ten years.

(b) Provision should be made for regular review of the Plan during its lifespan.

(c) Indication of the number and pattern of essential charges which the Presbytery hopes to achieve by the end of the specified period should be given.

(d) Presbytery should either indicate the specific congregations which will continue to be essential to the parish system or indicate how many congregations in a particular grouping might be essential in the long term.

(e) Indication should be given of those charges where the need for staff exceeds a parish minister, and details of the envisaged additional staff should be stated.

(f) Plans should reflect proposed substantial new housing developments."

2.5.2 The present position is that once a Presbytery "approves" a Presbytery Plan, it is the locus of the Committee on Parish Reappraisal to "agree" the Plan. This "agreement" is given defining the Plan as "a statement of intent of the Presbytery which does not infringe the rights of ministers in charges or the rights of congregations". Agreement at present is given for a ten year period but the Committee always stresses the need, even within that period, for continual reappraisal in the light of the changes in communities and in the Church as a whole.

2.5.3 The proposals now before the General Assembly in the Overture on Appraisal and Adjustment give even more strength to the planning process and direct Presbyteries to prepare and maintain "rolling" five-year Plans which facilitate the vacancy process.

2.5.4 Given the overwhelming support of Presbyteries to the possibility of "fast-tracking" vacancies when decisions taken are in accordance with agreed Plans the Committee has given thought to the development of Presbytery Planning to facilitate this process should it be agreed by the whole Church.

2.5.5 A crucial issue in future Presbytery Planning will be the availability of Ministers, Deacons, and other paid staff such as Youth Workers, Parish Assistants, and Community Development Workers with this availability being governed by both the numbers being recruited and trained as well as by the financial resources of the Church to pay for parish staff.

2.5.6 To be acceptable for the "fast-tracking" scheme Presbytery Plans should be drawn up in accordance with Sections 3 to 6 of Act x 2003. In order to be supportive to Presbyteries wishing to adopt the "fast-track" scheme without any delay (if The Overtures are approved by the 2003 General Assembly), the Committee would be willing from the autumn of 2002 to work with Presbyteries to develop existing Plans to meet the above guidelines.

2.6 Proposed Appointment of Rural Adviser.
As highlighted in the Report of Scottish Churches Industrial Mission (Appendix VII), the Board facilitated the secondment of Rev Dr Richard Frazer to support the response of the Church in Scotland to the Foot and Mouth Crisis.

Dr Frazer's involvement has highlighted the need for a Rural Adviser and has opened up possibilities of financial support for such an appointment from outwith the Church. The Board also reports the interest of the Board of Stewardship and Finance and the commitment of a special grant to assist with the appointment.

At the time of writing the Board has resolved in principle to make the appointment of a Rural Adviser and has undertaken discussions with appropriate bodies to ensure that finances are in place for such an appointment.

2.7 Retiral Age of Healthcare Chaplains
2.7.1 Part-time Healthcare Chaplains' Age Restriction

Sessional part-time chaplains are appointed by the Department to an "office" and do not receive Contracts of Employment. As a consequence, the statutory retirement age of 65 has not been applied. Nevertheless guidelines have been issued to Presbyteries by the Department stating that "an upper age limit of 70 should be respected" and "that a review, every three years, of all part-time chaplains' appointments should be undertaken in consultation with Trust representatives."

2.7.2 In the main part-time chaplaincy arrangements have worked but occasionally there have been difficulties especially when the recommended three-yearly reviews by Presbyteries have not been held. The Sub-Committee hopes that Presbyteries will undertake the recommended reviews.

2.7.3 The issue of appropriate training has been addressed by the recent appointment of the Whole-time Healthcare Chaplaincy Training and Development Officer. To ensure an adequate level of supervision and accountability, the Sub-Committee desires that Presbyteries be reminded by the General Assembly to review Part-time Healthcare Chaplaincy appointments every three years and to terminate the appointments where chaplains reach the age of 70. Where chaplains in post already exceed the age of 70 the review should be undertaken within the next 12 months. Such reviews should be able to ascertain if chaplains of retirement age (65+) are in sufficient good health to be capable of carrying out their duties and responsibilities.

2.8 Chaplaincy Contract with the Scottish Prison Service

2.8.1 In its report to the General Assembly of 2001 the Board introduced proposals for the development of Prison Chaplaincy to meet changes in ministry and the care of prisoners. These included the establishment of a "Contract" to provide chaplains. To this end an ecumenical joint working party was set up to plan and carry out the service provision to reflect its future ecumenical basis for delivery. During the last twelve months substantial progress has been achieved. All prisons in Scotland have been visited and discussions held with prison managers and chaplaincy teams to identify the optimum levels of chaplaincy required in the various jails. These visits highlighted a number of situations which required urgent attention for the recruitment of new, suitably qualified and trained personnel ahead of the conclusion of the "Contract" in April 2002. At the same time the appointment of two Prison Chaplaincy Contract Co-ordinators (one Church of Scotland and one Roman Catholic Church) also became a priority.

2.8.2 It is pleasing to report that in January 2002, in consultation with the Scottish Prison Service, the Rev Stuart Fulton was appointed as the Church of Scotland Co-ordinator with responsibility for the chaplains of other denominations, excepting the Roman Catholic Church, and other faiths. Father Brian Gowans was appointed to the corresponding position with the Roman Catholic Church. Their primary tasks are to co-ordinate, encourage and motivate chaplains serving in penal establishments on the basis of team working to meet the religious and pastoral needs of prisoners and staff. In February 2002 the Rev Colin Reed, of the Scottish Episcopal Church, was appointed as the first full time chaplain to HM Prison Edinburgh. This was followed by the appointment of Rev William Moore, of the Presbyterian Church in Ireland, as a Throughcare Chaplain at HM Prison Low Moss in partnership with the Glasgow Lodging House Mission. Appointments at HM Prison Perth and HM Young Offenders Institution Polmont are likely to be announced prior to the 2002 General Assembly.

2.8.3 At the time of writing the Board has received the formal "Invitation to Tender" document from the SPS and the joint working party is progressing diligently through the detail. A response to the document is anticipated but it seems unlikely that the "Contract" will be concluded by the original target date of April 2002. However satisfactory agreement has been reached with the Scottish Prison Service regarding the funding of the new appointments described above until the "Contract" is in force. A further round of visits to prisons is being undertaken, ostensibly for the purposes of the contractual arrangements, but also to maintain contact with chaplaincy teams to explain developments and to offer support and encouragement during this period of change and some uncertainty.

2.9   Scottish Church Attendance Census 2002 and Statistics for Mission:

2.9.1 Scottish Church Attendance Census 2002
2.9.1.1   The Board is committed to providing quality statistical resources to support congregations, Presbyteries, and the whole Church in rising to the challenges of the missionary task in Scotland today. With this in mind the Board reports a new initiative and continue progress with another.

2.9.1.2 By the time of the General Assembly the Scottish Churches Census 2002 will have taken place on Sunday 12th May 2002. This census has been encouraged by the Board working collaboratively with the other Churches in Scotland and with "Christian Research". It will offer to the Church information about Church attendance that will build on statistics gleaned at similar censuses in 1984 and 1994. Once preliminary results are available in the autumn of 2002 a series of focus groups will be organised to assist in understanding the statistics. When the full results are published in 2003 a series of roadshows will be organised to make the statistical analysis available as an encouragement for mission.

2.9.2 Statistics for Mission:
2.9.2.1   The 2001 General Assembly welcomed the initiative of the Board to obtain accurate statistical information on every parish in Scotland based on the results of the 2001 National Census. The Board reports steady progress on obtaining the postcodes necessary as

a basis for the work and also on discussions with other denominations in Scotland to enable the results to be widely used. The statistics will be available during 2003 and will not only provide a useful resource in themselves but will also assist in the interpretation of the results of the Scottish Church Census 2002.

3.   Report:

3.1   Responding to Change ... in the staffing of parishes:
3.1.1 The staffing of the parishes of Scotland is the responsibility of the Committee on Parish Reappraisal which works in close co-operation with the Committees on Parish Assistance and New Charge Development.

3.1.2 The Committee on Parish Reappraisal reports that in its ongoing work it is seeking to assist congregations, Presbyteries, and the whole Church in responding to change. Much of the Committee's work is giving consideration to decisions of Presbyteries taken under Acts IV 1984 and V 1984 and a full record of decisions taken is given in the Tables in Appendix IV. During 2001 the Committee concurred with 64 unrestricted calls, 38 calls with restricted tenure, 9 bases of union and 8 bases of linking.

3.1.3 The Committee always seeks as much information as necessary to make its decisions. In requests for concurrence with unrestricted calls the Committee always requests completed Congregational Survey Forms. When such forms are incomplete the Committee often defers a decision and so the importance of fully completed Survey Forms being submitted with decisions of Presbyteries cannot be over-emphasised.

3.1.4 In order that decisions regarding vacancies are not taken in isolation the Committee continues to stress the value of Presbytery Planning. At the end of 2001 41 Presbyteries had Agreed Plans with the Committee and all other Presbyteries were engaged in the process of planning. When the Committee agrees a Plan with a Presbytery it is stated that "the Plan is a statement of intent of the Presbytery which does not infringe the rights of ministers in charges and the rights of congregations". As Scotland and the Church of Scotland continues to change, planning has become an ongoing process and throughout 2001 the Committee has been involved at the request of Presbyteries in many discussions on planning.

3.1.5 The Committee continues to work closely with the General Trustees in the fulfilment of the Regulations for Control of Work at Ecclesiastical Buildings. In 2001 58 requests for work over £50,000 were considered and the Committee records warm appreciation to the General Trustees for their co-operation in the fulfilment of the Regulations.

3.1.6 Warm appreciation is also expressed by the Committee to many others who have assisted in its work. Presbytery Conveners and Clerks have facilitated effective communication; the Committee has been greatly assisted in the process of the revision of Acts IV 1984 and V 1984 by the Depute Secretary to the Board of Practice and Procedure, Rev Marjory A. Maclean.

3.1.7 In the course of 2001 the Committee has noted an increased interest in the Church in team ministries serving areas covering several parishes and involving greater participation by members of congregations enabled by a multi-disciplinary team. While recognising that considerable challenges still exist in the formation, financing, and support of such teams, the Committee is positive about these developments and has included such possibilities as a form of readjustment in the revision of Act IV (1984).

3.1.8 Remit from 2001 General Assembly:
3.1.8.1 The 2001 General Assembly approved the following section of the Deliverance of the Board of National Mission relating to the work of the Committee:

"In the light of the declining numbers of ministers in the Church urge the Committee on Parish Reappraisal to give consideration to the preparation of guidelines for the strategic deployment of ministers across the Church, these guidelines to include (1) an indication of the size of charge and circumstances

where they would be unlikely to concur with the appointment of a full-time minister; (2) an indication of the size of charge and circumstances where they would recommend additional pastoral assistance and to report to the General Assembly of 2002."

3.1.8.2 The Committee has given considerable consideration to this remit but has concluded that it would be impractical to undertake this task at a time when the need for flexibility is of the essence. Furthermore to base guidelines solely on population or geography would lead to unworkable anomalies throughout Scotland. The Committee believes it is not possible to equate a town population of a certain size with a county population of the same size and say that each requires only one minister. Likewise the Committee believes that when a large geographical rural area with one minister is translated into an urban setting, it would not be possible for one minister to serve the large population resident there. The Committee believes that the way in which it currently works using Presbytery Planning, Reappraisal Congregational Survey forms, visits where required, with a sensitivity to local issues such as congregations in the same town of different theological and cultural traditions, leads to the fairest possible distribution of ministers.

3.1.9 Ministry among Deaf People:
3.1.9.1 The Committee was greatly encouraged with the decision of the 2001 General Assembly to resolve that the Scheme of Ministry with Deaf People becomes an ongoing part of the ministry and mission of the Church of Scotland. The Committee continues to provide the support group for the three ministers engaged in Ministry among Deaf People and is currently seeking a number of ways in which this area of work can be developed.

3.1.9.2 A significant development has been the move by the Albany Deaf Church, Edinburgh, from the Church at the premises of the Edinburgh and East of Scotland Deaf Society to Greenside Church, Edinburgh. The congregation of Greenside Church have warmly welcomed the move and have created a chapel in the sanctuary using the furnishings of the Albany Deaf Congregation. The chapel was dedicated by Rt Rev Dr

John Millar, Moderator of the General Assembly, at a service on Sunday 3rd February 2002.

3.1.10 Summer Student Appointments:
3.1.10.1   Each summer the Committee appoints students to serve in a number of rural and UPA parishes in a scheme entitled "Summer Student Appointments". Students are paid at 60% of the current minimum stipend and accommodation and travel costs are met.

3.1.10.2   Those appointed give invaluable support to ministers and congregations in the most remote and the most hard-pressed parishes of Scotland. The students from the Scottish Divinity Faculties – some not yet accepted for ministry in the Church of Scotland -are complemented by students from Partner Churches world-wide and in 2001 24 appointments were made. A new venture in 2001 was the appointment of a student, Dr Robin Hill, to work in Edinburgh Prison as part of the chaplaincy team.

3.1.11 Guidelines for Reviewable and Terminable Tenure Charges:
3.1.11.1   The Committee gave a commitment at the 2001 General Assembly to prepare a national database of reviewable and terminable tenure charges and to prepare guidelines for the review of these charges. The Committee reports diligence and that a database of reviewable and terminable tenure charges was circulated to Presbytery Clerks in December 2001 and that guidelines (Appendix V) have been prepared, circulated, and are in use.

3.1.12 Conference for Ministers in Part-time Charges:
3.1.12.1   At the 1994 General Assembly authority was given to the Committee to approve of part-time charges and since then regular reports on this new development have been brought before the General Assembly. At present there are 11 part-time charges in the Church of Scotland and ministers in such charges were invited to attend a conference on 14th and 15th June 2001. Overall those attending were positive about part-time ministry with one of the few concerns being that some appeared

not to have a copy of their Basis of Part-time Ministry. Fresh copies of bases prepared by Presbyteries have been circulated to all ministers in part-time charges. Given the assurance coming from the conference that there is a place for part-time ministry where a charge was necessary for territorial purposes (e.g. some island situations) or in a team context, the Committee has resolved to continue to concur with reasonable requests from Presbytery for the establishment of part-time charges.

3.1.13 Unions with at least three places of worship:
Following receipt of correspondence from a minister of a united charge with a number of places of worship, the Committee has sought to compile a list of unions in which there are at least three places of worship in use every Sunday. At the time of writing the list is being completed and the intention is to seek the completion of a questionnaire inviting comment on the challenges and opportunities of such charges with the possibility of a conference for ministers in such charges being arranged.

3.1.14 "New Forms of Parish Ministry":
There are now only fourteen ministers serving in the category of "New Forms of Parish Ministry" with seven serving as Associate Ministers and seven serving as Community Ministers. One significant development has been the establishment of the chaplaincy at Braehead Shopping Centre, Glasgow, by Rev Mike Edwards and a highlight was the presentation of a thought-provoking drama "The Pram in the Crib" prepared in consultation with the Netherbow Centre, Edinburgh, in the period leading up to Christmas 2001.

3.1.15 National Mission Appointments:
3.1.15.1   By December 2001 the Committee on Parish Assistance of the Board was supporting 73 full and part-time members of staff in parishes and projects from the Shetland Islands to Dumfries, Carlisle and Corby. Of these, 16 are in posts created to assist the development of particular projects. Besides these openings for new mission opportunities, there remains a considerable demand from large urban parishes for parish assistance to share in the regular and ongoing mission of the Church. At the turn of the year there were seven vacant posts.

Two were being publicly advertised and five more, available only to existing members of staff and Deacons in training, remain vacant.

3.1.15.2 The Committees on Parish Reappraisal and Parish Assistance expressed their deep concern that the Board has had to take the decision as reported in the "Future Strategy" section of the Report (sec 2.1.5) to restrict fresh National Mission Appointments, other than of Ministers, and Deacons currently in training, to existing members of staff. The Committees recognise fully the reasons that have led to the decision but such recognition is accompanied by deep concern for ministers, congregations, and parishes where necessary support will in the future be limited.

3.1.16   Annual Reports:
Teams of ministers and parish assistants working together in parishes and projects complete an Annual Team Report, which is forwarded to the Board through their Presbytery. This procedure gives the Presbytery an opportunity to understand the value of the National Mission Appointments that have been requested and agreed, and to support the staff concerned. A new form of report has been introduced that will give more scope to teams to reflect on their own circumstances. It is hoped that this system of reporting will also assist all involved to plan for the future.

3.1.17   Personal Appraisal:
3.1.17.1   The 2000 General Assembly approved the following instruction to the Board of National Mission:

> "Instruct the Board to formulate guidelines of criteria for the five yearly review of all National Mission Appointments and establish a procedure for personal appraisal to run alongside these reviews".

3.1.17.2   At the 2001 General Assembly the Board reported that "Five Year Reviews" were no longer appropriate in the light of the new regulations for National Mission Appointments but that discussions would continue concerning a procedure for personal appraisal. The Committee on Parish Assistance now reports that a scheme is in place involving:

—Self-appraisal being included in team training.
—The maintenance of staff profiles with the approval of staff members and checked annually by staff.
—A visit to each staff member twelve months prior to the end of a period of appointment for personal appraisal and to look at future options for staff members, such as personal development and training
—Contacts made by the Committee with staff through visits, telephone contact, annual conferences and information days.

3.1.18   Study Leave:
The Committee on Parish Assistance continues to encourage the professional and personal development of members of staff, particularly through a flexible study leave programme. During 2001 study leave was granted to, among others, deacons attending the World Diakonia Conference in Brisbane, Australia, and also the UK Urban Congress.

3.1.19   Team Training:
To assist a collaborative approach to ministry, an annual training occasion for new ministry teams is provided by a group comprising representatives from the Boards of National Mission, Ministry and Parish Education, and the Board of Mission of the Scottish Episcopal Church. This group also offers support through a number of team consultants who make themselves available to meet with established teams in their own situations.

3.1.20   Lay Missionaries:
In 1998, when the General Assembly closed the office of Lay Missionary to new entrants, the Board promised the Assembly that a book would be published to celebrate the achievements of Lay Missionaries. This research has recently been completed by Rev Dr Frank Bardgett and a book, "Devoted Service Rendered: The Lay Missionaries of the Church of Scotland" will be published during 2002, a year that marks the centenary of the appointment of Lay Home Missionaries by the General Assembly.

3.2   Responding to Change … in New Charge Development:
3.2.1   The Committee on New Charge Development

continues to be encouraged by the development of new charges throughout Scotland and currently there are eleven new charges and nine Church Extension charges. The Committee undertakes its work in terms of Act XIII 2000 and Regulations for Church Extension Charges approved at the same General Assembly. The Act not only provides the legal framework to allow Presbyteries, with the concurrence of the Committee on Parish Reappraisal, to establish new charges but also gives the Committee the responsibility for general oversight of such charges.

3.2.2 The Committee is responsible for the provision of a manse for the charge and every endeavour is made to find a suitable house within the designated parish or as close as possible. The Committee seeks always to follow the guidelines used by the Church on the size of manses but, because in new housing developments houses tend to be smaller than traditional manses, this is not always possible. The Committee has, therefore, adapted or added to some houses to allow them to be used as a manse. The problem of the minister's home being also, at least at first, the only building available to a charge is one which the Committee is looking at with some urgency and the purchase or letting of office accommodation, where possible, is being pursued. This has meant that in one new charge, Robroyston in the Presbytery of Glasgow, a former shop and the adjacent house have been purchased and are being converted into a worship centre for the growing congregation. It must be pointed out, however, that such conversions are by no means always possible and that the importance of involving the Committee at as early a stage as possible in the planning of a new charge is vital as sites quickly become unavailable to the Church. The new charge at Cove, Aberdeen, is still without a building after almost five years and this is a concern to both local parties and to the Committee.

3.2.3 2001 has seen the completion of two new buildings. That in Kilwinning for the congregation of Mansefield Trinity was opened for worship and dedicated in the Spring while that for Riverside, Perth, was available for use just in time for Christmas. Both buildings were conceived and the design assisted with input from those who will actually use the building. A building for a new church has to be adaptable, flexible and orientated towards mission. It is merely a tool, albeit an important one, for the mission of a local congregation.

3.2.4 The Committee provides a budget, currently £5,500, over a five year period, for mission purposes to each new charge to encourage imaginative and creative programmes of outreach and evangelism. Each new charge also has a Commission made up of representatives of the local Presbytery and nominees of the Committee. The Commission has the legal status of a Kirk Session but it is also the body that encourages and supports the minister and the new congregation as they seek to serve the parish in Christ's name.

3.2.5 The Committee believes that: "People should come to believe that the power which has the last word in human affairs is represented by a man hanging on a cross. The only answer, the only hermeneutic of the Gospel, is a congregation of men and women who believe it and live by it". (Lesslie Newbigin) This is a task for our time. Throughout Scotland, as the Church and its teaching are being marginalised in society, the need is not for a withdrawal by the Church into itself or a detachment by local Christians from the world but an awareness by the local Church of the culture that surrounds it and engagement with that culture for Christ's sake. In establishing new charges in recent housing areas and post-war housing schemes the Committee seeks to create communities that will not impose themselves upon the people but grow out of the area which they serve to become the Church in the midst.

3.2.6 The Committee is pleased to report the establishment of three new charges with the introduction of Rev. Jim Redpath, Interim Minister, to Paisley: St. Ninian's Ferguslie on 1st May 2001, the induction of Rev. Douglas Wallace and Rev. Jim Wilson to East Kilbride: Stewartfield on 12th November 2001 and Dundee: Whitfield on 21st November 2001 respectively. A fourth new charge at Gilmerton in Edinburgh was created on the last day of 2001 and a Commission is responsible for the drawing up of an initial mission design prior to a minister being appointed. Two Church Extension Charges, Cove and Oldmachar (Presbytery of Aberdeen) changed status to New Charge Developments under their sitting Ministers in 2001. The Committee places on record thanks to all who serve as members of New Charge Commissions and would commend the work of New Charge Development, the ministers and members of Commissions to the prayers of the whole Church.

3.3 Responding to change ... in Mission and Evangelism Resourcing:

3.3.1 The Mission and Evangelism Resources Committee (MERC) of the Board is charged with developing vision for the work of mission and evangelism in Scotland and its promotion by means of research, development and training. It operates at both parish and national level. The local parish church is recognised as the principal agent of mission and great emphasis is placed in the Committee in responding with appropriate resourcing to the context in which this work is conducted. The Report of the Special Commission anent Review and Reform to the General Assembly of 2001 echoed principles with the Committee would identify and would wish to reinforce. 'The local congregation is the space where Christian life is nurtured in practical discipleship, earthed in the concrete realities of local life. The congregation shows the way by serving alongside the community and inviting others to become followers of Christ.' Then: 'For reasons of theology and missionary strategy, we affirm the local Christian congregation as the primary expression of the church.' (Reports to the General Assembly 2001, 36/19)

3.3.2 Moreover, the Committee recognises the need to ensure that its staff and the resources made available to it are deployed in ways that encourage and enable the Church to be missionary and evangelistic. Particularly in the light of the on-going deliberations within the Church at large on the recommendations made by the Special Commission anent Review and Reform, this is a process of reflection that the Committee is constantly engaged in with a view to ensuring that the local parish church is adequately resourced and supported.

3.3.3 Important though the local is, the Committee is also responsible for 'identifying, originating and supporting projects which are advancing mission and evangelism in key areas of life in Scotland'. Hence its involvement in the relationship between religion and science and technology in the SRT Project, and engagement with arts and culture at The Netherbow, and its participation in the Asian Information and Advice Centre at The Well in an ethnically diverse part of Glasgow.

3.3.4 Responding to Change ... in Advisers in Mission and Evangelism

3.3.4.1 The Advisers in Mission and Evangelism report having discovered a renewed surge of interest in matters relating to church development and outreach in the course of this past year. In response to the demand for resources that will enable local congregations to wrestle with the issues facing the church today, in particular the Church Without Walls report, the Team has developed and is in the process of presenting 'a six-month "focus" package'. This will take place in Scone from October 2001 to March 2002. So great was the interest that it was fully booked within ten days of publicity going out. The Team has no doubt that there is a real desire for support in responding appropriately to the challenges facing the church today. The 'focus' will feature the major themes of Spiritual Journey, Discipleship, Ministry of the Whole People, Partnerships, Alternative Models of the Church and Eldership. It is pleasing to note the extent of co-operation and partnership that this initiative has generated with significant contribution being made by staff from Parish Education, Stewardship and Finance, the Scottish Churches Open College and others in the preparation and delivery of the materials.

3.3.4.2 Responses received to date have been overwhelmingly favourable and plans are afoot to present broadly the same in other places and according to the following timetable:

Edinburgh	—	September 2002 – March 2003
Newton Stewart	—	September 2002 – March 2003
Inverness	—	April 2003 – November 2003
Aberdeen	—	April 2003 – November 2003
Glasgow	—	January 2004 – June 2004

3.3.4.3 A number of booklets have also been produced designed to help ministers, elders and other office-bearers and church members to consider the issues arising and so come up with **their own particular strategy** for church development and effective outreach.

3.3.4.4 Furthermore, after consultation the Team is preparing with the assistance of Pathway Productions, to produce a video summarising the main themes referred to earlier. It will contain discussion material for Kirk Sessions and its distribution and usage will help raise the prominence of mission and evangelism as part of the Church's agenda over the next few years.

3.3.4.5 The Team of Advisers report: 'We ascertain that **each situation is absolutely unique**. All of these resources are simply starting points which come with the offer of one of the Team to journey with your congregation for a while if you think that would be helpful. **However the new life is breaking through "bottom-up" and not "top-down".** One of our most important jobs in these days has been – spreading the good news, letting others know about some of the really good things that are happening where God is using **ordinary people to achieve extraordinary things** as they discover how to be A Church Without Walls.'

3.3.4.6 The Team has been developing more effective links with other mission agencies and organisations. One of the most rewarding has been with "Springboard" – the Archbishops' Initiative to encourage, renew and mobilise the Church of England for evangelism. The Director of Springboard (Martin Cavender) has now helped the Team set up the first course of its kind in Scotland and the content relates well to the process of reflection arising from the Special Commission's Report "A Church Without Walls". The first presentation of "Leading Your Church into Growth" will be held in September 2002. Depending on the success of the initial conference the intention is to make this available on a regular basis in different parts of the country.

3.3.4.7 In their work with very different congregations all over the country the Team has picked up important changes which congregations must be aware of for their own work in outreach and evangelism. Some of the key themes were very helpfully summarised by Robert Warren (one of the Springboard team in the Church of England and well-known author and conference speaker) as outlined below:

From Event to Process. This is the biggest shift emerging out of the decade of evangelism. It is a movement in the normal context of evangelism - from a single event to one of "accompanying people on the journey of faith", as in the widespread use of courses like Emmaus and Alpha, or similar.

From Speaking to Listening. Whereas the starting point has often been simply that of "telling the Good News", greater prominence is now given to the context in which we operate, so as to discern what God is calling the church to do and say.

From Doctrine to Spirituality. There is less emphasis on framing in a set of propositions the truth about God, more on encounter with and experience with God in Jesus Christ. At that point there then follows exploration of what Christians believe, so as to make sense of the experience of God.

From Bolt-on to Bloodstream. Outreach activities added to the over-active life of a church may increase its problems rather than enlarge its numbers. Instead, where a church is a living, engaging community of faith, others are drawn to it and to Christ who is at the centre of such communities. Healthy evangelism functions in the context of a church which is itself good news.

From Life-changing to Life-enhancing. In today's culture "spirituality" focuses on the mentality "What's in it for me?" But the gospel has traditionally been seen as a call to obedience, self-sacrifice and service. How can we start from the self and show that self finds fulfilment in self-giving love to the Other and to others? What is our Gospel in this context?

From Authority to Authenticity. The Gospel has often been proclaimed on the basis of an appeal to a higher authority. For example, "The Bible says..."

But today what commends the gospel to our culture are the lives of people who believe and live by the values of the Good News embodied in Christ. This is about "walking the walk as well as talking the talk".

3.3.4.8 The team reports: 'Our sense is that God's Spirit is truly moving in our land – the Spirit of renewal and upheaval. Local congregations are beginning to discover once again that at the heart of reformation and renewal is – not the minister, not tradition, not impressive church buildings, not Presbyterianism - but ordinary people like you and me responsive to God's calling in our own unique way in our own area.'

3.3.4.9 The team bade farewell in September 2001 to Paul Beautyman, who departed to begin a course of post graduate study at Strathclyde University. As Missions Co-ordinator Paul put a tremendous amount of energy and enthusiasm into his work – recruiting and leading mission teams, encouraging Youth workers, developing Schools' missions and new initiatives, such as Sports missions. It was not just fellow "Impact" workers who held him in the highest regard for his commitment to and inventiveness in this post, but many others too.

3.3.5 Responding to Change ... in Projects in Evangelism
3.3.5.1 The Rev Jim Stewart, parish minister at Perth: Letham St Mark's, was approved as part time evangelist by the General Assembly of 2001. A support group is in place and meets regularly for the purposes of reflection and review. Mr Stewart reports:

'Over the past 12 months I have worked 46 days as the part-time evangelist. The areas covered have been from Troon to New Deer with a rich diversity of different people being exposed to the Gospel of Christ. The challenge always is to make Christ real, relevant and relishing to the people I meet. It has been a very great challenge and privilege to see people make that step of faith and commitment and then subsequently grow into a local church. This is a very exciting position to have and one that should be considered as stepping stone to more part-time evangelists within the Church of Scotland.'

3.3.5.2 The Committee continues to monitor this exciting development and a number of issues are already beginning to emerge that may change the shape and focus of this ministry over the next few years.

3.3.5.3 Moreover, the Committee played a part in facilitating a visit by many Scottish church leaders involved in evangelism to the Billy Graham Training Centre in North Carolina. This took place from 22nd -30th April 2002 and had as its purpose allowing participants to focus directly on the ministry of evangelism through prayer, listening, interaction, worship, and planning and developing strategy for the years ahead. The Committee will report further on what emerged in due course.

3.3.5.4 One of the priorities of the Committee is the development of Youth Mission. In 2001 two High School projects were organised and ran very successfully in Penicuik and Burntisland. During the summer hundreds of young people served in Impact teams in many locations country-wide. In partnership with local churches the venues included Kirkcudbright and Colvend to the south and Blairgowrie, Boat of Garten, Mearns Coastal and Arbroath further north. A positive sign emerging in the development of this youth ministry were the instances in 2001 of local churches that had previously hosted Impact teams assuming the major responsibility themselves for recruiting, resourcing and programming their own summer projects.

3.3.5.5 As successor to Paul Beautyman the Committee welcomed in January 2002 Philip Wray. He was formerly a teacher and worked latterly as Project Development Woker with the West London YMCA.

3.3.5.6 The Committee has been experimenting with the development of a web-site. It is recognised that professionally designed and regularly updated it could prove to be a very useful tool in supporting, informing and resourcing congregations and parishes preparing to engage in new initiatives in mission and evangelism.

3.3.5.7 In recent times the Committee has contemplated how best to fulfil and develop its remit, and this process is set to continue for a time. Its Convener notes:

'The work of the Committee goes on and there has been of late a renewed sense of enthusiasm. There are interesting and exciting projects in the pipeline, we hear of many good news stories from congregations and groups across the length and breadth of Scotland. We have had the privilege of sharing in some of those stories ourselves and we look to the future challenges with faith and enthusiasm.'

3.3.6 Responding to Change ... The Rural Committee

3.3.6.1 The Rural Committee, as part of its remit within the Board, endeavours to be aware of developments in rural Scottish life, to discover and share models of good practice in mission and evangelism in rural Scotland, and to develop new initiatives in supporting rural parishes in their life and outreach. It communicates principally through its newsletter, The Rural Spirit, that is produced and distributed on a regular basis.

3.3.6.2 Sadly this past year has seen a further downturn in rural life with the Foot and Mouth crisis affecting many livelihoods. This not only affected our common thinking in relation to agriculture and crofting but had great implications for tourism and forestry and rural life in general across the land. Only a few agricultural shows were held in 2002. The largest - The Royal Highland Show - was a casualty, but the Committee intends to be represented at it in 2002. The Committee, however, was able to lend advice and support to the local Presbyteries jointly in attendance at the Dumfries Show, and the presence of the Church as a mark of solidarity with the community of the South West at a difficult and fraught time was noted and appreciated.

3.3.6.3 The Committee has established in recent time a theology group to explore the application of the Biblical concept of Year of Jubilee and the Sabbatical Year to modern fishing and agricultural practice which will be a means of feeding into the new and ongoing debate regarding food production in Scotland.

3.3.6.4 Consultation has been – and will be for time to come – a feature of the way in which the Committee has

been operating. It launched as a pilot project in the Presbytery of Abernethy a consultation with rural churches and similar ventures are likely to follow in the light of this promising beginning.

3.3.6.5 As part of its role in supporting congregations serving rural parishes the Committee is now well advanced in its plans for a Rural Church Conference on 1st – 2nd November 2002 at Tulliallan Police College. Delegates will be drawn from rural Presbyteries and will be able to contribute from their experience to the emerging emphases of the Committee and help shape its future policy. The keynote address at the Conference will be given by a prominent member of the Scottish Parliament, Ross Finnie MSP.

3.3.6.6 Reference is made elsewhere in the Report to the appointment of a Rural Adviser and the Committee has engaged fully in the deliberations on longer term support to Rural communities still affected by the consequences of Foot and Mouth Disease. In those discussions the Committee has emphasised that the rural economy is larger than the traditional 'farming, fishing and forestry' and urged recognition of leisure and tourism as significant sectors properly to be taken into account.

3.3.7 Responding to Change ... The Urban Priority Areas

3.3.7.1 The pace of change within the inner city communities and peripheral housing schemes continues. While there are some indications that the quality of life for some of Scotland's most vulnerable groups is improving, for many, life remains intolerable. Over 30% of children in Scotland are still growing up in poverty, and government policy continues to over emphasise physical regeneration and on reducing the levels of unemployment as the key mechanisms for lifting communities out of poverty.

3.3.7.2 Over 110 representatives from UPA congregations met at Carberry Tower for their National UPA Consultation in November. This is a bi-annual consultation, which this year was responsible for helping to draft the Board of National Mission's report on UPAs

– Sharing the Pain, Holding the Hope. The UPA Committee have been fully involved over the last three years in the preparation of this report, which it commends to the prayers and urgent attention of the whole Church. The crisis, which many in the wider Church are now acknowledging, has been present within UPAs for a number of years. Without a major realignment of priorities and resources many UPA congregations will die.

3.3.7.3 Two of the participants at the National UPA Consultation were the Moderator of the General Assembly, the Rt Rev John D. Miller and his wife Mary. During his year in office, the Moderator and his wife have spent seven weekends in some of Scotland's most vulnerable communities, meeting with local people from the churches and wider community. These weekends have done a great deal to affirm people and the UPA Committee is immensely grateful to the Moderator and Mrs Miller for making these visits a priority within such a busy year.

3.3.7.4 Congregations in Scotland's housing schemes and in its run-down inner cities often sense that they have more in common with poor congregations in the rest of the world than they do with their rich neighbours in this country. In the past, however, there have been relatively few opportunities for dialogue. Through the Board of World Mission this situation is now changing. In May 2002 representatives from the Boards of World Mission and National Mission held a one-day gathering to consider how links could be strengthened. A Faithshare visit to the Evangelical Church of the Czech Brethren is already planned for later in the year.

3.3.8 Responding to Change ... The Why Believe? Committee
3.3.8.1 Why do we believe, not only that God exists, but that he has made himself known in Jesus Christ? Why do we believe that he takes away the sins of the world, and restores us to fellowship with him forever? Why do we believe that this faith gives purpose to human life and is the basis of goodness, beauty and morality? It is the task of the 'Why Believe?' committee to help Church members to be confident of the answers to these questions

so that they can be strengthened in their own faith and bear witness to Christ in an often spiritual yet sceptical society. It is in these modern times a daunting task, yet the Committee has set about it with imagination and enthusiasm.

3.3.8.2 The Committee is currently engaged in setting up a Web site engaging with the many questions a sceptical public frequently asks. Under the heading 'Agnostics Anonymous', this can be accessed at http://www.srtp.org.uk/aa.htm. There are plans to make available in tape or CD format longer versions of the short Web site articles that are supplied by way of response to enquirers. This will form in time 'Facing the Issues 2', the next part of an apologetics resource that was produced by the Committee a few years ago.

3.3.8.3 The Committee approved the establishment of a response team to be on the alert for articles or items in the press suitable for further comment or observation. Members report as individuals and it is clear that the responses that are submitted do not carry the authority of the Committee. There is an attempt made, too, to be pro-active and the response team has provided articles for the press especially prior to the main Christian festivals of the year. So far several letters and articles have been published.

3.3.8.4 The Committee was represented at the Evangelical Alliance Assembly in Cardiff in early November 2001. It provided much stimulation under the banner 'Reasons for Hope'.

3.3.9 Responding to Change ... The Netherbow
3.3.9.1 In 2001 The Netherbow brought together the work of the Church's cultural centre and the mission of every Scottish parish in a new training and resource package. Art of the Parish is issued in sections and during the year three parts were released: Enabling Worship, Shaping Stories and The Christian Year.

3.3.9.2 Storytelling was the major programme theme in 2001 with over 10,000 people participating in the Scottish International Storytelling Festival and approximately 200,000 people in storytelling sessions and events across Scotland. Sixty of these events took place on the First National Tell-A-Story Day organised by The Netherbow on Friday, 26th October. This included programmes in a cave, a barge, prison, in a children's hospice, on radio and on television. Also in 2001 the StoryMakers project supported by The Scottish Arts Council piloted new ways of affirming children as the makers and tellers of stories.

3.3.9.3   Drama also played its part with the Puppet Animation Festival, Common Force Community Theatre's revival of The Guid Sisters and the first Saltire Society Season of Theatre, all at the Centre. Wee Stories Theatre for Children's Treasure Island proved a Festival highlight. Out and about, The Netherbow staged a dramatic commemoration of Alexander Men, the Russian martyr and a street nativity "Crib in a Pram" at Braehead Shopping Centre. The visual arts, too, were consistently in demand with a stream of small scale exhibitions at the Centre and an increasing use of visual creativity across Church and community.

3.3.9.4   Perhaps, however, 2001 was as significant for what was planned as for what was achieved. Agreement was reached with The Scottish Storytelling Forum and The Scottish Arts Council for future development of The Netherbow as The Scottish Storytelling Centre, heralding a new identity and role for a new century. In addition, the first substantial grants were received towards the plan, approved in principle by the General Assembly of 2000, for physical expansion and development of the Centre around the needs of children, schools, families and older people. Much fund raising remains to be done but an encouraging start has been made.

3.3.9.5   In 2001, The Netherbow also played its full part as an ambassador in the wider world of Scottish culture. The Director, Dr Donald Smith, chaired the Independent Working Group on the Scottish National Theatre which reported in May, and was elected chair of the Literature Forum for Scotland. On 2nd October 2001, Allan Wilson MSP, the Scottish Executive's Minister for Culture, launched a book by the Director, Storytelling Scotland: A Nation in Narrative at the Royal Scottish Museum.

3.3.10   Responding to Change ... The Well
3.3.10.1   The Well is the Asian Information and Advice Centre run by the Presbytery of Glasgow, with Catriona Milligan deployed by the Board as one of the two full-time community workers based there. The other is Sardar Hassan Ghauri from the Diocese of Peshawar in Pakistan, co-sponsored by the Church Mission Society and the Presbytery of Glasgow.

3.3.10.2   It is fair to say that to many people in Scotland the context in which The Well exists may seem remote from their own experience. However, the events of 11th September 2001 and the collapse of the twin towers of the World Trade Centre highlighted anew the reality of the multi-faith context in which we live, whether that be as a neighbourhood or as a nation.

3.3.10.3   The attacks on that day had a profound effect on the people served by The Well. In the days immediately afterwards The Well was very quiet as people gathered round televisions watching how the events would impact on Pakistan. Many people reported being verbally abused. It was a very tense few weeks but punctuated with acts of kindness by people keen to build links at a time of division. Some women from a local church handed in flowers with a message of support for their Asian neighbours and a Muslim customer made a point of coming to sit and grieve with Ghauri when the news broke of the Christians murdered while attending worship in Pakistan. That The Well was already well-established meant that Christians and Muslims living locally did not need to start from scratch to communicate with one another.

3.3.10.4   In 2001 approximately 5000 people visited The Well. Many of those were refugees housed in emergency accommodation nearby. In November The Well Management Committee held a vision-building morning to discern whether to extend the focus of the Centre to include refugees or to continue it concentration on the settled Asian communities. The outcome of those deliberations was to maintain the present emphasis but to welcome refugees as they presented themselves at the Centre requesting help and assistance. At present there is a strong feeling to nurture and maintain those relationships that have been developed over many years.

Catriona Milligan highlights the challenge in evaluating any activity undertaken at The Well on the basis of whether or not it builds relationships. 'We try to offer as professional an advice service as possible but if it doesn't allow people to meet and build relationships then we are no different from any other advice centre.'

3.3.10.5 In publicity material produced by the Board the following comment is made: 'A missionary church travels across boundaries to people we may not know, people we may not understand, people we may not like, because God knows them, God understands them, God loves them'. The prayer of the staff and volunteers at The Well is that the Centre and its neighbours are able to make that journey together, and can help others to do the same wherever they are.

3.3.11 Project Rejoice!
3.3.11.1 Closely associated with the work of the Committee on Mission and Evangelism Resources, but responsible directly to the Board through an ecumenical committee is "Project Rejoice!"

3.3.11.2 The Convener of the Committee, Mrs Fiona Campbell, reports:

"2001 has been a challenging year for Rejoice. However, good ideas, themes and artwork can only be transformed into mission resources with the help of IT and print professions, and when difficulties arose in these areas this year, Rejoice customers experienced delays and disappointment. For that we are truly sorry, and thank our customers for their patience.

To balance this, everyone who has seen the Rejoice CD-ROM has been enthusiastic about its use, and already 258 are in circulation, fulfilling Rejoice's stated aim, to not simply provide churches with mission resources, but to stimulate and encourage local creativity. As local skill increases we hope to work ourselves out of a job!

The Rejoice CD-ROM does this by providing "raw materials" of text and image, which anyone can reformat to suit local needs.

Partnership has always been high on Rejoice's agenda, and for a 2001/2 – as the first part of our 3-year *Celebrate Life!* Programme – we have worked together with the Board of Parish Education on *Year of the Child*. Over the summer of 2001, artwork was submitted from Holiday Clubs and from this, four designs by children were selected for Christmas, Easter and Pentecost resources. Building upon this, our planning for 2002/3 focuses on the 16-30 age group, and we are unrolling an artwork competition through School Chaplaincy, Art magazines and web-sites. By engaging in this kind of process we hope to bring the spiritual insights of young people to the eye and mind of the wider church ... which may prove to be a challenging experience, not just for Rejoice, but for us all!

Our greatest challenge continues to be the physical distribution of our materials. Rejoice has joined forces with the Boards of Social Responsibility, World Mission and Parish Education, and with The Guild to provide 'retail opportunities' in selected towns in the month of October. However, we are keen to reach more parts of the country with our resources and would welcome the involvement of local church or Presbytery offices where materials could be displayed and shared orders received and distributed."

3.4 Responding to change …. In Chaplaincies.
The Committee meets three times per year and provides a point of contact at which the Conveners and some Committee members of the three Sub-Committees may meet to exchange views and collaborate on areas of mutual interest. As well as this, the Committee is examining its remit and the role of the Chaplain within his or her organisation (University, Hospital, Prison or Industry) which may be largely secular in nature. A major conference on Chaplaincies is being planned for the spring of 2003. This would also include chaplaincies in the Armed Forces and Schools and would seek to support chaplains and address issues which these specialised ministries are facing.

3.4.1   Universities

3.4.1.1   At their annual conference there was a full attendance of whole time university chaplains who greatly appreciate the opportunity provided by the Board for meeting, thinking and sharing which the conference provides. Led by the Sub-Committee Convener, participants reflected together on the priorities of their ministry to students and staff - the pastoral, the prophetic and the apologetic. With the help of two of their number who are studying in their spare time for MBA degrees, they considered how best to plan and organise their work and the 'tools' available to assist them. After a talk on 'Support for Chaplaincy' given by Chris Levison who has worked as both a university and hospital chaplain, there followed a fruitful discussion of the necessity of personal support in ministry and of the relative advantages and disadvantages of different ways of obtaining it. The Sub-Committee at their request has agreed to ask that Universities not already doing so should fund the provision of regular personal supervision for full-time University Chaplains.

3.4.1.2   The university chaplains are a most talented and committed group of people serving in some of the key academic institutions across Scotland. The church has good reason to be proud of them.

3.4.2   In Hospitals and Health Care

3.4.2.1   Chaplaincy in a Changing Health Service
The NHS is an arena in which one encounters both the best and the worst of human experience. Healthcare chaplains and their colleagues work close to the making and breaking of life; they are exposed to the reality of suffering and death as few of their contemporaries are; they also share in the exhilarating pleasure and satisfaction felt when patients, responding well to the sophisticated treatments and superb care which are widely available in today's health services, return to their homes and their normal routines renewed in body, mind and spirit.

3.4.2.2   Every working day chaplains minister to the sick, injured, disabled and dying of many faiths and none; to their closest relatives and friends; and to the staff who care for them. Serving in hospital and primary care NHS Trusts, they are expected to support, from cradle to grave, those whose illness or injury requires admission to a hospital bed or sustained care in the community. They will meet patients who have suffered sudden catastrophic collapse or prolonged degenerative illness; they will be asked to comfort relatives in circumstances of unspeakable anxiety, numbing grief and agonising self-doubt; they will work alongside staff at all levels, who in circumstances which may be less than ideal and which are continually changing, carry responsibility for the future health, wellbeing, and sometimes indeed the very survival of those entrusted to their care.

3.4.2.3   Healthcare chaplaincy is one of the most difficult and demanding of ministries: it is also one of the most rewarding. Chaplains, perhaps more frequently than most, 'rejoice with those who rejoice and weep with those who weep'. Almost always they work in secular settings, 'outside the camp'. It is a 'Kingdom' ministry rather than an ecclesiastical one. It is exercised in settings in which the immediacy and grace of God's presence and rule in His world are witnessed, identified and embodied both in the lives of patients and the skill and care of staff. The life, teaching and compassionate example of Jesus who devoted himself to relieve the suffering of others yet was ready to suffer himself is inspirationally relevant to everyday situations in the NHS. The presence of chaplains is generally widely welcomed but, if they are to survive and flourish, they must reach deep into the well of their personal and professional resources and must be able to call upon the friendship, understanding, encouragement and goodwill of the whole church.

3.4.2.4   A Most Significant Year
The past year has been a most significant one for NHS chaplaincy in Scotland. The need for spiritual and religious care has been recognised by the Scottish Executive Health Department in a number of important ways:-

1.   Continued funding of health care chaplaincy through NHS Boards and Trusts.
2.   The establishment of a 'Spirituality in the NHS' Steering Group on which faith communities and chaplaincy professional associations are represented.

3. The establishment of a Working Party charged with the task of revising Trust guidelines for the provision of chaplaincy and spiritual care.

4. The creation and funding for a minimum of three years of the post of Whole-time Healthcare Chaplaincy Training and Development Officer for Scotland.

5. The creation of the Healthcare Chaplaincy Training and Development Group whose purpose, having put in hand the appointment of the whole time Training Officer, is to offer supervision and support to the appointee, to arrange the necessary facilities and with the Officer to promote training and development initiatives in religious and spiritual care in the NHS in Scotland.

6. The appointment of the Rev Christopher Levison, Chaplain to the Victoria Infirmary in Glasgow to the post of Whole-time Healthcare Chaplaincy Training and Development Officer from 8th October 2001 for three years.

7. A conference held in Stirling in November on the theme 'Spirituality in Health and Community Care'.

8. A further two-year appointment of an Assistant Co-ordinator working with Mr Levison to advise Boards and Trusts as they develop and implement a strategy for the provision of spiritual and religious care.

The Convener of the Hospitals, Healthcare and Universities Sub-Committee and the Chaplaincies Administrator have been and still are fully involved in these initiatives, as are representatives of chaplaincy and the faith communities in Scotland.

3.4.2.5 The Work of the Sub-Committee

It is in this positive climate that the Sub-Committee continues to discharge its responsibilities for the recruitment, employment, support and review of chaplains and for the promotion of healthcare chaplaincy. In this, the Sub-Committee acknowledges the contribution of chaplains themselves, their professional associations - The Scottish Association of Chaplains in Healthcare, The College of Health Care Chaplains (Scotland Branch) and the Association of Hospice Chaplains (Scottish Branch), all three of which have representatives in attendance at the Sub-Committee - and

the remarkable Journal of Healthcare Chaplaincy, now in its fourth year.

Issues which have exercised the Sub-Committee in the past year include:-

(a) **Whole-time Personnel**
In December 2001 the Rev John Banks, Chaplain, Ailsa Hospital, Ayr and Chaplaincy Co-ordinator for Ayrshire and Arran Primary Care NHS Trust retired after 13 years' outstanding service in the development of mental health chaplaincy.

Rev Elizabeth Crumlish resigned from her post in Inverclyde Royal Hospital, Greenock in February 2002 to move to Parish Ministry. During her five years' service she achieved eminent success in developing the new whole-time chaplaincy service and raising its profile within the hospital community.

The Sub-Committee has been pleased to welcome the following new Chaplains and Chaplains' Assistants during the last 12 months:

Chaplain's Name	Location
Rev Alister Bull	Yorkhill NHS Trust
Rev Hilda Smith°	Yorkhill NHS Trust
Rev Patricia McDonald°	North Glasgow University Hospitals NHS Trust
Rev David Gordon	Tayside University Hospitals NHS Trust
Rev Carrie Upton°	Lothian University Hospitals NHS Trust
Rev Lorna Murray	Lothian Primary Care NHS Trust
Rev Iain Whyte° (50% whole-time equivalent)	Lothian Primary Care NHS Trust
Rev Patricia Allen° (50% whole-time equivalent)	Lothian Primary Care NHS Trust
Rev Sheila Mitchell	Ayrshire and Arran Primary Care NHS Trust
Rev Iain Reid	South Glasgow University Hospitals NHS Trust (three-year appointment)

°New post

(b) **Bi-ennial Reviews**

The Sub-Committee has carried out evaluation and assessment of whole-time appointments for more than 10 years. These are now undertaken bi-ennially and involve members of the Sub-Committee and appropriate NHS staff. Recently where chaplaincy teams are in place reviews have been held on a team basis with provision for individual consultation.

In its desire to ensure that the review system is effective and valued by chaplains and NHS Trusts the review process was itself reviewed by a small Working Party. Recommendations were submitted towards the end of last year and the following description summarises the revised system adopted.

(i) In preparation for each review proforma reports will be completed by chaplains and NHS Trust staff members.

(ii) Reviews will continue bi-ennially but on an individual basis. A separate informal discussion with the Chaplaincy Team can take place as relevant. Channels of communication are to remain open to pick up and deal with important issues between the reviews.

It is hoped that this revised system will prove to be more supportive of chaplains and promote the service they deliver. The participation of Trust Officers is vital in this process.

(c) **Part-time Healthcare Chaplains' Age Restriction**

Consideration has been given to an age restriction for part-time Healthcare Chaplains and details are contained in Section 2.7 of the Report.

(d) **Off Duty Cover**

Adequate off duty cover arrangements are a matter of concern for all single handed whole time chaplains and the Sub-Committee has been encouraging Trusts to ensure that all chaplains are able to take uninterrupted time off and that cover is provided for holidays, sick leave, study leave and weekly time off. Regrettably, this has not always been possible, mainly because of the budgetary constraints which inevitably restrict the pace of expansion and require the setting of priorities.

(e) **Study Leave**

Six whole time chaplains have been granted study leave with the approval of their Trusts and have used the time to develop their knowledge and understanding of a significant range of topics closely related to their work e.g. bereavement support for families facing loss in pregnancy, neo-natal and childhood death; recognition, assessment and primary management of individuals following exposure to traumatic events; community mental health chaplaincy; PhD research into chaplains supporting families following perinatal death; MA. studies in healthcare chaplaincy. Since a report is required, the whole chaplaincy enterprise stands to benefit from these studies.

3.4.2.6 In Conclusion

3.4.2.6.1 The Working Party Report referred to in item 3.4.2.4 above and the guidelines for Trusts which are expected to be issued early this year may well have important implications for the Church of Scotland Board of National Mission, for Presbyteries and for faith communities with an interest in religious and spiritual care in the NHS. They are likely to impinge on arrangements for the recruitment and employment of chaplains and on the range of responsibilities of the Sub-Committee. Although not known at the time of writing, they will probably be known by the time the Assembly meets. One thing is clear - that the tide is flowing in favour of chaplaincy and spiritual care in the NHS and that all the faith communities and chaplains themselves must be ready to respond imaginatively and co-operatively to the initiatives currently under way. The spiritual health of our nation and the wellbeing of vulnerable patients, devoted carers and committed staff across the NHS depend upon it.

3.4.3 In Prisons

3.4.3.1 Chaplaincy Contract with the Scottish Prison Service (SPS)

Full details of the discussions taking place with the Scottish Prison Service concerning a Contract for the provision of Chaplaincy are given in Section 2.8 of the Report.

3.4.3.2 Communication with and support of part time chaplains

3.4.3.2.1 The Sub-Committee recognises that maintaining effective communication with chaplains is very important. Two-way channels must remain open to facilitate exchange of information and to establish meaningful support systems as required. Examples of this are the visits to prisons described above and the organising of bi-ennial conferences, at modest cost, the first of which was held in March last year. The Very Rev Dr Andrew McLellan gave an uplifting and encouraging address reflecting on aspects of prisons and prison ministry following his Moderatorial tour of Scottish Prisons. Chaplains were given the opportunity to discuss the proposed developments in chaplaincy. They expressed concerns about industrial relations in the SPS and also recommended closer working relationships amongst the Church authorities involved in chaplaincy.

3.4.3.2.2 The Sub-Committee has taken steps to form a small support group which will work with the Prison Chaplaincy Contract Co-ordinator to provide appropriate pastoral care for chaplains. It is planned that this will become fully effective with the implementation of the "Contract."

3.4.3.3 Throughcare for prisoners and ex-offenders

3.4.3.3.1 In recent years the SPS has taken significant initiatives in the provision of "Throughcare" which can be briefly described as the care of prisoners leading to their effective rehabilitation in society following their release from custody. It requires prisoners to address their offending behaviour and for many it is the first step towards breaking the revolving door of offending – custody – release and re-offending. It is no easy task and the Sub-Committee became aware that a small number of congregations, independently, were offering an after care service within their own local areas.

3.4.3.3.2 In an attempt to build up an overview of existing care, to raise awareness within the Church and to encourage more congregations towards positive action a Day Consultation on Throughcare was held in the Orbiston Neighbourhood Centre in October 2001.

Representatives from the SPS, faith communities and other agencies already providing throughcare were invited. The key note address was given by the Moderator of the General Assembly, the Right Rev Dr John Miller. He observed that "a real resource is provided by the prison end of the religious structure, but that resource is not drawn upon back in ordinary community life."

3.4.3.3.3 Following workshop discussions and a plenary session a steering group was formed with an extensive remit which included the question of how to stimulate positive action by the churches through partnership, networking and co-ordination. The report of the consultation was circulated to all congregations in January 2002 and the steering group is meeting regularly and making plans for development of this challenging and important work.

3.4.3.4 Behind Closed Doors

These past twelve months have witnessed periods of frenetic activity in the development of prison chaplaincy. At the same time the ongoing service in Scotland's prisons has been faithfully maintained by dedicated teams of chaplains. It is right and proper that this hidden work "behind closed doors" is given the recognition it deserves within this report. To all of you – thank you!

3.4.4 In the world of work.

The Board supports the work of Scottish Churches Industrial Mission through the appointment of 5 whole-time Industrial Mission Organisers and through administrative support. A full report of the work of Scottish Churches Industrial Mission is contained in Appendix VII.

3.5 Responding to Change … in specific areas

3.5.1 Residential Centres Executive

3.5.1.1 St Ninian's Centre, Crieff:

3.5.1.1.1 Decisions of the 2001 General Assembly led to the closure of St Ninian's Centre, Crieff, and the last guests were received at the centre on 9th August 2001.

3.5.1.1.2 At its meeting on 6th June 2001 the Board unanimously agreed to:

"(a) Recognise the service of Rev Dr Adrian Varwell, Miss Pauline Greenaway, and all staff, especially for their commitment to the centre during the recent years of uncertainty.

(b) Welcome the Deliverance of the 2001 General Assembly in these terms:

"Give thanks for all who have worked at St Ninian's during the last 43 years for the magnificent work they have accomplished for the Lord, and acknowledge the great debt the Church has to the visionary men and women who have enriched the Church through the witness of St Ninian's."

3.5.1.1.3 The Board places on record its deep appreciation to Mr George B.B. Eadie, Personnel Manager, and all staff of the Personnel Department for the care and sensitivity shown to staff of the centre and officers of the Board during the extended period of uncertainty and at the time of closure. All former staff have been supported as a new chapter in life beyond service in St Ninian's has been opened and the role of the Personnel Department in this transition has been deeply appreciated.

3.5.1.1.4 The Board is now in the process of disposing of the properties of the St Ninian's Centre according to the instruction of the 2001 General Assembly.

3.5.1.2 Badenoch Christian Centre, Kincraig

3.5.1.2.1 2001 was an encouraging year at the Badenoch Christian Centre, Kincraig, with occupancy levels the highest since 1992 and finances reflecting the positives level of use.

3.5.1.2.2 Open now for some 25 years, the Centre is a self-catering facility which can accommodate up to 36 people in comfortable bunk rooms of 2 to 4 people. There is also a self-contained family suite which can accommodate 4 to 6 people.

3.5.1.2.3 It provides a resource for congregations and groups and enquiries about bookings should be directed to Mrs Di Lamb (Tel 01540 651373).

3.5.2 Refugees:

3.5.2.1 The 2001 General Assembly approved the following section of Deliverance on the Report of the Committee on Church and Nation:

"Commend the many congregations who have worked so hard to make refugees welcome in Scotland and remit the matter of financing to the Board of National Mission for consideration."

3.5.2.2 As an immediate response to this request the Board awarded a grant of £2,000 from Special Mission Trusts to the "Glasgow – The Caring City" project.

3.5.2.3 The Convener and General Secretary then met with Rev Neil Galbraith, Minister of Glasgow: Cathcart Old, who is deeply involved in "Glasgow – The Caring City" project and at the meeting of the Board in September 2001 further consideration was given to the request.

3.5.2.4 In the light of the conversation with Mr Galbraith the Board agreed:

(a) To invite the Committee on Church and Nation to support Mr Galbraith in opening "the doors of the Scottish Executive and Glasgow City Council".

(b) That a welcome be given to discussions taking place within the Presbytery of Glasgow in meeting the needs of refugees arriving in the city.

(c) That the Presbytery of Glasgow be invited to keep the Board informed about the developing situation.

(d) That conversations take place at an early date with representatives of the Board of Social Responsibility concerning the situation.

3.5.2.5 The conversations referred to in (d) have taken place and both Boards affirm a willingness to develop their support for work among refugees within the present constraints of staffing and finance.

3.5.3 Scottish Mission Studies Centre:

3.5.3.1 At the 2001 General Assembly the Board

reported on discussions which had taken place concerning the establishment of the Scottish Mission Studies Centre with the following remit:

— To enable the Board of National Mission to fulfil its Vision Statement
— To assist the Board in auditing and evaluating its work
— To be aware of current missional theology at home and abroad
— To be abreast of new models of mission
— To encourage the interchange of ideas and action.

3.5.3.2 The 2001 General Assembly noted the initiative and the Board has progressed its thinking. A day conference was arranged at which further thought was given to the structure and staffing of the project as well as consultation with representatives of Scottish Divinity Faculties and other Boards and Committees.

3.5.3.3 At its meeting on 5th December 2001 the Board resolved to finance the project and to establish a steering group. At the time of writing the steering group was being established and it is hoped that the first Director of the Scottish Mission Studies Project will be appointed in 2002.

3.5.4 Communication:
3.5.4.1 As can be seen from the detail of this Board Report, the committees and staff of National Mission have engaged in a dynamic way with the exciting process of change moving through the Church. If *they* are **Responding to Change**, then the task of those of us charged with the Board's communication has been to *celebrate* that response and carry the news into the pews and beyond.

3.5.4.2 2001 has seen the unrolling of a Communication Strategy, seeking in its first phase, to ensure not only that our Congregational Link volunteers are well-informed about National Mission's work, but that congregational members receive first-hand news on a regular basis. To involve them in the Church's task of mission, we now produce **Link Update** every second month. A lively

newspaper with topical reports, interviews and staff news, its current circulation is 6,000 and rising. Link Update is a two-way process so every congregation is encouraged to order enough copies to gain a working knowledge of National Mission, and - just as important - to contribute local mission stories.

3.5.4.3 You will see from the Mission and Evangelism Resourcing section of the main report, that stimulating and supporting congregational outreach is an important part of the Board's work. Practical mission resources are produced by the team of Advisers, the UPA and Rural Committees and Project Rejoice! so the Communication team is working on a single comprehensive **Resources Catalogue** to ensure that congregations are aware of the range of what is available. New in 2002 will be a **National Mission Sunday Wizard** with outline ideas and materials.

3.5.4.4 Over the last year the Board has completed a series of Life & Work adverts and the next phase of the Communication Strategy moves the focus to local and national media, to carry news of a dynamic Church in action to the wider population of Scotland. This began in October 2001 with a *Meet the Media* training day for our Congregational Links and interested church members. Participants worked on preparing articles for local press and radio, and met the Church of Scotland Press Officer who outlined her role in relation to the Links' work. Further plans under the working title **Christianity - Spirit of Scotland** are under discussion, and will be followed through by Fiona Campbell (Vice Convener) and the Board's first Communication Officer - Mrs Laura Vermeulen. Appointed in January, Laura's post was newly created to service the developing strategy, and in recognition of the increasingly important need for the Church to tell Scotland what it is doing! National Mission's greatest resource is its people who daily share their faith, and that's a news story that the whole country *needs* to hear.

3.5.5 Staffing:
3.5.5.1 Changes in staffing in the varied areas of the Board's work are contained separately in the Report.

Particular mention is made here however of changes in the administration staff. Three particular changes in 2001 are of note:

— The appointment in March 2001 of Rev Alex M. Millar as Secretary-Depute. Mr Millar brings to this challenging task experience in two parishes including a Church Extension Charge, a period as Clerk of the Presbytery of Perth, and of mission work throughout Scotland.

— The retiral in October 2001 of Mrs Norma Henderson, Secretary-Depute (Parish Staffing). Following Mrs Henderson's decision – which meant she retired on the same day as her husband, John, the Board resolved to reduce the number of Secretaries-Depute from two to one. The continuation of Mrs Henderson's work in parish staffing was ensured by the appointment (and welcome return!) in December 2001 of Rev Dr Frank Bardgett as Parish Staffing Administrator on a one year contract.

— The decision by Mrs Georgina Payne to resign from her post as Congregational Links Administrator to enable her, along with her husband Brian, to undertake service in Africa with the Board of World Mission. The development of the work undertaken by Mrs Payne will be undertaken by Mrs Laura Vermeulen who has been appointed as the Communications Officer of the Board and she began service in January 2002.

3.5.5.2 The Board is deeply appreciative of the service of both retired and serving staff.

3.5.6　Property and Safety:

The Board is committed to the professional management of the properties for which it has responsibility and to the continued development of a Health and Safety Policy and its implementation.

One of the properties that the Board maintains and insures, houses the work of the Glasgow Lodging House Mission in East Campbell Street, Glasgow. The Board affirms the work of the Mission and is currently seeking ways in which to be supportive at a time of development.

APPRECIATION

At the 2002 General Assembly three Vice-Conveners complete their three terms of service:

— Mr Noel Glen completes a term as Vice-Convener of the Committee on Parish Reappraisal. His legal training, attention to detail, warm personality, and ready wit proved of great value to the Committee in many challenging situations. The collection of photograph he has taken and poems he has written following deputation visits will serve as a continual reminder of his sterling contribution.

— Rev T. Stewart McGregor completes a term as Vice-Convener of the Committee on Chaplaincies and Convener of the Sub-Committee on Hospitals, Healthcare and Universities. With many years of experience in hospital chaplaincy, Stewart brought a deep concern for those areas of work and for individual staff. Through his involvements there are have been significant developments in Healthcare Chaplaincy and the whole Church is in his debt for a lifetime of commitment to this frontier area of ministry.

— Mr Jamie Greig completes a term as Vice-Convener of the Committee on Chaplaincies and Convener of the Church and Industry Committee. His understanding of the Scottish Industrial scene, his deep interest for many years in Scottish Churches Industrial Mission, and his gracious manner have all contributed to the way in which his Convenership has strengthened this area of work. During his term he has also continued to serve as the representative of the Board on the Committee on Church and Nation and this way has brought together two vital areas of interest.

In the name of the Board

JAMES M. GIBSON, *Convener*
JOHN C. MATTHEWS, *Vice-Convener*
FIONA M.H. CAMPBELL, *Vice Convener*
DOUGLAS A.O. NICOL, *General Secretary*
ALEX M. MILLAR, *Secretary-Depute*

APPENDIX I

Revisions to the Constitution of the Board of National Mission

In the Constitution of the Board of National Mission as from 31st May 2002:

In Section 2.2(a) delete "aided by the reflection on the deliberations of a regular National Mission Conference"

In Section 5.2 delete "one member of, and appointed by, the Board of Parish Education"

APPENDIX II

Overture anent Appraisal and Adjustment of Charges

The General Assembly adopt the Overture the tenor whereof follows, and transmit the same to Presbyteries for their consideration under the Barrier Act, directing that returns be sent to the Principal Clerk not later than 31 December 2002.

1   Interpretation

For the purposes of this Act the following terms shall be deemed to have the meanings hereby assigned to them:

(a) A "charge" shall mean a sphere of pastoral duty to which a minister is inducted;

(b) A "congregation" shall mean a company of persons associated together in a parish whose names are on the Communion Roll and who are under the pastoral oversight of a minister or ministers and a Kirk Session, for Christian worship, fellowship, instruction, mission and service;

(c) A "Financial Board" shall mean the body responsible for managing the finances of a congregation, e.g. Congregational Board, Deacons' Board, Committee of Management, etc.;

(d) "The Assembly's Committee" shall mean the committee of the Board of National Mission responsible for matters of presbytery planning, adjustment of charges and vacancy issues;

(e) "The Presbytery" shall mean the Presbytery of the bounds of the charge concerned;

(f) A "vacancy" shall mean the state in which a charge finds itself when it is without an inducted minister;

(g) "Basis [of Adjustment]" shall mean the written terms upon which adjustment is implemented.

2   Introduction of the Scheme

(1) All Presbyteries shall within three years of the passing of this Act prepare a Presbytery Plan, as defined in sections 3 to 5 of this Act.

(2) The Assembly's Committee shall consider each Plan and intimate to the Presbytery whether they concur with all or part of the Plan.

(3) The provisions of section 8 of this Act shall apply to charges within Presbyteries, or parts of Presbyteries, in respect of which the Presbytery and Assembly's Committee have agreed that such a plan exists. The provisions of sections 2 to 7 inclusive of Act IV 1984 shall apply to all other Presbyteries, or parts of Presbyteries.

THE PRESBYTERY PLAN

3   Appraisal

(1) The Presbytery shall undertake an annual appraisal of the deployment of all ministries in charges within its bounds, and shall agree a plan which shall narrate in respect of each charge the outcome of the appraisal conducted.

(2) The Presbytery shall submit to the Assembly's Committee by 31 December each year a list of amendments made to the Plan during the year just ending.

(3) Concurrence shall require to be obtained from the

Committee every five years, or whenever the Presbytery alters the plan in such a way as to increase the staff complement or other resources allocated to any charge.

(4) Presbyteries shall provide the Assembly's Committee with extract minutes of all actions taken in terms of this section of this Act.

(5) On receiving intimation of the concurrence or non-concurrence of the Committee, the Presbytery shall intimate the same to all Kirk Sessions within twenty one days.

(6) Any congregation directly involved in or named in any change to the Plan shall be cited to appear for their interests at any meeting of the Presbytery at which a decision is to be made in terms of this Act.

4 Content of the Plan

The plan should include the following information about the Presbytery area as a whole:

(a) The period of time for which the Plan is made should be specified, this period to be not less than ten years and to remain not less than ten years as the plan is updated in each subsequent year:

(b) Indication of the number, nature and pattern of charges and all other appointments which the Presbytery considers necessary at the end of the specified period.

(c) Indication of likely substantial housing or other developments and their effect on the plan.

5 Outcomes of Appraisal Process

In respect of each charge, the plan shall contain one of the following appraisal outcomes:

(a) That no adjustment is foreseen during the lifetime of the plan.

(b) That adjustment in a form specified from amongst those described in section 10 below shall be effected immediately.

(c) That adjustment in a form specified from amongst those described in section 10 below shall be effected when the charge next falls vacant.

(d) That adjustment in a form specified from amongst those described in section 10 below shall be

necessary, but shall not be effected until after the next vacancy: the Presbytery may combine this decision with a decision to seek an Interim Ministry appointment when the charge next falls vacant.

(e) That appraisal, and the determination of any adjustment, shall be deferred until the charge next falls vacant.

6 Appeal against Appraisal Decisions

(1) Upon receiving intimation from a Presbytery of the content of a plan or amendment of an existing plan, any Kirk Session within the bounds may within twenty one days intimate to the Presbytery Clerk its intention to appeal against all or part thereof.

(2) Upon receiving intimation that the Assembly's Committee has concurred or has not concurred with a plan or any part thereof, a Presbytery or any Kirk Session within its bounds may within twenty one days intimate to the Assembly's Committee its intention to seek determination of the matter by the Commission of Assembly, and to any such process the Kirk Session, Presbytery and Committee shall all be parties.

(3) Except where the Presbytery judges that appeal (intimated in terms of subsection (1) above) or a request for determination (intimated in terms of subsection (2) above) requires to be disposed of immediately for the advancement of the whole plan or in the interests of fairness to other congregations, such appeal or request shall be submitted to the Commission of Assembly at the point at which the relevant part of the plan falls to begin to be implemented and after the negotiation of a Basis of Adjustment.

(4) Subsections (1) and (3) above shall apply *mutatis mutandis* to the right of dissent-and-complaint by any member of the Presbytery against a decision of the Presbytery.

7 Implementation of the Plan

The Presbytery shall proceed, as far as possible, to implement a completed or amended plan, subject to the rights of appeal, dissent-and-complaint and determination described in section 6 above. All adjustment effected in implementation of a plan, and any instruments for adjustment and future planning deployed in terms of this Act, shall be intimated to the Assembly's Committee and by them to the relevant Boards and agencies of the General Assembly.

8 Presbytery Plans and the Right to Call a Minister

(1) A vacant charge in respect of which an agreed plan exists may be given permission to elect a minister, subject to the provisions of Act x 2003 Anent Vacancy Procedure, and further provided that

(a) the plan clearly provides that no adjustment is required before a new minister is inducted, or

(b) the adjustment described in the plan has been fully implemented, or

(c) the Presbytery has already negotiated a basis for the adjustment described in the plan and is able to implement it before sustaining a call and there is no outstanding appeal, dissent-and-complaint or request for determination.

(2) A vacant charge shall not be given permission to elect a minister if

(a) a basis of adjustment has not yet been agreed between the Presbytery and the congregation, and/or

(b) there is any outstanding appeal, dissent-and-complaint or request for determination to be heard by the Commission of Assembly, and/or

(c) appraisal requires to be conducted in terms of this Act or Act IV 1984.

9 Suspension of the Implementation of the Plan

On cause shown, and subject to the right of immediate appeal, dissent-and-complaint or determination, the Presbytery or the Assembly's Committee may suspend the implementation of the plan or part thereof. The cause of the suspension shall be resolved among the parties as soon as possible by further appraisal and amendment of the plan.

ADJUSTMENT

10 Forms of Adjustment

The Presbytery plan may specify any of the following forms of adjustment of charges:

(1) *Union*

Two or more congregations may be united to form one congregation, and such union shall involve the union of charges, parishes, Kirk Sessions, Financial Courts, property and funds and, except in special circumstances where provision is made to the contrary in the Basis of Union, all congregational agencies and organisations.

(2) *Linking*

Two or more charges may be linked to form one charge, so that the congregations are served by one ministry, the constitutions of the said congregations being in no other way affected.

(3) *Deferred Union or Deferred Linking*

(a) When for any reason it is not possible to unite a vacant congregation with another congregation under the minister of the other congregation, the Presbytery may decide to unite them on the understanding that the implementation of such decision shall be deferred until that minister's interest has terminated.

(b) The Basis of Deferred Union shall provide (i) that the congregations to be united shall elect a minister who shall be inducted in the first instance as minister of the vacant congregation, and (ii) that on the termination of the other minister's interest the Union shall immediately be effective under the minister so elected and inducted.

(c) If another vacancy occurs in the originally vacant congregation before the termination of the other minister's interest the basis of Deferred Union shall remain in force and the congregations shall elect another minister as in (b) above; subject to the *proviso* that the Presbytery may decide to recall the Basis of

Deferred Union with a view to making another adjustment decision.

(d) A linking may be deferred in the same manner as a union in terms of subsections (a) to (c) above.

(4) *New Charge Development*

A new charge may be established in terms of Act XIII 2000.

(5) *Transportation*

(a) The Presbytery may move a congregation from one place of worship to another, and where that involves a change of parish it shall be designated 'transportation'.

(b) Where transportation is effected, the Presbytery shall take such steps of adjustment as may be necessary to ensure that the parishes involved are allocated to defined charges.

(6) *Parish Groupings*

The Presbytery may declare that two or more charges shall have responsibility for a single area. The Basis of such an adjustment shall determine the extent to which the charges shall operate as a Parish Grouping, for instance in the sharing of worship, personnel, education resources, mission initiatives, congregational organisations etc.

(7) *Dissolution*

(a) A charge may be dissolved by the Presbytery of the bounds.

(b) The Basis of Dissolution shall provide, *inter alia,* for the issuing of certificates of transference to all the members of the congregation, the allocation of the parish to another charge or charges, the destination of the property and funds, and for the transfer to the General Trustees prior to dissolution of any heritable property held by or for behoof of the congregation, title to which is not already vested in the General Trustees.

(8) *Alteration in number of ministers*

The Presbytery may determine, in respect of any charge, the amount of ministerial time required by any charge, and the number and nature of appointments necessary, provided that (except in the case of job-sharing) the Presbytery shall identify one ministry as that of minister of the charge and moderator of the Kirk Session.

(9) *Other Form of Ministry*

After consultation with the Assembly's Committee, the Presbytery may devise a new form of adjustment or ministry, provided that such form is not inconsistent with this Act or any other Act or deliverance of the General Assembly.

11 Agreement to Union or Linking under an Incumbent

(1) When an explicit provision of a Basis of Union or Linking is that the minister of one of the charges involved shall be the minister of the united or linked charge:

(a) no such Basis of Union or Linking shall be published without the written consent of the minister

(b) all congregations involved, at the time when the Basis of Union or Linking is put to the vote in terms of section 13 below, shall be asked to approve separately by secret ballot
 (i) the union or linking of the congregations, and
 (ii) the appointment of the minister to be minister of the united or linked charge:

(c) if any congregation votes against the appointment in terms of (b)(ii) above, the Presbytery shall not approve the Basis of Adjustment, but shall renegotiate a Basis of Deferred Union or Deferred Linking.

(2) In the case of a minister who becomes minister of a united or linked charge in terms of a Basis of Deferred Union or Linking, the united or linked charge shall be regarded as a modification of the charge to which he or she has already been inducted so that no further induction

shall be required; but in all such cases the Presbytery shall conduct a service of introduction.

12 Instruments for Adjustment and Future Planning

(1) (a) The Presbytery may utilise in any charge any of the instruments for future planning described in subsection (2) below, subject to a right of appeal or dissent-and-complaint, which shall be heard by the Commission of Assembly at the point at which the Presbytery's decision would otherwise take effect.

(b) Where the use of such instruments is anticipated, the intentions of the Presbytery shall be narrated in the Presbytery plan but shall not require the concurrence of the Assembly's Committee.

(2) (a) *Reviewable Tenure*

In respect of any charge, the Presbytery may decide that its next minister shall be inducted on condition that the Presbytery may terminate the tenure of the minister at any time and for any reason which may seem good to the Presbytery, on terms specified in the Basis of Adjustment. On the date of termination the minister shall be deemed to have demitted his or her charge.

The minister shall be free to seek to demit or be translated as in the ordinary case of any minister inducted to a charge, provided that, if the reviewable tenure relates to his or her first charge, this tenure constitutes exceptional circumstances in terms of Act x 2003 Anent Vacancy Procedure section 4.

Before proceeding to induct a minister in terms of this section, the Presbytery shall submit to him or her the Basis of Reviewable Tenure, and shall obtain and record his or her written acceptance thereof.

(b) *Continued Vacancy*

(i) The Presbytery may decide that the vacancy should continue indefinitely without permission to call a minister, the charge remaining under an Interim Moderator.

(ii) At the request of the Kirk Session, or on the initiative of the Presbytery, the Presbytery shall consider whether to recommence vacancy procedure in terms of Act x 2003 Anent Vacancy Procedure, subject to the right of appeal or dissent-and-complaint.

(iii) The Presbytery planning process shall continue annually in terms of this Act in respect of such a charge.

(c) *Transference*

(i) A parish and charge may be transferred from the bounds and jurisdiction of one Presbytery to the bounds and jurisdiction of another with the agreement of both Presbyteries.

(ii) In the event of disagreement between the two Presbyteries the Presbytery desiring the transference may petition the Commission of Assembly and shall notify the other Presbytery of its Petition.

(iii) Transference shall be a necessary preliminary to union or linking of congregations which are not within the bounds of one Presbytery.

(d) *Demission in the Interests of Adjustment*

(1) When the demission of a minister facilitates adjustment such demission may be regarded as a demission in the interests of adjustment, provided that procedure, terms and conditions are in accordance with the following provisions:

(2) Procedure

(a) When, in the course of pursuing the question of adjustment, it appears that the demission of a minister or ministers would facilitate adjustment the appropriate Committee of the Presbytery shall confer with such a minister or ministers thereanent.

(b) When the Presbytery Clerk receives intimation of desire to demit on grounds of age or infirmity from any minister, the Presbytery Clerk shall inform the appropriate Committee of the Presbytery, who shall consider whether such demission would facilitate adjustment, and, if so advised, shall confer with the minister thereanent and also with any other minister or ministers whose demission might facilitate the same adjustment.

(c) In the case of any minister or ministers being willing to demit in the interests of adjustment, the Convener of the appropriate Committee as above shall confer with the Boards of Ministry and National Mission with a view to preparing the draft terms and conditions of such demission.

(d) The draft terms and conditions, once agreed among the Presbytery and the Boards of Ministry and National Mission, shall then be submitted to the minister or ministers. The minister or ministers concerned, if willing to accept the draft terms and conditions, shall intimate such acceptance, in writing, to the Board of Ministry.

(e) These terms and conditions, in so far as they affect the financial or other responsibilities of the congregation or congregations concerned, shall be incorporated in the Basis of Adjustment before it is presented to the congregation or congregations involved.

(f) The terms of this section are not to be construed as conferring a right on any minister whose demission facilitates adjustment, to have such demission regarded as being in the interests of adjustment, and, in particular, no minister who has declined to demit in the interests of adjustment shall be entitled to have his or her demission so regarded at a later date.

(g) An offer by any minister to demit in the interests of adjustment by any procedure other than that outlined above shall be disregarded.

(3) <u>Terms and Conditions</u>

(a) The sole provision which may be made for any minister demitting in the interests of adjustment shall be a capital amount which may be made available by either or both of

(i) The Financial Court or Courts of the congregation or congregations concerned, and

(ii) the Board of Ministry,
subject to the consent of the Presbytery and the Assembly's Committee and provided that:

(b) No financial provision may be made for any minister who has not reached his or her 60th birthday;

(c) A Basis of Adjustment is formally agreed by all parties prior to the date of demission of the minister concerned;

(d) The capital amount may as an alternative to or in addition to the sum in terms of (f) below be a sum according to the Table appended hereto made available to the minister by the Financial Court or Courts concerned; any such sum shall be paid after the date of demission, ordinarily within seven days thereof, or otherwise by agreement between the minister and the Financial Court or Courts concerned;

(e) Any sum provided by a Financial Court in terms of this Act may be refunded to such Board out of the proceeds of sale of relevant heritable property, subject always to the terms and conditions of the titles thereof, and to the approval if necessary, of the General Assembly or the General Trustees;

(f) The capital amount may as an alternative or in addition to the sum in terms of (d) above be a sum made available by the Board of Ministry for the purchase of an early enhanced retirement pension from the Church of Scotland Pension Scheme for Ministers and Overseas Missionaries. Any enhanced early retirement pension would be payable from the minister's date of demission and would require not to exceed the pension which the minister would have received had he or she continued in service to the appropriate birthday according to the Table appended hereto and then retired but would require to be based on the level of Standard Annuities applying at the date of demission and assuming no increase in the minimum stipend between the date of demission and the appropriate birthday according to the Table appended hereto and ignoring the effects of any Social Security Revaluation of Earnings Factors Orders coming into force after the date of demission and ignoring any change to the Lower Earnings Limit for National Insurance purposes after the date of demission. Notwithstanding this, the Deduction for State Pension as described in Regulation 107 of the aforesaid Scheme shall not be made before the minister's sixty-fifth birthday.

The cost of any enhanced early retirement pension would be payable to the Church of Scotland Pension Trustees at the date of the minister's demission in accordance with the Regulations of the Scheme;

(g) No provision of any kind shall be made available to or for the benefit of any minister other than the sum or sums which may be made available by (1) the Financial Court or Courts concerned or (2) the Committee on the Maintenance of the Ministry, or both, in terms of the foregoing paragraphs (d) and (f) respectively.

TERMS OF INDUCTION	MAXIMUM POSSIBLE FINANCIAL PROVISION	MAXIMUM POSSIBLE PENSION ENHANCEMENT
Inducted in terms of Act IV 1995	On a Sliding Scale from a sum equivalent to twice the Minimum Stipend at age 60 to a sum equivalent to the Minimum Stipend at age 64; or if retirement in the 65th year the proportionate balance of a sum equivalent to the Minimum Stipend until age 65.	Pension enhanced as if service was to 65.
Inducted in terms of Act III 1972	Same as above to age 64; the sum equivalent to the Minimum Stipend then continuing to be available up to the 69th birthday; and if retirement in the 70th year the proportionate balance of a sum equivalent to the Minimum Stipend until age 70.	Pension enhanced as if service was to 70.
Inducted prior to 23rd May 1972	Same as above to age 64; then a sum equivalent to the Minimum Stipend on retiral thereafter.	Pension enhanced as if service was to 70. There would be no enhancement of pension if a minister, inducted prior to 23rd May 1972, retired on or after age 70.

Note: "The sum equivalent to the Minimum Stipend" relates to the level of Minimum Stipend at the date of Demission.

13   Achievement of Adjustment

(1) When the Presbytery decides to negotiate a Basis of Adjustment in a charge in accordance with a plan, it shall remit to the appropriate Standing Committee, or to a committee appointed for the purpose, the task of conferring with local parties, provided that:

    (a) Conference with local parties shall be with the ministers and with the elders and the members of the Financial Board (if any) of the congregations which may be involved in adjustment, and may include consultation with other members of a ministry team;

    (b) No proposed adjustment involving the rights of the minister shall be discussed with the office-bearers of the congregation as in (a) above without his or her consent in writing;

    (c) All meetings of office-bearers under this section shall be called by the Presbytery's Committee and a minister, deacon or elder, appointed by the said Committee shall act as Convener for the purposes of conference. In no case shall a minister preside at or attend any meeting called under the terms of this Act where matters in which his or her interests are involved are discussed or decided.

(2) A detailed basis of adjustment shall be negotiated with the office-bearers involved, and afterwards voted upon by the congregation or congregations involved, before the matter is put to the Presbytery for decision. Those entitled to speak and vote at such a meeting shall include those who have been formally recognised by the Kirk Session as adherents of the congregation. For the avoidance of doubt, no other form of decision-making shall be valid.

The Presbytery shall have regard to the decisions arrived at by the respective congregations, provided always that:

No basis affecting the rights of a minister shall be presented to his or her, or any other, congregation without his or her written consent;

Any congregation directly involved in and named in any proposed basis shall be cited to appear for their interests at any meeting of the Presbytery at which a decision is to be made in terms of this Act.

Notwithstanding the provisions of this section, while it shall be the duty of the Presbytery to make every effort to secure approval of the congregations involved, the right of the Presbytery to effect adjustment in terms of this Act is hereby affirmed, subject to the consent of any minister or ministers whose rights are involved.

The negotiation and approval of a Basis of Adjustment shall be without prejudice to any outstanding appeal against the outcome of appraisal in terms of section 6 above.

(3) If the Basis of Adjustment agreed by the Presbytery differs from the outcome agreed in the current Presbytery plan, the concurrence of the Assembly's Committee shall be required before the adjustment can be implemented, and the concurrence or otherwise of the Assembly's Committee shall be intimated to the Presbytery at its next ordinary meeting and to the congregation immediately thereafter.

14   Appeal against Adjustment Decisions

(1) The right of appeal, dissent-and-complaint or request for determination against Bases of Adjustment shall be as in section 6 above, except that intimation must be given immediately at the meeting at which the decision of Presbytery is made or at the meeting at which the concurrence or otherwise of the Assembly's Committee is formally intimated.

(2) The Commission of Assembly shall, except as provided in section 6 above, consider at the same time appeals etc on matters of appraisal and appeals etc relating to Bases of Adjustment; in no case shall the Commission review its own decision or give judgement twice on the same question.

(3) Act VI 1997 shall be construed in conformity with this Act.

15   Members of Ministry Teams

(1) This section shall apply to individuals other than inducted parish ministers, whether part-time or whole-time, and whether ordained or not, who exercise paid leadership in the worship and pastoral life of the congregation.

(a) In particular, this section shall apply to assistant ministers, deacons, youth workers and such appointments deemed by the Presbytery to be comparable for the purposes of this section.

(b) For the avoidance of doubt, this section shall not apply to Church secretaries, Church officers and organists

(2) Appointments referred to in subsection (1) shall be made either

(a) under the terms of a Presbytery Plan agreed in terms of this Act or

(b) by a congregation or congregations with the prior approval of the Presbytery of the bounds.

(3) In relation to appointments approved in terms of this section the Presbytery shall

(a) ensure that a statement of terms and conditions is agreed (in the case of an ordained minister of the Church of Scotland) or a contract of employment is entered (in the case of all other appointments)

(b) satisfy itself as to the status and good standing of any minister of another denomination appointed in terms of this section

(c) notify the Assembly's Committee of such an appointment

16 Repeals and Amendments

(1) Act IV 1984 is hereby repealed with the exception of sections 2 to 7 inclusive which are retained for the purposes referred to in section 2 above and subject to the following amendment: in section 2 delete 'Act V of 1984' and substitute Act x 2003 Anent Vacancy Procedure.

(2) Acts XXII 1932 and VI 1998 are hereby repealed.

(3) In Act VI 1997 section 5(d)(ii) delete 'Act IV 1984 (as amended by Acts III 1988; III 1989; and II 1992; VI 1994; X 1996; IV 1997 and IX 1999)' and substitute Act x 2003 Anent Appraisal and Adjustment.

(4) In Act III 2000 section 33, delete 'Section 18 of Act IV 1984' and substitute Act x 2003 Anent Vacancy Procedure section 30(4).

(5) Notwithstanding subsection (1) above, the repeal of Act IV 1984 as amended shall not affect the operation of the said Act (or Deliverances of the General Assembly in pursuance thereof) prior to the repeal of the said Act, or anything done or suffered under the said Act or Deliverances; and any rights or obligations acquired or incurred thereunder shall have effect as if the said Act had not been repealed.

APPENDIX III

OVERTURE ANENT VACANCY PROCEDURE

The General Assembly adopt the Overture the tenor whereof follows, and transmit the same to Presbyteries for their consideration under the Barrier Act, directing that returns be sent to the Principal Clerk not later than 31 December 2002.

1 Vacancy Procedure Committee

(1) Each Presbytery shall appoint a number of its members to be available to serve on Vacancy Procedure Committees and shall provide information and training as required for those so appointed.

(2) As soon as the Presbytery Clerk is aware that a vacancy has arisen or is anticipated, he or she shall consult the Moderator of the Presbytery and they shall appoint a Vacancy Procedure Committee of five persons from amongst those appointed in terms of subsection (1), which committee shall (a) include at least one minister and at least one elder and (b) exclude any communicant member or former minister of the vacant charge or of any constituent congregation thereof. The Vacancy Procedure Committee shall include a Convener and Clerk, the latter of whom need not be a member of the Committee but may be the Presbytery Clerk. The same Vacancy Procedure Committee may serve for more than one vacancy at a time.

(3) The Vacancy Procedure Committee shall have a quorum of three for its meetings.

(4) The Convener of the Vacancy Procedure Committee may, where he or she reasonably believes a matter to be non-contentious, consult members individually, provided that reasonable efforts are made to consult all members of the committee. A meeting shall be held at the request of any member of the committee.

(5) Every decision made by the Vacancy Procedure Committee shall be reported to the next meeting of Presbytery, but may not be recalled by Presbytery where the decision was subject to the provisions of section 2 below.

2 Request for Consideration by Presbytery

Where in this Act any decision by the Vacancy Procedure Committee is subject to the provisions of this section, the following rules shall apply:

(1) The Presbytery Clerk shall intimate to all members of the Presbytery the course of action or permission proposed, and shall arrange for one Sunday's pulpit intimation of the same to be made to the congregation or congregations concerned, in terms of Schedule A.

(2) Any four individuals, being communicant members of the congregation or full members of the Presbytery, may give written notice requesting that action be taken in terms of subsection (3) below, giving reasons for the request, within seven days after the pulpit intimation.

(3) Upon receiving notice in terms of subsection (2), the Presbytery Clerk shall sist the process or permission referred to in subsection (1), which shall then require the approval of the Presbytery.

(4) The Moderator of the Presbytery shall in such circumstances consider whether a meeting pro re nata of the Presbytery should be called in order to avoid prejudicial delay in the vacancy process.

(5) The Presbytery Clerk shall cause to have served upon the congregation or congregations an edict in terms of Schedule B citing them to attend the meeting of Presbytery for their interest.

(6) The consideration by Presbytery of any matter under this section shall not constitute an appeal or a petition, and the decision of Presbytery shall be deemed to be a decision at first instance subject to the normal rights of appeal or dissent-and-complaint.

3 Causes of Vacancy

The causes of vacancy shall normally include:

(a) the death of the minister of the charge
(b) the removal of status of the minister of the charge or the suspension of the minister in terms of section 20(2) of Act III 2001
(c) the dissolution of the pastoral tie in terms of Act I 1988 or Act VI 1984
(d) the demission of the charge and/or status of the minister of the charge
(e) the translation of the minister of the charge to another charge
(f) the termination of the tenure of the minister of the charge in terms of Act X 2000

4 Release of Departing Minister

The Presbytery Clerk shall be informed as soon as circumstances have occurred that cause a vacancy to arise or make it likely that a vacancy shall arise. Where the circumstances pertain to section 3(d) or (e) above, the Vacancy Procedure Committee shall

(1) except in cases governed by subsection (2) below, decide whether to release the minister from his or her charge and, in any case involving translation to another charge or introduction to an appointment, to instruct him or her to await the instructions of the Presbytery or another Presbytery.

(2) in the case of a minister in the first five years of his or her first charge, decide whether there are exceptional circumstances to justify releasing him or her from his or her charge and proceeding in terms of subsection (1) above

(3) determine whether a vacancy has arisen or is anticipated and, as soon as possible, determine the date upon which the charge becomes actually vacant, and

(4) inform the congregation or congregations by one Sunday's pulpit intimation as soon as convenient.

(5) The provisions of section 2 above shall apply to the decisions of the Vacancy Procedure Committee.

5 Demission of Charge

(1) If a ministerial member of Presbytery demits his or her charge or resigns an appointment on the ground of age or infirmity, he or she shall retain a seat in Presbytery unless in terms of Act III 2000 he or she elects to resign it.

(2) In the case where it is a condition of any basis of adjustment that a minister shall demit his or her charge to facilitate union or linking, and the minister has agreed in writing in terms of the appropriate regulations governing adjustments, formal application shall not be made to the Presbytery for permission to demit. The minister concerned shall be regarded as retiring in the interest of readjustment and he or she shall retain a seat in Presbytery unless in terms of Act III 2000 he or she elects to resign it.

(3) A minister who demits his or her charge without retaining a seat in Presbytery shall, if he or she retains status as a minister, remain under the supervision of the Presbytery which accepted the demission unless and until he or she moves into the bounds of another Presbytery, in which case he or she shall without delay lodge any current practising Certificate with the Clerk of that Presbytery, and he or she shall then come under its supervision. In all such cases the provisions of sections 5 to 15 of Act II 2000 regarding practising certificates shall apply.

6 Appointment of Interim Moderator

At the same time as the Vacancy Procedure Committee makes a decision in terms of section 4 above, or where circumstances pertain to section 3(a), (b), (c) or (f) above, the Vacancy Procedure Committee shall identify an Interim Moderator for the charge and make intimation to the congregation subject to the provisions of section 2 above. The Interim Moderator shall be a ministerial member of the Presbytery in terms of Act III 2000 or Act V 2001 and shall not be a member of the vacant congregation. The name of the Interim Moderator shall be forwarded to the Board of Ministry.

7 Duties of Interim Moderator

(1) It shall be the duty of the Interim Moderator to preside at all meetings of the Kirk Session (or of the Kirk Sessions in the case of a linked charge) and to preside at all congregational meetings in connection with the vacancy, or at which the minister would have presided had the charge been full. In the case of a congregational meeting called by the Presbytery in connection with adjustment the Interim Moderator, having constituted the meeting, shall relinquish the chair in favour of the representative of the Presbytery, but he or she shall be at liberty to speak at such a meeting. In consultation with the Kirk Session and the Financial Court he or she shall make arrangements for the supply of the vacant pulpit.

(2) The Interim Moderator appointed in a prospective vacancy may call and preside at meetings of the Kirk Session and of the congregation for the transaction of business relating to the said prospective vacancy. He or she shall be associated with the minister until the date of the actual vacancy; after that date he or she shall take full charge.

(3) The Interim Moderator shall act as an assessor to the Nominating Committee, being available to offer guidance and advice. If the Committee so desire he or she may act as their Convener, but in no case shall he or she have a vote.

(4) In the event of the absence of the Interim Moderator, the Vacancy Procedure Committee shall appoint a ministerial member of the Presbytery who is not a member of the vacant congregation to fulfil any of the rights and duties of the Interim Moderator in terms of this section.

8 Permission to Call

When the decision to release the minister from the charge has been made and the Interim Moderator appointed, the Vacancy Procedure Committee shall consider whether it may give permission to call a minister in terms of Act x 2003, and may proceed subject to the provisions of section 2 above. The Vacancy Procedure Committee must refer the question of permission to call to the Presbytery if:

(a) shortfalls exist which in the opinion of the committee require consideration in terms of section 9 hereunder

(b) the committee has reason to believe that the vacancy schedule referred to in section 10 below will not be approved

(c) the committee has reason to believe that the Presbytery will, in terms of section 11 below, instruct work to be carried out on the manse before a call can be sustained, and judges that the likely extent of such work warrants a delay in the granting of permission to call, or

(d) the committee has reason to believe that the Presbytery may wish to delay or refuse the granting of permission for any reason.

Any decision by Presbytery to refuse permission to call shall be subject to appeal or dissent-and-complaint.

9 Shortfalls

(1) As soon as possible after intimation of a vacancy or anticipated vacancy reaches the Presbytery Clerk, the Presbytery shall ascertain whether the charge has current or accumulated shortfalls in contributions to central funds, and shall determine whether and to what extent any shortfalls that exist are justified.

(2) If the vacancy is in a charge in which the Presbytery has determined that shortfalls are to any extent unjustified, it must not resolve to allow a call of any kind until:

(a) the shortfalls have been met to the extent to which the Presbytery determined that they were unjustified, or

(b) a scheme for the payment of the unjustified shortfall has been agreed between the congregation and the Presbytery and receives the concurrence of the Board of Ministry and/or the Board of Stewardship and Finance for their respective interests, or

(c) a fresh appraisal of the charge in terms of Act x 2003 has been carried out, regardless of the status of the charge in the current Presbytery plan:

(i) During such appraisal no further steps may be taken in respect of filling the vacancy, and the Presbytery shall make final determination of what constitutes such steps.

(ii) Following such appraisal and any consequent adjustment or deferred adjustment the shortfalls shall be met or

declared justifiable or a scheme shall be agreed in terms of subsection (b) above; the Presbytery shall inform the Board of Ministry and the Board of Stewardship and Finance of its decisions in terms of this section; and the Presbytery shall remove the suspension of vacancy process referred to in sub-paragraph (i).

10 Vacancy Schedule

(1) When in terms of sections 4 and 6 above the decision to release the minister from the charge has been made and the Interim Moderator appointed, there shall be issued by the Board of Ministry a Schedule or Schedules for completion by the responsible Financial Board(s) of the vacant congregation(s) in consultation with representatives of the Presbytery, setting forth the proposed arrangements for stipend and payment of ministerial expenses and for provision of a manse, and showing the amount of aid, if any, to be given to, or to be received from, the Minimum Stipend Fund, with details of any endowment income. The Schedule(s), along with an extract minute from each relevant Kirk Session containing a commitment fully and adequately to support a new ministry, shall be forwarded to the Presbytery Clerk.

(2) The Schedule(s) shall be approved by the Vacancy Procedure Committee and thereupon transmitted to the Board of Ministry by the Presbytery Clerk. The Vacancy Procedure Committee or Presbytery must not sustain an appointment and call until the Schedule(s) have been approved by them and by the Board of Ministry, which shall intimate its decision within six weeks of receiving the schedule from the Presbytery.

(3) The provisions of this section shall be repeated every six months until a call has been sustained.

11 Manse

As soon as possible after the manse becomes vacant, the Presbytery Property Committee shall inspect the manse and come to a view on what work, if any, must be carried out to render it suitable for a new incumbent. The views of the Property Committee should then be communicated to the Presbytery which should, subject to any modifications which might be agreed by that Court, instruct the carrying out of the work. No induction date shall be fixed until the Presbytery Property Committee has again inspected the manse and confirmed that the work has been undertaken satisfactorily.

12 Advisory Committee

(1) As soon as possible after intimation of a vacancy or anticipated vacancy reaches the Presbytery Clerk, the Vacancy Procedure Committee shall appoint an Advisory Committee of three subject to the following conditions:

(a) at least one member shall be an elder and at least one shall be a minister

(b) the Advisory Committee shall contain no more than two members of the Vacancy Procedure Committee

(c) the Advisory Committee may contain individuals who are not members of the Presbytery

(d) the appointment shall be subject to section 2 above

(2) The Advisory Committee shall meet:

(a) before the election of the Nominating Committee, with the Kirk Session, or Kirk Sessions both separately and together, of the vacant charge to consider together in the light of the whole circumstances of the parish or parishes, what kind of ministry would be best suited to their needs

(b) with the Nominating Committee before it has taken any steps to fill the vacancy, to consider how it should proceed

(c) with the Nominating Committee before it reports to the Kirk Session and Presbytery the identity of the nominee, to review the process followed and give any further advice it deems necessary

(d) with the Nominating Committee at any other time by request of either the Nominating Committee or the Advisory Committee.

In the case of charges which are in the opinion of the Presbytery remote, it will be adequate if the Interim Moderator (accompanied if possible by a member of the Nominating Committee) meets with the Advisory Committee for the purposes listed in paragraphs (a) to (c) above.

13 Electoral Register

(1) It shall be the duty of the Kirk Session of a vacant congregation to proceed to make up the Electoral Register of the congregation. This shall contain (1) as communicants the names of those persons (a) whose names are on the communion roll of the congregation as at the date on which it is made up and who are not under Church discipline, (b) whose names have been added or restored to the communion roll on revision by the Kirk Session subsequently to the occurrence of the vacancy, and (c) who have given in valid Certificates of Transference by the date specified in terms of Schedule C hereto; and (2) as adherents the names of those persons who, being parishioners or regular worshippers in the congregation at the date when the vacancy occurred, being at least eighteen years of age, and not being members of any other congregation, have claimed (in writing in the form prescribed in Schedule D and within the time specified in Schedule C) to be placed on the Electoral Register, the Kirk Session being satisfied that they desire to be permanently connected with the congregation and knowing of no adequate reasons why they should not be admitted as communicants should they so apply.

(2) At a meeting to be held not later than fourteen days after intimation has been made in terms of Schedule C hereto, the Kirk Session shall decide on the claims of persons to be placed on the Electoral Register, such claims to be sent to the Session Clerk before the meeting. At this meeting the Kirk Session may hear parties claiming to have an interest. The Kirk Session shall thereupon prepare the lists of names and addresses of communicants and of adherents which it is proposed shall be the Electoral Register of the congregation, the names being arranged in alphabetical order and numbered consecutively throughout. The decision of the Kirk Session in respect of any matter affecting the preparation of the Electoral Register shall be final.

(3) The proposed Electoral Register having been prepared, the Interim Moderator shall cause intimation

to be made on the first convenient Sunday in terms of Schedule E hereto that on that day an opportunity will be given for inspecting the Register after service, and that it will lie for inspection at such times and such places as the Kirk Session shall have determined; and further shall specify a day when the Kirk Session will meet to hear parties claiming an interest and will finally revise and adjust the Register. At this meeting the list, having been revised, numbered and adjusted, shall on the authority of the court be attested by the Interim Moderator and the Clerk as the Electoral Register of the congregation.

(4) This Register, along with a duplicate copy, shall without delay be transmitted to the Presbytery Clerk who, in name of the Presbytery, shall attest and return the principal copy, retaining the duplicate copy in his or her own possession. For all purposes connected with this Act, and for all purposes connected with adjustment, the congregation shall be deemed to be those persons whose names are on the Electoral Register, and no other.

(5) If after the attestation of the Register any communicant is given a Certificate of Transference, the Session Clerk shall delete that person's name from the Register and initial the deletion. Such a Certificate shall be granted only when application for it has been made in writing, and the said written application shall be retained until the vacancy is ended.

(6) When a period of more than six months has elapsed between the Electoral Register being attested and the congregation being given permission to call, the Kirk Session shall have power, if it so desires, to revise and update the Electoral Register. Intimation of this intention shall be given in terms of Schedule F hereto. Additional names shall be added to the Register in the form of an Addendum which shall also contain authority for the deletions which have been made; two copies of this Addendum, duly attested, shall be lodged with the Presbytery Clerk who, in name of the Presbytery, shall attest and return the principal copy, retaining the duplicate copy in his or her own possession.

14 Appointment of Nominating Committee

(1) When permission to call has been given and the electoral register has been attested, intimation in terms

of Schedule G shall be made on two Sundays that Nominations of possible members of the Nominating Committee shall be received by the Kirk Session from members of the congregation. When this intimation is made there shall also be read an exhortation impressing upon the congregation the importance of their responsibilities in nominating persons representative of the whole life of the congregation, including younger persons.

(2) Within one week of the close of Nominations in terms of subsection (1) above, the Kirk Session and the Advisory Committee shall meet together (separately where more than one Kirk Session is involved) to appoint the members of the Nominating Committee. The decision of that meeting or those meetings shall be final.

If your committee feels that it should revert to the congregational election of the Nominating/Vacancy Committee, we would revert to something akin to the original wording of the 1984 Act in place of subsections (1) and (2) above. However, I am minded to keep subsections (3) to (6) as below in either event, as it would represent some progress even if the election is substantially in the current regime. Subsections (1) and (2) could read:

(1) When permission to call has been given and the electoral register has been attested, intimation in terms of Schedule G shall be made that a meeting of the congregation is to be held to appoint a Committee of its own number for the purpose of nominating one person to the congregation with a view to the appointment of a minister.

(2) (a) The Interim Moderator shall preside at this meeting, and the Session Clerk, or in his or her absence a person appointed by the meeting, shall act as Clerk.

(b) The Interim Moderator shall remind the congregation of the number of members it is required to appoint in terms of this section and shall call for Nominations. To constitute a valid Nomination the name of a person on the Electoral Register has to be proposed and seconded, and assurance given by the proposer that the person is prepared to act on the Committee. The Clerk shall take a note of all Nominations in the order in which they are made.

(c) When it appears to the Interim Moderator that the Nominations are complete, they shall be read to the congregation and an opportunity given for any withdrawals. If the number of persons nominated does not exceed the maximum fixed in terms of subsection (4) below there is no need for a vote, and the Interim Moderator shall declare that these persons constitute a Nominating Committee. If the number exceeds the maximum the Interim Moderator shall submit the names one by one as they appear on the list to the vote of the congregation, each member having the right to vote for up to the maximum number fixed for the Committee, and voting being by standing up. In the event of a tie for the last place a vote shall be taken between those tying.

(d) The Interim Moderator shall announce the names of those thus elected to serve on the Nominating Committee, and intimate to them the time and place of their first meeting, which may be immediately after the congregational meeting provided that has been intimated along with the intimation of the congregational meeting.

(3) Where there is an agreement between the Presbytery and the congregation or congregations that the minister to be inducted shall serve either in a team ministry involving another congregation or congregations, or in a designated post such as a chaplaincy, it shall be competent for the agreement to specify that the Presbytery shall appoint up to two representatives to serve on the Nominating Committee.

(4) Where the number of names on the electoral roll of the congregation is smaller than 750 the total membership of the Nominating Committee shall be no more than seven; where the number on the electoral roll is 750 or greater the total membership of the Nominating Committee shall be no more than nine.

(5) When the vacancy is in a linked charge, or when a union or linking of congregations has been agreed but not yet effected, or when there is agreement to a deferred union or a deferred linking, or where the appointment is to more than one post, the Vacancy Procedure Committee shall, subject to the provisions of section 2 above determine how the number who will act on the Nominating Committee will be allocated among the congregations involved, unless provision for this has already been made in the Basis of Union or Basis of Linking as the case may be.

(6) The Nominating Committee shall not have power to co-opt additional members but the relevant Kirk Session shall have power when necessary to appoint a replacement for any of its appointees who ceases, by death or resignation, to be a member of the Nominating Committee, or who, by falling ill or by moving away from the area, is unable to serve as a member of it.

15 Constitution of the Nominating Committee

It shall be the duty of the Interim Moderator to summon and preside at the first meeting of the Nominating Committee, which may be held at the close of the congregational meeting at which it is appointed and at which the Committee shall appoint a Convener and a Clerk. The Clerk, who need not be a member of the Committee, shall keep regular minutes of all proceedings. The Convener shall not have a casting vote. If the Clerk is not a member of the Committee, he or she shall have no vote. At all meetings of the Committee only those present shall be entitled to vote.

16 Task of the Nominating Committee

The Nominating Committee shall have the duty of nominating one person to the congregation with a view to the election and appointment of a minister. It shall proceed by a process of announcement in a monthly vacancy list, application and interview, and may also advertise, receive recommendations and pursue enquiries in other ways.

The Committee shall give due weight to any guidelines which may from time to time be issued by the Board of National Mission or the General Assembly.

17 Eligibility for Election

The following categories of persons, and no others, are eligible to be nominated, elected, and called as ministers of parishes in the Church of Scotland, but always subject, where appropriate, to the provisions of Act x 2002 [anent Admission and Readmission of Ministers and Others]:

(1) A minister of a parish of the Church, a minister holding some other appointment that entitles him or her to a seat in Presbytery or a minister holding a current Practising Certificate in terms of Section 5 of Act II 2000.

(2) A minister of the Church of Scotland who has retired from a parish or appointment as above, provided he or she has not reached his or her 65th birthday.

(3) (a) A licentiate of the Church of Scotland who has satisfactorily completed, or has been granted exemption from, his or her period of probationary service.

(b) A graduate candidate in terms of sections 26 and 27 of Act V 1998 (as amended).

(4) A minister, licentiate or graduate candidate of the Church of Scotland who with the approval of the Board of World Mission, has entered the courts of an overseas Church as a full member, provided he or she has ceased to be such a member.

(5) A minister, licentiate or graduate candidate of the Church of Scotland who has neither relinquished nor been judicially deprived of the status he or she possessed and who has served, or is serving, furth of Scotland in any Church which is a member of the World Alliance of Reformed Churches

(6) The holder of a Certificate of Eligibility in terms of Act x 2002 [anent Admission and Readmission of Ministers and Others].

18 Ministers of a Team

Ministers occupying positions within a team ministry in the charge, or larger area including the charge, and former holders of such positions, shall be eligible to apply and shall not by virtue of office be deemed to have exercised undue influence in securing the call.

19 Ministers of Other Churches

(1) Where a minister of a church furth of Scotland, who holds a certificate of eligibility in terms of Act x 2002 [anent Admission and Readmission of Ministers and Others], is nominated, the nominee, Kirk Session and Presbytery may agree that he or she shall be inducted for a period of three years only and shall retain status as a minister of his or her denomination of origin.

(2) Upon induction, such a minister shall be accountable to the Presbytery for the exercise of his or her ministry and to his or her own church for matters of life and doctrine. He or she shall be awarded corresponding membership of the Presbytery.

(3) With the concurrence of the Presbytery and the Board of Ministry and at the request of the congregation the period may be extended for one further period of not more than three years.

20 Nomination

(1) Before being asked to accept Nomination, the Interim Moderator shall ensure that the candidate is given an adequate opportunity to see the whole ecclesiastical buildings (including the Manse) pertaining to the congregation and shall be provided with a copy of the constitution of the congregation, a copy of the current Presbytery Plan and of any current Basis of Adjustment or Basis of Reviewable tenure, and the most recent audited accounts and statement of funds, and the candidate shall acknowledge receipt in writing to the Interim Moderator.

(2) Before any Nomination is intimated to the Kirk Session and Presbytery Clerk, the Clerk to the Nominating Committee shall secure the written consent thereto of the nominee.

(3) Before reporting the Nomination to the Vacancy Procedure Committee, the Presbytery Clerk shall obtain from the nominee or Interim Moderator evidence of the eligibility of the nominee to be appointed to the charge.

(a) In the case of a minister not being a member of any Presbytery of the Church of Scotland, this shall normally constitute an Exit Certificate in terms of Act V 1998 as amended, or evidence of status from the Board of Ministry, or a current practising certificate, or certification from the Board of Ministry of eligibility in terms of Act x 2002.

(b) In the case of a minister in the first five years of his or her first charge, this shall consist of an extract minute either from the Vacancy Procedure Committee of his or her current Presbytery, or from that Presbytery, exceptionally releasing the minister.

21 Preaching by Nominee

(1) The Interim Moderator, on receiving notice of the Committee's Nomination, shall arrange that the nominee conduct public worship in the vacant church or churches, normally within four Sundays, and that the ballot take place immediately after each such service.

(2) The Interim Moderator shall thereupon cause intimation to be made on two Sundays regarding the arrangements made in connection with the preaching by the nominee and the ballot thereafter - all in terms of Schedule H hereto.

22 Election of Minister

(1) The Interim Moderator shall normally preside at all congregational meetings connected with the election which shall be in all cases by ballot. The Interim Moderator shall be in charge of the ballot.

(2) The Interim Moderator may invite one or more persons (not being persons whose names are on the Electoral Register of the vacant congregation) to assist him or her in the conduct of a ballot vote when he or she judges this desirable.

(3) When a linking or a deferred union or deferred linking is involved the Interim Moderator shall consult and reach agreement with the minister or Interim Moderator of the other congregation regarding the arrangements for the conduct of public worship in these congregations by the candidate or candidates as in section 21(1) above. The Interim Moderator shall in writing appoint a ministerial member of Presbytery to take full charge of the ballot vote for the other congregation. In the case of a deferred union or deferred linking the minister already inducted shall not be so appointed, nor shall he or she be in any way involved in the conduct of the election.

23 Ballot Procedure

(1) The Kirk Session shall arrange to have available at the time of election a sufficient supply of voting-papers printed in the form of Schedule I hereto, and these shall be put into the custody of the Interim Moderator who shall preside at the election, assisted as in section 22 above. He or she shall issue on request to any person whose name is on the Electoral Register a voting-paper, noting on the Register that this has been done. Facilities shall be provided whereby the voter may mark the paper in secrecy, and a ballot-box shall be available wherein the paper is to be deposited when marked. The Interim Moderator may assist any person who asks for help in respect of completing the voting-paper, but no other person whatever shall communicate with the voter at this stage. The Interim Moderator, or the deputy appointed by him or her, shall be responsible for the safe custody of ballot-box, papers and Electoral Register.

(2) As soon as practicable, and at latest within twenty-four hours after the close of the voting, the Interim Moderator shall constitute the Kirk Session, or the joint Kirk Sessions when more than one congregation is involved, and in presence of the Kirk Session shall proceed with the counting of the votes, in which he or she may be assisted as provided in section 22 above. When more than one ballot-box has been used and when the votes of more than one congregation are involved, all ballot-boxes shall be emptied and the voting-papers shall be mixed together before counting begins so that the preponderance of votes in one area or in one congregation shall not be disclosed.

(3) If the number voting For exceeds the number voting Against the nominee shall be declared elected. Otherwise it shall be declared that there has been a failure to elect, and the provisions of subsection (5) below shall apply.

(4) If the number voting For is equal to or less than the number voting Against, the Interim Moderator shall declare that there has been failure to elect and that the Nominating Committee is deemed to have been discharged.

(5) After the counting has been completed the Interim Moderator shall sign a declaration in one of the forms of Schedule J hereto, and this shall be recorded in the minute

of the Kirk Session or of the Kirk Sessions. An extract shall be affixed to the notice-board of the church, or of each of the churches, concerned. In presence of the Kirk Session the Interim Moderator shall then seal up the voting-papers along with the marked copy of the Electoral Register, and these shall be transmitted to the Presbytery Clerk in due course along with the other documents specified in section 27 below.

24 Withdrawal of Nominee

(1) Should a nominee intimate withdrawal before he or she has preached as nominee, the Nominating Committee shall continue its task and seek to nominate another nominee.

(2) Should a nominee intimate withdrawal after he or she has been elected, the Interim Moderator shall proceed in terms of sections 23(4) above and 26(b) below.

25 The Call

(1) The Interim Moderator shall, along with the intimation regarding the result of the voting, intimate the arrangements made for members of the congregation over a period of not less than eight days to subscribe the Call (Schedule K). Intimation shall be in the form of Schedule L hereto.

(2) The Call may be subscribed on behalf of a member not present to sign in person, provided a mandate authorising such subscription is produced as in Schedule M. All such entries shall be initialled by the Interim Moderator or by the member of the Kirk Session appending them.

(3) Those eligible to sign the call shall be all those whose names appear on the Electoral Roll. A paper of concurrence in the Call may be signed by regular worshippers in the congregation over 14 years of age and by adherents whose names have not been entered on the Electoral Register.

26 Failure to Nominate

The exercise by a congregation of its right to call a minister shall be subject to a time-limit of one year; this period shall be calculated from the date when intimation is given of the agreement to grant leave to call. If it appears that an appointment is not to be made within the allotted time, the congregation may make application to the Presbytery for an extension, which will normally be for a further three months. In exceptional circumstances, and for clear cause shown, a further extension of three months may be granted. If no election has been made and intimated to the Presbytery by the expiry of that time, the permission to call shall be regarded as having lapsed. The Presbytery may thereupon look afresh at the question of adjustment. If the Presbytery is still satisfied that a minister should be appointed, it shall itself take steps to make such an appointment, proceeding in one of the following ways:

(a) (i) The Presbytery may strengthen the Advisory Committee which had been involved in the case by the appointment of an additional minister and elder, instruct that Committee to bring forward to a subsequent meeting the name of an eligible individual for appointment to the charge and intimate this instruction to the congregation. If satisfied with the recommendation brought by the Advisory Committee, the Presbytery shall thereupon make the appointment.

(ii) The Presbytery Clerk shall thereupon intimate to the person concerned the fact of his or her appointment, shall request him or her to forward a letter of acceptance along with appropriate Certificates if these are required in terms of section 27 below, and shall arrange with him or her to conduct public worship in the vacant church or churches on an early Sunday.

(iii) The Presbytery Clerk shall cause intimation to be made in the form of Schedule N that the person appointed will conduct public worship on the day specified and that a Call in the usual form will lie with the Session Clerk or other suitable person for not less than eight free days to receive the signatures of the congregation. The conditions governing the signing of the Call shall be as in section 25 above.

(iv) At the expiry of the time allowed, the Call shall be transmitted by the Session Clerk to the Presbytery Clerk who shall lay it, along with the documents referred to in sub-paragraph (ii) above, before the Presbytery at its first ordinary meeting or at a meeting in hunc effectum.

(b) Alternatively, the Presbytery may discharge the Nominating Committee, and a fresh committee shall be elected in terms of section 14 above. The process shall then be followed in terms of this Act from the point of the election of the Nominating Committee.

27 Transmission of Documents

(1) After an election has been made the Interim Moderator shall secure from the person appointed a letter of acceptance of the appointment.

(2) The Interim Moderator shall then without delay transmit the relevant documents to the Presbytery Clerk. These are: the minute of Nomination by the Nominating Committee, all intimations made to the congregation thereafter, the declaration of the election and appointment, the voting-papers, the marked copy of the Register and the letter of acceptance. He or she shall also inform the Clerk of the steps taken in connection with the signing of the Call, and shall arrange that, at the expiry of the period allowed for subscription, the Call shall be transmitted by the Session Clerk to the Presbytery Clerk.

(3) After the person elected has been inducted to the charge the Presbytery Clerk shall:

(a) deliver to him or her the approved copy of the Vacancy Schedule(s) referred to in section 10(2) above, and

(b) destroy the intimations and voting-papers lodged with him or her in terms of subsection (2) above and ensure that confidential documents and correspondence held locally are destroyed.

28 Sustaining the Call

(1) All of the documents listed in section 27 above shall be laid before the Vacancy Procedure Committee which may resolve to sustain the call and determine arrangements for the induction of the new minister, subject to (a) the release, if appropriate, of the minister from his or her current charge in terms of this Act and (b) the provisions of section 2 above. The Moderator of

the Presbytery shall, if no ordinary meeting of the Presbytery falls before the proposed induction date, call a meeting pro re nata for the induction.

(2) In the event that the matter comes before the Presbytery in terms of section 2 above, the procedure shall be as follows:

(a) The Call and other relevant documents having been laid on the table the Presbytery shall hear any person whom it considers to have an interest. In particular the Advisory Committee shall be entitled to be heard if it so desires, or the Presbytery may ask for a report from it. The Presbytery shall then decide whether to sustain the appointment in terms of subsection (1) above, and in doing so shall give consideration to the number of signatures on the Call. It may delay reaching a decision and return the Call to the Kirk Session to give further opportunity for it to be subscribed.

(b) If the Presbytery sustain an appointment and Call to a Graduate Candidate, and there be no appeal tendered in due form against its judgement, it shall appoint the day and hour and place at which the ordination and induction will take place.

(c) If the Presbytery sustain an appointment and Call to a minister of the Church of Scotland not being a minister of a parish, or to a minister of another denomination, and there be no ecclesiastical impediment the Presbytery shall appoint the day and hour and place at which the induction will take place.

29 Admission to a Charge

(1) When the Presbytery has appointed a day for the ordination and induction of a Graduate Candidate, or for the induction of a minister already ordained, the Clerk shall arrange for an edict in the form of Schedule O to be read to the congregation on the two Sundays preceding the day appointed.

(2) At the time and place named in the edict, the Presbytery having been constituted, the Moderator shall call for the return of the edict attested as having been duly served. If the minister is being translated from

another Presbytery the relevant minute of that Presbytery or of its Vacancy Procedure Committee agreeing to translation shall also be laid on the table. Any objection, to be valid at this stage, must have been intimated to the Presbytery Clerk at the objector's earliest opportunity, must be strictly directed to life or doctrine and must be substantiated immediately to the satisfaction of the Presbytery, in which case procedure shall be sisted and the Presbytery shall take appropriate steps to deal with the situation that has arisen. Otherwise the Presbytery shall proceed with the ordination and induction, or with the induction, as hereunder.

(3) The Presbytery shall proceed to the church where public worship shall be conducted by those appointed for the purpose. The Clerk shall read a brief narrative of the cause of the vacancy and of the steps taken for the settlement. The Moderator, having read the Preamble, shall, addressing him or her by name, put to the person to be inducted the questions prescribed (See the Ordinal of the Church as authorised from time to time by the General Assembly). Satisfactory answers having been given, the person to be inducted shall sign the Formula. If he or she has not already been ordained the person to be inducted shall then kneel, and the Moderator by prayer and the imposition of hands, in which members of the Presbytery, appointed by the Presbytery for the purpose, and other ordained persons associated with it, if invited to share in such imposition of hands, shall join, shall ordain him or her to the office of the Holy Ministry. Prayer being ended, the Moderator shall say, "I now declare you to have been ordained to the office of the Holy Ministry, and in name of the Lord Jesus Christ, the King and Head of the Church, and by authority of this Presbytery, I induct you to this charge, and in token thereof we give you the right hand of fellowship". The Moderator with all other members of Presbytery present and those associated with it shall then give the right hand of fellowship. The Moderator shall then put the prescribed question to the members of the congregation. Suitable charges to the new minister and to the congregation shall then be given by the Moderator or by a minister appointed for the purpose.*

(4) When an ordained minister is being inducted to a

charge the act of ordination shall not be repeated and the relevant words shall be omitted from the declaration. In other respects the procedure shall be as in subsection (3) above.

(5) When the appointment is for a limited or potentially limited period (including Reviewable Tenure, or an appointment in terms of section 19 above) the service shall proceed as in subsections (3) or (4) above except that in the declaration the Moderator shall say "I induct you to this charge on the Basis of [specific Act and Section] and in terms of Minute of Presbytery of date …"

(6) After the service the Presbytery shall resume its session, when the name of the new minister shall be added to the Roll of Presbytery, and the Clerk shall be instructed to send certified intimation of the induction to the Session Clerk to be engrossed in the minutes of the first meeting of Kirk Session thereafter, and, in the case of a translation from another Presbytery or where the minister was prior to the induction subject to the supervision of another Presbytery, to the Clerk of that Presbytery.

30 Service of Introduction

(1) When a minister has been appointed to a linked charge the Presbytery shall determine in which of the churches of the linking the induction is to take place. This shall be a service of induction to the charge, in consequence of which the person inducted shall become minister of each of the congregations embraced in the linking. The edict regarding the induction, which shall be in terms of Schedule P, shall be read in all of the churches concerned. There shall be no other service of induction, but if the churches are far distant from one another, or for other good reason, the Presbytery may appoint a service of introduction to be held in the other church or churches. Intimation shall be given of such service, but not in edictal form.

(2) In any case of deferred union or deferred linking the minister elected and appointed shall be inducted "to the vacant congregation of A in deferred union (or linking) with the congregation of B" and there shall be no need for any further act to establish his or her position as

---

* See Acts III and IV 1999 regarding Induction.

minister of the united congregation or of the linked congregation as the case may be. The Presbytery, however, shall in such a case arrange a service of introduction to the newly united congregation of AB or the newly linked congregation of B. Intimation shall be given of such service, but not in edictal form.

(3) When an appointment has been made to an extra-parochial office wholly or mainly under control of the Church (community ministry, full-time chaplaincy in hospital, industry, prison or university, full-time clerkship, etc.) the Presbytery may deem it appropriate to arrange a service of introduction to take place in a church or chapel suitable to the occasion.

(4) When an appointment has been made to a parochial appointment other than that of an inducted minister, the Presbytery may arrange a service of introduction to take place within the parish. If ordination is involved, suitable arrangements shall be made and edictal intimation shall be given in terms of Schedule P.

(5) In all cases where a service of introduction is held it shall follow the lines of an induction except that instead of putting the normal questions to the minister the Moderator shall say to him or her, "Mr or Ms ...., on the occasion of your ordination you solemnly vowed that, believing in one God, Father, Son and Holy Spirit, and accepting His Word in Holy Scripture and the fundamental doctrines of the faith contained in the Confession of Faith of this Church, you would seek the unity and peace of the Church, and that, inspired by zeal for the glory of God, by the love of Christ, and by a desire for the salvation of all people, you would lead a godly and circumspect life and would cheerfully discharge the duties of your ministry – do you now reaffirm your adherence to this vow?" In the declaration the Moderator in place of "I induct you to ....." shall say, "I welcome you as ....".

31 Demission of Status

If a minister seeks to demit his or her status as a minister of the Church of Scotland, any accompanying demission of a charge will be dealt with by the Vacancy Procedure Committee in terms of section 4 of this Act without further delay, but the question of demission of status shall be considered by the Presbytery itself. The Moderator of Presbytery, or a deputy appointed by him or her, shall first confer with the minister regarding his or her reasons and shall report to the Presbytery if there appears to be any reason not to grant permission to demit status. Any decision to grant permission to demit status shall be immediately reported to the Board of Ministry.

32 Miscellaneous

For the purposes of this Act intimations to congregations may be made (a) verbally during every act of worship or (b) in written intimations distributed to the whole congregation provided that the congregation's attention is specifically drawn to the presence of an intimation there in terms of this Act.

For the purposes of this Act attestation of all intimations to congregations shall consist of certification thereof by the Session Clerk as follows:

(a) Certification that all intimations received have been duly made on the correct number of Sundays shall be sent to the Presbytery Clerk before the service of induction or introduction.

(b) Certification that any particular intimation received has been duly made on the correct number of Sundays shall be furnished on demand to the Vacancy Procedure Committee or the Presbytery Clerk.

(c) Intimation shall be made immediately to the Presbytery Clerk in the event that intimation has not been duly made on the appropriate Sunday.

33 Repeals and Amendments

(1) Act V 1984 as amended is hereby repealed; it is hereby provided that all other legislation prior to this Act shall be construed in conformity with this Act

(2) Earlier Acts and Regulations are amended as follows:

(a) In Act XVIII 1932, ss. 2 and 7, delete the latter sentence of section 2 and all of subsection 7(b)

(b) In Act IV 1999 delete 'Act V 1984 section 25(3)' and substitute 'Act x 2003 Anent Vacancy Procedure section 29(3)'

(c) In Act II 2000 s. 19(2) delete 'section 2(3) of Act V 1984' and substitute 'Act x 2003 Anent Vacancy Procedure section 7'

(d) In Act X 2000 s. 8 delete 'in terms of Act V 1984 paragraph 27'

(e) In Act XIII 2000 s. 12(i) delete 'sections 6-8 of Act V 1984' and substitute Act x 2003 Anent Vacancy Procedure section 13

(f) In Regulations II 1996 delete reference to Act V 1984 and substitute Act x 2003 Anent Vacancy Procedure

(3) Notwithstanding subsection (1) above, the repeal of Act V 1984 as amended shall not affect the operation of the said Act (or Deliverances of the General Assembly in pursuance thereof) prior to the repeal of the said Act, or anything done or suffered under the said Act or Deliverances; and any rights or obligations acquired or incurred thereunder shall have effect as if the said Act had not been repealed.

34 Interpretation
For the purposes of this Act the Interpretation section of Act x 2003 will apply.

SCHEDULES

A INTIMATION OF ACTION OR DECISION OF VACANCY PROCEDURE COMMITTEE – Section 2(1)
To be read on one Sunday
The Vacancy Procedure Committee of the Presbytery of ……… proposes [here insert action or permission proposed]……. Any communicant member of the congregation(s) of A [and B] may submit to the Presbytery Clerk a request for this proposal to be considered at the next meeting of the Presbytery: where such requests are received from four individuals, being communicant members of the congregation(s) or full members of the Presbytery, the request shall be met. Such request should be submitted in writing to [name and postal address of Presbytery Clerk] by [date seven days after intimation].
A ………. B ………. Presbytery Clerk

B EDICT CITING A CONGREGATION TO ATTEND – Section 2(5)
To be read on one Sunday
Intimation is hereby given that in connection with the [anticipated] vacancy in this congregation a valid request has been made for the matter of [here insert action or permission which had been proposed] to be considered by the Presbytery. [The proposed course of action] is in the mean time sisted.
Intimation is hereby further given that the Presbytery will meet to consider this matter at ………. on ………. the ………. day of ………. at ………. o'clock and that the congregation are hereby cited to attend for their interests.
A ………. B ………. Presbytery Clerk

C PREPARATION OF ELECTORAL REGISTER – Section 13(1) and (2)
To be read on two Sundays
Intimation is hereby given that in view of the [1]anticipated vacancy the Kirk Session is about to make up an Electoral Register of this congregation. Any communicant whose name is not already on the Communion Roll as a member should hand in to the Session Clerk a Certificate of Transference, and anyone wishing his or her name added to the Register as an adherent should obtain from the Session Clerk, and complete and return to him or her, a Form of Adherent's Claim. All such papers should be in the hands of the Session Clerk not later than ………. The Kirk Session will meet in ………. on ………. at ………. to make up the Electoral Register when anyone wishing to support his or her claim in person should attend.
C ………. D ………. Interim Moderator
[1] This word to be included where appropriate – otherwise to be deleted

D FORM OF ADHERENT'S CLAIM – Section 13(1)

I, [1] .... of [2] ...., being not under eighteen years of age, being a regular worshipper in the Church of ....
and not being a member of any other congregation in Scotland, claim to have my name put on the Electoral Register of
the parish of .... as an adherent.

Date ....   (Signed) ....…….

[1] Here enter full name in block capitals
[2] Here enter address in full

E INSPECTION OF ELECTORAL REGISTER – Section 13(3)

To be read on one Sunday

Intimation is hereby given that the proposed Electoral Register of this congregation has now been prepared and that an
opportunity of inspecting it will be given today in .... at the close of this service, and that it will be open for
inspection at .... on .... between the hours of .... and .... each day. Any questions regarding entries
in the Register should be brought to the notice of the Kirk Session which is to meet in .... on .... at ....
o'clock when it will finally make up the Electoral Register.

C .... D .... Interim Moderator

F REVISION OF ELECTORAL REGISTER – Section 13(6)

To be read on two Sundays

Intimation is hereby given that more than six months having elapsed since the Electoral Register of this congregation
was finally made up, it is now proposed that it should be revised. An opportunity of inspecting the Register will be given
in .... at the close of this service, and also at .... on .... between the hours of .... and .... each
day. Anyone wishing his or her name added to the Electoral Register as a member should give in a Transference
Certificate, or as an adherent should give in a Form of Adherent's Claim (copies of which may be had from the Session
Clerk) not later than .... The Kirk Session will meet in .... on .... at o'clock when it will finally make up
the Revised Register.

C .... D .... Interim Moderator

G INTIMATION OF ELECTION OF NOMINATING COMMITTEE – Section 14(1)

To be read on two Sundays

Intimation is hereby given that the Kirk Session and the Advisory Committee of the Presbytery of .... will meet
on [date] to appoint a Nominating Committee for this vacancy. The total number of persons serving on the committee
shall be [total number, according to section xx] and the number to be appointed by the Kirk Session of this congregation
is [number determined by the VPC].

Letters recommending individuals for appointment should reach the Session Clerk [here details of contact] before the
above date.

C..........D............Interim Moderator

If section 13 reverts to the 1984 system, Schedule G should be replaced by Schedule F of the 1984 Act suitably adapted,
perhaps as follows:

Intimation is hereby given that a meeting of this congregation will be held in the Church[1] on Sunday .... at the
close of Morning Worship for the purpose of appointing a Nominating Committee which will nominate one person to
the congregation with a view to the appointment of a minister.

C .... D .... Interim Moderator.

[1]Where other arrangements are deemed appropriate particulars should be given here.

H   MINUTE OF NOMINATION BY NOMINATING COMMITTEE – Section 21

To be read on two Sundays

(1)   The Committee chosen by this congregation to nominate a person with a view to the election and appointment of a minister, at a meeting held at .... on .... resolved to name and propose[1] .... and they accordingly do name and propose the said ....

Date .... E .... F .... Convener of Committee

[1]   The name and designation of the person should at this point be entered in full

(2)   Intimation is therefore hereby given that the Nominating Committee having, as by minute now read, named and proposed Mr/Ms A .... B ...., arrangements have been made whereby public worship will be conducted in this Church by him or her on Sunday the .... day of .... at .... o'clock; and that a vote will be taken by voting-papers immediately thereafter; and that electors may vote For or Against electing and appointing the said Mr/Ms A .... B .... as minister of this vacant charge.

C .... D .... Interim Moderator

I   VOTING-PAPER – Section 23

FOR Electing Mr/Ms A .... B	
AGAINST Electing Mr/Ms A .... B.......	

Directions to Voters – If you are in favour of electing Mr/Ms A .... B .... put a cross (+) on the upper space. If you are not in favour of electing Mr/Ms A .... B .... put a cross (+) in the lower space. Do not put a tick or any other mark upon the paper; if you do, it will be regarded as spoilt and will not be counted.

Note: The Directions to Voters must be printed prominently on the face of the voting-paper

J   DECLARATION OF ELECTION RESULT – Sections 23(5)

First Form (Successful Election)

I hereby declare that the following are the results of the voting for the election and appointment of a minister to the vacant charge of .... [1] .... and that the said Mr/Ms .... has accordingly been elected and appointed subject to the judgement of the courts of the Church.

Date .... C .... D .... Interim Moderator

[1]   Here enter details

FOR Electing Mr/Ms A .... B	
AGAINST Electing Mr/Ms A .... B.......	

Second Form (Failure to Elect)

I hereby declare that the following are the results of the voting for the election and appointment of a minister to the vacant charge of .... [1] .... and that in consequence of this vote there has been a failure to elect, and the Nominating Committee is deemed to have been discharged. [Continue in terms of Schedule F as appropriate.]

Date .... C .... D .... Interim Moderator

[1]   Here enter details

FOR Electing Mr/Ms A .... B	
AGAINST Electing Mr/Ms A .... B.......	

K   THE CALL – Section 25(1)

Form of Call

We, members of the Church of Scotland and of the congregation known as ………., being without a minister, address this Call to be our minister to you, ………., of whose gifts and qualities we have been assured, and we warmly invite you to accept this Call, promising that we shall devote ourselves with you to worship, witness, mission and service in this parish, and also to the furtherance of these in the world, to the glory of God and for the advancement of His Kingdom.

Paper of Concurrence

We, regular worshippers in the congregation of the Church of Scotland known as ………. concur in the Call addressed by that congregation to ………. to be their minister.

N.B. The Call and Paper of Concurrence should be dated and attested by the Interim Moderator before they are transmitted to the Clerk of the Presbytery

L   SUBSCRIBING THE CALL – Section 25(1)

To be read on at least one Sunday

Intimation is hereby given that this congregation, having elected Mr/Ms A ………. B to be their minister, a Call to the said Mr/Ms A ………. B ………. has been prepared and will lie in ………. on ………. the ………. day of ………. between the hours of ………. and ………. when members may sign in person or by means of mandates. Forms of mandate may be obtained from the Session Clerk.

A paper of Concurrence will also be available for signature by persons of fourteen years of age or over who are connected with the congregation but are not communicant members.

C ………. D ………. Interim Moderator

M   MANDATE TO SIGN CALL – Section 25(2)

I, ………. of ………., being a person whose name is on the Electoral Register of the congregation, hereby authorise the Session Clerk, or other member of Session, to add my name to the Call addressed to Mr or Ms A ………. B ………. to be our minister.

(Signed) ………..……….

N   CITATION IN CASE OF NOMINATION BY PRESBYTERY – Section 26(a)(3)

To be read on one Sunday

Intimation is hereby given that Mr or Ms X ………. Y ………. whom the Presbytery has appointed to be minister of this congregation will conduct public worship in the Church on Sunday the ………. day of ………. at ………. o'clock.

Intimation is hereby further given that a Call addressed to the said Mr or Ms X ………. Y ……….. will lie in ………. on ………. the ………. day of ………. between the hours of ………. and ………. during the day and between the hours of ………. and ………. in the evening, when members may sign in person or by means of mandates, forms of which may be had from the Session Clerk.

Intimation is hereby further given that the Presbytery will meet to deal with the appointment and Call at ………. on ………. the ………. day of ………. at ………. o'clock and that the congregation are hereby cited to attend for their interests.

A ………. B ………. Presbytery Clerk

O   EDICTAL INTIMATION OF ADMISSION – Section 29(1)

To be read on two Sundays

Whereas the Presbytery of ………. has received a Call from this congregation addressed to Mr/Ms A ………. B ……….. to be their minister, and the said Call has been sustained as a regular Call, and has been accepted by him/her;[1]

And whereas the said Presbytery, having judged the said Mr/Ms A ………. B ………. qualified[2] for the ministry of the Gospel and for this charge, has resolved to proceed to his or her[3] ordination and induction on ………. the ……… day of ………. at ………. o'clock unless something occurs which may reasonably impede it:

Notice is hereby given to all concerned that if they, or any of them, have anything to object to in the life or doctrine of the said Mr/Ms A ………. B ………. they may appear at the Presbytery which is to meet at ………. on ………. the ………. day of ………. at ………. o'clock; with certification that if no relevant objection be then made and immediately substantiated, the Presbytery will proceed without further delay.

By order of the Presbytery

A ………. B ………. Presbytery Clerk

[1]   add, where appropriate, "and his or her translation has been agreed to by the Presbytery of …..."
[2]   omit "for the ministry of the Gospel and" if the minister to be inducted has been ordained previously
[3]   omit, where appropriate, "ordination and"

P   EDICTAL INTIMATION OF ORDINATION IN CASE OF INTRODUCTION – Section 30(1)

To be read on two Sundays

Whereas [narrate circumstances requiring service of introduction]

And whereas the Presbytery, having found the said Mr/Ms A ………. B ………. to have been regularly appointed and to be qualified for the ministry of the Gospel and for the said appointment has resolved to proceed to his or her ordination to the Holy Ministry and to his or her introduction as [specify appointment] on ………. the ………. day of ………. at ………. o'clock unless something occur which may reasonably impede it;

Notice is hereby given to all concerned that if they, or any of them, have anything to object to in the life or doctrine of the said Mr/Ms A ………. B ………. they may appear at the Presbytery which is to meet at ………. on ………. the ………. day of ………. at ………. o'clock; with certification that if no relevant objection be then made and immediately substantiated, the Presbytery will proceed without further delay.

By order of the Presbytery

A ………. B ………. Presbytery Clerk

APPENDIX IV
Committee on Parish Reappraisal Tables

TABLE I
NO CHANGE

1	Edinburgh: Corstorphine Craigsbank	Edinburgh
2	Edinburgh: Marchmont St Giles'	Edinburgh
3	Edinburgh: Corstorphine Old	Edinburgh
4	Edinburgh: Corstorphine St Anne's	Edinburgh
5	Edinburgh: Portobello St James'	Edinburgh
6	Dalkeith: St John's and King's Park	Lothian
7	Haddington: St Mary's	Lothian
8	Bonkyl and Preston linked with Chirnside linked with Edrom Allanton	Duns
9	Carlisle: Chapel Street linked with Longtown: St Andrew's	Annandale and Eskdale
10	Anwoth and Girton linked with Borgue	Dumfries and Kirkcudbright
11	Dalry: St Margaret's	Ayr
12	Irvine: Relief Bourtreehill	Irvine and Kilmarnock
13	Crosshouse	Irvine and Kilmarnock
14	Largs: St Columba's	Ardrossan
15	Stevenston: High	Ardrossan
16	Kilwinning: Abbey	Ardrossan
17	Saltcoats: North	Ardrossan
18	Douglas: St Bride's linked with Douglas Water and Rigside	Lanark
19	Lanark: St Nicholas'	Lanark
20	Port Glasgow: Hamilton Bardrainney	Greenock
21	Inverkip	Greenock
22	Giffnock The Park	Glasgow
23	Glasgow: Merrylea	Glasgow
24	Glasgow: Netherlee	Glasgow
25	Glasgow: Possilpark	Glasgow
26	Airdrie: New Monklands linked with Greengairs	Hamilton

27	Uddingston: Burnhead	Hamilton
28	Bellshill: West	Hamilton
29	Newmains: Coltness Memorial linked with Bonkle	Hamilton
30	Rhu and Shandon	Dumbarton
31	Dumbarton: Riverside	Dumbarton
32	Old Kilpatrick Bowling	Dumbarton
33	Cumbernauld: Kildrum	Falkirk
34	Cumbernauld: Abronhill	Falkirk
35	Sauchie and Coalsnaughton	Stirling
36	Burntisland	Kirkcaldy
37	Tulliallan and Kincardine	Dunfermline
38	Markinch	Kirkcaldy
39	Largoward linked with St Monan's	St Andrews
40	Cupar: Old and St Michael of Tarvit	St Andrews
41	Ardler, Kettins and Meigle	Dunkeld and Meigle
42	St Martin's linked with Scone: New	Perth
43	Perth: Kinnoull	Perth
44	Crieff	Perth
45	Muthill linked with Trinity Gask and Kinkell	Perth
46	Abernyte linked with Inchture and Kinnaird linked with Longforgan	Dundee
47	Dundee: Trinity	Dundee
48	Kirriemuir St Andrew's linked with Oathlaw Tannadice	Angus
49	Aberdeen: South Church of St Nicholas, Kincorth	Aberdeen
50	Aberdeen: St George's Tillydrone	Aberdeen
51	Portlethen	Kincardine and Deeside
52	Inverurie: St Andrew's	Gordon
53	Turriff: St Ninian's and Forglen	Buchan
54	Bellie linked with Speymouth	Moray
55	Lossiemouth: St James	Moray
56	Lossiemouth: St Gerardine's	Moray
57	Laggan linked with Newtonmore	Abernethy
58	Kiltarlity linked with Kirkhill	Inverness

59	Strath and Sleat	Lochcarron-Skye
60	South Uist	Uist
61	Knock	Lewis
62	Kirkwall: St Magnus' Cathedral	Orkney
63	Lerwick and Bressay (Shetland Arrangements)	Shetland
64	Corby: St Ninian's	England

TABLE II
REVIEWABLE TENURE

1	Edinburgh: Drylaw	Edinburgh
2	Edinburgh: Kirk o' Field (Further review approved)	Edinburgh
3	Musselburgh: St Andrew's High	Lothian
4	Ettrick and Yarrow	Melrose and Peebles
5	Kilbarchan: East	Paisley
6	Greenock: Ardgowan	Greenock
7	Glasgow: Drumchapel Drumry St Mary's	Glasgow
8	Glasgow: Rutherglen Stonelaw	Glasgow
9	Glasgow: Rutherglen Wardlawhill	Glasgow
10	Banton linked with Twechar	Glasgow
11	Glasgow: Mosspark	Glasgow
12	Glasgow: Renfield St Stephen's	Glasgow
13	Cambuslang Trinity St Paul's	Glasgow
14	Glasgow: Castlemilk West	Glasgow
15	Glasgow: Toryglen	Glasgow
16	Blantyre: Livingstone Memorial	Hamilton
17	Kilberry linked with Tarbert	South Argyll
18	Kirn	Dunoon
19	Glenorchy and Innishael linked with Strathfillan	Lorn and Mull
20	Appin linked with Lismore	Lorn and Mull
21	Laurieston linked with Redding Westquarter	Falkirk

22	Airth	Falkirk
23	Cowie linked with Plean	Stirling
24	Alloa: North	Stirling
25	Glenrothes: Christ's Kirk	Kirkcaldy
26	Abdie and Dunbog linked with Newburgh	St Andrews
27	Dundee: Lochee Old and St Luke's	Dundee
28	Aberdeen: Denburn	Aberdeen
29	Banchory Ternan East	Kincardine and Deeside
30	Fintray and Kinellar linked with Keithhall	Gordon
31	Echt linked with Midmar	Gordon
32	Buckie: South and West linked with Enzie	Moray
33	Resolis and Urquhart	Ross
34	Barvas	Lewis

TABLE III

TERMINABLE TENURE

1	Strathaven : West	Hamilton
2	Dundee: Broughty Ferry St Aidan's (Further review approved)	Dundee

TABLE IV

AGE RESTRICTION

1	Old Cumnock: Crichton West and St Ninian's (not under 55 years)	Ayr
2	Baldernock (not under 50 years)	Dumbarton

TABLE V

UNIONS

1	Ettrick and Yarrow	14th December 2001
2	Kirkpatrick Irongray and Lochrutton and Terregles (IRONGRAY, LOCHRUTTON AND TERREGLES)	6th June 2001
3	Bargrennan and Newton Stewart: Penninghame St John's (PARISH OF PENNINGHAME)	22nd April 2001
4	Glasgow: Yoker Old and Yoker St Matthew's (YOKER)	1st November 2001
5	Blairgowrie: St Andrew's and St Mary's South (BLAIRGOWRIE)	29th January 2002
6	Drumoak and Durris (DRUMOAK-DURRIS)	1st January 2002
7	Grange Church and Keith: St Rufus and Botriphnie Church (KIRK OF KEITH: ST RUFUS BOTRIPHNIE AND GRANGE)	29th June 2001
8	Keith: North, Newmill and Boharm and Rothiemay (KEITH: NORTH, NEWMILL, BOHARM AND ROTHIEMAY)	18th January 2002
9	Berneray and Lochmaddy and Trumisgarry (BERNERAY AND LOCHMADDY)	22nd February 2001

TABLE VI

LINKINGS

1	Kilmarnock: St Ninian's Bellfield and Kilmarnock: Shortlees	29th May 2001
2	Lochranza and Pirnmill and Shiskine and Lamlash	1st November 2001
3	Clydebank: St Cuthbert's and Duntocher Trinity	12th September 2001
4	Connel and Coll	
5	Gargunnock linked with Kincardine in Menteith linked with Kilmadock	29th March 2001
6	Blair Atholl and Struan linked with Tenandry	
7	Bendochy linked with Coupar Angus Abbey	7th February 2002
8	Nesting and Lunnasting and Whalsay and Skerries	24th June 2001

TABLE VII
SEVERANCE OF LINKING

1	Abercorn and Dalmeny	31st October 2001
2	Bendochy and Blairgowrie: St Mary's South	
3	Grange linked with Rothiemay	29th June 2001
4	Delting linked with Nesting and Lunnasting	20th April 2001

TABLE VIII
DEFERRED UNION

1	Maybole: Old in deferred union with Maybole: West	Ayr
2	Buckhaven and Denbeath	Kirkcaldy

TABLE IX
DEFERRED LINKING

1	Fisherton in deferred linking with Kirkoswald	Ayr
2	Whiting Bay and Kildonan in deferred linking with Kilmory	Ardrossan
3	Buckhaven united with Denbeath and Methilhill	Kirkcaldy
4	Monquhitter and New Byth linked with Turriff: St Andrew's	Buchan

TABLE X
JOINT MINISTRY

1	Lochs in Bernera and Community Ministry	Lewis

TABLE XI
BASIS OF NEW CHARGE

1	Edinburgh: Gilmerton (Change of Status)	31st December 2001
2	Paisley: St Ninian's Ferguslie (Change of Status)	1st May 2001
3	Dunfermline: St Paul's East	

TABLE XII

RESTORATION TO FULL STATUS

1	Edinburgh: Craigmillar Park	Edinburgh
2	Gardenstown	Buchan

TABLE XIII

PART-TIME MINISTRY

1	Fergushill linked with Kilwinning: Erskine (50%)	Ardrossan
2	Gigha and Cara (50%)	South Argyll
3	North Knapdale (70%)	South Argyll
4	Shapinsay (50%)	Orkney

TABLE XIV

TRANSFER OF CONGREGATION

	Abercorn was transferred from the Presbytery of Edinburgh to the Presbytery of West Lothian	1st November 2001

ARTHUR P. BARRIE, *Convener*
C. NOEL GLEN, *Vice-Convener*
DOUGLAS A.O. NICOL, *General Secretary*

APPENDIX V

GUIDELINES FOR REVIEW OF TERMINABLE OR REVIEWABLE TENURE CHARGES

1. At the time the Terminable or Reviewable Tenure is agreed there should be clear, written information available about the nature of the Tenure, the reason for it, and the date and purpose of a Review.

2. This information should be included in the Parish Profile of the vacant Charge and should be made available to all Ministers expressing an interest in the Charge. The Minister called to the Charge should be asked to sign a statement that the information has been understood.

3. A database in the Department of National Mission will include reference to all Bases of Terminable or Reviewable Tenure in which a Review Date is detailed and 12 months prior to that date a reminder will be sent to the appropriate Presbytery.

4. The Review Process should not begin before the specified date and should if at all possible be completed and a report made to Presbytery within three months of the date.

5. A small group (minimum 3, maximum 5) should be appointed by the Presbytery and at least one should be a member of the Presbytery Committee responsible for Reappraisal business. The names on the nominated Group should be vetted by the Presbytery Clerk to avoid conflict of interest. The Group should be given a clear remit.

6. The congregation(s) should be asked to complete a *Reappraisal Congregational Survey Form* (available from the Department of National Mission) and this should be used as a basis for discussion, jointly and severally, with the Minister and office-bearers. Discussion should also take place on the original stated purpose of the Terminable or Reviewable Tenure.

7. The Presbytery shall ensure that a clear Record Note is kept of all discussions.

8. During the Review Process pastoral support should be offered to the Minister in the Terminable or Reviewable Tenure Charge, and where appropriate, the Manse family.

9. It is important that throughout the process it is stressed that it is the Charge (rather than the incumbent) which is being reviewed.

10. Consultation when appropriate with a body outwith the Church, such as a local prison or NHS Trust, should be undertaken after full consultation with the Minister and office-bearers concerned.

11. If any of the issues raised during the Review relate to specific legislation in the Church, the appropriate procedures must be pursued prior to the Review being concluded.

12. The Review Group should report to the Presbytery Committee responsible for Reappraisal matters and when a report is given to Presbytery the reasons for decisions should be clearly stated.

13. The Committee may recommend to the Presbytery:

    — (a) that the ministry under the terminable or reviewable tenure be continued for a further specified period

    — (b) that the restriction on the Minister's tenure be removed

    — (c) that the Minister's tenure of the charge be terminated, with an accompanying recommendation on the future of the vacant charge.

In the case of (a) and (b), the concurrence of the General Assembly's Committee on Parish Reappraisal is required. In the case of (c), Presbytery is required to give the Minister six months' notice in writing.

APPENDIX VI

COMMITTEE ON NEW CHARGE DEVELOPMENT STATISTICS

Statistics

1. New Charges

During the year 2001/2002 6 New Charge Commissions were created

Paisley: St Ninian's Ferguslie
Aberdeen: Oldmachar
Aberdeen: Cove
Hamilton: East Kilbride: Stewartfield
Dundee: Whitfield
Edinburgh: Gilmerton

2. Sites

2.1 At the time of writing, negotiations for the acquisition and the purchase of several sites at various stages were ongoing. These sites are for the purpose of erecting suitable places of worship.

Glasgow: Gorbals
Aberdeen: Cove
Hamilton: Ravenscraig
Dundee: North East
Hamilton: East Kilbride: Stewartfield
Greenock: East End

2.2 The Committee has also been invited by the Committee on Parish Reappraisal to enter into discussions to establish the nature of new developments which may require a place of worship in the following areas:

Hamilton: Ravenscraig

3. New Buildings

3.1 During the year the following buildings were completed:

(a) Ardrossan: Kilwinning Mansefield Trinity completed for a contract sum of approximately £550,000.
(b) Perth: Riverside completed for the contract sum of £660,000

The Committee is also in the process of completing and constructing a new church in the following location: Glasgow: Robroyston (on site)

3.2 Other projects, at the design stage, include:

Glasgow: Gorbals
Dunfermline: Bellyeoman
Inverness: Inshes

4. Acquisition of Buildings

4.1 The Committee has acquired or is in the process of acquiring the following properties:

(a) New manse for Dundee: Whitfield
(b) New manse for Dunfermline: East St Paul's
(c) Manse for Edinburgh: Gilmerton
(d) New manse for East Kilbride: Stewartfield
(e) At Edinburgh: Gilmerton the Church building is in the process of being transferred to the Committee.

5. Repairs

The Committee continues to assist with repairs of existing Extension Charge buildings and has developed a comprehensive property management system throughout its entire property portfolio, including cyclical maintenance and Health and Safety.

6. Finance

6.1 The Committee is grateful to the Presbytery of Aberdeen, for a generous donation of £54,974.95 from the dissolution of Nigg Parish Church towards the provision and maintenance of any building used by the New Charge at Aberdeen: Cove.

The Committee is grateful for the receipt of a number of legacies during the year amounting to £941,025.

6.2 As a consequence of the receipt of these legacies, the surplus for 2001 in the general fund of the Committee on New Charge Development amounted to £596,620.

7. Arbitrations

During the year under review, no Arbitrations took place.

ANDREW RITCHIE, *Convener*
JOHN K. COLLARD, *Vice-Convener*
WILLIAM JOHN MACDONALD, *Secretary*

APPENDIX VII

REPORT OF THE SCOTTISH CHURCHES INDUSTRIAL MISSION

The mission of the whole church

We describe industrial mission as being part of the whole mission of the church and part of the mission of the whole church. It is a way of trying to say as succinctly as possible that our tasks are complementary to those of parish ministry and that we work in an avowedly ecumenical way, coming to workplaces as neither catholic nor protestant, but simply as Christians.

It has always been a feature of industrial mission in Scotland that each practitioner has taken seriously their denominational responsibilities. We are ministers, priests, deacons and lay women and men who contribute to the wider work of the churches that nurture and sponsor us. As a new constitution comes into operation that takes Scottish Churches' Industrial Mission slightly more at arms length from the denominations, our commitment and involvement with our parent churches will remain an important cornerstone for each of us.

"Peace to the world?"

In the light of the massacre of women and men going about their daily work in New York on the bright autumn morning of the eleventh of September; in the light of women and children being driven from their homes in Nablus and other West Bank towns as bulldozers smash the buildings to the ground; in the light of the destruction of the cities of Kabul and Khandahar, it seems almost crass to talk about the impact upon world trade. Yet world trade is at the very heart of the crisis. Who can doubt the significance of the September 11th targets – the World Trade Centre, symbol of global capitalism; the Pentagon, the symbol of the military complex that defends it; the chosen weapons, commercial airliners? Who can be blind to the obscene gulf between ostentatious wealth and grinding poverty? Who can hear the parable of Dives and Lazarus?

The Director-General of the Confederation of British Industry said at their annual conference in Birmingham in November that he saw 'a very difficult winter ahead for business'. One in three companies polled by the CBI said a significant number of orders had been cancelled since 11th September with estimates that profits would be anything up to 20% lower this year. There were he said, "Worrying signs of investment being put on hold because of economic uncertainty." He implored the Chancellor not to come back to business with more taxes for 'there was no room to raise business taxes.' Far from being bold, private investment is timid and would do well to learn the lesson of Jeremiah's purchase of the field at Anathoth. If the 'great captains of industry' truly believe they are worthy of the rewards they draw down and the respect they crave, then it is in the difficult times we expect them to show their worth, show they have a belief in the future, show in that future they have a vision of economic renewal and justice.

At the heart of the churches' task is to tell of the consistent theme that beats throughout scripture of God's demand for justice for the poor and the excluded and the oppressed; to tell of the possibility of the mending of broken relationships; to tell of the rebuilding of community; to sound again the angels' song of peace to the world.

Ours is an incarnational faith and so the life of the church is to be found in the midst of the life of the world. This is at the heart of the Kirk's pursuit of being 'a church without walls'. It is of the essence of the task of industrial mission. It is *at* the workplace we listen to the stories of living; it is *at* the workplace we tell our stories of faith. It is in the promises of reconciliation and redemption by the grace of the risen Christ that we unambiguously affirm our belief in the future.

Peter Donald, chaplain in Arbroath reflects that 11th September has widely been described as 'the day that changed the world'. He says that though the world will certainly never be the same again the day that really changed the world was the day of the birth of Jesus, the first Christmas Day. Reflecting on issues of the day in the light of faith experience is where engagement deepens. Peter is a former businessman who felt called to Christian service in the economic sphere. An excellent working partnership has been developed in Arbroath. He is now well established as chaplain to the Arbroath staff of Angus Council and in local private sector companies.

Workplace – touching place

In the past year there has been further expansion of our chaplaincy services to local authorities. There are new chaplaincies to Perth and Kinross Council (Rev. Liz Brown) and Angus Council (Mr Peter Donald). The appointment of Peter Donald marks what we believe is an exciting development (see above)

The work of Rev. Bill Rayne in Edinburgh City Council and Rev. Elisabeth Spence in Glasgow City Council has been expanded. The chaplaincy at Dundee City Councils continue.

Consequent upon a meeting with airport managers at Glasgow Airport, new chaplaincies at Dundee and Aberdeen have been set up and the chaplaincies at Glasgow and Edinburgh developed. In a joint venture with the Church of Scotland's Board of National Mission a chaplaincy was begun at the new Braehead Shopping Centre near to Glasgow Airport. At Cameron Toll two voluntary chaplains have been appointed by Newington Churches Council (NCC) in partnership with South East Edinburgh Churches Action Together (SEECAT) and the chaplains at the Gyle and Buchanan Galleries centres remain greatly valued.

Our Victorian forebears gave us a legacy that improved the health of the nation with their extensive water and sewerage systems. In the drive towards a water and sewerage system able to cope with modern demands a single water authority covering all of Scotland. SCIM looks forward to building relationships with the new Authority like those pioneered by Lewis Rose DCS, chaplain to the North of Scotland Water Authority, who has for the past three years 'walked with water' across Grampian, the Highlands and the Islands.

The General Assembly heard last year that when Foot & Mouth disease began to grip Scotland's farming communities, thanks to the availability of IM Trust money we were able to take the innovative step of inviting the secondment of Rev. Dr Richard Frazer, the minister of St Machar's Cathedral to a two month appointment as farming chaplain. This was timely and right as witnessed by the amazing response to Richard's terrific efforts. In partnership with the Scottish Executive, the Board of National Mission is now building on that work with the establishment of a post of Rural Adviser.

It has been a hard year (isn't it always) on the Clyde and Rev. Alister Goss' chaplaincies in the Bae Systems' yards at Scotstoun and Govan remains hugely valued.

We have extensive chaplaincies in the power and utility industries, Oil, Gas, Electricity, Water and Nuclear. The office of the Oil Industry Chaplain has moved. When the TOTAL-FINA Oil Operating Company purchased the North Sea Assets of Elf-Aquitaine in 2001, the original TOTAL FINA offices had to be enlarged and refurbished for the enhanced administrative staff. It soon became apparent that office-space was limited. Perhaps after seven years the Chaplaincy should 'pitch its tent' elsewhere.

However the new Managing Director insisted that the Chaplaincy should be given the same office-space in the new refurbished TOTAL FINA ELF Complex as it had in the original ELF offices. Maybe the work and nature of chaplaincy commended itself to this man also in another way. He insisted that the Chaplain conducted a 'Service of Blessing' for the new North Sea 'Elgin-Franklin' Development in September 2001. Many and wonderful are the technological achievements of this latest North Sea Development. Yet on the day of its inauguration the faith and the message of the Church were given a special place in the day's proceedings.

We continue to support a number of organisations with our time and expertise. Among them are Unity Enterprise, Church Action on Poverty and Scottish Refugee Council. We participate in the Civic Forum, local Chambers of Commerce and in the Scottish Council for Development and Industry. Rev. Erik Cramb was appointed an Independent Assessor of Public Appointments this year, reflecting the respect and value put on the work of industrial chaplains by the wider community. We continue to promote an annual Safety Lecture for International Workers' Memorial Day and the Wallace Lecture in memory of the Rev. Cameron Wallace.

Webpage and IMAgenda. Lewis Rose DCS has been part of a new editorial team that has re-vamped "IMAgenda" the UK monthly for Industrial Mission practitioners. As well as keeping up to date with new discoveries in the Bio-sciences and the challenges and opportunities that come from the possibilities in genetic modification, the magazine also contains worship and spirituality resources. We would also commend our webpage to the church. (www.scim.org)

Summary

The demands upon the small team of chaplains and the faithful 70 or so ministers and priests who do workplace visiting as an extension of their parish work remains intense. Although the greatest limitation to expansion lies less in finance than in the ability to find busy colleagues willing to take on further commitments, critical to recent expansion has been the money made available through the IM Trust to promote part-time appointments. Scottish Churches Industrial Mission and our supporting churches are very grateful for the work of the Trust. The Methodist Church continues to fund the ministry of the Edinburgh Area Organiser, Rev. Bill Rayne. Nothing however has been more crucial to the beginnings, the sustaining and the development of the on-going work and the contribution that Scottish Churches' Industrial Mission has been able to make to the economic life of Scotland than the support of the Church of Scotland through the Board of National Mission. Not only has the Kirk been the major funder of chaplains, it has also provided all the essential administrative support to SCIM.

APPENDIX VIII

REPORT OF JOINT FAITHS ADVISORY BOARD ON CRIMINAL JUSTICE

1.   The Board in its second year has sought to build relationships with institutions, organisations and individuals with the aims of raising its profile and making its purpose known within the Criminal Justice System. To this end, representatives of the Board met with the Justice Minister, Mr Jim Wallace QC MSP in October 2001. During discussions the Board's representatives outlined their general remit and shared particular interests in Throughcare of prisoners and ex-offenders, Drugs Courts, dealing with sex offenders and Human Rights. The Minister welcomed the Board's contribution to the Criminal Justice debate and acknowledged its unique multi-faith stance.

2.   The Board has been concerned about issues in Scotland's prisons and recognised that an Estates Review was being undertaken by the Scottish Prison Service. At the time of writing the report of this comprehensive exercise is in the hands of the Justice Department and the Board looks forward with anticipation to its publication. Media reports suggest that there is much to be improved in the Scottish Prison Service but the Board is aware that positive developments are ongoing and have not all been postponed pending the issue of the Estates Review.

3.   One such development has been the proposal to contract out chaplaincy services to the Church of Scotland and the Roman Catholic Church in Scotland. The Board has been party to the process of negotiations between the Churches and the Scottish Prison Service and has had the opportunity to express the importance it attaches to consultation with all interested parties, in order to ensure that the selection procedures for new appointments in chaplaincy are transparently ecumenical, and that the needs of religious minorities are respected.

4.   The plight of asylum seekers and refugees in Scotland has troubled the Board, especially, those held in the non-custodial centre within the buildings of the former Dungavel Prison in Lanarkshire. The Board was anxious that those detained there were provided with religious and spiritual care appropriate to their faith. Communication was made with the Home Office and the National Asylum Support Service and, after some initial misgivings, information was received that basic access to chaplaincy and religious services was being made available by the company managing the centre on behalf of the Home Office.

5.   The Board was pleased to be invited to be represented at the Scottish Ecumenical Assembly in September and at the Conference of the Scottish Association for the Study of Delinquency in November.

By participating in these events the Board is able to make its voice known and network with others in criminal justice and related fields. A further example of this are developing links with the Churches Criminal Justice Forum, a network of Churches Together in Britain and Ireland, based in London.

6. During its formative years the Board has been grateful for the assistance of the Scottish Churches Parliamentary Officer, the Rev Dr Graham Blount, whose advice and gentle steering has been valuable on several occasions.

In the name of the Board

BRUCE F NEILL, *Convener*
JOHN K THOMSON, *Secretary*

APPENDIX IX

SCOTTISH CHURCHES COMMUNITY TRUST

MAY 2002

1. Introduction
1.1 The Scottish Churches Community Trust completed its first full year of operation at the end of 2001. Eight denominations are working in partnership to combat poverty. The eight participating churches are:- the Baptist Union, the Congregational Federation, the Methodist Church, the Religious Society of Friends, the Roman Catholic Church, the Scottish Episcopal Church, the United Free Church and the Church of Scotland.

2. Applications
2.1 During the year the Trust considered 72 applications and awarded 27 grants totalling £304,117.

3. Grant Policy
3.1 The Trust will support the following types of work:-

- Work directly developed by local churches and motivated by a clear faith perspective.
- Work developed by community or non-church groups, but which is actively supported by local churches.
- Work which meets real and identified needs in either a local community or amongst particular groups of disadvantaged people.
- Work which is primarily developed on a partnership basis by local churches and community groups working together to meet these needs.
- Work which encourages local people to identify and tackle problems themselves, bring about change and develop their own skills and knowledge.

Priority is give to churches and other organisations with minimal resources operating in areas of greatest disadvantage(urban and rural).

4. Projects Supported
4.1 Some examples of the projects supported during the year are listed below. They illustrate the breadth of work in which congregations are involved.

4.2.1 Emmaus Family Project, Drumchapel, Glasgow
A drop-in-centre which provides educational and social activities for mothers and play facilities for children.

4.2.2 Lismore Island Minibus Project
Assistance with the running costs and maintenance of community minibus.

4.2.3 Starter Packs, Dundee
Provides assistance for recently homeless or needy individuals and families who have been given tenancy of a house, but cannot afford basic household goods. Supplies are donated through local churches.

4.2.4 Town Centre Youth Project, Fort William
Churches have formed a partnership with local authority and police following closure of a Youth Café. Assistance was given to local churches to provide funding to match contribution from Scottish Executive.

4.2.5 Acorn Youth Centre, Leith, Edinburgh
Based at the Methodist Church in Leith, the Centre runs an after-school homework club 4 days per week, a half-day activities club on Fridays and the 'Big Breakfast' on

Sunday mornings. The Centre staff also work closely with local primary schools on anti-bullying, drugs and alcohol and environmental awareness.

4.2.6 Support for long-term Mental Health in the Community, Edinburgh

This is a drop-in service based at the Eric Liddell Centre in Edinburgh for people experiencing long-term mental health problems. Many of the people using the Centre have been residents at the Royal Edinburgh Hospital.

4.2.7 Gallowgate and Calton Children's Project, Glasgow

The purpose of this project is to develop self-esteem in children aged 5-12 through education, creative and leisure opportunities. The programme runs a series of funshops in different centres in the area and showcases these for family and friends thereby involving families.

4.2.8 Rosebery Centre Sitter Service, Livingston

Based at St. Paul's Church in Livingston the Centre serves people with dementia and their families. The grant will provide "sitters" to give respite to carers.

4.2.9 Richmond Outreach Child Support, Craigmillar, Edinburgh

Assistance provided for a play therapy unit to support children who have lost a parent or sibling through substance abuse or related causes.

4.2.10 Orbiston Out of School Care, Bellshill

In an area of high unemployment, low income and poor health, the centre seeks to extend after-school care places to up to six children with disabilities (out of 24) and to include the 12-14 age group. The programme involves a range of creative and educational activities in a safe and stimulating environment for children across denominational boundaries.

4.2.11 Castlemilk Refugee Centre, Glasgow

This project was initiated by Churches Together in Castlemilk to respond to the expressed needs of refugees and asylum seekers in the area. The grant helps to provide items not usually donated, but which the beneficiaries would be unable to provide for themselves from allowances.

5. Grants

5.1 Grants are normally in the region of £3,000-£5,000 per annum and may be non-recurring or for a period of one to four years. The trust does not normally support more than one-third of the cost of a piece of work.

6. Grant Applications

6.1 Application packs are available from the Trust's Office at 200 Balmore Road, Possilpark, Glasgow G22 6LJ. Applications are considered four times a year by the Board. Closing dates for the receipt of applications are the end of January, April, July and October.

6.2 The Trust's Development Co-ordinator, John Dornan, not only processes applications, but is also available to assist and advise congregations and groups wishing to develop and initiate projects.

7. Training

7.1 Every grant automatically attracts an additional sum for training purposes. This is normally 25% of the grant, up to a maximum of £750. The Trust is anxious that members of management committees, staff and volunteers should be assisted in accessing appropriate training for the work which they wish to carry out locally.

7.2 A day 'gathering' for representatives of projects already in receipt of grants was held at the Trust's office in Possilpark in June 2001. Twenty people from Lismore to Leith attended. The day was facilitated by the training organisation -"Working Together for Change" and the comments from one exercise have been used to develop a simple questionnaire for local projects. This will help in the planning of programmes for future support/training events.

8. The Board

8.1 The Board has completed the appointment of its three co-opted directors. They bring expertise in the areas of the voluntary sector, financial management and rural affairs. They serve alongside the eight directors appointed by the participating churches.

8.2 In November the Board shared in a seminar on "Risk Management". 'Risks' can include anything that can threaten the achievement of any of the Trust's objectives eg lack of awareness among supporting churches, lack of staff resource, or over reliance on a few funding sources.

8.3 Thanks to a generous grant from Lloyds TSB Foundation, the Board has begun to work on a 'Capacity Building' programme. This will enable the Board to develop a co-ordinated Business Plan with the help of an independent consultant.

8.4 An experienced Grants Group has been established. It examines applications and makes recommendations to the Board. Two Board members serve on the group along with a number of experienced people from the participating churches.

9. Promotion and Networking
9.1 The Trust's publicity leaflet has been distributed widely among all the participating churches, particularly those which rely on special offerings in individual congregations for their contribution to the Trust.

9.2 A series of presentations to Church of Scotland Presbyteries is now under way and it is hoped that most Presbyteries will receive a visit during the next few years. Board members and the Development Co-ordinator are available to speak to groups and congregations about the work of the Trust.

9.3 Nicholson Square Methodist church in Edinburgh has decided to 'adopt' the Trust as a special project for a year. Contacts with projects supported by the Trust in Edinburgh, are being arranged so that small groups from Nicholson Square can visit and learn more about the work. This has already generated £500 for the Scottish Churches Community Trust and it is hoped that it could be developed into a model for other congregations.

10. Finance
10.1.1 The Trust is grateful to the Church of Scotland for its contribution of £150.000 for the year 2001 (£100.000 from the Mission and Aid Fund and £50.000 from money given by the former Priority Areas Fund). The Trust continues to administer the payment of grants to projects whose payments from the Priority Areas Fund still have to be completed. The Trust also monitors these projects and supervises the use of training allowances.

11. Church of Scotland Representation
11.1.1 The General Assembly of 2001 re-appointed Rev Ian Moir as the Church of Scotland's representative on the Board of the Trust. He also serves as the Chair of the Trust. It is recommended that Ian Moir be appointed as the Church of Scotland's representative for a further year.

11.2 The Trust does not exist to set up particular projects itself, but to respond to the visions coming from local churches and communities. The Trust believes that it is in the context of service and shared community that the encounter between God and humanity takes place.

APPENDIX X

REPORT OF THE SOCIETY, RELIGION AND TECHNOLOGY PROJECT

SRT Assistant Director Post
In September the Board of National Mission agreed to create a new post of Assistant Director of the Society, Religion and Technology Project. This exciting development in SRT's 32 year history reflects the enormous increase in opportunities which have opened up for the Project in the past few years. Technology has emerged as a mainstream question for society in many areas. SRT's pioneering work on GM food and animal issues, risk, patenting, and on especially cloning and stem cells, which grew from our contacts with the Roslin researchers, have together propelled the Project into the forefront of national and international debate on biotechnology. This has led to unparalleled activity in the life of SRT and to opportunities, often at the highest levels, that for the past 2 years have exceeded the limits of our human resources. We are delighted at the affirmation of the strategic importance of SRT's mission for the Church of Scotland which this new post will represent. The new post will focus on SRT's long standing work on environment, which have been taking an

unwelcome back seat, and also on the wider dissemination of SRT's work in the church and ecumenically. It will enable SRT to address some forthcoming issues in relation to renewable and nuclear energy policy and climate change.

GM Food and Labelling : Developments in Europe and USA

This report gives some examples of these opportunities as SRT's mission in the UK, European and world arena. In July 2001 the European Commission published proposals which would require that all GM foods be labelled as such, not merely by their content, but even if a GM process had been used in growing or preparing the food. These are welcome and go a long way to addressing the 1999 General Assembly's deliverance over consumer choice about GM food. They would overcome the present unjust situation that labelling as "genetically modified" is only required where the product contains measurable amounts of the relevant genetic material or its products. However, the UK Government, following the advice of the Food Standards Agency (FSA), has opposed the EC proposals. FSA sees it as impractical and open to abuse to make a requirement for something which cannot be tested on the product, but can only be verified by its traceability back to source. The SRT Project along with the main UK consumer organizations has criticized the FSA position, saying that its concern for regulatory water-tightness is much less important in this case than giving consumers a proper choice, either to have or to avoid a GM foodstuff. A second concern is that the FSA's alternative proposal, for labelling as "GM free", could lay the burden of the additional costs incurred by segregation and traceability on to those who want to buy non-GM food, instead on GM food. It is normally the innovator who should bear the costs implicit in bringing a novel variety to market, not the providers of what has been hitherto the normal product. Consumers ought to have the right to choose GM food if they wish, but they should not have to pay *more* for conventional food because of labelling it as non-GM.

The issue may also reignite US-EU tensions over GM issues. In the USA GM crops are not seen as such a major issue and European concerns tend to be perceived as trade issues or hysteria. The technical and commercial developments are very much US-led, and in this context the SRT Director Dr Bruce was invited to be the European representative in a series of ethical discussions with the US biotechnology industry and with the US National Academy of Sciences. One meeting began on the morning of September 11 and was rapidly abandoned. Stranded as a group in Philadelphia, our shared humanity in response to the awful events of those days has added a new dimension to our discussion of the future for food technology and GM crops. At this crucial time for global issues such contacts are strategically important. SRT's experience in these issues has played an important contribution here and is a witness to the relevance of the gospel to the real world.

SRT has been working with other church groups on these issues. Dr Bruce drafted a report on GM food for the Church and Society Commission Conference of European Churches, and chaired an Evangelical Alliance study which produced the book "Modifying Creation", published by Paternoster Press in November 2001. We are also preparing a second edition of SRT's own book 'Engineering Genesis', updating especially on GM food risk, organic agriculture and the global context.

Biotechnology as a Social Contract

Another area of opportunity was an invitation to Dr Bruce to address the World Life Sciences Forum, Biovision, in Lyon in February 2001, to give an ethical vision for biotechnology to some of the key players in the biotechnology industry, policy makers and the research community. His paper laid out the idea of biotechnology has an invisible social contract with civil society. People are prepared to accept novel technologies to deliver certain benefits, and will accept and the changes and risks they may bring, provided a set of conditions are fulfilled.

- Values : does it uphold or challenge basic values?
- Familiarity : is the technology familiar and understood, socially embedded?
- Comparison : if it is unfamiliar, has something like it gone wrong before or proved reliable?
- Control : how much do we feel in control of the technology or the risks?

- Trust : how much do we trust those who are in control?
- Vision : how much do we share their values, motivations and goals?
- Choice : is it a voluntary or imposed risk?
- Frequency of risk : if it's too frequent it's unacceptable
- Magnitude of risk : there is a much greater aversion to high consequence risks
- Immediacy of risk : is it noticeable or does it creep up insidiously?
- Benefit : does it offer realistic, tangible benefits to the consumer?
- Profile : has it been given a positive or negative image in the media?

If several of these factors are not fulfilled, the technology is unlikely to be accepted, as was dramatically illustrated in the UK public reaction to food products derived from imported US GM soya and maize, which failed most of the conditions. Dr Bruce has since presented this analysis to members of the Agriculture and Environment Biotechnology Commission (AEBC) at a special joint meeting it held in Edinburgh with members of the SRT's Engineering Genesis working group in April 2001, where it was well received, and to the Biotechnology Research Council in June. SRT was also invited to Brazil in March as part of a British Council delegation to the state of Parana, a major grower of soya and maize. This was an exciting opportunity to discuss the ethical issues with a key developing country which is currently debating whether or not to go down the GM crops route, and how to engage the public with the issues.

GM and Cloned Animals and Ethics

SRT was also invited to meet with the AEBC to discuss the ethics of GM animals, in the light of the 2001 Assembly report. We also made two submissions to the Home Office - about the use of cost-benefit analysis in weighing up animal harm and human benefit and about the new ethical review process under the Animals (Scientific Procedures) Act. The Home Office assessor asked to meet with Dr Bruce to hear about his experience as ethical advisor on animal issues with the Scottish Agricultural College and PPL Therapeutics plc. Dr Bruce

stressed the importance of other organizations learning from SAC and PPL's examples of opening ethical issues within the organization and to wider scrutiny in the public domain.

The combination of arthritis in Dolly the cloned sheep and the creation of a set of cloned "knockout" piglets by PPL's US subsidiary gave SRT prime media exposure, with interviews as the first item on Channel 4 TV news and on BBC Scottish news. SRT was already well aware of the issues and had indeed foreseen this very debate a year before in presenting them to the 2001 General Assembly. The removal of the function of a particular gene in an animal is a serious intervention which should not be done without a very good reason. Overcoming an immune rejection to enable pig organs be transplanted into human patients might constitute such a reason, but only provided the prospects for saving life were considerable. It is worthwhile continuing research but only as long as viable solutions seem likely to problems of rejection and the risk of virus transfer.

Dolly's arthritis was exaggerated in the media as throwing the concept of cloning into doubt. While giving rise to concern, several factors indicate this conclusion to be premature. It is a single result on a unique animal. To be statistically significant, diseases associated with old age would need to be found several more times in cloned animals. Although Dolly shows evidence in her chromosomes as if she were "older" than normal, some other cloned farm animals show the opposite effect, appearing to be "younger". This indicates how much remains unclear in the underlying science of cloning. Dolly was by no means the first cloned animal, but her novelty was in being cloned by reprogramming *adult* cells. Her arthritis might be associated with this method of cloning rather than all cloning. Most animal cloning uses a more efficient method starting from reproductive cells. By this means Roslin and PPL have sheep both of 4 years old and one a year older than Dolly, which do not show arthritis. Both organizations use animal cloning primarily as a means to do novel genetic modifications. Once a "founder" GM animal is produced, they no longer need to clone, and breed by normal mating. The major practical doubts about animal cloning remain the welfare problems at birth in sheep and cattle (though not in pigs). SRT has repeatedly said that these problems would need to be resolved for the technique to be used regularly on animals.

Human Cloning Legislation
The media fascination with cloning has given unmerited attention to spurious claims for the imminent production of cloned babies. The scientists concerned have drawn universal condemnation from their professional communities, on ethical grounds and because of the serious risks involved. This did, however, prompt the UK Government finally to legislate to ban it in December 2001. SRT had first questioned the Government in 1997 whether the Human Fertilization and Embryology Act of 1990 really did outlaw the cloning of human beings, and had several times urged specific legislation. The Government eventually promised this in August 2000, but gave it no priority. In November 2001 a judicial review ruled that creating cloned human embryos lay outwith the strict definition of embryos in the Act. This left both reproductive and therapeutic uses of nuclear transfer cloning unregulated, and so led to an emergency Bill specifically to ban human reproductive cloning. While this is welcomed, it is a sad reflection that it took a political embarrassment to rush legislation which could have been carefully planned four years earlier. The Appeal Court has since overturned the judicial review, so that the use of cloned human embryos for research into stem cells once more comes under the HFE Act. Guidelines still need to be set, however, to ensure that embryo research is only done when there really is no alternative, and to ensure that alternative, non-embryonic methods are also fully researched.

Wider Ethical Debate on Embryonic Stem Cells and Therapeutic Uses of Cloning
The UK Parliament's decision to allow embryonic stem cell research and cloned embryos has aroused much controversy in continental Europe, especially in Germany. The SRT Director was invited to speak at a number of high level discussions on the issue by the British Embassy in Berlin, Humbolt University in Berlin, and the European Molecular Biology Laboratory in Heidelberg. He wrote an article in the leading German newspaper the Frankfurter Allgemeine Zeitung. He was also asked by the European Commission to speak at its major conference on stem cells in Brussels in December 2001, and by the European Parliament to discuss these issues with members of its Human Genetics Committee when it visited Edinburgh in November. He also presented objections to the patenting of stem cells at a hearing of the European Commission's ethical advisory group, on behalf of European churches.

In these various discussions, much bafflement has greeted the General Assembly's 2001 position that cloned embryos could be used to produce stem cells for treating degenerative diseases, but that spare IVF embryos should be not be used for this purpose, because God intends embryos only for reproduction. Many leading ethical bodies such as the EC's ethical advisory group have argued the opposite. It has been contended that it would be illogical to forbid the use of "spare" embryos to make stem cells on the particular grounds that this would frustrate the intention for them, because in practice the fate of the thousands of spare embryos will not be to produce babies but to be destroyed. It has been also argued that cloned embryos are not of less of human status than IVF ones, but present more ethical problems because of the physical risks and making it easier to perform reproductive cloning. SRT considers there is some validity to these arguments.

Science and Society
"Trust me I'm a Scientist" was the provocative title of a day session about scientists and their sometimes strained relationship with society, at the annual Festival of British Association for the Advancement of Science in Glasgow in September. Dr Bruce spoke on the church's role in science, describing how SRT has provided a unique, creative space to bring scientists together with specialists in ethics, social sciences and other disciplines, often before issues became points of contention. He was an expert witness in a public debate on "Should we trust scientists?", arguing that we should, if they prove trustworthy, but not if they merely dismiss public concerns as ignorance or promote science as answering all problems. He also spoke on the new Scottish Science Strategy, arguing that it needs a much greater emphasis on ethical issues in setting science policy.

Energy Policy and Risk Issues

SRT has continued a watching brief on climate change and energy policy issues in relation to the review of energy policy, the development of renewable sources and the future of nuclear power. It hopes to begin a major study on these issues later in 2002. A new dossier on climate change is also available through the European Christian Environment Network of which SRT is a member. SRT continues its important work on value issues relating to technological risk, in biotechnology, mobile telecommunications, waste disposal and energy.

The 2002 World Summit on Sustainable Development, Johannesburg : "Rio + 10"

In 1992 the Earth Summit in Rio de Janeiro put environment high on the global agenda in 1992. Ten years on what have we to show for it? The world's leaders will gather again at the World Summit on Sustainable Development in Johannesburg from 25 August to 4 September 2002. As they take stock of the present and consider where we go in future, the UK churches have a variety of initiatives to keep our responsibility for care for God's creation to the fore in our local congregations and communities, and to our Governments. ACTS have already contributed to the joint input made by the Scottish Civic Forum and the Scottish Executive to the formal UK submission to the Summit. Individual congregations are encouraged to hold special services before or during the Summit focusing on creation and sustainability. Study material and sermon outlines will be available via SRT's website. Here is also a good opportunity to reach out into the community by holding a public debate focusing on one of the themes under discussion, perhaps with other local groups.

Eco-Congregation Resource Packs Available

Probably the best way for churches to get involved locally is to join the Eco-Congregation Programme. This was set up jointly in 2000 by Churches Together in Britain and Ireland and the government's Going for Green initiative, to help congregations across Britain find practical ways of caring for God's creation. Following its successful launch in Scotland at Dunblane Cathedral in March 2001, all congregations which have received introductory packs are now being encouraged to register formally with the programme. This will enable them to receive the full range of a dozen excellent resource modules which were published in November 2001. These are available in ring binder form free of charge to churches which register with the scheme. Fresh inquiries from congregations are also welcomed. Further information is available by contacting Eco-Congregation Enquiry, Elizabeth House, The Pier, Wigan WN3 4EX, freephone 0800 783 7838. With good material now available, it would be an opportune time also to extend the concept of a full environmental audit to 121 George Street and other central church premises.

Dr Donald Bruce, of the Society, Religion and Technology Project

APPENDIX XI

SUPPLEMENTARY REPORT OF THE SOCIETY, RELIGION AND TECHNOLOGY PROJECT ON "SUSTAINABLE AGRICULTURE"

1.   Introduction

In the three years since the SRT Project reported to the General Assembly on genetically modified crops and food in 1999,[1] there has been widespread discussion about the methods and technologies we should use in our future agriculture. "How should we make our food better?" is a question on the lips of lay person and expert alike. We are all concerned about food. In reaction to pesticides, BSE and the GM food controversy, there has been a growing interest in what are called sustainable agricultural practices, and in particular in "organic" methods and products. Does this, as some believe, represent the trend for the agriculture of tomorrow, majoring more on health

---

[1] Church of Scotland (1999), *The Society, Religion and Technology Project Report on Genetically Modified Food*, Reports to the General Assembly and Deliverances of the General Assembly 1999, pp 20/93-20/103, and Board of National Mission Deliverances 42-45, p 20/4.

and environmental care than production efficiency, or is just trendy, strong on a lifestyle and imagery but short on practicality, as others argue? SRT has contributed to the working group of the Church and Nation Committee which is reporting to this Assembly on some of the wider lessons learned from the foot and mouth outbreak of 2001. The present SRT report focuses on the particular question of what represents a sustainable approach to agriculture.

There has been a tendency to polarise the answer as though it were a simple question of alternatives - organic or GM. In reality it is more complex, with many factors to take into account. In weighing these up, which underlying principles should take priority? There are three main criteria and corresponding approaches, each with their advocates. In a highly competitive international climate, one argument maintains that it is essential to continue intensive methods, focused on high inputs, efficiencies and yields in order to compete on the global market? A second sector sees the future requiring a far greater emphasis on environmental protection with alternative sustainable approaches, for example using greatly reduced chemical inputs, sensitivities to soil quality, and careful habitat management. A third group regards such changes as insufficient, agriculture needing instead a revolution to break the mould of the past 50 years, by moving to a different philosophy of agriculture altogether, as embodied in organic farming methods. These three approaches are broadly described as intensive, integrated and organic.

Are these either/or questions, or is the best policy way forward some combination of all of them? Amongst these various approaches, what is the part, if any, for a range of emerging biotechnologies like targeted genetic modification, plant and animal genomics, marker assisted selection, and sophisticated new approaches to soil science? This report examines each of three methods in turn with their good and bad points, but examines organic agriculture in more depth in view of its particular claims.

This report draws upon SRT's detailed involvement with agricultural biotechnology since 1993, and its wider insights on theology and environmental care,[2][3][4][5] food and agriculture over the past 25 years. SRT has been involved in numerous discussions on sustainable agriculture before and since its 1999 report. Its

Engineering Genesis working group has focused especially on these issues in preparing the new edition of our book.[6] They featured prominently in a parallel study for Evangelical Alliance chaired by the SRT Director, recently published in the book "Modifying Creation".[7] SRT has close ongoing links with the agricultural sector, for example through membership on the Care for the Protection of the Environment Committee of the Scottish Agricultural College (SAC). It is in continuing discussions on research and policy in the fields of organic agriculture, reduced environmental impacts and genetic modification, and has taken part in a number of conferences and consultations on sustainable agriculture.

2. High Input, High Output Intensive Farming
The current debate has arisen against a background of half a century of application of industrial methods to crop agriculture, which arose out of the situation at the end of the Second World War. There was not enough food to go round and people were all too aware of the fragility of food supply. This led to the impetus to produce more home-grown food, and to increase yields by use of breeding technologies, chemical inputs, mechanisation and systems management. Very large increases in yields were achieved. For example by the late 1980s improved wheat varieties enabled bread to be produced from British-grown wheat, with a marked reduction in imports.

Intensive arable farming follows a linear model, which typically puts in high fertiliser levels, protects seed from

---

[2] SRT Project (1986), *While the Earth Endures*, SRT Project, Edinburgh

[3] Somerville, Charles (1994), *Seeing Scotland from the Summit - Sustainable Development in Scotland after Rio*, SRT Project, Edinburgh.

[4] EECCS (1995), *The Dominant Economic Model and Sustainable Development: Are they Compatible*, European Ecumenical Commission for Church and Society, Brussels

[5] EECCS (1999), *Sustainable Development and the Market Economy*, European Ecumenical Commission for Church and Society, Brussels

[6] Bruce, D. and Bruce, A. (eds) (2002), *Engineering Genesis*, Earthscan, London, in preparation.

[7] Bruce, D. and Horrocks, D. (eds) (2001), *Modifying Creation*, Paternoster Press, Carlisle

disease before planting with a fungicide, removes weed competition from the field with a herbicide, uses disease-resistant varieties. A farmer may spray five or six times in a growing season. There may be prophylactic use of agrichemicals as an economic precaution in order to maximise yields. To recoup the high input costs of chemical inputs and machinery, high yields of good quality crops are indeed essential to this approach. The driver is to compete at global market prices. This requires maximisation of unit size, the externalisation of costs to the environment, and a narrow focus on production. Unless they are cost-effective in themselves, environmental features tend to be viewed as externalities which might be funded by grants. GM crops would be worth the additional cost of seed if they provided for control of pests, weeds and diseases using less chemical inputs, and the farmer would argue that it also reduced the environmental impact by comparison with multiple spraying.

In a globalised context, this approach is seen by some as the only one likely to be able to compete in major commodity crops in the international markets. This approach is more typical of regions of England like East Anglia and Lincolnshire than Scotland, where the soil quality and climate are less favourable, but there are nonetheless some significant Scottish users. Compared with the pre-war situation, intensive agriculture has led to very much higher yields and cheaper food, but at what wider cost? In parallel with this, cheap and rapid transport and sophisticated sourcing and distribution systems have also brought a much wider diet to the tables of many people.

These same trends have however also been seen as the root of the present agricultural crisis. The domination of a 'production and efficiency' mind set has caused serious negative impacts on the environment and wildlife which have for many prompted a re-examination of our ways of practising agriculture. It has brought a considerable loss in biodiversity. Insect and weed seeds, which provide food for many birds, have been greatly reduced. Hedges have been removed to make room for larger machinery, yet non-crop plants often provide important habitats. There are high levels of waste and nutrient loss into the water courses. Soil organic matter content has decreased.

Erosion can also be a problem. Such effects have also been exacerbated by a round about of EC subsidies and quotas, and a constant pressure to reduce prices and lower overhead costs. This in turn has meant less people on the land and concerns about the long-term viability of the rural areas with poorer yielding sectors. In combination these various factors have led many Christians to see this approach as incompatible with care for God's creation. The Currie Commission report on the future of agriculture after foot and mouth disease comments "Beyond any doubt the main cause of this decay has been the rise of modern, often more intensive farming techniques." [8] Its recommendation of a major change to sustainable alternatives reflects a broad feeling that we cannot continue the intensive route unchecked.

3. Integrated farming

The name embraces a wide variety of arable farming systems which have been developed within the context of mainstream agriculture, but which aim to be sustainable in one way or another. The contention is that present systems of agriculture are capable of adaptation in much more environmentally sustainable ways, without necessarily calling for so complete a revolution as that entailed in the organic approach. Quite a lot of the broader claims which have popularly become associated with the word "organic" would apply to these methods also. The high media profile given to organic systems and their claims to the moral high ground, have tended to mean that there is less public awareness of integrated farming methods, but in agricultural terms they may prove to be of greater significance. The environmentalist, Jonathan Porritt, has predicted that "the boundaries between what we now describe as 'organic', 'chemical' or 'GM', are likely to soften; whatever the descriptor, all production systems will be bound by the same discipline of sustainability".[9]

Integrated systems aim to produce food profitably,

[8] Currie D. (ed) (2002), *Farming and Food: A Sustainable Future*, Report of the Policy Commission on the Future of Farming and Food, p.68, Cabinet Office, London.
[9] Porritt, J. (2000) *Playing Safe: Science and the Environment*, p.90, Thames & Hudson, London.

whilst safeguarding the environment by a balanced and holistic approach to farming, which considers all aspects of food production. This includes the site and landscape, the nutrient status and structure of the soil, crop rotation, variety choice, pest, weed and disease control, conservation, energy use, waste disposal, and also the management, auditing and monitoring of the entire farming process. In principle, its scope of its practical application is as wide as organic, but it sets out from a different starting point and philosophy.

Plant varieties are carefully chosen for disease resistance, aiming to reduce pesticide usage to when outbreaks occur. This contrasts with a high input system, where spraying is used as an insurance, just in case. Soil is analysed for its nutrient status and a field analysed into zones. More controlled amount of fertiliser added accordingly, reducing the surplus run-off. Particular attention is paid to the conservation of wildlife on the farm, including hedge and pond management, and woodland conservation. By careful monitoring inputs it aims to use inputs with precision and wasting nothing. Whereas organic agriculture formally proscribes transgenesis, integrated methods would allow GM crops if there was merit in doing so. GM crops could be used which targeted specific nutritional, health or environmental improvements. For example, engineered traits might be favoured which improved nutrient uptake or conferred resistance to particular fungi, but not GM crops tolerant to broad range herbicides.

Integrated agriculture has many different expressions including agri-environment schemes promoted by the Government. For example, since 1993 Scottish Natural Heritage has promoted the TIBRE project (Targeted Inputs for a Better Rural Environment) to use the best of new technology to reduce environmental impacts of intensive systems. Such systems claims to be more flexible than organic farming and need not have a long conversion period. This may be an attraction for many farmers. Because it is not governed by a tight set of 'rules' it can also be harder to regulate and to market, since integrated systems do not have one all-embracing label equivalent to "organic". The Currie Report found some integrated approaches pitched at too high level to achieve large penetration into mainstream farming practice. It argued

that they are appropriate as a "top tier" for especially sensitive environments, but are rather too expensive and cumbersome for more general uptake in the farming community. It recommended major financial investment to enable a lower level "entry point" into a less demanding system, which may be made gradually more sustainable later on.

For some Christians, integrated farming represents a suitable alternative to intensive agriculture on the one hand and the more radical and uncertainties aspects of organic farming. It still allows such methods as chemical inputs and genetic modification. At best it would aim to go with the best of agricultural methods and technology and avoid the worst. It might be criticised for remaining too close to intensive systems and merely ameliorating some of their excesses. For some, this would not go far enough, and a more revolutionary path would be seen as the way ahead.

4.　Organic Agriculture
i.　What is organic farming?

Organic farming lies at the opposite end of a spectrum of approaches from intensive agriculture, but has some radical distinctions from all the others. While it shares some similar practical aims with integrated farming, organic agriculture it is qualitatively different. It is not so much about not using synthetic pesticides and fertilisers, as representing a different philosophy of agriculture. It is a holisitic, integrated system of farming based on the management of the natural ecosystem and its processes, so that crop production is in balance with the ability of the soil to release nutrients. Synthetic fertilisers are unnecessary because of the way organic methods manage the soil, its microbes and nutrients, as summed in the phrase 'feed the soil and let the soil feed the plant'.[10] Indeed, soluble "inorganic" fertilisers which directly feed the plant are seen as impoverishing the soil. Instead of fertilisers, wastes from crop residues and manure become nutrients for crop products. Thus, unlike intensive arable systems, most organic farming includes livestock as an integral part of the system. Rotating the

---

[10] E. Balfour (1943), *The Living Soil,* Faber and Faber, London.

use of a field with carefully chosen species enables nutrients to be recycled within the system. Crop health is to be maintained by natural systems of pest, weed and disease control, using rotations, mechanical weeding and various ingenious planting patterns which exploit the natural pest and disease resistance of certain plant combinations.

It is a more human-intensive approach. To maintain such a system requires considerable care on the part of the farmer. The above description is an ideal and it is not always achieved. At times the system fails, and under such circumstances organic farmers are allowed to use some specified older pesticides as a last resort, for example to control potato blight. Initially the potential use of genetically modified organisms (GMO's) was unclear, but a decision was made in 1996 explicitly to reject them. The main grounds are ideological. A sharp ethical line is drawn between selective breeding and genetic modification. The former is said to present a more natural way of agriculture, respecting the distinctions of species which have evolved. GM is seen as a disruption of inherent balances which was intrinsically wrong regardless of any apparent benefits. The second is that mixing genes across species is seen as inherently more risky than selective breeding, or that not enough is known to predict the long term implications of GMO's. This argument is not primarily evidential - it would be very difficult to prove - but conceptual, associating one type of agricultural intervention with higher risks than another.[11] Organic organisations have been actively campaigning for the eradication of all use of GMOs and oppose the current farm scale trials programmes. There are some, however, who are sympathetic to organic agriculture but who question the long term wisdom of rejecting all GM applications in principle.

Organic farming aims to produce good yields without needing artificial inputs, while emphasising harmony with nature, biodiversity, soil health, energy conservation, food quality, farm animal welfare, and the avoidance of environmental pollution. Its origins date back to pioneering work in the 1930s and 1940s of Sir Albert Howard, Lady Eve Balfour and others. The term organic defines a particular form of production process rather than a product as such. Unlike integrated or intensive farming, it has developed into a system which is quite strictly defined by a set of minimum rules set by the UK Register of Organic Food Standards (UKROFS). These have to be adhered to allow the use of the term "organic". Within these rules, there are several approaches, regulated by different bodies, of which the most prominent is the Soil Association. It is a system to which the farmer has to "convert". This is a process requiring a minimum of two years, usually with grants available, before the farmer can gain accreditation to sell produce labelled as "organic", and is subject to monitoring thereafter. While aiming to be pure according to its own definitions, organic produce has to accept the reality that it may contain traces of pesticides and foreign gene constructs because of the proximity of other farmed systems and there are appropriate levels set in the rules.

ii.   Evaluating Organic

On the face of it these are some very good ideas and concepts, compatible with many Christian concerns about the environment and much else. One major problem is how effective is would be on a large scale. It is generally harder to obtain a high predictable yield of good quality using these systems. Supermarkets are also geared to a continuous supply concept which is less sensitive to small scale production and seasonal effects. Organic food frequently costs more in the supermarket because it tends to have more variable yields and be significantly more expensive to run that current conventional systems. There is an argument that the comparison is distorted because the conventional crops appear artificially cheap because they do not include their costs to the environment and to health. Most people buy by the price at the shelf, however, rather than the full life cycle costs. It is also not clear that this correction would be enough in itself to make organic the more economic option. On the other hand there seems considerable scope for research investment into organic methods to give substantial improvements in yield. One recent comparative US study of intensive,

---

[11] Bruce, D. M. and Eldridge, J. T. (2000), *The Role of Values in the GM Debate*, in "Foresight and Precaution", M. P. Cottam, D. W. Harvey, R. P. Pape and J. E. Tait (eds), pp. 855–862, Balkema, Rotterdam.

integrated and organic apple production showed that encouraging yields were possible.[12] The Government should therefore put priority into significantly increased research effort in the organic sector.

A main practical attraction for farmers is that it is a crop which carries a premium because some people are prepared to pay more for what they regard as better food or food grown in better ways. Indeed public demand for organic products has risen considerably since the late 1990's, and the trend looks fairly stable. If demand increased very greatly the premium may fall, but at present the organic sector remains a relatively small part of the UK agriculture. Organic proponents are uncomfortable with the fact that large amounts of organic food are at present imported to meet consumer demand, because of environmental impacts from the transportation and because it sits awkwardly with the concept of food produced in the local environment. This indicates that there is considerable scope for expansion of this sector. How much is open to debate. Proponents say the aim should be that 30% of UK agriculture is organic by 2010, and eventually 100%.

Such an uptake would, however, represent a major change for the organic system from a radical alternative run by committed enthusiasts to a mainstream farming system, and introduce significant uncertainties. It is a common experience in technology generally that scaling up may generate unexpected problems. The concept of organic farms is small, local and sensitively managed. Would the concept survive being operated at something akin to industrial scale and by perhaps less committed farmers? Organic systems tend to be less tolerant of neglect and poor practice. There are also significant economic and supply risks. No one knows if 56 million people could be fed organically or whether we could afford whatever this would cost. These are unknowns which must be taken into account. Applying the precautionary principle implies some caution about seeing organic systems as the whole future. As with all systems, scaling up would need to be applied stepwise and with careful monitoring for problems.

iii. Is Organic Really Better for us?
Because of the nature of the claims which are made about

the superiority of organic food, some discussion is necessary. The environmental claims of organic agriculture seem to have definite merit, certainly by comparison with intensive agriculture. In a Scottish context, whether it is markedly better for biodiversity, pollution levels and general environmental good than well managed small scale mixed farming or integrated systems is at present less clear, but the general environmental picture is good, as would be expected for an approach which gives this top priority.

At present there is little evidence one way or the other for the claim that organic food is necessarily safer or better for health, however. Such comparisons are very difficult to make. It is claimed to be more healthy because it uses an intrinsically better way of growing crops, and that synthetic chemicals make food inherently worse. The philosophy of organic agriculture speaks of concepts like "vitality", which are difficult to define in any meaningful scientific sense. There are tests such as the pattern of crystallisation of copper chloride salts which are said by proponents to indicate the better vitality of crops grown by organic rather than conventional means. The problem is that such claims as these are at the borderline of the conventional scientific way of evaluation. Indeed some scientists regard it as well beyond the borders. As with the church authorities in Galileo's time there is a danger of saying that our dogma says certain things are so, therefore the scientific evidence will prove it. It will be difficult to determine whether they represent anything more than a faith statement of what believers believe about a system, or something which has a more objective validity.

Some people buy it because they feel that it is more "natural". As all farming systems are artificial when compared with the original landscape of Britain, the 'natural' argument is only relative and perhaps somewhat nostalgic. Organic farming is not a return to pre-war farming. It is a different system. It makes use of good quality, up-to-date cultivars, and even allows some limited use of older pesticides in certain situations. The notion

---

[12] Reganold, J. P., Glover, J. D., Andrews, P. K. and Hinman, H. R. (2001), *Sustainability of three apple production systems*, Nature vol. 410, 19 April 2001, p.926.

of natural food may simply express a sense that recent intensive methods have gone too far in their intervention, without asking too many questions about *how* natural food is supposed to be. Organic farming does not by definition imply 'pure' products, and is facing some safety questions of its own from the Food Standards Agency, for example over micro-organisms in manure and mycotoxins in grain. There is an undoubted appeal for many people that organic food represents a more attractive and sustainable concept than food produced by intensive methods.

5.   Organic ideology and the spiritual dimension
Whilst many farm organically because they see it as a better way of farming, and some even because it is a promising niche market to get into, for some organic is truly a movement with an ideological thread, a political goal, or a spiritual expression. Its pioneers saw it as an alternative to the political philosophies and cultural decrepitude of the inter-war years with a 'revivified' rural life.[13]   Today it is being promoted as a post-industrial, holistic alternative to the over-application of reductionist science. It finds common cause with the environmental movement, which generally regards it as being the best expression of the principles of environmental sustainability within the field of agriculture.

A seminal paper by Lady Eve Balfour also reveals that although the organic movement has some Christian roots, it also drew on the anthroposophical ideas of Rudolf Steiner and similar movements earlier last century.[14]   It included concepts like vitality, energy flows and balances which are speculative and sit awkwardly both with scientific and biblical understandings. Lady Eve claimed that 'The energy manifesting in birth, growth, reproduction, death, decay and rebirth can only flow through channels composed of living cells, and when the flow is interrupted by inert matter [meaning in this case inorganic fertilisers] it can be short circuited with consequent damage to some parts of the food chain.' Such notions have strong parallels with the cluster of beliefs commonly called New Age. While would certainly be an exaggeration to describe the organic agriculture as New Age as such, there are many for whom its underlying values represent the motivation in seeking to demonstrate a valid and viable alternative. For them, the ideology is

much more explicit and integral.

There have been many environmental theologies advanced as the basis of care for God's creation in the 30 years. SRT has itself played a pioneering role, notably in Ruth Page's concept of companionship with nature as a necessary corrective to the sometimes too "top down" view of environmental stewardship.[15]   In recent years we have addressed the challenge of technology and environmental care in terms of a balance of intervention and conservation between two contrasting and complementary pictures in Genesis 1 and 2.

Genesis 1 describes the creation in elemental terms with the strong language of dominion to describe human relations with the creation. Men and women are commanded by God to 'fill the earth and subdue it' and to 'rule over' fish, birds, livestock, creeping creatures, and 'all the earth' (Gen. 1:26-28). This stresses God's calling to humankind, made in God's image, to express God-given gifts and creativity in transforming the natural world. Thus we may say that to practice technology, in its broadest definition of the 'practical arts', is a fundamental part of being human. This is expressed in passing in numerous ways throughout the Old Testament – in agriculture, irrigation, building, mining, metallurgy, ship-building, and all kinds of skilled crafts. Genesis 2 counterbalances this picture of intervention by describing human relationship to creation within the subtler context of a garden which we are to work and to care for (Genesis 2:15). Cultivation implies work and intervention, but it places more emphasis on the horizontal dimension. We are fellow creatures, in a good garden of which God is the owner. Care for our fellow creatures and the overall systems of what God has created should thus act as a restraint on human ambitions.

Thus in these creation accounts we find a creative tension between notions of development and conservation, which does not have a simple resolution. God calls us to work to find a dynamic balance between

---

[13] P. Conford, Introduction, in P. Conford, (ed.), *The Organic Tradition*, Bideford, Devon: Green Books, 1988, pp.14-15.

[14] E. Balfour, *Towards Sustainable Agriculture – The Living Soil*, IFOAM Conference, Dornach: Switzerland, 1977.

[15] SRT (1986), *While the Earth Endures, op cit.*

the two as one of the tensions of the Christian life on earth. There is a further dimension that human beings are also fallen from the relationships which God intended - with God, our fellow humans and also with the creation. Our stewardship and companionship of the earth has been spoiled and the whole creation groans as a result. It will not be restored to a contemporary environmental idyll or social utopia, but awaits God's final salvation in the parousia.

Christians should therefore beware of two opposing secular pressures. One is the drive of determinism which promotes scientific rationality as an idol, autonomous from the guidance of God's laws and wisdom. Christians rightly oppose a "technicist" attitude which sees things only for their functional or economic value, or as nothing more than a reductionist scientific description. Many see this error expressed in intensive agriculture, in which an unmitigated dominion over fellow creatures expressed in an efficiency and production orientation which ought to have been restrained the parallel responsibility of care for God's wider creation.

Less familiar is the opposite concern reflected in a rise of what some have termed neo-pagan views which sees nature as quasi-divine instead of created, and not to be tampered with lest 'she' strike us back. Even if not reverting to mother goddess terminology, it rests on an assumption that 'nature knows best' holding an exaggerated concept of pristine nature which tends to be static and fatalistic. A cultural trend in this direction has been noticed before in what people mean by 'God'.[16] Human intervention and scientific endeavour is flawed unless it stays close to natural patterns. In contrast a Christian view of nature is morally ambiguous, perhaps fallen, and on occasion dangerous to human well being. It is not necessarily a good guide

Thus a Christian understanding has mixed views about the basis for organic agriculture. Many of the concepts involved in both integrated and organic agriculture resonate with a Christian understanding of care for God's creation. These include respect for the natural world, care of the soil, health and wholeness, holism and connectedness, permanence, the recycling of wastes and responsibility for future generations. On the other hand, the more speculative claims about organic agriculture are

problematical. Acting in harmony with nature's patterns and to 'balance the energies' against disruptions by inorganic chemicals seem to play down the validity of human creativity against an idealised view of nature. They borrow terminology like 'patterns' and 'energies' from science, but give them very different meanings. There is also an implicit idealism about human solutions, which it shares with some secular ecological thinking, which fails to take sufficient account of human fallenness. Christians may differ quite strongly with some of the movement's interpretation of such concepts and the world view they fit into. But we should see this is as an opportunity to bear witness to Christ and engage in dialogue concerning the spiritual dimension in agriculture and environment, rather than something to steer clear of. From Old and New Testaments, the patterns of the natural world furnish any number of examples and pointers to God and to care for creation, yet humans can also intervene to adapt them to our purposes under God. This is not exclusive to organic methods. Organic should not be seen as necessarily more ethical than any integrated methods of farming. Both reflects a desire to do things better, reacting to the over-technologisation of food production.

6. Some Conclusions about Sustainable Agriculture

Food is fundamental to human survival and well being. We have to eat to live and we have to produce food to eat. Producing food is therefore fundamental to any community of people. To the extent that we do not grow our food ourselves, we are in a dependent situation on others outside the community. To function properly this requires stability, trust and a measure inter-dependence. Food is also connected with health and poverty. Too much, too little, and the wrong balance of nutrients in the diet all affect human health, as do good or bad food processing and preparation. These are linked to poverty and how much we can afford to spend on food. In past generations a large proportion of the population spent much of their energy and lives in providing food. Trends over centuries means that in the UK, hardly anyone now

---

[16] Church of Scotland (1996), *Understanding the Times*, Edinburgh: St Andrew Press.

earns a living from growing food, though a significant number do so in processing, transport, retail and catering in the food sector.

All food is derived from God's creation. In God's rich provision for human needs, we are given the creation to use, but within limits. The efficient use of God's creation, soil, water, crops, nutrients, minerals, livestock makes for good stewardship of creation, husbanding it well for the poor as well as the rich. But the too ready import of industrial motifs from mechanical and chemical production processes has brought a functional view of agriculture and its resources, which sits awkwardly with the concept that God's creation, its creatures, processes and ecology, have intrinsic value. Providing food involves parts of God's creation being both products of nature and products of human industry, but a proper balance has been lost between them. The functional, formulaic approach of the physical sciences fits less well with complex living systems. We have concentrated on certain features of food security, efficiency and lowered costs which have been the main drivers since the Second World War graphically brought home the perils of food insecurity. These trends seem to many to have gone too far. It is probably the case that we cannot afford for food to stay as cheap as it is, because it costs too much in other ways.

Farming has always impacted on the environment. Intensive agriculture has increased the impact, and is high in its use of non-renewable energy, is highly interventionist and produces substantial wastes. Some consider it 'violent', reflecting the traditional view that farming is a struggle against the forces of nature. They advocate a paradigm shift to what they regard as more benign, lower energy, information-rich sustainable farming systems, inspired by a belief in the possibility of farming in harmony with nature. For some these ideals find partial practical expression in organic farming. Others do not see the need for so radical an alternative, and look to see how conventional methods can be adapted to achieve results that might be equally good in terms of sustainability.

The words sustainable, integrated and organic have all come to mean several things. They are in danger of becoming Humpty Dumpty words which mean whatever the speaker wants them to mean. Sustainability of *what*,

we may ask? Each of the different approaches sees different priorities for what needs sustaining. The word "organic" has several definitions including a particular class of chemicals or the defined system of agriculture described above. But it has also become a connotation word which conveys a general impression or a lifestyle choice, which embraces things which go far beyond the practices and ideals of organic agriculture. Farmers markets, locally grown produce and food boxes are not the sole preserve of any one form of agriculture. It is also quite a problem to disentangle what is truly a characteristic of organic agriculture from a range of other sustainable methods of agriculture which aim at rather similar things, and might claim to be equally "natural". A lot that is claimed for organic would be equally true of several other methods.

Organic as a practical system well worth trying on a larger scale and seeing how sustainable it is in economic practical and environmental terms. If it were a substantial percentage, say 30%, it would raise some new problems of scale and widening its practice from a relatively small group of dedicated enthusiasts to the wider farming community which may compromise the standards in practice. In general it would be environmentally a good thing, but its nutritional and health claims are much more uncertain. These may be a question of what you believe to be the case rather than things that can be proven, though it is worth trying to test the claims scientifically as far as possible. The system is not infallible because soils, local pests, diseases, weather, and the practice of the farmer all represent great variability. There also remains the risks that it may not prove economically viable on a large scale or provide enough food. These are unknowns, but precaution suggests we should expand the rate of uptake at a level from which we could draw back if its undoubted promises proved to be seriously hampered by its potential concerns.

Rather than embrace organic agriculture as the exclusive choice, the conclusion of this report is to advocate the range of alternatives which could be defined as environmentally sustainable and which have hopes of proving economically and socially viable. This would certainly include organic methods, and encourage their much greater development in Scotland and the UK generally, but it would also embrace a range of alternatives described above. These offer a more flexible approaches which would not adopt a fundamental rejection of chemical inputs or genetic modification under the right circumstances. Indeed, the absolute prohibition of GMO's by organic systems is seen by some as a mistake. It is argued that some of the cultivars currently approved for organic use have had no less invasive origins, and in some cases GM technology could, in the view of some, achieve things very helpful to organic systems.

For the Christian consumer who is concerned about where our food is coming from and wants to have a more ethical approach to food purchasing and consumption, buying organic food will have strong attractions. Christians should be aware that less radical alternatives also exist, which may be equally good. The picture is not simple. Organic products tend to be expensive, which puts them effectively out of the reach of the poor. While demand exceeds UK supply, a lot of organic produce has unfortunately to be flown in from abroad. It would also be misleading to imply that simply by buying organic

'you've done your bit'. There are other important ethical considerations, such as sourcing fairly traded goods, eating products primarily in season, buying locally, not shopping at out-of-town supermarkets.

Even if the underlying ideals and ideologies may differ from those of Christian exponents. Organic systems and integrated farming both offer alternatives of sustainable agriculture, and a means of expressing Christian environmental responsibility and social justice more than conventional intensive approaches. In the case of organic agriculture, Christians should be wary of the conceptual package and its philosophical undergirding and quasi-religious elements. But the same applies to all farming approaches and movements where they deviate from Christian principles. While integrated farming may not have an explicit ideology, it too has its more subtle assumptions, which also need to be evaluated in a biblical light. The challenge is to develop approaches that enable Christians to farm in a way that reflects Biblical principles yet remain in farming, and provide a basis for a stronger prophetic voice in the agricultural arena.

BOARD OF THE IONA COMMUNITY
MAY 2002

PROPOSED DELIVERANCE

The General Assembly

1. Receive the report and thank the Board.

2. Commend the Iona Community's faithful commitment to its purpose of seeking 'new ways to touch the hearts of all' through the renewal of worship and the pursuit of an approach to spirituality that integrates devotional concerns and action for justice and peace-making.

3. Express appreciation of the contribution of the Wild Goose Resource Group to the life of the churches and encourage them in developing their future strategy.

4. Congratulate Rev Kathy Galloway on her election to be Leader of the Community from 1 August and wish her well; and thank Rev Norman Shanks for his service over the past seven years.

REPORT

General

1. The Board is pleased to report that the Community has had another good year. The Community's programmes at the three residential centres on Iona and Mull and the mainland activities have again attracted much interest and support, as the Community has pursued, faithfully and creatively, its concern for the renewal of worship, the promotion of increased ecumenical understanding, and an approach to spirituality that embraces witness for peace and justice. This generally positive situation is reflected both in the membership figures, with the number of Members and Associate Members continuing to rise, and in the state of the Community's finances: whereas a deficit budget had been prepared for 2001, in fact expenditure only narrowly exceeded income, owing to the season on Iona being better than expected and significant savings being made across the range of the Community's work. Financial planning for 2002 has gone ahead on the basis of a break-even budget and increased attention is being given to fund-raising strategy.

2. Three major themes have dominated the life of the Community in the course of the past year. In September two months' notice was given that, owing to lack of funding, the Pearce Institute in Govan, within which the Community's administrative offices and most of the mainland staff were located, would close at the end of November. Particularly in view of its links with the Community's origins the Community was sorry to leave Govan after around twenty years there, but the Board has been particularly impressed by the speed with which new offices, highly suitable in terms of both space and accessibility, were found on Sauchiehall Street and by the commitment of the staff in completing the move so smoothly and settling into the new premises so effectively.

3. Throughout the past year the Community has been pursuing a 'leadership discernment process' with a view to electing a successor to Norman Shanks, whose seven-year term as Leader ends during Community Week on Iona at the end of July. Through extended discussion within local Family Groups, at Community Week last summer, and at a special meeting of Family Group representatives last September, consideration was given to the task, direction and different models of leadership. In the course of the process several important issues, relating to strategy and priorities, were identified, and

these will be followed up as appropriate. The eventual decision was to retain the single-post model, and at the beginning of March it was announced that Rev Kathy Galloway had been elected as the next Leader, to take up responsibility on 1 August during this year's Community Week.. The Board wishes Rev Kathy Galloway well and expresses warm thanks to Norman Shanks for all that he has done these past seven years.

4.   The third major theme relates to the Community's political witness, and commitment to action for justice, peace-making and social change as integral to Christian discipleship. Members of the Community were active in the Scottish Coalition for Justice not War following the horrific events on September 11 and the subsequent war in Afghanistan. Many Members and other supporters of the Community have been involved in the continuing opposition to Britain's Trident nuclear weapons system, through events at Faslane in October and February and other activities. And the Community's commitment to economic justice and combating poverty both within Britain and overseas was expressed through involvement, for instance, with a range of activities of Church Action on Poverty and Christian Aid's 'Trade for Life' campaign.

Islands Work

5.   During the 2001 season, despite the difficulties for tourism generally, particularly through foot-and-mouth disease, occupancy levels at all three centres compared very favourably with previous years.   Guests, both individually and in groups, and staff came from many different countries to share in the weekly programme under the general theme – 2001: a Faith Odyssey. Bookings for the 2002 season are encouraging, although a matter of continuing interest and concern is the relatively low level of Scottish bookings. There are plans for a visit by the Moderator in April, during his time with the Presbytery of Lorn and Mull.

6.   Brian Woodcock completed his term as Warden in August and moved to a United Reformed Church charge in St Albans. He was succeeded by Jan Sutch Pickard, until then Deputy Warden, who was Vice-President of

the Methodist Conference in 1997; and Nancy Cocks, a minister of the Presbyterian Church of Canada, started in January as Deputy Warden in charge of the MacLeod Centre.

7.   In April 2000 Historic Scotland, through an interim arrangement with the Iona Cathedral Trustees, took over responsibility (until then exercised by the Trustees' own management company, Iona Abbey Limited) for the management and maintenance of Iona Abbey and the other historic buildings in the Cathedral precincts. The cy-pres action in the Court of Session, completing the formal transfer to Historic Scotland, is under way at present.   The working arrangements between the Community and Historic Scotland continue to operate generally satisfactorily. Plans are being drawn up for the provision of refreshment facilities in the building that was the Community's coffee-house and is now its shop, just outside the Abbey grounds, thus restoring the dimension of the Community's ministry of hospitality that was lost when Historic Scotland took over the shop in the Abbey cloisters.

8.   The main outstanding issue with Historic Scotland relates to how Historic Scotland, 'present', reflect and recognise (both in their published material, wherever Iona is referred to, and in what their guides on Iona say) the significance of the Community's presence on Iona, including the value and impact of their witness and commitment there as a contemporary Christian community.   But the Board is encouraged to hear the Community's view that, by talking about this issue and through the deepening of the working relationship, this matter can be satisfactorily resolved.

9.   Although the start of the season was delayed owing to foot-and-mouth disease, Camas too had a good year, with a very committed and skilful staff team, and the distinctive outdoor opportunities were appreciated by a range of groups mostly from disadvantaged backgrounds. With the assistance of a grant from the Rank Foundation the business plan for the centre is now being put into effect; certain building works were carried out over the winter; and the architects who have been engaged to

develop and improve the facilities further are carrying out preliminary consultations prior to drawing up plans, the implementation of which is likely to require a fundraising initiative that may be combined with the development of the shop-building on Iona.

Mainland Work

10. The work of the Wild Goose Resource Group has continued to make a significant impact on the life of the churches throughout Scotland and far beyond, through the songs, liturgies and other material they produce and the workshops and other events they take part in. Following extended discussion and consultation about priorities and the future nature and focus of their activities, a new monthly Sunday evening event – *Holy City* – has been started in Glasgow and has attracted much interest; and the Wild Goose Worship Group (the volunteers who assist the Resource Group in their work) has been reshaped. There have been significant changes too within the membership of the Resource Group itself: Alison Adam will cease full-time work in July, following her marriage and move south, and Mairi Munro left the Group in April to take up a post with the Scottish Churches Open College. The Board wishes the Group well in evolving a strategy and structure for the future to enable it to respond to the considerable interest in and demand for its work.

11. Wild Goose Publications has had another outstanding year. The new edition of the *Iona Abbey Worship Book* and the new video about the work of the Community – *Today's Challenge, Tomorrow's Hope*, both produced around the time of last year's General Assembly - have sold very well. The latest Wild Goose collection of songs *One is the Body* was released in cassette and CD form last year and the accompanying book is to be published shortly. Other publications over the past year include *A Need for Living – signposts for the journey of life and beyond* (reflections by Tom Gordon on his experience as a hospice chaplain), *Iona Abbey Cloisters* (a compilation of photographs and reflections on the cloister capitals), *Lent and Easter Readings from Iona*, *Daily Readings from George MacLeod* and Ron Ferguson's biography *George MacLeod* (both originally published by Collins), and an encouragingly popular *A Book of Blessings*.

12. The Community's youth work has also progressed satisfactorily. This year's Youth Festival on Iona was full to capacity, catering for a younger age-group (14-18) than previously. Mainland events have taken place, the process of networking with other youth organisations has continued, and there has been further involvement with ACTS and the corresponding British and English ecumenical bodies. The placement of a volunteer through Jesuit Volunteer Communities has opened up a new field of possibilities for work in schools. And the activities of the Community's Youth Associates have continued to flourish and develop in creative ways.

13. After twelve years' distinguished service Kathy Galloway has been succeeded by Ruth Harvey as editor of the Community's bi-monthly magazine *Coracle*. Under the guidance of a newly appointed editorial group a readership survey is being carried out and the possibility of a re-launch with a new design is under consideration.

Membership

14. The membership of the Community continues to increase. There are currently 245 Members, 1550 Associate Members and 1434 Friends. Nine New Members were hallowed into full membership at Community Week last summer, and there are 26 on the New Members programme at present. The Community's five-fold Rule and integrated approach to spirituality (combining political engagement with a commitment to the renewal of worship and a personal devotional and economic discipline) continue to attract much interest.

15. Over the past year, alongside Community week on Iona, there were four other plenary meetings: at Drumchapel in June the Community's AGM included also discussions with local people involved in the ecumenical Drumchapel Churches partnership; in October there was a meeting in Edinburgh focusing on Northern Ireland (with input from the convener of the Church and Nation Committee, the Irish Vice-Consul, and a representative

of amnesty International), and the same weekend Community Members and staff shared in a very worthwhile '50-a-side' meeting with the Corrymeela Community at Ballycastle exploring matters of common interest; and the programme for the March meeting in Stirling reflected the Community's interest in issues relating to human sexuality.

16. At least twenty Members of the Community, representing a range of different denominations and other groups, were present at the Scottish Ecumenical Assembly in September, and there is a continuing demand, which is fulfilled as far as resources of time and human energy allow, for input by Members, whether in a personal capacity or more formally on behalf of the Community, into a wide range of events both throughout Britain and overseas. The opportunity for contributing to the work of the Assembly Council on spirituality and the Board of Ministry's conferences for probationers has been particularly appreciated.

17. Since its foundation the Community's purpose has been essentially missionary, in the conviction that God's transforming purpose embraces both social and personal renewal and that action for social change is an important part of Christian discipleship. The Board recognises that this continuing commitment is expressed not only through all that Members are doing in their own local situations but also by the Community's association with other organisations pursuing similar objectives; and the Board was therefore pleased that the Community was able to respond positively to an invitation to become a member of the Scottish Churches Housing Agency.

TOM GORDON *Convener*
JEAN WILLIAMS *Secretary*

BOARD OF SOCIAL RESPONSIBILITY
MAY 2002

CONTENTS

PROPOSED DELIVERANCE

The General Assembly:

1. Receive the Report of the Board and note with appreciation the work of the Convener, Vice-Conveners, Members of the Board and all Staff.

2. To encourage the Board to continue to monitor changes in service needs and provision using a variety of methodologies.

3. Note that as a result of positive intervention by the Scottish Executive a more appropriate rate of financial supplement has been agreed for residents in homes for older people who require public support.

4. Approve the Board's Strategic Development Plan for the next 3 years.

5. Note with satisfaction the continuing interest in the Ministry of Health and Healing and commend forthcoming national and area conferences on health and healing.

6. Note with interest the Board's initiative in seeking research into the issue of social capital and await with anticipation the independent research on the contribution made by Church of Scotland Congregations to their communities.

7. Note the Board's approach to Sex Selection and
    (i)   Commend further study and a report to a future General Assembly
    (ii)   Affirm that children are God's gift, and are to be loved for themselves;
    (iii)   Appeal to society as a whole not to place prospective parents under pressure to have a child of a particular sex;
    (iv)   Recognise that sex-selection may be acceptable when it is done in order to preclude serious sex-linked disease, but reject sex-selection when it is done to give parents a child of their preferred sex;
    (v)   Endorse the current legal ban on sex-selection by selective insertion of IVF embryos, except to preclude serious sex-linked disease;
    (vi)   Encourage HMG to monitor the sex ratio of live births closely, and to consult with the public on the way ahead if sex-selection significantly changes the sex ratio;
    (vii)   Encourage HMG to keep records of sex-selected children, and to commission an ongoing study to determine if children of the "wrong" sex are more likely to be rejected, mistreated, or aborted.

8. Commend the Board of World Mission for its initiative on HIV/AIDS and note the Board's commitment to responding to HIV/AIDS in Scotland.

9. Note the publication of the leaflet on "Human Genetics" and the now widely circulated pack on HIV/AIDS and encourage comments from Presbyteries and congregations (Kirk Sessions and ministers) on these documents.

10. Note the retirement of Ian D Baillie CBE, from his post as Director of Social Work, and record appreciation of his service.

1. Introduction

Extracts from Report of Committee on Social Service **50 years ago** (1952):

"Again and again the Committee has had to hesitate to undertake fresh commitments, being rightly concerned about the financial drain on its funds, but at each stage it has been constrained to go on by evident tokens of Divine approval"

"Enough has been written to show that the marvellous growth of the work of the Committee on Social Service is not something devised by men, but the weaving of a pattern designed by God. Into that tapestry has been woven a remarkable variety of strands, each with a colour and character of its own. Instead of modern legislation stifling the work of the Church in the realm of Social Service, it has in fact been the means of revealing new avenues of opportunity and providing indirectly new sources of funds."

Extract from Report of Social Responsibility Committee **25 years ago** (1977):

"It is right to observe that, as the largest Voluntary Social Work Agency in Scotland, the Social Responsibility Committee should take the lead in a critical time. In this inflationary situation so much work for so many people is being put at risk that the Church must take an initiative to ensure that a concerted approach is made by voluntary bodies at both Regional and National level, not to safeguard the interests of agencies, but those of people in need who are at grave risk now, and likely to be even more at risk in the long term."

At the end of yet another difficult financial year for the Board, it is good to look back to see what our predecessors wrote in reporting to the General Assembly. Today we believe that still we are being guided by God, that new opportunities are presented to us, and that people are still in need and respond to the services which the Board offers. New legislation is now upon us and it is imperative that it is used to ensure that the work done in the service of Christ continues to reflect the quality and care expected of us.

The work of the Board during the last fifty years has grown and changed in ways that perhaps were not envisaged then. Through it all can be seen the moving of the Holy Spirit, as the pattern changes lives and services, but the weave remains strong. This Report will reflect even more changes occurring now, or anticipated in the future, but it also reflects the steadfast commitment to our Lord and His work.

As in past years this Report seeks to achieve the Practice and Procedure Board's objective of "presenting a Brief Report and making use of Appendices whenever feasible". **Part One** of the Report provides sufficient material to report diligence to the General Assembly and give a general overview of the work during the past year. **Part Two** of the Report provides much more detailed accounts of the wide range of work undertaken in Christ's name throughout Scotland. Please make the time to read both parts.

PART ONE: AN OVERVIEW

2. The life of the Department of Social Responsibility in 2001

The General Assembly will be aware that much can be learned from re-reading Reports submitted to the General Assembly in previous years. It is possible to observe trends and developments, areas of work which create excitement, concerns over resources and people, records of service given to Christ over many years; within such reporting is the evidence of regular commitment to the sometimes apparently mundane task of providing high quality services for 365 days every year. **For those staff** who endeavour to provide such service with freshness and with God's grace we give thanks; **to those Staff** the Church records its thanks.

The Board is conscious that it is this determination to deliver high quality services with freshness that removes much of the mundane nature of the task. Always there is an individual receiving a particular service that must be shaped towards the needs of that individual. When the task relates to the ever increasing "paper mountain" of consultation and policy papers, there is the knowledge that all the effort is directed towards improving services for people in need. This past year is one in which a major part of the staff effort has been to take forward the proposals that were in the pipeline and were indicated to the General Assembly last year.

- The Human Rights Act, 1998 with all its aspects including ethnic and gender issues.
- Application of the Tendering Manual and the Quality Assurance System ("Towards Quality").
- The Regulation of Care (Scotland) Act incorporating National Standards and single care homes.
- A Scottish Social Services Council (Operational as from 1 October 2001).
- A new Scottish Commission for the Regulation of Care (operational as from 1 April 2002) and
- The Board's determination to move towards enabling and facilitating more local involvement in the delivery of social caring services in the name of the Church.

All the while, direct caring services continue to be delivered, managed, assessed and evaluated; but, *most important*, the services are used by people in need.

During the year the Board received around 30 **official consultation documents** for comment, mostly from the Scottish Executive. These are listed in **Appendix 1**.

The Regulation of Care (Scotland) Act received Royal assent in July 2001. The Act is now in the process of implementation and for the Board will mean, *inter alia*:

- The Board's residential homes and day centres will be registered and inspected by staff of the new Scottish Commission for the Regulation of Care.
- Residential care homes and nursing care homes will now be monitored by the same Commission (rather than by local authority social work departments and by health authorities).
- Standards of care will, for the first time, be measured against National Standards of Care as identified by the Commission. Publication of National Standards, eighteen sets to cover all client/service user care groups, commenced in January 2002.
- Social workers and social care workers will require to be registered with the new Scottish Social

Services Council. The regulations detailing registration requirements are pending.

- The Council will also issue Codes of Practice to which adherence will be required by employers and employees; details are awaited.

It is important for the Board to ensure that the staff and Board members are kept up-to-date not only as to the contents of consultation documents and legislation, but also with trends in social work and social care. To this end certain senior staff within the department are given a "Lead Role" for a particular service or client group; their task is to attain a level of expert knowledge in that topic and to provide information and advice to the Director of Social Work for appropriate dissemination. As an example of such information, the following are extracts from, or comments on, written reports provided at the end of 2001.

- The report on **alcohol abuse** provides some comparative figures which indicate current trends; it comments on the increasing ready availability of alcohol; that although reflecting satisfactory results, residential rehabilitation facilities are not being used to their full potential; comments on the need for a national alcohol policy similar to the national strategy for drug misuse (Tackling Drugs Together); and refers to the Alcohol Abuse Reference Group set up by the Board to consider ways in which the Board's services could be developed or changed.
- The report on **older people** begins with statistical information, then comments on the Scottish Council on Ageing, which is a new fledgling organisation seeking to act as a voice for older people, and a new MORI poll reflecting some research into ageing and health expectations. The report then gives advice on current literature and comments on the main issues concerning older people being considered within political circles in Scotland.
- The report on **mental illness** gives an update on the Adults With Incapacity (Scotland) Act and the Review of the Mental Health Act, and then confirms the trend of seeking care in the

community solutions for individuals rather than residential facilities either in small groups in the community or in hospital settings. The report also highlights the new awareness within the National Health Service for spirituality to be understood and facilitated.

- Similar extracts could be given from reports on **learning disabilities, child care, drug dependency, counselling, offenders, homelessness, dementia, home support, HIV/ AIDS,** and **physical disability**. It is hoped that these few examples indicate one of the ways in which the Board is kept aware of trends in the care sector, enabling a comparison with the Board's own service delivery.

In an area of service which demands regular changes in both the nature of services and the way in which they are delivered, it is essential to ensure that there are readily available and appropriate **training opportunities** for staff. The Department offers training in a variety of forms. Scottish Vocational Qualification is the major training opportunity for care staff who are not in a position to secure the Diploma In Social Work (or choose not to do so because vocational training is personally more appropriate). The Board now has 95 staff who hold the SVQ at level 2, 169 at level 3, and 4 at level 4; in addition there are a further 142 candidates active in securing level 3 or 4. This is an excellent development and confirms that the care being provided in our homes and projects is such that staff are able to use their everyday operational experience to achieve their qualification. Training staff will now require to take cognisance of the requirements of the new Scottish Social Care Council to ensure continuity of the progress made to date. The Board's thanks to the Training Staff and to all those who assist is recorded with grateful appreciation.

In addition to the processing of Vocational qualifications, in the calendar year 2001 Training staff offered 100 in-house training courses on a wide variety of subjects. The main thrust of in-house training has, however, been directed at the department's new Quality Standards (which inter-face with the new National Standards issued by the Scottish Executive). Seminars

have been organised for all grades of staff in a variety of geographical locations throughout Scotland; these seminars have been highly successful and there is now an enlightened awareness of the Quality Standards expected by the Board, by external inspectors, and by service users.

The General Assembly has been advised in past years of the development of an **Advisory Forum** on which staff and management meet to discuss issues germaine to staff and to the operational practices within the department. The Forum continues to progress and the department can now see clear developments which have arisen as a result of discussion at the Forum. In addition the Board has been able to offer three new employee benefits for those who are interested – a preferential banking package with the Board's bankers, involvement in the Scottish Council for Voluntary Organisations Credit Union, and a Childcare Voucher scheme to assist employees with childcare costs.

In recent years it has not been possible to report to the General Assembly without a major comment on the **Financial Care Gap** which arose because local and central government failed to fund properly the residential care of older people. As has been explained regularly, the only resolution to the problem was a major review of the funding provided through the public purse; the alternatives to such a review were that the Church required to carry the deficit or decide to close the Boards 28 homes, making up to 1,000 old people homeless and up to 1600 staff unemployed. The Church, through its Christian responsibility, determined to accept the deficit while protesting to government and trying to secure a change in funding. The Church should recognise the major contribution it has made through the Board to the poorest older people in Scotland over the last ten years, directly as a result of this decision.

In June 2001 it was decided by the Board that the Church had fulfilled more than its responsibility and that the deficit funding at the existing level could not continue.

Fortunately, in September 2001, following threats and action to withdraw residential care opportunities by the private sector, the Scottish Executive set up a **National Review Group** consisting of representatives from the NHS in Scotland, COSLA, Scottish Care (*a private sector body*), the Voluntary Sector and the Scottish Executive "to conduct a review of the costs associated with providing nursing and residential care for older people in Scotland and to determine appropriate fee-funding levels for application from 1 April 2002", including a mechanism for future review of rates.

The Board's Director and a Depute Director were involved in the work of this Group and an agreed "Report on Care Home Costs for Older People in Scotland" was presented to the Minister for Health and Community Care by the independent Chairman, Owen Clarke CBE, in November 2001. In February 2002, following a meeting of the Scottish Executive and the Convention of Scottish Local Authorities on this issue, the Minister for Health and Community Care, Malcolm Chisholm MSP, wrote to the Board:

"I understand that there will be frustration within the Church of Scotland that progress has not been quicker. I too am disappointed that we are not yet in a position to give you full details of increased funding from April this year. However, the Executive's commitment to resolving this, in terms of both effort and finance, is considerable. Raising care homes fees is a priority for us and I wanted to see that reflected in increased fees for care homes in both the voluntary and independent sectors, and a secure future for older people, as soon as possible.

First, let me highlight for you the important new developments. There was a commitment by everyone round the table to ensure that funding for care homes, for the future, is sustainable. We want a solution for the long–term that stops this kind of dispute arising in the future.

Furthermore the fee levels recommended by the National Review Group on which we are all agreed, suitably uplifted, will be paid in full from 1 April 2003."

At the time of writing the Scottish Executive have committed an additional £24 million to be applied as from 1 April 2002; in addition £11 million has been added to an earlier £10 million in order to pay a level of back-dated fees to 1 July 2001. The Convention have agreed to an additional £3 million pound.

Further details will be provided to the General Assembly if they are properly settled by then.

In 1998 the Board produced its first three year **Strategic Development Plan**; it was presented to the General Assembly in 1999. The Board can report to the General Assembly that the six Aims have been diligently pursued and the 52 Objectives identified have been achieved or have been commenced.

The Board is happy to present to this General Assembly the Strategic Development Plan for the three years commencing 1 June 2002. The Aims for this Plan have been increased to seven; the new Aim (No. 5) states:

"To actively seek opportunities with other Boards of the Church of Scotland and other Christian denominations to maximise the Christian churches' ability to use resources."

The original Aim 6 which stated "To further incorporate volunteers into the work of the Board" has been amended to read:

Aim 6: To work with Presbyteries and local churches to find ways of meeting local needs while continuing to encourage volunteer activity.

The seven Aims break down into 64 Objectives which will be pursued throughout the work of the Board over the next three years.

The Strategic Development Plan is produced in full at **Appendix 2**. The Church will wish to note that as well as the very particular Aims and Objectives, the first essential part of the Plan sets out clearly the background to the Board, the value base against which work is done, and the future trends which result in the Aims and Objectives being as they are.

It can be seen from this Strategic Development Plan that the priority areas of service which the Board hopes to address and progress during the next three years include: development of the Home Support service, a re-introduction of short respite care breaks (now referred to as Short Break services), to continue the move to more localised services within communities, to develop more creative family support services, and to facilitate the growth of Care Homes which provide both care and nursing care (formerly referred to as Single Care Homes). Two further initiatives which warrant mention are the furtherance of work with Carers, primarily through local congregations, and the expansion and development of work through the Congregational Contact system.

In 1994 after discussion with other Boards and Committees, the General Assembly decided to leave responsibility for the **Ministry of Health and Healing** with this Board. The remit given to the Board in the area of Health and Healing was:

(a) *to promote ways of encouraging ministers and congregations to accept healing as a part of their ministry and mission to individuals and to their community;*

(b) *to promote reflection on theological issues relating to the exercise of the ministry of healing within the Church.*

The Board determined that the prime objective should be to promote this ministry within the Church by continuing the organisation of an annual conference. These conferences, held at Carberry Conference Centre, have proved very popular and informative. Many ministers, and others, are now comfortable with, and informed about, a healing ministry, and seek to put into practice the ministry of healing. This has resulted in a demand for additional more locally organised conferences; this is proceeding. The Board gives thanks to God for the enlightenment that has come to many through the teaching and experiences of the Carberry conferences. A full report on the 2001 Conference is included as **Appendix 3**. The General Assembly is also reminded of the Board's publication "Health and Healing: A Christian Perspective" published in 1998 and still available from the Board.

The Board's Report to the General Assembly last year included an appendix reflecting the Board's Christian Commitment Policy. It states clearly that the Christian faith should permeate the whole of a person's life and should be evident in their lifestyle. Prayer is integral to such a lifestyle and to the staff groups in our offices, homes and projects. The **Board's Prayer Letter** now has a circulation of 9,000 copies. The Letter comprises a prayer for each day, the prayers being prepared by staff, by service users and by Friends, in the Board's offices, homes and projects throughout Scotland. These prayers are very moving and tell so much about the daily lives of those who receive this service in Christ's name. The Board would also like to record its grateful thanks to all those who lead or assist in worship services in our offices, homes and projects; we are indeed fortunate in the service we receive from so many people.

The Board has regularly reported on its commitment to **partnership working**. Nowhere is the need for this greater than within the Church itself, a point made explicit within last year's major report "A Church Without Walls". The Board has always endeavoured to work and co-operate with other Boards, Committees and Departments, and this last year greater effort has been made through the Five Boards Group (consisting of the Conveners and Secretaries/Directors of Ministry, National Mission, Parish Education, Social Responsibility and World Mission). Efforts are being made to develop pilot examples of Team Ministry involving the five Boards as appropriate, with the possibility of including other Boards or Committees as inclusion is indicated by local need. This is time consuming and often delicate as systems and practices are identified which may require to be changed or eradicated. The Board has tried also to give greater attention to ecumenical opportunities, again dealing with sensitive issues in order to progress joint work. Examples of such initiatives would be the new development in Buckie (Solid Rock), the developing work with children and families in Glasgow (PACT), the National Counselling Services, and the developing work with young people in Uist.

A priority for development work for the Board is to take forward **greater liaison with Presbyteries and local congregations**. This is hampered by resources at this moment in time but it is hoped to be able to make some progress in the forthcoming year. However, it should be noted with thankfulness, the wonderful way in which congregations are seeking to serve their local communities. This is evidenced in the Computer Data Base created and maintained by the Communications Officer (Congregations) which now records over 1180 local social care services delivered by congregations. This database enables congregations who "have an idea" of beginning a service to contact Church people who have been through that stage and are now delivering a service.

The database asks congregations to place their community services within one of the following categories: Advice centre, after school club, coffee meetings, day care, holiday club, lunch club, parent and toddler group, pastoral care, play group, social club, support group, transport service, worship, and youth activity.

Some examples of the more interesting services to promote social inclusion in communities include:

- The Henderson Cybercafe for over 50's run by Henderson Parish Church, Kilmarnock.
- A web design group at St. Andrew's Bo'ness.
- A Breakfast Club run by members of St Ninians, Dunfermline, which serves breakfast to schoolchildren.
- Launch Pad, run by Crown Church, Inverness, which provides grants to those who are long term unemployed for hobbies or preparation for work.
- A monthly ME Support Group at New Cathcart Church, Glasgow.
- Coal delivery to those with real fires by Beith High Church of Scotland.
- The Ecumenical Murrayfield Dementia Project in Edinburgh.
- The Castlemilk Refugee Centre, run by Castlemilk East Church, and providing a twice weekly drop-in centre with English classes for refugees living in the community.
- The Lighthouse Help Centre, an advice centre run by St Michael's Church of Scotland and St Johns Evangelical Church, Linlithgow.

This year the Board, as a result of discussions initiated through the Planning and Development section, commissioned research through **Glasgow University Urban Studies Department** to seek to independently identify the contribution Church of Scotland congregations make to their communities. The Research is entitled "The Impact of Churches on Social Capital in Scottish Communities" and was begun in the second half of 2001. "Social Capital" is described as "the ability of people to work together for common purposes in groups and organisations" (Fukayama 1995). The subject has been receiving considerable government comment and it is hoped that the results of the research will provide the Board with independent evidence of the value of the Church within local communities. The following is an interim report received in January 2002:

"In the UK the potential contribution of faith communities towards achieving policy goals appears to be enjoying increasing recognition across the political spectrum, including the Prime Minister and other senior members of the government. This reflects the growing understanding that faith communities both directly deliver a wide range of social support services to individuals, and also that through their values, activities and organisational structures, they are a valuable source of social capital in local communities. Social capital refers to the levels of trust, participation and associational networks that exist within communities and help to sustain and maximise investment in human and physical capital. Policy in the UK has highlighted the important role of faith communities working with socially excluded individuals and deprived neighbourhoods.

Despite this growing UK interest in the linkages between faith communities, civic engagement and community wellbeing, and much anecdotal evidence, there is little understanding about the actual processes through which faith organisations contribute to neighbourhood renewal and community development. A number of major studies in the US have demonstrated the important contribution of faith organisations towards social capital. However, there has been no such research carried out within Scotland, which has its own geographical, historical, political and religious contexts.

The Church of Scotland Board of Social Responsibility has sought to inform the understanding of these community processes in Scotland through commissioning the Department of Urban Studies, University of Glasgow, to conduct a research project evaluating the linkages between Church of Scotland congregations and their local communities. The research aims to quantify the contribution that congregations make to social capital and community development. The research will establish the number and range of activities that congregations are engaged in and the impacts of these activities upon social capital in their communities. In addition it will explore how the structures of the Church and the interventions of local and national government influence the ability of congregations to contribute to their local communities.

The research involves a postal survey of all the Church of Scotland congregations in Scotland (and England);

interviews with key actors, detailed vignettes of particular congregational activities and case studies of four congregations including interviews, focus groups and residents surveys.

The first two phases of the project, the postal survey of congregations and key actor interviews have been completed. There were over 440 completed survey returns, representing over a 40 percent response rate and ensuring that over one in three congregations in Scotland are included in the findings. Encouragingly, multiple responses have been received from all 46 presbyteries, enabling a representative geographical coverage of the country.

The data from these surveys is currently being processed. Some early indications are that congregations are involved in a very wide range of activities that contribute to social capital. Analysis of the survey returns also suggests that members of congregations make substantial contributions within their local communities in a number of ways that are not easily measured through formal organisational activity. The importance of faith as a motivating factor in engaging in community networks is also a predominant theme of the survey returns. Responses reveal that the majority of ministers see churches as having an important role in a range of partnerships with other voluntary and government agencies that seek to reduce social exclusion and strengthen local communities. There is a spectrum of views about the exact nature of the relationships congregations should establish with other organisations. The surveys have also highlighted a number of issues relating to the role of individual congregations within the overall structures and processes of the Church.

The next phase of the research, involving vignettes and case studies is now under way. The final report of the research findings should be produced by the end of May this year."

The Board continues to have an involvement in social caring issues on an **international front.**

World Mission are reporting this year on **HIV/AIDS** in a major way; the Board are pleased to be represented on the World Mission Task Force on HIV/AIDS by John Wyllie, Social Work Divisional Manager. The Board has been involved in this issue for many years and has contact with the World Council of Churches' Advocacy Alliance which is concentrating a major part of its focus on this issue. At home, current information about HIV and AIDS was provided to all churches for use on or around World AIDS Day which is held each 1st December. An article to help people understand AIDS is produced at **Appendix 4** and the Board's new Information Pack on HIV and AIDS has now been sent to all Parish Ministers. Copies can be purchased from Charis House.

The Red Ribbon is the international symbol of HIV and AIDS awareness. This is why UNAIDS has chosen to incorporate the ribbon into its own logo. It stands for:

Care and Concern: It is worn by many people around the world to show their care and concern for those living with HIV, for those who are ill, for those who have died and for those who care and support people directly affected.

Hope: It is intended to be a symbol of hope – that the search for a vaccine and cure to halt the suffering is successful and the quality of life improves for those living with the virus.

Support: It offers symbolic support for those living with HIV, for the continuing education for those not infected, for maximum efforts to find effective treatments, cures or vaccines and for those who have lost friends, family members or loved ones to AIDS.

But wearing a Red Ribbon is not enough; it is only a useful symbol in the long run when attached to words and deeds that actually make a difference.

The Board continues to be active within **Eurodiaconia** and was represented at the AGM and Conference held in Jarvenpaa, Sweden in September 2001. The conference (A European Diaconal Forum) was organised jointly by four European organisations: The Conference of European Churches, The European Federation for Diaconia-Eurodiaconia, The Churches' Commission for Migrants in Europe, and The European Contact Group for Urban and Industrial Mission. This Forum, which was a follow-up to the first pan-European consultation on diaconia in 1994 which produced the "Bratislava Declaration", was a space for dialogue, networking, analysis and reflection on the new challenges which have emerged for the churches' social action within the rapid changes in Europe. It was organised in four thematic groups around the topics of the value of work and employment, migration and mobility, building sustainable communities and seeking quality of life for all. Three round tables focused on the relationship between diaconia and the churches, between diaconia and civil society, and the tasks of diaconia in relation to the changing role of the state and of the European institutions. The Forum identified a series of projects and strategies which will be pursued through individual organisations and through the sponsoring bodies.

The Board has been involved as a founder member of the **International Christian Federation** for the prevention of alcoholism and drug addiction (ICF) for 25 years. For many years ICF had a major role of raising awareness within the churches of the issue of alcohol addiction and of the healing and supportive role that churches could adopt. In more recent years many other organisations have taken up similar roles, some on a UK basis, others on the wider European or World arena. In the last few years in particular, ICF has worked very closely with the World Council of Churches and it is this role which is receiving greater attention at this time. The two major WCC themes being addressed are "Justice and Addiction Concerns" and "Violence as related to Addiction".

3. Financial Overview

It will be noted from the Statement of Financial Activities (SOFA) that the funds of the Board have reduced to £29.275 million (2000 £34.631 million). Due to the continuing difficulties in securing adequate funding for care of older people the Board has again used reserves to maintain homes and the services provided. Similarly the Board has traditionally financially supported services such as counselling, home support, women and children and holiday homes for older people in addition to meeting costs of upgrading and improvement to properties.

During the course of the year the Board's income amounted to £33.875 million (2000 £34.971 million) a reduction of £1.096 million (3%). Income derived from service delivery increased marginally (1%) but income received from other sources dropped by £1.359 million when allowance is made for deferred income. In the course of one year this level of reduction is very significant and one which is being given very serious consideration. The Board did not receive any significant grants from Councils or Trusts towards the costs of renovations. Also the process of marketing and selling a number of properties had not been completed as speedily as anticipated therefore the gain on sale of properties is lower than in the previous year.

Expenditure on service delivery increased by £1.983 million during the year, a 6% increase against the previous year. Within this increase is the cost of new services commenced in terms of home support, day care and services to people with learning disabilities.

The result of the reduction in income and the increase in costs is that expenditure exceeded income by £3.919 million (2000 £958,000).

STATEMENT OF FINANCIAL ACTIVITIES
FOR THE YEAR ENDED 31 MARCH 2001

	Unrestricted Funds £'000	Restricted Funds £'000	Permanent Endowment Funds £'000	Total 2001 £'000	Total 2000 £'000
Income and Expenditure					
Incoming Resources:					
Income from Service Delivery	0	31,403	0	31,403	31,140
Donations	8	322	0	330	1,278
Legacies	180	987	40	1,207	1,455
Gain on sale of assets	0	39	0	39	612
Investment Income and Interest Received	235	661	0	896	1,015
Less: Deferred Income	0	0	0	0	(529)
Total Incoming Resources	**423**	**33,412**	**40**	**33,875**	**34,971**
Expended Resources:					
Direct Charitable Expenditure:					
Expenditure on Service Delivery	0	35,616	0	35,616	33,633
Support costs	0	1,693	0	1,693	1,817
Other Expenditure:					
Fundraising & Publicity	0	167	0	167	184
Management & Administration of the Charity	0	318	0	318	295
Total Expended Resources	**0**	**37,794**	**0**	**37,794**	**35,929**
Net Added/(Expended) Resources for the year	**423**	**(4,382)**	**40**	**(3,919)**	**(958)**

The Statement of Recommended Practice "Accounting and Reporting for Charities" requires the Church's Financial Statements to include a section on Risk Management. A seminar and workshop on "Risk Assessment" was held in November for the Board's Executive Committee and senior staff. The workshop identified the major risks relating to the central operations and finances of the Board and agreed that suitable systems are in place to mitigate against exposure to these risks. The General Treasurer of the Church has been notified of this position.

The budgeting process for 2002/2003 is being re-addressed as a result of unavoidable major increases in costs which have come to light and in response of the failure of local authorities to recompense the Board appropriately for the cost of residential care for older people as from 1 April 2002. It is likely that once this exercise is complete a Supplementary Report will be prepared for the information of the General Assembly.

4. Social Interests

The Board has a Social Interests Committee which meets four times a year, and *inter alia* receives reports from the Human Genetics Liaison Group; the Committee deals with all matters relative to the moral issues aspects of the Board's remit. Enquiries arriving in the department would normally be dealt with by the Director or by the Social Interests Secretary who for this year has recorded around 450 enquiries. These enquiries could be a single telephone call, extended correspondence on a particular issue, or an enquiry from a school or university student seeking information on the view of the Church on a particular issue.

Other matters which also have received major attention include official responses being prepared to consultation documents on "Gaming Machines: Method of Payment", "The Gambling Review Report", "Review of Liquor Licensing Law in Scotland", and the "Keep Sunday Special: Proposed Family Days (Protection) Bill".

The Committee has maintained an interest in activity around the schools sex education guidelines, although this is seen as primarily a matter for the Church's Education Committee with whom the Board has regular contact. The Committee also gave consideration to the proposals by Edinburgh District Council, on the advice of Lothian and Borders Police Authority, to set up "tolerance zones" within which prostitutes would be allowed to trade without interference from the Police. The Committee's primary interest would be to offer alternative life styles to those women presently offering themselves in prostitution. It was agreed that if prostitution is practised then it is important to ensure personal safety for all citizens.

A short report on the subject of **Begging** was included in the Board's Report to last year's General Assembly. The Board is continuing to pursue this issue and will report progress in due course.

A small group of Board members have been studying the ministry of deliverance, a particular aspect of health and healing ministry. The Board will consider this work and determine whether a full study is required or other action would be more appropriate.

The Human Genetics Liaison Group. Over the last year, the Group as a whole responded to the Nuffield Council on Bioethics' Public Consultation Document "Genetics and Human Behaviour: the ethical context". The Group has also considered the implications of genetics for insurance, but has decided, for the present, merely to watch the situation.

Individual Board members of the Group have been following-up last year's Deliverance on human cloning. A leaflet has been produced outlining the thinking behind the Board's position (available from Charis House). This was sent to all MSPs, and has also been sent to Board congregational contacts. An article covering the same area was published in the February 2002 "Life and Work" and a brief response to adverse comment by Bishop Mario Conti upon the deliverance was published in the "Scotsman" Letters column.

In addition, Board members of the Group have responded to requests from the press for comment on new results in the field of human genetics. One such concerned sex selection, which the Group as a whole considered, and which is dealt with in the following brief comment.

"Sex Selection

The issue of 'sex selection' - choosing whether to have a boy or a girl - was brought to the General Assembly in 1996 through the Board of Social Responsibility's Report on Human Fertilisation and Embryology[1]. The General Assembly of that year accepted the Report's 12th conclusion, and agreed that it 'oppose[d] sex selection,

---

[1] This Report was published as "Preconceived Ideas - A Christian perspective on IVF and Embryology", Saint Andrew Press, Edinburgh, 1996.

except to prevent sex linked genetic disease'[2]. Since that time, however, there have been important developments.

In 1996, sex selection was only possible following conception, either by aborting foetuses of the undesired sex, or by not inserting IVF embryos of the undesired sex into the mother's womb (which implies destroying them). Each method raises ethical issues which are arguably more immediate than sex selection as such; and each was, and remains, illegal in the UK, except to prevent sex-linked genetic disease. But the Report's compilers foresaw that sooner or later, parents would be able to choose whether to conceive a boy or a girl[3]. Since this wouldn't involve destroying foetuses or embryos, the major ethical concern would be sex selection as such.

What was foreseeable in 1996 is now available commercially in clinics in Glasgow and elsewhere[4]. (Sex selection as such for personal preference has never been the subject of UK legislation.) The method used is sperm selection. The father-to-be provides a sperm sample, from which another sample is prepared containing a higher proportion either of Y-bearing sperm (to make a son more likely) or of X-bearing sperm (to make a daughter more likely), with which the mother-to-be is then inseminated. The cost of this treatment is around £3000, and the success rate is claimed to be around 80%. This might seem a high price; but since many people spend more than this annually on holidays, a couple who strongly preferred a child of a particular sex might think it a worthwhile investment. Pre-conception sex selection, then, is a matter upon which ministers may be asked for pastoral advice.

The Assembly's view is clear. Since the 1996 Deliverance does not distinguish between pre-conception and post-conception sex selection, it opposes both when done for personal preference. What's more, by affirming "the sanctity of the human embryo from conception"[5], the Deliverance implicitly opposes any activity, such as post-conception sex selection, which involves destroying IVF embryos without compelling reason. In two recent high-profile cases, this allowed an authoritative, reasoned response from first principles. In one, it was possible to argue that a couple shouldn't be allowed to have a daughter by IVF, on the ground that male embryos shouldn't be destroyed merely because the parents preferred a girl. In another, it was possible to argue that parents shouldn't be allowed to have a child of a particular genotype by IVF, on the ground that embryos shouldn't be destroyed merely because a child of their genotype would be unable to help a sibling.

But the 1996 Report and Deliverance weren't so useful when the Press invited comment upon sperm selection. The body of the Report does offer arguments for and against sex selection as such - that is, before or after conception - but it doesn't evaluate them; and it rejects sex selection for personal preference specifically when accomplished by abortion, infanticide, or selective non-insertion of embryos[6], that is, after conception. So while the Report's 12th Conclusion and the Deliverance oppose sex selection for personal preference whether before or after conception - and the Convener of the Study Group which produced the Report affirms that this was the Study Group's view – the Report itself doesn't argue against sex selection before conception. In particular, the Report doesn't explain why a couple would be wrong to change the odds in favour of having a child of the sex they'd prefer. This is in no sense a criticism of the Report: as the Report's Summary states, it could 'only offer at best a snapshot in time'.

Since sperm selection is now available, it seems worthwhile to ask the Assembly to affirm that it is opposed to sex selection for personal preference even by means which do not involve destroying foetuses or embryos. If the Assembly does affirm this, it should say how opposed it is: would it wish to see legislation against all forms of sex selection? or would it merely advise couples not to employ it?

Much has been written on sex selection. Arguments in favour of permitting it include:

- People should be permitted to do what they like, provided that it doesn't harm others. None of the potential difficulties with sex selection amounts to direct harm.

---

[2] Board of Social Responsibility Deliverance 11.11 (1996).

[3] "Preconceived Ideas" p76.

[4] See, for example, www.genderclinic.co.uk; www.childselect.com

[5] Board of Social Responsibility Deliverance 11.4 (1996).

[6] "Preconceived Ideas" p77.

- Sex selection is likely to benefit children, since more children would be of the preferred sex, and a child of the preferred sex is less likely to be rejected.
- Sex selection would allow a couple to ensure that any future children were unaffected by a sex-linked disease, such as haemophilia. (But it should be noted that sex selection would have to be 100% effective for this purpose, which rules out the sperm selection method used by the Glasgow clinic.)
- Some couples have more children than they'd prefer solely because they want a child of a particular sex, or a child of each sex. If sex selection were available to such couples, they would have fewer children. This would be a painless way to reduce or reverse population growth.

Arguments against permitting sex selection include:

- Sex selection is a form of genetic selection, and arguably opens the door to 'designer babies'.
- Unless sex selection were 100% reliable, children of the 'wrong' sex would still be born, and might still be rejected. In fact, they might be rejected more deeply, since the more reliable the sex selection process were, the greater the parents' dismay would be at having a child of the 'wrong' sex.
- Sex selection is likely to change the parent-child relationship. In the past, a couple couldn't influence which child they had, so that if a child turned out to be a disappointment, they couldn't reasonably feel that the child might have been different if they'd done something different. Parents who had the option of sex selection would know that they could, with fair certainty, have had a child of the opposite sex from the one they did have; and hence a child who would have been very different. This can only make it more difficult for parents to love their child for itself.
- The availability of sex selection will expose couples to greater family pressure to have a child of a desired sex.

- Commercial sex selection is likely to be available only to the better-off, and so be inequitable and socially divisive.

Christian arguments against using sex selection include:

- Children are a gift from God, not a commodity to be bought. We should desire children for their own sake, as God desires us, not to meet our own agenda; and we shouldn't seek to have a child unless we mean to cherish it however it turns out.
- We should not do what we would not wish everyone to do. If every potential parent chose to have a child of the sex we'd prefer to have, the result would be a shortage of people of the opposite sex to be our child's partner, and to parent our hypothetical grand-children. Society as a whole would also depart from the plan which God gave in Genesis 2:24 and which Jesus endorsed, which presupposes roughly equal numbers of men and women."

This report was fully discussed and accepted by the Board.

In concluding this Social Interests Section, the General Assembly may wish to note that the Medical Research Council plans to assemble a 500,000-subject genetic database, and the Group hopes in the near future to learn more about this. The Group will also keep an eye on such developments as the production of synthetic sperm by the "haploidisation" of mature cells, and the production of parthenogenetic embryos.

5. Staff

5.1 Thanks to Staff

In response to people in need, the Board is served by supportive and caring staff. The Board commends staff at all levels and in all areas of work, and gives thanks to God for their service and commitment.

5.2 Staff in the Employ of the Board
at 1st February 2002

	Full-time		Part-time		Total		Full-time Equivalent	
	2002	2001	2002	2001	2002	2001	2002	2001
Operations Staff	735	783	843	808	1578	1591	1239.76	1254.47
Executive, Office & Support Staff	73	69	6	12	79	81	76.14	74.48
					°1657	1672	1315.90	1328.95

*In addition there are 777 people employed as Home Support/Relief Care Workers.

6. Operations

6.1 Introduction

This part of the Board's report reflects the ways in which direct caring services are provided in Christ's name, throughout Scotland, on behalf of the Church of Scotland. It also reflects the work activity throughout the year for the sections of the department which are so necessary if the direct caring services are to be effective. It contains much detail and is largely drawn from annual reports prepared by staff for line managers. It is what the work of the department, delivery of service and management, is all about.

6.2 Child Care

The Board continues to develop its work with children and their families. In 1999/2000 the Board's Report on **'Social Inclusion'** helped to sharpen the focus of attention on the encompassing love of Jesus Christ in action.

At the same time, the Scottish Executive report 'Social Justice – A Scotland Where Everyone Matters' set out their commitment to delivering social inclusion in Scotland. These two reports brought together within the Board an active political agenda together with the Board's social inclusion agenda for change.

The Board's strategic plan identifies that best value in its child related work will meet or exceed national Child Care standards, develop inclusive services which offer seamless care between residential and community-based care and work in partnership with other service providers, the children, their families and local communities. At a time when the Board had completed major service adjustments and physical improvements at Geilsland residential school and was moving to develop Ballikinrain residential school, the strategic plan for the school set out how the Board would not only make a significant investment in providing the physical, experiential and environmental standards expected but would also invest in developing new partnership services that address the needs and aspirations of children and families whilst in the community or while benefiting from the learning and living opportunities at Ballikinrain Campus.

To this end **Ballikinrain** adopted the motto of **'Include Me In'**, signifying that where children had been excluded, by society or their families, or by their own actions, the school's objectives would encompass social inclusion policies and practices which would enable children to say 'Include Me In'.

For this reason, Ballikinrain Residential School in Balfron is undergoing both major physical and programme development. It now offers five new Include Me In partnership services:

- 'What Works!' Intervention Programmes
- Back to Learning
- Crisis Response
- Family Support
- Residential School

'What Works!' Intervention 'Include Me In' Programmes are being developed in conjunction with the Scottish Institute for Residential Child Care, leading academic institutions and practitioners, specifically designed for the needs of children involved in the Ballikinrain 'Include Me In' child services. These programmes are being developed on the basis of research, with explicit inputs and measurable results. An initial effectiveness study of the Ballikinrain 'Include Me In' child services has already been commissioned.

The 'Back to Learning' 'Include Me In' curriculum considers the child, his strengths and his skills and is guided by the principles of 5-14 and Higher Still teaching requirements. It teaches sociability, citizenship and skills for educational career development. This will be achieved through small class sizes, individual work on numeracy, literacy, personal and social development, information technology and problem solving. Other supports in this learning process include family work, group work, parents support group, activity based programmes, supported college placements and work experience.

The Crisis Response 'Include Me In' Programme is still being developed. This programme will seek to support identified families in the community through times of crises with responses to suit the particular situation. It may include temporarily accommodating a member, or members, of the family at the school or in a partner environment.

The Family Support 'Include Me In' Service will work in partnership with families and Social Work

Departments in order to improve the quality of life of the immediate family who have a young person living at Ballikinrain.

The objectives are:

1. to improve relationships within the family;
2. to reduce the severity of behavioural and emotional difficulties presented by the young person;
3. to facilitate maximum appropriate family contact; and
4. where possible to work towards the young person's return home or to alternative family.

An important aspect of the service offered is providing parents/carers with the opportunity to work through some of their own issues and not just those connected to their child. This could involve looking at the impact of their own past experiences on family life:

1. anger management work;
2. parenting skills;
3. behavioural modification programmes;

all of which can contribute to building up a parent's self-esteem and coping skills.

The work will involve full assessment followed by planned, solution-focused intervention. This will include planned evening and weekend work as required, complimenting the services provided by local authorities.

Possible future developments of the Family Support Service will include outreach work with Early Intervention Teams to reduce the risk of young people becoming accommodated and secondly developing a Throughcare & Aftercare Service to provide time-limited support to young people when they return to the community.

The Residential School 'Include Me In' services are the core work of the school. The school living accommodation consists of five living areas, each of which includes its own kitchen and dining facilities, lounges and play area. One of the Board's key values is to give the children back their childhood and within the school's supportive framework of well understood routines there is adequate opportunity for play, exploration, making mistakes, learning and lots of fun. Property improvements will make the living accommodation more personal and adjusted staffing arrangements are based as much as possible on the day-to-day needs of each child

This targeted 'Include Me In' approach has struck a chord with Local Authorities who now see a clearer purpose and range of integrated services being offered. This development is motivated by the Board's concern that children who have been excluded, or who have excluded themselves, should be offered services that directly afford the opportunity to say: "Include me In".

The Board wishes to acknowledge the part played by staff in moving ahead these important child-centred developments and Local Authorities, as the purchasers of services at Ballikinrain, for showing their commitment to improving service, assisting with programme development and agreeing increases in weekly charges to cover revenue requirements and £2m of the capital development costs over the next twelve years. The School had a royal visitor in September when Princess Anne spent a morning touring the facilities and meeting staff and pupils. The Princess Royal arrived by helicopter and during her 90 minute visit she was shown the results of the ongoing £3 million refurbishment programme which so far includes a new sports hall and classrooms. The Princess took time to present certificates to some of the boys and to speak to them in an unscripted speech that showed how much she had learned about the school and its function: "Sadly there will always be a need for a school like Ballikinrain, but that is the only sad thing about it. The atmosphere proves that so much that is positive can be done. I am perfectly sure that no-one wants to be here too long, but make the best of it while you are here."

The Board has the encompassing motto of its **Mission Statement** "In Christ's Name we seek to retain or regain the highest quality of life which each person can achieve at any given time." In addition, the various services also adopt various mottos from year to year to help all involved to keep a sharp focus on the nature and reasons for the work.

Although not using the Ballikinrain motto "Include me In", **Geilsland Residential School** in Beith, through its package of care and education, strives to accept, care for and work with each young person with similar inclusive objectives in order to maximise his quality of life, development and future potential. Last summer, one of the boys won a poetry competition which was subsequently set to music composed by the school Music Teacher. The competition was organised by Who Cares? (Scotland) for young people in care in Scotland.

CARE-FREE?

My life has been taken over again
But not to worry, I will still remain
Here where I'm cared for
And shown the way

Chorus
I'm looking ahead to a better day
I'm looking ahead
To the end of my stay
In a place of care

I'll listen to what people say
Because I hope to find my own way
And one day I long to be
Care-free

Chorus
So I long to be care-free
And fly away
Who will be there
To catch me when I fall

Chorus

Brian Knowles, Summer 2001

The School maintains close links with the local community and with Christian groups such as: Youth with a Mission; Loaves and Fishes; the Prison Fellowship; the Christian Motor Bike Association and with the school Chaplains. A new educational timetable has been introduced to offer an enriched curriculum, in part facilitated by the Board's prompt and full implementation of the guidance given in the McCrone Report, a national review of teachers' pay and conditions. The Lomond Unit is now in its third pilot year with the Research and Education Project expected to be completed by September, 2002. and will be reported to the 2003 Assembly. A book chapter has been written on "Working with Sexually Aggressive Young People" by Professor A Kendrick, who leads the research study, and R Mair, Head of School. This chapter is for a book entitled "Work with Young Sexual Abusers" edited by Martin Calder and to be published by Russell House Publishing early in 2002. Martin Calder is a recognised authority on juvenile sexual offending and child protection. Both Schools continue to provide much needed services to some very damaged and vulnerable young people.

Other child care services, including The Mallard in Glasgow and Keith Lodge in Stonehaven, continue to develop their work for young people with serious disabilities and their carers. Despite the high demand from carers for such residential, respite and outreach services the referral rate, particularly in Glasgow, remains sluggish. Service Managers continue in discussions with referring Social Work Departments, but the main restriction appears to be lack of funding rather than an increase in local community and carer support.

The **Women and Children Project in Dundee** is working well from its new base in the Forth Valley and North East Division office in Kandahar House, Dundee, while a similar project, **PACT (Parents and Children Together)**, Glasgow, is being established from its base in the rebuilt Renfield St Stephen's Church. Both projects are well placed to use their bases and outreach centres to support vulnerable families.

The **Post Natal Depression Project (PND)**, based in Edinburgh, operates from six sites in Granton, Joppa, the City centre, Sighthill, Linlithgow and Galashiels, as well as joint work with a Health Visitor and Community Education in North Berwick. The main focus for PND is offering a counselling and support service for new mothers, their families and children, with 35 trained listeners and various other supports such as art therapy. The service operated in 2001 under its motto:

God is our refuge and strength
A very present help in trouble
Therefore we will not fear.

Psalm 46:1.2

Quotes from service users include:

"It was good to know that there were other people in this position; that I wasn't unique; that there was help."

"I found it rewarding when the baby started to show enjoyment and connect with me. I feel better about myself."

The Board is grateful to *Sure Start* for a further year's funding to retain the Infant Massage Teacher and a counsellor/development worker. Thanks are also due to *Children in Need* for a grant to ensure the appointment of trained crèche workers. It should also be noted that **Number 21 Counselling Service**, based in Edinburgh city centre and with various outreach points, as well as having an adult service, has a well established counselling service for children and young people, using a variety of approaches including the use of art, play and drama. **Lifestyle in Stornoway** plays a multi-faceted role in the centre of the town, including its "Want to Talk" sessions and other ways of allowing young people to reflect, using individual and group work. **AXIS**, referred to in last year's report as "Project Plus", in Mid and East Lothian is in its first year of offering support to those aged 16 and over who are seeking to move beyond substance misuse. This includes supporting individuals to return to employment, training, education and leisure in their community. In the first year, 54% of clients reached their agreed goals. Using twelve meeting points, this service operates under a Service Level Agreement between Midlothian and East Lothian Health and the Board. While this service would not strictly come under the description of 'Child Care', many of the presentations relate to influences while under age 16. This applies also to the contract with Lothian Health and NCH (Scotland) which **Simpson House Counselling and Related Services** operates in Edinburgh city centre.

Solid Rock Cafe and drop-in centre in Buckie for teenagers is proving a popular venue with strong local community support. Opening times have progressively increased as the volunteers have gained confidence; from two to three and now four evenings a week. Weekend opening is now being planned. The Café is well used and attracts quite considerable numbers each night. It is hoped to appoint a part-time local Co-ordinator soon to relieve the volunteer managers of some of the burden and to give a professional base on which to build. Plans are now in hand to address another objective – the provision of support to very young mothers in the town. Safe affordable crèche facilities will be provided during the day in the coming year.

In recognition of the importance of existing Child Protection Procedures, the Board's own Child Protection Policy, referred to in the report to the General Assembly last year, is now complete. This means that the Board will be fully compliant with the child care requirements of the incoming Scottish Commission for the Regulation of Care which takes effect in April 2002.

6.3 Counselling and Support Services

In addition to Lifestyle, PND, PACT and the Dundee Women and Children Project which have a bearing on child care and related work, other mainstream counselling services continue to operate and develop. **Number 21 Counselling Service** has had a significant year, with the Deputy Manager requesting a six month sabbatical in Armenia disseminating counselling and supervision skills and supporting an agency which was developing counselling work. This she duly did, after a spell of successful fundraising for her trip. Later in the year, a very public and well attended launch of the art therapy service took place at which Richard Demarco spoke most generously and entertainingly. Number 21 continues to promote an expansion of the idea of counselling in ways which can make the concept of healing-through-relationship more accessible. Closer links with other Board services are being considered, such as sharing the Families and Children Therapist post with PND. The existing postholder already works with Saheliya, a Black and Asian women's organisation, so the expansion of service is lateral and broad-based. The Board is grateful for the continuing service offered by the trained counsellors in all its counselling services. In Number 21 alone 46 counsellors and 7 art therapists give of their time, with 420 people being supported. A high level of satisfaction is shown from questionnaires. Those seeking counselling presented with the following identified problems:

	2000	2001
	%	%
Depression/Anxiety/Stress	30.6	35.9
Not Clear	5.5	21.2
Relationships/Confidence/Self-esteem	20.2	19.7
Loss/Bereavement	4.9	6.6
Marital/Partnership	20.2	3.5
Alcohol/Gambling/Drugs	2.7	2.5
Anger/Violence	2.7	2.5
Sexual Abuse/Rape	2.2	2.5
Diagnosed Mental Health Difficulty	3.3	1.5
Personal Growth	1.1	1.5
Eating Disorder	0.0	1.5
Work Related	2.4	0.5
Sexual Difficulties	2.2	0.5
Financial	2.6	0.0
Other	9.6	0.1

The age range of clients:

	2000	2001
Under 16	1.6%	2.0%
16-18	1.3%	5.0%
19-30	24.6%	32.2%
31-45	29.0%	31.7%
46-55	12.6%	6.5%
56-64	2.7%	3.0%
65 +		19.1%
Not Known		2.2%

Comments from clients included: *"Well relieved; like a weight lifted from my shoulders"* and *"I like myself a bit better"*.

Case Histories

"Sally"

17 year-old Sally was referred by Couple Counselling and at the initial meeting talked about her bottled up feelings and unhappiness since her parents split up six months earlier "quite out of the blue". Her school work was being affected and she needed to get good grades to get into a media studies course in Glasgow. She had thought her unhappy feelings would disappear when she and her mum moved into their own home, having been living with her grandparents. This hadn't happened.

Her relationship with both parents was affected. She appeared quite depressed. Sally was an only child, but her parents used to foster children. At first they were like brothers and sisters for her, and then she came to regard herself as a carer to them. She had learned to take on an adult role and needed permission to be a teenager.

Themes of loss and change emerged as Sally expressed feelings of hurt and sadness, but also angry feelings, which were more difficult to express without feeling bad. Sally expressed feelings of relief in the first session at being able to talk freely and have someone to listen who would not get upset. She then chose to take up a contract of five counselling sessions starting straight away, rather than having to wait for the possibility of a longer term programme.

In the time of the five sessions, Sally changed from a withdrawn, quite depressed teenager, lacking in confidence and blaming others for making her life difficult, to a more mature young person with a greater understanding of herself and how she relates to others. She was able to be assertive and take responsibility for herself. Her relationships with family and friends improved and her energy to tackle her school work was renewed. She was very responsive to the counselling and was surprised at the changes that had happened in a relatively short time."

"Josephine"

This woman came to art therapy following a breakdown and long period of depression. Permission to acknowledge and express negative feelings had not been part of her early nurture, and whilst part of her wanted to comply and please her parents, another part of her was very angry because they had not been able to "see" her. A consequence was that she became entrapped by her extreme hurt and anger and her first pictures expressed this painful and intolerable situation.

She made a very large number of images, almost

without exception on the same size of paper and with the same materials and this seemed to reflect the confines of her emotional 'landscape'. Her fear of seeing beyond her pain, whilst intolerable, was known and reliable, unlike her parents whom she had experienced, and continued to experience, as unavailable. Gradually she became open to other possibilities and as the horizons in her pictures altered, sometimes very distant, sometimes very close, so did her ideas about herself. Her vision very noticeably expanded. It was as if she saw the therapy room with 'opened' eyes, the wealth of materials available became, for the first time, visible to her. As she moved familiar symbols and motifs around the paper she became able, gradually, to revise some of the narratives which she clung to because they were all that she had and to discover new ones.

She had grown to believe in her own capacity to be an effective agent of change in her own life when the therapeutic relationship concluded."

The **Older Persons Counselling Group** meets weekly to offer support to twelve older women who have depression, suffer from anxiety or who are isolated. It is planned to set up a Day Care Group using nearby local church premises in Edinburgh. While this is a small project, it is well appreciated, and over the year assisted 20 older people.

The **Tom Allan Centre in Glasgow** continues to offer a very valued service. The Service Manager describes 2001 as being "a time of consolidation, yet one that has seen new challenges as we continue to meet the demands asked of us." These demands include 6,573 appointments for 1,347 clients, seen by 61 trained counsellors (12 men and 49 women), 24 of whom are registered by the United Kingdom Register of Counsellors. The Board is a sponsoring agency for the UKRC and is also a member of the Confederation of Scottish Counselling Agencies (COSCA), the British Association of Counsellors (BAC) and the Association of Christian Counsellors (ACC). One of the 18 external organisations using the Tom Allan Centre premises is a support group for families of children who have been murdered. This group has a long-standing connection with the Centre and the Board is pleased to have its facilities used in this way by other support groups. In addition to the day-to-day counselling programme, TAC staff also provide COSCA 'Certificate in Counselling Skills' modules for Board staff and external purchasers of course time. The Board considers it essential that staff in all its homes and projects undertake at least a course on an "Introduction to Listening Skills". In response to one of the TAC objectives for 2001: "To support and encourage the development of client evaluation and research within the Centre and the other counselling projects", one of the trained volunteer counsellors engaged in an MSc in Counselling at Abertay University is researching "The Client at the Heart of Therapy: An Investigation into People's Experience of Counselling". The Board expects that the results of this research and that being pursued at the NCS in Dundee will provide valuable indicators for its counselling provision.

The **National Counselling Service** (NCS) is now halfway through its five year development programme. At the beginning of the year counselling services had been established in Edinburgh, where NCS is based, Dunfermline and Dundee, between them offering 4000 appointments a year. During 2001, **Connections**, based in Dunbar with an appointment service in Tranent, Prestonpans and Musselburgh, came fully under the NCS umbrella and a new service was opened in Kyleakin with the total appointments rising to 4,334.

A client from the Connections service wrote:

"I would like to thank you for all your help and understanding when I couldn't help myself. Talking helped to put a lot into perspective and I do think my counselling sessions were what really made the difference. I would like to thank Connections for all your help and if there is ever a time when you wonder if what you do is making a difference I would like you to know that it does."

As the service begins to move into more rural areas, one of the major challenges is supervising the counselling services and the counsellors. An interactive video conferencing system will greatly assist with this, the concept having been brought forward through the NCS link with the Highland Theological College. It is important to check that services achieve their various aims. "Outcome measurement" now forms part of the task of all Board services. Counselling is no exception. Bearing in mind that all the Board's counselling work is free at the point of delivery, there is a continuing need for the Board to know that using its reserves in providing such services is an appropriate expenditure. Similarly, when approaching other funders and trusts it is vital to be able to demonstrate value for money and positive outcomes. However, the Board lives with the uncertainty of obtaining external funding for rent, utilities and administrative support; an uncertainty which staff have to learn to manage. In Dundee, two University research students will carry out an external evaluation of the NCS service in that city, devising a questionnaire to help measure service outcomes. The NCS Dundee, or Number 10 as it has become known locally, continues to be the busiest NCS centre. Meantime the written responses of clients give some indication of the benefits of professional Christian counselling:

"I found all aspects of the service uplifting and encouraging. I was made to feel relaxed and optimistic. A first class service".

"For the first time I felt that my problems could be resolved".

"I felt as if someone was really listening to me and I felt hope for the future".

6.4 Drug and Alcohol-related Work

While the Board had placed a strong emphasis on making its counselling services more widely available, counselling skills are also needed for all other staff who assist service users to become more able to make the most of life's opportunities and challenges. This is particularly relevant in the residential rehabilitation services for those with drug and alcohol-related problems at Ronachan, Victoria View, Malta House, Beechwood, Deeford and Rainbow. It is also a basic theme in the supported accommodation projects of Whiteinch, Cale House, Lewis Street and Rankeillor Initiative, as well as day services at Simpson House, AXIS and Lifestyle. As what has worked before does not necessarily work now, there is a constant need to evaluate effectiveness, and so the Board has a rolling programme of formal service reviews to ensure the

continuing relevance and good standards of work.

It was with thanks to God that the Board learned that no-one had been injured in the fire at **Rainbow House** in Glasgow in November 2001. Rainbow offers residential rehabilitation programmes for those dependent on substance misuse. The fire damage was severe enough to require that the service be transferred elsewhere until the building was again available in April 2002. Those on the programme were incorporated into the core work at **Victoria View** and **Ronachan** while others who were nearing completion of the rehabilitation programme left. Staff were incorporated into vacancies in the Board's other services. At the time of writing, repair work is starting and the opportunity is being taken to retrain and refresh staff before returning to the repaired Rainbow with a revised programme. During the year residents at Rainbow were incorporated into an initiative backed by Sir Tom Farmer where people on rehabilitation programmes can learn working habits and skills in realistic working conditions. The initial and successful result was that those on the Real Work scheme succeeded in gaining employment. Other schemes are planned throughout Scotland. This innovative scheme by Scotland Against Drugs (SAD) is proving to be enhancing for those who are keen to re-establish themselves in the community and the Board is delighted to be associated with SAD in this project.

Ronachan House in Argyll has completed a review of its service and continues to seek the most suitable form of programme to meet changing needs and the expectations of local authorities who remain the main purchasers of service. Ronachan has been offering an alcohol rehabilitation service for 24 years. One result of the review of service was that the Board would remain committed to residential placements as a preferred option to meet individual needs, because the person may need time out from his or her home environment, with complex and inter-related problems that can best be addressed in a residential setting. Placement in such a supportive temporary environment can provide an opportunity for the person to receive intensive assistance for change, including physical, social, emotional and spiritual care. The revised programme has been improved with a more individual focus on a 1 to 6 month stay. In the same way that the Rainbow programme is linked to real work opportunities, Ronachan reviews evidence about effective ways to support alcohol and drug misusers into education, training and employment. Finding and sustaining a job on the open market can be a challenge, even in times when work is more plentiful. It can be more so during times when vacancies and opportunities are not so available. Similarly, finding a full-time place in education or training can be a particularly difficult and distant goal for service users. To assist, the programme includes confidence building, personal and social skills development, debt counselling and basic skills training. Alongside this, the internet is proving useful to access learning programmes and funders. Attempts are maintained to keep contact with those who have moved on from Ronachan and at the Open Day in August 2001, eighteen former residents attended, which was an encouragement both to staff and to those currently on a rehabilitation programme. Nonetheless, despite the benefits of residential care, referral by Social Workers remains at a low level, compared with the damage to individuals and families as a result of alcohol abuse. Extracts from letters by former service users illustrate satisfaction with their achievements:

John wrote:

"It was lovely to be back in Argyll last August for the Open Day. By the grace of God and AA (Alcoholics Anonymous) I will be three years and eight months sober on 4 December. Ronachan gave me that chance."

Alex also wrote:

"Still no sign of work for me, but I've not given up hope. I have completed a college course for pipe fitting and welding and have actually gained an SVQ Certificate: a first in the whole of my life and I am really getting quite proud, as I have never achieved any qualifications at all, never even at school."

The past approach to alcohol abuse has been varied and the Board has commented on this over many years. The Board therefore welcomes the move towards a national strategy on alcohol established by the Scottish Executive and hopes to be able to play its part in discussions as the largest provider of residential rehabilitation facilities in the country. Whilst the Government accepted the need for a national strategy - "Tackling Drugs Together" - no such policy has yet been developed for alcohol abuse. It is hoped that, following the consultation undertaken by the Scottish Executive, it might adopt many of the points identified in the **European Charter on Alcohol** which was published in 1995, i.e.:

- **All** people have the right to a family, community and working life protected from accidents, violence and other negative consequences of alcohol consumption.
- **All** people have the right to valid impartial information and education, starting early in life, on the consequences of alcohol consumption on health, family and society.
- **All** children and adolescents have the right to grow up in an environment protected from the negative consequences of alcohol consumption and, to the greatest extent possible, from the promotion of alcoholic beverages.
- **All** people with hazardous or harmful alcohol consumption and members of their families have the right to accessible treatment and care.

Over the past year the residential rehabilitation units operated by the Board have, in general, suffered from a definite lack of referrals. There is no evidence to support that there has been a decrease in the number of people who would benefit from such help. The trend appears to be to offer support through community-based programmes. While this may be an appropriate treatment for some addicts, it will not be for all. Concern arises that the community-based programme is currently preferred to residential programmes because of financial restrictions on local Council Social Work Departments, rather than their being more effective. Concern must be raised at the current use of the Board's residential rehabilitation units where, in the present financial year, percentage occupancy has varied from 33.3% at worst to 97.2% at best, the average occupancy for all the units throughout this period being 63.9%. Given the enormity of the problem throughout Scotland, even taking into account that the residential option is not appropriate for everyone, it still begs the question "Why?" This is a service which is under review.

6.5   A Homely Environment

In 1991, the Board approved the move from registered institutional care to more ordinary living where this was possible. Over these ten years there has been considerable movement towards using ordinary or adapted housing from twenty-three housing providers. With the issue by the Scottish Executive of "The Same as You", this trend has been underlined. This Report emphasised the importance of people with a learning or complex disability having the same opportunities as anyone else to experience life in an ordinary house, using local shops and community supports in the same way as others in local communities. Central Government has enabled this progress through greater application of Interim Housing Benefit, Disability Living Allowance and the Independent Living Fund to provide the levels of housing support required to sustain a tenancy, while the local Social Work Department can contribute towards direct care costs. This package can ensure that available support is individually planned and applied, with minimum intrusion into a person's life and property, unlike the traditional residential registered care model which has inbuilt institutional elements. It remains to be seen how the new registering Commission starting in April 2002 will approach this.

In recognition of the changes of theory and practice in this area of work the Board established a Member/Staff Group on Learning Disability to prepare a report for the Board during 2002; the remit given to the Group is:

1. To review the Scottish Executive document "The same as you?", associated literature, and other appropriate documentation, and
2. To identify the ways in which the Board can fulfil the objectives of such literature.
3. To identify a variety of service delivery styles for individuals with learning disabilities, giving due attention to the views of service users
4. To make comment on the appropriateness of each service style and its suitability for use by the Board, and

5. To identify new styles of service which should be considered by the Board.

Over the years, the Board has striven to minimise the institutional effects of registration, by moving services from large premises into ordinary housing or by adapting large premises into flats or bedsits. Examples of this are found at **Belmont Castle** in Meigle, **Clashfarquhar** in Stonehaven, **Cumnor Hall** in Ayr and **Tollcross** in Glasgow, where more individual services are offered for older people.

This has also been done for young disabled people at **Keith Lodge**, Stonehaven and **The Mallard**, Glasgow and for people with various needs at **Lewis Street** in Stornoway, **Cale House** in Inverness, **Whiteinch** in Glasgow and the **Rankeillor Initiative** in Edinburgh. Further such work has been completed at most of the registered and other housing services with support for adults with learning and other disabilities and the Board's mental health work.

One of the benefits of using Interim Housing Benefit and the arrangements of its successor, Supporting People, which comes into force in 2003 is that each person can have tenancy security, with the benefit of greater personal choice, dignity and as ordinary a life as possible. Having moved along this path for some years, the Board is presently in discussion over life-mapping and person centred planning with the 8 people living in **Dunforth** and the 11 at **Wolfson** in Edinburgh, along with their relatives, staff and Social Work Department staff, to prepare for each person to move on to community-based housing. Although the Board has now completed such work on many occasions, for each individual and their relatives it is normally the first time, and can be an alarming prospect. Saltmarket in Glasgow hosts the base for a service which moved from an 18 place hostel into ordinary houses. The Unit Manager, in his Annual Report, commented:

"I am very pleased with the progress and development made since the move from the Sutherland Hostel. I feel we have developed a better quality and more progressive service for adults with a learning disability. Service users have a far more appropriate service for their needs and wishes and a much higher

quality of life. Each person has their own individual flat with their required support and easy access to community facilities."

Janet, who is supported in one of the flats, said: *"I like the privacy of my own flat. It's better than being at Sutherland House"*, while Andrew remarked: *"It's OK. I like staying here. Workers help me a lot."* Similar comments could be repeated in relation to other residential services which have been incorporated into local communities in ordinary, anonymous housing. This is a reflection of the motto chosen by Florentine dispersed flats in the South Side of Glasgow, where 24 adults with a learning disability are supported in 9 houses and flats, and Alligan Day Service, managed by Florentine staff, which offers 14 day care places in Govanhill Neighbourhood Centre:

"Since God chose you to be the holy people whom he loves, you must clothe yourselves with tender-hearted mercy, kindness, humility, gentleness and patience. You must make allowance for each other's faults and forgive the person who offends you. Remember, the Lord forgave you, so you must forgive others."

Colossians 3: 12-13

The homelessness accommodation of **Cunningham House** and **McGregor House** in Edinburgh, the Rankeillor Initiative previously mentioned, **Kirkhaven** in Glasgow and Cale House in Inverness similarly reflect attempts to support individuals back into everyday life. Cunningham House takes as its motto Joshua 1:9:

"I have commanded you, be strong and courageous, do not tremble or be afraid, because the Lord your God is with you wherever you go."

With financial support from the Social Work Department, the Housing Department, Scottish Homes Resettlement Grant and the Board, and with the commitment of staff under God's command and strength, 178 people were supported and accommodated from Cunningham House this year. Resettlement was sustained at a high level, but a concerning feature was the repeated high level, at 30%, of referrals of people who were being looked after in care before age 16. As a founding member

and funder of the Scottish Throughcare and Aftercare Forum, this failure of suitable aftercare support is of concern to the Board. Discussions are in hand with various authorities to see how the Board could assist with better provision of aftercare and support.

One other concerning feature of the Board's homelessness services is the apparent need for an alternative to being locked up for being drunk and incapable. The Board already manages such a service, the 8 person Designated Place (DP) which forms part of the **Beechwood** campus in Inverness. The DP has been successfully operating for 10 years, yet despite this there has been a reluctance on the part of local authorities for this successful venture to be repeated. The Board is currently discussing with various Councils how this concept could be developed within the context of the unfolding national alcohol strategy.

6.6 Older People

The Board's services for older people are still heavily weighted towards residential homes although a priority in development terms is support to people in their own home through the Home Support Service. The Board provides residential services for older people in 28 homes and for those with dementia, 4 specialist homes and 2 specialist units within homes. Over the past decade the building upgrading that had commenced required to slow down as the finance was being used to meet revenue deficits. The Regulations coming from the new Scottish Commission for Care will mean that upgrading will require to be addressed again and a programme of upgrading agreed. Occupancy levels in our homes in general have remained high.

A major challenge to our residential homes will be the introduction of (**Single) Care Homes** from 1 April 2002 within which care and nursing care can be provided. The new regulations remove the different registration authorities for care and nursing care, all responsibility now passing to the Commission. This will be a time for change and learning and it is hoped that the Board's input to training opportunities will again bear fruit.

The proposed development of **Crosbie Tower in Troon** will provide a short break or longer stay for people of any age including older people. The refurbished facility will help people to relax and enjoy their break, providing a safe haven with friendliness and comfort, away from the routine stresses and strains of everyday life. An established link with a Northern Ireland Trust will ensure that families from there who need respite will be able to benefit from the resource, as well as people from throughout Scotland. When completed Crosbie Tower will provide 8 single bedrooms, 2 twin rooms and 6 family rooms, all with private facilities. 5 lounges will be available, including 1 for smokers. To achieve maximum flexibility, the annexe will provide 3 self-catering flats for families of 4, and 2 self-catering flats for families or groups of 8.

6.7   Home Support

Throughout the year, the **Home Support Service** has continued without significant growth, pending publication of the Audit Commission's Report on such services. While the Report indicated that 73% of home support services were provided by local authorities, the trend towards more care in the community means an opportunity for the Church to develop further its home support through the Board. At present, 4,939 hours a month are being provided and if the average for Threshold is included this gives a total average of 5,026 hours of home support per month. A small working group has been meeting to review focus and costs which it is hoped will lead to an expansion of this service.

6.8   Divisions

The 5 operational Divisions continue to establish themselves in their geographic areas, with good contacts being made locally with statutory, voluntary and local churches. The resultant improvement in local knowledge is leading to better targeted work, opportunities for engagement in small projects and smoother communications on some matters. The Divisions were established 3 years ago with basic staffing and the development of the workload, overloaded with new legislation, regulations and evolving good practice, meant that much work would have remained undone without some relief being provided. Accordingly, the Board considered and approved that the hours available in each

Division for professional development should be increased, together with half-time clerical hours. While the clerical posts have not yet been released because of funding limitations, the increased Planning and Development hours have already resulted in more locally based initiatives being explored. The Board therefore continues to move into positions where it can be more of a resource in partnership with or to facilitate local churches to reach out within their parishes.

7.   Planning and Development

Whereas the operational work of the Department is changing and developing all the time, being easily seen to be alive through its reporting of service delivery and human interest recordings, it is much more difficult to reflect the consistent hard work, planned and directed, which is required to provide the platform on which so much of the operational work can then be built. The Planning and Development role is seeking to provide systems that support the service delivery, and on many occasions planning for future services or standards before they are on the ground. This year there is evidence of Planning and Development taking forward issues that are essential to the long term development and stability of the Board. For example considerable time and effort has been invested in taking forward our quality assurance work systems – Towards Quality, while time is also being spent grappling with possible future family based services which can be implemented locally and with the involvement of individual congregations. Effective consultation is time consuming but the reward is in seeing services develop from a sound base and by staff who understand the objectives of the service.

This can best be illustrated in the work on the "**Towards Quality**" initiative. Following the launch in January 2001 of the Board's standards, staff have been encouraged to think about how these standards can be measured. This is essential as it is not acceptable to **believe** that standards are being met; they must be **shown** to be being met. Laudable as this is, a balance must be maintained to ensure that the measurement system does not become a paper chase. The best people to consult are those who will apply the system. This has been done by inviting every service to submit its views and by engaging with a representative staff group who have reviewed the work of the quality assurance working party.

As a result, front line services are now engaged in reviewing their work and identifying how well they meet the Board's standards. This is an ongoing task as the title "Towards Quality" suggests. By self assessing, greater ownership of the standards will be achieved and service delivery improved.

This system will fit into the external inspection applied by the newly set up Scottish Commission of the Regulation of Care, a completely independent body tasked to regulate all providers against national standards. These standards have been published in December 2001 and January 2002 and are themselves the product of consultation. The Board's standards, when met, will exceed the minimum standards set by the Commission. It is important for the Board to monitor its own practice against its standards and it is anticipated that, as services review their performance, and write development or improvement plans, individual staff will be encouraged and re-affirmed in the task they undertake.

Staff are the most important resource of the Board and play a large part in any development. Last year, it was reported that **policies and procedures** had been reviewed. This year additional policies have been needed to reflect the complexity of needs of service users and staff. Consequently, staff have been involved not only in writing but also in checking the policies and procedures to make sure they are manageable.

Two-way communication is aided by the divisional structure and this has been demonstrated by the consultation process used when devising the new **strategic plan**. Once the Board agreed the aims these were given to each service in order that realistic objectives could be set by the services. These were reviewed by the divisions who in turn set their divisional objectives. These were then analysed at a national level and influenced the final objectives set for the Board.

The whole exercise starting in March and concluding in December involved a review of previous aims and objectives. As well as staff consultation the Planning and Development Committee was also involved in giving its perspective. While time consuming, it is hoped that this experience helps individuals influence the direction of the work and feel part of it.

In the course of setting the aims, it has become more evident that the divisional staff have been successful in working closer with individual congregations in helping meet local needs. "Solid Rock" in Buckie is the culmination of local church partnerships working together with help from the Board and other local organisations to provide a service to young people which would not have been achieved if any one party had worked alone. There is growing evidence of successful consultative work between the Board and local churches resulting in local issues being explored and met. One of the Board's aims for the next three years is "To work with presbyteries and local churches to find ways of meeting local needs while continuing to encourage volunteer activity". This will give even greater impetus to this style of co-operative work.

A further development of working with congregations is the **Social Capital** survey carried out by the University of Glasgow to test how local congregations contribute to the social capital of their communities. The results of this will be of interest to the whole church as it looks at its place within Scotland. It is reported upon in Part One of this Report.

It is hoped to interview significant elements of each local community with a view to commenting on how church congregations contribute to their local communities. These results will help direct the future shape of the Board's work as it enters the early years of the new millennium. The Board and local congregations have much to contribute one to the other as we seek to act out our privilege of being the Body of Christ.

The work on **health and healing** has continued to be fruitful seeking to promote, support and develop the ministry of healing throughout the church.

During 2001, each presbytery has been asked to appoint a health and healing contact who can be informed of forthcoming events, thus promoting the health and healing ministry. It is hoped that this person will also keep the advisory group informed about local needs and that localised support for individuals interested in taking forward this ministry will grow as the role of the contact develops.

7.1 Press & Publicity
7.1.1 Media Enquiries

In 2001, there was a continual stream of questions and requests for interviews or articles from all sectors of the media. In the twelve months, there were a total of 156 telephone requests from radio and television stations or newspapers. These were dealt with in the first instance by the Communications Officer (Media) and, where appropriate, passed on to the Board's Convener or the relevant member of staff. One area of growth came from web and text-based news providers such as BBC Online and Teletext. There was also a marked increase in stories originating from News Agencies across Scotland who then sell it to other press outlets. To emphasise the range of subjects that the Board was asked to comment on, here is a selection:

- Allowing co-habiting couples to live in HM Forces accommodation
- A clinic in Glasgow which lets couples choose the sex of their baby
- The morning after pill being made available in schools to over 16s
- BBC programme called 'Son of God' that had created a computer image of Jesus
- An Edinburgh Festival show featuring erotic dancers
- Internet advertising of wedding services
- Child prostitution in Edinburgh
- Billy Connolly's film: 'The man who sued God'
- A television and billboard advert for a new soup
- 200 IVF couples in Korea who were being prayed for
- A proposed 'opt-out' scheme for organ donation

Two of the major issues from the previous year still resulted in the largest number of enquiries – funding for care of older people in Scotland, and human cloning.

Quotes from 2000/2001

In **January**, Church leaders accused the Scottish Executive of taking a 'cavalier' approach to the importance of marriage in sex education classes. The then Board Convener Ann Allen told the *Edinburgh Evening News* that results of a survey found that 92% of young people saw marriage as their ultimate goal: "The Executive are ignoring the general response of many young people on the issue of marriage." Also in January, Mrs. Allen condemned the sale of an 'offensive' T-shirt in a Glasgow music store. Speaking to the *Sunday Herald* she said: "I am horrified that anyone would want to wear blasphemous material like this." In the same edition, the Convener also hit out at a new reality television show called Temptation Island which was due to hit British TV screens. She described the show as 'sinking to new depths of depravity' and added: "The couples taking part in this would have to be either motivated solely by the fame and publicity or else be very confident in the commitment they have to one another. Given the manipulative nature of TV I reckon it would be the former. Nothing surprises me any more about the morality and opportunism of programme makers. No-one can be surprised at their willingness to plumb the depths of human behaviour."

In **February**, *The Herald* reported on a 20 year-old patient who had undergone 300 operations for a rare bowel disorder and wanted to die if his next operation was not successful. The Board's Communications Officer Hugh Brown said: "We are not in favour of euthanasia and I don't think that position will alter. We don't believe there is a situation where euthanasia could be an acceptable way forward. 95% of conditions can now be effectively controlled with pain relief."

Funding for care of older people never left the headlines, and in **June** the Board's new Convener, Rev. Jim Cowie, wrote a feature for the *Scottish Daily Mail* 'The Price of Dignity'. This sparked off a number of articles including one in *The Scotsman* 'Kirk in elderly care cash crisis'. The Board's Convener stated: "At the moment the Executive says it gives the necessary funding to local authorities but it is simply not filtering through to the homes. We want to see the money ring-fenced to ensure funding is going straight to the homes." An editorial in *The Herald* – 'Stop dithering over care' – made the case for implementing the Sutherland Report: "The Kirk has provided a service in caring for the elderly. This has clearly been at a financial cost that seems to be rising. It is not in the business of holding guns to heads, particularly where care for the needy is involved, but its patience has been sorely tried. The Kirk's appeal for proper resources, taken with Scottish Care's warning that the present arrangements for publicly funded places cannot be tolerated, must leave central and local government in no doubt that they cannot continue to prevaricate."

The *Edinburgh Evening News* carried a story about church leaders concern over sex advice services in a youth pamphlet. Hugh Brown said: "We generally feel it to be responsible to educate young people about these resources. But due to the wide target age range it may be slightly unwise to include details of organisations and groups which deal with specifically adult issues." **July** also saw the first of many advances towards the possibility of human cloning. *The Herald* said that a church leader had voiced fears about parents paying for 'designer babies' after it emerged that a company in the US could help British couples choose the sex of children. Board member Rev. Dr. Richard Corbett said he feared that people would choose the sex of their children 'for selfish reasons'.

'First human embryo cloned' was a headline in The Herald in **November**. Scientists in America have cloned a human embryo, raising fears that it could lead to the birth of a cloned baby. Despite reassurances that it would not be used to create a human clone, it provoked a storm of protest from ethical groups. Rev. Dr. Richard Corbett said that the Kirk was uncomfortable with therapeutic cloning (to produce embryonic stem cells for research) but not opposed to it. "If scientists can avoid making an embryo the Church would much prefer that."

The Scotsman reported that the Edinburgh Dungeon visitor attraction had replaced Santa's sleigh and reindeer with a coffin pulled by skeletons. Jim Cowie was quoted as saying that parents should be aware of what they are taking their children to see. "If people take it seriously it could attract devil worshippers." Not printed was the rest of his sentence: "However people will not take it seriously as it is a blatantly commercial venture."

7.1.2 'Circle of Care' Newspaper
Social Responsibility's free newspaper is one of the most successful ways of spreading the message about the Board's work. Circulation continues to increase and it now prints 47,000 copies three times a year. The main recipients are Congregational Contacts who then distribute them to their church members. However, there are also mailings to church newsletter editors, mission partners and Social Work Directors. 'Circle of Care' has been entered for a national competition – the 2001 Charity & Public Service Publishing Awards sponsored by Charity Times and popcomm. This independent set of awards acknowledges the high standards achieved by the publishers of public service and charity publications. At the time of writing, it is not known how 'Circle of Care' fared in the two categories – The Newsletter of the Year and The Totally in-house Edited and Designed Publication of the Year.

7.1.3 'Circle of Care' Calendar
In a growing marketplace for calendars, the 'Circle of Care' calendar continues to be amongst the top sellers in Scotland – and beyond. The 2002 edition, which retained the style and shape of recent years with only minor alterations, has increased its sales to around 21,000 copies. These are not only sent to people in Scotland, but are posted to family and friends around the world.

7.1.4 Christmas Cards
This year's Board card has been the biggest ever seller with 30,000 cards printed and sold in a very short space of time. The winning design came from a resident at Cornerstone in Wishaw, Francis Pinchbeck, who was assisted by his key worker Frances Shaw. Francis has learning disabilities and has stayed at Cornerstone since 1993. The card depicted the material gifts we receive at Christmas but also reminds us of God's best gift – Jesus Christ. The front cover says: "God gave just the right gift." The story of the Christmas card along with a photograph appeared in the local paper the Wishaw Press. Having listened to comments from customers, it was decided to produce one size of card instead of two as in previous years, and to put 10 cards in each pack rather than 6. The cost however stayed at £2.50 per pack. This was possible due to an increased print run and by using the Church's Design Services to manufacture the card it meant that production costs were kept to a minimum.

7.1.5 Merchandise
The sales of Board merchandise are encouraging and a valuable method of promotion. The range has been

expanded to include pencils, rulers and badges. These low cost items – along with key rings and pens – sell the largest number and have to be reordered on a regular basis. 900 'Lights for Christ' have been sold and due to an error by the manufacturer there are now another 300 available, but as a well-known supermarket says: "When they're gone, they're gone!" Based on the success of the large light, a miniature version has been commissioned which will contain a tea light. Another new project in preparation is an address book, which is being produced in association with Donald Ford, who is one of the photographers whose work regularly appears in the 'Circle of Care' calendar. The book, which will include over 60 beautiful Scottish scenes, will also have pages for 'special days' and a Christmas card list and should be on sale in time for the General Assembly.

7.1.6 HIV/AIDS Resource Pack

During the year work continued on the production of a new HIV/AIDS Resource Pack. It has been over five years since the last Board pack on HIV and AIDS which was widely praised. This new pack has been edited by one of the Divisional Managers, John Wyllie, who has a lead role within the Board for HIV and AIDS. The pack, which is A4 in size and contains a resource book, cassette, activity sheets and an evaluation questionnaire, was sent to every parish minister in January 2002.

7.1.7 Other Publicity Material

New display boards were produced which show the types of service that the Board offers. These are available for churches to borrow for use at information days or for special services. A leaflet called 'Why Care?' gives 10 frequently asked questions (and answers) about the Board and its work. These have proved to be very popular with one Ayrshire minister asking for 300 so he could distribute them with his church magazine. Because of the growing interest in human genetics, a new leaflet was produced with the help of Board member Rev. Dr. Richard Corbett. It outlines Social Responsibility's views on In-Vitro Fertilisation, Stem Cell Research and Human Cloning. 'Circle of Care' Tape number 8 was edited at Pathway Productions and sent out to Congregational Contacts. In addition to the normal cassettes, this audio resource was available on Compact Disc for the first time.

7.1.8 General Assembly Seminars

Because the 2001 General Assembly was held in the Usher Hall, it was decided to make use of the additional space by holding a series of lunchtime seminars in the area behind the public gallery. Social Responsibility took three of the slots; Board member Rev. Neil Galbraith explained the workings of the charity 'Glasgow – the Caring City'; 'HIV and AIDS – the latest picture' was led by John Wyllie who updated what is happening in Scotland, whilst Walter Dunlop from the Board of World Mission gave a picture of the situation in Africa. Dr. Dorothy Logie told the tragic story of her husband Sandy who died while working as a doctor in Zambia after he was accidentally infected by the virus following a needlestick injury. The third seminar saw the launch of a new pack: 'Social Inclusion – A Study Pack for Churches'. The special guest was Jackie Baillie MSP, then minister for Social Justice. She told the large audience: "The role of individuals in addressing social exclusion is very important. As I see it, this is what makes the Study Pack for Churches different. It encourages individuals to examine their own attitudes towards social exclusion and towards those who are marginalised in our society. This is a good start and will help to give everyone a better understanding of the true nature of exclusion and why we must work together to eliminate it. I applaud the Board of Social Responsibility's decision to produce this pack and I'm sure that it will be well used by congregations throughout Scotland." The pack is still available from Charis House at a cost of £4 plus postage.

7.1.9 Press Releases

During the year nine Press Releases were issued on behalf of Social Responsibility by the Media Relations Office at 121. Amongst the topics were the Princess Royal's visit to Ballikinrain, the Social Inclusion seminar at the General Assembly and three joint releases with the Kirk's Society, Religion and Technology Project on cloning.

In September the Board's Communications Officer (Media) worked with his opposite number in the Glasgow Archdiocese, Ronnie Convery, on a release about the launch of a Glasgow Charter. It said: "A new Glasgow

Churches Social Action Alliance will be launched to offer a 'one-stop-shop' to public bodies who wish to harness the energy and commitment of thousands of Christians of 11 denominations all over the city whose quiet voluntary work is rarely publicised, and whose expertise and experience is rarely utilised. Scottish Executive Minister for Social Justice Jackie Baillie MSP, Lord Provost Alex Mosson, Moderator of the General Assembly the Rt. Rev. John Miller and Administrator of the Archdiocese of Glasgow, Monsignor John Gilmartin will sign the declaration committing themselves to work together in future on new social inclusion projects. The launch had been timed to allow the participation of the late Cardinal Tom Winning, who backed the initiative from the start."

Throughout the year, the Board has been assisted in its dealings with the media by the staff at the Media Relations Unit at 121 to whom thanks are due.

7.2 Congregational Liaison
7.2.1 Introduction
The role of the Communications Officer (Congregations) has encompassed many new areas of work over the past year involving closer working with other Boards and Committees of the Church and discussions about how the Board can better support congregations who are working to prevent social exclusion in their communities.

7.2.2 Congregational Contacts – basic statistics and facts
There are 1090 Congregational Contacts who keep congregations advised of developments in the Board's work. Where there is no congregational contact the only form of communication is via a copy of 'Circle of Care' in the minister's mailing 3 times each year.

In February and March of this year the Board undertook a major updating of its Congregational Contact database, correcting entries, updating information, collecting e-mail addresses and ensuring that all people named on the database were aware of its existence and purpose, in line with data protection good practice guidelines.

7.2.3 The Work of Congregational Contacts
Congregational Contacts undertake their role in a variety of ways dependent on the support available to them, the size and type of congregation and the skills and time available which they can bring. They provide current, correct and appropriate information to their Church. They often act as distributors for the Circle of Care newspaper and they act as agents for the Board's calendar, Christmas Card and merchandise sales. In line with the Scottish Executive Active Communities Strategy the extent of voluntary work undertaken by these and other volunteers is fully recognised by the Board.

The vital role played by Congregational Contacts within their community means that an opportunity to meet face to face with representatives from local units, divisional teams and Charis House representatives is very important. During the past year Congregational Contacts have met with the Communications Officer (Congregations) and Divisional Team members at organised meetings on at least one occasion. Meetings were held in Glasgow, Dumfries, Edinburgh, Aberdeen, Dundee, Polmont and Inverness.

Topics discussed at these meetings included: an update on the Carer's Questionnaire; a talk on the "Caring For You" rose; a workshop on the Social Inclusion Pack and the importance of churches tackling the issues of social exclusion in their communities. The meetings also allowed for discussions on the work of the local Division and the future development of the Congregational Contact role. The opportunity was taken to receive feed back from Contacts as to how they could be better helped to fulfil their role. Suggestions included: smaller posters for churches with small notice boards; pre written newsletter articles on a variety of issues; more frequent meetings and advance agendas for meetings (to allow for preparation in local churches prior to attending).

Divisional offices arranged additional meetings and open days throughout the year to allow an extra opportunity to share local updates with Congregational Contacts.

7.2.4 Work with other Boards
The Communications Officer (Congregations) works with representatives from other Boards of the Church of Scotland seeking to assist all Boards to provide a co-ordinated approach to congregations looking for

information and assistance. The main focus has been to understand, streamline and advance the nature of work between the different Boards. This work has included, sharing of information, arranging and attending joint meetings of advisors and discussing protocols for referring churches to other Boards and committees of the Church where expertise in an area lies outwith our Board e.g. a need for youth work training would be referred to Parish Education. This work falls within the Board's stated objective of 'establishing links with other Boards of the Church of Scotland to explore joint working thus maximising resources'.

Joint working with other Boards has also allowed for the Social Responsibility calendar outlets across the country to develop into Church wide "resource fairs" where this year Social Responsibility was joined by representatives from World Mission, National Mission, Parish Education Publications and the Guild. It is hoped that next year, these Fairs will be supported by other Boards and Committees of the Church and will encompass more of the Church's work in local communities.

There is also a working party of representatives from within the Board of Social Responsibility and from other boards and committees of the Church who are looking into the concept of Church of Scotland 'Shopfronts'. These would be information, advice and service delivery units on the main shopping streets of our major towns and cities. The hope would be to prove that the central church can work without walls and be where people are in their communities and not just in the buildings where the church is expected to be. From these 'shopfronts' the church may be in a better position to help those who would otherwise not look to the church in their times of need.

7.2.5 The Website
Another project for the Communications Officers, both Media and Congregations, has been the updating of information on the Board's pages of the Church of Scotland web site and preparing up to date information about each of the units and services for inclusion on the World Wide Web at a later date. This work highlighted the need for consistent and corporate information about the services provided. A contracted IT specialist has been working with the Communications Officer (Congregations) to ensure that a centralised source of unit brochures containing all the information requirements of the Regulation of Care (Scotland) Act exists prior to the Scottish Commission on Care commencing in April 2002. The Board is represented on the Internet Forum which is the Church wide discussion forum for issues relating to how Boards use the Church of Scotland website and how this might be developed to better serve all Boards' needs.

7.2.6 Crossover 2001
As part of its ongoing work with young people in congregations and church related groups, Social Responsibility was part of Crossover 2001 again in June. All staff and volunteers involved in the weekend had a busy time but also plenty of fun (despite the rain!). Over 800 young people aged 12–18 came to the weekend festival and enjoyed activities, games, worship, live bands and workshops. Social Responsibility had a marquee with a staged area and tables and chairs for coffees/teas and 'Beat the Street' – an interactive homelessness game. It was estimated that around a quarter of those attending came into the tent at some point through the weekend and that 50–100 either played the Beat the Street game, looked at information or attended one of the sessions.

Outside the tent, sideshows were used to encourage the young people to come to the area and find out more about the Board. There was a selection of skills based games for all ages including a coconut shy, a beat the goalie game, a 'float a penny' challenge, and face painting.

A programme of interactive sessions called 'The Weakest Link?' aimed to challenge young people's perceptions of society's perceived 'losers'. Using 'true' and 'false' questions, a 'who wants to be a millionaire?' game and breakout groups doing creative writing, arts and crafts and drama, the issues of homelessness, HIV/AIDS and addictions were addressed.

A ceilidh was organised in the main venue on the Saturday night as had been done in previous years. Again this event proved to be a huge success with many of the leaders and young people enjoying the opportunity to mix in this way.

7.2.7 Social Responsibility Worship Resource Pack

This year, for Social Responsibility month a working group of the Planning and Development Committee in conjunction with the Communications Officer (Congregations) produced a pack of worship resources. The pack was a set of photocopyable A4 sheets which could be used within worship services of a variety of format. Resources included suitable hymns and readings, a sermon, children's talks and a crossword and wordsearch.

Feedback forms were issued in August and the response from congregations was particularly positive. It is anticipated that update/additional sheets for the pack will be issued in June of next year.

7.2.8 About the Rose

Last August, the rose was launched at Cockers in Aberdeen.

Many people ordered roses in 2000 and all last year's stock was sold with several orders being carried forward to this year.

This year a targeted publicity campaign has been undertaken to ensure that as many churchgoers as possible know about the rose and have an opportunity to purchase some. We worked with James Cocker and Sons to design the front cover graphic for their 2001 catalogue.

Local Authorities have received a letter, order form and 2001 catalogue and Cockers will inform the Board of any trade orders arising from this. They also received a follow up letter in September to remind them as they were budget planning for next year and will be reminded again when their year end budgets are drawn up in February.

Congregational Contacts, Ministers and Guild members received a flyer in their August Mailings and a copy went into every issue of Circle of Care and Life and Work. An article about the rose was in Circle of Care and in the Guild Newsletter and there have been several requests for a newsletter and article and digital photos to be sent direct to church newsletter editors. An advert about the rose was featured in the Sunday Times in September, highlighting its suitability as a Christmas gift.

Congregational Contacts heard about the rose and discussed ways to sell it to their congregation and church groups at their meetings in the autumn.

There are still several thousand roses to sell before the planting year ends in April and the Communications Officer (Congregations) has been preparing additional flyers and information to go to churches via their mailings.

7.3 Fundraising

The Board has a firm belief in the value of people; as users of the services and as supporters. The relationships we forge with recipients of, and donors to, these services are of great value and are vital to our work. Relationships are the key to our fundraising – a Relationship Fundraising Strategy.

In order to help the homes and projects within Social Responsibility with ideas for fundraising it was decided to produce a 'How to' manual explaining different concepts and giving some fresh ideas. It was decided that a consultative process would ensure a variety of experiences and the view of people from a broad range of jobs.

The result is the **Fundraising Cookbook**. It comes in two sections: the first contains an aid to planning, a section on how to agree what to raise funds for, and where the likely finance is to be found. The second section contains the Rough Guides with practical ideas about a fundraising venture. For example how to organise a fashion show, arrange and make money from river rafting or prepare a medieval banquet. It is written in simple straightforward language and contains ideas that should be accessible to every Social Responsibility project.

Two-thirds of Social Responsibility gifted income is from **legacies**. In 1994 it amounted to £850,000, rising to reach its highest level to date in 1998 at £1,915,000. In 1999 legacies amounted to £1,445,000.

One of the sections in the Fundraising Cookbook is about legacies. With initial training being planned, there will be the prospect of recruiting and training local people as volunteers to assist in a legacies campaign. The Board's legacies document covers:

- Giving thanks to donors or prospective donors
- How to gather information
- How to advertise
- Training people to respond to requests for information
- Monitoring the results.

Gift Aid is an important and growing development in tax efficient giving. Initial training in recording and promoting Gift Aid has been given to all Divisions. Separate single days of training have been organised for individual projects that requested it. Those who took the individual training (mainly the counselling projects) have had a very positive response and have seen the number of Gift Aid donations increase dramatically. (In one project over 100 people have signed a new Gift Aid form this year.) The job of processing these donations is growing.

We have received £18,300 of Gift Aided donations, yielding a further £5,124 of revenue.

One of the facets of the Relationship Fundraising Strategy is the approach to **Companies and Grant-making Trusts**. This has proved less successful this year.

The major fundraising project has been to raise money for family work, principally for **PACT** (The Parents and Children Together project in Glasgow) and also for the **Dundee Women and Children Project**.

PACT is a development to provide assistance, support and advice for parents and children who have little practical, emotional or financial support. It will be run in partnership with Renfield St Stephen's Church centre where high quality accommodation – in a non-stigmatised environment – is provided.

Money is required to run the project and pay for core costs and staffing. It has not been easy to attract such funds. Work with the **Dundee Women and Children** has meant gaining a greater understanding of how the project works and the services it provides. As well as flagging up similarities with the new PACT project it has provided the means to produce an audiotape which will be used to promote the existing work in Dundee and the new work in Glasgow.

As part of our commitment to Relationship Fundraising, a Prayer Letter is produced to inform supporters of the work and to encourage interest in prayer. The **Prayer Letter** circulation continues to grow. We now distribute 9,000 copies which is very encouraging.

7.3.1 Beat the Street – design competition

One of the outcomes from the Crossover last year was the production of the interactive game 'Beat the Street' (A new name is now required.) designed to encourage young people to try to win a home for themselves and get 'off the street' it put them through some of the difficulties and frustrations of trying to get anywhere against the system.

It is proposed that we develop the game for use in schools and church youth groups. A market survey has still to be taken, but with a view to its development we offered a prize for a new design of the game materials. This was taken up by Telford College as a final year project for design students. We were pleased with all the entries and it helped all to see the potential of the game. We are now at the stage of assessing the development and production costs. If the market survey is positive it should be possible to produce a number of copies during the coming year.

8. Central Services

8.1 Finance and Administration

Within Finance, I.T, Health & Safety, and Technical (the latter covering buildings, supplies, and aspects of general administration), significant pieces of work have been the development of Performance Standards and the preparation of material concerning aims and objectives for integration into the Board's Strategic Plan.

Detailed below are indications of some of the other features of the last year specific to the specialist areas concerned.

Considerable time and work is involved in providing information about the Board, its structures, its service objectives, its operating standards, its finances, and insurances to local authorities reviewing their Approved Service Provider's Lists for particular services and in ensuring acceptable detail on contracts with local authorities and others.

8.1.2 Finance

The Section was handicapped for the first half of the year due to difficulties in recruiting into a vacant Assistant Accountant position, this problem finally being resolved in the summer.

Work on identifying new Accounting software and providing for increased compatibility with the Payroll system has been given a high profile and is well under way, with planning geared to the implementation of a new system from April 2003.

In the meantime the use of electronic forms has been introduced for regular input from Units with the Finance and IT Sections providing training for staff in the operational Projects as required; senior section staff have also undertaken further training in the use of specialist budgeting software.

Following on from the circulation last year of a Financial Procedures Manual tailored to the needs of all operational units and projects, a commitment was made to take account of comments and of new developments by way of an annual update. The first of these Updates has been completed.

The provision of ad hoc financial information to incorporate into tenders for new services or to assist in other service development initiatives continues to be an important part of working with staff in the field - as does the ongoing liaison with local authorities on rate and grant negotiations, and on the provision of financial statistics as required.

As usual of course such considerations have to be set alongside the ongoing annual cycle of budget preparation, financial monitoring, Final Accounts production, audits, and training of operational staff – not forgetting the day-to-day important and mandatory routines of financial receipts, transfers, and payments, bank reconciliations, cash-flow and investments.

8.1.3 Information Technology

Arising from the earlier review of IT structure and staffing steps have now been taken to establish a Help-desk facility to provide a front-line response to Units in resolving practical problems as they are encountered on a day-to-day basis.

Further work has been carried out to complete the installation of new PCs and develop access to e-mail facilities for Units.

A review of how IT Training needs might most effectively be identified, provided, and monitored in operational staff's own locality is nearing completion and will form an important part of the Board's future overall IT Strategy.

8.1.4 Health & Safety

The main emphasis this year has been on Health & Safety Training.

A needs assessment was carried out, and this formed the basis of a tendering exercise through which external specialist agencies were invited to submit proposals for providing training on Moving and Handling, Food Hygiene, First Aid, Fire, and General aspects of Health & Safety.

Through this process the Providers for the different specialisms were identified, terms agreed with them, and training programmes set up which were put into effect in September. Responses from staff attending courses held to date have been extremely positive.

The Board's Health & Safety Officer continues to help Units as required in the important work of Risk Assessments, and to carry out a programme of Heath & Safety Audits.

8.1.5 Buildings, Supplies, and General Administration

'Best-value' reviews continue to be carried out in relation to contracts for equipment and services.

Divisional Managers have had presentations on the developing content of the Property Database, relevant parts of which have now been installed in each Divisional Office. It will be periodically updated by the Section as additional content becomes available.

A system using computers to generate Purchase Orders electronically was developed by the Section and has been piloted successfully in Charis House with a view to wider application in other locations.

The Section is also establishing a programme of formal training for drivers of minibuses attached to the Board's Units.

Ongoing activity has as usual included the putting into effect of work provided for within the Board's Capital Program – with the major developments at Ballikinrain School being the largest single project - and also reviewing and co-ordinating expenditure on a Planned Maintenance Programme.

Within Charis House itself a review of the catering arrangements has resulted in improvements being made to the Dining Room and its equipment, and the introduction of an external catering organisation to provide the service on a day-to-day basis; this year we have welcomed a new Reception team to HQ, and discussions are also nearing completion with a view to upgrading the telephone system serving the building.

The new Stores building developed in the grounds of Charis House has also successfully been brought into operation with the staff concerned now re-located from Malta House to Charis House.

8.2 Personnel and Payroll

A number of initiatives have taken place during the past year.

8.2.1 Staff Questionnaire

In order to update the computerised Personnel and Payroll database and to assist in the development of a Workforce Plan a Staff Questionnaire was issued to all employees. The Questionnaire sought information on qualifications, personal information and information relating to equal opportunities. The information is being processed in order that a computerised analysis can be made of the workforce.

8.2.2 Quality Standards

Following implementation of the Quality Standards a working group comprising of Personnel, Payroll and Training Staff was set up to write Quality Standards for the work which is undertaken in Charis House.

8.2.3 Payroll Forms

Following discussion with the Accounts Section it was agreed that new Payroll forms should be implemented. The information required on the forms enables detailed costings to be provided on each of the individual areas of service.

8.2.4 New Maternity Guidelines

Following changes to legislation covering maternity benefits and leave revised maternity guidelines have been drafted and issued. These provide employees with all the information which they require in such circumstances along with pro-formas which they complete in relation to maternity leave and pay.

8.2.5 Staff Advisory Forum

The work of the Staff Advisory Forum has continued to make an impact on the work of the department. The commitment and enthusiasm of the Forum members has resulted in a range of matters being discussed over the past years such as Give as You Earn, Friends Groups, Quality Assurance, Communication and a wide range of conditions of service matters.

8.2.6 Discipline and Grievance

The Board has long recognised Trade Unions for the purposes of accompanying staff to Disciplinary and Grievance procedures. During the past year the Board has extended this right to representatives from Professional Associations being mindful that a number of the Board's staff were members of such associations and would welcome the opportunity to be accompanied by such a representative.

A seminar was organised with the Board's Employment Lawyers for all Senior Managers on the Board's Disciplinary Procedures. This seminar was highly successful and resulted in the knowledge base of such Managers being widened in this important area of work.

8.2.7 Training
8.2.7.1 Practice Teaching Unit (PTU)

A year of change within the PTU and to a certain extent a time of uncertainty for Practice Teachers with the demise of Central Council of Education and Training in Social Work (CCETSW) and the Scottish Social Services Council taking over responsibility for the regulation of Education and Training. Initially funding for PTUs had not been guaranteed beyond March 2002 but that was later extended to 2004.

Three members of the Boards staff gained a Practice

Teaching Award and in line with CCETSW's reaccreditation requirements two members of staff have gained their 5 year Agency reaccreditation certificates.

One member of staff in Division 2 is currently working towards their Practice Teaching Award and three members of staff are undertaking Social Work training through Robert Gordon's University Distance Learning Route – one of the Social Work students is taking advantage of the free training offered by Scottish Institute of Residential Child Care.

8.2.7.2 Scottish Vocational Qualification (SVQ) Assessment Centre

The Centre continues to provide quality work; however due to staff vacancies as a result of a significant reconsideration of the training function in Divisions, the number of staff presenting completed SVQ portfolios has dropped although the number of senior staff achieving an Assessor Award has remained more or less the same.

We did not expect many level 4 completions before February of 2002; it would seem that 18 to 20 months is the least time for candidates to complete at this level but others may need longer. Much depends on the candidate's own ability to consider reflective practice and think more broadly about the situations that they encounter. The details about theory have to be learned but the worker's actual practice is essentially personal and it is getting the fusion of what they have learned and their individual practice onto paper that can sometimes prove difficult.

8.2.7.3 European Social Funding Bid

We were advised in October that our partnership bid for ESF funding was not successful on the ground that we did not meet the requirements to have 50% split of beneficiaries from small to medium sized employers. (SMEs)

Although this was disappointing news we were advised that the bid was marked and scored quite well and the next opportunity to make another bid will be May 2002.

8.2.7.4 Staff Induction Package

The Staff Induction Working Group have continued to meet over the past year adding to the activities workbook and information handbook. The meetings held in the Dewar Centre, Perth, to consult with approximately 20 members of staff in February was particularly helpful to fine tune the staff induction checklists, work activities and information handbook. We are now ready to pilot the package and arrange for filming of the video. A draft script has been prepared in readiness for this last piece of the jigsaw.

Such a rounded piece of work could not have been produced until the Boards Standards document and Policy and Procedures manuals were in place.

The introduction of the staff induction pack is an exciting and challenging first stage in the process of training for staff.

Employees will have the opportunity to learn about the organisation and work practices and to gain knowledge and understanding of their role and responsibilities within the workplace, in a friendly but structured way.

Involvement in their own learning situation will enable individuals to feel valued and confident within their role from an early stage in their career with the Board of Social Responsibility. This will have a positive impact on service delivery from a well informed, confident and competent member of staff.

8.2.7.5 Electronic Portfolio Pilots

These are pilots which SQA are running with the Church of Scotland, Glasgow City Council and the UKCCPO Centre to test the use of an all electronic paper-free version of the SVQ Candidate Portfolio. The purpose of the pilots is to trial two electronic portfolio products: one established product and one product in the latter stages of development.

The overall aim is to develop and provide a simple user friendly tool for candidates which could also offer both financial and time savings, and a robust quality assurance process.

For the initial pilot the Boards participating site is Achvarasdal House (Reay). The first pilot should be concluded by March 2002, by which time we should know whether it can be developed as a model for assessment centres.

8.2.7.6 Regulation of Care (Scotland) Act 2001 - Video

Following a series of meetings it was agreed the Scottish Executive Video & Television Production Unit would produce a video which was required to explain and raise awareness of the key elements of the Regulation of Care Act and its implications for the heads and senior members of the staff of care homes.

The Board's Senior Training Officer was the Boards representative on the Video Working Group.

The first edit of the video has already been produced and interviews with members of the Commission and Council filmed on 19th December. The programme will be ready for showing early in 2002 with Shereen Nanjiani as presenter. St. Margarets House, Polmont was one of the six care homes chosen for filming and the work of the Board and the practice of St. Margaret's is well represented on the video.

In the name of the Board,

JAMES M COWIE, *Convener*
GILBERT C NISBET, *Vice Convener*
DAVID L COURT, *Vice Convener*
IAN D BAILLIE, *Director of Social Work*

ADDENDUM

RETIRAL OF DIRECTOR OF SOCIAL WORK

The Board was advised at its meeting in February that the Director of Social Work, Ian D Baillie CBE, had intimated his intention to retire early with effect from 30 June 2002. Mr Baillie joined the Board as its Director of Social Work on 3 December 1990 following a long period of service with the former Strathclyde Regional Council latterly as Depute Director. The Board gives thanks to God for Mr Baillie's service and prays that he will have a long and happy retirement.

The Board wishes to acknowledge Mr Baillie's professionalism, insight and commitment to the development of social services within Scotland and particularly within the Church of Scotland. The Board is grateful to the personal and leadership qualities shown by Mr Baillie in developing the Church's social work department during his 11 years as Director. The 1990's and early part of this millennium has been a time of great change both nationally and within the Church and Mr Baillie has been instrumental in heralding the need for review, change and continuing development.

We look forward to building on these foundations as we develop services for the future.

In the name of the Board

JAMES M COWIE, *Convener*
REV. GILBERT C. NISBET, *Vice-Convener*
DAVID L COURT, *Vice-Convener*

APPENDIX 1

CONSULTATION DOCUMENTS 2001

Date Received	Title
18 December 2000	**Hague Convention on Children 1996**
8 February 2001	**Scottish Executive: Plan for Action on Alcohol Misuse**
19 February	**Scottish Executive: Changing Children's Services Fund**
22 February	**Scottish Executive: Supporting People: Quality & Monitoring**
26 February	**Scottish Executive: Regulation of Care**
March	**Home Office: Gaming Machines: Methods of Payment**
20 March	**City of Edinburgh Council: Rehousing Review Consultation**
April	**Volunteer Development Scotland: Volunteering in Education for Citizenship: Opportunities and Challenges**
2 April	**Scottish Executive: Plan for Action on Alcohol misuse**
19 April	**Scottish Executive: Better Care for All our Futures**
19 April	**Scottish Executive: Care Development Questionnaire**
2 May	**Scottish Executive: Draft National Care Standards 2nd Tranche**
17 May	**Health Tech. Board for Scotland: Assessment of Prevention of Relapse etc.**
18 May	**Scottish Executive: Review of Funding for the Voluntary Sector in Scotland**
June	**Nuffield Council on Bioethics: Genetics and Human Behaviour: The Ethical Context**
15 June	**Scottish Executive: Identifying Housing Support Service costs**
June	**Scottish Executive: Adults with Incapacity (Scotland) Implementation, part 5**
18 July	**Scottish Executive: Criminal Justice Accommodation Services Review**
July	**Greater Glasgow Health Board: Delivering Integrated Drugs Services and a Review of the Methadone Service**
31 July	**Greater Glasgow Health Board: Modernising MH Services**

Date received	Title
August	**Scottish Executive: Complaints Procedure**
8 August	**Glasgow City Council: Impact on Disability Draft Strategy**
August	**Department of Culture, Media and Sport: The Gambling Review Report**
16 August	**Scottish Executive: Review of Liquor Licensing Law in Scotland**
31 August	**Scottish Executive: Supporting People; Definitions of Housing Support Services**
15 September	**Scottish Executive: National Care Standards & Costs: Daycare/Adults**
October	**Scottish Commission for the Regulation of Care Registration: Policy and Procedures**
October	**Keep Sunday Special: Proposed Family Days (Protection) Bill**
5 October	**Scottish Law Commission: Age of Criminal Responsibility**
5 October	**Scottish Executive: Observation of Acutely Ill Patients in Hospitals**
10 October	**Scottish Executive: National Framework for the Prevention of Suicide and Self Harm**
6 December	**Scottish Executive: Care & Welfare of Boarding Pupils: National Care Standards and Costs**
13 December	**Scottish Executive: Early Education & Childcare Standards/ costs & input standards**

APPENDIX 2

THE BOARD OF SOCIAL RESPONSIBILITY

STRATEGIC DEVELOPMENT PLAN

Summary

As a Christ-centred organisation focusing on people, the Board of Social Responsibility must always review its work to find how it can best serve the people of Scotland. Whilst the message of hope and new life in Christ remains unaltered, the Board's outworking in styles of care has to be relevant to the current day and age. It is in seeking to find the best channel of service for the Board that the strategic document is written.

With greater emphasis on value for money and care in the community, the Board's balance of care provision will change. It will seek to provide quality measurable service outcomes no matter how or where the service is delivered. It will continue to face the financial drive to lower costs and will decide on a level of contribution which it feels appropriate.

There will be greater partnership working between Boards and denominations as a matter of good stewardship. It is expected that there will be a growing number of church initiatives which are assisted by the Board through staff consultation time. More decentralisation will occur and greater flexibility of service delivery will be expected by purchasers of services. The service which we provided will be publicised on the WEB and work to clearly defined outcomes.

Value Base

Vision Mission and Value statement "In Christ's name we seek to retain and regain the highest quality of life which each individual is capable of experiencing at any given time."

Implicit in this mission statement lies the core values of the organisation, and large though it is, every activity undertaken in the name of the Church of Scotland Board of Social Responsibility, finds a route to at least one element of the mission statement.

The vision of the Board as it begins to operate in a new millennium has not materially changed. It is to deliver services throughout Scotland, making significant impact on the lives of service users. These services will be at the cutting edge of service provision either in terms of the client group; the style of provision; the complexity of needs being met; or a combination of these components.

The services will be appropriately funded and be delivered to high standards of care and practice, by Christian staff. Both internal and external measurements will be in place to contribute to the continual striving for excellency. In the endeavour to remain at the cutting edge, the voices of users, carers, purchasers and the wider church will be sought and heard. This is the vision as the Board prayerfully seeks to act as a vehicle of God's love in Scotland.

The core values that underpin this vision and mission statement are as follows:

- **Individual Worth**
  As a Christian organisation, all the Board's caring work is rooted in the belief that each individual is of intrinsic worth being created in the image of God. He or she is of equal value irrespective of age, gender, sexual orientation, ability or social situation. As such, each will be afforded love, respect and dignity. This value will permeate the Board's service delivery, its attitude in business and its attitude to staff.

- **Ordinariness**
  Ordinariness is the concept of each individual having access to the opportunities and aspects of daily living available to the wider population. Based on the uniqueness of each person, the Board believes in delivery of services tailored to the individual's need to live as a full member of the community.

- **Involvement**
  The Board believes that only through evaluation and change can services continue to be appropriate and effective; therefore, it is committed to listening to all involved in providing, using, purchasing it services and to all significant others who have contact with the Board.

- **Quality**
  To achieve a quality service resources must be made available. The Board recognises that its greatest resource is its staff and their personal Christian commitment which endorses the intrinsic value and equality of all human life. The Board is committed to reflecting its value of staff through working terms and conditions as well as through appropriate management, support, and training opportunities.

- **Value for Money**
  Value for money is a priority for the Board. It is expected by purchasers and also is an indication of good stewardship. The Board continues to seek appropriate levels of funding through old and new channels in order to meet current and emerging service needs.

The Organisation's Background

The Board of Social Responsibility has carried out the formal social work of the Church of Scotland for over 130 years. It is a registered charity and is responsible to the General Assembly of the Church of Scotland and is charged by constitution to:

(i)   provide specialist resources to further the caring work of the Church;

(ii) identify existing and emerging areas of need;

(iii) guide the Church in pioneering new approaches to relevant problems;

(iv) study and present essential Christian judgements on social, moral and ethical issues arising within the area of the Board's concern.

In discharging this remit it has an equal opportunities policy and employs 2,434 staff, with headquarters in Charis House, Edinburgh, and five divisional offices which manage and develop the work in homes and centres throughout Scotland.

As one of the largest voluntary social care organisations in Scotland, the Board currently offers support to:

- people with alcohol and drug dependency
- physically frail older people
- mentally frail older people
- children with behaviour problems
- adults with mental health problems
- children and adults with learning disabilities
- adults with epilepsy
- adults who have offended
- homeless people
- adults and children in need of counselling

The Board, over its years in operation, has continually adjusted its management structure and its delivery of services to meet the social care needs both existent and emerging in Scotland. The creation of five Divisional offices, in Inverness, Paisley, Glasgow, Edinburgh and Dundee, has allowed for closer local consultation with churches, social work departments and health authorities, thereby influencing the future developmental thinking of the Board. Every effort is made to ensure that decisions are made nearest to the service and its users.

As a people-focussed body, the Board continues to direct resources towards training for staff. Despite financial constraints, the Board has maintained a high training profile and is an accredited social care training organisation. It is also an SVQ (Scottish Vocational Qualification) assessment centre. This commitment to training is critical to quality service delivery, and to meeting the requirements of the newly-appointed Scottish Social Services Council and the Scottish Commission for the Regulation of Care.

Training and retraining play an essential role in enabling the Board to fulfil its aim of providing a wide range of social care interventions all aimed at meeting the needs of vulnerable people in the most appropriate way while reinforcing the principle of Social Inclusion.

Future Trends

The major strategic statements enshrined in the NHS Care in the Community Act 1990 continue to drive the delivery of social care. The agenda laid down in the government publication *Modernising Community Care: An Action Plan* continues to be worked out. The then Scottish Office Minister for Health, Social Work and the Arts, said he expected

"People to be cared for at home wherever possible by:

- shifting the balance from institutional forms of care to caring for people at home;
- developing more flexible home care services and suitable housing; and
- encouraging health and social care services to work side by side in the community."

We expect to see five changes in support of people at home spanning the social work, health and housing sectors. These are:

- a shift towards home care services;
- better and more flexible home care services, supported by suitable housing;
- more flexible respite services and training to support carers;
- community-based health services to support the shift to home or community-based care; and
- more cost effective services.

Within this framework the emphasis is on:

- care at home
- flexibility of service
- cost effectiveness.

These principal objectives are endorsed by the Scottish Executive.

This does however still leave the question of how much institutional care will be required and how this will be funded.

The Regulation of Care (Scotland) Act (2001) sets out minimum physical standards for current residential and nursing homes giving a five-year timescale for compliance. It further states that individuals once in care should not be moved out when their care needs increase. This has implications not only for buildings but for skill mix and funding.

Free care for older people adds another layer of complexity to the funding packages and the working out of the financial solution will significantly affect the shape and balance of care between institutional models and care at home models.

The Scottish Social Services Council set up in October 2001 and the Scottish Commission for the Regulation of Care set up in April 2002 result from the Regulation of Care (Scotland) Act 2001. Their purpose is to protect vulnerable people through monitoring of national standards of care and individual codes of practice to which staff and employers are expected to adhere. At the same time, there has been a national recognition of problems in workforce recruitment and retention in the field of social work and social care.

The emphasis on child care reflects a growing expectation of accountability, security for the child and the child's needs, opinions and wellbeing being central in all services.

Thus government initiative, users' voices, the issue of who will do the work, all combine to necessitate closer working relationships between local authorities, health bodies and providers.

Within church structures, a move for decentralisation is growing and the Board's decentralised management will help respond to the trends within local congregations.

Thus the Board's stakeholders continue to look for more flexible care which still reflects quality standards at a local level. It is against this background that the aims are identified based on the following assumptions:

- The Board of Social Responsibility will remain part of the Church of Scotland.
- The Board will continue to have a Christian employment policy.
- The Board, as part of the Church of Scotland, will work closely with congregations and Presbyteries.
- The Board will work more closely with other Boards and Committees of the Church of Scotland.
- The Board will be prepared to work across Scotland and across all age groups.
- The Board will continue to seek to find different ways in which it can deliver services to the most vulnerable.
- Individuals will expect care to be provided locally.
- There will be a rising demand for care for individuals with challenging behaviour.
- Day care and short breaks opportunities will be in more general demand than residential care.
- Tailored packages of care available in the community will be preferred to long-term residential care.

- Fees payable by Local Authorities will be restricted due to national stringencies.
- The necessity to be able to show quality will increase.
- Purchasers will continue to demand value for money

The priorities of the Board for the duration of this plan are –

- to consolidate its financial position
- to expand community-based services
- to work co-operatively with local churches and presbyteries in the field of social care
- to increase home support services
- to reduce the revenue deficit

Aims and Objectives

AIM ONE: *To continue to provide measurable, high quality, affordable care through Christian staff to those in need*

OBJECTIVES

1.1 To introduce and implement "Towards Quality", the Board's quality assurance system, throughout all services.

1.2 To implement Personal Quality Development Plans for all employees.

1.3 To continue to update all practice and service delivery manuals.

1.4 To implement the staff induction programme throughout all services.

1.5 To develop and update appropriate training programmes.

1.6 To produce a Workforce Plan in order to achieve the Board's aim of an appropriately qualified workforce.

1.7 To implement guidelines to determine the future training needs of staff across all aspects of their work.

1.8 To develop the function of the Staff Advisory Forum as part of the Board's staff support system.

1.9 To actively promote staff development through work exchange programmes

1.10 To continue with regular, structured supervision of all staff.

1.11 To continue to explore and identify flexible staffing models appropriate to service users' needs and available finance.

1.12 To continue to apply the Board's Christian recruitment policy

1.13 To devise a national and local awareness-raising strategy to promote recruitment

AIM TWO: *To ensure that the Board's financial contribution allows support of appropriate work both current and new*

OBJECTIVES

2.1 To devise national and local awareness-raising strategies to promote the work of the Board

2.2 To devise and implement a marketing strategy for Board services

2.3 To implement the Board Fund Raising Pack

2.4 To administer tax efficient giving schemes in order to maximise the value of individual donors' gifts

2.5 To apply to appropriate Grant making Trusts and to Companies for funding for specific schemes

2.6 To ensure that absenteeism is reduced to acceptable levels according to the Board's Guidelines

2.7 To maximise the accuracy of budget information

2.8 To continue to monitor performance against budgets

2.9 To continue to seek appropriate fees through purchasing bodies for contracted services

2.10 To work with individual services on energy conservation

2.11 To continue to monitor occupancy/usage levels against individual service targets

2.12 To continue to show Best Value through sound governance by implementing the Board's Financial Standards

2.13 To review the use of land owned by the Board

2.14 Maximise the return received on investment and regularly review investment performance.

AIM THREE: *To continue to review and develop a portfolio of different styles of service delivery for current and new client groups in order to meet present and emerging needs within a changing legal framework*

OBJECTIVES

3.1 To continue service reviews in the light of current trends and legislation

3.2 To facilitate individual services to conduct an Annual Review of their service provision

3.3. To establish Home Support services where there is a proven need

3.4 To increase the provision of Short Break services

3.5 To create a programme which enables the transition from current residential provision to single care provision as appropriate

3.6 To transfer services to a non-registered Supported Living model where appropriate

3.7 To pursue opportunities to create Family Support and Counselling services

3.8 To review and evaluate Drug and Alcohol rehabilitation programmes to ensure maximum effectiveness

3.9 To implement systems which ensure carers and service users have a voice in the development of new and existing services

3.10 To develop initiatives for supporting children and families in line with the Children's Act

3.11 To review and develop the Board's work within criminal justice services

3.12 To evaluate and respond to the implications of the introduction of the Scottish Commission for the Regulation of Care and the Scottish Social Services Council

AIM FOUR: *To develop co-operative structures to enable the Board to maximise its resources to continue its caring work*

OBJECTIVES

4.1 To establish national and local links with the Scottish Commission for the Regulation of Care and the Scottish Social Services Council

4.2 To continue to seek opportunities for partnership working with other agencies where appropriate

4.3 To progress benchmarking through improved links with Europe

4.4 To forge professional relationships with statutory bodies

4.5 To increase networking and co-operation between Board services

AIM FIVE: *To actively seek opportunities to work with other Boards of the Church of Scotland and other Christian denominations to maximise the Christian churches' ability to use their resources appropriately*

OBJECTIVES

5.1 To continue to develop the Five Boards Group working together initiative.

5.2 To explore ways in which the Board can establish ecumenical projects/initiatives

5.3 To offer other Boards accommodation in Divisional Offices

5.4 To continue to strengthen links between Field Officers of all Boards to ensure co-operative working at local level

AIM SIX: *To work with presbyteries and local churches to find ways of meeting local needs while continuing to encourage volunteer activity*

OBJECTIVES

6.1 To produce Guidelines on how the Board, within its constitution, can assist presbyteries and local churches develop imaginative ways of meeting local needs

6.2 To ensure the availability of appropriate material

on what the Board currently provides in each community

6.3 To establish Guidelines on how the Board's expertise at local level may be accessed by churches and presbyteries

6.4 To develop the Divisional Newsletters with a view to becoming thrice yearly in line with Circle of Care and the Prayer Letter

6.5 To develop occasional briefing papers for Congregational Contacts and Presbytery Representatives

6.6 To ensure that all Congregational Contacts have the opportunity to attend at least one meeting within their Division each year

6.7 To produce a Board Prayer Letter three times each year

6.8 To consult with stakeholders on the role of Friends Groups

6.9 To continue to update the community services database

AIM SEVEN: *To continue to study social, moral and ethical issues arising within the area of the Board's concern and present and promote a Christian perspective*

OBJECTIVES

7.1 To ensure relevant publications are available to all services

7.2 To encourage open discussion on social and moral issues as part of training initiatives

7.3 To continue to review and comment on human genetics, cloning and associated topics

7.4 To develop and use the Social Interests Digest

7.5 To pursue meaningful communications with persons in the Church to identify new subjects for study

7.6 To encourage the participation of all staff in daily devotions

7.7 To further explore the role of chaplains in relation to service delivery

Implications

As the aims and objectives are implemented there will be implications that will require to be managed at Board and staff levels. The following are some of the more obvious implications:

- the need to identify a timescale for implementing change.
- training to ensure that any change is understood and that staff are supported.
- acceptance of the need to move from the known and tried ways of service delivery to greater flexibility and diversity.
- acceptance that there may be a drop in demand for residential services.
- the need to develop re-skilling packages for current staff.
- that an increase in partnership arrangements will be expected by purchasing agencies.
- greater ecumenical activity can be expected in providing support in pursuing social interest matters.
- the possibility that access to public funds may be restricted for the Board due to its employment policy.
- the need for good communication systems in order to keep staff, users and purchasers fully informed of any change.
- greater emphasis on fund-raising.

Financial Implications

As each aim and objective is worked through either by staff or by Committee, or both, the financial implications will become more obvious. The following are some of the anticipated implications that will need to be addressed and resolved.

- cost of training staff to agreed levels
- cost of any additional staff
- any cost to the Board of partnerships that may mean taking greater risks with capital
- deciding on a specified sum of money to be set aside to enable new projects with, for example,

- local churches
- the funding of any transitional costs incurred when changing services
- capital implications of new work and any refurbishment of current buildings.

CONCLUSION

The Board is in the midst of one of the greatest change periods in recent social care history. The future cannot be predicted with certainty, as local and central government in Scotland determine the boundaries of their responsibilities in this field and seek to deliver Scottish policies to meet the needs and aspirations of the Scottish people.

The Board believes it is in a position to confront the challenges ahead and with God's direction, to deliver the desired outcomes evident in this Strategic Development Plan.

APPENDIX 3

REPORT ON THE CARBERRY HEALTH AND HEALING CONFERENCE NOVEMBER 2001

The Board's thirteenth Annual Christian Healing Conference, a meeting of faces familiar and new, under the banner "How healthy is the Church's Healing Ministry Today?" was held at Carberry Tower in November 2001. In excess of 80 attended, including ministers (some taking advantage of study leave) and medical doctors. Most delegates were ordinary church members and included delegates from Holland and Switzerland. A high percentage of delegates sought Christian Healing ministry, either at thirty-minute interview by appointment or through coming forward at the healing service for the laying on of hands. Movingly, a good number of the delegates shared on the last morning of the Conference what God had been doing among them during memorable days of togetherness.

Conference days opened and closed with times of worship led by several of the ministers attending the conference. These worship times of teaching and quiet reflection were particularly appreciated, with the praise being led by piano, guitar and instrumental accompaniment. The healing service on the second evening of the conference was particularly memorable, with everyone present afforded opportunity to come forward for the prayers and the laying on of hands by two others.

Principal Speaker at the Conference was Canon John Gunstone, co-author of the publication for the Anglican House of Bishops entitled "A Time to Heal" (published Church House Publishing 2000). During two sessions led by Canon Gunstone, conference delegates were taken through the contents of this valuable contribution to the Church's healing ministry today.

In between times there were hour-and-a-half seminars on offer to delegates looking at a variety of topics on the Christian healing ministry. Each delegate was able to attend two seminars. The six seminar subjects are summarised:

Against all opposition Many inside and outside the church look at the Christian Healing Ministry with a measure of scepticism. A minister of the Scottish Episcopal Church in this seminar looked at the problems faced in introducing the Christian healing ministry in its fullness in the congregational setting.

Children This seminar, led by a Minister of the Church of Scotland, looked at children and Christian healing ministry, and about how to effectively and sensitively minister. The holding of special services of Christian healing for children was also spoken about.

Deliverance One of the Church of Scotland's ministers spoke in a most informed and informing way, drawing on examples from his own parish experience, about the church's occasional need in the parish situation to minister in Jesus' name in situations where people need deliverance from oppression and possession by evil.

Divine appointments – This seminar, led by a Minister of the Church of Scotland, focused on how circumstances in an individual's life come together in a way in which

God's hand can be seen, bringing them and God's chosen ministers together to that place of effectual prayer and ministry being offered for them in healing.

Spiritual gifts – A seminar led by a Minister of the Scottish Episcopal Church, looked at God's gifting of the Christian for specific ministries, including the ministry of healing, which is a supernatural work of God carried out in a quite natural way.

Street healing This seminar, led by a Minister of the Vineyard Church in Glasgow, focussed on the need to take the healing ministry of the Church out into the streets of the city and housing areas. In this street ministry, healing in Jesus' Name is being offered effectively and powerfully today in Glasgow in a secularised, hardened-to-the-Gospel environment.

These seminar topics led to full discussion in discussion groups numbering around ten persons, to which delegates were allocated. The group discussion sessions also gave opportunity for delegates to share their own experience in the healing ministry and to ask questions not otherwise raised in the seminars. Some of the discussion group sessions ended with delegates praying for one another.

Opportunity was afforded on the last morning of the conference, as in the previous year, to allow delegates to share how they had experienced healing from God during the course of the conference. One spoke of the "Lord's having lifted a heavy burden", another who had lived with constant pain in his jaw shared how following a time of ministry, during which the pain had become more, he was now pain-free. A delegate whose toes on one foot had not touched the ground for forty eight years was healed of this infirmity at the healing service through the laying on of hands. Another delegate spoke of having been released from dizziness, others of release from guilt and anxiety. The occasion of the sharing of each testimony was concluded by delegates spontaneously singing a chorus "Alle, alle, alleluia". Delegates got most practised in the words and tune of this chorus, indicative of how many people had shared testimony of God's healing!

The conference concluded with a Communion service in the Chapel, during the course of which people brought forward, written out on pieces of paper, hurts and sins they wished to off-load. These were all consigned to burning, with the pall of heat smoke that arose bringing to mind the emissions of the chimney of a crematorium, underlining the dying to the old self and past and the rising to newness of life in Jesus Christ. After receiving Communion, each delegate came forward to the front and had their hands anointed with oil as each was commissioned anew to God's ministry of healing in Christ.

This was a joyous conclusion to our time at Carberry of envisioning and commissioning anew of the Lord. We had a renewing of our conviction and commitment to Christ's bidding not only to preach good news, but in His Name also to heal the sick and cast out demons. Surely needed work for Christ's Kingdom today!

A report by the Chairperson of the Conference

"HOW HEALTH IS THE CHURCH'S HEALING TODAY?"
- A REVIEW OF CURRENT TRENDS –
THE MINISTRY OF HEALING CONFERENCE 19-21 NOVEMBER 2001

Monday, 19th November 2001

1000 – 12.30	Arrival and Registration
1130 – 1230	Meeting with Rev Canon John Gunstone, Seminar and Group Leaders
1300 – 1400	Lunch
1400 – 1430	Introduction to the Conference with opening worship: Rev Douglas Irving
1430 - 1530	"To Heal as Jesus Healed": Rev Canon John Gunstone
1530 – 1600	Refreshments
1600 – 1730	First meeting of Discussion Groups
1800 – 1900	Dinner
1915 – 2045	Seminars: *Deliverance* Rev D Ross Mitchell
	Against all Opposition Rev Canon Philip Noble
	Children Rev William Kelly
	Street Healing Rev James Waters
	Divine Appointments Rev Douglas Nicol
	Spiritual Gifts Rev Robin Anker-Peterson
2100 – 2130	Evening Prayers in the Chapel
2145 – 2215	Supper

Tuesday, 20th November 2001

0800 - 0830	Morning Worship in the Chapel
0845 – 0915	Breakfast
0930 – 1030	"Spiritual Gifts and Institutional Traditions" – Rev Canon John Gunstone
1030 – 1100	Refreshments
1100 – 1230	Seminars: Repeat Seminars as listed for Monday.
1300 - 1400	Lunch
1400 - 1600	Optional: two showings of the video made by the Burrswood Christian Centre for Healthcare and Ministry *A Whole Approach to Healing*
1645 – 1745	Second meeting of Discussion Groups
1800 – 1900	Dinner
1930 – 2130	Worshipful Healing Service directed and led by Canon John Gunstone, Rev Douglas Irving, Rev Ross Mitchell, Canon Philip Noble, Rev James Waters and Rev Douglas Nicol
2145 - 2215	Supper

Wednesday, 21st November 2001

0800 - 0830	Morning Worship in the Chapel
0845 – 0915	Breakfast
930 – 1045	Question and discussion time with Conference Panel of Rev Canon John Gunstone and the seminar leaders
1045 – 1115	Refreshments
1115 – 1230	Holy Communion – celebrated by Rev Douglas Irving
1300 – 1400	Lunch
1400 – 1500	Individual and group requests for guidance, informal conversations and departures

APPENDIX 4

UNDERSTANDING AIDS

What is AIDS, and how do you get it?

AIDS (or Auto-Immune Deficiency Syndrome) is the result of infection with the Human Immunodeficiency Virus (HIV), and also the result of other 'opportunistic' infections which invade the body as a result of its diminished capacity for resistance. HIV is passed on through body fluids, the commonest avenues for transmission today being sexual intercourse with an infected partner, shared needles used for drug-injecting, and transmission from mother to child during pregnancy or breast-feeding. In Europe and North America, the earliest cases were identified among male homosexuals, and in these parts of the world HIV was originally thought of as 'the gay disease'. In Africa and Asia, the overwhelming majority of infections take place as a result of sexual intercourse between heterosexual men and women. In global terms, the ratio of women to men infected is now 47/53, with the fastest rate of increase occurring in women between the ages of 19 and 25.

What happens when you become infected with HIV?

HIV is not like malaria or meningitis, which have distinctive symptoms and for which treatments are available. HIV gradually destroys the body's immune system and makes the individual progressively more and more vulnerable to other infections. A person with HIV may be well for many years, then begin to suffer from skin complaints chest infections, diarrhoea and other problems. Eventually, illnesses become more and more frequent, weight loss becomes impossible to ignore, it becomes increasingly difficult to live a normal life, and the person will be described as suffering from AIDS.

Can you cure HIV/AIDS?

There is currently no cure for HIV, although there are medications which can prolong the period of 'normal' healthy life. In addition, there is plenty of evidence that good nutrition, a reasonable quality of life, a positive attitude and belonging to a supportive community can delay the onset of symptoms and mitigate their severity. Good basic health care is crucial, backed up by the availability of standard treatments for opportunistic infections. Conversely, poverty, malnutrition and hopelessness can hasten the progress of the disease, while frequent attacks of illness are debilitating, and in situations where adequate primary health care is not available, they may prove fatal. In Europe and North America, where health care is adequate and drugs available for treating HIV itself, it has been observed that HIV is no longer a terminal condition. In the developing world, where 95% of all HIV-infected people live, good nutrition and effective primary health services are an impossible dream for the vast majority of the people.

Is there any treatment for HIV/AIDS?

People with HIV are reliant on the availability of treatments for opportunistic infections like pneumonia and tuberculosis. In addition, most HIV positive people in Europe today have access to specialist combination therapies which enable them to live normal lives by delaying the breakdown of the immune system. The problem is that these therapies remain expensive and so are less relevant in the developing world, where basic painkillers, antibiotics and diarrhoea drugs may be unavailable, and lack of continuity in the supply of medicines to treat tuberculosis is leading to an alarming increase in the incidence of drug-resistant TB.

What are the elements in the problem?

One of the most striking things about the HIV epidemic is that the current situation has developed out of a phenomenon which was generally recognised as recently as the early eighties. The size of the problem is demonstrated by the absolute numbers living or dying from HIV/AIDS; by the percentage of young adults affected in different places; by the number of unsupported survivors, who included elderly parents and grandparents as well as orphaned children; and by the economic effects of the loss of productive people. It urgency is demonstrated by the rapid increase in the number of infections in all but a very few countries in the developing world.

THE SIZE OF THE PROBLEM

- 36.1m people, globally, are HIV+
- 25.3m live in Sub-Saharan Africa, 5.8m in South and South-Asia, 1.4m in Latin America. In parts of Africa, 36% of adults are HIV+
- 4.3m individuals were newly infected in 1999 of whom 42% were women.
- 13.2 children have been orphaned since the beginning of the epidemic.

Sources: Norwegian Church Aid and UNAIDS)

BOARD OF WORLD MISSION

MAY 2002

PROPOSED DELIVERANCE

The General Assembly:

1. Receive the Report, and thank the members and staff of the Board.

2. Give thanks for the life and witness of overseas staff who have died, salute those who have completed their period of service overseas, and uphold in prayer all mission partners who continue to serve overseas.

3. Affirm the five strategic commitments which have been made by the Board for the years 2001-10.

4. Commend the Board on the management consultancy exercise which it has completed and on its strategy for the pastoral care of its staff.

5. Adopt the HIV/AIDS Project outlined in the Report as a response from the whole Church to the challenges posed by the pandemic, instruct the Board to implement the project forthwith, and encourage all congregations and church members to play their part in it.

6. Call on HM Government to accelerate the process of debt relief for highly indebted poor countries, especially those which are severely afflicted by the HIV/AIDS epidemic.

7. Pass an Act amending Act VI, 2001 as set out in Appendix II.

8. Assure partner churches around the world, at this time of heightened international tension, of the commitment of the Church of Scotland to stand united with them in the love of Christ and to offer all possible solidarity and support.

REPORT

"As the Father sent me, so I send you." John 21:20

Introduction

Seeking to discover what part the Church of Scotland should play, at the beginning of the 21st century, in the global mission of Jesus Christ, the Board has sought to chart a clear direction. The first part of this Report is devoted to the five Strategic Commitments which the Board has made for 2001 to 2010. Particular attention has been given to developing an appropriate response from the Church to the HIV/AIDS pandemic and a major section of this Report sets out the Board's proposals. The results of a management consultancy exercise and of consideration of the question of pastoral care are also set out below. Finally, brief indication is given of the Board's

implementation of the new Act anent Overseas Charges and its response to the "Church without Walls" Report received by last General Assembly.

1. Strategic Commitments for 2001–2010

1.1. Finding Strategic Direction

In fulfilment of the remit received from the 2001 General Assembly, the Board has been seeking to "discern priorities and form policies to guide the Church of Scotland's ongoing worldwide participation in God's transforming mission, through the gospel of Jesus Christ". As well as drawing on the biblical basis for mission and the historic overseas involvement of the Kirk over two centuries, the Board has prayerfully taken account of our contemporary context, seeking to read "the signs of the times". While each local context is distinctive and mission strategy must be formed in light of the particular characteristics of each, there are also global trends which an overall world mission strategy must take into account. For the first decade of the 21st century, the Board has identified five contemporary challenges and has responded to each with a commitment to action. This Report indicates the commitments made and some of the work already underway to put them into effect.

1.2. Good News to Share

1.2.1. *The Context*
Geographically, ethnically and culturally, Christian faith has spread further and faster in this generation than ever before – between 1970 and 2001 church membership increased from 1,236 million to 2,025 million. Within this dynamic spread of the faith, there are areas which are marked by particularly rapid church growth. Certain societies appear to be at a point today where they are ripe to respond to the gospel of Christ. People are becoming Christians in large numbers, many new congregations are being established, and Christianity is becoming a force to be reckoned with at all levels of national life. Young, fast-growing churches provide new capacity for evangelism among the many people who have not heard the gospel in a meaningful way. Such is the vigour of their engagement with the biblical gospel that these new movements generate a freshly minted faith, recovering the joy, hope and love which arise from a knowledge of Christ. The whole church rejoices with them and seeks to benefit from this renewal of Christian faith in our time. Yet it also poses formidable challenges for mission. Often the opportunities for evangelism extend far beyond the areas where the church's resources allow it to operate effectively. Fast-expanding needs for Christian nurture and pastoral care stretch the church leadership to the limit and beyond. Development of theological education at all levels is an urgent requirement.

1.2.2. *The Commitment*
The Board recognises that it has a role to play in making Jesus Christ known and in inviting people everywhere to follow him. The Foreign Mission Committee's 1950 *Statement of Policy* made it clear that its "primary emphasis" was "the possession of great and good news which it is our privilege and duty to share, believing, as we do, that it is God's will that the Gospel should be proclaimed to all until the Kingdom of God comes in all its fullness". This heritage was reaffirmed by the representatives of 26 partner churches gathered with the Board at St Andrews in 1999 when they agreed that continuing partnership should be focused on evangelism– "helping one another to create new models and launch new initiatives to take the Gospel to all people".

While conscious of the danger of becoming over-extended, the Board is sensitive to strategic new opportunities for making Christ known which emerge in our time. In the last decade this has led to new work in post-war Mozambique, work which the Board seeks to sustain even with the current lack of mission partners. An exciting new partnership is being developed with the Presbyterian and Reformed Church in Cuba which has entered a time of great opportunity as a new openness to the gospel brings many young people into the life of the church. The Board has offered practical help with motorcycles for pastors and support for new churches. In Malawi, Helen Scott serves as a deacon in her local congregation and has seen the church grow through two four-day evangelism events which resulted in a number of conversions to Christ. The renewal of links with Nigeria gives the opportunity to share in the church-planting initiatives of the Presbyterian Church of Nigeria in areas where historically there has been little Christian presence. The Board has supported the Synod of the Nile in the development of church extension projects in Egypt.

The appointment of Roderick Campbell to work on capacity-building with the church in southern Sudan and the appointment of Mike and Jane Fucella to work in a border area of Thailand where there are many Karen refugees, are among the new initiatives which the Board has recently taken. At the request of the Waldensian Church, Rob Mackenzie has been appointed pastor of its English congregation in Turin where there is need for ministry to the growing number of English-speaking immigrants. Partnership with the Evangelical Church of Czech Brethren has found a focus in support for a church extension project in a densely populated area on the south side of Prague. The Board's links with the extensive outreach of the Korean churches have been strengthened by the recent appointment of Elinor Gordon to work with the Korean Christian Women United in Seoul.

The rapid urbanisation which is apparent worldwide is a particular focus in the Board's thinking. Congregations in European cities are on the cutting edge of the development of urban ministry. Often they learn lessons from which all can learn, e.g. their rapid turnover of membership means involving newcomers very quickly in taking responsibilities within the life of the congregation. Gifted ministers continue to offer for service in charges overseas. The end of 2001 was marked by the retirement of Colin Westmarland after twenty-seven years of fruitful ministry in Malta. Under the ecumenical arrangements for the charge the Board welcomes the appointment of the Rev David Morris of the Methodist Church as the new minister. The Board also welcomes the proposal in the Report of the Board of Practice and Procedure (see p. 1/22) that Malta become a sanctioned charge within the Presbytery of Europe.

Another primary call on the Board's attention is the need for capacity-building in churches which are undergoing rapid growth. Noting the priority which was accorded to theological education, as a focus for partnership, by the St Andrews Consultation, the Board seeks to be a resourceful partner in the development of lay and ministerial training to provide for the needs of growing churches. A review of the bursary programme aims to ensure that training provided for members of partner churches is fitted to their needs. In 2001-02 there are nine bursars from nine different churches and countries studying in Scotland. Strategic placement of mission partners, such as the recent appointment of Bruce Ritchie as Lecturer in Systematic Theology at Zomba Theological College in Malawi, continues to be a priority for the Board. It is hoped that a mission partner will be appointed to a teaching post at Trinity Theological College in Singapore.

At the same time the Board seeks to enable the Church of Scotland to be strengthened for its mission through drawing on the resources of partner churches overseas. New energy continues to come to the witness of churches in Scottish parishes through the appointment of Faithshare partners. This year Joanny Capellan of the Dominican Republic, through partnership with Christian Aid, served in the Presbytery of Stirling, Daniel Etim of Nigeria in the Presbytery of Buchan, Levi and Ruth Nyondo of Malawi in the Presbytery of Dunkeld and Meigle, Arpad and Zsuzsanna Szabo of Hungary in the Presbytery of Kirkcaldy, while Margaret Kyeame of Ghana was hosted by the Presbytery of Dumbarton and had a special role nationwide in the Boys Brigade. The highly appreciated work of Faithshare partners Sardar and Violet Ghauri at The Well in Glasgow has been extended for a further two years. The Coordinating Forum, at its September Conference, benefited from the perspectives of three representatives from partner churches overseas– the Rt Rev Dr Jesse Kamau of Kenya, the Rev Dr Jong-Wha Park of South Korea, and the Rev Dr Ofelia Ortega of Cuba.

1.3. The Ministry of Reconciliation

1.3.1. *The Context*

The end of the Cold War in 1989-90, far from ushering in the hoped-for time of peace, marked the emergence of a sharply divided world. In almost every part of the world people are asserting their identity in aggressive ways which can easily descend into violence. In particular, ethnic and religious identity often defines the opposing sides in a situation of tension and conflict. Besides many local and regional conflicts, there is also the widening gap between the affluent north and the impoverished south, which increasingly gives rise to violence, both direct and indirect. Churches in many parts of the world have been caught up in conflict and working for justice and peace has become a prominent part of their agenda. The Board's thinking in this area received terrible confirmation with the attacks on the World Trade Centre and the Pentagon in the USA and the subsequent war in Afghanistan. The Board has been active in expressing solidarity with partner churches most affected by the conflict, such as the Presbyterian Church (USA) and the Church of Pakistan.

This experience has led the Board to appreciate the importance of "being a good partner" to churches which are most affected by the division and conflict of our time.

1.3.2. *The Commitment*

The Board is driven by the mandate that Christ's people, being reconciled to God, become agents of reconciliation in every situation of conflict. In the deployment of staff and resources, priority is given to seeking to strengthen the witness of the church in situations of division, conflict and oppression. Offering a ministry which is accessible and challenging to both sides of the divide in Israel and Palestine is the difficult task undertaken by Clarence Musgrave and Fred Hibbert. The new centre in Tiberias will give fresh opportunities to develop and enhance the Church's historic ministry of reconciliation amongst Israeli and Palestinian; Christian, Muslim and Jew. A new initiative by the Board is the appointment of Bryson and May Arthur to the Mar Elias Educational Institutions in Ibillin – an indigenous Christian foundation with a remarkable vision for reconciliation. Support is offered to the Middle East Council of Churches and the Sabeel Ecumenical Liberation Theology Centre as these bodies give expression to the protest of Palestinians over the illegal occupation of their land and the accompanying oppression. Keith Russell reports on a situation of potential Christian-Muslim polarisation with the good news that the Archbishop of Sudan publicly embraced the deputy Grand Sheikh of Al Azhar University in a moving meeting at Cairo Cathedral where both men committed themselves to seek reconciliation between their two faith communities.

The Board has added its voice to those of others who have protested over the willingness of multinational oil companies to benefit from the scorched earth policy pursued by the Khartoum government in the oil fields of Sudan and the free flow of oil revenue which allows the government to pursue its war on the south with scant regard for any humanitarian considerations. Through the Ecumenical Women's Solidarity Fund the Board plays a part in initiatives such as health clinics, an interfaith choir, ballet dancing and legal representation which help people to rebuild their lives after the terrible conflicts in the Balkans. The Board cherishes its links with the Center for Pastoral Studies in Central America which continues to act as a force for justice and peace in Guatemala. In Sri Lanka Tony McLean Foreman is engaged in theological formation in one of the rare institutions where Sinhala and Tamil live and study together. In Nepal the massacre of the royal family and increased Maoist insurgency led to the imposition of a state of emergency in November which has inhibited the work of the United Mission to Nepal in some areas. Moira and Alasdair Murray saw their local church at Lal Gadh destroyed by people hostile to Christian faith but courageously rebuilt by the local believers.

The Board also seeks to be a source of solidarity and encouragement to partner churches which witness as minorities in societies where another faith predominates. The Church of Scotland, as one of the "mother churches" within the Reformed tradition, has a special responsibility to share its life and witness with churches seeking to nourish the roots of their Reformed identity. The Board took a painful, but correct, decision to withdraw all its staff from Pakistan before the start of the Afghan War. Tragically this was soon followed by the massacre of 17 members of the Church of Pakistan congregation at Bahawalpur – a chilling reminder of the vulnerability of a Christian minority at a time of international tension. Special efforts have been made to remain in solidarity with the Church of Pakistan through difficult days, e.g. a service of prayer was held in Edinburgh on the day of the Bahawalpur massacre. The return of mission partners to their work in Pakistan in March 2002 demonstrated the Board's continuing commitment to active solidarity. In Bangladesh, following the election of a strongly Islamic coalition government, Christians and other minorities have experienced serious repression and the tiny Church of Bangladesh greatly needs our love and prayers. The Board has also renewed its links with the Presbyterian Church in Burma/Myanmar at a time when such solidarity is greatly appreciated.

The Board seeks, wherever possible in its mission engagement, to participate in the formation of international, multi-ethnic, multi-racial teams which demonstrate the reconciliation and unity which is Christ's gift in the gospel. From Egypt to Thailand, from Pakistan to Malawi, mission partners are to be found serving on such teams and having a remarkable impact for Christ.

1.4. The Scandal of Poverty

1.4.1. *The Context*

While economic globalisation has brought rapidly increasing prosperity to some, there are many in today's world whose experience is one of deepening impoverishment. While 40 wealthy countries have sustained average per capita income growth of more than 3% a year since 1990, 55 poor countries have had declining per capita incomes. Today some 1.5 billion people live in absolute poverty. Under such economic pressure societies begin to corrode. Schools, hospitals and other institutions begin to collapse, eating the heart out of the society. Law and order breaks down. Crime and terror dramatically increase. National governments lose their grip and authority is assumed by gangsters and warlords. There is a rapid increase in the spread of sexually transmitted diseases. Local culture disintegrates under the pressure of the all-conquering Western consumer culture. The natural environment is stripped of its resources with no thought for the future. United Nations Development Programme Reports speak of "parallel worlds": security, affluence, power in the one; violence, poverty and disintegration in the other. Many of the Board's partner churches are located in the latter "world" and its experience of increasing poverty.

1.4.2. *The Commitment*

Recognising God's priority for the poor, the Board seeks to be a channel of support, both human and financial, to the partner churches which are most painfully afflicted by the deepening poverty of our time. The economic marginalization of Africa has led to a marked increase in absolute poverty throughout that continent. Seeking to be a faithful partner to churches in the eye of this storm is a great challenge for the Church of Scotland at this time and the Board seeks to give prominence to the needs of African churches and communities.

In order to give expression to the part which the Church of Scotland plays in the work of Christian Aid, co-branded projects in Bosnia, Mozambique and Haiti will be given special focus during 2001-2004. The Guild Project to support the Rainy Hospital Nursing School in Chennai has brought the attention of many to the important contribution made by the churches to healthcare in India. The presence of mission partners in the world's poorest communities continues to be a valued part of the Church of Scotland's outreach. Jane Petty in southern Zambia reports that changes favourable to urban workers are working to the severe disadvantage of unemployed rural people who see the cost of staple foods almost doubling in price while their resources remain static. The Joint Relief Ministry in Cairo serves Sudanese refugees both by pressing for justice on their behalf and by offering relief to their grinding poverty.

The Board aims to raise consciousness in Scotland about issues of global justice. This involves making common cause with others who share its concerns to work for greater justice in the global economy. The Jubilee Scotland coalition, which takes forward the work of Jubilee 2000, is a forum within which the Board works with others to advance the cause of the cancellation of the unpayable debt of poor countries. Together with other churches and agencies, the Board is involved in a dialogue with HM Government about the United Nations 2015 poverty reduction targets. The Board also joined with the Church and Nation Committee to make representations to the Secretary of State for Trade in regard to the interests of poorer countries within the work of the World Trade Organisation.

1.5. The HIV/AIDS Epidemic

1.5.1. *The Context*

A unique feature of this generation is the rapid spread of the HIV/AIDS epidemic. It has been suggested that every now and then something comes along which changes the way we think about everything; and that the HIV/AIDS epidemic is in this category. The scale of the suffering which it is bringing can be gauged by the estimate that more than 40 million people worldwide are currently infected by the virus. Over the next few years their health will collapse and they will lose their lives. Since the great majority of those infected are young adults, their illness and death will be very painful also for their children and parents. The loss of many of the most economically productive members will debilitate the whole society. Furthermore, the effects of the disease are accentuated by the fact that it is distributed unevenly – it is heavily concentrated in the poorest countries of sub-Saharan Africa and Asia. Churches there are faced by a situation where individuals, families and communities are experiencing suffering and deprivation on an unprecedented scale. Since both social conditions and individual behaviour greatly influence the spread of the disease, the need for moral formation is urgent.

1.5.2. *The Commitment*
Recognising that HIV/AIDS is a defining issue for the church in this decade, the Board gives prominence to the epidemic both in its consciousness-raising and in its deployment of resources. In solidarity with the partner churches most deeply afflicted, the Board aims to have a significant number of staff engaged in providing care for those suffering from AIDS, in developing programmes to resist the spread of HIV, and in generating the theological and spiritual resources which enable the church to bring its distinctive contribution to the crisis. The Board also seeks to engage the concern, prayer and action of congregations in Scotland so that as many church members as possible may become involved in a Christ-like response to the spread of the epidemic. Given that many of those most affected by HIV/AIDS are found in poor and easily ignored communities, the Board seeks to play a part in keeping the epidemic high on the international agenda.

The project proposal found below on p. 23/13 indicates the next steps which might be taken in this area. Meanwhile, mission partners continue to be actively engaged both with the medical and the educational response to the crisis. Newly-appointed medical doctor Alex Maclean is working at Embangweni Hospital in northern Malawi in a situation where many of his patients are HIV-positive. In South Africa Sandra Duncan has met with an overwhelming response as she has offered training to students and church leaders on church action in relation to HIV/AIDS. In Thailand Jane Fucella offers a ministry of care to those infected or affected by the epidemic.

1.6. Local Involvement in Global Mission

1.6.1. *The Context*
The transport and communication revolutions of the late 20th century have generated a culture of immediate contact and direct involvement. The peoples of the world are in contact with one another as never before. People are using these new opportunities to make their own global connections and are no longer satisfied with second-hand experience of the wider world. This is accompanied in Western culture by disenchantment with large, formal institutions and a lifestyle which finds social expression in informal and transitory networking. Concomitant to this is suspicion and fear of long-term commitments and a clear preference for direct experience and immediately demonstrable results. Despite the shock of the events of 11 September it is likely that these underlying trends will continue.

1.6.2. *The Commitment*
Recognising that local churches today are seeking more immediate involvement in global mission and greater direct accountability for contributions which they make, the Board seeks to be an encouraging and resourceful centre for all congregations aiming to make fruitful connections with the world church. In shaping the Church of Scotland's engagement in mission worldwide, the Board seeks to respond, on the one hand, to the aspirations of congregations in Scotland and, on the other, to the needs and opportunities indicated by partner churches overseas.

Direct links have recently been forged between the Presbytery of Lothian and the Church of North India Diocese of Eastern Himalaya and between the Presbytery of Abernethy and the Diocese of North East India. A group from Barclay Church in Edinburgh made a visit to mission partners Mike and Jane Fucella in western Thailand in autumn 2001. Pathhead Church in Kirkcaldy linked with mission partner Gillian Rose to sink a tube well which has transformed the water supply in Karpasdanga in Bangladesh. St Cuthbert's Church in Edinburgh has made a link with the Scots International Church in Rotterdam which is already proving to be mutually challenging and enriching. The Board seeks to encourage and facilitate such direct involvement in overseas mission on the part of congregations.

Recognising that in today's society people do not always express Christian commitment through the formal structures of the church, the Board seeks to break new ground in promoting awareness of the global dimension of the church's mission amongst the people of Scotland. This has led to a fresh appearance to Board publications – the quarterly *Insight*, the regular partner plan letters and a variety of innovative resources communicating in new ways the work of the Board. Outlet days in different parts of the country gave an opportunity to co-operate closely with other Boards in promotional work. People remain a primary means of communication – not only the Board's overseas staff but also Board members and Presbytery Conveners who return from overseas visits with infectious enthusiasm. This has been evident in the work done, e.g., by Valerie Allen of the Presbytery of Angus, Ian Stirling of the Presbytery of Ayr, Duncan Macpherson of the Presbytery of Annandale and Eskdale, Donald Martin of the Presbytery of Buchan, Kitty Campbell of the Presbytery of Ross, Neil Urquhart of the Presbytery of Irvine and Kilmarnock and Dennis Rose of the Presbytery of Dumfries.

1.7. In Summary

During 2001–2010 the Board proposes to be committed to:

- Working with partner churches on new initiatives in evangelism
- Working for justice, peace and reconciliation in situations of conflict or threat
- Resourcing the church to set people free from the oppression of poverty
- Contributing meaningfully to the struggle against the HIV/AIDS epidemic
- Increasing the involvement of Scottish Christians in the world church.

2. Responding to the HIV/AIDS Pandemic

2.1. A Commitment to Action on HIV/AIDS: the General Assembly of 2001

The following points were established in the Board of World Mission's Report to the General Assembly of 2001:

- The HIV/AIDS pandemic is "a tragedy of unprecedented proportions" (Nelson Mandela), with 36.1 million people infected worldwide, 25.3 million in sub-Saharan Africa (now 40m and 28.1m respectively).
- Not only are many lives being lost, there is a devastating impact on families, communities, social institutions and national economies.
- The spread of HIV and AIDS, while global, is massively concentrated in poor countries and poor communities – those least equipped to resist.
- Since the disease is spread predominantly by sexual contact, there are cultural, social, moral and spiritual questions posed for the church.
- Faith in Jesus Christ and membership of his church involve a commitment to act in solidarity with those afflicted by HIV and AIDS.
- For the Church of Scotland this means standing alongside partner churches in areas where the pandemic is most heavily concentrated.
- It is time to develop a strategy which will engage every congregation in meaningful participation in the struggle to roll back the advance of the epidemic.

Accordingly the General Assembly:

- expressed deep concern, in Christ, for all those affected by the rapid spread of the HIV/AIDS pandemic, particularly partner churches in the worst-affected areas;
- recognised that confessing faith in Christ and being part of the body of Christ involves, in today's context, both an active engagement in the battle against the disease and a loving solidarity with those infected; and
- instructed the Board of World Mission to consult with other Boards of the Church and concerned agencies in order to develop an appropriate response to the HIV/AIDS pandemic, and report back to the General Assembly of 2002.

2.2. Developing an Appropriate Response: Project Development 2001-02

In response to this instruction from the Assembly, during 2001–02 the Board of World Mission:

- Convened a day conference on the HIV/AIDS situation in June 2001 with participation from Boards and Committees of the Church, other churches and concerned agencies, and facilitators with first hand experience.
- Established a task force, convened by Shirley Brown, to design a project proposal for submission to the General Assembly of 2002.
- Established a consultative group with representation from other Boards and Committees of the Church, and from other churches and concerned agencies.
- Published and circulated an abridged version of the 2001 General Assembly Report, entitled "Confessing Faith in Christ in the Context of the HIV and AIDS Pandemic".
- Consulted with all overseas partner churches by correspondence and, when opportunity arose, by conversation.
- Held two residential Consultations with project staff of selected partner churches – one in southern Africa (at Blantyre) and the other in south Asia (at Delhi).
- Made HIV/AIDS the lead theme for a Local Involvement Conference for Presbytery Conveners.
- Contributed to Presbytery Conferences with a focus on HIV/AIDS in Aberdeen and Dumfries and Kirkcudbright.
- Ran pilot projects in four congregations: Kelso Old and Sprouston, Glasgow Williamwood, Edinburgh Murrayfield, and Thurso West.
- Made HIV/AIDS a feature in articles published in *Life and Work* and *Insight*.

It is out of the above process that the Board now proposes that in order to appropriately respond to the HIV/AIDS crisis, the Church of Scotland should:

- break the silence on HIV/AIDS
- stand together with partner churches
- offer practical support
- speak up for the voiceless
- involve every member.

This Report indicates what is involved in each of these steps and concludes with a concrete plan of action.

2.3. Break the Silence on HIV/AIDS

In many societies the initial reaction to HIV/AIDS has been to stigmatise and isolate those affected. Gideon Byamugisha, an HIV-positive Anglican priest in Uganda, has commented: "In HIV/AIDS, it is not the condition itself that hurts most (because many other diseases and conditions lead to serious suffering and death), but the stigma and the possibility of rejection and discrimination, misunderstanding and loss of trust that HIV-positive people have to deal with. How important it is to reach out in recognition of common humanity. How important it is that those of us who are HIV-positive continue to live rather than waiting to die." It is here that the church's recognition of HIV-positive members and their active inclusion in church worship and programmes gives a very powerful signal to the wider community.

It has to be acknowledged, however, that the church has usually found it very difficult to name the issues raised by HIV/AIDS. In particular, the whole area of sexual health and fulfilment is one which has tended to be excluded from the worship and teaching of the church. Participants at a Global Consultation on the Ecumenical Response to the Challenge of HIV/AIDS in Africa held in Nairobi in November 2001 observed that: "As the pandemic has unfolded, it has exposed fault lines that reach to the heart of our theology, our ethics, our liturgy and our practice of ministry. Today, churches are being obliged to acknowledge that we have – however unwittingly – contributed actively and passively to the spread of the virus. Our difficulty in addressing issues of sex and sexuality has often made it painful for us to engage, in any honest and realistic way, with issues of sex education and HIV prevention. Our tendency to exclude others, our interpretation of the scriptures and our theology of sin have all combined to promote the stigmatisation, exclusion and suffering of people with HIV or AIDS. This has undermined the effectiveness of care, education and prevention efforts and inflicted additional suffering on those already affected by HIV. Given the extreme urgency of the situation, and the conviction that the churches do have a distinctive role to play in the response to the epidemic, what is needed is a rethinking of our mission, and the transformation of our structures and ways of working."[1]

At the World AIDS Day celebration in the Roman Catholic Cathedral in Bujumbura in 1995, the priest said, in the course of his sermon, "We must have compassion for people with AIDS because they have sinned and because they are suffering for it now". At that point something propelled Jeanne Gapiya to rise from her pew and walk up to the front of the church. "I have HIV," she declared, "and I am a faithful wife. Who are you to say that I have sinned, or that you have not? We are all sinners, which is just as well, because it is for us that Jesus came." Out of that moment there grew Burundi's Association of Seropositive People. Those who come to the Association often feel that they want to pray, but fear they are too wicked for God to hear. "But suffering is the face of God," says Jeanne, "it is for this moment, when you turn to him in need and fear, that God has been waiting and longing."[2]

Just as Jesus came not to call the righteous but rather sinners to repentance, so the church is called not to be reserved for the "respectable" but rather to be a space to which people come to find forgiveness for their sins and healing for their wounds. In today's context this means taking HIV and AIDS into the vocabulary of the church. Then our worship and witness will signal that those afflicted by the epidemic are affirmed, accepted and embraced. Dr V.I. Mathan, a senior consultant in the Indian Government Ministry of Health and Family, at the Delhi Consultation called on churches "by the example of their communities" to show the nation "how the marginalised can become the central point to the community". De-stigmatising those who are HIV-positive will not only make a world of difference to their own experience but will also create an environment in which the challenges posed by the epidemic can be realistically faced by others. For all of us, openly addressing the issues raised by the epidemic creates a field within which we may discover a wider and deeper knowledge of God.

2.4.   Stand Together

No one in today's world is unaffected by HIV/AIDS. Everyone is at risk of being infected – though the level of risk varies greatly. Everyone has played a part in creating the conditions in which the epidemic spreads. Everyone suffers as the human community loses so many of its young, creative and productive members. In the church we proclaim ourselves members together of the body of Christ and "if one part suffers, every other part suffers with it". We therefore cannot look on HIV/AIDS as "someone else's problem". It is an issue for all of us and calls upon us to stand together.

Such solidarity finds particular expression for the Church of Scotland in its relations with its partner churches, especially those which witness in the most heavily affected areas. At Consultations held in Africa and Asia, partner churches expressed deep appreciation that the Church of Scotland is conscious of their pain and is listening to their concerns as they face the epidemic. Living in traumatised societies, they need the friends who come with a listening ear, with gentle solidarity and with an unyielding commitment to stand together in adversity.

The courage and faith which we encounter as we enter into this solidarity is often a profound inspiration to us. The Africa Consultation heard the story of a 13-year old girl whose mother and father had died. She was solely responsible for her two younger brothers. She had given up school to care for them. After the death of their parents, relatives had come and removed everything from the house, even the animals. When visited by a church member the girl said: "Please don't cry for us because you make us feel hopeless. Even without anything, the Lord is sustaining us. I have seen the hand of the Lord leading us." When asked how she manages, she responded: "God loves and leads us."

The challenge of HIV/AIDS is leading the churches to look together at some of the most intimate aspects of human life and some of the most sensitive cultural issues. Overcoming embarrassment and unnecessary reserve gives the opportunity to be more open with one another and achieve a more authentic shared discipleship. Girls at a refuge run by the United Mission to Nepal say that

[1] "Plan of Action: The Ecumenical Response to HIV/AIDS in Africa", World Council of Churches Global Consultation on the Ecumenical Response to the Challenge of HIV/AIDS in Africa", Nairobi, Kenya, 25-28 November 2001, p. 2.

[2] Gillian Paterson, *AIDS and the African Churches: Exploring the Challenges*, London: Christian Aid, 2001, p. 12.

they can cope with their HIV-positive status because of the care and compassion with which they are treated.

An important aspect of "standing together" is collaboration and coordination among those within Scotland who share this common concern. Through the Consultative Group this proposal has been developed in conversation with a range of social agents. This collaborative approach should be maintained. The Church of Scotland should make its resources available to sister bodies and should remain open to learning from their experience. Collaboration with Christian Aid, the churches' own relief and development arm, is central. The response here proposed for the Church of Scotland is in line with Christian Aid's statement: "The church is in a unique position to provide spiritual, moral and practical leadership; challenge social stigma; extend compassion; and provide spiritual and practical support and guidance to those infected and affected".[3] Resources produced by Christian Aid are prominent among the materials being commended for congregational use. In order to link the global approach to the local situation in Scotland, the project development has benefited from the input of the Board of Social Responsibility and the pioneering work which it has done.

For partner churches most directly affected there is great value in coordination and pooling of resources, at national level through such bodies as the churches' National AIDS Secretariat in Zimbabwe. There is also value in comparing experiences among churches from different countries – as was apparent at the Africa Consultation.

2.5. Offer Practical Support

Our partner churches have made it abundantly clear to us that there is a huge amount to be done in terms of practical care. Since the impact of the disease is felt in every dimension of the life of a society, the practical care needed is multi-faceted.

2.5.1. *Caring for People Living with AIDS*
The churches have often been in the forefront in the development of palliative care for those whose health collapses as a result of AIDS. For example, the Home Based Care Programme of Ekwendeni Hospital in Malawi

aims to "provide care and support to chronically and terminally ill patients so that they spend their last days of life and die in comfort, dignity and hope". The Home Care Programme of the Church of Christ in Thailand based in Chiang Mai lays emphasis on inclusion of those with and affected by HIV/AIDS within their home community, supported by a team of trained volunteers. A recent development has provided small homes for three or four people to live together for extra support and fellowship. Effective training and support for carers and the supply of the basic necessary equipment are the key to the success of such a programme. Otherwise there is the danger that "home based care" turns out to be "home based neglect".

2-5.2. *Providing for Orphans*
In Malawi alone there are more than a million orphans and the number is rising daily. "Religion that God our Father accepts as pure and faultless is this: to look after orphans and widows in distress" (James 1:27) Given this biblical mandate, the responsibility to offer care and support is one which the church cannot evade. Some of our partner churches have already begun to offer excellent programmes and, again, there is a clear need for resources and a part to be played by concerned partners.

2.5.3. *Keeping HIV-negative People Negative*
While those who are HIV-positive are a necessary focus of concern, no less important are those who are HIV-negative and the question of how they can retain that status. HIV/AIDS is a preventable disease. It is possible for a community to develop patterns of behaviour which markedly reduce the incidence of transmission, as has been demonstrated in such countries as Uganda, Senegal and Thailand. Partner Churches in Africa and Asia are actively promoting the importance of abstinence before marriage and faithfulness within marriage as means of countering the spread of the epidemic. However, there are barriers of stigma and silence which inhibit the delivery of effective educational programmes. Hence there is need for a highly intentional effort before people

---

[3]"Towards a Christian Aid Policy on HIV/AIDS", London: Christian Aid, July 2001, p. 3.

will have access to the information they need to remain HIV-negative. Some countries, like Nepal, have at present a relatively low incidence and low profile for the disease but are aware that this gives a "window of opportunity" to equip people to remain HIV-negative. One model which may have wide application both in Africa and Asia is peer-to-peer education. The Church of Scotland is part of the United Mission to Nepal which has been asked by the Government to develop a national strategy for HIV/ AIDS.

2.5.4. *Education for Church Leaders*
Given the special role which the church can have in equipping people to deal with the epidemic, it is particularly important that clergy and lay leaders are offered appropriate training. A relatively modest investment at this point could have a major effect for good. As partner churches, we have much to learn from each other in this fast-changing field. Providing the structures for the sharing of successful models and good practice would be a very effective resource which could be offered through partnership at this time.

2.5.5. *Supporting Key Institutions*
Certainly in some African countries the impact of the disease is now so serious that there is a danger of what Mulanje Mission Hospital medical director Bram Sizoo described as "social chaos and total breakdown". In order to resist this destructive force, support for key institutions has strategic importance. Among these are the churches and their programmes, so support from the Church of Scotland for partner churches facing this crisis has high value. In the Asian context now is the time when church programmes can seize the opportunity to offer education to the rising generation before it is too late.

2.6. Speak up for the Voiceless
2.6.1. Since it is predominantly the poor and the powerless who are directly affected by the AIDS crisis, it is often passed over in silence. As the advocate for the voiceless, the church has a responsibility to talk often and forcefully about the epidemic. As the community responsible to articulate in worship the concerns and the prayers of contemporary society, the church cannot evade its obligation to give AIDS its due place in evangelism, preaching and catechesis. This means speaking openly about subjects often regarded as taboo in such areas as sexual behaviour, gender issues and cultural practices.

2.6.2. *Poverty, Unpayable International Debt and the Spread of AIDS*
The United Nations estimates that for 17 countries in Africa the costs of providing basic prevention and care for HIV/AIDS are $1.4 billion a year: exactly what these countries will spend to service debts. Funds are diverted from the delivery of basic health and educational services to service the debts owed to wealthy nations. In some countries, more is being spent on debt service than on health. The average per capita health budget in sub-Saharan Africa has declined to just over £4.00 per annum.[4] This leaves the population of many heavily indebted countries very vulnerable to HIV infection. High rates of infection, with the resultant ill-health and premature death, lead to economic decline thus making the debt burden even more difficult to bear. Poor health and widespread illiteracy ensure ever higher rates of HIV infection and in this way the debt burden causes the early death of large numbers of people in the poorer countries. Only a multi-sectoral response will meet the demands made by the epidemic. This will not be achieved without much more rapid progress on debt cancellation and firm steps towards meeting the UN target of 0.7% of the GNP of wealthy countries being dedicated to international development. A realistic level of contribution from the wealthier countries to the United Nations Global Health Fund is another imperative of our time. Though their financial resources are limited, the churches in the rich world can give an important moral lead by responding with sacrificial generosity to the suffering caused by HIV/ AIDS.

2.6.3. *Provision of Medicine*
In many poor countries the prices of drugs which could save lives and reduce suffering are too high for either

---

[4]World Bank, *Can Africa Claim the 21st Century?*, Washington DC: World Bank, 2000.

individuals or governments to afford. This includes drugs for infections associated with HIV/AIDS, like resistant tuberculosis, meningitis and thrush. Poor countries should be able to access key drugs for HIV at dramatically lower prices than rich countries and far more research and development should be targeted towards drugs for diseases of the south. While current world trade rules allow countries to break patents in public health emergencies, poor countries often find this difficult to do because of economic pressure from the rich ones.

Access to the new anti-retroviral drugs between rich and poor people is grossly unfair. Even with recent price cuts, they remain largely unaffordable for the vast majority of people in the south. Anti-retroviral drugs have significantly prolonged the life and alleviated the suffering of many millions in the north (though they do not cure). In many poor countries, not only are the drugs unaffordable, but the back-up health services required for their safe use is not in place. Bringing pressure to bear on governments, drug companies, and international organisations in order to increase availability of these drugs, and to ensure the medical infrastructure for their safe delivery, is a key plank in the strategy to combat AIDS.

2.6.4. *Preventing Mother-to-Child Transmission.*

In poor countries, the transmission of HIV from mother to child, during childbirth and by breast-feeding, accounts for 5 to 10% of all new infections. One quarter to one third of babies born to infected mothers are HIV positive. Cheap ways of reducing this transmission are now available, by providing drugs like nevirapine (which can cut mother-to-child transmission by a half for just £2.50 per treatment). But this is still not being widely used as the drugs are unavailable, and as many women do not know they are HIV positive (and may not wish to know because of the stigma). Giving artificial feeding to babies at risk is not a viable option for most mothers in developing countries. And the considerable problems of orphan care remain. In a landmark judgement in South Africa in December 2001, a South African court ordered the government to distribute niverapine to HIV-positive pregnant women to halve the likelihood of the baby becoming infected.

2.6.5. *Gender Inequity*

Just as in most situations of poverty it is women who bear the brunt of the suffering, so women are often more vulnerable than men to the effects of HIV/AIDS. Under conditions of poverty, women are vulnerable to sexual exploitation and abuse. In order to feed themselves or their children, they may seek work in the informal sector where unregulated jobs, like beer brewing or commercial sex work, are physically and sexually dangerous. In many societies women face male power which restricts their capacity to protect their sexual health. Tragically many women have "died of trust" as they have been infected with HIV by their husbands whom they mistakenly believed to be faithful sexual partners. Equally when there is illness and debilitation as a result of the onset of AIDS it is women on whom most of the demands for care are placed. When parents die and the question arises as to who will care for the orphans it is most often the grandmothers who provide the answer. For these reasons the empowerment of women and girls is one of the most effective steps which can be taken in the struggle against HIV/AIDS. Correspondingly there is urgent need for men's self-understanding, expectations and behaviour to be reformed. "You can try to empower women all you like," Dr V.I. Mathan told the Delhi Consultation, "but they cannot control the men. Where the work needs to go is with the male population." Migrant working, limited economic opportunities and cultural sexual practices all contribute to establishing patterns of behaviour which lead to the spread of HIV and AIDS.

2.7. Involve Every Member

2.7.1 While the church raises a prophetic voice calling for action from national governments and international organisations, the integrity of this call will be demonstrated by the action which we ourselves take. In sub-Saharan Africa the churches provide 40-70% of health care. What the situation would be like without this effort from the churches does not bear thinking about. While we salute their courage and initiative, we cannot leave them to fight this battle alone. Many of the efforts of churches in sub-Saharan Africa to mount effective programmes in this area are handicapped by the deepening poverty in which they operate. As an expression of partnership, every member of the Church of Scotland should be given an opportunity to contribute to a special fund which will provide grant support for church programmes that meet best-practice guidelines. Courageous and talented members of our partner churches are ready to act against the HIV/AIDS pandemic. Well-targeted grants will enable them to put well-designed programmes into effect. Every member of our Church can help to make this a reality. This was reflected in reports from the four pilot congregations, in the programmes they devised for different age-groups and congregational organisations. These included special services, guest speakers, Bible studies, focus evening displays, games and campaigning activities. They were encouraged and amazed at the willingness of the congregations to speak and to learn about HIV/AIDS, to increase their awareness, and to be motivated to act locally and globally.

Financial provision, however, is only part of the answer. The onset of HIV and AIDS invites us to join with those most affected in an adventure of faith. Remaining informed about the general context and linking directly with a particular situation are opportunities which can be offered by the Board of World Mission as it develops our partner church relationships in the areas most affected. Partner churches have also pled for our Church to use its campaigning strength to support measures which will better enable poorer communities to resist the spread of the epidemic. The following proposed lines of action show how a practical response can be offered by the Church of Scotland.

2.8. The Shape of a Church of Scotland HIV/AIDS Project

2.8.1. *Raising awareness of HIV/AIDS in Congregations in Scotland.*

In collaboration with other Boards and Committees of the Church:

- Development of a congregational resource pack,
  —factual and statistical information,
  —true life stories from partner churches,
  —activities geared for all ages,
  —display material,
  —contact details for further information e.g. internet addresses.
- Plan and conduct an intensive awareness-raising campaign at Presbytery and congregational levels to include:
  —meetings,
  —discussions,
  —consultations,
  —workshops.
- Introduce HIV/AIDS information at all World Mission events.
- Encourage individual congregations to identify ways in which they can support partner churches overseas, e.g. development of congregational links with a view to understand the effect of HIV/AIDS on the lives of individuals, communities and nations, by building up partnership links through prayer, mutual communication and exchange visits.
- Encourage all congregations to take part in World AIDS Day on Sunday 1st December 2002.
- Provide an opportunity of bringing representatives from partner churches to work alongside congregations.
- Give financially to the common fund, which would be administered by the Board to ensure partners benefit according to their needs.
- Encourage congregations to take part in advocacy activities, e.g.
  —lobbying governments for new money for the Global Health Fund,
  —cancellation of debt
  —provision of health care including basic needs such as nutrition and clean water
  —provision of anti-retroviral drugs where appropriate.

2.8.2 *Support for Partner Churches.*
- Priorities for partner churches highlighted in the consultations include
  —training at all levels,

—education, structured and unstructured, including church leaders.
—development of resource material,
—support for orphan care schemes
—support for home based care activities,
—breaking the silence,
—reducing stigma and
—providing networking opportunities.

- Request for project proposals from partner churches in line with set priorities.

- Make funds available for proposals that fit the criteria.

- Offer specifically designed short programme for people working with HIV/AIDS projects in Partner Churches, at St Colm's International House, these would encompass provision of skills such as project proposal writing, visiting Scottish congregations and south-south linking opportunities.

2.8.3. *Structures for Management of the Project.*
Human Resources

- Appointment of a project co-ordinator by the Board to work alongside the Assistant Secretary (Local Involvement) and the Assistant Secretaries within the Partnership Team.

- Set up a management group to establish policy and guide the formation of work relating to HIV/AIDS. The group will give support to the co-ordinator.

- The co-ordinator and the management group will develop the project by sustaining and strengthening the network of concerned churches and agencies which has emerged in Scotland.

Financial Resources

- Apply to the Board of Stewardship and Finance for a special grant to provide initial funding for the project.

- Subject to the approval of the Board of Stewardship and Finance a Special Appeal will be made to all members of the church.

- Seek opportunity for matching funding.

- Explore available grants.

- Draw up project goals in line with the plan of action,
- A detailed funding proposal will be collated.
- Develop criteria for the distribution of funds.

2.9. Conclusion

In conclusion, let us hear the call of the Christian Conference of Asia, issued from a Consultation on HIV/AIDS held at Chiang Mai, Thailand, in November 2001:

This then is the time

- to heal,
- to care, not only by providing services, but also by standing alongside with love
- to build a community of belonging and acceptance
- to transform prejudice into compassion, healing and understanding
- to overcome injustice and discrimination
- to live with hope and to die with dignity.

To us who live and profess our faith in Christ in the age of the HIV/AIDS epidemic, this call comes. The above project proposal maps a path by which the Church of Scotland could play its part in responding in Christ's name to this great crisis of our time.

2.10. Acknowledgements

The Board acknowledges with gratitude a grant of £5,000 from the Erskine Cunningham Hill Trust towards the costs of the project development phase and is also very grateful to congregations which made unsolicited contributions when they heard of the work being done.

3. New Ways of Working

The Report of the Special Commission anent the Board of World Mission, received by the General Assembly of 2000, recommended that the Board undertake a management consultancy exercise. The Board engaged McKinsey & Co (on a *pro bono* basis) and the McKinsey team prepared a report which was adopted by the Board in December 2000. A major exercise in the following year was the implementation of the recommendations of the Report. Action has been taken to introduce new ways of working in the following areas:

3.1. Clear Strategic Direction

The Board was challenged to become an organisation with a clearly articulated, and commonly held, strategic direction. This has been done by:

- preparing a new remit which was approved by the General Assembly of 2001,
- adopting a 15-point statement of identity and purpose,
- establishing five strategic commitments for 2001-10 (as above, section 1),
- charging committees and groups to work on specific strategic initiatives to give effect to the overall strategic commitments,
- publishing a Handbook of Board Policy which provides clarity on the details of the Board's approach to its task.

3.2 Clear Roles for All

The Board was challenged to become an organisation where every individual, both on the Board and among the staff, has a clear role to play and understands how they fit into the big picture. At Board level this has been done by:

- removing a middle layer of committees so that all committees and working groups report directly to the Board,
- introducing a Business Committee which has no executive authority but is responsible for arranging the flow of business within the Board,
- increasing slightly the size of working groups and committees by the appointment of co-opted members with specific expertise and interest,
- giving detailed terms of reference to all committees and working groups,

- introducing an annual performance review for all committees and working groups,
- providing clear guidelines on the responsibilities of Board members,
- setting out the responsibilities of co-opted members of committees and working groups,
- establishing an induction process for new Board members and co-opted members of committees and groups.

At Departmental level this has been done by:

- clarifying the role and responsibilities of the General Secretary by the adoption of a new job description,
- reorganising all staff into teams, each focussed on a specific field of work,
- preparing up-to-date and comprehensive job descriptions for all members of staff,
- setting out realistic and well-defined management responsibilities,
- physically relocating staff to make the different teams more obvious and workable,
- establishing a code of best practice for office procedures and communications,
- extending the system of staff appraisal (staff development) to include all staff,
- providing relevant training opportunities for all staff,
- holding regular meetings of all staff to nurture a shared vision of the Board's work.

3.3 Clear Decision-making Procedures

The Board was challenged to have efficient and effective decision-making and reporting processes which are well understood by all Board members and staff. This has been done by:

- providing Board members and staff with the information necessary for responsible decision-making,

- defining the relationship and respective responsibilities of Board members and Departmental staff, and of conveners and secretaries,
- setting out procedures which establish the level at which any given decision ought to be taken,
- ensuring best practice in the preparation of written materials and in the flow of information within the various structures of the Board,

3.4. Clear Communication

The Board was challenged to have strong and well understood systems of communication so that Board members, Departmental staff and overseas staff are provided timeously with all the information necessary for the effective fulfilment of their respective roles. This has been done by:

- arranging for Board meetings to be held at regular intervals throughout the year,
- dividing Board meetings between conference-style sessions which examine the larger issues facing the Board and business sessions with a highly focussed agenda of matters requiring decision,
- maintaining a schedule under which committees and groups regularly report to the Board,
- keeping Departmental staff abreast of developments through regular meetings and circular emails,
- introducing systems to ensure that all communications from overseas staff are promptly acknowledged and that they are kept informed about progress in addressing any issues which they have raised,
- keeping overseas staff informed about the work of the Board and ensuring that they are consulted on matters which will affect them,
- monitoring the outworking of gospel values in all areas of the Board's life and work.

Evaluation exercises have suggested that these measures have been widely appreciated by all who are involved in the work of the Board. Nevertheless, efforts continue to be made to refine the new structures and processes and to respond effectively to changing conditions.

4. Review of the Pastoral Care of Overseas Staff

4.1. Introduction: the Nature of Pastoral Care

Care and caring are universal attributes and characteristics of humankind. "Glasser maintains that persons have only two essential personality needs – to love and be loved, and to feel that one is worthwhile to oneself and others. I would reduce these to a single indispensable need – to experience authentic love in a dependable relationship. An individual's personality hungers are all met to the degree that he (sic) participates in a relationship characterised by mutual sensitivity and responsiveness to the needs of others." (Howard Clinebell).[1] Care becomes pastoral care when it is informed and undergirded by the Christian faith and is discharged in the context of some aspect of the life of the church. It is a ministry, a "cure of souls", and it "consists of helping acts done by representative Christian persons, directed toward the healing, sustaining, guiding and reconciling of troubled persons, whose troubles arise in the context of ultimate meanings and concerns." (Clebsch and Jaekle).[2] All which follows here in terms of the responsibility borne by Board and Department for its Mission Partners rests upon and stems from the foregoing definitions.

Pastoral Care is therefore the promotion and maintenance of the well being of each individual member of staff (and family) from the time of initial inquiry to the date of termination of contract. All that is done to equip and enable the member of staff to undertake his/her responsibilities as well as ensuring an environment of general care is Pastoral Care. Pastoral Care may also take the form of assisting staff in times of crisis or need. Pastoral Care in its broadest context encompasses all spiritual, medical, professional and practical aspects of life.

---

[1] Basic Types of Pastoral Counselling, p. 18, Nashville Abnigdon 1962

[2] Pastoral Care in Historical Perspectives, p. 4 Aronsen 1994

4.2. **The Responsibility of Mission Partners and of the Board**

4.2.1. The Pastoral Care needs of each person are as individual as the person himself or herself. The Board thus provides a variety of options of Pastoral Care and it is for individuals to decide what best suits them. It is also important to realise that each individual has to undertake some responsibility for their own Pastoral Care and should seek to develop their own support networks. Mission Partners are thus encouraged to keep in contact with their 'home' congregation and minister for spiritual support, if spiritual support is felt necessary. Once overseas, where possible, Mission Partners are encouraged a) to meet together, if they so desire, for mutual support and wellbeing and b) to utilise the resources of their Partner Church or Institution.

The Board has a responsibility for Pastoral Care towards the following:

a) Enquirers
b) Mission Partners and families in training
c) Mission Partners and families when overseas (and non-accompanying families)
d) Mission Partners and families on interim leave
e) Mission Partners and families on final leave

The following is classed as falling within the realm of Pastoral Care and is already taking place. It is worth remembering that some Pastoral Care is carried out quietly, unobtrusively and, of necessity, confidentially.

4.2.2. *Spiritual*

a) Access to Board appointed chaplains while preparing for, during and after overseas service.
b) Provision of opportunity for a funded period of retreat when on leave.
c) Support from the Association of Returned Overseas Staff (AROS).

4.2.3. *Medical*

a) Board medical provisions:
  Full medical and option of personal debrief with Elphinstone International Health Centre, the Board's Medical Officers. This before appointment, during leave, at the end of contract and with the availability of advice during time overseas.
b) Provision of emergency medical insurance / evacuation.
c) Opportunity for personal debrief and counselling and follow up, if necessary, through Elphinstone International Health Centre when returning to the UK.

4.2.4. *Professional*

a) Provision of opportunity for funded study and career development. This includes assistance with funding for courses undertaken by non-employed spouses which would enable them to carry out voluntary work with the Partner Church / Institution.
b) Opportunity to apply for help with re-training once service with the Board is completed.
c) Career counselling is available on request for mission partners who have completed their period of service with the Board.

4.2.5. *Practical*

a) Implementation of the McKinsey Report general recommendations in respect of the communication process, in particular the acknowledgement of Enquirer and Mission Partner communications.
b) Provision of opportunity to utilise the Board's furlough house accommodation while on leave (Board and private visits).
c) Facilitating a thoughtful and caring interview process to ensure, as far as is possible, that the appropriate person is selected for the post.
d) Training programme for Mission Partners customised to suit their needs (and the needs of the Partner Church / Institutions) with regular meetings between Mission Partner and Board staff scheduled. Some elements of training are offered to the non-employed spouse of the Mission Partner as a support for the transition to life overseas. Core elements of training for a mission partner, regardless of placement, include:

- Personal / spiritual development
- Culture and orientation to country of service
- Language training (prior to departure if possible, if not in country of placement)
- Knowledge of the Church of Scotland
- Presentation skills training
- Acquaintance with Partner Presbyteries

e) The Board seeks to ensure the provision by the Partner Church / Institution of an appropriate orientation course for new Mission Partners.

f) Three month questionnaire sent to newly positioned Mission Partners seeking feedback on how they feel they are in their new post.

g) Annual report required from each Mission Partner providing the formal opportunity to report on their circumstances.

h) In depth work debriefing session with relevant Group representatives, with notes kept which are available to all concerned.

i) Regular communication / meetings with non-accompanying spouses.

j) Résumé of Board Minutes sent to Mission Partners.

k) Invitations to Mission Partners to attend the conference session of Board meetings.

l) A regular review of the Handbook for Overseas Staff (revision currently underway).

m) Visits to Mission Partners, while in post, by Area Secretaries and Board Members.

n) Invitation to all new Mission Partners and those on leave to attend an all staff Departmental meeting. This is a good opportunity for the whole Department to meet and hear about the mission partner's life and work.

o) Offer of pre-retirement courses where appropriate.

p) Practical advice and support on resettling in Great Britain from the Association of Returned Overseas Staff (AROS).

q) All Mission Partners retiring, resigning, home on leave or in training at the time of the General Assembly are invited to a meal with representatives of the Board and Department on the Friday evening. They are then presented to the General Assembly.

The issue of the pastoral care of the departmental staff was held to be outwith the remit given to the Working Group.

5. Overseas Charges–Implementing the New Act

In terms of Act VI 2001 Anent Overseas Charges, the Board has established anew its Overseas Charges Committee to implement its Presbyterial responsibilities to the five charges, which are in the Bahamas (two charges), Bermuda, Sri Lanka and Trinidad. Secretarial support is provided by the Board of Practice and Procedure, while the relevant Assistant Secretaries of the Board of World Mission implement the policies of the Board in this area of its work. The work in this first year has been characterised by the development of policies and processes. Accountability by congregations to the Committee has been put in place in respect of finance and property in terms of the Act. A regular process of superintendence visits has begun, and the Committee has the impression that the provision of improved presbyterian oversight is appreciated most where congregations have faced local crises and been supported by the Committee and its staff. The General Assembly welcomes representation from overseas charges for the first time. The Committee's work has been made more burdensome by vacancies in three out of the five charges, and personnel questions in others. The challenge has been to bring the support that might be expected from a Presbytery, and already the Committee has begun to form views on the future improvement of the Act, and to produce guidelines for local parties to help their implementation of the current scheme.

One small amendment to the Act would greatly assist the Committee in its work, and would improve the recruitment process. Since the passing of Act VI 2001 several ministers of other denominations have been seeking appointment to overseas charges. Some of them have been discouraged on discovering the presumption that an appointee would always become a minister of the Church of Scotland. At a time when it is proving difficult to recruit Church of Scotland ministers to overseas charges, the Board would like to find a way to maximise the interest shown in each appointment by suitable applicants and to overcome the disadvantages of the current system. A minister belonging to a compatible denomination and called to serve in one of the overseas charges may have no wish permanently to transfer status to the Church of Scotland. He or she may see this period of service as fitting naturally into a ministry otherwise belonging entirely to his or her home church, and that may be a church with which we have close associations. In practical terms, a transfer of status, even if reversed after a few years, may have a prejudicial effect on things like pension entitlement or social security contributions and make such an appointment inconceivable for the individual.

The Committee, in its appointments policy, recognises the usefulness of section 13(11) of Act V 1984. This special scheme enables ministers to be called from sister-churches without loss of status in their own denominations but with all due accountability for ministry to the authority of the Church of Scotland and the provision has been utilised already in the Committee's work. The Committee proposes to adapt that provision to meet its own needs – and to reflect the already time-limited nature of its appointments – by means of the Act set out in Appendix II. It has modelled this amending Act, *mutatis mutandis*, on the new version of section 13(11) that is to be found in the Overture anent Vacancy Procedure brought by the Board of National Mission to this General Assembly. As all ministers appointed under this new provision would have to obtain a certificate of eligibility in the same way as ministers from other churches applying for charges in Scotland, the General Assembly can be confident that anyone so appointed would meet the standards required by the Church of Scotland. It is anticipated that this change in the Act will lead to a reduction in the time taken to make appointments.

6. Church Without Walls

On receiving the Report of the Special Commission anent Reform and Renewal, the General Assembly of 2001 instructed the Board of World Mission "to involve Partner Churches in the study of the Report, to invite their comments, and to share insights and experiences thus gained with the Church through the Board of Practice and Procedure and the Assembly Council, and in other appropriate ways". On the basis of an "invitation to conversation" drafted with the help of the Convener of the Special Commission, this exercise has begun and is being built into the Board's regular interaction with partner churches around the world.

7. Disposal of Property

In terms of section 38 of the Deliverance of the 2000 General Assembly on the Report of the Board of World Mission, the Board has successfully transferred ownership of the property at Khaira Gali to the nearby Murree Christian School, an institution which plays a key role in supporting the mission community in Pakistan and which the Board has supported for many years through the appointment of staff.

8. Secretariat

Katy Laidlaw

Katy Laidlaw had already made a notable contribution to World Mission, as a Board member and Vice-Convener, when she joined the Department as Local Involvement Secretary in 1991. She then quickly established herself as the face and voice of World Mission in Presbyteries throughout the country and directed a significant renewal of the local involvement programme. Her friendship and counsel have been greatly valued by mission partners as she has skilfully managed the partner plan scheme. Ever resilient and resourceful, she has been an unshakeable rock for the Department, as for the Board as a whole, in a period of many challenges and changes. This led her latterly to play a key role in the administrative reform of the Department and to lay important foundations for the future. In her constant travels throughout the country she enjoyed the unfailing support of her late husband George whose death in the summer of 2001 is widely mourned. Katy's unreserved and selfless commitment brought a distinctive quality to her service. For this the

Board is deeply grateful and extends to Katy on her retirement its warmest good wishes for the future.

Carol Finlay

The Board is pleased to report that, on the completion of ten years service as a mission partner at Ekwendeni in Malawi, Carol Finlay took up the post of Assistant Secretary (Local Involvement) in November 2001.

In the name of the Board

ALAN MAIN, *Convener*
ALAN GREIG, *Vice-Convener*
ELISABETH CRANFIELD, *Vice-Convener*
KENNETH R ROSS, *General Secretary*

.

ADDENDUM

Very Reverend Professor Alan Main

The Very Reverend Professor Alan Main has given hugely of his time, energy and talents during the past two years as Convener of the Board of World Mission. To this challenging role he has brought outstanding gifts, great wisdom and deep pastoral sensitivity. Following the report of the Special Commission to the General Assembly of 2000, Professor Main has played a pivotal part in helping the Board clarify its objectives and reform its organisation. He has actively encouraged Departmental staff, overseas staff and Board members to share and pursue a common vision of strengthening relationships with our Partner Churches. In particular the Board has benefited from the experience and skills Professor Main has brought to its Working Group on the Pastoral Care of Overseas Staff and to its HIV/AIDS Task Force. The Board owes a deep debt of gratitude to Alan Main for his immense and distinguished contribution during his time of service as Convener. The Board also greatly appreciates the support Anne Main has given to her husband during this very busy time. We thank them both and wish them a long and happy retirement.

ALAN GREIG, *Vice-Convener*
ELISABETH CRANFIELD, *Vice-Convener*
KENNETH R ROSS, *General Secretary*

Rev Alan Greig

Rev Alan Greig concludes his term of office as Vice-Convener of the Board and in recording the Board's appreciation of his excellent service, the Board note with satisfaction his willingness to continue service through his acceptance of nomination as Convener of the Board.

ALAN MAIN, *Convener*
ELISABETH CRANFIELD, *Vice-Convener*
KENNETH R ROSS, *General Secretary*

APPENDIX I

Members of the Board of World Mission HIV/AIDS Task Force

Mrs Shirley Brown (Convener)
Ms Eildon Dyer (Christian Aid)
Ms Carol Finlay
Mrs Katy Laidlaw
Dr Dorothy Logie
Very Rev Prof Alan Main
Rev Prof Ken Ross
Mr Sandy Sneddon
Mr John Wylie (Social Responsibility)

Churches, Agencies, Boards and Committees invited to the Consultative Group

<u>Church of Scotland Boards and Committees</u>

Church and Nation
Communication
Ecumenical Relations
General Treasurer
Guild
Ministry
National Mission
Parish Education
Church of Scotland Trust
Stewardship and Finance
Social Responsibility
Worship, Doctrine & Artistic Matters

Other Churches and Agencies

ACTS
Baptist Union of Scotland
Congregational Federation in Scotland
Elphinstone International Health Centre
Free Church of Scotland
Jubilee Scotland
Methodist Church
Positive Steps Partnership
Religious Society of Friends
Roman Catholic Church in Scotland
Salvation Army
Scottish Bible Society
Scottish Parliament International Affairs Committee
Solas, HIV/AIDS Resource Centre
Scottish Episcopal Church
Tearfund
T B Alert
United Free Church of Scotland
United Reformed Church
Waverley Care Trust

Partner Churches Participating in Residential Consultations

Church of Central Africa Presbyterian, Malawi (Synods of Blantyre, Livingstonia, Nkhoma)
Evangelical Church of Christ in Mozambique.
Uniting Presbyterian Church in Southern Africa
United Church of Zambia
Church of Bangladesh
Church of North India
United Mission to Nepal
Church of Christ in Thailand
Methodist Church, UK (Observer)

APPENDIX II

Act Amending Act VI 2001

The General Assembly enact and ordain that Act VI 2001 is hereby amended as follows:

Renumber section 3 as section 3(1).

Add a new section 3(2) as follows:-

(a) Notwithstanding the provisions of section 3(1) above, where a minister of a church furth of Scotland, who holds a certificate of eligibility in terms of Act xx 2002 Anent Admission and Re-admission of Ministers and Others, is offered an appointment in terms of Schedule C hereof, the candidate, Kirk Session and Overseas Charges Committee may agree that he or she shall retain status as a minister of his or her denomination of origin.

(b) Upon introduction, such a minister shall be accountable to the Board for the exercise of his or her ministry and to his or her own church for matters of life and doctrine.'

APPENDIX III

Staff Selected and Preparing to take up Appointment from 01.01.01 to 31.12.01

Rev John Fraser
Rev Elinor Gordon
Rev William McCulloch
Mr Alasdair Murray
Mrs Moira Murray
Mr Brian Payne
Mrs Georgina Payne

APPENDIX IV

New Appointments between 1 January 2001 and 31 December 2001

Rev Dr Bryson Arthur, Head of Department of Religion, Mar Elias Educational Institutions, Israel
Mrs May Arthur, Lecturer in Midwifery and part-time TEFL Teacher, Mar Elias Educational Institutions, Israel

Rev Roderick Campbell, Training and Capacity Building Co-ordinator, Uganda/Sudan

Rev Maxwell Craig, Interim Minister, St Andrew's Church of Scotland, Rome, Italy

Rev Bruce Gardner, Locum Minister, St Andrew's Church, Colombo, Sri Lanka

Mrs Marianne Karsgaard, Tutorial Group Leader, United Mission to Nepal, Kathmandu, Nepal

Rev Rob Mackenzie, Mission Partner to the Waldensian Church, Turin, Italy

Dr Alexander Maclean, Medical Officer, Embangweni Hospital, CCAP, Livingstonia Synod, Malawi

Rev Ian Manson, Minister, Church of Scotland, Geneva, Switzerland

Mr Michael Nolan, English Language Teacher, Coptic Evangelical Organisation for Social Services, Cairo, Egypt

Miss Jane Petty, Agricultural Development Co-ordinator, Mwandi Hospital, Mwandi, Zambia

Rev Bruce Ritchie, Lecturer in Systematic Theology, Zomba Theological College, Zomba, Malawi

New Contracts between 1 January 2001 and 31 December 2001

Rev Alan Garrity, Minister, Church of Scotland, Christ Church, Warwick, Bermuda

Rev Frederick Hibbert, Minister and Liaison Person, St Andrew's Galilee, Tiberias, Israel/Palestine

Miss Helen McMillan, Lecturer, United Bible Training Centre, Gujranwala, Pakistan

Rev Thomas Pitkeathly, Minister, St Andrew's Church, Brussels, Belgium

Mr Alexander Sneddon, Development Officer, Peshawar Diocese, Church of Pakistan, Pakistan

Dr Alison Wilkinson, Doctor, PCEA Chogoria Hospital, Chogoria, Kenya

APPENDIX V

Staff and family members overseas during 2001

ASIA

Church of Bangladesh

Miss Gillian Rose, Midwifery Manager, Bollobhpur Hospital (ecumenical appointment)

Mr Andrew Symonds, Theology Teacher, St Andrew's Theological Seminary, Dhaka (ecumenical appointment)

Mrs Rosemary Symonds, Dhaka Development Office (ecumenical appointment)

Rev John Bennett, Minister, Church of Bangladesh (ecumenical appointment)

Mrs Rita Bennett, Administrative Assistant, Dhaka Diocese (ecumenical appointment)

Miss Ann Tuesley, Nursing Tutor, Nursing Institute, Christian Mission Hospital, Rajshahi (ecumenical appointment)

Church of South India

Rev Eileen Thompson, Communication Consultant, Church of South India Diocesan Office, Madras (ecumenical appointment)

United Mission to Nepal

Mrs Marianne Karsgaard, Tutorial Group Leader, Kathmandu

Miss Christine Stone, Educationalist, Kathmandu

Mr John Ross, Pharmacist, Patan Hospital, Patan

Nepal Leprosy Trust

Mrs Moira Murray, Nurse, Lalgadh Hospital, Lalgadh - until August

Mr Alasdair Murray – until August

Church of Pakistan

Rev Paul Burgess, Lecturer, Gujranwala Theological Seminary, Gujranwala

Mrs Catherine Burgess

Mrs Elizabeth McKee, House-Parent and Teacher, Murree Christian School

Miss Helen McMillan (study leave in UK), Teacher, United Bible Training Centre, Gujranwala

Mr William Seaman, Teacher, Murree Christian School – until July

Mrs Catherine Seaman – until July

Mr Alexander Sneddon, Development Officer, Peshawar Diocese

Mrs Marie Sneddon, Alison, Duncan and Andrew

Sri Lanka

Rev Bruce Gardner, Locum Minister, St Andrew's Church, Colombo – until November

Rev Anthony McLean-Foreman, Lecturer, Theological College of Lanka, Kandy

The Church of Christ in Thailand

Mrs Jane Fucella, Church Development Worker, Sangklaburi

Rev Michael Fucella, Church Development Worker, Sangklaburi

Rachel and Aylie

AMERICAS

Bahamas

Rev Dr James Berger, Minister, St. Andrew's Presbyterian Kirk, Nassau

Mrs Patricia Ann Berger

Rev Douglas Jenkins, Minister, Lucaya Presbyterian Kirk, Freeport – until May

Rev Jan Jenkins, Minister, Lucaya Presbyterian Kirk, Freeport – until May

Bermuda

Rev Alan Garrity, Minister, Church of Scotland, Christ Church, Warwick

Mrs Elizabeth Garrity

The United Church of Jamaica and the Cayman Islands

Miss Maureen Burke, Staff Associate, Mel Nathan Institute, Kingston

Mrs Jane Dodman, Research and Training Officer, Mel Nathan Institute, Kingston

Rev Roy Dodman, Minister, Shortwood Parish Church, Kingston

Rev Margaret Fowler, Minister, Negril Parish Church, Montego Bay

Trinidad

Rev Harold Sitahal, Minister, Church of Scotland Greyfriars – St Ann's and Sangre Grande, Port of Spain

Mrs Ruth Sitahal, Richard and Roxanne

MAINLAND AND CONTINENTAL EUROPE

Belgium

Rev Stewart Lamont, Executive Secretary, Church and Society Commission, Conference of European Churches, Brussels

Mrs Larisa Lamont

Rev Thomas Pitkeathly, Minister, St Andrew's Church, Brussels

France

Rev William Reid, Minister, The Scots Kirk, Paris

Mrs Esther Reid

Gibraltar and the Costa del Sol

Rev John Page, Minister, St Andrew's Church, Gibraltar and the Costa del Sol

Mrs Janet Page

Hungary

Rev Bertalan Tamas, Ecumenical Officer, Hungarian Reformed Church, Budapest

Mrs Elizabeth Tamas

Rev Kenneth MacKenzie, Minister, St Columba's Church, Budapest and Mission Partner to the Hungarian Reformed Church

Mrs Jayne MacKenzie, Mairi, Catriona, Ruaridh and Kirsty

Italy

Rev Maxwell Craig, Interim Minister, St Andrew's Church of Scotland, Rome, Italy

Mrs Janet Craig

Rev David Huie, Minister, St Andrew's Church, Rome – until June

Mrs Margaret Huie – until June
Rev Rob Mackenzie, Mission Partner to the Waldensian Church, Turin, Italy
Mrs Anne Mackenzie

Malta
Rev Colin Westmarland, Minister, St Andrew's Church, Valetta – until December

Netherlands
Rev Robert Calvert, Minister, The Scots International Church, Rotterdam
Mrs Lesley-Ann Calvert, Simeon, Zoe, Benjamin and Daniel
Rev John Cowie, Minister, The English Reformed Church, Amsterdam
Mrs Gillian Cowie, Matthew, Sarah and Ruth

Portugal
Rev Gordon Oliver, Minister, St Andrew's Church, Lisbon – until December
Mrs Jenny Oliver and Sarah – until December

Romania
Rev Celia Kenny, Lecturer, Protestant Theological College, Cluj

Switzerland
Rev Ian Manson, Minister, Church of Scotland, Geneva
Mrs Roberta Manson, Andrew, Robert and David
Rev Douglas Murray, Minister, The Scots Kirk, Lausanne
Mrs Sheila Murray
Rev Paraic Reamonn, World Alliance of Reformed Churches, Geneva
Mrs Rowena Reamonn

MIDDLE EAST & NORTH AFRICA

Egypt
Mr Michael Nolan, English Language Teacher, Coptic Evangelical Organisation for Social Services, Cairo – from January
Mrs Margaret Nolan

Dr Keith Russell, Medical Administrator/Co-ordinator, Joint Relief Ministry, Cairo
Dr Lai Fun Russell, Mhairi and Katharine

Israel
Mrs Karen Anderson, Teacher, Tabeetha School, Jaffa
Rev Dr Bryson Arthur, Head of Department of Religion, Mar Elias Educational Institutions – from September
Mrs May Arthur, Lecturer in Midwifery and part-time TEFL Teacher, Mar Elias Educational Institutions – from September
Miss Emma Given, Manager, St. Andrew's Hospice, Jerusalem – until December
Rev Frederick Hibbert, Minister and Liaison Person, St Andrew's Galilee, Tiberias
Mrs Diana Hibbert
Miss Lynda Keen, Teacher, Tabeetha School, Jaffa – until August
Mr Christopher Mottershead, Head Teacher, Tabeetha School, Jaffa
Mrs Susan Mottershead
Rev Clarence Musgrave, Minister, St. Andrew's Church, Jerusalem
Mrs Joan Musgrave
Miss Irene Wilson, Teacher, Tabeetha School, Jaffa

Lebanon
Mr David Kerry, Librarian, Near East School of Theology, Beirut

SUB-SAHARAN AFRICA

Presbyterian Church of East Africa, Kenya
Rev Dr Bryson Arthur, Theological Lecturer, Nairobi – until April
Mrs May Arthur – until April
Dr Elizabeth Borlase, Doctor, Kikuyu Hospital
Mr Kevin Borlase and Hannah
Dr Angus Grant, Doctor, Chogoria Hospital – until November
Dr Elizabeth Grant, Rebecca and Catriona – until November

Rev Elaine McKinnon, Lecturer, Pastoral Institute, Kikuyu
Dr Alison Wilkinson, Doctor, Chogoria Hospital

Church of Central Africa Presbyterian, Malawi
Mrs Lesley Balaj, Sister Tutor, Ekwendeni Hospital – until September
Mr Nelu (Ioan) Balaj – until September
Miss Carol Finlay, Sister Tutor, Ekwendeni Hospital – until July
Dr Andrew Gaston, Doctor, Ekwendeni Hospital
Mrs Felicity Gaston and Katy
Dr Alexander Maclean, Medical Officer, Embangweni Hospital, CCAP, Livingstonia Synod
Mrs Carolyn Maclean, Allison, Kirsty and Alexander
Rev Bruce Ritchie, Lecturer in Systematic Theology, Zomba Theological College
Miss Helen Scott, Teacher, Ekwendeni Girls' Secondary School

United Church of Zambia
Mr Martin Harrison, Accountant (ecumenical appointment) – until June
Miss Bridget Kellett and Reuben – until June
Rev Colin Johnston, Minister, Lusaka
Miss Jane Petty, Agricultural Development Co-ordinator, Mwandi Hospital

South Africa
Rev Graham Duncan, Lecturer, Fort Hare University
Mrs Sandra Duncan, Faculty Secretary/Administrator, Fort Hare University

Episcopal Diocese of Sudan
Rev Roderick Campbell, Training and Capacity Building Co-ordinator, Uganda

APPENDIX VI

Staff – Retired or Not Returning Overseas between 1 January 2001 and 31 December 2001

ASIA

Pakistan
Mr William Seaman, Teacher, Murree Christian School, Jhika Gali

Sri Lanka
Rev Bruce Gardner, Locum Minister, St Andrew's Church, Colombo

AMERICAS

Bahamas
Rev Douglas Jenkins, Minister, Lucaya Presbyterian Kirk, Freeport
Rev Jan Jenkins, Minister, Lucaya Presbyterian Kirk, Freeport

MAINLAND AND CONTINENTAL EUROPE

Italy
Rev David Huie, Minister, St Andrew's Church, Rome, Italy
Mrs Margaret Huie

Portugal
Rev Gordon Oliver, Minister, St Andrew's Church, Lisbon, Portugal
Mrs Jenny Oliver and Sarah

Malta
Rev Colin Westmarland, Minister, St Andrew's Church, Valetta, Malta

MIDDLE EAST AND NORTH AFRICA

Israel, Church of Scotland
Miss Lynda Keen, Teacher, Tabeetha School, Jaffa
Miss Emma Given, Manager, St Andrew's Hospice, Jerusalem

SUB-SAHARAN AFRICA

Church of Central Africa Presbyterian

Mrs Lesley Balaj, Sister Tutor, Ekwendeni Hospital, Malawi

Miss Carol Finlay, Sister Tutor, Ekwendeni Hospital, Ekwendeni, Malawi

Mr Martin Harrison, Accountant (ecumenical appointment)

APPENDIX VII

In Memoriam

	2001
Rev R M MacDonald, Calabar	8 August

	2002
Miss Elisabeth S Alexander, Kenya	5 February
Mrs Margaret Rae, India	14 January

APPENDIX VIII

Appointments

Ministers	23
Other church workers (religious, education, consultancy)	6
Teachers, lecturers, educationalists	21
Doctors	5
Nurses	4
Pharmacists	1
Administration	4
Community Development Workers	2
Ecumenical Appointments	8
Spouses	35
Children	21
Total Appointments	74
Total Overseas	130

APPENDIX IX

Teachers in China with the Amity Foundation

Long Term Teachers

Anne and Mick Kavanagh, Nanping Teacher's College, Fujian

1998–2002

Richard Brunt, Tai'an Teacher's College, Shandong

2000–2002

Sarah Ker, Jiujiang Teacher's College, Jiangxi

Mark McLeister, Changwei Teacher's College, Weifang

2001–2002

Stuart Craig Tai'an Teacher's College, Shandong

Eileen Brodie, Ganzhou Teacher's College, Jiangxi

Richard Lester, Changwei Teacher's College, Weifang

Vera Vicente, Changshu Teacher's College, Jiangsu

APPENDIX X

Faithshare Partners 2001/2002

Ms Akua Tabuaa-Aforo, Presbyterian Church of Ghana, community work in the Presbytery of Hamilton, April to September 2001

Ms Joanny Peralta Capellan, Roman Catholic Church, Dominican Republic, community work with the Presbytery of Stirling and with Christian Aid, Scotland, May to December 2001

Rev Daniel Eyo Etim, parish work in the Presbytery of Buchan, September 2001 to March 2002

Rev Sardar and Mrs Violet Ghauri, Church of Pakistan, Peshawar Diocese, Assistant Community Worker at the 'The Well' Asian Information and Advice Centre in the Presbytery of Glasgow, 2001–2003

Ms Margaret Kyeame, Presbyterian Church of Ghana, community work in the Presbytery of Dumbarton and the Boys Brigade, Scotland, October 2001–March 2002

Rev Levi and Mrs Ruth Nyondo, Church of Central Africa, Presbyterian (Livingstonia Synod), parish work in the Presbytery of Dunkeld and Meigle, September 2001 to March 2002

Mr Arpad and Mrs Zsuzsanna Szabo, Reformed Church in Hungary, community work in the Presbytery of Kirkcaldy, September 2001 – March 2002

Bursars 2001–2002

Rev Nii Armah Ebenezer Ashittey, Presbyterian Church of Ghana, MTh in Theology, Ethics and Communication, University of Edinburgh

Rev Timothy Nyasulu, Church of Central Africa, Presbyterian, MTh in New Testament, University of Glasgow

Mr Benson Njobvu, Uniting Presbyterian Church of Southern Africa (Zambia), MSc in Library and Information Services, University of Strathclyde

Mr Daniel Rugut, Reformed Church of East Africa - nominated by WCC, post graduate Masters in Pastoral Studies and Applied Theology, University of Aberdeen

Fr Noel Dionicio Dacuycuy, Philippine Independent Church - nominated by WCC, MTh (by research) in Theology, Culture and Development, University of Edinburgh

Miss Matild Györi, Reformed Church in Slovakia, Diploma in Hebrew and Old Testament, University of Aberdeen

Mr Alessandro Spanu, Baptist Church of Milan, MTh in Theology and History, University of Edinburgh

Mr Ladislav Havelka, Evangelical Church of the Czech Brethren, Practical Theology and Systematic Theology (Non-graduating), University of Edinburgh

Rev Elvis Elahie, Presbyterian Church of Trinidad & Tobago, MTh in Christianity in the Non-Western World, University of Edinburgh

Pastorally responsible for:
Rev. Dave Hazle, United Church of Jamaica and the Cayman Islands, 3rd year of a PhD in Christian Ethics and Practical Theology, University of Edinburgh

APPENDIX XI

World Exchange Volunteers 2002

Andrew Birch	Malawi
Katy Bean	India
Rachel Clark	Malawi
Arthur Currie	India
Emma Dones	Malawi
Sara Fitzhenry	Guatemala
Kirsten Forsyth	Malawi
Gail Gaston	Malawi
Lynda Gow	India
Ben Goldstraw	India
Stuart Greenhill	India
Laura Hall	India
Isla Hislop	India
Peter Kirwan	India
Gill Lobo	Rwanda
Jane Lowe	Malawi
Katherine Merry	Rwanda
Rachel Moffat	Guatemala
Mary Muir	Kenya
Caroline Musgrave	Rwanda
John McDiarmid	Malawi
Ellen Purves	Malawi
Abigail Robertson	India
Barney Ross	India
Fran Rout	Malawi
Matthew Smith	India
John Sharp	Malawi
Sarah Tointon	Malawi

The following volunteers will be departing in July
(placements not confirmed)

Nicola Arney
Sioux Baker
Aileen Campbell
Sheralee Docherty
Marianne Gillion
Anne Glover
Laura Hood
Carmelita Lazatin
Bernadett McFadden
Ian Macaulay
Alison Macleod
Lisa Mbull
Alistair Moir
John Taylor
Sarah Walpole

PROPOSED DELIVERANCE

The General Assembly:

1. Receive the Report and thank the Convener, Vice-Convener and Committee members for their work.

2. Welcome the impetus provided by the Scottish Ecumenical Assembly for the Churches to seek to do more work together and commend the Statements produced for use throughout the Church (par. 4 & Appendix III)

3. Instruct the Church of Scotland members of the SCIFU Group to take into account the specific comments received from Presbyteries and others consulted in the preparation of the final report in 2003 (par. 8)

4. Note the report of the ACTS Review Group set out in Appendix IV; reaffirm the Church of Scotland's commitment to the Churches Together principle and support the implementation of the new structure of ACTS.

5. Commend the valuable opportunities available at the World Council of Churches' Institute at Bossey for those interested in pursuing theological training (par. 14.2)

6. Encourage congregations to use the Charta Oecumenica imaginatively to promote better ecumenical relations in their area (Appendix V)

7. Approve the appointment of delegates to other churches' assemblies, synods and conferences as listed in Appendix I.

8. Approve the appointment of representatives to Ecumenical Bodies listed in Appendix II.

REPORT

OVERCOMING THE BROKENNESS

1. Introduction

1.1 The on-going work of the Committee
The Committee on Ecumenical Relations has had a busy and stimulating year. It has continued to build up its picture of what is happening ecumenically throughout the Church of Scotland. It has done this through two of its teams - the Local Involvement Team and the Liaison Team. The Local Involvement Team, once again, offered the opportunity for people throughout presbyteries and presbyterial councils to come together in October to share their stories and to be encouraged and challenged by guest speakers. The Liaison Team has continued to meet with representatives of Boards and Committees about the extent to which ecumenical thinking is shaping the on-going work of the whole Church of Scotland.

1.2 In addition, the Committee has continued to be represented at the Co-ordinating Forum. It responded positively to an invitation from the Board of World Mission to explore the setting up of a project on HIV/AIDS. It also took up an invitation from the Board of Social Responsibility to attend a seminar on the Churches' Role on the Social Capital of Communities. It is currently working with the Assembly Council on an interdepartmental group looking at issues relating to Call and Tenure.

1.3 The Committee has produced and distributed its first video and study guide – Patterns of Partnership. This has been well received and is being widely used.

2. Relations with other Churches

2.1 The Church of England

In 2001 a small group of ten from the Church of Scotland and the Church of England met in Wyedale, Yorkshire to explore the possibility of bilateral talks on faith and order issues. These preliminary talks proved useful and it has been agreed to meet again in 2002 with more substantial

> **The aim is to seek agreement on faith and doctrine that would allow recognition, though not reconciliation of ministry.**

papers about each other's traditions. The Committee on Ecumenical Relations is still anxious that the talks should not move from this preliminary stage without an invitation being extended to the Scottish Episcopal Church and the United Reformed Church to participate with us. The aim is to seek agreement on faith and doctrine that would allow recognition, though not reconciliation, of ministry.

2.1.1 Plans were also set in place for the next event in an on-going series of broad bilateral meetings with the Church of England to take place in April 2002. Topics were identified in the areas of ministry, national mission, church and society and ecumenical relations.

2.2 Four Nation Reformed Consultation

In December 2001, postponed from April because of the Foot and Mouth epidemic, a four way meeting took place at the United Reformed Church Centre in Windermere. This brought together the Church of Scotland, the Presbyterian Church in Ireland, the Presbyterian Church of Wales and the United Reformed Church. It provided the opportunity to explore issues relating to partnership in mission, relations between church and nation, and our Reformed identities. This was the first time these four

churches had met. It proved to be a very important meeting as each in the process learned from the others' traditions and perspectives. The extent to which our contexts have shaped us sharpened the differences between us.

2.2.1 Yet there was a sense of a family gathering, a shared language and a common concern to witness to the Gospel in a way that is relevant

> **... there was a sense of a family gathering**

to today's world. Often it was our Christian identity that found precedence over any contribution we might make as specifically 'Reformed' churches.

2.2.2 Each of us from our different settings put much stress on the need to work together with others in a broader ecumenical context. Odair Matheus, the Study Secretary of the World Alliance of Reformed Churches and Jet den Hollander of the Mission in Unity Project sponsored by WARC and the John Knox Centre in Geneva acted as external reflectors. They were able to put our domestic conversations within the broader context of Reformed relations.

3. The Duncan McClements Trust

The Trust continued to draw in contributions throughout 2001. Once application forms have been drawn up the Committee will begin to advertise for applications to the fund. The Committee is gratified by the level of donations. This has proved an attractive way of commemorating the life and work of Duncan McClements, the Committee's first Convener.

4. The Scottish Ecumenical Assembly

4.1 Much hope was placed on the Ecumenical Assembly held in Edinburgh in September 2001 – the first of its kind. Four hundred people gathered from across Scotland, from every part of church life and from community organisations as well, to explore the theme *Breaking New Ground*. The vision was to draw up statements on seven sub-themes, which would outline broad areas of policy that could shape the agenda of the churches together over the next five years.

4.2   The weekend was intensive, driven from the outset by the need to produce statements. For many it was their first experience of a large gathering, their first encounter with people of different Christian traditions at the level of relating faith to witness and their first involvement in a church decision-making process of any kind. Many people commented on how denominational labels were set aside as people explored their faith together and discovered their common Christian heritage and calling. There were painful exchanges on issues of disagreement, which were seldom denominational disagreements, but ones stemming from differences of theological tradition or personality.

4.3   The worship was for many a highlight of the weekend and few will forget the sermons and reflections of **Prof. James Dunn** of Durham University:

4.3.1   From the beginning he set the challenge from Jeremiah chapter 1 – the commission 'to uproot and to break down, to destroy and to overthrow, to build and to plant' (1:10). Breaking down he said was not a sign of failure, but recognition that society changes and we require fresh ways of living in it and speaking to it. What breaking down is necessary at this stage in our common and individual church lives? He used the image of breaking up the land so that seeds can penetrate the land and take root, finishing with the need to break down the dividing walls of hostility and push out beyond the old boundaries to the new.

4.3.2   To what extent this challenge will be taken up still remains to be seen. James Dunn warned about the "default mode" we have as individuals and as churches, which prevent us changing and doing new things. The seven statements on poverty, a new enlightenment, alienation, work, spirituality, science and

> *Ecumenism is not about finding the lowest common denominator ...*

technology, and being church have been received by the Churches and are published in **Appendix III**. They have been circulated to every Board and Committee with encouragement not only to look at how they relate to our on-going agendas within the Church of Scotland, but how they can be taken forward ecumenically. The Central Council of Action of Churches Together in Scotland and its various commissions are also looking at how the statements can be developed as the churches continue to seek ways of working together effectively. Ecumenical statements can sometimes appear bland and it is worth exploring what lies behind the blandness. Was it that there were very difficult issues raised which ought to be revisited with more time and space? Ecumenism is not about finding the lowest common denominator, but enjoying the space to share differences of opinion with growing respect and understanding. The Ecumenical Assembly was an important step in an on-going process.

4.4   Those who attended the Assembly from local congregations have been asked to share the experience and encourage local reflection on the themes. The Committee has already heard how the Ecumenical Assembly has provided impetus to local thinking in Falkirk as the churches seek to do more of their work together. It is hoped that this might be repeated in many places across Scotland.

5.   Local Ecumenism

5.1   The main focus of the Committee on local ecumenism comes in the annual October conference. Contacts from presbyteries and presbyterial councils come eagerly to share their news, their concerns and frustrations and to find something to inspire them for their continued work.

5.2   Last year's conference was no exception. The keynote address by **Rev Flora Winfield** of the Church of

> *"The only reason for engaging in ecumenism is because the brokenness of the Church is a state of sin. We are less than the Church because we are divided from each other."*
>
> *Rev Flora Winfield*

England's Council for Christian Unity gave much food for thought, of which the following points are worth sharing:

- **Ecumenism is not a denial of difference.** Rather it is about being realistic about differences and embracing diversity cheerfully. The only reason for engaging in ecumenism is because the brokenness of the church is a state of sin. We are less than the Church because we are divided from each other.
- The 'C Scale' – this recognises different ways of coming together – **conflict, coexistence, conversation, co-operation, commitment and communion**. It is possible to be in conflict and in conversation at the same time.
- **Some, perhaps most, are in the comfort zone of coexistence, which requires no engagement and no change.** Churches live out a programme of events – Week of Prayer for Christian Unity, Lent Groups, Hunger Lunches, World Day of Prayer, Walk of Witness on Good Friday, Easter Praise, Christian Aid Week, Harvest/One World Week, Carol Singing, Week of Prayer…..
- These "cyclical" events need to belong to the churches and not solely to groups of people interested in ecumenism. Programmes within congregations often continue as though the ecumenical programme does not exist.
- At present, Churches are engaged in an ecumenism of exception. There is a need to arrive at a stage where being together is the norm.

6.   Groundswell

6.1   A new Communication and Resources team within the Committee on Ecumenical Relations has begun an occasional letter, Groundswell, which puts together stories of good ecumenical practice for information and, hopefully, inspiration. The Committee is aware that there are many stories waiting to be heard. Too often people do not realise that what seems to be normal in their local church life could in fact be of great encouragement to others who may feel isolated and unsure of what is possible.

6.2   This team is also reviewing worship-related materials. Reviews are to be placed at regular intervals on the website for easy accessibility.

7.   Local Ecumenical Partnerships

7.1   An awareness of the growing community in **Livingston**, and the establishment of a large new town-centre, led the Ecumenical Parish Council to seek assistance from the Church of Scotland's Board of National Mission. This triggered a full review of Livingston. The Ecumenical Parish, Livingston Old and St Andrew's Deans, the Presbytery of West Lothian and the Sponsors' Council met with representatives of constituent Committees of the Board of National Mission over several meetings. All were agreed that there needed to be changes in how the churches minister in Livingston. While some questions remain to be answered, not least the number and location of buildings, the process brought the Ecumenical Parish Council and the Kirk Sessions of Livingston Old and St Andrew's Dean round the same table. There is now a commitment that the two parishes will seek ways of co-operating in mission to the town as a whole and the new town centre, while recognising the integrity of the identity of each parish.

7.1.1   In the meantime, the Ecumenical Parish is being served well by a team that works with energy and imagination, ably supported by the Parish Council and a growing team of trained lay people. The Scottish Episcopal Church has been able to continue support for the appointment of a Community Ministry Co-ordinator. The Sponsors' Council has continued to give encouragement and support. It has been kept fully informed of the review process.

7.2   Three Church of Scotland congregations in **Barrhead** and Barrhead United Reformed Church have continued to move steadily towards the point of forming a multi-centred union in the town. A Shadow Parish Council was set up to see how what was being proposed might work, and a Sponsors' Council has brought together local, regional and national interests to accompany the process.

7.3   Likewise, in **Aberdeen**, the Kirk o' St Nicholas and the St Nicholas United Reformed Church have been pursuing the possibility of uniting to become the Kirk o' St Nicholas, Uniting. In this case, the building, which has been shared for many years, would become the building of the uniting congregation. A group bringing together local, regional and national representatives was set up to assist the process towards union. The minister of the United Reformed Church is currently serving as Interim Minister in the Kirk o' St Nicholas, a first for the Church of Scotland and an interesting ecumenical development of a new form of ministry.

7.4   In **Dundee** the discussions about union between Mid-Craigie and Linlathen (Scottish Episcopal Church) which had been making encouraging progress earlier (and had been included in the video), were discontinued at the final stage, owing principally to structural factors. While this outcome was disappointing to many, it is a salutary indication that the process towards union, once started, is not inexorable.

8.   Scottish Church Initiative for Union (SCIFU)

8.1   Update

8.1.1   The SCIFU Group has continued the work that was entrusted to it in 1996. The Group has spent much time reflecting on how to communicate the vision of SCIFU. It was felt not enough emphasis had been put on answering 'why union?' and too much on the 'how' of the union process. The result had been an over-stress on the mechanics and structures and not enough on the principles involved.

> **People...are looking to the churches to speak more about God**

8.1.2   Extensive revision was made to the appendices of the Second Interim Report on the work of the bishop. The Church of Scotland's Reflection Panel took an active role in suggesting amendments to the text, most of which were happily accepted by the SCIFU Group. The Working Group on the Diaconate produced a paper on *the Spirituality of the Diaconate*, which the Group has sought to publish as a separate paper available to the widest possible readership. The SCIFU Group recognised in this paper a valuable contribution to the national and international ecumenical discussions currently taking place on the Diaconate. It was also immediately passed to the Board of Ministry, members of the Church of Scotland Diaconate and the Warden of the Methodist Diaconate Order for their information. An Ordinal Working Group has been working on the rubrics and actions of the Ordination Service and the question of who should participate if the ordination is to be recognised as valid by all the participating churches. Further work requires to be done on who should lay on hands at ordination as practice varies between the churches and, in the case of the Church of Scotland, is actively under discussion. A group has also started to look at nomenclature. The First and Second Interim Reports are in the process of being collated and adapted in the light of discussion and responses from the churches as preparation for a final report from the SCIFU Group in 2003.

8.1.3   At a further meeting, the Group looked again at the process and the remit in the light of responses from the churches. This was a very positive meeting in which the context of SCIFU was placed within the wider setting of a contemporary culture in which people are seeking spiritual experiences and are looking to the churches to speak more about God. Some responses suggested that the case of a united church as an effective instrument of mission had not been proven. It was agreed that this should form the basis of a document which would be brought to the churches either on its own or as part of the final report in 2003.

8.2   Church of Scotland Responses

8.2.1   In 2000 the General Assembly instructed Presbyteries to study the *Second Interim Report* of the Scottish Church Initiative for Union (SCIFU), seeking views of Kirk Sessions, and to send responses to the Ecumenical Relations Committee by 30th April 2001. It also commended the *Second Interim Report* to Kirk

Sessions and local Churches Together groups and invited comments to be sent by 30th April 2001. In addition, it instructed all Boards and Committees to study the report and send comments by the same date.

8.2.2 The Committee is grateful to those presbyteries, 41 in all, who responded, to the 209 Kirk Sessions who sent in comments and to the Assembly Council, the Education Committee and the Board of Stewardship and Finance for their remarks.

8.2.3 The task of analysing the responses has proved very difficult because of their nature and range. Because the Second Interim Report, like the first, was a consultation document, it was to be expected that there would be critical remarks, even from those who broadly speaking support the initiative. It was also to be expected that these areas of concern would also appear in responses from those who were completely negative in their response.

8.3 Kirk Session Responses

8.3.1 A small proportion of Kirk Sessions responded directly to the Committee on Ecumenical Relations. The smallness of the numbers can be accounted for to some extent by the fact that some responded to their presbyteries, but the detail of their responses was not sent on to the Committee. Details were sometimes incorporated into the presbytery reports. We also know of other Kirk Sessions who have studied the report but who sent in no responses. Where responses were received, the different ways in which Kirk Sessions reported on their discussions means that no issue was commented on by all Kirk Sessions.

8.3.2 It is therefore impossible to give a completely accurate picture of what Kirk Sessions are thinking. It is, however, the case that the same issues stand out as are highlighted by the presbytery responses. Some Kirk Sessions expressed gratitude for being given the opportunity to discuss the issues. Fifty of the respondents, while all criticising some aspects, expected the discussion

to continue, 11 expressly encouraging continuation; 30 respondents believed the talks should cease. Out of the 209 Kirk Sessions, 129 expressed no specific view about the way the process should be taken forward. Of these, 23 requested more information.

8.3.3 The Kirk Session responses gave a picture of good co-operation between the denominations at local level. This is particularly encouraging and is taken up in many of the presbytery responses.

8.4 Board and Committee Responses

8.4.1 Board of Stewardship and Finance welcomed and encouraged the aim of uniting four denominations as something that should mean 'better deployment of resources, a reduction of duplication and more effective communication of the unity and mission of the Church to the people of Scotland.' However, it had a number of reservations about specific proposals (some shared by presbyteries) – whether too many buildings might result, the dangers of further schism and the possibility of increasing the complexity of structure. The Board sees a greater number of successful local ecumenical partnerships as a catalyst for greater unity at a national level.

8.4.2 The Board of Stewardship and Finance also drew attention to the need to face questions about authority and hierarchy, much expressed in the Church. They also point out that within the Church of Scotland, there is a significant number who would incline more towards the Baptist Church and independent fellowships than towards the participant churches in the SIFU talks. (Some of the presbytery responses made the same point but with reference to the Free Church and the Associated Presbyterian Churches.)

8.4.3 The Board of Stewardship and Finance also gave some helpful comments on the possible cost of uniting. These comments are crucial for the financial work that would need to be done by experts from all four participating churches ahead of any union being effected.

8.4.4 The Assembly Council warned against creating a new church that was retrospective in structure rather than having the flexibility envisaged in many recent initiatives in the Church. It appreciated the sections on *The Nature and Purpose of the Church, Why Union?* and *What is the meaning of mission?* as attempting to establish a vision for the future. It gave the reminder that bottom-up change has to be matched by a legitimate top-down initiative. 'The key is in finding the right balance, so as to affirm local initiatives and at the same time lead the way forward.' The Council then shared some of the responses it has heard as it has consulted with Presbyteries and made mention of places where positive ecumenical initiatives are taking place.

8.4.5 The Education Committee in its report helpfully commented on certain sections and suggested where more work needs to be done. The Ecumenical Relations Committee was disappointed not to receive responses from any other Boards or Committees.

8.5 Presbytery Responses

8.5.1 Because of the differing ways in which the presbyteries approached the matter, there was no single issue that was covered by all 41 respondents.

8.5.2 Of the 41, 19 – in spite of making critical comment – clearly expected that the talks would continue, while only 7 called for a halt to the process. On the other counts, 18 found more to criticise than to praise, while 17 looked forward to proposals for union – albeit different from those currently before the Church. .

8.5.3 Issues of Concern

Several concerns emerged from Presbyteries:

- Unity in Diversity. Many presbyteries felt that union was not an appropriate expression of the unity of the Church and in fact confused unity with uniformity. For some it was clear that Christ's gift of unity is a spiritual gift, which somehow did not need to find expression in church structures. 'Would it not be better to look for unity in mission, rather than unity in structure?' Some suggested that the different denominations were part of God's gift of diversity. On the other hand, one presbytery noted that 'disunity between denominations does not endear people to the Church.'

- The eldership. Eight felt that the eldership was being eroded, while three expressed gratitude for the guarantee that the eldership would have a central role.

- The role of the Bishop. Sixteen presbyteries expressed anxiety over the role of the bishop. Eight were not averse to such a role, but pleaded for a word other than 'bishop' to be used. One stated that 'the word 'Bishops' seems to send most people into orbit', while another said, 'The pastoral role of the Bishop to other pastors is welcomed, as is the wider perspective that a Bishop would bring to a co-ordinating role (especially in mission).' Again, another wrote, 'On balance, we believe that there is potential benefit to the church to be derived from introducing episcopacy in the form of an area ministry of humble, respected pastors, as long as safeguards are implemented.' This presbytery goes on to define eight safeguards.

- Structures. Many found the proposed structures cumbersome. This was usually expressed in terms like 'overly bureaucratic'. Nevertheless, some did welcome the maxi-parish. From the Central belt: 'The concept of "maxi-parishes" commands the support of Sessions, but the practical concerns… need to be further addressed by SCIFU.' From one rural area: 'The maxi-parish is seen as a way forward. [It] would help break down the sense of isolation from the wider church felt by rural parishes.' Another rural area at the other end of the country also stated: 'There is much to be welcomed in this document; maxi-parishes for example.' On the other hand, there was this very strong statement: 'Team ministry would not work within the Northern Isles.'

- Bottom-up approach best. While several presbyteries used the term 'imposed' both of episcopacy and of the maxi-parish structure, by far the largest response (23 in all) indicated that there are many initiatives going on at local level which they wished to commend and to give room to grow. For them the best way forward was to allow these initiatives, suitably encouraged and supported, to determine the nature and pace of change. Thus, one presbytery commended 'all ecumenical sharing within the presbytery at local level' and encouraged 'congregations on an inter denominational basis to do together everything which is not required to be done separately.'

- <u>Time scale</u>. Thirteen indicated that the time scale was unrealistically short. This was coupled in some responses with a plea for more information and opportunities for learning about each other's denominations.
- <u>Fragmenting the Church</u>. Fourteen presbyteries reckoned that the outcome of union would lead to a split in the Church of Scotland. For example, 'The disunity that will be manifested as many in the Church seek alternative spiritual homes or form a Church of Scotland Continuing will be more divisive than the present happily tolerant and co-operative separation.'
- <u>Buildings and Costs</u>. Seven presbyteries raised issues about buildings and 5 about cost.
- <u>Doctrine and The Westminster Confession of Faith</u>. Some presbyteries wished for more doctrinal clarification. There was unease at the amount of things that seemed to be left for clarification after union. Five presbyteries expressed alarm that a Confessional Statement could be left until after union. Two presbyteries were happy to leave the drawing up of a statement to the united Church and to the involvement of a broader spectrum of churches. However, the impression overall was of an unease that it was not clear what people would be asked to sign up to.
- <u>What are young people saying?</u> Two Presbyteries pointed to the need to consult young people. One wondered whether their views had been sought. The

> *It is striking to note that the SCIFU Report received overwhelming support from the 2000 Youth Assembly.*

other pointed to the contribution of the young people in the debate in the 2000 Assembly. 'We ignore God's speaking through them at our peril.' It is striking to note that the Committee on Ecumenical Relations did take SCIFU to the Youth Assembly in 2000 and received overwhelming support for the initiative.

8.6 **Where do we go from here?**

8.6.1 **Local Relations**. The Committee on Ecumenical Relations has been involved in encouraging local initiatives wherever possible. In fulfilling this part of its remit, it sees as part of its role the sharing of good ecumenical practice. It was clear from some of the responses that there is still a lot more sharing to be done. There is a lack of awareness of the degrees of ecumenical engagement that are possible within current church structures. There is already a flexibility, which could be more widely tapped.

8.6.2 However, it is clear that while there was no real enthusiasm for the road SCIFU had taken, many, and in particular the overwhelming response of young people, did take seriously the need to seek union as a means of expressing something of our unity in Christ and wanted to feel part of the process. It is necessary to heed the cry that, no matter how many good ecumenical relations there may be on the ground, these have not led to a groundswell of opinion that the present proposals offer the best way forward at this stage. It will be important to ensure that this response was not used simply as an avoidance mechanism, but was an expression of a real desire in local communities to take forward the ecumenical agenda in a way that is dynamic and allows room for change and growth.

8.6.3 It will be important that those Kirk Sessions who were waiting for union at national level as the signal for them to take the next stage in their ecumenical journey with neighbouring congregations are enabled to feel encouraged and supported to travel that journey now. In order that this can happen there will need to be the cultivation of an open attitude in presbyteries that is ecumenically regional and relational.

8.6.4 It can be argued that it was one of the major shortcomings of both the *Church Without Walls* report and the report of the Joint Boards Group on Presbytery Boundaries (presented at the General Assembly in 2001) that neither gave sufficient acknowledgement to the ecumenical dimension. Yet in many places, it would be impossible to be local and relational and ignore relations with other churches. Likewise, for presbyteries to be most effective, they too need to be able to develop relationally in a way that brings a much-needed ecumenical dimension to the regional life of the Church. It is also hard to see how the model of collaborative ministry outlined in the Board of Ministry's report of 2000, *Ministers of the Gospel* – the group practice – can be implemented in many places without it involving ministers and priests of other denominations.

8.6.5 The Nature and Purpose of the Church. The responses suggest that more work in this area would be welcome to assist further reflection. In particular, there needs to be more thinking around the understanding of the ministry of the whole Church, exploring within that the place of the laity, the eldership and the ministry of Word and Sacrament. And as this is not a peculiarly Church of Scotland reflection, it is something that would be most profitably explored in an ecumenical context, wherever that is possible. There is a feeling of uncertainty and unsettlement in all denominations

> *The fundamental question of what the Church is for and who it is for and how it relates to the society in which it is set is a question none of the churches can properly face on its own.*

at present. The fundamental question of what the Church is for and who it is for and how it relates to the society in which it is set is a question none of the churches can properly face on its own. This discussion is unlikely to be simply a local discussion, but if it is not informed by local thinking, it will remain rootless and unconvincing.

8.6.6 National Level. The responses suggested that there should be continued talking at national level. If the momentum is to come from the 'grassroots', it will be important that work has been done at national level to enable appropriate resourcing of the local. The ground needs to be prepared so that local ecumenical partnerships can acquire national recognition and, in some instances, a new legal framework. There needs to be understanding and a close working relationship across the denominations among those who resource ministry, mission and education. Once again, this national discussion needs to have fed into it the experience and needs of local communities and vice versa.

8.7 Continuing the Process

8.7.1 It is clear that while the SCIFU Group had been anxious to engage in a process of consultation, which would move back and forth rather than be 'top-down', this has not been fully appreciated. It would seem that the Church as a whole has still to get used to a consultative approach. This will mean the overcoming of distrust. There is a distrust that if something appears vague or incomplete, there is a hidden agenda. Sometimes there seems to be a fear that decisions have already been taken. 'The report is the aim of a pressure group within the Church seeking to propagate and impose goals on the whole Church.' 'There is a perceived lack of sensitivity in that what is presented might be viewed as a *fait accompli*.' With the SCIFU process a feeling of distrust was exacerbated by the fact that many felt that their comments had not been heard following the first Interim Report. 'It is essential that the grassroots (Kirk Sessions) are being heard.' The SCIFU Group is committed to seeking improvement in the way in which consultation takes place and it is hoped that there can yet be the development of trust between the SCIFU Group and local communities.

8.7.2 It will be important that thinking continues both locally and nationally. Working together as churches and reflecting together on faith issues need to be held together and neither locally nor nationally can the working together and reflecting together stop short of challenging our structures. Local initiatives will continue to be encouraged and local discussion can still be generated around key issues of how best we can engage in mission in the twenty first century. A number of responses commented favourably on the nature of the debate that has been generated by the *Interim Report* and it is hoped that some of the issues raised will continue to be pursued in local congregations and churches together groups. Local initiatives will continue to give encouragement in the national and international contexts of church life and witness.

8.7.3   Nationally it will be important to look more closely at how different Boards and Committees relate to one another when they are pursuing related matters. Ministers of the Gospel (Ministry 2000), A Church without Walls (Special Commission 2001), Presbytery Boundaries (Inter-Board Report 2001) and the continuing brief of the Assembly Council all have overlapping concerns with SCIFU which need to be recognised, with more effort made to ensure better lines of communication and sharing of thinking.

8.7.4   Also nationally, more work needs to be done on the reconciliation of ministries between the participating churches. Locally and nationally there is still need for more work on the healing of memories. Working together gives a false sense of well-being while deep hurt and distrust, prejudice and misinformation continue to exist beneath the surface.

8.7.5   The commitment of the Church of Scotland remains a commitment to seek the unity of Christ's Church. We continue to have an obligation to seek union with other churches - as long as we have our Articles Declaratory. But perhaps most crucially of all, is the commitment we made in 1990 to the 'Lund Principle' to act together in all matters except those in which

> **LUND PRINCIPLE:**
>
> **Whether the churches should not act together in all matters except those in which deep differences of conviction compel them to act separately.**

deep differences of conviction compel us to act separately. In today's world, the areas of deep difference between denominations are fewer than ever before. It is this commitment that remains to be more fully explored by all those who asked for time and space to develop ecumenical relations locally.

8.7.6   The Committee on Ecumenical Relations is conscious that, although the time scale has proved problematic, it did have the effect of generating debate. It is proposed that the time between now and 2010 should be used to allow local relations to grow and deepen, to work more closely with other Boards and Committees and to continue the process of consultation between those at local and national level in a way that continues to raise issues of how best to engage in mission in the twenty first century and clarify the nature and purpose of the Church.

8.7.7   The 'church without walls' is a church that lives and acts ecumenically. In a church without walls God's gift of unity in Christ shapes our structures as well as our hearts. The church is local and it is universal. It is always relational.

9.   Action of Churches Together in Scotland (ACTS)

9.1   The Central Council initiated a major Review of the life of ACTS at a special meeting called for the purpose in February 2001. A review process, 'Discerning the Future for ACTS' was established to reflect on what the Churches had learnt in the first decade of being 'churches together' in Scotland and, in the light of the changes in the ecumenical landscape since ACTS' inception in 1990, to identify the most appropriate way ahead. The Central Council was conscious of the new impetus which would be given to the churches' common engagement by the Scottish Ecumenical Assembly. Three Working Groups were set up. One on staffing has had to wait until current matters relating to staff have been resolved. A second was set up to look at the future of Scottish Churches House. This Working Group has reported to the Central Council and more work has been asked for before the churches can take any decisions. A third looked at the structures and ethos of ACTS. It was decided that the groups would themselves be established on a 'churches together' model. This third presented a major report to the June meeting of the Central Council. The report strongly reaffirmed the 'churches together' model while acknowledging that it has taken time for the churches to grow in awareness of its demands, and brought forward proposals for a lighter, more dynamic structure for ACTS itself. With minor amendments it was sent out to churches for their reactions.

9.1.1 The Committee on Ecumenical Relations discussed the proposals and was happy to see the process move forward along the lines suggested, though it did register some concern, particularly in the area of how ACTS relates to civic institutions and whether it can have a representative role, something not touched on in the review report. The points raised were to be taken up again by the Working Group early in 2002. The report, which was circulated to the Churches, is in **Appendix IV**. The Working Group is currently working on the fine detail of how the new structure will work in the light of the comments received from the Churches.

9.1.2 The restatement of the Churches Together Principle that:

- churches would take decisions, not a council separate from the churches
- statements would be made by the churches, not by a council
- more people would be involved who would have authority from their churches and access to the relevant communication channels to ensure that information was shared with the right people

and the renewed pattern to the work of ACTS presents us with a new opportunity to reaffirm our commitment to work, wherever possible, with the Lund Principle: 'whether they (i.e. the churches) should not act together in all matters except those in which deep difference of conviction compel them to act separately.'

9.1.3 The Committee on Ecumenical Relations commends the new structure to the Assembly. It is intended that the new Scottish Churches Forum will replace the Central Council. Together with the 4 Networks (made up of trustee and associate members – Church Life, Faith Studies, Church & Society, and Mission – to replace the three commissions) it is envisaged that the new structure will come into existence from January 2003 once the full complement of ACTS staff is clear. The Committee has therefore brought to the General Assembly nominations for the Churches' Forum and their alternates. (Appendix II) The Committee is keen to stress that the four people and their alternates should form a group who will meet before each meeting of the Forum. In this way, those who attend the Forum will do so with a broader spectrum of Church of Scotland thinking. In determining the categories of people involved, the Committee gave consideration to continuity with the current Central Council, particular remits within the Church of Scotland's Boards and Committees, which allow a general overview of its life and work, and individual expertise, which would be valuable in a bidding process.

9.1.4 Membership of Networks will be sought in consultation with particular Boards and Committees according to the remit of each Network. The Committee on Ecumenical Relations wishes to reaffirm that the success of the work of the Networks will depend on the appointment of key people and an agenda that is relevant to their areas of work. It is hoped very much that the use of task groups will help to make the working together of the churches more manageable for people with already heavy agendas.

9.2 The Local and Regional Unity Committee of ACTS was asked to look at how Local Ecumenical Partnerships (LEPs) could be better supported and encouraged. It gathered representatives of the member Churches of ACTS and other interested churches to explore the idea of setting up a **national sponsoring body**. It had become apparent that, although there are comparatively few LEPs in Scotland, the number that require sponsoring or advisory bodies is such that the Churches are finding it difficult to supply the number of people required. The Committee on Local and Regional Unity also invited representatives of LEPs to a consultation where the idea could be explored with them. The result of each of the consultations was a positive response.

9.2.1 From the point of view of the denominations, a national sponsoring body would act as an enabling group, which is both supportive and advisory. It will involve key representatives of the churches in a way that signals to those involved in LEPs that their pioneering work is valued. It also offers a necessary forum for smoothing out problems that can arise when different denominations have different expectations of congregations involved in LEPs and to do this in a way that does not put an unnecessary burden on the local people. The national sponsoring body would have, as its primary task, the drawing up of agreed guidelines for those seeking to deepen ecumenical relations in local areas. At present, there is no consistency of advice and no agreed models for those congregations who wish to unite across denominational boundaries. The emphasis is on support and encouragement, ensuring accountability to parent denominations and ownership by parent denominations. It is the intention that within the guidelines each LEP will be able to develop its own distinctive character according to its own particular needs.

9.2.2 From the point of view of the LEPs there is the possibility of being brought into a network of others who are also exploring exciting ways of being the Church and who can so often feel rather isolated. Experience has shown us that those who work in LEPs are greatly encouraged both by the interest of an advisory or sponsoring body and by opportunities for sharing with others in similar but distinctive initiatives elsewhere in the country.

9.2.3 The proposal is ambitious but the Committee on Ecumenical Relations supports its implementation should it find approval among the member Churches of ACTS, believing that this will provide a positive way forward in an area of the Church's life that has been steadily expanding over recent years. The body will come under the auspices of ACTS, but will appeal to churches that are outside membership of ACTS.

10. Churches Together in Britain and Ireland (CTBI)

10.1 CTBI continues to bring together representatives from the four nations and the two jurisdictions in these islands in the areas of international affairs, church and society and church life. Three CTBI Commissions continue to do likewise in the fields of Mission, Inter Faith Relations and Racial Justice. All three Commissions have sought ways of strengthening the four-nation profile of their work. The Boards of National Mission and World Mission have been working with the Churches Commission on Mission. The Committee on Church and Nation has been working with the Churches Commission on Racial Justice and the Scottish Churches Agency for Racial Justice for a renewed relationship between the two bodies. The Committee on Ecumenical Relations has been working with the Churches Commission on Inter Faith Relations and the Churches Agency for Interfaith Relations in Scotland (CAIRS) (see par. 15.3 below)

10.2 Four Church of Scotland representatives attended a consultation planned by the Church Life Liaison Group to look at **ecumenical methodology**. This provided an opportunity to take a look at various methods being used throughout Britain and Ireland to bring churches institutionally closer together. The request for such a consultation had come from the last CTBI Assembly in 1999. Contributions came from those engaged in formal and informal discussions and also from those who are not, as matter of principle, engaged in any talks e.g. the Salvation Army and the Religious Society of Friends. There were significant differences of approach between the four nations, many, if not all, due to our different histories. Dr Turid Karlson Seim from Norway, Vice Moderator of the World Council of Churches Faith & Order Commission gave a keynote address towards the end of the consultation. Summing up at the end of the consultation, Bishop Barry Rogerson from Bristol asked that we remember to hold certain things together:

- Discussion and action about the Unity of the Church and the Nature and Purpose of the Church as an open and welcoming community
- The Unity of the Church and the Renewal of Human Community

- Unity and Mission
- Unity and Social Action
- Training together for clergy and lay people
- Administration and financing
- Revising Liturgy together
- To develop the Diaconate together and to consider together the place of Elders and to do both by revisiting Scripture and allowing new guides to lead us.

The papers from this Consultation in Woodbrooke Quaker Centre, Birmingham, are to be made more widely available among the Churches.

10.3 Preparations were also made for the **CTBI Assembly** held at the end of February 2002 with the theme *In Search of Common Ground*. The Ecumenical Relations Committee sought to ensure that alternates were appointed for those who in the end could not attend. It also made arrangements for the representatives to gather for a briefing session prior to the Assembly. This allowed as many as possible to have knowledge of the variety of things that are happening throughout the Church of Scotland as local churches seek to find the common ground between the Church and those who are seeking spiritual nourishment in different ways and different places.

11. Conference of European Churches (CEC)

11.1 In April 2001 the Conference of European Churches and the Council of European Bishops' Conferences (CCEE) held an Ecumenical

> **Ecumenical encounter in Strasbourg:-**
>
> **200 church 'leaders' met with 200 young people**

Encounter in Strasbourg:- 200 hundred 'Church leaders' met with 200 young people. In the course of the Encounter the *Charta Oecumenica* was adopted and signed by the Presidents of the two Church bodies. The *Charta* was then distributed to all member churches. It provides 'Guidelines for the Growing Co-operation among the churches in Europe' and is specifically to be adapted in ways appropriate to each part of Europe. It is designed to promote an ecumenical culture of dialogue and co-operation at all levels of church life, and to provide agreed criteria for this. It is a tool for ecumenical good practice. In many ways much of what is contained in the *Charta* is already accepted ecumenical practice in Britain and Ireland. However, there are some issues, perhaps those relating to the role of majority churches in relation to minority churches, that might be a touching place for the Church of Scotland. The Ecumenical Relations Committee set up a small group to consider the document in the Church of Scotland context and to feed into an ecumenical discussion within ACTS. The text of the Charta Oecumenica is printed in **Appendix V**. Local churches together groups are encouraged to use it and adapt it for use in their area.

11.2 The next CEC Assembly is to be held in Trondheim, Norway in 2003. Invitations have been received and the Committee on Ecumenical Relations has nominated four people to attend. The theme is *'Jesus Christ heals and reconciles – our witness in Europe.*

12. Leuenberg Fellowship of Churches

The Leuenberg Fellowship of Churches held its General Assembly in Belfast in June 2001. A report on Law and Gospel has been sent to the member churches for comment prior to a final document being produced. The completed texts of two other studies, *Church & Israel* and *Church-People-State-Nation* were adopted by the Assembly. These were passed to the Board of World Mission and the Committee on Church and Nation for them to note.

12.2 In addition, the General Assembly approved two further areas for doctrinal discussion – *the Form and Shape of the Protestant Churches in a Changing Europe* and *The Missionary Task of the Churches in Europe*. With reference to the latter, the task is to reflect on what role the churches of the Leuenberg Church Fellowship might assume within this common task.

12.3 On the basis of the fellowship in word and sacrament which has already been achieved in some

European countries between the Anglican, the Lutheran and the Reformed churches (Porvoo, Meissen, Reuilly), the General Assembly of the Leuenberg Church Fellowship has requested dialogue to be held between the Leuenberg Church Fellowship and the Anglican Communion at European level.

13. The World Alliance of Reformed Churches (WARC)

13.1   **The European Area Council** is to be held in Oradea, Romania in August 2002. The overall theme is *Fullness of life: Global Vision-Local Action*. This links with the theme adopted for the 2004 General Council in Ghana *That all may have life in fullness*. Sub themes will look at the relation of majority to minority churches, coping with the past and covenanting for justice.

13.2   **Covenanting for Justice in the Economy and on the Earth.**
WARC, with the co-operation of other world ecumenical bodies, has been engaged in a series of consultations around the world on economic justice. In 2001 there was a meeting in Budapest for eastern and central European churches. In June 2002 in the Netherlands there is to be a consultation for the churches in western Europe. By the time of the General Council in Ghana in 2004 WARC hopes that all churches will be able to brief their delegates on whether or not a stance should be taken on the grounds of faith against the injustice done to the poor through global economics and environmental damage. The basis for such a stance would be the Christian belief in God as creator and the responsibility given to human beings for stewardship of the creation. The Committee on Ecumenical Relations is working with the Committee on Church and Nation and the Board of World Mission on this issue. It is hoped that the Church of Scotland will be represented at the consultation in the Netherlands.

> *...acting together churches and aid gencies can influence government policies...*

13.3   Already names are brought to the Assembly for the **2004 General Council** in Ghana. WARC has asked for early nominations so that there can be a process of preparation involving member churches and their delegates.

13.4   WARC published two reports of international theological dialogues in 2001. The first is the Report of the Theological Dialogue between the Oriental Orthodox Family of Churches and the World Alliance of Reformed Churches (1993-2001). Rev Peter McEnhill represented the Church of Scotland on this dialogue. It covered the following areas: An Agreed Statement on Christology, Convergences and Divergences on Tradition and Holy Scripture, Theology, Church and Mission, Priesthood/Ministry and Sacraments. The seven sessions of the dialogue represent the first time these two traditions have engaged in dialogue with each other. They are seen only as a beginning. The hope now is for the document to be studied by the member churches of WARC.

13.4.1 The second report is the Final Report of the International Dialogue between Representatives of the World Alliance of Reformed Churches and Some Classical Pentecostal Churches and Leaders (1996-2000). This was the first time these traditions had been in dialogue. The report is entitled *Word and Spirit, Church and World*. It has as its main focus the person, doctrine and experience of the Holy Spirit. It deals successively with the Spirit and the Word of God, the Spirit and the Church, the Spirit and Mission and the Spirit and the Kingdom of God. It addresses significant contemporary pastoral issues such as the presence of the Holy Spirit in human history, in various cultures, the importance of the healing of the sick, of the gift of tongues and of other gifts of the Spirit in the life of Christian churches today. Again, the hope is that this report will be studied by the member churches of WARC.

13.4.2 The dialogue between the World Alliance and the Orthodox Church continued to make progress. It is anticipated that there will be one further meeting in September 2002 in Romania at which the fruits of this discussion will be drawn together in a final report.

14. The World Council of Churches (WCC)

14.1 The past year the WCC has set up the Advocacy Alliance. Two specific topics have been chosen by member churches – HIV/AIDS and globalisation. The Boards of Social Responsibility and World Mission and the Committee on Church and Nation have expressed an on-going interest in these issues – Social Responsibility and World Mission for HIV/AIDS and World Mission and Church and Nation for globalisation. The hope is that by acting together churches and aid agencies can influence government policies following the example of the effective campaign on debt relief by Jubilee 2000.

14.2 The WCC's Decade to Overcome Violence continued to provide a perspective and framework within which to develop thinking on appropriate issues, primarily with the Church and Nation Committee in the lead. There was a disappointing response to an invitation to a meeting in Edinburgh in October with Professor Ioan Sauca, the Director of the WCC's residential educational centre, the Bossey Institute in Switzerland; but those present had a lively and worthwhile discussion. It was clear that there was considerable scope for promoting within Scotland the valuable opportunities available at Bossey a range of theological and biblical courses within an international ecumenical community. Plans are being made for an ecumenical group, including staff from several Church of Scotland departments, to visit the Ecumenical Centre at Geneva in November to strengthen the working links with the WCC and exchange up-to-date information on matters of common interest.

14.3 In the aftermath of September 11th, the WCC has provided information on statements from churches, agencies, other faith communities and governments. This has given a helpful picture of solidarity and has highlighted areas of tension.

15. The Inter Faith Forum

15.1 The Ecumenical Relations Committee continues to host an interdepartmental forum for inter faith relations. Following September 11th, when it became apparent that there was a wave of anti-Islamic feeling in this country, letters of solidarity were written to the chairmen of the Glasgow and Edinburgh Central Mosques.

15.2 Inter Faith Story Telling Project

The Forum gathered sufficient funds to run a three-month pilot study. Rev Linda Bandelier, a Methodist minister and professional storyteller, undertook to gather stories from local people about their perceptions of people of other faith communities. She was also able to get one story from someone of another faith community of his experience of the Christian community. Linda put together a short presentation. It is clear from the information already gathered that there is scope for a full project, using a wider cross section of stories and including the voices of children as well as adults. Unfortunately, the Forum has not succeeded in securing funding for this year long project. The Forum is clear that the end product would be for use in local churches and is essentially a look at how Christians relate to people of other faiths.

15.3 Churches Agency for Inter-faith Relations in Scotland (CAIRS)

15.3.1 Negotiations took place between CAIRS and the Churches Commission for Inter Faith Relations (CCIFR), the CTBI Commission. It has been agreed that the two bodies will work more closely. While CAIRS will keep its Scottish focus, funding from the churches in Scotland will go direct to CCIFR. CAIRS will set a budget for its work each year and will bid for funding from CCIFR for particular projects. The effect, it is hoped, will be a clearer four-nation dimension to the work of CCIFR while being able to continue developing experience within the Scottish context through CAIRS. The funding churches from Scotland will make one payment and will no longer in effect pay twice for Scottish work.

15.3.2 The CAIRS Committee has continued to organise a **Christology Conference** to be held in June 2002. The Conference is to be held in Pollock Halls, in Edinburgh. The keynote speakers are to be Dr Clark Pinnock, Prof Perry Schmidt-Leukel, Dr Helen Bond and Dr Edward Kessler. Between them they will look at two of the 'difficult texts' – John 14.6 and Acts 4.12.

15.4 The Scottish Inter Faith Council. The Church of Scotland continues to be represented by the Convener of Ecumenical Relations on the Scottish Inter Faith Council. In the course of last year the Inter Faith Council met with the First Minister to discuss matters of common concern to the faith communities.

15.5 Council for a World Parliament of Religions, Scotland

The Church of Scotland was approached along with other Churches in Scotland to support a bid from Scotland to bring the Council for a World Parliament of Religions to Scotland in 2005. The Committee on Ecumenical Relations gave this serious consideration and kept in close touch with representatives from the other churches through CAIRS. The Committee is currently unconvinced that a major gathering in two cities would give the kind of sensitive support and encouragement required but will continue to monitor the situation.

15.6 An Inter Faith Adviser

The Inter Faith Forum is pursuing the possibility of the Church of Scotland appointing an inter faith adviser. The need for such an adviser is growing as more and more ministers and kirk sessions are exploring how best to maintain a presence in areas where the Christian population is becoming a minority. There is need for networking and sharing of ideas among those who sometimes feel isolated. If anything, the events of September 11th have increased our awareness of the need to pay more attention to inter faith relations and to deepening our understanding of each other across the faith boundaries. This is a developing work and, in this regard, the Church of Scotland lags behind most of the major churches in the UK.

16. Conclusion

The Committee was saddened by the death of Rev David Anderson last November. David had been a faithful member of the Committee despite his heavy commitments as the General Secretary of the Evangelical Alliance in Scotland. His incisive mind, his quick sense

of humour and his interest in the deepening of relations between Christians across the denominational spectrum while holding fast to his Presbyterian heritage made him a valued member of our Committee and of the SCIFU Reflection Panel. He will continue to be missed by all who worked with him and the sympathy and prayers of the Committee remain with his family.

In the name of the Committee

THOMAS MACINTYRE, *Convener*
CHRISTINE TAIT, *Vice-Convener*
SHEILAGH M KESTING, *Secretary*

ADDENDUM

Rev Thomas Macintyre retires as Convener of Ecumenical Relations. Under his leadership the Committee has continued to develop its work, not least in the field of communication and publication. His own personal commitment and enthusiasm for the work of the Committee was infectious and fed his desire to ensure that the work of the Committee was well publicised and that local stories were shared for the benefit and inspiration of others. As Convener, he built good relations between the Committee and its Presbytery and Presbyterial Council contacts as well as at national level between the Church of Scotland and our sister churches in Scotland and beyond. The Committee records its gratitude for the way he encouraged them in their work and for the inspiration he brought from his own personal experience.

In the name of the Committee

CHRISTINE TAIT, *Vice-Convener*
SHEILAGH M KESTING, *Secretary*

GLOSSARY OF TERMS

ACTS Action of Churches Together in Scotland
CAIRS Churches Agency for Interfaith Relations in Scotland (Agency of ACTS)
CCEE Council of European Bishops Conferences
CCIFR Churches Commission on Inter-faith Relations (CTBI Commission)
CEC Conference of European Churches
CMEE Commission on Mission, Evangelism and Education (ACTS Commission)
CTBI Churches Together in Britain and Ireland
LEPs Local Ecumenical Partnerships
NEWS Network of Ecumenical Women in Scotland
SCARJ Scottish Churches Agency for Racial Justice (Agency of ACTS)
SCIAF Scottish Catholic International Aid Fund
SCIFU Scottish Church Initiative for Union
WARC World Alliance of Reformed Churches
WCC World Council of Churches

APPENDIX I

DELEGATES TO OTHER CHURCHES

The following have been appointed as delegates to the Assemblies, Synods and or Conferences of other Churches:-

Presbyterian Church in Ireland – The Moderator, Chaplain and Elder
Presbyterian Church of Wales – The Moderator
United Reformed Church – The Moderator, Mrs C Tait
Church of England – Rev. H Davidson
United Reformed Church Scotland Synod – Rev. D Nicol
Scottish Episcopal Church – Rev. T Macintyre
Methodist Synod – Rev. E Cramb
United Free Church of Scotland – Rev. R Mitchell
Baptist Union of Scotland – Mrs H McLeod

APPENDIX II

ECUMENICAL BODIES

The following serve on assemblies and Committees of the ecumenical bodies of which the Church is a member:-

World Council of Churches
Eighth Assembly (September 1998)
    Rev. G Elliot, Rev. N Shanks, Mrs C Tait, Mrs V Ott, Rev. Dr R Page
Central Committee
    Rev. N Shanks
Faith and Order Commission
    Rev. Dr P H Donald

World Alliance of Reformed Churches
24th General Council (July 2004)
    Mrs S Brown, Rev. W Brown, Dr F Burnett, Rev. A G Horsburgh, Miss C Whiteford
European Area Council
    Mrs S Foote, Rev. A G Horsburgh

Conference of European Churches
12th Assembly (June 2003)
    Dr A Elliot, Rev. G Maclean, Rev. D Nicol, Miss M Ross
Central Committee
    Dr A Elliot
Church and Society Commission
    Dr A Elliot

Churches Together in Britain and Ireland
Assembly
    Miss F Brooker, Rev. D Brown, Rev. W Brown, Miss S Brown, Rev. E Cranfield, Rev. M Cuthbertson, Dr A Elliot, Mrs K Galloway, Mrs M Gordon, Mrs F S Gordon, Mrs E Kerr, Rev. T Macintyre, Rev. M MacLean, Rev. G Maclean, Miss J Martin, Mrs H McLeod, Rev. M Millar, Rev. A Newell, Rev. D Nicol, Rev. K Petrie, Rev. J Purves, Rev. M Scott, Rev. D Shaw, Mrs A Twaddle, Mrs J Young
Church Representatives Meeting
    Mrs H McLeod, Rev. S M Kesting, Rev. Dr F A J Macdonald
Steering Committee
    Rev. S M Kesting

Action of Churches Together in Scotland

Scottish Churches' Forum

Convener of the Committee on Ecumenical Relations (alternate: representative from the Guild), Convener of the Assembly Council (alternate: representative from the Board of Practice and Procedure), General Secretary of the Board of National Mission (alternate: Secretary of the Committee on Church and Nation), Secretary of the Committee on Ecumenical Relations (alternate: General Secretary Board of Ministry)

Central Council

Rev. W Brown, Dr A Elliot (Vice-Convener), Miss H Hughes, Rev. S M Kesting, Rev. Dr F A J Macdonald, Rev. T Macintyre, Rev. G Maclean, Rev. F Marshall, Rev. S Mitchell, Rev. D A O Nicol, Rev. D Shaw, Mrs P Stewart, Mrs A Twaddle

Commission on Unity, Faith and Order

Rev. Dr P H Donald, Rev. D Galbraith
Rev. M MacLean, Mrs E Templeton, (vacancy)

Commission on Mission, Evangelism and Education

Rev J H Brown, Mrs E Cranfield, Rev. A Greig,
Rev C Sinclair, Mr I Whyte,

Commission on Justice, Peace, Social and Moral Issues

Rev. Y Atkins, Miss M Donaldson,
Rev. E Cramb, Rev. A McDonald,
Rev. Dr D Sinclair

Committee on Communication

Mr R J Williamson

Committee on Local and Regional Unity

Miss M Cameron, Mrs N Summers

Network of Ecumenical Women in Scotland

Rev. V Allen, Mrs E McVie

Committee on Scottish Churches House

Rev. A A Moore

Youth Action

Mr A Adam

Churches Commission on Mission

Mrs F Campbell, Rev. E Cranfield, Very Rev Prof A Main, Rev. K L Petrie, Rev. D A O Nicol, Rev. Prof. K Ross

Joint Liturgical Group

The Very Rev. G I Macmillan, Rev. D Galbraith

APPENDIX III

STATEMENTS FROM THE SCOTTISH ECUMENICAL ASSEMBLY

GROUP 1 – POVERTY

Here in Edinburgh on 23 September 2001, we, the first Scottish Ecumenical Assembly, commend to the Churches and the Nation the following statements:

1. The Church recognises that to "break out of" poverty, we should first repent and put our own house in order by:

 • acknowledging that individually and corporately we share in Society's addiction to wealth. Poverty becomes an inevitable consequence, a symptom of a deeper malaise;

 • acknowledging our personal and collective responsibility for the misuse of the abundance of God's creation;

 • redistributing Churches' resources long term to address the needs expressed in poorer areas;

 • giving people in poor churches a key role in the decision-making of the Church;

 • reviewing Church practice in light of our commitment to social inclusion;

 • personal commitment to change lifestyles;

 • encouraging local parishes and congregations to co-operate in surveying and targeting the true needs of their communities;

 • changing hearts and minds via an educational programme that converts the Church to engage in issues around poverty;

2. Recognising the new opportunities for contributing to public policy in Scotland, and the shared commitment of the Church and our political leaders to deliver social justice, we call upon HM Government, the Scottish Executive and all public authorities in Scotland, in partnership with people experiencing poverty, urgently to:

 • move the emphasis from indirect to progressive, **direct taxation** to achieve a fairer distribution of resources;

- promote and monitor practical policies to deliver **equality** in health, education and the public services;
- **empower** communities in areas of urban and rural deprivation to eradicate poverty of opportunity, hope and aspiration by allocating adequate resources directly to them;
- establish a Royal Commission to review with the utmost speed the benefits system in order to **ensure** that those on benefit have the resources to live in dignity;

3. We call on the Churches to campaign along the lines of the Jubilee 2000 model for income re-distribution and we challenge people to play their part in narrowing the income gap

4. We recognise that global and domestic poverty are intimately linked. As Churches, we learn from our partners the realities of World poverty and we are together committed to the remission of debt and the establishment of fairer economic relations. We can and must unmask and confront the structures of debt and global inequality. We call on all people to reflect on how far they contribute to the impoverishment of other people, their communities, other nations and the created World.

GROUP 2 – ENLIGHTENMENT

1. We affirm the need to identify and remove all that diminishes human potential and to challenge the dominant economic, social and environmental models in the light of the sanctity of human life and the love and wisdom of God.

2. We should explore anew what it means and what it costs to be communities of teaching, learning and enquiry, committed to integrated, balanced, life-long development of the whole person (in body, mind, emotions and spirit), enabling and empowering all for life, action and service.

3. Celebrating the interdependence of church and society, we commit ourselves to recognise, support and work in partnership with all who nurture fullness of life and work for the common good; including those who work through families, places and agencies of education and communities of faith.

At the start of the World Council of Churches' "Decade to Overcome Violence", we commit ourselves to the renewal of our appropriate use of language and imagery for God, from the depths of our traditions, by reshaping the language to that which better expresses the love, wisdom, and humour of God.

4. We commit ourselves to the more effective promotion and nurture of Christian values, an active and serving citizenship and inclusive social policies.

We will constantly pursue more effective ways to participate in the worlds of politics, media, information technology, arts and culture, industry and other spheres of public life. The church should commit itself to work on the renewal of its language and imagery in dialogue with contemporary culture.

5. We strongly affirm the uniqueness of each person and the need to include differently-abled people and their perspectives in our church communities of teaching, learning and enquiry, recognising that we are diminished without their contribution.

GROUP 3 – ALIENATION

Here in Edinburgh on 23rd September 2001, we, the first Scottish Ecumenical Assembly, commend to the Churches and the Nation the following statements:

We call upon the Churches

1. to stand in solidarity with our sisters and brothers of all faiths, races and cultures particularly when they face harassment, threats, intimidation and violence.

2. to commit ourselves to learning and working more alongside people of other faiths and cultures.

We invite those of all faiths and cultures to join with us in this dialogue towards increased understanding of one another and of our joint responsibility for the welfare of our multi-faith and multi-cultural society.

Racism

We in the Churches acknowledge our past and present share of responsibility for racism – in, for example, our historic links with colonialism and our failures to welcome the presence and the gifts of those who come to our shores.

We give thanks for those who work to overcome all forms of racism and to promote respect, mutual recognition and justice both within and outwith the Church. We the Churches should continue to work together towards the elimination of racism and other forms of discrimination in our society.

We call on all Church members to challenge racist policies, language and actions as and when they occur.

Migration and Asylum

Migration is an historical fact of human existence which can enrich community and promote economic well-being. Barriers which have been erected to the movement of people around the world have caused unnecessary suffering and hardship. Many of these barriers have been overtly or covertly based on race and colour and as such are unacceptable to the basic tenets of the Christian faith. Furthermore, those who seek safety among us are entitled to asylum by international treaty and common humanity.

We call for the replacement of the present system for asylum seekers which humiliates and devalues people who seek refuge in the United Kingdom with a system which recognises and fulfills the UK's commitments under United Nations conventions. In addition to calling for these changes, the Churches should work to provide appropriate arrangements at a local level for those in need.

Generous welcome and hospitality ought to be the mark of our dealings with those who come as strangers.

Sectarianism

Churches in Scotland acknowledge that we have our own problems with alienation. This is evidenced by the sectarian divide. We hope that this is diminishing, but we know how much we have contributed to it in the past.

Churches and church members have a responsibility to overcome hatred and division and to emphasise commonality while respecting diversity;

Challenging Alienation

Alienation in our society comes in many forms. We therefore call on all church members, beginning with ourselves, to challenge alienating policies, language and actions, and for forms of Church life which:

- are relevant to the community in which they are set;
- promote inclusiveness through education, information and example;
- acknowledge and celebrate the expression of different identities;
- affirm the right of each person to realise the image of God within their lives;
- develop ways to live alongside those who differ from us;
- proclaim the oneness of humanity;
- establish contacts with all faiths and cultures at local level.

GROUP 4 – WORK

Breaking into a New Understanding of Work

Here in Edinburgh on 23 September 2001, we the first Scottish Ecumenical Assembly, commend to the Churches and the Nation the following statements

1. That together we recognise that:

   - Work is part of God's purpose for the human race whereby we exercise responsibility for and benefit from the earth's resources for the good of all.
   - Work is meant to be an expression of worship
   - God is with us in a creative partnership wherever we work
   - Work impacts on the whole of God's creation
   - Work is essential to the world in which we live
   - While at the level of the individual the worker can give dignity to the work we know too that at the level of structures work can be demeaning.
   - Work may be paid or unpaid, based at home, in the community or workplace

2. We ask that the churches together express the regret that they have not given the proper attention to or fully engaged in where people work. We have to

improve our empathy and service to people who are in work and those people who are not in work.

- When we witness to work as an opportunity for companionship we know too that work can also be a place of exclusion.
- When we witness to work as creative we know too that it can be destructive
- When we witness to work as made for people we know too that people are not made for work

3. We ask that the Churches together take action to:

- commend those who have implemented sound ethical working practices
- commend the work of Industrial Chaplains and encourage a new vision for others to be "chaplains" in the workplace.
- raise awareness about the negative impact of consumerism and the benefits of ethical management, globally, organisationally and individually.
- move towards best practice in all of its dealings with those who give of their time and talents in the service of the Church.
- urge others to take up and continually develop good practice particularly in relation to work and life balance.
- encourage and support Christians to exercise their ministry in the workplace, that through their actions they will demonstrate Christian ethics and values
- explore the challenges of a future in which money, status and satisfaction may need to be derived from sources other than paid employment
- further develop support networks for those under stress either in the workplace or through redundancy or through unemployment
- Share information about workplace issues

GROUP 5 – SPIRITUALITY

We give thanks for the ecumenical journey and prayer that has given us this new opportunity to listen to one another and share God's gifts of diversity and unity in Christ in the power of the Holy Spirit.

We recommit ourselves to deepen and widen our journey and prayer together by listening to God:

in each other,
in our own church traditions
in other faiths,
in the world,
in day to day living and
in the desire for peace and justice.

To this end, we encourage the peoples of the church to continue to pray together and ask the churches to support this by building up an ecumenical prayer network across Scotland.

We also re-affirm the Lund Principle, urging that we do nothing separately, which can, in conscience, be done together.

We challenge our churches to reduce resources used separately and so increase the resources, people and finance, used for common purposes.

GROUP 6 – SCIENCE AND TECHNOLOGY

Science and faith need have nothing to fear from each other. Both seek to deal with issues of truth and external reality. Both are on journeys of discovery and can complement each other. There is a need for mutual education of Scientists and Theologians.

We ask churches, universities and schools to respond to the need for education on issues in science, technology and theology.

Science and technology do not operate in a moral vacuum. Church and Scientific communities are urged to promote discussion at every level on the ethical issues arising, such as in genetic modification, cloning, climate change and information technology.

We recognise the Society, Religion and Technology Project as a model which provides an effective forum for addressing these issues, and for formulating criteria for moral decision making. Its remit and range of topics could be extended and its profile raised in both church and community.

We encourage a wider ecumenical involvement in the Society Religion and Technology Project through Action of Churches Together in Scotland (ACTS).

We are concerned at the trend towards the privatisation of scientific knowledge. We encourage the practice and development of free and unencumbered access to the results of scientific research. The Human Genome Project is a good model of this practice.

There is deep concern over the use of patents to secure disproportionate private gain from discoveries that should be to the benefit of humanity and the rest of creation.

We urge the Scottish Executive and Her Majesty's Government to take more account in the priorities for science & technology of the needs of the vulnerable and socially excluded and of developing countries.

We support International initiatives to enable affordable access to pharmaceuticals in the Third World to address such major issues as HIV/AIDS, malaria and tuberculosis.

SRT website www.srtp.org.uk

GROUP 7 – CHURCH

Let the power of God work through the people of God

We call the Church to be confident – to believe in the distinctiveness of its message about the person, life and teaching of Jesus to all people in Scotland today.

Therefore, we commit ourselves afresh to listen together for the truth of the Gospel and to live it.

Let the love of Christ be our strength

We call the Church to be compassionate - to live out its faith in the suffering and risen Christ, through working together in the joys and sorrows of our world.

Therefore we commit ourselves

* *to form local groups in which people of all faiths and none can share vulnerability and hope,*
* *and to strive for justice and peace in a fearful world.*

Let the Holy Spirit renew us

We call the Church to be creative – to recognise the Spirit active in the lives of people, and to model a culture of faithful community, overcoming divisions, in and for the wider world.

Therefore we commit ourselves to develop a variety of imaginative ways of

making the Church accessible,
nurturing those within it,
and reaching out beyond it,
so that people can discover faith and share it.

APPENDIX IV

ACTS Review 2001
Proposals for a Renewed ACTS

I   Summary

1.   Introduction

The ACTS Central Council at its meeting on 7–8 February 2001 reviewed the working of ACTS. Both the strengths and the weaknesses of ACTS since its inception in 1990 were identified. The review provided the opportunity to re-think ACTS, to reconsider the 'churches together' model of ecumenism and, if necessary, suggest another model for the twenty first century. The Central Council set up three working groups to take forward the thinking begun at the meeting. Working Group 3, sometimes known as 'the ethos group', brought its report to the meeting of Central Council on 23rd June 2001. The Central Council warmly welcomed the report as an important step in the recovery of the vision which had led to the creation of ACTS.

2.   Brief

2.1   The third Working Group was asked to look at the work, ethos, staffing requirements and location of ACTS. In the light of 'Churches Together in Pilgrimage' (BCC 1989) usually referred to as 'the Marigold Book' and subsequent experience it was to look at:

* The role of the Central Council
* The existing model of commissions and committees
* The role of the Executive

2.2 It was to draw out the implications of its recommendations for staffing and the location of the ACTS office.

2.3 Because of circumstances beyond its control, the Working Group has not been able at this stage to look at the staffing implications to which it will return in due course.

2.4 As with all the working groups it was expected that there would be appropriate consultation and, if required, the use of outside consultancy.

3. Summary of findings

3.1 The 'churches together' model has not been properly tried because of a tendency of the churches still to think of a 'council of churches' model. The 'churches together' model was an imaginative one for the 1990s. It was to mean:

- churches would take decisions, not a council separate from the churches
- statements would be made by the churches, not by a council
- more people would be involved who would have authority from their churches and access to the relevant communication channels to ensure that information was shared with the right people.

As a result

- work would be slower to ensure the greatest degree of consultation and consensus between the churches
- ACTS as a body should be almost invisible, as it creates the necessary space for the churches to consult and to work together. It is not ACTS that does the work. Rather ACTS enables the churches to work together.

3.2 Because this shift of emphasis has not always been adequately grasped, some churches feel excluded. Some feel that the particular mode of working in ACTS does not take into account their particular ecclesiology. Decisions are taken without the envisaged consultation and consensus. Others, particularly from the smaller churches, feel that the way has not opened up for them as they hoped to allow them to participate in issues that on their own they cannot do.

3.3 Poor attendance at ACTS Commissions and Committees, makes continuity and development of work difficult and raises the question of whether the churches are really committed to one another through ACTS.

3.4 Two-way communication between the churches and the commissions and committees is poor which raises questions of accountability.

3.5 The relation of the associate members of ACTS requires examination to ensure that the churches benefit from the knowledge and expertise of the associate members in a way that allows the authority for ACTS work to remain with the churches.

3.6 There is a serious gap between local ecumenism and national ecumenism, flowing from the dynamic within as well as between the churches.

3.7 People with already full diaries will be more likely to give of their time and energy for specific, focused, time-limited pieces of work.

4. Key recommendations

It is recommended:

i) **that the churches need to recommit themselves to work with one another as Churches Together**

ii) **that there be two categories of membership – Trustee Membership and Associate Membership**

    a) **Trustee Membership to describe those churches that originally convenanted together and other churches that subscribe to the Aims and Basis of ACTS.**

    b) **Associate Membership to cover three categories: churches that are not trustee members though eligible, bodies in association and a new category of ecumenical agency.**

    c) **The new category of ecumenical agency to include NEWS and Youth Action.**

iii) **that ACTS be restructured with**

    a) **a smaller Scottish Churches' Forum made up of trustee members**

    b) **four networks made up of trustee and associate members – Church Life, Faith Studies, Church & Society, and Mission – to replace the three commissions**

    c) **three standing committees – Scottish churches House (retained), Finance (retained) and Personnel (newly established).**

iv) **that a new pattern of working be established using bidding, setting priorities and review**

v) **that ACTS staff remain located at Scottish Churches House.**

II   The Purpose of ACTS

5.   Purpose

The 'Marigold Book' stated that the purpose of ACTS is

"to further the mission and realise the unity of the Church universal by providing a national focus for Inter-Church counsel and action". (page 49)

6.   Basis and Commitment

The Basis and Commitment of ACTS were also set out in the 'Marigold Book'.

"Action of Churches Together in Scotland (ACTS) unites in pilgrimage those churches in Scotland which, acknowledge God's revelation in Christ, confess the Lord Jesus Christ as God and Saviour according to the Scriptures and in obedience to God's will and in the power of the Holy Spirit, commit themselves

to seek a deepening of their communion with Christ and with one another in the Church, which is His Body, and

to fulfil their mission to proclaim the Gospel by common witness and service in the world

to the Glory of the One God, Father, Son and Holy Spirit."

III   Introduction and Background

7.   The ACTS Review

7.1   ACTS underwent a review in 1995. This review made no structural readjustment to ACTS, nor did it affect the way in which the churches sought to work together in ACTS. It did, however state that another review should take place after five years.

7.2   As a setting for the current review the General Secretary brought a paper to the October 2000 meeting of the Central Council, 'Discerning the Future for ACTS'. In it he reflected on the ecumenical landscape and raised questions about location, structures and staffing requirements. In the light of this, the Central Council agreed to meet for a special overnight meeting in February 2001 for the sole purpose of reflecting on the nature, purpose and shape of ACTS. A reflection group was set up to plan the meeting. This group included those who had no working knowledge of ACTS.

7.3   At the February meeting members of the Central Council engaged in SWOT analysis.

8.   The Strengths of ACTS

Strengths were identified which included:

- ACTS provides a forum for the churches to meet
- ACTS works well where people who carry similar responsibilities within their churches meet and where the agenda is set and focused
- The production of Lent study material
- ACTS provides opportunities for worshipping together
- ACTS has staff with creative skills
- Scottish Churches House provides a place for cross-fertilisation with other groups
- ACTS can facilitate emergency statement by church leaders

9.   The Weaknesses of ACTS

Weaknesses were identified which included:

- A lack of communication with local level
- ACTS is an 'added' extra for church representatives on commissions and committees

- Key people are not being appointed to commissions and committees, leading to a side-lining of ACTS
- ACTS has become a talking shop
- There is poor attendance at meetings
- There is a lack of co-ordinated cover in the ACTS office
- Procedures set up are not followed through
- Theological differences are not being explored
- The timings of meetings are proving difficult for some

10. Opportunities and Threats

The Central Council was clear that there were many opportunities presenting themselves to the churches for joint reflection and work, including engagement with non-member churches in Scotland, other ecumenical groupings in Scotland and beyond and secular agencies. As always, vision and opportunity can be diluted to the point of extinction by threats, often external to the instrument itself. Potential threats include:

- Too high levels of expectation
- Pressure for self-preservation in the churches
- Lack of resources
- Apathy

11. Making ACTS an effective instrument

11.1 From the analysis it was clear that there was need to consider the structure of ACTS. Any restructuring would require a radical look at the commissions and committees and how they succeed or fail to further the purpose of ACTS. Methods of working would need to be refined in order to assist the churches to deepen their commitment to one another, to keep the ecumenical discussion open and to ensure that the churches engage with those with particular experience and expertise. The Working Group understood that it had the freedom to go back to the drawing board, to examine whether or not the 'churches together' model was still appropriate at the beginning of a new century and to seek more effective ways of working together which would create centres of energy.

11.2 In the process of clarifying its thinking, the Working Group held two consultations. Initial thinking was shared with the current conveners of ACTS Commissions and Committees. The first draft of a proposed new structure was shared with associate members of ACTS as it was recognised that the emerging proposals had particular implications for them.

11.3 The Working Group wishes to record its thanks to those who met with it under almost impossible time constraints. (See Annex II) While this report necessarily highlights those aspects of ACTS that have not worked as well as hoped, it would be wrong to suggest that ACTS has served no useful purpose. This is clearly not the case, and the following proposals are offered as a way of building on the strengths of ACTS and those methods of working that have proved fruitful.

IV Proposals

12. Restating the Principles

12.1 The Working Group felt that the 'churches together' model still provided the best model for working out the purposes of ACTS. The structure did not fail, nor the people animating them, but the churches have yet to respond to the challenge and discipline, which the model implies. There is still a tendency to expect decisions to be taken in ACTS along the lines of a council of churches. The result has been that, because of their particular ecclesiologies, some member churches have felt unable to own decisions taken by commissions and in some instances there has been a sense of exclusion. The decision-making processes have militated against the inclusion on the agenda of items of particular concern to one church tradition, which might prove tricky for others. The result has been that sensitive issues have not been dealt with in a way that allows the member churches to share their positions in an atmosphere of trust and respect and without the need to reach a common mind.

12.2 In the light of this, the Working Group wishes to restate the churches together principles on which ACTS is founded.

- The Aims of ACTS should be reaffirmed as
  —Seeking oneness
  —Growth in understanding an common life
  —Unified action

(Marigold Book page 50)

These aims should be promoted in four fundamental ways that can be applied at all levels of ecumenical engagement:

Worshipping together
Studying together
Serving the community together
Proclaiming together

ACTS should be clearly recognised as an expression of the commitment of the churches to one another.

13. Membership
Full membership should remain, as at present, open to those churches that are committed to the Basis of ACTS, including those that on principle have no credal statements, but that manifest faith in Christ as grounded in Holy Scriptures and are committed to the aims and purposes of ACTS and to working in the spirit of the Basis. The Working Group recommends that this category be known as Trustee Members. These include those churches which originally covenanted themselves to the Churches Together model.

13.2 **Associate members** should be defined under three categories:

- Churches, which are eligible, but do not wish at this stage to enter full membership: currently the Lutheran Council of Great Britain, the Orthodox Church
- Bodies in association: currently Christian Aid, Commonweal, Feed the Minds, the Iona Community, the Scottish Bible Society, the Scottish Catholic International Aid Fund (SCIAF), The Scottish Churches Housing Agency (SCHA), the Scottish Churches Open College (SCOC), the Scottish Churches Parliamentary Office (SCPO), the Student Christian Movement (SCM), Unity Enterprise, World Day of Prayer, YMCA, YWCA.
- Ecumenical agencies: Churches Agency for Inter-faith Relations in Scotland (CAIRS), Scottish Churches Agency for Racial Justice (SCARJ), NEWS, Youth Action, each of which has a funding relationship with the ecumenical instruments.

13.3 Observer status may be mutually acceptable for any church, Christian tradition or other Christian body not in sympathy with the Aims or the Basis of ACTS.

14. Structure
14.1 The Working Group agreed that the current structure was weakened by a dissipation of energy between the Central Council and the Commissions. It considered carefully the frustrations voiced at the February meeting of the Central Council that the commissions were not fulfilling the expectations that were held for them in terms of places of energy, joint action and deepening commitment. It was concerned to ensure that any new structure for ACTS should make clear the churches together model.

14.2 The proposal is for a simplified decision-making structure – one place where the churches would decide on the work priorities for a particular period. This would be called the Scottish Churches' Forum (The Forum). It would be a smaller body than the current Central Council and would comprise only trustee church representatives. Decisions on the churches' common agenda would be taken on the basis of

a) properly presented bids put together by Networks of people from the churches and other Christian bodies in associate membership with shared interests and experience;
b) initiatives from other ecumenical bodies at British and Irish, European or world levels;
c) and other suggestions from the General Secretary from his contacts with other agencies, including secular agencies.

14.3 The Working Group is clear that in making this proposal the churches are being asked to ensure that those who are appointed to this Scottish Churches' Forum should broadly fit the 'church leader' category in that they will need to have a good overview of the current concerns, practices and procedures of their church. However, they will also need to be people who are able to encourage imaginative proposals. The proposed new structure will not work if the Forum is perceived as a place where people like to say 'No!'. The Forum will need to contain a mixture of those who are interested in the broad picture and those who are expert in handling intricate detail. The Forum must carry the confidence of the churches and of the Networks that are striving to develop the ecumenical vision to which the churches are committed.

14.4 To fulfil the proposed remit for the Forum, a pattern of four meetings a year, two of which would be overnight is suggested. The Working Group is conscious that this is a heavy commitment, but believes that the task merits this degree of commitment from the member churches. It is confident that if the envisaged energy is generated, with a sense that there are specific outcomes to the work of ACTS, this commitment will not be burdensome.

14.5 The Working Group expresses the hope that at one of the evening sessions of the overnight meetings the opportunity is taken to hold a gathering of associate members. Extended meetings would also present an opportunity for member churches and associate members to display publications and resource material.

15. The Scottish Churches' Forum (The Forum)

15.1 The Working Group suggests that the Scottish Churches' Forum should be made up of representatives appointed by each trustee member church:

4 from the Church of Scotland
4 from the Roman Catholic Church in Scotland and
2 representatives from each of the other member churches
conveners of Networks (see below) unless otherwise present

15.2 Balances of gender, age, ordained and lay should be observed wherever possible. It is proposed that each member churches should appoint an alternate for each representative. This will allow for continuity of commitment and communication in the member churches.

15.3 A convener and two vice-conveners should be appointed according to the present custom – one Church of Scotland, one Roman Catholic and a third elected by the other member churches. The Convenership should continue to be by rotation.

15.4 The Working Group felt that with a smaller body, meeting more frequently, there would be no need for an Executive Committee. The convener and vice-conveners should work with the General Secretary to plan meetings of the Forum and to undertake the executive function between meetings.

- The **aim** of the Forum should be 'to discern priorities and give overall guidance for common action'. (Marigold Book p. 53)
- Its **task** would therefore include:

a) taking up the challenge of how the national relates to the local and vice versa
b) taking up the challenge of how the churches inter-relate regionally in Scotland
c) engaging with wider regional (i.e. European) and world ecumenical bodies and agendas
d) arranging to hear bids from the various Networks and deciding which priority issues from the churches should find their way onto the common agenda (see par 17 below)
e) commissioning work to be done, indicating the remit, time-limit and the resources available
f) receiving the completed work from task groups
g) ensuring a balance between issues on which co-operation will be easy and more sensitive issues
h) seeking nominations from the churches for Task Groups
i) organising one-off studies, seminars and occasional conferences
j) having overall responsibility for ensuring that the ecumenical conversation is kept open to all churches whether members of ACTS or not and other organisations
k) organising occasional, national events (e.g. Christian Gatherings, ecumenical Assemblies)
l) developing mechanisms for co-ordinating responses to papers e.g. from the Scottish Executive.

The Working Group strongly recommends that the Forum invites an external 'reflective observer' to review the work of the Forum against its stated aims and functions. This should be done every second year to ensure not only the setting up of a model of good practice, but also the continued flow of dynamism into and through the work of ACTS.

16. Modes of Working

A commonly asked question has been: What does ACTS do? With few exceptions it is hard to point to a product. In so far as ACTS is a relational body, any product can be hard to measure. However, in so far as joint action is envisaged and enabled, then it is realistic to expect some measurable outcome. The proposal from the Working Group is that the modes of working would include: Networks, Task Groups, one off consultations and seminars. It is here that the Working Group envisages the most creative encounters between the member churches and other churches, Christian organisations, secular agencies etc. will be. It is here that the conversation is to be kept open.

17. Networks

17.1 The Working Group is recommending that the main locus for both the relational work and the drawing up of proposals for action should be the Networks. To follow through the churches together model, the Networks should have a core membership of church appointed people with particular interest and/or experience in broad areas of church life and witness.

17.2 There will be no distinction between the authority of those church representatives on the Forum and those on the Networks. They will each carry the authority of their churches. The Networks are given the responsibility of doing work which will go back to the churches. A member church unable to accept the completed work will not make the work less important or valid for those that do accept it. Where there is disagreement it is expected that others will understand better the reasons for that disagreement. It is not the task of Networks to find the lowest common denominator of agreement. It is a fundamental principle of ACTS' function to broker communication between the churches. Networks will not speak as networks. Only churches together can speak. Networks are essentially a method of work. They are not ecumenical agencies.

17.3 The Working Group considered different configurations for Networks. The danger of a small number is that there is not sufficient focus to hold the interest of busy people. The danger of a larger number of Networks is that it would provide too great a burden on ACTS staff. No matter how many Networks there might be, it would be important that there is a constant sensitivity to where issues are shared across the Networks. Equally it is expected that each of the Networks will do its work within the context of prayer, theological reflection, mutual learning, mission and with an eye to how best and with whom to communicate, i.e. proclaim, its work. The Working Group recommends four Networks, each being clearly linked to one of the four fundamental ways of promoting the aims and purposes of ACTS.

- The aim should be the sharing of information and the identifying of areas of common work.
- The **tasks** would therefore include:
  a) sharing current issues on the denominational agendas
  b) identifying areas of common concern
  c) preparing bids for the Forum, indicating the nature of the work, its cost and its projected time scale. This could include a bid to undertake a feasibility study
  d) advising, with others, on the composition of task groups

17.4　Church Life Network

The Church Life Network would bring together the core concerns of common spirituality, worship, local churches together etc. It would cover 'Worshipping Together'.

17.5　Faith Studies Network

The Faith Studies Network would bring together the core concerns of the nature, purpose and unity of the Church. It would cover 'Studying Together'.

17.6　Church & Society Network

The Church and Society Network would bring together core concerns of justice & peace, social and moral issues and public issues relating to the Scottish and UK parliaments. It would cover 'Serving the Community Together'.

17.7 Mission Network

The Mission Network would bring together the concerns of mission and evangelism and all forms of communication. It would cover core concerns in 'Proclaiming Together'.

17.8 Each Network would be expected to undertake an annual review as part of its preparation for reporting to the Forum. Each Network would ensure that a small scoping group would prepare the bids for the Forum and would monitor the progress of the work for the Network. The Forum will need to decide whether to run a rolling programme of review with one Network reporting at each meeting of the Forum. It is also suggested that a remit is produced which will outline what is expected of each Network.

18. Task Groups

18.1 The Working Group identified models of working within the current structure, which appear to have worked well. These were most apparent when groups were formed to undertake a specific purpose, which was time limited, clearly defined and costed. It was felt that people already stretched by the demands of their denomination were more likely to give time to ACTS when the time commitment and the remit were clear.

18.2 It is suggested that churches would opt to be part of a Task Group. It may well be that a church, perhaps a smaller church, would be happy to have the work done by others, while interested to make use of the finished product. It could also be the case that a church may simply not wish to be associated with a piece of work.

18.3 As with the Networks, it would be essential that Task Groups can draw on the experience and expertise of appropriate associate members. It is proposed that the Networks will bring nominations for the Task Groups to the Forum for reception and approval.

- The aim of the Task Groups is to undertake work agreed by the Forum following the bid process.
- The tasks would therefore include:

  a) bringing together people of particular expertise

  b) fulfilling the remit given by the Forum

  c) presenting the outcome, including any minority report, in an appropriate form for reception by the Forum and the interested churches

19. Standing Committees

ACTS requires three Committees to progress its structural concerns and to conform to statute.

- The Scottish Churches House Committee
- The Finance Committee
- The Personnel Committee

V Resources

20. Financing ACTS

The Working Group believes that its proposals are unlikely to cost the churches less than they currently pay to ACTS. It accepts that ACTS must live within the financial constraints of the budget, which to a degree mirror the financial situation within the member churches themselves. The finance made available to ACTS will determine what the Churches can do together through ACTS. There will be hard choices to be made by the Forum as it determines the priority issues and as it seeks a balance between smaller and larger pieces of work, and ecumenically easy and sensitive areas of work. The Working Group is clear that there needs to be a realistic balance between these different types of work and that there should be no habit which seeks always the easy or the cheapest options. It will also be important that there is at least one piece of work from each Network at any one time, so that no Network is made to feel less important to the churches working together.

21. Friends of ACTS

Friends of ACTS offers the opportunity for all interested people to support and encourage the work of ACTS. It is envisaged that this should continue as part of the way in which the ecumenical commitment of the churches can be communicated widely within the Scottish community.

22. Location of ACTS

22.1 The Working Group gave careful consideration to the location of ACTS. In particular, it was sensitive to the difficulty in reaching Dunblane by public transport, particularly from the North of Scotland. However, it was clear that any move away from Dunblane would have significant on costs, not least in terms of rental of premises. The Working Group was made aware that the Churches are unlikely to find new money for this kind of expense and that therefore the funding of any relocation would restrict the work and staff of ACTS.

22.2　The Working Group also felt that pressure to see Edinburgh as the centre for everything should be resisted, lest we fell into the same trap that says all meetings must take place in London! There is good reason to insist that people, including those involved in government, need to move out from Edinburgh

22.3　The Working Party was also made aware of the kind of proposals that are likely to come to the Central Council later in 2001 concerning the future of Scottish Churches House.

22.4　In the light of all these factors, the Working Group recommends that in future the ACTS staff should continue to be located in Scottish Churches House, Dunblane.

23. Transition Period

The Working Group recognises that the process required to progress these proposals through the decision-making structures of the trustee member churches will require time during which there will be an increasing demand on ACTS staff. It is appreciated that good work already being undertaken should not cease. It therefore offers some guidelines for the transition period and asks that the Executive in particular is particularly watchful so that the burden does not become too great. (Annex III)

24. Conclusion

The Central Council, having considered the proposals of the Working Group now offer this report and the detailed proposals set out in Annex I for the consideration of the churches and the associate members. It does so in the belief that what is offered can bring dynamism and flexibility to the working of ACTS, while retaining the importance of the churches together model.

Membership of the Working Group

John Coultas (Roman Catholic Church)
Christine Davis (Religious Society of Friends)
Col. John Flett (Salvation Army)
Bob Fyffe (Scottish Episcopal Church)
Sheilagh Kesting (Church of Scotland)
Ross McLaren (United Reformed Church)
Stephen Matthews (United Free Church)
Kevin Franz (ACTS General Secretary, in attendance)

ANNEX I　　A Proposed New Structure for ACTS
ANNEX II　 A list of those consulted by the Working
　　　　　　 Group
ANNEX III　Guidelines for the Transitional Period.

ANNEX I

ACTS – Proposed New Structure

1. Preamble

The Central Council of ACTS, following its special meeting in February 2001, asked for a Working Group to be set up to bring forward proposals about the shape and ethos of ACTS, its staffing requirement and its location. After a period of intense consultation, the Working Group presents the following proposals for consideration by the member churches of ACTS on the shape, ethos and location of ACTS. It will return to staffing requirements after the embargo has been lifted.

2. Basis & Commitment (Churches Together in Pilgrimage – usually referred to as 'The Marigold Book' – page 49f)

Action of Churches Together in Scotland (ACTS) unites in pilgrimage those churches in Scotland which, acknowledge God's revelation in Christ, confess the Lord Jesus Christ as God and saviour according to the Scriptures and in obedience to God's will and in the power of the Holy Spirit, commit themselves

> to seek a deepening of their communion with Christ and with one another in the Church , which His body, and

to fulfil their mission to proclaim the Gospel by common witness and service in the world

to the Glory of the One God, Father, Son and Holy Spirit.

3. **Aims**

These were also set out in the Marigold Book' (page 50) under the headings:

*   Oneness
    —to become a fuller realisation of the unity that Christ wills, in accordance with the prayer, "that they all may be one; even as thou, Father art in me, and I in thee, that they also may be in us, that the world may believe that thou has sent me" (John 17:21);
    —to express the degree of unity that is already theirs by Christ's gift; their commitment to one another, and their resolve to continue as Pilgrims Together;
*   Growth of understanding and Common Life
    —to grow into a greater unity of mind and heart through experience of each other's living tradition of spirituality and worship;
    —to co-operate through prayer, theological reflection and consultation, at local and national levels, in all that concerns their common life, especially the nature, purpose and unity of the Church;
    —to work through joint study towards a Christian evaluation on moral and social issues.
*   Unified Action
    —to co-operate as far as possible in proclaiming the gospel so as to evoke a personal commitment to Christ and his Church;
    —obeying the Gospel in practical response to the life and needs of the community, the nation and the world;
    —witnessing to Christian moral and social values, in a critical phase of human history;
    —bringing Christian perspectives on the above matters into dialogue with the secular authorities.

3.2   These aspects can be promoted in four fundamental ways:

*   **Worshipping Together,** an expression of our need at all times to pray together to the Lord and including the experiencing of each other's living tradition of spirituality and worship
*   **Studying Together** – beginning with Scripture, through prayer, theological reflection and consultation co-operating in all that concerns the common life of the churches, especially the nature, purpose and unity of the Church at local and national levels and issues of social and moral concern
*   **Serving the Community Together** –identifying projects to support or initiate which can demonstrate Christian witness, including education and justice and peace issues.
*   **Proclaiming Together** – so as to evoke a personal commitment to Christ and his Church in ways that respond to the life and needs of the community, the nation and the world including press releases, publications and church representation in the national sphere.

3.3   The Churches Together model asks of the Churches that they hold out what is important to them in the expectation that that will be respected. Divisions are acknowledged but are not allowed to impede those things that can be done together. Authority lies with the churches and is expressed differently by the churches. Unless this is taken seriously, ACTS will continue to be a source of frustration. Put at its most simple, **ACTS is an expression of the commitment of the churches to one another.**

4.   **Membership**

ACTS hopes for the widest possible active participation of the Christian community of Scotland.

4.1   Trustee membership belongs to those churches that have covenanted together to form ACTS and is open to churches which are committed to the Basis and Aims of ACTS.

4.1.1   Any church which on principle has no credal statements in its tradition and therefore cannot formally subscribe to the statement of faith in the Basis, may nevertheless apply for and be elected to full membership provided it satisfies the members churches which subscribe to the Basis, that it manifests faith in Christ as grounded in Holy Scriptures, that it is committed to the Aims and purposes of ACTS and that it will work in the spirit of the Basis.

4.2   **Associate Membership** is open to

—**churches** which, though eligible, do not wish at this stage to enter into full membership e.g. the Lutheran Council of Great Britain, the Orthodox Church

—**bodies in association** which confirm their commitment to the Basis and Aims e.g. Christian Aid, Commonweal, The Iona Community, Feed the Minds, The Scottish Bible Society, The Scottish Churches Open College, The Scottish Churches Parliamentary Office, The Scottish Churches Housing Agency, SCIAF, The Student Christian Movement, Unity Enterprise, World Day of Prayer, YMCA, YWCA

—**ecumenical agencies** which confirm their commitment to Basis and Aims and are funded from the core budget of ACTS e.g. CAIRS, NEWS, SCARJ, Youth Action

4.3   If however any church, and Christian tradition, or any Christian body were not in sympathy with the AIMS or Basis of ACTS these forms of membership would not be appropriate although observer status may be mutually acceptable, e.g. the Scottish Unitarian Association.

5.   Structures

5.1   The structures of ACTS maintain the authority of the churches, and enable as many members of the churches as possible to engage in common activity to further the Aims. Local co-operation will continue to be central to all the work of ACTS. All churches are encouraged, in making appointments at all levels of ACTS, to hold wherever possible to the ecumenical Guidelines for Resource Sharing, particularly regarding the participation and representation of women, young people and lay people.

NOTE:
The Ecumenical Guidelines referred to, developed by the

World Consultation on Resource Sharing at EL ESCORIAL recommend, among other things that there should be 'at least 50% women, 50% lay people and 20% young people' in the appointment of representatives.

5.2   Local
5.2.1   Many ecumenical initiatives at local level have happily taken root in various parts of Scotland. These include sharing in prayer and worship, in study and learning, and in witness and service. They represent a growth in fellowship and in warmth of relationships. Much however remains to be done to encourage such activity throughout the land. The challenge to ACTS is to support and make known these initiatives, without seeking in any way to take them over or control them; the need is for promotion, communication, resource-sharing and co-ordination.

5.2.2   In addition to the growth of local inter-church groups, and the continuing work of local councils of churches and clergy fraternals, an increasing number of congregations are entering into some form of association with one or more neighbouring congregations. Such associations are commonly known as 'Local Ecumenical Partnerships' or 'Ecumenical Parishes'. They vary greatly in form and scope, depending on local needs, opportunities and preferences. All involve some sharing of activities or projects; many include the sharing of buildings, or to a measure of team ministry. Where possible, this close association of congregations is expressed in a 'covenant' as a sign of the seriousness of the mutual commitment which is involved.

5.2.3   Focal points in the year for local ecumenical activity include the Week of Prayer for Christian Unity, the World Day of Prayer, Holy Week, Christian Aid Week and One World Week.

5.3   Regional
Discussion is taking place within member churches concerning their regional structures. It is important that ACTS keeps a watch on developments with a view to seeking suitable complementary structures. In the meantime, attention is drawn to the model being

developed in the Glasgow conurbation with the appointment of an ecumenical officer by Glasgow Churches Together, a model which is being followed in Edinburgh. With the appointment of an Ecumenical Officer, Churches Together in Glasgow has someone who is able to provide a link between local churches together groups in Glasgow and the surrounding area. This model is commended as being suitable for adaptation in other urban areas across Scotland.

5.4 National

5.4.1 At national level the Scottish churches continue to commit themselves progressively to plan and act together in every appropriate area of their life and witness. They therefore understand the proposed structures not as complete expressions of their commitment to one another but as a means of deepening their commitment.

5.4.2 In particular a National instrument must enable work to be done in a way that takes into account the development of local and regional activity. At National level it is proposed to have a Scottish Churches' Forum, which will enable the churches to deepen their commitment to one another. It is envisaged that they will work together through Networks and Task Groups of people with particular interest and expertise.

5.5 The Scottish Churches' Forum (The Forum):

Aim:

'the discernment of priorities and overall guidance for common action'. (Marigold Book p. 53)

5.5.1 The task of the Forum would be:

a) to take up the challenge of how the national relates to the local and vice versa
b) to take up the challenge of how the churches interrelate regionally
c) to engage with wider regional (i.e. European) and world ecumenical bodies and their agendas.
d) to arrange for hearing bids from the various Networks (see below) and deciding which priority issues from the churches and associate members could find their way onto the common agenda

e) to commission work to be done, indicating the remit, the time-limit and the resources available
f) to review and receive the completed work of the Task Groups (see below) and any other commissioned work
g) to ensure a balance between issues on which co-operation will be easy and more sensitive issues
h) to seek nominations from the churches and associate members for Task Groups
    i) to organise one-off studies, seminars and occasional conferences
j) to have overall responsibility for ensuring that the ecumenical conversation is kept open to all churches, whether members of ACTS or not and other organisations
k) to organise occasional national events (e.g. Christian Gatherings, Ecumenical Assemblies)
l) to develop a mechanism for co-ordinating responses to papers e.g. from the Scottish Executive

5.5.2 Composition:

In a restructured ACTS it is proposed that the Forum should be composed of Church representatives from trustee member churches:

> two from the smaller churches
> four from the Church of Scotland and the Roman Catholic Church
> conveners of Networks unless otherwise present

The trustee member churches will be expected to appoint representatives who broadly fit the category of 'church leader'. Each should have a good overview of the current concerns, practices and procedures of their church and should have clear lines of accountability.

It will be important that wherever possible the usual balances or gender, age, ordained and lay will be observed. Each trustee member church should ensure the appointment of alternates when representatives are unable to attend meetings.

5.5.3 Convenership:

The Convenership should operate along the lines currently used. A three year appointment, following a rotation of Church of Scotland, Roman Catholic Church, other trustee member church of ACTS.

The Convener and two vice conveners would work with the General Secretary to plan meetings and to undertake the executive function between meetings.

5.5.4 Frequency of meetings:
To enable it to develop the character of the life of churches together the Forum would meet at least four times a year, of which two will be overnight.

5.6 Networks:

Aim:

To encourage the sharing of information and identify areas for common work.

5.6.1　Networks would be composed of key people in their churches, and associate members.

5.6.2 The task of a Network would be:

a) to bring together key people
b) to share current issues on the denominational agendas
c) to identify areas of common concern
d) to prepare bids for the Forum, indicating the nature of the work, its cost and its projected time scale
e) to advise, with others, on the composition of Task Groups.

5.6.3 Composition:

The core membership of the Networks will be appointed by the trustee member churches at the invitation of the Forum. It should include those with particular expertise and engagement in the member churches. Care should be taken to ensure representation from the smaller member churches. The Forum should encourage representation from associate members and should work with the Networks to ensure the balance rests with the church representatives.

Efforts should be made in the Networks to keep the conversation open with non-member churches of ACTS and other ecumenical partners and alliances. Invitations from the Networks can be made after consultation with the General Secretary and reported subsequently to the Forum.

All Networks need to remember their responsibility to be inclusive in their membership.

Each member of the Network should ensure the appointment of an alternate when unable to attend meetings.

5.6.4 Conveners:

Each Network would have co-conveners appointed by the Forum on the recommendation of trustee member churches on a rota to be devised.

5.6.5 Frequency of meetings:

There would be one major agenda setting meeting a year. Other meetings would ensure the building up of trust, the preparation of bids and the monitoring of work.

ACTS staff would be responsible for bringing the task groups together, taking minutes and undertaking appropriate research. Until the new structure is in place and the staffing situation is clear, such work will need to be done from within the membership of the Networks. (See Annex III.)

5.6.6 Review:

Each Network will undertake an annual review for presentation to the Forum. This will indicate work in progress, work completed and evaluation of outcomes.

5.6.7　The following Networks are recommended, each of which would be expected to work within the context of prayer, theological reflection, mutual learning, proclaiming and mission:

- **Church Life Network.** This would bring together core concerns of common spirituality and worship. It would cover 'Worshipping Together' (see par. 3.2 above). It would bring together those involved in promoting spirituality, the development and promotion of seasonal worship material for local use, the development of an ecumenical prayer calendar, and the identification of the difficult or neuralgic question related to common worship.

- **Faith Studies Network.** This would bring together the core concerns of the nature, purpose and unity of the Church. It would cover 'Studying Together' (see par 3.2 above). It would bring together those who will explore the faith through Lent Studies, WCC and Vatican documents, and will include the proper sharing of how churches engage in moral and ethical decision-making. It will also include engagement with other faith communities. Matters relating to education and ministerial formation will be located here.

- **Church & Society Network.** This would bring together the core concerns of justice and peace, social and moral issues, together with issues relating to the Scottish and Westminster Parliaments. It would cover 'Serving the Community' (see par 3.2 above). It would bring together those involved in racial justice, homelessness issues, the work of the Parliamentary Office and other Parliamentary Officers, engagement in the Civic Forum and public questions, education in its public policy dimension. It will also bring together those involved in diaconia/social responsibility work.

- **Mission Network.** This would bring together concerns of mission, evangelism and communication. It would cover 'Proclaiming Together' (see par 3.2 above). It would ring together both those who will communicate from ACTS and those who will enable the provision of material to encourage local ecumenical bodies, but also those involved in evangelism and broader mission strategies such as 'Building Bridges of Hope'.

5.6.8   While each of the Networks has a particular area of responsibility, it is recognised that some issues will require cross boundary co-operation. The Forum, the Networks and the ACTS staff should be vigilant for opportunities of this nature. It is also suggested that it may be appropriate from time to time to have one issue discussed in all four Networks in order to gain a more integrated understanding.

5.7   **Task Groups**:

Aim:

To undertake work agreed by the Forum

5.7.1   Task Groups would not only draw on people with relevant experience in the trustee member churches, but would also ensure the inclusion of representatives from appropriate associate members. The gathering of nominations would be channelled through the Forum, thus ensuring that the work done will be owned by all the churches in trustee membership that decide to participate in the piece of work. It is not necessary that every member church participate in every piece of work. A church may choose not to participate in a piece of work, trusting others to do the work for all, or it can choose not to participate because it does not want to be associated with the particular piece of work.

5.7.2   Tasks:

a)   to bring together people of particular expertise from as many member churches as wish to be involved and from associate members with a particular interest and expertise in the field of work

b)   to fulfil the remit given by the Forum from the bids presented by the Networks

c)   to present the outcome of their work, including any majority report, in an appropriate form for reception by the Forum and those churches who have opted to be part of the work

d   )to bring reports that are realistic and honest and not afraid to show where there is genuine disagreement. It is not necessary always to find consensus.

5.7.3   Composition:

It will be important that Task Groups draw on the wide experience of associate members. This is one area where the challenge to the trustee member churches from groups with particular expertise and knowledge should be most visible. Attention will need to be paid to the balance between trustee church appointed representatives and those from other interested bodies. It is important that the outcome is owned by the churches. The usual facility for the appointment of alternates should be applied to ensure the fullest participation of member churches as the work progresses.

5.7.4 Convenership:

The Task Groups should be convened by someone appointed by the Forum, on the recommendation of the Networks.

The convener should work with ACTS staff in planning the agenda for the meetings and in overseeing the implementation of the work agreed. The Convener should report as necessary to meetings of the Network(s) with interest in the agreed task, using the Networks as useful reference groups for the progress of the work. The convener of the Network will ensure reports on progress to the Forum.

6. **Membership**: At all times the usual balances of gender, age, ordained and lay will be observed.

7. **The outcome/products of ACTS** would be various and would be fed back into the churches. These would included:

- A report to the churches
- Resources for worship and study
- Information for the equipping of LEPs
- Seminars on particular issues

8. **Staffing Requirements**
   EMBARGOED UNTIL FURTHER NOTICE

9. **Scottish Churches House**

Scottish Churches House was established more than 35 years ago as a Conference Centre and Meeting Place for all the churches in Scotland. For much of that time it has also been the main office of first the Scottish Churches Council and then ACTS, to whom the house belongs. It is in constant use by all kinds of church groups and many secular bodies. It is also used by ACTS Commissions and Committees and for consultations on topics of importance for the church or the nation. The contribution of the house to the unity and mission of the Scottish churches cannot be over-estimated and it is a much-loved place of meeting and retreat. The House continues to support and underpin many of these activities and provides a meeting place for ACTS.

9.2 After consideration of the drawbacks of Dunblane as the location for ACTS, particularly its inaccessibility for those travelling from the North, the possibility of relocation was considered. It is clear that ACTS could not afford the cost of relocating without decreasing both possible work and staffing. It is therefore recommended that, subject to the consideration of proposals from the House Working Group about future development of the House, the ACTS staff remain located in Dunblane.

10. **Standing Committees**

ACTS requires two Committees to progress its structural concerns and to conform to statute with an additional committee in the Personnel Committee.

10.1 **Scottish Churches House Committee**

The Scottish Churches House Committee will comprise the Convener of ACTS, the General Secretary, one representative of each trustee member church and who have experience in managing buildings and amenity.

10.2 **The Finance Committee**

The Finance Committee will comprise the Treasurer (to be appointed by the Forum), the Bursar, the General Secretary and one representative from each of the trustee member churches not represented by the Convenor and the two vice-conveners. The Convenor will be appointed by the Forum following consultation with trustee member churches and should be experienced in financial matters.

10.3 **The Personnel Committee**

The Personnel Committee will comprise the Convenor of the Scottish Churches House Committee (see below), three members appointed from the trustee member churches and who have personnel experience, one of whom will act as convener.

11. Finances

The trustee member churches will make regular annual financial contributions to a collective budget, to cover the costs of the Forum, Networks, Task Groups, staff of ACTS and other appropriate bodies.

11.2 ACTS will co-operate with Churches Together in Britain and Ireland in agreeing and presenting a combined asking, for all trustee member churches, which covers members of both instruments. This will be done every three years to cover the following three years period.

11.3 Associate member churches, associate members and bodies in association will be asked for appropriate contributions.

11.4 If two or more churches judge that new work requires to be undertaken in any field and also judge it would be wise to undertake this new work together, they will finance it from their own budgets, as they would if the new work were undertaken separately. Such work undertaken together will not entail greater expenditure and may require less expenditure than if it were undertaken separately.

11.5 Similarly, if two or more churches agree to undertake together work which at present they undertake separately, there will be no additional expenditure.

11.6 Thus the quality of the commitment asked of the churches will continue to be expressed, not in any increase in their contributions to the combined budgets of the ecumenical bodies, but in their progressive willingness to use their resources together or in common strategy, in all appropriate areas of their common life and witness.

12. Ensuring Complementary Structures

It is essential that there should continue to be integration between the ecumenical bodies. As before this will be assured in a number of ways:

12.1 The staff of ACTS should be in regular contact with the equivalent co-ordinating staff of Churches Together in Britain and Ireland.

12.2 At the level of the Forum in Scotland and the Assembly and Church Representatives Meeting in Britain and Ireland, the churches should ensure that there is overlap of membership.

12.3 In the case of ACTS Networks and equivalent bodies in Churches Together in Britain and Ireland (CTBI), the same argument might apply. As an alternative however the Scottish churches might consider some joint representation on some Commissions and Networks of CTBI. This could help integration, save considerable resources, help the smaller churches to feel better represented, and could also represent the reality of a situation where the Scottish churches are often able to speak with a common voice on many issues.

13. Review Process

It is strongly recommended that the Forum itself is subject to a regular review process. It is proposed that every second year a 'reflective observer' should attend a meeting of the Forum. The observer would be asked to measure the work of the Forum against its intended aims and functions. This process would enable the Forum not only to model the good practice it expects of the Networks, but would also ensure a continued dynamism flowing through the work of ACTS.

14. Conclusion

The Working Group presents these proposals as a means of embodying what has been good in the past and of building on what has been vital and good in order to take these into the future. It believes that the proposals remain true to the vision of the Inter-Church Process, are flexible, capable of adaptation, and can be an effective means by which the Scottish Churches can give substance to their commitment to one another, and their common commitment to the one God, Father, Son and Holy Spirit.

ANNEX II

Consultations

The Conveners of ACTS Commissions, Committees and Networks

Those who attended a meeting on 2nd April were:

Major Josephine Davies (Communications)
Mr Chris Docherty (Youth Action)
Dr Alison Elliot (Justice, Peace, Social & Moral Issues)
Mrs Norma Henderson (Mission, Evangelism and Education)
Mr Steve Mallon (Youth Action)
Mrs Elizabeth Templeton (Unity, Faith & Order)
Mr John Coultas (Scottish Churches House Committee and member of the Working Group)
Rev Ross McLaren (local and Regional Unity and member of the Working Group)
Alison Clarke (NEWS) responded by telephone

The Associate Members and Agencies

Those who attended a meeting on 24th May were:

Mr Stanley Bonthron (Feed the Minds)
Rev Dr Graham Blount (Scottish Churches Parliamentary Office)
Mr Alastair Cameron (Scottish Churches Housing Agency)
Very Revd Protopresbyter Columba Flegg (Orthodox Church)
Mrs Helen Hood (YWCA)
Rev Norman Shanks (Iona Community)
Sr Isabel Smyth (CAIRS)
Rev John Wylie (Christian Aid)

Member Churches of ACTS not represented on the Working Group

Rev John Butler (Congregational Federation)
Rev Andrew McKenzie (Methodist Church)

ANNEX III

Transition to New Structures

Should the Central Council agree to commend the proposed new structure to the churches, there will be a quite lengthy transition period before these can be implemented. There will be the follow up to the Scottish Ecumenical Assembly. The General Secretariat will need time to respond to the needs of the new structures. It is not the intention that good work already in process should cease. It will be important that the Executive are aware of the increasing burden that is likely to fall on the staff in this period and to ensure that it does not become unbearable. In addition, the Working Group offers the following Guidelines to the Central Council to assist with the process of transition from the current structure to the new structure, should it prove acceptable to the churches.

1. **Work to continue**

It is not the purpose of the restructuring to cease doing work that is effective. Work in the Commissions should continue with assistance in minute taking from within the Commissions, in collaboration with the General Secretary. Likewise, the Committee on Local & Regional Unity should continue to organise its annual conferences.

NEWS and Youth Action will have their own transitional arrangements as they become ecumenical agencies of ACTS.

There is need to look closely at the communications and publications strategy. Currently ACTS lacks a coherent policy, which in practice means that too much is left to the decision of staff. The Working Group strongly recommends that there is a clear policy in place by the time the new structure comes into operation.

2. **Time Scale**

The Proposals are to be presented to the Central Council in June 2001. Assuming that they are broadly approved by the Central Council, they will be sent to member churches for comment and decision. As the decision-making processes differ from church to church, it is unlikely that the opinions of the churches will be known before the February 2002 meeting of the Central Council.

It is then suggested that if the proposals are accepted by the member churches nominations for the new Forum and Networks should be processed by the end of June 2002, so that the new structures can be introduced by 1st July.

This may mean that some member churches will have to prepare their appointments in advance so that if and when the decision is made to go ahead, there is no delay in bringing forward names by the proposed date.

APPENDIX V

Charta Oecumenica
Guidelines for the Growing Co-operation among the Churches in Europe

The Charta Oecumenica is a significant document, the outcome of long and deep discussion and prayer on the part of the Conference of European Churches and the Council of European Catholic Bishops' Conferences. It has three brief sections.

The first section invites us to respond to Paul's call to unity in the Spirit that we find in Ephesians, viewed in the wider context of the Creed and Trinitarian faith. The second section offers five different ways of expressing this fundamental unity - proclamation of the gospel, reconciliation, action together, prayer and dialogue. The third section offers six tasks for the churches in contemporary Europe, - building wider European unity, reconciliation, the safeguarding of creation, closer community with Judaism, dialogue with Islam and with other religions.

The Charta Oecumenica does not tell us what to do. It recognises that churches are co-operating more and more, particularly at the local level. But it then goes on to offer us pointers to where we can extend that co-operation further and deepen our commitment to each other. It raises important questions for us all as we try to follow through what the Scriptures say about unity.

The Charta Oecumenica has emerged from co-operation among churches throughout Europe. It invites us to explore what it means to have a common European home. As the Church of Scotland, encouraged both by our history and by contemporary reflections, we should be able to respond readily to this.

The challenge to us, quite simply, is to give expression to that unity which by faith is ours already through Jesus Christ, in the power of the Holy Spirit, to the glory of God the Father. How can we do that in ways that have life in them and fit the needs of today? The Charta can help us, whether by prompting discussion among local churches, by suggesting how to map further areas of co-operation, or as a set of guidelines for action together.

I

WE BELIEVE IN
"ONE HOLY CATHOLIC AND APOSTOLIC CHURCH"

"Make every effort to maintain the unity of the Spirit in the bond of peace. There is one body and one Spirit, just as you were called to the one hope of your calling, one Lord, one faith, one baptism, one God and Father of all, who is above all and through all and in all" (Ephesians 4:3-6)

Called together to unity in faith
With the Gospel of Jesus Christ, according to the witness of Holy Scripture and as expressed in the ecumenical Nicene-Constantinopolitan Creed of 381, we believe in the Triune God: the Father, Son and Holy Spirit. Because we here confess "one, holy, catholic and apostolic church" our paramount [1] ecumenical task is to show forth this unity, which is always a gift of God. Fundamental differences in faith are still barriers to visible unity. There are different views of the church and its oneness, of the sacraments and ministries. We must not be satisfied with this situation. Jesus Christ revealed to us on the cross his love and the mystery of reconciliation; as his followers, we intend to do our utmost to overcome the problems and obstacles that still divide the churches.

---

* To the Conference of European Churches (CEC) belong almost all Orthodox, Protestant, Anglican, Old-Catholic and independent churches in Europe. In the Council of European Bishops' Conferences (CCEE) are represented all Roman Catholic Bishops' Conferences in Europe.

We commit ourselves
to follow the apostolic exhortation of the letter to the Ephesians and persevere in seeking a common understanding of Christ's message of salvation in the Gospel;
in the power of the Holy Spirit, to work towards the visible unity of the Church of Jesus Christ in the one faith, expressed in the mutual recognition of baptism and in eucharistic fellowship, as well as in common witness and service.

II

ON THE WAY TOWARDS THE VISIBLE FELLOWSHIP OF THE CHURCHES IN EUROPE

**"By this everyone will know that you are my disciples, if you have love for one another"
(John 13:35)**

Proclaiming the Gospel together
The most important task of the churches in Europe is the common proclamation of the Gospel, in both word and deed, for the salvation of all: The widespread lack of corporate and individual orientation and failing away from Christian values challenge Christians to testify to their faith, particularly in response to the quest for meaning which is being pursued in so many forms. This witness will require increased dedication to Christian education (e.g. catechism classes) and pastoral care in local congregations, with a sharing of experiences in these fields. It is equally important for the whole people of God together to communicate the Gospel in the public domain, which also means responsible commitments to social and political issues.

We commit ourselves
—to discuss our plans for evangelisation with other churches, entering into agreements with them and thus avoiding harmful competition and the risk of fresh divisions;
—to recognise that every person can freely choose his or her religious and church affiliation as a matter of conscience, which means not inducing anyone to convert through moral pressure or material incentive, but also not hindering anyone from entering into conversion of his or her own free will.

Moving towards one another
In the spirit of the Gospel, we must reappraise together the history of the Christian churches, which has been marked by many beneficial experiences but also by schisms, hostilities and even armed conflicts. Human guilt, lack of love and the frequent abuse of faith and the church for political interests have severely damaged the credibility of the Christian witness.

Ecumenism therefore begins for Christians with the renewal of our hearts and the willingness to repent and change our ways. The ecumenical movement has already helped to spread reconciliation.

It is important to acknowledge the spiritual riches of the different Christian traditions, to learn from one another and so to receive these gifts. For the ecumenical movement to flourish it is particularly necessary to integrate the experiences and expectations of young people and actively encourage their participation.

We commit ourselves
—to overcome the feeling of self-sufficiency within each church, and to eliminate prejudices; to seek mutual encounters and to be available to help one another;
—to promote ecumenical openness and co-operation in Christian education, and in theological training, continuing education and research.

Acting together
Various forms of shared activity are already ecumenical. Many Christians from different churches live side by side and interact in friendships, in their neighbourhoods, at work and in their families. Couples in interdenominational marriages especially should be supported in experiencing ecumenism in their daily lives.

We recommend that bilateral and multilateral ecumenical bodies be set up and maintained for co-operation at local, regional, national and international levels. At the European level it is necessary to strengthen co-operation between the Conference of European

Churches and the Council of European Bishops' Conferences (CCEE) and to hold further European Ecumenical Assemblies.

In the event of conflicts between churches, efforts towards mediation and peace should be initiated and/or supported as needed.

We commit ourselves
—to act together at all levels of church life wherever conditions permit and there are no reasons of faith or overriding expediency mitigating against this;
—to defend the rights of minorities and to help reduce misunderstandings and prejudices between majority and minority churches in our countries.

Praying together

The ecumenical movement lives from our hearing God's word and letting the Holy Spirit work in us and through us. In the power of this grace, many different initiatives now seek, through services of prayer and worship, to deepen the spiritual fellowship among the churches and to pray for the visible unity of Christ's Church. A particularly painful sign of the divisions among many Christian churches is the lack of eucharistic fellowship.

In some churches reservations subsist regarding praying together in an ecumenical context. But we have many hymns and liturgical prayers in common, notably the Lord's Prayer, and ecumenical services have become a widespread practice: all of these are features of our Christian spirituality.

We commit ourselves
—to pray for one another and for Christian unity;
—to learn to know and appreciate the worship and other forms of spiritual life practised by other churches;
—to move towards the goal of eucharistic fellowship.

Continuing in dialogue

We belong together in Christ, and this is of fundamental significance in the face of our differing theological and ethical positions. Rather than seeing our diversity as a gift which enriches us, however, we have allowed differences of opinion on doctrine, ethics and church law to lead to separations between churches, with special

historical circumstances and different cultural backgrounds often playing a crucial role.

In order to deepen ecumenical fellowship, endeavours to reach a consensus in faith must be continued at all cost. Only in this way can church communion be given a theological foundation. There is no alternative to dialogue.

We commit ourselves
—to continue in conscientious, intensive dialogue at different levels between our churches, and to examine the question of how official church bodies can receive and implement the findings gained in dialogue;
—in the event of controversies, particularly when divisions threaten in questions of faith and ethics, to seek dialogue and discuss the issues together in the light of the Gospel.

III

OUR COMMON RESPONSIBILITY IN EUROPE

"Blessed are the peacemakers, for they will be called children of God"
(Matthew 5:9)

Participating in the building of Europe

Through the centuries Europe has developed a primarily Christian character in religious and cultural terms. However, Christians have failed to prevent suffering and destruction from being inflicted by Europeans, both within Europe and beyond. We confess our share of responsibility for this guilt and ask God and our fellow human beings for forgiveness.

Our faith helps us to learn from the past, and to make our Christian faith and love for our neighbours a source of hope for morality and ethics, for education and culture, and for political and economic life, in Europe and throughout the world.

The churches support an integration of the European continent. Without common values, unity cannot endure. We are convinced that the spiritual heritage of Christianity constitutes an empowering source of inspiration and enrichment for Europe. On the basis of our Christian faith, we work towards a humane, socially conscious Europe, in which human rights and the basic values of peace, justice, freedom, tolerance, participation and solidarity prevail. We likewise insist on the reverence for life, the value of marriage and the family, the preferential option for the poor, the readiness to forgive, and in all things compassion.

As churches and as international communities we have to counteract the danger of Europe developing into an integrated West and a disintegrated East, and also take account of the North-South divide within Europe. At the same time we must avoid Eurocentricity and heighten Europe's sense of responsibility for the whole of humanity, particularly for the poor all over the world.

We commit ourselves
—to seek agreement with one another on the substance and goals of our
social responsibility, and to represent in concert, as far as possible, the concerns and visions of the churches vis-a-vis the secular European institutions;
—to defend basic values against infringements of every kind; - to resist any attempt to misuse religion and the church for ethnic or nationalist purposes.

Reconciling peoples and cultures
We consider the diversity of our regional, national, cultural and religious traditions to be enriching for Europe. In view of numerous conflicts, the churches are called upon to serve together the cause of reconciliation among peoples and cultures. We know that peace among the churches is also an important prerequisite for this.

Our common endeavours are devoted to evaluating, and helping to resolve, political and social issues in the spirit of the Gospel. Because we value the person and dignity of every individual as made in the image of God, we defend the absolutely equal value of all human beings.

As churches, we intend to join forces in promoting the process of democratisation in Europe. We commit ourselves to work for structures of peace, based on the non-violent resolution of conflicts. We condemn any form of violence against the human person, particularly against women and children.

Reconciliation involves promoting social justice within and among all peoples; above all, this means closing the gap between rich and poor and overcoming unemployment. Together we will do our part towards giving migrants, refugees and asylum-seekers a humane reception in Europe.

We commit ourselves
—to counteract any form of nationalism which leads to the oppression of other peoples and national minorities;
—to strengthen the position and equal rights of women in ail areas of life, and to foster partnership in church and society between women and men.

Safeguarding the creation
Believing in the love of the Creator God, we give thanks for the gift of creation and the great value and beauty of nature. However, we are appalled to see natural resources being exploited without regard for their intrinsic value or consideration of their limits, and without regard for the well-being of future generations.

Together we want to help create sustainable living conditions for the whole of creation. It is our responsibility before God to put into effect common criteria for distinguishing between what human beings are scientifically and technologically capable of doing and what, ethically speaking, they should not do.

We recommend the introduction into European churches of an Ecumenical Day of Prayer for the Preservation of Creation.

We commit ourselves
—to strive to adopt a lifestyle free of consumerism and a quality of life informed by accountability and sustainability;-
—to support church environmental organisations and ecumenical networks in their efforts for the safeguarding of creation.

Strengthening community with Judaism
We are bound up in a unique community with the people Israel, the people of the Covenant which God has never terminated. Our faith teaches us that our Jewish sisters and brothers "are beloved, for the sake of their ancestors;

for the gifts and the calling of God are irrevocable" (Rom 11.28-29). And "to them belong the adoption, the glory, the covenants, the giving of the law, the worship and the promises; to them belong the patriarchs, and from them, according to the flesh, comes the Messiah" (Rom 9.4-5).

We deplore and condemn all manifestations of anti-Semitism, all outbreaks of hatred and persecutions. We ask God for forgiveness for anti-Jewish attitudes among Christians, and we ask our Jewish sisters and brothers for reconciliation.

It is urgently necessary, in the worship and teaching, doctrine and life of our churches, to raise awareness of the deep bond existing between the Christian faith and Judaism, and to support Christian-Jewish co-operation.

We commit ourselves
—to oppose all forms of anti-Semitism and anti-Judaism in the church and in society;
—to seek and intensify dialogue with our Jewish sisters and brothers at all levels.

Cultivating relations with Islam
Muslims have lived in Europe for centuries. In some European countries, they constitute strong minorities. While there have been plenty of good contacts and neighbourly relations between Muslims and Christians, and this remains the case, there are still strong reservations and prejudices on both sides. These are rooted in painful experiences throughout history and in the recent past.

We would like to intensify encounters between Christians and Muslims and enhance Christian-Islamic dialogue at all levels. We recommend, in particular, speaking with one another about our faith in one God, and clarifying ideas on human rights.

We commit ourselves
—to conduct ourselves towards Muslims with respect;
—to work together with Muslims on matters of common concern.

Encountering other religions and world views
The plurality of religious and non-confessional beliefs and ways of life has become a feature of European culture. Eastern religions and new religious communities are spreading and also attracting the interest of many Christians. In addition, growing numbers of people reject the Christian faith, are indifferent to it or have other philosophies of life.

We want to take seriously the critical questions of others, and try together to conduct fair discussions with them. Yet a distinction must be made between the communities with which dialogues and encounters are to be sought, and those which should be warned against from the Christian standpoint.

We commit ourselves
—to recognise the freedom of religion and conscience of these individuals and communities and to defend their right to practise their faith or convictions, whether singly or in groups, privately or publicly, in the context of rights applicable to all;
—to be open to dialogue with all persons of good will, to pursue with them matters of common concern, and to bring a witness of our Christian faith to them.

Jesus Christ, the Lord of the one Church, is our greatest hope of reconciliation and peace. In his name we intend to continue on our common path in Europe. We pray for God's guidance through the power of the Holy Spirit.

"May the God of hope fill us with all joy and peace in believing, so that we may abound in hope by the power of the Holy Spirit." (Rom 15.13)

COMMITTEE ON EDUCATION
MAY 2002

PROPOSED DELIVERANCE

The General Assembly:

1. Receive the Report.

2. Commend the Committee's continuing professional support to the Church's Representatives on local authorities. (2.1)

3. Commend the Committee's continuing support for the work of School Chaplains and encourage the Committee to devise quality indicators for use in the self-evaluation of Chaplaincy in schools and develop training materials for Chaplains and Headteachers. (3.2)

4. Commend the Committee's efforts to support Chaplaincy in Scottish Colleges through consultations and the development of a handbook. (4.1)

5. Encourage the Committee to continue to promote the partnership of parents and carers with teachers in the development and implementation of sex education programmes in Scottish schools. (5.1)

6. Instruct the Committee to monitor the response to the Standards and Quality in Secondary Schools: Religious and Moral Education 1995–2000 (HMIE, 2001). (6.1)

7. Invite the Youth Assembly to consider the remit of the Review Group on Religious Observance in Scottish Schools and offer views to the Committee. (8.3)

8. Instruct the Committee to continue to monitor the implementation of the agreement "A Teaching Profession for the 21st Century". (9.1)

9. Approve the Committee's view on joint campuses, and spiritual provision in Public Private Partnership education projects. (13.1)

REPORT

1. Introduction

1.1 The continuing task of the Committee on Education is to apply the insights of the Christian faith to the processes and procedures of educational provision.

> ***1.1.1*** *A Christian vision of education is rooted in the wider vision of what it means to be a human being within God's creation. Our relationships to one another and to the environment are of fundamental importance. Education is not just about the whole person as an individual it is also about that person in community and relationship.* A Christian Vision for Scottish Education (ACTS Education Group) - 2000.

1.2 Following the report of the Special Commission anent the Department of Education considered at the 2001 General Assembly, the Committee on Education appointed Ms Susan M Leslie as Secretary to the Committee. Ms Leslie, formerly Headteacher, Colinsburgh Primary School, Fife, took up her appointment on 22 October, 2001.

1.3 One of the final tasks of Rev John Stevenson who, after official retirement served the Committee as Secretary till August 2001, was to see to the arrangements for the Conference of the European Forum of Teachers of Religious Education (EFTRE). The EFTRE

Conference "Handling Truth Claims in Religious Education" took place from 30 August to 2 September last year at Pollock Halls, University of Edinburgh. Some 150 delegates attended from 26 European countries. The Rev John Stevenson chaired the conference. (Report on web site HtmlResAnchor http://re-xs.ucsm.ac.uk/eftre)

1.4 In the three years of the Scottish Parliament there have been three ministers responsible for school education. Jack McConnell succeeded Sam Galbraith and in turn was succeeded by Cathy Jamieson as Minister for Education Culture and Sport. Responsibility for Teachers and Schools now falls within the remit of the Deputy Minister, Nicol Stephen. Wendy Alexander continues to be responsible for Enterprise and Life Long Learning and deals with Community, Further and Higher Education.

1.5 There is no indication that the pace of change and adjustment to educational provision is slowing. At the beginning of the year the Scottish Parliament Committee on Education Culture and Sport began an inquiry into *The Purposes of Education* and Cathy Jamieson, Education Minister announced that a National Debate on School Education would be launched in March 2002. In February 2002 HM Inspectors (Education) issued a revision of *How Good is our School?* It is widely acknowledged that this publication provides a constructive basis for school self-evaluation.

2. Church Representatives on Local Authority Committees dealing with Education

2.1 The thirty-two Church of Scotland Representatives continue to do valuable work on behalf of the Church on the local authority committees dealing with education. Our Representatives are full voting members of these committees.

2.2 In October the Committee issued a questionnaire to our Representatives about the range and nature of their work. Representatives reviewed the result of the questionnaire at the start of the two day residential conference held at Scottish Churches House, Dunblane, in November 2001.

2.3 A question about how the new Sex Education guidance was being implemented brought a variety of responses that informed ongoing action by the Committee (See paragraph 5.1)

2.4 Our Representatives reported that disruptive behaviour in the classroom continues to be a major concern at local level. However, they were able to share experiences of different local authorities responding to the particular issues they faced. Responses to disruptive behaviour ranged from reviewing procedures like exclusions, behaviour management and codes of conduct, to setting up off-campus units and employing additional staff and initiating further outreach work. The report of the Task Group, chaired by Jack McConnell, the then Minister for Education, *Better Behaviour, Better Learning*, initiated further work at local level and there has been additional support and resources provided by the Scottish Executive. An action plan to implement the report has now been produced and this will be monitored by our Representatives at local level.

2.5 It was evident from the questionnaire that all local authorities are responding to broadly similar issues: Special Educational Needs, school buildings and Public Private Partnership (PPP) projects, Raising Attainment, Social Inclusion and budget issues. The Committee was able to offer particular support to the Scottish Borders' Council Church Representative during the Inquiry into budget issues in that authority, submitting written evidence to the Parliamentary Inquiry.

2.6 Speakers from the Scottish Executive (Mike Ewart), the General Teaching Council Scotland (Matt MacIver), Her Majesty's Inspectorate (John Brown HMIE), Scottish Churches Parliamentary Officer (Graham Blount) and the Healthy Respect Project (Dona Milne) also addressed the Dunblane conference.

2.7 It continues to be a high priority for the Committee to offer assistance and support of such quality on current educational developments and initiatives in order that both our Church Representatives and our Committee are well-informed and pro-active in their work for the Church.

2.8 A further meeting is to be held at the beginning of May for Church of Scotland, Roman Catholic and third Representatives. Prof. Gordon Kirk, Edinburgh University, will speak about the development of the Chartered Teacher Programme.

3. Chaplaincy in Scottish Schools

3.1 There is a real and important role for Chaplains to play in Scottish schools, but no one should minimise the difficulties facing those who try to ensure that they make a positive contribution to the life of the school. Today it is all the more essential that Chaplains should be clear about the role they have to play and that they should fulfil it with understanding, conviction and commitment.

3.2 The success of a Chaplaincy depends on good relationships being built with the staff. The relationship between the Headteacher and the Chaplain is crucial. Every aspect of the work is dependent on these relationships. Such working relationships do not simply happen. They must be worked at and developed by all concerned over a period of time.

3.3 A new course for School Chaplains has been designed and was delivered in Shetland in February 2002. The course, for Chaplains and Headteachers, covers the development of working relationships based on knowledge of the Scottish education system and the three core roles of the School Chaplain: Religious Observance, Pastoral Care and Resource Person. Advice about Religious Observance will be reviewed in light of any new guidance from the Scottish Executive Review Group. (See paragraph 8.1)

3.4 The course also examines indicators of effective school Chaplaincy and ways of maintaining good quality in School Chaplaincy. This work is closely linked to the process of self-evaluation used by schools, 'How Good is our School' 2002.

4. Chaplaincy in Scottish Colleges

4.1 The group formed to support Chaplaincy in Scottish Colleges has continued to meet.

4.2 The Committee hosted a conference for Chaplains and college staff in October 2001. The conference gave participants the opportunity to share different experiences of Chaplaincy across the widely differing size, composition and locations of Scotland's Colleges of Further Education. Contributions to the conference from Chaplains, staff and students allowed participants to appreciate Chaplaincy from all perspectives.

4.3 The workshop session of the conference focussed on: -

What can Chaplaincy offer the college?
What can the college offer the Church?

4.4 The following points are an extract from a summary conference report which was sent to the Principals of Scottish Colleges.

4.5 What can the Church/Chaplaincy offer the college:-
- pastoral/spiritual care
- presence of church & contact with the wider church communities
- independent support/advice on issues and links to other agencies
- host families
- justice/peace/equality issues and concern for values
- a spiritual dimension
- participation in college life - music/sports
- an independent voice on appeals committees
- encouragement/affirmation/sense of worth
- a sense of balance & calmness to a stressful place
- a valuing of the work of the college and the people within it

4.6 What colleges can offer the Church/Chaplaincy:-

- space and facilities
- communication via Student Handbook, prospectus, web site and Fresher's Fayre
- training and staff development opportunities for Chaplains
- offering a role at graduations
- contact with a broad spectrum of society
- opportunity to discern and meet community and individual needs
- helping to develop the skills of Chaplains
- interdependence of other professional bodies with the college
- awareness of marketing, competition and environmental and ethical issues
- an understanding of the pressure of the workplace and the balance of work and home commitments.

4.7 The summary Conference Report sent to college Principals has generated interest from several colleges with which the Committee had not previously had contact. This increased interest will form the basis of further work in this area in 2002. A further conference is planned for September 2002.

5. Sex Education in Scottish Schools

5.1 The Committee has continued to monitor Sex Education programmes in Scottish schools and had asked Church Representatives about the distribution of the *Sex Education in Scottish Schools, A Guide for Parents and Carers* produced by the Scottish Executive. The responses from the Representatives were varied and raised concerns about the manner in which parents were or were not being consulted about Sex Education.

The Committee promotes three underlying principles in the guidance on Sex Education introduced by the Scottish Executive in March 2001.

5.2 The first principle.

5.2.1 The partnership of parents and teachers in the process of planning and providing young people with education about sex and relationships. Parents have a right to be consulted when a programme is being planned or altered. This establishes a vital safeguard to what, when and how sex education is taught. If a parent decides the programme is unsuitable for the child, the parent has the right to withdraw the child. However, there are positive advantages to the process of consultation, because in reality the parent can ensure that the child has positive support at home when matters about sexuality and relationships feature in school. Many teachers are also parents and are aware of the issues involved in talking to children about sex in the home.

5.3 The second principle.

5.3.1 That programmes of sex education have to be appropriate for the age and stage of development of the young people. This means that a careful balance has to be struck between children learning too much too soon, or too little too late. From quite a young age, pupils today are exposed to all kinds of publicity through TV, magazines and advertising which highlight sexual attractiveness and sexual activity as if these were the main aims in growing up. Much of this publicity underplays the importance of stable family life and relationships. The Committee is clear about the need to ensure young people have a proper knowledge and understanding of the physical aspects of human sexuality at appropriate times.

5.4 The third principle.

5.4.1 That sex education must include moral education in which questions are honestly faced and discussed. The guidance on sex education in schools requires that due attention is given to the beliefs and values of home, church and other faith groups. There is a need to ensure that young people are encouraged to understand the responsibilities that their developing sexuality requires of them in their relationships, for their personal well-being and the well-being of society. Young people need to know the legal aspects of sexual behaviour in our society, but they also need to develop their own moral stances to guide them with sensitivity and responsibility in this vital area for life.

5.5 The past year has seen expressions of public concern for the kind of materials that might be recommended or used in school sex education programmes. Much of the concern has focussed on a document produced by Learning and Teaching Scotland on 5 - 14 National Guidelines on Health Education and in particular on the list on page 77 of the booklet for Teachers and Managers entitled 'Resources'. Members of the Committee discussed the issue in September 2001 with MSPs of the Scottish Parliament's Committee on Education, Culture and Sport.

5.6 The Committee has no evidence of inappropriate materials actually being used in schools. Nevertheless the Committee has made representations to the Education Minister asking the Minister to distance herself from the list or to clarify its nature and purpose. In response Cathy Jamieson wrote on 14th December 2001:

"... For the record, there is no Scottish Executive endorsed or recommended list of resources for sex or drug education. National advice and guidance refers to materials which it is believed schools have found helpful, in whole or in part, in delivering the health education curriculum, in particular about sex and drugs. However such a reference does not constitute an endorsement of any particular resource material. There is a wealth of resources and materials available, some produced by commercial publishers, some health promotion companies and also other sources. Responsibility for the development and management of the curriculum rests with education authorities and decisions about the choice of materials used to support the curriculum are made by those education authorities and schools. Whatever materials are used, schools will take account of the statutory guidance and national advice: the age, understanding and maturity of the pupils, and the views of parents and pupils in developing their education programmes. ...
Perhaps even more worryingly, resources that were never designed for use in schools have been highlighted and presented as though they were. ..."

5.7 The Committee takes the view that more attention should be given to helping parents to play their part. It is appreciated that parents and their children do not always find it easy to talk together about these important issues. A leaflet has been produced by the Committee to offer parents information and suggestions of how they can take an active part in supporting one another and encouraging positive sex education programmes in schools. It has been distributed along with a School Chaplains' Bulletin in an issue of Manse Mail and distributed to Local Authorities and MSPs. The feedback about the approach taken has been very positive. At a meeting in February 2002, the Committee raised these issues with Nicol Stephen, Deputy Minister.

5.8 Consultation between parents, carers and schools will continue to be the focus for ongoing discussions with the Scottish Executive, Ministers and Civil Servants.

6. Standards and Quality Report

6.1 Last autumn HM Inspectors of Education issued a Standards and Quality Report on Religious and Moral Education. (RME) The report records progress in Religious and Moral Education in the past few years. The number of pupils opting for presentation for Standard Grade and Higher Religious Studies continues to grow. However the report raises concerns about aspects of the 5-14 programme and the overall provision in S3/S4. There are still issues raised by the report concerning the amount of time made available for RME if a learning experience of reasonable quality is to be provided for all young people. When representatives of the Committee met with Nicol Stephen, the Deputy Education Minister, they asked for a programme of inservice courses similar to those that followed other Standards and Quality Reports. As a result of this request, we understand that action has been taken and that in-service courses are being planned.

7. Resources for RME

7.1 In response to the need for teaching resources raised at the Assembly last year the Committee has embarked on a programme to provide practical help for teachers. The resources we are planning will offer suggestions to teachers on how to use Personal Search targets alongside Christianity targets. It is planned to include materials that children can access directly on the Church's website. The Committee is also supporting a project by the Religious and Moral Education Department of the Faculty of Education, Strathclyde University (formerly Jordanhill). The project will create resources from a local context designed to inform learners about beliefs and practices within the Church of Scotland in a style that will encourage engagement and interaction.

8. Religious Observance

8.1 The Standards & Quality Report on Religious and Moral Education included a special note on Religious Observance. Many Headteachers face important issues in determining how best to provide worthwhile experiences in Religious Observance that meet the needs of increasingly diverse school communities. HM Inspectors report that nearly two thirds of secondary schools do not follow the guidelines of Circular 6/91. The Education Minister has established a working group to explore issues about Religious Observance. The Minister invited the Church to nominate a representative to this group and the Committee has asked the Secretary to fulfil this role.

8.2 The remit of the group is:-

8.2.1 "*To review current guidance on arrangements for religious observance in schools taking account of the views of interested bodies and individuals including religious organisations, teachers, parents and pupils; to make recommendations to Ministers on any changes which are required to ensure that revised guidance to schools is relevant and appropriate for pupils, that it fulfils the requirements of the 1980 Act and also provides practical advice on religious observance.*"

8.3 The Committee has sought views within the Church and is grateful to the many ministers and School Chaplains who returned a short questionnaire to furnish the Committee with their views. In conjunction with Parish Education Year of the Child initiative, plans are in

hand to consult with young Christians, using the Children's Forums. We hope that the Youth Assembly might also offer views on Religious Observance.

9. A Teaching Profession for the 21st Century

9.1 April 2001 saw a landmark agreement between the Scottish Executive, the teachers' unions and Cosla called *A Teaching Profession for the 21st Century*. This document forms the agreement which was reached following the recommendations made in the McCrone Report. The first part of the agreement, pay rises of 10% for all teachers and the introduction of a 35 hour week, came into effect in April and August 2001 respectively. One immediate and welcome change is the guarantee of a one year training place for all new teachers with a supported induction to the profession which should see them achieve the *Standard for Full Registration* in one year.

9.2 The Agreement is wide-ranging covering 5 areas; Career Structure, Conditions of Service, Pay, Developing and Supporting the Profession and Future Negotiating Machinery. It will be many years before all of the agreement is in place. There are roles for the Scottish Negotiating Committee for Teachers (SNCT), the GTCS, the Scottish Executive, Local Authorities and schools in delivering the Agreement.

9.3 The Committee is well placed to appreciate the implications of the agreement and monitor its implementation because the Secretary in her previous appointment was heavily involved in the negotiating process which led to the Agreement.

10. Scottish Qualifications Authority (SQA)

10.1 The Committee continues to take an interest in the work of the Scottish Qualifications Authority (SQA) and shares with many others the relief that almost all exam candidates received accurate results in August 2001. This is due in no small part to the hard work invested in the system by teachers, school administrative staff and council staff. However, although many difficulties have been overcome, the Committee believes that there should be no complacency about the future of the SQA.

10.2   While we welcome the return to an exam system which delivers effectively, there is also a need to look to the future. This was reflected in the publication by the Scottish Executive of a consultation document on the Scottish Qualification Authority Bill. The Bill sets out a package of measures to retain the SQA as an Executive Non-Departmental Public Body (NDP), with a reformed Board, stakeholder involvement and improvements to the management and organisation.

10.3   The Committee, in its response to the consultation paper in November 2001, agreed that the SQA should retain its status as an Executive NDP, and that the new Board should be smaller. We also welcome the recommendations about transparency and accountability and the provision to set up an Advisory Council to the SQA Board in order that all stakeholders have input to the work of the SQA. The Bill also emphasised the necessity of delivering the Board's key functions and effectively monitoring this process, which the Committee is happy to support.

11.   Higher Still

11.1   The Committee responded to the Review of Assessment within the New National Qualifications in December 2001. The demands of assessment, internal and external have been a major contributing factor in the difficulties in the implementation of the Higher Still programme. The National Qualifications Task Group (NQTG) is co-ordinating action to address the range of assessment issues across the board, and in specific subject areas. In its response, the Committee endorsed the work being undertaken by the NQTG and stated that we saw a continuing role for it in monitoring progress and informing debate, as changes are planned and implemented. There is no doubt that the current system of assessment places an unnecessarily heavy burden on learners and teachers and further work is necessary to lighten the burden across subjects.

11.2   The Review put forward two options for change to the current assessment system;

Option A - where candidates could achieve a course award by success in the external exam, with unit assessment as an added possibility, and;

Option B - where candidates could achieve an ungraded award by completing all the course units and unit assessments.

11.3   It was the view of the Committee that neither option would meet the needs of all learners, teachers and users of qualifications. However, if change were to be made it should be along the lines of Option A. We would be opposed to any return to the divisive system of Scottish Examination Board (SEB) and Scottish Vocational Education Council (SCOTVEC) where external exams were held in higher esteem than internal assessment. Option B should also be available to candidates particularly in Colleges of Further Education.

12.   State Funding for school based Youth and Children's Work

12.1   Last year the Assembly agreed as follows:
In the light of the growth of Youth and Children's Ministry, instruct the Committee in consultation with the Board of Parish Education to investigate the possibility of state funding for schools based youth and children's work and report to the General Assembly of 2002.

The Committee and the Board of Parish Education have investigated the possibility of funding from the Scottish Executive for this work. The Scottish Executive has increased its funding for schools considerably but is unable to fund work of this nature for single-faith organisations.

13.   The Public Private Partnerships

13.1   The Committee on Education considered Public Private Partnerships (PPP) so far as they relate to education. A briefing paper was sent out to Church representatives on Local Authorities because many Local Authorities are actively looking at PPP

13.2 In addition the Committee took a view on two specific issues.

13.2.1 First, there is the issue of joint campuses. Some authorities have indicated, as part of the rationalisation proposals linked to PPP developments, that they wish to develop joint non-denominational/ denominational school buildings. In such proposals there are essentially still two schools with two Headteachers. However, there are economies gained in relation to certain shared facilities such as a single kitchen. Additionally it may be argued that such a development is a step on the road to integration and that the very fact of sharing a single campus potentially will ease some tensions. The Committee, in accordance with the Church's stated position of fully integrated state schools, welcomes the proposal of joint campuses as a step in the right direction.

13.2.2 Second, there is the issue of spiritual provision. Local authorities generally accept that, in denominational secondary schools, oratories with a chaplaincy office are provided. Thus in the nearly completed Glasgow PPP Project all of the new denominational secondary schools were provided, at significant cost, with such a facility. No such provision was made for non-denominational schools. It is the Committee's view that this disparity is ill-founded and that the spiritual needs of pupils, staff and parents in non-denominational schools should also be met. This could be undertaken by providing a "contemplation" area such as that being developed in the Midlothian PPP Project bringing together Dalkeith High and St David's High into a single building but where each has a spiritual area. The Committee takes the view that all non-denominational secondary schools should have such provision.

14. Work In Partnership With Other Organisations

14.1 The Committee has been actively involved in the work of the Scottish Joint Committee on Religious and Moral Education and along with the Educational Institute for Scotland supplies the joint-secretary to the SJCRME. This commitment was renewed after review in 2001. SJCRME has produced a leaflet on Religious Studies to provide information for pupils and parents. A conference on "The Place of RME in a crowded curriculum" is planned for September 2003.

14.2 Representatives of the Committee participate in the Religious Education Movement, Scotland and in the past year have been pleased to be associated with *'Education for Mutual Understanding'* a programme combating sectarianism and racism through drama and art programmes that bring pupils together from a variety of backgrounds.

14.3 The Forum on Scottish Education has, since its inception in 1988, been supported by the Church. The Committee has undertaken administrative support for the Forum. The Forum brings together a wide range of representatives from the Educational establishment in Scotland. However, in the light of the developments of the Scottish Parliament, the Forum is currently undertaking a fundamental review of its role and methods of working.

15. Consultations

15.1 Between May 2001 and Feb 2002 the Committee has made responses to the following: -

- Collaborative Review of Initial Teacher Education in Scotland.
- Higher Education Review Group First Consultation
- Education (Disability and Pupil Records) Act
- GTCS Standard for Full Registration
- SQA Bill
- Review of Assessment within new National Qualification
- Review of Education for Work and Enterprise

- Chartered Teacher 2nd Consultation
- GTCS Codes of Practice
- Guidance on the Circumstances in which parents may choose to educate their children at home.

In the name of the Committee

JOHN J LAIDLAW, *Convener*
WILLIAM T WEATHERSPOON, *Vice Convener*
SUSAN M LESLIE, *Secretary*

ADDENDUM

Mr William T Weatherspoon has served for three years as Vice-Convener of the Committee on Education. The Committee has enjoyed the benefit of his wide experience in education and the Church. His gentle courtesy, shrewdness and good humour provided support and encouragement to members of the Committee and particularly to the Convener and the staff. We thank him for his commitment to education and the time given to this job now completed.

JOHN J LAIDLAW, *Convener.*
SUSAN M LESLIE, *Secretary.*

PARISH EDUCATION
MAY 2002

PROPOSED DELIVERANCE

The General Assembly

1. Receive the Report
2. Affirm the place of education at the centre of Christian life (1.5)
3. Welcome the appointment of Regional staff as an indication of the Board's desire to deliver its services more locally (3.3)
4. Encourage the Board to explore further such local delivery of its services
5. Commend the work of the Year of the Child to the whole Church (3.6)
6. Instruct the Board of Parish Education in consultation with the Board of Ministry to review the arrangements for the supervision of, elders and others who operate as worship leaders in congregations (3.4.1)
7. Amend Act ii, 2000, to include as a category of worship leader, "Elders who have satisfactorily undertaken a course of training under the auspices of the Board of Parish Education" (3.4.2)
8. Welcome the strengthening of partnerships reflected in the relationships between Scottish Churches' Open College, Napier University and its members bodies (4.9)
9. Encourage further development of the ecumenical commitment to the educational and corporate governance of the Scottish Churches' Open College (4.9)
10. Instruct the Board to explore ways in which the Church of Scotland can continue to provide core financial support for the Scottish Churches' Open College (4.10)
11. Urge discussions to take place between the Board of Parish Education, the Board of Ministry and the Scottish Churches' Open College with regard to developing collaborative educational provision for ministry training in its widest sense (Appendix)
12. Instruct the Board to invite the Youth Assembly of 2002 to bring to the Board a view on the nature and priority of church education and training services (Appendix)

REPORT

1.   Introduction

1.1   Christian Education has a history as long as that of the Gospel.

When the first disciples accepted Jesus invitation to "Follow Me", they embarked on a journey which was at once challenging and demanding. Jesus the Rabbi, the teacher, taught them all that they knew. Drawing on his insights into scripture and history and his relationship to God, Jesus showed his disciples a new and better way.

1.2   We live in the inheritance of Jesus teaching. The Reformers brought the vision of a "Kirk and a school in every Parish". They also brought the Catechisms, where the elements of the Christian faith were taught by questions and answers. Times change. Methods change. The Good News of Jesus Christ remains the same. Thus, all of us bring, from our relationship with God through Jesus Christ, the values of the Kingdom to Christian Education, which must address, in a meaningful and genuine way, everyone's educational needs; no matter age, background or ability; no matter the place where an individual is on his or her own faith journey.

1.3   The General Assembly of 2001 received the report of the Special Commission Anent Review and Reform. Reflection on this document leads to the inevitable conclusion that times and methods are changing. The somewhat dry and cumbersome title of the Commission tends to obscure the fact that the refreshing, challenging and reflective nature of the report gave our great institution a chance to face up to and to overcome many of the issues that have tended to depress and de-motivate us in the past.

In the memorable words of one senior minister, we had been given the chance to "grasp the nettle and run with it"!

1.4   For the Board of Parish Education, the Commission's report and its more expressive sub-title, "A Church Without Walls" came as a breath of fresh air…a welcome insight into the well-recognised problems of our church, but for once with a confident and evangelical expression of both a willingness and an ability to do something about them.

1.5   Above all, the Board of Parish Education found the report welcome insofar as it offered affirmation of the place of Christian education in our church and of the need to give our people confidence in and understanding of their faith and its relevance to the world; to recognise the need for the people of God to see themselves as exactly that, through worship , service and example.

If a new church, a "Church Without Walls", is to emerge, then by definition we must educate ourselves to be a part of it.

1.6   For the Board of Parish Education, that means a pivotal role in equipping individuals and congregations for the types of worship and service that will manifest that Church.

For the church as a whole, it demands a prioritisation of, and investment in, education (in every sense of that word) that has not been the case up to now.

2.   Themes for the work of the Board of Parish Education

The Church "works where people join together, building relationships with each other and the community to which they belong. It is through these relationships that the Gospel is spread. In each place the Church is different. There is no one model that fits all. We rejoice in the diversity within the Church. We celebrate and encourage it".

Report of the Special Commission

2.1   In the past year, the Board of Parish Education has considered much about its work. Recognising the issues raised by the Church Without Walls (CWW) report and recognising how closely they fit with our own intentions has been exciting. It has also demanded a strategic re-consideration if what we do on behalf of the Church of Scotland.

2.2   It is not enough for us to adjust what has always been done to fit a new framework. We need instead to look at the contemporary Church and its environment and ask what kind of educational service it needs to thrive within that framework.

In that context, three themes have emerged against which the Board can assess its present work and plan for the future.

2.3   These themes are:

- **Local Church**
- **Leadership**
- **Inclusion**

3.   Local Church

'The storm is so serious, I believe that it marks the end of "business as usual" for the Churches and marks the need for us to begin again building the church from the ground up.'

Report of the Special Commission

3.1 The local church is the place where the Church of Scotland is rooted. The worshipping congregation is the basic unit of the living church. It is there that commitment, relationships and faith are conceived and nurtured. It is clear that without thriving local churches there would be no national church.

However, it is also clear that the value of a national church, of the pooling and sharing of every type of resource, can feed and enhance the local situation.

3.2 In this symbiotic relationship, the central Boards must recognise and respond to the needs of the local church. In its turn, the local church must value the role of the national in terms of its own development and also of the role of that national church in the wider society here in Scotland and throughout the world.

In other words, the two are parts of the same body, working in partnership to the greater benefit of the work of God.

In seeking to work more closely with the local church, the Board of Parish Education has become involved in a series of major initiatives.

3.3 Regional Staff

The Board of Parish Education has been saying for many years now that it needs to be able to develop and deliver services in a way that takes account of local situations.

3.3.1 In the past few months, we have gone some considerable way towards that by introducing Regional Development Workers, initially on a pilot basis, who will work closely with local groups to develop educational strategies and to raise awareness of the value of education and training to the congregations in their areas.

At present there are three of these workers, funded for three years from the reserve funds of the Board. They are based in :

- **Inverness**
- **Tayside**
- **South West**

3.3.2 The initial response has been positive and the staff themselves report a welcome from those with whom they are in contact and a recognition that they are able to building relationships in the ground that allow for the resources of the Board of Parish Education to be channeled more effectively back into local situations.

3.3.3 The Board believes strongly that this is an important step forward in how it relates to the local church and will be monitoring the use of and response to this service so that it can consider how to extend it beyond the pilot areas and the pilot period.

3.4 Elder Training

The Eldership Working Party has been involved in a range of new ideas to work at the local level. Working on such areas as:

3.4.1 Peoples' vision of and for the Eldership:

- **Developing prayer life**
- **Encouraging team ministries involving Elders**
- **Participating and Leading worship**
- **Discussions on the spiritual and pastoral roles of the Elder**
- **Youth Eldership and the Elders' response to the Year of the Child**
- **Helping Kirk Sessions think about their response to the CWW report**

All of these are exciting developments that begin to address some of the hard questions that face Elders and Sessions in a difficult time.

3.4.2 If the local church is the focus of our work, then the Eldership is at the very heart of that and we need to allow Elders to be equipped to do the job and to do it with confidence and imagination if they are to be energised to face the new context of their work.

3.5 Publications

3.5.1 One of the functions of the Board of Parish Education has always been to provide published resources that help people do the tasks that they are given by the

Church. Increasingly, that has been interpreted by the Board as a role that is best met by offering a wide range of resources that fit different times and places.

This approach has led to the publication of materials that are aimed at a wide range of educational contexts and at different groups and individuals.

In the Appendix to this report there are listed the new items available.

3.5.2 It is hoped that the emerging church will benefit from these resources, but also that it will engender new ideas and produce material from within the wider church that can be brought to the attention of others. The communication of good practice is always desirable and this is one area in which the Board of Parish Education can act as a conduit for the wider community of the Church of Scotland and its partners.

3.6 Year of the Child

The Year of the Child process and project has been the biggest development of the work of the Board of Parish Education in the last year.

3.6.1 The Assembly of 2001 adopted a Vision Statement that challenged the church to look at how it dealt with children in terms of every aspect of its work. The project aims to raise the profile of children in our churches and to give the church the chance to find ways of communicating with children that allow a dialogue between the generations to be established and for the church to be better informed about its young people and the experience they have of the church.

3.6.2 The Year of the Child is about children, but not only about them. It is about relationships and leadership and community and is directly related to all three of the main themes listed earlier in this report.

3.6.3 From all of the areas mentioned here, we can find ways in which the Church can grow and become a stronger witnessing and worshipping community. Diversity and flexibility can be encouraged as our church seeks to take risks and to be invigorated by the challenges that it faces.

The role of the Board of Parish Education in this is to be a channel for good ideas, a promoter of good practice and a partner in the coming adventure.

4. Leadership

> 'We need leadership. We need...vision and flexibility...there needs to be an honest appraisal of the gifts and callings of our elders (leaders)
>
> **Report of the Special Commission**

4.1 Whilst ministers have clear responsibility for the leadership and oversight of the life of the congregation, leadership itself takes many forms. Theological; moral; spiritual; practical leadership and so on are all essential to our church life. Also possible are worship leadership; children's leaders; mission leaders; youth leaders; Guild leaders.

In all of these we must equip people to take on their roles and to recognise the value of good leadership, be that individual or collective.

4.2 Across the whole range of work undertaken by the Board of Parish Education, leadership is a central theme. To foster and develop the many elements of the local church described earlier, we need to support leaders. To play a part in the sustaining and rebuilding of our church, we need to identify the leadership roles that are required and the skills, understandings and resources implied to allow that leadership to flourish.

4.3 In the training of Elders, Readers, Youth Workers, Children's Workers, Guild Educational Representatives; leaders in Uniformed Organisations and the rest, the Board of Parish Education is already at the forefront of leadership development. However, we cannot fall in to the trap of assuming that whilst all of these are important what we are doing in detail is either the correct priority or entirely relevant to the contemporary situation.

4.4 It is essential that we keep under review the nature of the tasks being undertaken by the leaders with whom we are already working and that we are willing and able to adjust services in line with changing needs and expectations.

Where, for example, the model of Eldership changes, Elder training must change too.

4.5 Beyond that, however, there exists the further issue of emerging forms of leadership. Where congregations find themselves worshipping in new ways; serving their parishes in new ways; meeting social challenges to their work and working outside their walls, new tasks will emerge and new systems of support will be required.

4.6 In other words, if we are to become a Church Without Walls, we will see a very different church from the one that many people experience now and if we are to enjoy and celebrate that, we need to have confidence in what we are doing and in our ability to do it.

4.7 Already we can see this being worked through in the training of youth workers and children's workers. Experiments in training elders involved with worship. The support of young people in the Youth Assembly and the General Assembly. The leadership of Children's Forums and the leadership being recognised in children. All of these are crucial.

4.8 The prospectus of the Scottish Churches' Open College is another major contributor to this. The opportunity for people to study for Higher Educational qualifications that will provide a pool of expertise and leadership for the church is surely of immense value.

4.9 A summary of the work of the College for the past year and some information about its programmes is contained in the Appendix to the report. It can be seen there that the relationship between SCOC and Napier University is a fruitful one and is allied to the ecumenical nature of the College to provide a valuable resource for the Churches in Scotland.

4.10 The Board recognises the role of the Open College and seeks to continue to support its work through the provision of funding and other resources

5. Inclusion

> *'The aim of the Board of Parish Education is to provide a variety of Christian educational opportunities for people, irrespective of age, gender, ability or location.*
>
> **Board of Parish Education**

5.1 If education is not inclusive, we are missing the point. The work of the Board of Parish Education needs to offer opportunities to an enormous range of people from a wide range of circumstances doing a wide range of jobs.

5.2 The Church of Scotland has a constituency of at least 700 000 people. If we can see the opportunity for leadership, service and mission that figure represents, then we can unlock boundless energy in the work and witness of our church.

If we can also find ways of helping the church speak to others in the communities it serves, then we will truly see God's work on the march and not in retreat.

> *We recommend that the Church recover the lost art of Christian friendship. This lost art is not about being a "friendly church", but being a church that makes its friends beyond 'those that salute you'.*
>
> **Report of the Special Commission**

5.3 Again, what is said here is at the heart of much of what the Board of Parish Education is doing.

- Child Protection
- Year of the Child
- Youth Assembly
- Counselling Training
- Learn to Live Programme
- Learning Disabilities

5.4 All of these address and face up to issues of inclusion that must be central to the development and integrity of a genuine sense of community within and around our congregations, where each person is welcomed, encouraged, nurtured and affirmed.

5.5   Within the church, we have already seen how youth work, when addressed in ways that allow our young people to be a part of rather than apart from our work, can change the face of what we do and how we think. Youth Representatives have challenged and refreshed our General Assembly. The Youth Assembly has provided a forum where our young people can share their views and draw support from their peers.

The Year of the Child is beginning to do the same kinds of things for younger people still.

Yet these are internal things that build on what we know.

5.6   The bigger challenge is to work with and for those who are less familiar to us and who are crying out for a lead and a voice from the church that welcomes them and gives them support.

5.7   The Board of Parish Education is looking at headings like relationships; social inclusion; other faiths; gender attitudes and so on to see what educational imperatives and directions they might offer the church. Our publications, our conferences and events, our course materials, our office bearer training, need all take account of these issues and are already doing so.

5.8   The church needs to deal with these issues. Finding them difficult does not mean we can leave them aside. Discussing them and thinking about them does not imply a viewpoint, but helps us to work towards one and that is of the essence of a healthy educational perspective.

The exciting thing for the Board of Parish Education is to look ahead to new places and to work with the wider church as it wrestles with them.

6.   Conclusion

6.1   The past year has seen the Board of Parish Education move in many ways. Physically, we have moved to new premises. Educationally, we have begun to move in ways that reflect a need for the church to respond

constructively and imaginatively to the ideas, so wholeheartedly supported by the last General Assembly, that have emerged from the Special Commission report.

The belief of the Board of Parish Education is that education and training play an absolutely fundamental role in the process of change that is upon us.

If the Church of Scotland is to survive, let alone thrive, we must accept that view.

6.2   The Board of Parish Education regrets the financial deficit recorded for the year to 31 December 2001 which it views as unacceptable. The preliminary Budget for the current year presented an equally dismal prospect. A full review of the Board's work and associated costs is now in progress in an attempt to achieve, as quickly as is reasonably possible, a balanced Budget which does not require us to continue to make unsustainable calls upon the Board's reserves.

6.3   However, the Board is conscious of the expectations which its broad educational role within the Church has raised. It recognises also that to operate within its core income will inevitably mean either a reduction or elimination of some of those functions.

6.4   That will demand innovation and new practices. It will also demand a significant increase in the priority given to the nurture, education and training of the whole people of God to be the people of God

6.5   That will cost time, talent and money, but an investment in our people can reap rewards in terms of commitment, service, mission and, in short, in the work of Christ's Kingdom.

REV JOHN C CHRISTIE, *Convener*
MRS LORNA PATERSON, *Vice-Convener*
MR IAIN WHYTE, *General Secretary*

Appendix

The Board of Parish Education 2001-2002

Children's ministry

- **Year of the Child**, *a major initiative for the Church of Scotland. Supported by over 700 congregations and giving a voice to our children. Launched by the Board in December at an event addressed by the First Minister, Jack McConnell. Year of the Child is sponsored by Children First and Christian Aid*

- **Children's Forums**, *over 70 local councils of children working together on national agendas and speaking to the church from a child's perspective.*

- **CHoK newsletter**, *offering support to children and their leaders as they find their way through the year of the child and into new ways of working*

- **Ambassadors**, *28 young people representing their peers at national events organised by the Church of Scotland, including the General Assembly*

- **National training course in children's ministry** *revised*

- *Transition of post of Presbytery Adviser to Trainer instigated, focussing the work of the Board locally on the support of volunteers and in the meeting of local training needs*

Child Protection

- *Continued work in this area, including much development on police checks and the beginning of looking at the church's response to offenders*

Youth Work

- **Youth Assembly** *planned for September in Glasgow*

- **General Assembly Youth Night** *in two locations in Edinburgh and Glasgow, June 1 and 2. Details are available from the Board's offices*

- **Crossover Festival,** *arts and events for young people in conjunction with Board of Social Responsibility, BB, GB, and Christian Aid. Held in West Linton in June, this event has achieved increasing success over the past four years and has found a significant place in the calendar for many young people*

- **Representation at World Youth Day** *in Canada along with meeting with Presbyterian contemporaries in Canada*

Adult Education

- **Development of Odyssey programme**, *first downloadable programme from the Board of Parish Education*

- **Work with Guild Educational Representatives**, *including their annual conference, thereby supporting one of the organisations in our Church that has a long tradition of education and learning*

- **The annual Board Conference** *held at the Scottish Police College in Tulliallan in February and bringing together 170 people involved in our work to discuss and develop what we offer to the church*

Readership Training

- **48 Readers in training** *on the SCOC "Living Worship" Programme*

- **280 active Readers in service**, *being supported with a programme of in-service training and an annual conference*

Elder Training

- **39 trainers in 27 Presbyteries** *who worked with over 3300 people in the last year.*

- *6 more trainers in training*

- *Co-operation with 3 trainers in the* **United Free Church of Scotland**

- **Over 100 Session Clerks** *attended training courses run by the Board of Parish Education*

- *Working with the Assembly Council and others to examine the spiritual role of Eldership, prayer life and team ministry involvement*

Publications

- *Move to a more commercial approach, with* **name change to Scottish Christian Press**

- **Catalogue with a circulation of over 7000** *continues to develop and diversify*

- **Catalogue available on the web**

- *Warehousing and sales now being handled by Book Source on behalf of the Board, allowing orders to be processed and paid for by credit card*

- **Church Without Walls report** *and discussion book published, both in great demand*

- *New publications to be launched at the Assembly*

…**KiK** *series edited by Doug Swanney, head of the Board's Youth and Children's Ministry section*
…**Let There be Light**, *a song book by Iain Whyte*
…**Hear our Voice**, *the Year of the Child song and other musical publications now available on listen only format on the Board's website@* www.parisheducation.org.uk

- *Other forthcoming resources*
…**Beyond the Walls**, *a series of practical guides on the working out of the Church Without Walls agenda*
…**Bite the Bullet**, *a challenging adult education series on areas such as domestic violence, sexuality*
…**Guide to the Gospel of Mark**, *by Leith Fisher*

Information Technology

- *The Board has agreed to increase the use of IT as a means of internal communication and for the servicing of Committees*

- **The Board's web-site**, www.parisheducation.org.uk, *offers information, forums and ideas for people to become involved in and with the work of the Board*

Scottish Churches' Open College 2001-2002

- **SCOC is an ecumenical theological college** *that represents a major extension of the work of the Board. All the main denominations in Scotland plus some agencies are member bodies of SCOC. This partnership is unique in Scotland and relies on the continuing commitment of each of its member bodies to ecumenical theological education. The Church of Scotland is a member body and is represented by Mr. Iain Whyte (Director, Board of Parish Education) and Rev Sheilagh Kesting (Ecumenical Relations). In 2001-2, the College has revised its curriculum, re-positioned itself, and designed its own business plan for the first time.*

- **A new Collaborative Partnership Agreement with Napier University** *was also signed, indicating the level of renewed commitment between these two respective institutions.*

- *In May 2001 SCOC's new theological honours degree programme was successfully validated through Napier University. It is called the Learn to Live Programme and offers an innovative route to theological study. Students can choose to study for one module (ten weeks' duration) or towards an award (CertHE; DipHe; BA; BA[hons]). The emphasis is on doing theology within our current socio-political context using resources from past and present Christian tradition but not at the expense of contemporary experience. It is a learner-centred, experiential but nonetheless academic approach to theological learning. In this first year of delivery there have been 90 students on the programme and it is hoped that this will increase steadily over the next two years. This is the programme through which Readers-in-Training are prepared for Readership in the Church of Scotland.*

- On June 6th, SCOC held a **Launch event at Dynamic Earth**, Edinburgh. About 120 attended the day which included students, denominational representatives, Napier University representatives, and other interested parties. Workshops making use of the exhibition areas within Dynamic Earth were on offer and the official launch took place over lunch. Alasdair Morrison, MSP, had hoped to attend, but was unable to do so because the General Election was due to take place the next day. His written greetings were received and presentations from Professor John Mavor (Principal of Napier University), Rev Jayne Scott (Principal of SCOC) and Mr. Iain Whyte (Board of Parish Education) formed the basis of the lunch-time event.

- **The Training for Learning and Serving (TLS) programme** which had, for eight years offered foundational theological education to many who otherwise would not have ventured into theological study, was drawn to a close in Scotland. The programme was due to be reviewed and reconsidered as part of the validation processes with Napier University. Whilst there continue to be some features in the Learn to Live Programme which are reminiscent of the TLS course it has now been superceded by the Learn to Live Programme.

- The materials and copyright for the Foundation Course and the Worship and Preaching Course which were part of the TLS course have now been sold to the United Reformed Church for use as lay preachers' training in England and Wales.

- Validated through the professional body, COSCA, (Confederation of Scottish Counselling Agencies), there is also the Advanced Diploma in Counselling, which is validated by both COSCA as a professional qualification and Napier University as an academic award. This programme includes extensive placements with counselling agencies and, more particularly, with PF Counselling which is also a member body of SCOC. This course will be revalidated through Napier and COSCA this coming year as a Graduate Diploma. It will continue to be a three-year part-time course.

- **The Certificate in Higher Education (CertHE) for Working with People in the Church and Community** is a two-year part-time distance learning course which is validated by CeVe (Community Education Validation and Endorsement) and Napier University. Offered as a basic course in community education it is well suited for those who are involved either on a paid or unpaid basis as youth, children's or community workers in the church context. There are currently 22 students on this course and it is expected that the next two years will see some significant growth in numbers as increasingly church-based youth and community workers look for suitable training. In December, the Roman Catholic Bishops' Conference agreed to use this course in future as the route for training their youth workers in Scotland.

- With the introduction of its own Business Plan, SCOC has indicated its desire to take more responsibility for its own affairs. This is a step which would not have been possible without the continued support both strategically and financially from the Board of Parish Education.

- In order to support SCOC in this, the Board has planned to offer core funding of £325,000 (fixed) in each the first three years of its Business Plan (2001-2004). After this three year period, it is hoped that funding would be available from a wider base than simply through the Board of Parish Education. The work of SCOC is wholly consistent with the work of the Board in terms of educational methods, ecumenical commitment and breadth of provision. Therefore, the Board sees it as important in the light of the Church Without Walls Report for the Church of Scotland to continue financial support for SCOC. However, the financial restraints facing the Board mean that the level of funding offered to the College may need to be reviewed with implications for the business planning and strategy of the College.

Funding from other sources (eg, denominations, agencies, and trusts) is also being sought, but the College has no capital or cash assets upon which it can draw so annual costs have to be met through annual revenue.

- *Church of Scotland funding for SCOC through the Board of Parish Education currently contributes about 70% towards the cost of running the College. The remaining 30% is made up from fees, partners' subscriptions and other grants.*

- *The sale of Annie Small House, Inverleith Terrace, has meant that SCOC has now moved its location to 22 Colinton Road, Edinburgh. It is hoped that the United(SCOC) Library will move to the same location in the near future. This move in the middle of the first year of delivery of its Learn to Live Programme has meant more disruption for the staff, but the move is considered to be beneficial in the longer-term. The location places SCOC closer to the main campuses of Napier University and the PF Counselling agency. It also helps to address some of the difficulties which have been faced regarding library use, teaching space, access and parking.*

BOARD OF COMMUNICATION
MAY 2002

PROPOSED DELIVERANCE

The General Assembly

1. Receive the Report

2. Thank the Board members and staff for their work throughout the year

3. Affirm the changes to and the development of the Board's services following the independent Best Value Audit (2, 3)

4. Welcome the restructuring of Pathway Productions (4)

5. Commend the Board on its good stewardship of resources in significantly improving its year on year budgetary position through savings, and investment in areas of the Board's work leading to increased income (5, 8, 9, 10, 12)

6. Encourage the continuing development of a single, integrated website for the Boards and Committees of the Church of Scotland, with the Board of Communication acting as lead Board in co-ordinating this service (6.2 - 6.7)

7. Welcome the development of Life & Work magazine and note the positive impact that this is having on subscriptions and advertising sales (8)

8. Note the production of user guides to the website, Saint Andrew Press and Design Services in order to help service users to get the best service

9. Acknowledge the achievement of Saint Andrew Press and Pathway Productions in the successful launch of the new Professor William Barclay materials (10)

10. Receive the report on the use of multimedia in worship (14)

REPORT

SUPPORTING MISSION AND MINISTRY

1. Introduction

1.1 The Board of Communication continues to strive to support the mission and ministry of the Church of Scotland with the best possible communication services.

1.2 Responding to constant change, the Board is seeking to develop creatively its services which include media relations, video and audio production, book and magazine publishing, design and the Internet.

1.3 Some of the Board's operations such as Saint Andrew Press are principally run as revenue earning businesses while Media Relations and the Internet are purely service based. Others, such as Pathway Productions, have both elements present.

1.4 Performance is very important since, unlike most other Boards, the bulk of the Board of Communication's budget comes from earnings. There are real challenges and tensions in this given the volatility of markets over recent times and the increasing requirements to direct resources into the provision of services – Internet development, for example - being placed on the Board.

1.5 This has happened against a back-drop of decreasing proportional provision from Mission and Aid which places greater pressure on other methods of funding the Board's work, including generation of income from external sources or using reserves. The Board is seeking to develop its commercial potential while remaining sensitive to its central ethos of service to and for the Church of Scotland.

BEST VALUE AUDIT

2. Continuing change and development

2.1 This year the Board has continued the process of change and development in pursuit of delivering the best possible communication services to the Church. A main challenge has been responding to the independent Best Value Audit report which the Board commissioned from Scott-Moncrieff, the Church's Internal Auditors.

2.2 Every part of the Board's work was subjected to intensive scrutiny over a period of several months in the early part of the year. The Director and Section Heads, in consultation with their staff, submitted answers to detailed questions in a series of templates covering all aspects of the Board's planning, operations, finance and accountability.

2.3 In August Scott-Moncrieff delivered their report to the Board. The Auditors' report was positive and provided the Board with:

2.3.1 An independent analysis of its present position and recommendations for the future;

2.3.2 A picture of future excellence to aim for and practical suggestions to help achieve and maintain this. This has already helped to inform and enrich the present round of planning;

2.3.3 A series of measures aimed at helping the Board's short-term financial position.

2.4 The Board hopes that, in responding to the report, it will be able to move towards greater financial stability and the opportunity for growth.

2.5 As well as making its main recommendations the report implicitly endorses the Board's present plans and takes the view that they should be given the opportunity to bear fruit.

2.6 It identifies impressive existing levels of initiative in the pursuit of best value services.

2.7 The report offers an opportunity to learn from constructive criticism and directs the Board and its managers towards building continuous improvement into every aspect of policy making and operations. In doing so, the report highlights areas requiring improvement - especially the related areas of customer focus, planning and target setting, performance monitoring, financial accountability and responsibility and internal communications.

3. Main points of the Best Value Audit

3.1 At the time of writing, the Board is finalising its business and service plans, which incorporate its responses to the recommendations of the audit report. The main points are:

3.2 *A significant restructuring of Pathway Productions* aimed at further improving productivity and cost-effectiveness, and reducing overheads (see section 4 below).

3.3 *Review of recovery of costs for services* in the light of the Auditors' finding that the Board was operating very competitively compared with market rates whilst not recovering costs at a sufficiently realistic level of overheads (see section 5 below).

3.4 *Longer term and more detailed planning.*

3.5 *Increased commitment to reporting on performance* against agreed targets.

3.6 *Finance training for managers* to further improve accountability to the Board.

3.7 *More resources put into marketing* the Board's products and services both externally and internally.

3.8 *Customer services post discontinued* in order to reduce costs.

3.9 *Provision of handbooks* in order to help customers get the best out of the Board's services.

3.10 *The creation of an administration pool* in order to service the support requirements of the Department in a flexible and efficient way.

KEY ACHIEVEMENTS AND CHALLENGES

4. Restructuring Pathway should result in savings of around £100k per year

4.1 One of the most important practical outcomes of the Audit is that the Board has agreed to a significant restructuring of Pathway.

4.2 These changes will reduce Pathway's costs by around £60,000 in 2002 and this should be increased to the c. £100,000 mark in following years. Savings in 2002 are reduced by the costs of moving Pathway.

4.3 At the time of writing, Pathway is in the process of moving out of its Colinton Road premises and into a new suite of offices in the office complex on George Street. Apart from major cost savings, this move will have the benefit of bringing Pathway into closer contact with an important part of its customer base as well as the rest of the Communication Department.

4.4 In line with the Audit recommendations Pathway is being split. Laurence Wareing, Director of Pathway Productions, and Simon Jones, Audio Visual Producer, will deliver the production element of this service and John Williams – now re-designated Technical Support Manager - is being attached to the Media Relations Unit and will report to the Head of Media Relations. This has the effect of brigading all the Board's Assembly support services. John Williams will still work for Pathway for about forty per cent of his time but this time will, in effect, be bought from Media Relations via an internal market arrangement.

4.5 Derek Speirs' short-term contract in the post of Technical Assistant will end in June of this year. Work carried out within this post will either be absorbed into existing staffing capacity, bought in on a project by project basis or, where necessary, discontinued.

4.6 Pathway will retain some equipment and editing facilities in-house but in line with the Audit recommendations, it will extend its use of bought-in resources. This will make costs easier to track and will help to give a clearer picture of effectiveness and efficiency, and allow the utilisation of the latest technologies without having to invest capital in equipment.

4.7 As well as continuing its commitment to core business such as video production and media training, Pathway is continuing to develop the potential for webcasting. This year's Assembly is once again being broadcast live on the Church's Internet site.

5. Fast growth in Design Services

5.1 Design Services is one of the fastest growing areas of the Board's work. With over 400 jobs completed this year, output has virtually doubled over the past two years. The Board has piloted a new service-accounting model in this Unit, designed to give an accurate measure of costs and value.

5.2 It costs £25 per hour to run the in-house Design service.

5.3 The Best Value Audit report found that the average cost for a similar service in the marketplace is currently around £75 per hour.

5.4 At present the Board recovers £5 per hour through charges – an 80% discount on costs and a fraction of the market value.

5.5 Following consultation with the General Treasurer, the Board has agreed that a rate of £15 per hour be set for Boards and Committees. This represents a discount of 40% against the actual cost and is still very competitive against the market rate. The Board has agreed to set a standard hourly rate of £40 for external clients. Congregations, presbyteries and outside bodies connected to the Church will be offered a rate of £30.00 per hour (equivalent to a 25% discount against the standard rate).

5.6 The Board intends to review this policy in one year's time and, at that point, to consider moving to a charging policy for Boards and Committees that would fully recover costs at £25 per hour.

5.7 In the meantime, Design Services is developing a new on-line ordering and monitoring system. This will allow the design team to keep close track of each job and to ensure that customers are kept informed of progress. In fact, according to last year's records only two jobs were delivered late – both because of difficulties at the print stage. However, Design Services is aware that this is not always how the service is perceived and they are working hard to provide customers with up-to-date information at every stage in the job cycle.

5.8   A greater commitment to working with parishes, congregations and presbyteries forms part of Design Services plan for this year.

6.   Website hit rate increased to three million in past year

6.1   Interest in the Church's website – run as part of the Board's Media Relations Unit - continues to grow significantly. Projecting on the basis of the figures gathered so far, since the last Assembly the site's hit rate has virtually doubled to a total of more than three million - an average of around 250,000 hits per month.

6.2   The Board of Communication has agreed that there should be a single, integrated website for the Boards and Committees of the Church of Scotland, with the Board of Communication acting as lead Board in co-ordinating this service. An integrated site would avoid unnecessary duplication of resources and enable the development of core expertise and flexible service provision.

6.3   It is also important to remember that the Church of Scotland will be held publicly accountable for any service provided in its name. This is a particular concern when dealing with potentially vulnerable groups or situations. Examples might include children in a chat room who could be prey to unwelcome attention or spiritually or emotionally needy people seeking guidance or advice from a Church source.

6.4   The Board is concerned that there should be no fragmentation of the site otherwise there could be a serious dilution of the quality of the service. Boards and Committees have widely divergent levels of Internet interest and expertise.

6.5   The challenge is to strike a balance between the need for quality, consistency, ease of use and security at 'corporate' level with the desire of many within the Boards and Committees to be directly involved in the development of their part of the site. This is particularly (but not exclusively) true when considering the involvement of younger people who are generally more media aware and web literate.

6.6   In order to meet that challenge a new Website Guidebook has been drafted - with active participation from interested Boards and Committees – and has been circulated to all Boards and Committees for consultation. Areas covered by the Guidebook include general information relating to text, design and graphics; guidelines for people who will be updating pages via the website editor; and more technical information for "coders" – people who will be using specialist technology to create and update pages.

6.7   Additionally, the Board is setting up a training programme that it is hoped will offer a degree of autonomy to service users, within the context of the guidelines.

6.8   Given its current levels of human and financial resources it is clear that the Board of Communication is not able to satisfy all the Church's requirements for developing an integrated site. It is worth noting in this context that the development of the site to date has been achieved within the existing resources. The Board agreed that it was essential that the Church of Scotland should have a presence in this vital new medium. However, the additional strain that this has placed on the Board's finances has been a significant factor in the deficit budgeting of recent years.

6.9   Funds are being raised for the website by the Guild as part of their projects scheme. However, to date, the level of support for this project has yet to reach target.

6.10   At the suggestion of the Co-ordinating Forum, the Board has submitted a bid for a special grant to take forward important development work on the site and thereby encouraging one of the fastest growing areas of the Church's involvement in Communication.

6.11 The Board is carefully examining how best to use the existing skills base in order to develop the Internet service from within the Communication Department.

7. Successful development of Moderator's media role

7.1 One of the important elements of the Board's strategy for the Media Relations Unit is to develop the Unit's work with the Moderator and those staff who support this role. In a year of particularly high media activity there has been a significant development of this aim. The Unit has assisted the Moderator in identifying and maximising opportunities for promotion of the Church of Scotland's message.

7.2 In 2002 the Media Relations Unit plans to work alongside Presbyteries in helping to develop and train the network of local media contacts.

8. Successful Development for Life & Work

8.1 A promotional initiative for Life & Work is now being rolled out across Scotland following the success of a pilot project in Stirling Presbytery. An extremely encouraging forty nine out of fifty of the local churches in the Presbytery participated in the promotion in which non-subscribing churchgoers were offered a free copy of the magazine. The pilot ran over November and December of 2001.

8.2 Over many decades the trend has been for a steady year-on-year decline in Life & Work readership. The statistical pattern has been an average drop of around seven or eight per cent. However, following the promotion, Stirling Presbytery is registering a slight overall increase in the number of subscribers. This means an effective increase of over eleven per cent within the promotional area, more than achieving the Board's target of holding the level of subscription steady.

8.3 This provides an encouraging basis for the Board's proposed three-year approach to rolling out the promotion across Scotland targeting a mix of urban and rural areas. The next areas to be targeted are Glasgow, Dundee, the Borders and Renfrewshire.

8.4 Against the trend of the market, Life & Work advertising income has performed very strongly over the past year and the Board has approved an increase to advertising rates as part of its approach to developing this important source of revenue.

8.5 The Board wishes to underline its commitment to its existing policy of keeping the price of the magazine as low as possible for present and future subscribers within the Church context.

8.6 In line with the recommendation of the Best Value Audit, Life & Work's cover price has gone up to £1.00 this year.

8.7 However, the Board has set a three-year target for getting Life & Work on to the news stands and a review of pricing policy and discounts is needed in order to achieve potential commercial viability in the high street. In a commercial context outwith the Church, the magazine might have to have a higher cover price in order to create sufficient margins of profit for retailers or wholesalers.

8.8 Along with the independent findings of two commercial marketing agencies, the Audit estimated that Life & Work has a commercial shelf-price in the region of £1.50 to £2.00. This will be an important consideration when putting the magazine on to the news stands in the endeavour to reach readers who are not regular churchgoers.

8.9 As part of its plans to develop the magazine further, the Board has appointed Muriel Armstrong (interim editor for ten months prior to Rosemary Goring's appointment) to the role of Life & Work Promotions Manager. Muriel will continue to have an editorial role in the magazine.

8.10 A new post of features writer has been set up in order to continue the Board's commitment to improve the quality of the magazine. Funding for this post has come primarily from savings through production efficiencies and higher earnings from advertising revenue. The new post has had a neutral effect on the budget.

8.11 Mr Bob Ross, recently retired from his job as a

journalist with The Herald, has agreed to be the Convener of the Life & Work Advisory Group. Other members of the Group are: Dr Lesley Orr-McDonald, Mr Dick Williamson, The Rev Shelagh Kesting, The Rev Ron Ferguson, Mr Tom Gray, The Rev Dr Finlay AJ Macdonald, Director of Communication, Editor of Life & Work.

9. Saint Andrew Press expects to achieve over 50,000 sales within the Christian book market this year

9.1 Book publishing has always been at the very heart of Christian communication. Its very first great purpose, in the 15th century, was to make the Bible available to the masses. Unlike any other medium, books enable in-depth, direct communication. The investment of time and intellect that book reading requires makes the experience of reading a well-written book very powerful indeed. As the Church of Scotland's publishing house, Saint Andrew Press plans to continue this important tradition and serve the Church by:

9.1.1 Informing and challenging Church members;

9.1.2 Reaching out to those outwith the Church.

9.2 Saint Andrew Press's infrastructure has been completely overhauled over the past year in order to build the foundations for the Board's aim of making Saint Andrew Press a stronger force in religious publishing. This process has involved a radical revision of every aspect of the Press's way of operating in order to position it strongly in a very demanding and competitive market place.

9.3 A large number of inherited projects – most notably the revision of the Barclay Daily Study Bible series – has been successfully completed. This opens the way for future development.

9.4 The Best Value Audit strongly endorsed the Saint Andrew Press business plan which concentrates on two key aims:

9.4.1 Robust marketing of the existing list of titles;

9.4.2 Focused development of a new list.

9.5 In support of the first aim, Saint Andrew Press has introduced price increases for its back-list. It is

anticipated that this will bring in an additional £20,000 over the course of the year.

9.6 Saint Andrew Press expects to achieve over 50,000 sales within the Christian book market this year, against the backdrop of one of the worst global trade recessions that the publishing industry has experienced in recent memory.

9.7 The Board now has a Marketing and Publicity Manager who plays an important role in supporting the Press's efforts to maximise sales of existing titles.

9.8 In support of the second aim, Saint Andrew Press is building up a network of advisers throughout Scotland both within the Church of Scotland and in the wider community. As well as helping to shape the policies of growth and development, the Board hopes that this network will enable the Press to identify potential new authors within the Scottish context as well as developing existing talent.

9.9 Further afield, Saint Andrew Press is seeking to appoint a part-time commissioning editor who will be based in England. This appointment should enable the Press to identify and develop new authors and marketing opportunities. The Board hopes in time to appoint a second commissioning editor to be based in the USA.

9.10 Savings within the existing budget are paying for new investment in this area of Saint Andrew Press's development.

9.11 In order to deliver the best possible publishing service, Saint Andrew Press has developed a Handbook giving comprehensive information on every aspect of its operations for all those whose work it publishes. This includes a guide to the timescales and standards of quality that Saint Andrew Press has set.

9.12 Given the long development time for book publishing, the Board recognises that it will be two to three years before a clear picture emerges of the success of the Saint Andrew Press plan. However, the early indications are encouraging, not least the strong initial sales of the revised Barclay materials which the Board hopes will act as an important factor in driving the regeneration of the Church's publishing house.

10. Strong initial sales following launch of new Barclay materials

10.1 The new Barclay Daily Study Bible materials were successfully launched on 1 November 2001 in the Royal Concert Hall, Glasgow. A revised version of Professor Barclay's commentary on the Gospels in six volumes formed the centrepiece of the launch. Pathway provided new versions of four recently discovered archive television lectures under the title "Barclay at the BBC". Although almost a quarter of a century old, the full colour lectures are still broadcast quality standard. A series of talks has also been released on CD and audio cassette as part of the package of new material.

10.2 Early sales of the material have been encouraging. For example, some of the books are selling at double the volume of the old stock.

10.3 Series editor, Linda Foster, who has a masters degree in New Testament Studies and has many years' experience in theological publishing, has already begun work on producing the next five volumes of revised books which are due to be published in the Autumn of this year. The final six volumes are scheduled for the Autumn of 2003.

11. Editor of Year Book

11.1 The Rev Ronald Blakey has agreed to edit the Church of Scotland Year Book for a further three years.

11.2 This year's edition came out in advance of its 1 October deadline. The Board wishes to record its appreciation of the excellent work being done by Mr Blakey in his editorial role.

FINANCE

12. Improving budgetary position

12.1 In the financial year 2001 the Board improved on its budget target by delivering, after accounting for deferred income, a final figure of £239,000 against the proposed deficit of £266,000 as reported in the Board's report to the General Assembly in 2001. This represents a favourable variance of £27,000 against that target and is an encouraging outturn based on the Board's decision to invest in the development of its services.

12.2 The Board is projecting this trend into 2002/2003, forecasting a reduction in deficit of over £100,000 for 2002 followed by a further improvement in 2003. This means, in 2002, that the Board expects the deficit to be reduced to £135,000, falling to a deficit of £49,000 in 2003. This improving trend will considerably reduce the pressure on the Board's reserves and is an encouraging indicator for the future beyond 2003.

12.3 Alongside its programme of investment, the Board spent much of 2001 responding to the Best Value Audit (section 3). In the process the Board has been able to plan reductions in expenditure through savings and has also been able to introduce planned increases in income, as outlined elsewhere in this report (see sections 5 and 8).

12.4 The Board's commitment to transparency in its accounting practices and in demonstrating the value delivered through its services will continue. After being successfully piloted in Design Services, this model is being rolled out to include Pathway Productions and Saint Andrew Press.

SPECIAL REPORTS

13. Report from the Rev Alan Sorensen, Radio Adviser

13.1 This year has seen ongoing changes in local radio services, the further development of digital broadcasting, proposals for large-scale regulatory change and changes in key personnel.

13.2 As the areas served by new radio stations becomes ever more local the opportunity for Presbyteries, congregations and individuals to influence the initial bid applications and the station's output is increasing. With every new technology and with every new broadcast source, there is the opportunity and the challenge to us in the churches to support and resource those who make programmes.

13.3   The Church of Scotland is represented on the Churches Advisory Council on Local Broadcasting (CACLB). During the year the Council appointed a new General Secretary, Mr. Peter Blackman, who will undertake also the task of guiding CACLB as it seeks to transform itself into a body which relates to all areas of the communications industry, not just local broadcasting.

13.4   Most broadcasters and broadcasting bodies have spent much of the year considering the Government's white paper "A New Future for Communication." Among many wide-ranging changes envisaged is the amalgamation of the Broadcasting Standards Commission, the Independent Television Commission, the Office of Telecommunications, the Radio Communications Agency and the Radio Authority into one body, OFCOM. This would simplify the regulation of broadcasting and it is to be commended that these various authorities have already begun to work together in anticipation of their "union and readjustment".

13.5   Much of the thrust of the white paper is the continued relaxation of the regulatory framework for broadcasting, while still maintaining strict guidelines, further relaxation of the rules governing ownership of radio stations and cross media ownership.

13.6   One of the more imaginative proposals is for local radio to become even more local. Building on the success of many Restricted Service Licensed services (RSLs) the government is proposing the creation of Access Radio, very small scale, local broadcasting which could also include television. The benefits to communities and the possibilities for the church to interact more closely with those around it are immense.

14.   Multimedia in Worship: Report of joint Board of Communication/Panel on Worship consultation group

14.1   The General Assembly of 2000 encouraged the Board in consultation with the Panel on Worship to begin to explore ways of developing partnerships with parishes exploring multimedia as part of their witness and worship.

14.2   A joint consultation group was formed. As well as initiating conversations with individuals engaged in multimedia projects, a key element of the group's investigation was the commissioning of a survey of local congregations, distributed through the Monthly Mailing.

14.3   Just over 320 congregations responded to the Survey. Three key factors emerged from the findings:

14.3.1 Though many activities may be regarded as "multimedia", nevertheless, the term most usually refers to the integration of video and slide materials, audio effects, live music and drama, and normally implies the use of technological support in worship.

14.3.2 Overwhelmingly, the survey indicated that those engaged in experimenting with multimedia develop home-produced resources, drawing upon taped materials, the Internet and bought-in materials. Congregations rarely turn to Church Boards for assistance.

14.3.3 The group was clear from the responses that congregations generally are concerned about the quality and relevance of their worship services and might explore multimedia contributions to worship were it not for the lack of knowledge and confidence to do so. Often such diffidence arises from a fear of technology, a worship space that does not easily lend itself to experimentation, and a lack of human and material resources.

14.4   The consultation group recognises that appropriate criteria are required to ensure that the use of such media contributes well to the enrichment of worship. Just as "traditional" liturgy requires to be used sensitively, taking all circumstances into account, so with technology-based media.

14.5   The most common requests emerging from the survey were for:

14.5.1 training;

14.5.2 equipment made available locally for hire;

14.5.3 ready made resources (e.g. downloads from the Internet);

14.5.4 money to fund experiments.

14.6 The consultation group recognises that some requests are easier to respond to than others. It sees within the Board of Communication the potential to *facilitate* the interest in developing worship-centred multimedia at local level and to encourage increased contact between congregations. In line with the Board's Communication Strategy, presented to the General Assembly of 2000, the consultation group therefore proposes that the Board of Communication will respond to the needs and interests of local congregations in the following ways:

14.6.1 Identify, within existing staffing levels, a central contact person whose role will be to advise and provide information on technical and equipment matters. The role will be based in the Board's Media Relations Unit and monitored, in the first instance, on a 6-month trial basis.

14.6.2 Encourage networking among interested congregations and provide support information via the Church of Scotland website and through print-based publications such as *Good News*.

14.6.3 Explore the possibility of creating, in conjunction with the Panel on Worship, a print-based resource with ideas for using multimedia contributions in worship; information about hiring equipment; useful website addresses; and illuminating case studies.

STAFFING MATTERS

15. Staff changes

15.1 Last year a number of staff retired after long service to the Board. Ian Dunnet worked 44 years with Saint Andrew Press, latterly as warehouse manager. Maureen Auld was the Board's accounts supervisor for 29 years and Bill Reid was assistant accountant for 24 years. Derek Auld also left the Board's service after 24 years principally as production manager in Saint Andrew Press.

16. Life & Work Editor

16.1 Earlier this year Rosemary Goring resigned from her position of Editor of Life & Work to join The Herald as Literary Editor. In just under two years of editing Life & Work, Rosemary Goring managed to improve significantly the editorial quality of the magazine and to lead the move to a fresh, modern layout and design. In addition, she raised the profile both of the magazine and the editorship, bringing a rigorous and challenging edge to its coverage of Church affairs. Many readers warmly appreciated this approach, which has doubtless contributed to the first signs of resurgence in the magazine's readership that have been seen for many years. There were some others who were not always so comfortable with Rosemary Goring's editorial stance. However, there was almost universal acknowledgement of her fairness, openness and skill as an editor.

16.2 The Board wishes to record its appreciation of the excellent work done by Rosemary in helping to set a new benchmark for Life & Work.

17. Personnel Statistics

17.2 At the end of 2001 the Board employed 27 full time staff. There are currently no ministers on the Board of Communication staff.

In the name and by the authority of the Board.

Jean B Montgomerie, Convener
Peter Graham, Vice Convener
Brian McGlynn, Director and Secretary

Joint Report of the Boards of Parish Education, National Mission, Social Responsibility, Practice and Procedure, Ministry and Stewardship and Finance on the Protection of Children and Young People in the Church

MAY 2002

PROPOSED DELIVERANCE

General Assembly

1   Receive the report.

2   Note the new systems for the checking of criminal records of volunteers and employees working with vulnerable adults (Section 2 and Supplementary Report).

3   Grant authority for the Joint Boards Group for Child Protection to maintain up to date guidance supporting the implementation of the Church's Child Protection Policy, when required. (Section 2.8).

REPORT

1. Introduction

Operating on behalf of the General Assembly, the Joint Boards Group is responsible for the creation and monitoring of policy with regard to matters of Child Protection.

The success of the Child Protection Unit over the past four years bears testimony to the co-operative work within the Joint Boards Group which has seen the Boards of Parish Education, National Mission, Ministry, Social Responsibility, Stewardship and Finance and Practice and Procedure work along with the Law Department to ensure the strategic interests of the Church are kept in mind as good practice and consistent standards of delivery are pursued.

2. Criminal Records Checks for People Working With Children and Young People in the Church of Scotland

2.1 The General Assembly of 2001 agreed the following:

a) that such checks for volunteers working at congregational level should be carried out only via the Church's Child Protection Unit

b) that the Joint Boards Group were authorised to take all necessary steps to effect registration on behalf of the Church with the proposed central registered body

c) that the Child Protection Unit will institute suitable procedures for the processing of applications for checks and the results thereof.

2.2 Despite significant delays, over which the Joint Boards Group had no control, the Joint Boards Group has progressed well down the route of registration with the Central Registered Body in Scotland (CRBS). The Boards directly involved with the recruitment of people to work with children or vulnerable adults have worked together to produce a clear set of guidelines and procedures for the administration of this process.

2.3 The introduction of this system will warrant a programme of seminars around the country for Child Protection co-ordinators and other relevant personnel, to ensure that everyone is aware of the introduction of these checks.

2.4 Although Criminal Records Checks for all volunteers will be free, it is anticipated that checks for paid staff will cost in the region of £12 - £15 per head. This cost has not yet been finalised. Checks for paid staff will also be processed via CRBS, but a charge will be levied, as outlined.

2.5 In order to comply with the registration requirements of the CRBS, the Church has been required to review its Code of Good Practice, which has now been in place for five years.

2.6 The amended Code of Good Practice and associated Guidelines and procedures for the Police Checks system, will be presented in a supplementary report. It has not been possible to include this information at this time because the guidelines cannot be finalised before information is available from the Scottish Executive. Each organisation wishing to register with CRBS will be required to adhere to a Code of Practice laid down by the Executive, and provide evidence of supporting policies already implemented. This Code of Practice has not yet been produced, and consequently any amendments to the Church of Scotland's existing Code of Practice cannot yet be made. It is intended that the Code of Good Practice will be a small reference document and the associated guidelines will be included in an update to the Child Protection Handbook, issued in October 2000. This document aims to help co-ordinators and Kirk Sessions implement the Code of Good Practice and contains information about most of the common enquiries addressed to the Unit.

2.7 It is of significant note that all other organisations working with children are in the process of adopting a system for the effective recruitment of people to work with children and vulnerable adults. The Church of Scotland has worked alongside other denominations and organisations to produce a system that parallels those of similar organisations.

A brief summary of the procedure for accessing these checks for volunteers is outlined below. This process is outlined in detail in the supplementary report

- A post is identified as being eligible for the incumbent to be police checked. Criteria for this decision and examples of such posts are included in the supplementary report.
- The application process is followed as at present
- The successful applicant signs a form giving their consent for any criminal record to be disclosed to the child protection unit or relevant board
- The form is countersigned by a local representative (usually a child protection co-ordinator) to verify that the person has provided suitable ID and is applying for an eligible post
- The form is sent to the Child Protection Unit or relevant Board for approval and forwarded to the CRBS
- The Criminal Records information is returned to the registered person within the Church of Scotland
- A duplicate copy of this information is forwarded to the applicant
- A decision is made, confidentially, on whether the person is suitable to work with children or vulnerable adults
- This decision is notified to the applicant and the local contact person in the organisation the person is hoping to work with
- The person will have a right of appeal as outlined in the supplementary report

A database administrator has been appointed to administer this system.

2.8 The Church's Code of Practice was originally approved by the General Assembly of 1997. As this system is implemented and information and advice is provided to the church from the Scottish Executive and CRBS, supporting guidance may require to be issued. This is likely to address such issues as retrospective checking, rate of review of checks for personnel etc. Such supporting guidance will effectively be an amendment to the Code, and therefore the Joint Boards Group seek the authority to amend the Code as required, from time to time to incorporate changes necessitated by the new checking procedures.

3 Circles of Support and Accountability

3.1 Initially piloted in Canada, Circles is a model which uses trained volunteers to work with sex offenders, in the community. The volunteers form a "circle" around each offender and provide daily support and spervision. The volunteers are drawn from the community in which the offender lives, are trained by professionals and work alongside Police and Social Work to ensure that the offender is held accountable at all times.

3.2 The ethos behind the idea is one of responsible and protective communities where people accept responsibility to work with those in their communities who might otherwise be driven out, difficult to monitor, unsupported and, therefore, present a greater risk to the community as a whole.

3.3 The concept is now being piloted in England. As a result of increasing awareness of the concept of Circles of Support and Accountability, among Statutory and Voluntary Sector Agencies in Scotland, a Steering Group was set up to explore the possibility of introducing Circles of Support and Accountability in Scotland.

This Group consists of representation from:

The Police, Sex Offenders Working Group
ADSW, Criminal Justice Working Group
SACRO
Church of Scotland
Quaker Society of Friends
Catholic Church
Episcopal Church

3.4 The Steering Group were of the opinion that the model of Circles of Support and Accountability offered a potential means of effective monitoring and support of sex offenders in the community, in conjunction with the statutory agencies. However, such an initiative must be introduced in a structured and well managed way, and only if it had support from referring agencies. Therefore it was decided to arrange a day conference on the 9th May to discuss the concept and explore the level of support.

3.5 The conference aimed
- to outline the concept of Circles of Support and Accountability and
- Explore whether this offers a viable option for the involvement of the community in the support and

monitoring of sex offenders, thus enabling us to move towards safer communities.
- If there is support for the initiative at the conference, the Steering Group would like to identify a way forward, probably through the identification of a management group to co-ordinate the initiative at a national level."

4. The Year of the Child

4.1 The Child Protection Unit has continued to jointly co-ordinate this initiative with the Children's and Youth Services Section of the Board of Parish Education. This initiative is an opportunity for the Unit to place an emphasis on good practice and protective ministry at the heart of its work and encourage congregations and Presbyteries to view child protection as an integral part of good children's ministry. The unit is also delighted by this opportunity to encourage children to participate actively in their own churches and communities, and learn to express their views and opinions in a constructive way. Evidence has shown that where organisations are actively engaged with children and respond to their opinions and views those organisations are less likely to develop cultures which can contribute towards abusive relationships. Further information about the Year of the Child is available in the report of the Board of Parish Education.

The name of the Joint Boards

REV G STEWART SMITH
Convener of the Joint Boards Group
Convener of the Board of Parish Education
REV DAVID LACY
Convener of the Board of Practice and Procedure
MR LEON MARSHALL
Convener of the Board of Stewardship and Finance
PROFESSOR WILLIAM STORRAR
Convener of the Board of Ministry
REV JAMES GIBSON
Convener of the Board of National Mission
MRS ANN ALLEN
Convener of the Board of Social Responsibility
MS GILLIAN SCOTT
Secretary of the Joint Boards Group

DELEGATION OF THE GENERAL ASSEMBLY

MAY 2002

PROPOSED DELIVERANCE

The General Assembly:

1. Receive the Report of the Delegation of General Assembly and thank it for its work.
2. Continue the appointment of the Delegation with the same powers as hitherto - the Principal Clerk of the General Assembly to be Chairman and the Depute Clerk of the General Assembly to be Vice-Chairman.

REPORT

The Delegation has to report that during 2001 it granted, in virtue of the powers conferred upon it by the General Assembly, ten additional Model Deeds of Constitution.

The present amended Model Deed of Constitution was approved and adopted by the General Assembly on 21 May 1994 for issue to each Congregation whose temporal affairs were then administered by a Congregational Board under the Model Deed and for granting to each Congregation thereafter adopting it. The total number of Congregations to which Model Deeds have been issued or granted up to the end of 2001 is now 1,198, of which 134 relate to new Parishes.

In the name and on behalf of the Delegation

FINLAY A J MACDONALD, Chairman

PROPOSED DELIVERANCE

The General Assembly:

1. Receive the Report.
2. Convert into a Standing Law of the Church the Overture anent Act V 1984 as printed in Appendix II.
3. Convert into a Standing Law of the Church the Overture anent Admission and Re-admission of Ministers as revised and printed in Appendix III

REPORT

As will be seen from the returns detailed in Appendix I both Overtures sent to Presbyteries by last year's General Assembly have received sufficient support, but a number of helpful comments have been received in respect of each.

I. Overture anent Act V 1984
Comments received, both from Presbyteries approving the Overture and from those disapproving it, expressed concern about the clarity of the wording proposed, reflecting perhaps the fact that it was raised from the floor of the General Assembly and drafted during the course of the debate. The problems about clarity included the number of people likely to be taking part in the laying on of hands, the definition of those associated with the Presbytery (their denomination, ordained status and so on), and the question of who would wish so to take part.

The Committee notes that the Board of National Mission brings to this General Assembly an Overture that would have the effect of replacing Act V entirely, and that the Board has adjusted the wording of that Overture to retain the substance of this amendment but enhance its clarity in these respects. The Committee recommends therefore that the current amendment be proceeded with as an interim measure, while its clarification is effected in due course as part of the Board's larger initiative. The Committee believes this may allay the fears of some of those who opposed the amendment.

Only one Presbytery based its disapproval entirely on a theological objection to the laying on of the hands of elders at the ordination of a minister. Others raised related issues, including the suggestions that the corollary of the passing of this amending Act should be a move towards (1) non-ministerial Moderators of Presbyteries conducting the whole of an ordination or (2) the laying-on of hands in the ordination of elders. Whilst these comments will be noted by the appropriate bodies, the Committee does not suggest any consequent alteration to the wording of the Overture in its passage into law.

II. Overture anent Admission and Re-admission of Ministers
The Committee has received comments relating to good practice in the implementation of the new legislation, and has passed these to the Board of Ministry.

Other concerns included the locus of final decision-making, the possible effect on eligibility for appointments, and the loss of privileged status for certain Presbyterian denominations.

The question was asked why Schedule A is empty. The Act is as comprehensive and inclusive as the Board of Ministry was able to make it, but experience suggests that in years to come there will emerge denominations beyond the World Alliance of Reformed Churches, but clearly sufficiently similar in polity and ministerial formation, that would suit the abbreviated procedure. The Board of

Ministry expects that, on the advice of the Committee on Ecumenical Relations, content will in due course be added to what is currently an empty (but useful) category.

It will be noticed that the Overture promoted by the Board of National Mission to replace Act V 1984 removes the complex and slightly anomalous provisions of section 13 of the existing Act. The Committee has accordingly amended section 5 of the Overture anent Admission and Re-admission to be consistent with the other piece of work, though the logic of this legislation does not rely on the passing of the newer Overture.

The Committee has adopted one Presbytery's suggestion that the term 's/he' be avoided, and has slightly adjusted terminology in one or two places to assist the internal logic or legal correctness of the text.

In the name and by the authority of the Committee

FINLAY A J MACDONALD, *Convener*

APPENDIX I

OVERTURE ANENT ACT V, 1984

No of Presbyteries		Members voting for	
Approving	*Disapproving*	*Approval*	*Disapproval*
36	12	1,836	613

OVERTURE ANENT ADMISSION AND RE-ADMISSION OF MINISTERS

No of Presbyteries		Members voting for	
Approving	*Disapproving*	*Approval*	*Disapproval*
42	6	2,432	165

APPENDIX II

OVERTURE ANENT ACT V 1984
Edinburgh, May 24 2001, Sess. 7

Adopt an Overture the tenor whereof follows, and transmit the same to Presbyteries for their consideration under the Barrier Act, directing that returns be sent to the Principal Clerk not later than 31 December 2001.

The General Assembly hereby enact and ordain that Act V 1984 anent Settlement of Ministers, as amended, is hereby further amended as follows:

In Section 25 (3), amend the words "in which all ministers present shall join" to read "in which members of the Presbytery and those associated with it shall join".

APPENDIX III

OVERTURE ANENT ADMISSION AND RE-ADMISSION OF MINISTERS
Edinburgh, May 24 2001, Sess.7

The General Assembly adopt the Overture the tenor whereof follows, and transmit the same to Presbyteries for their consideration under the Barrier Act, directing that returns be sent to the Principal Clerk not later than 31 December 2001.

1. In this Act the following definitions apply:

   (a) "Applicants" are persons who have submitted an application in terms of this Act

   (b) "The Board" is the General Assembly's Board of Ministry

   (c) "The Committee" is the Board's Assessment Scheme Committee

   (d) The "Review Panel" is a body appointed by the Committee but does not contain any of the Committee's voting membership. Its function is to assess the character and beliefs, education and experience, vocation, motivation and general suitability for ministry of those applicants referred to it by the Committee in terms of this

Act, and to make recommendation to the Committee about each application.

2. Applications in terms of this Act shall be submitted in the first instance to the Committee which is empowered, subject to the provisions of this Act, to make such Regulations for its procedure and to require such fees from applicants as it sees fit. The Committee shall issue a statement of such Regulations and Fees, the dates of the meetings of the Committee and the latest submission date for applications to be considered within a particular cycle of the Committee's meetings, for the guidance of applicants and for its own use.

3. Applications shall be presented in keeping with the style required by the Committee. They shall give full particulars as to the applicant's age, present Church connection, educational curriculum, medical history, ministerial career and other employment, together with a statement indicating the reasons for the applicant's wish to be admitted to the ministry of the Church of Scotland and the form of service which the applicant wishes to exercise. The application shall be accompanied by all the documents (originals, extracts or copies) necessary in the opinion of the Committee to substantiate the facts set forth, by the names of three referees, and by a statement indicating willingness to submit to a medical examination if this is considered necessary by the Committee.

Ministers— Standard Procedure

4. (1) Ministers referred to in section 4(2) shall have their application considered in terms of sections 6 and 7 below. It shall be the responsibility of the Committee to determine whether the applicant's ordination is recognised by the Church of Scotland before referring his or her application to the Review Panel. Such determinations shall be subject to the right of appeal set out in section 12 below.

(2) This section shall apply to the following categories of person: (a) Ordained ministers of other churches, except those specified in section 5 below (b) Former ministers of the Church of Scotland referred to in section 8 below.

Ministers— Abbreviated Procedure

5. (1) Ministers in the following categories shall have their applications considered in terms of section 6 below only:
   (a) Ministers of churches listed in Schedule A
   (b) A minister of any regularly constituted Presbyterian Church in the United Kingdom or of any Church which is a member of the World Alliance of Reformed Churches

(2) The provisions of section 4 above shall apply to any applicant who has ever attended one or more selection conference of the Church of Scotland without having been accepted as a Candidate, notwithstanding that he or she may also belong to one of the categories specified in section 5(1) above.

Consideration by the Committee

6. (a) It shall be the duty of the Committee to examine each application and such other documentation as it may require, to refer applications to the Review Panel as defined in section 1(d) above and receive its recommendation in respect of each applicant and to grant, with or without conditions, or refuse a Certificate of Eligibility. All decisions made by the Committee in fulfilment of this section shall be subject to the right of appeal set out in section 12 below.

(b) A "Certificate of Eligibility" entitles the holder to apply for charges, appointments open to ministers of the Church of Scotland and appointments to office outwith the jurisdiction of the Church of Scotland (provided such office is one which, if held by a minister of this Church, entitles the holder to membership of Presbytery in terms of Act III, 2000). Admission to the status of minister of the Church of Scotland shall take effect at the point of admission to membership of Presbytery. Certificates of Eligibility shall be valid for three years from the date of issue.

Consideration by Presbytery

7. (a) In respect of applications made in terms of section 4 above, following the interim decision of the

Committee, it shall be the duty of the Secretary of the Committee to inform the applicant of that decision and invite the applicant to determine whether or not he or she wishes to continue the application or appeal the decision.

(b)   When the Secretary of the Committee receives from the applicant an indication of her/ his desire to proceed with the application, he or she shall forward to the Presbytery of residence, or in the case of an applicant who has not resided in Scotland for three months prior to the date of the application to the Presbytery of Edinburgh, and to any Presbytery within whose bounds the applicant may have been permitted to be appointed as a minister pending the outcome of the application (a) a copy of the application in full (b) copies of any documents used by the Committee and (c) the interim decision of the Committee. The Secretary shall also intimate to all Presbyteries the applications that have been received, for their information and comment before the date of the meeting of the Committee at which the application is to be considered.

(c)   In the event that the interim decision of the Committee is not to allow the applicant to proceed, it shall be open to the applicant to appeal, as set out in section 12 below.

Ministers— Readmission Procedure

8.   An applicant who has been a minister of the Church of Scotland but who has resigned that status or been judicially deprived thereof, notwithstanding that he or she may also belong to one of the categories specified in section 5, shall make application in terms of this Act, which application shall be considered in terms of sections 6 and 7 above, subject to the right of any Presbytery to require that the decision of the Committee be confirmed by the Commission of the General Assembly, at which the said Presbytery shall be required to appear and be heard.

Licentiates and Graduate Candidates of the Church of Scotland

9. (1)   This section shall apply to the following categories of person:

(a)   Holders of an expired Certificate of Entitlement granted in terms of Act V 1985 (as amended) section 58,

(b)   Licentiates whose names no longer appear in the Roll of Probationers/ Licentiates maintained by the Board of Ministry,

(c)   Candidates in respect of whom more than three years have passed since any formal training was undertaken in terms of Act V 1985 (as amended) or Act V 1998 (as amended), or

(d)   Graduate Candidates in respect of whom a Graduate Candidate's certificate has been withheld by the Presbytery in terms of Act V 1998 (as amended) section 27

(2)   Act V 1998 (as amended) sections 3– 12 shall apply to those referred to in Section 9(1), and upon acceptance and nomination they shall be obliged to fulfil any training or familiarisation process determined by the Committee.

(3)   Upon completion of the requirements of section 9(2), those referred to in section 9(1) shall have the status, privileges and responsibilities of a Graduate Candidate as defined in Act V 1998 (as amended) sections 26 and 27.

Licentiates, ordinands, etc of other churches

10. Licentiates, ordinands, graduate candidates and those of comparable status, from Churches whose ordination is recognised by the Committee, shall be subject to the provisions of Act V 1998 (as amended) sections 3– 12. For the purposes of this Act the Committee shall determine how to apply those provisions to applications in terms of this section, subject to the right of appeal set out in section 12 below.

11. A successful applicant shall be admitted to the status of Graduate Candidate as defined in Act V 1998 (as amended) sections 26 and 27, subject to the completion (at the applicant's own cost) of such academic requirements, placements or other practical training, course work or conference work determined by the Committee, subject to the right of appeal set out in section 12 below.

Appeals

12. For the purposes of this Act, the Appeals Procedure shall be that set out in sections 6(e) and 12 of Act V 1998 (as amended), which shall for the purposes of this Act be construed in conformity with it. Recourse to the Panel of Arbiters shall for the purposes of this Act be available only in respect of appeals taken against the final decision of the Committee or any conditions attached to such decision, and shall not be available in respect of intermediate appeals.

Confidentiality

13. Each application and all procedure under this Act shall be taken in private by the Board and by Presbyteries.

The Diaconate

14. The provisions of this Act shall apply to members of the diaconal ministry of the Church of Scotland and other Churches. The Committee shall be responsible for determining the interpretation of this Act consistently with the provisions of Act VIII 1998 and Act IX 2001; such determinations shall be subject to the right of appeal set out in section 12 above.

Repeals and Amendments

15. (1)   Act III, 1995 and the Regulations appended thereto, are hereby repealed.
   (2)   Act V 1998 (as amended) section 28 is hereby repealed.
   (3)   The Act Anent Discipline of Ministers, Licentiates, Graduate Candidates and Deacons, 2001 shall be amended as follows: section 1(1)(h)(iii) shall be amended to read 'removal of status, subject to restoration only by application in terms of the Act Anent Admission and Readmission of Ministers and Others, 2002 section 8.'

Interpretation of Acts

16. Act XI 1994 shall be interpreted in conformity with this Act.

SCHEDULE A

This category is empty at the time of the passing of the Act, but is referred to in the body of the legislation for future use

COMMITTEE ON STAKEHOLDERS CONFERENCE

MAY 2002

PROPOSED DELIVERANCE

The General Assembly:

1.   Receive the Report.

REPORT

The General Assembly of 2001, on the Report of the Special Commission anent Review and Reform in the Church, resolved to appoint a planning group or seven persons to prepare a 'Stakeholders' Conference' in 2005 as a point of national celebration and a milestone of progress.

The group has met several times in the last year, and begun to monitor the reception of the *Church without Walls* report in local churches and Presbyteries. In consultation with other bodies engaged in the process, including the Assembly Council, it plans to assess in due course the sort of event best calculated to fulfil the intention of the General Assembly. It has begun to address the question of funding such a major initiative.

In the name of the Committee

ALEXANDER MCDONALD, *Convener*
MARJORY A MACLEAN, *Secretary*

INDEX